## SOUTH AMERICA

Pages 72–73

75

74

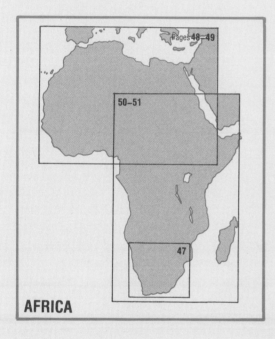

## AFRICA

Pages 48–49

50–51

47

## NORTH AMERICA

Pages 54–55

58–59

60–61

56–57

66

62–63

69

70

D1469740

## GENERAL MAPS

## AUSTRALASIA

Pages 32–33

34

35

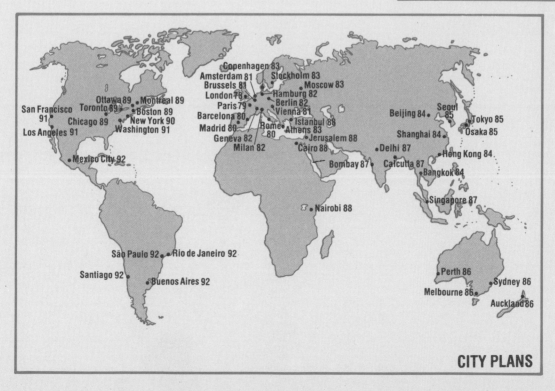

Copenhagen 83
Amsterdam 81    Stockholm 83
Brussels 81     Moscow 83
London 78       Hamburg 82
Paris 79        Berlin 82
Barcelona 80    Vienna 81
Madrid 80       Istanbul 88
Rome 80         Athens 83
Geneva 82       Jerusalem 88
Milan 82        Cairo 88
Ottawa 89       Montreal 89
Toronto 89      Boston 89
San Francisco 91
Chicago 89      New York 90
Los Angeles 91  Washington 91
Mexico City 92
Beijing 84      Seoul 85
Shanghai 84     Tokyo 85
                Osaka 85
Delhi 87        Hong Kong 84
Bombay 87       Calcutta 87
                Bangkok 84
Singapore 87
Nairobi 88
São Paulo 92    Rio de Janeiro 92
Santiago 92     Buenos Aires 92
Perth 86        Sydney 86
Melbourne 86    Auckland 86

## CITY PLANS

# The New York Times

# ATLAS

## OF THE WORLD

NEW FAMILY EDITION

Copyright © Times Books and Bartholomew 1992

*Maps and index prepared by* Bartholomew, Edinburgh

Published in the United States by Times Books, a division of Random House, Inc., New York.

This second edition was originally published in the United Kingdom by Times Books, a division of HarperCollins*Publishers*, London.

The first edition of this book was originally published in 1988 by Times Books, London.

All maps and other material were prepared under the supervision of the parties specified below.
The contents of this book have not previously appeared in *The New York Times*.

*Geographical Dictionary prepared by* Professor B.W. Atkinson

*Physical Earth Maps* Duncan Mackay

*Design* Ivan Dodd

*Printed and bound in Italy by* Mondadori, Verona.

*The Publishers would like to extend their grateful thanks to the following:*

Mrs J Candy, Geographical Research Associates, Maidenhead

Cosmographics, Watford

Flag information provided and authenticated by the Flag Institute, Chester

Additional information from the Flag Research Center, Massachusetts, USA

Mr. P.J.M Geelan, Place-name consultant

Mr Michael Hendrie, Astronomy Correspondent, *The Times*, London

Mr H.A.G. Lewis OBE, Geographical consultant to *The Times*

Mr R. Muhs, School of Slavonic & East European Studies, University of London

Swanston Graphics, Derby

Thames Cartographic Services, Maidenhead

Manufactured in Italy
9 8 7 6 5 4 3 2

First Times Books, New York Edition.

*The New York Times Atlas of the World, New Family Edition* is a reference work for use in the home, office or school, for those who travel the world and also those, like Francis Bacon, who journey only "in map and chart".

An index of no fewer than 30,000 entries, keyed to the main map plates, will aid those who, while familiar with the name of a place, are uncertain of just where it lies on the map.

It is by no means always easy to ascertain the correct title and status of a country as distinct from its everyday name used on maps. The list of states and territories gives in addition to name, title and status, the population and area, the national currency, the major religions and the national flag.

Maps, being an efficient way of storing and displaying information, are used to amplify the list of states and territories and the geographical comparisons of continents, oceans, lakes and islands. They form the basis of the section on earthquakes, volcanoes, economic minerals, vegetation, temperature, rainfall and population.

Maps are also, by nature, illustrative and a 14-page section shows the world's major physical features in the way they appear from space but with the names of the features added.

Among the statistical data contained in the Atlas is a listing of the major metropolitan areas with their populations. For the past several decades there has been, throughout the world, an accelerating flow of people from the land to towns and cities and especially the major cities, some of which now contain the bulk of the national population. Growth in air travel has turned those same cities into centers of tourism. Influx of population and the demands of tourism have enhanced the status of cities. Generous space has, therefore, been allocated to maps of major cities and their environs.

Geographical names in this Atlas are given in their anglicized (conventional) form where such a form is in current use. Other names are given in their national Roman alphabet or else converted into English by transliteration (letter-to-letter) or transcription (sound-to-sound). Because Roman alphabet letters, sometimes modified, are pronounced in a variety of ways, a brief guide to pronunciation has been included. The whole is supplemented by a dictionary of geographical terms.

In the names, in the portrayal of international boundaries and in the list of states and territories, the aim has been to show the situation as it pertains in the area at the time of going to press. This must not be taken as endorsement by the publishers of the status of the territories concerned. The aim throughout has been to show things as they are. In that way the Atlas will best serve the reader to whom, it is hoped, it will bring interest, benefit and continuing pleasure.

**H.A.G. Lewis, OBE**
Geographical Consultant to *The Times*

# AFGHANISTAN

STATUS: Republic
AREA: 652,225 sq km (251,773 sq miles)
POPULATION: 16,433,000
ANNUAL NATURAL INCREASE: 2.4%
CAPITAL: Kabul
LANGUAGE: Pushtu, Dari (Persian dialect)
RELIGION: 90% Sunni and 9% Shia Muslim
CURRENCY: afghani (AFA)
ORGANISATIONS: UN, Col. Plan

Afghanistan is a mountainous landlocked country in south-west Asia with a climate of extremes. In summer the lowland south-west reaches a temperature of over 40°C (104°F); in winter this may drop to −26°C (−15°F) in the northern mountains. Rainfall varies between 10 and 40cm (4–16in). The country is one of the poorest in the world with hardly 10% of the land suitable for agriculture. Main crops are wheat, fruit and vegetables. Sheep and goats are the main livestock. Mineral resources are rich but underdeveloped with natural gas, coal and iron ore deposits predominating. The main industrial area is centred on Kabul.

## ALAND

STATUS: Self-governing Island Province of Finland
AREA: 1,505 sq km (581 sq miles)
POPULATION: 24,231

## ABBREVIATIONS

| | |
|---|---|
| ANZUS | Australia, New Zealand, United States Security Treaty |
| ASEAN | Association of South East Asian Nations |
| CACM | Central American Common Market |
| CARICOM | Caribbean Community and Common Market |
| CFA | (Communauté Financière Africaîne |
| CFP | or Pacific franc (Communauté Française du Pacifique) |
| CIS | Commonwealth of Independent States |
| Col. Plan | Colombo Plan |
| Comm. | Commonwealth |
| ECOWAS | Economic Community of West African States |
| EC | European Community |
| EFTA | European Free Trade Association |
| G7 | Group of Seven Industrial Nations (Canada, France, Germany, Italy, Japan, UK, USA) |
| NATO | North Atlantic Treaty Organisation |
| OAS | Organisation of American States |
| OAU | Organisation of African Unity |
| OECD | Organisation for Economic Co-operation and Development |
| OIEC | Organisation for International Economic Co-operation |
| OPEC | Organisation of Petroleum Exporting Countries |
| UN | United Nations |
| WEU | Western European Union |

Codes, given in brackets, following the name of a currency are those issued by the International Standards Organisation.

# ALBANIA

STATUS: Republic
AREA: 28,750 sq km (11,100 sq miles)
POPULATION: 3,250,000
ANNUAL NATURAL INCREASE: 2.1%
CAPITAL: Tirana (Tiranë)
LANGUAGE: Albanian (Tosk, Gheg)
RELIGION: Religion officially banned from 1967-1990. Formerly 70% Muslim, 20% Orthodox and 10% Roman Catholic
CURRENCY: lek (ALL)
ORGANISATIONS: UN

Albania is situated on the eastern seaboard of the Adriatic. With the exception of a coastal strip, most of the territory is mountainous and largely unfit for cultivation. The country possesses considerable mineral resources, notably chrome, copper, iron ores and nickel, with rich deposits of coal, oil and natural gas. After decades of self-imposed political and economic isolation Albania shook off its own peculiar variant of communism in 1990. Administrative chaos and a massive fall in production ensued, notably in the (as yet collectivised) agricultural sector. Acute food shortages and economic backwardness have generated a desire for emigration among the younger members of the fast-growing population.

## ALEUTIAN ISLANDS

STATUS: Territory of USA
AREA: 17,665 sq km (6,820 sq miles)
POPULATION: 6,730

# ALGERIA

STATUS: Republic
AREA: 2,381,745 sq km (919,355 sq miles)
POPULATION: 24,960,000
ANNUAL NATURAL INCREASE: 3.1%
CAPITAL: Algiers (El-Djezaïr)
LANGUAGE: Arabic, French, Berber
RELIGION: Muslim
CURRENCY: Algerian dinar (DZD)
ORGANISATIONS: UN, Arab League, OAU, OPEC

Physically the country is divided between the coastal Atlas mountain ranges of the north and the Sahara to the south. Arable land occupies small areas of the northern valleys and coastal strip, with wheat, barley and vines the leading crops. Sheep, goats and cattle are the most important livestock. Although oil from the southern deserts dominates the economy, it is now declining. Economic policy has concentrated on encouraging smaller manufacturing and service industries. Tourism is a growth industry and now earns important foreign exchange.

# ANDORRA

STATUS: Principality under Franco-Spanish sovereignty
AREA: 465 sq km (180 sq miles)
POPULATION: 52,000
CAPITAL: Andorra la Vella
LANGUAGE: Spanish (Castilian, Catalan), French
RELIGION: mainly Roman Catholic
CURRENCY: French francs (FRF), Andorran peseta (ADP)

Andorra is a tiny alpine state high in the Pyrenees between France and Spain. Agriculture and tourism are the main occupations. Tobacco and potatoes are the principal

crops, sheep and cattle the main livestock. Important sources of revenue are the sale of hydro-electricity, stamps and duty-free goods.

# ANGOLA

STATUS: Republic
AREA: 1,246,700 sq km (481,225 sq miles)
POPULATION: 10,020,000
ANNUAL NATURAL INCREASE: 2.5%
CAPITAL: Luanda
LANGUAGE: Portuguese, tribal dialects
RELIGION: mainly traditional beliefs. Large Roman Catholic and Protestant minorities

CURRENCY: new kwanza (AON)
ORGANISATIONS: UN, OAU

Independent from the Portuguese since 1975, Angola is a large country south of the equator in south-western Africa. Much of the interior is savannah plateaux with rainfall varying from 25cm (10in) in the north to 60cm (24in) in the south. Most of the population is engaged in agriculture producing cassava, maize and coffee, but Angola is very rich in minerals. Petroleum, diamonds, iron ore, copper and manganese are exported with petroleum accounting for at least 50% of earnings. The small amount of industry is concentrated around Luanda. Most consumer products and textiles are imported.

## ANGUILLA

STATUS: UK Dependent Territory
AREA: 91 sq km (35 sq miles)
POPULATION: 7,019
CAPITAL: The Valley

# ANTIGUA & BARBUDA

STATUS: Commonwealth State
AREA: 442 sq km (171 sq miles)
POPULATION: 85,000
ANNUAL NATURAL INCREASE: 0.4%
CAPITAL: St John's (on Antigua)
LANGUAGE: English
RELIGION: Anglican Christian majority
CURRENCY: East Caribbean dollar (XCD)
ORGANISATIONS: Comm, UN, CARICOM, OAS

The country consists of two main islands in the Leeward group in the West Indies. Tourism is the main activity but local agriculture is being encouraged to reduce food imports. The production of rum is the main manufacturing industry.

# ARGENTINA

STATUS: Republic
AREA: 2,766,889 sq km (1,068,302 sq miles)
POPULATION: 32,610,000
ANNUAL NATURAL INCREASE: 1.4%
CAPITAL: Buenos Aires
LANGUAGE: Spanish
RELIGION: 90% Roman Catholic, 2% Protestant, Jewish minority
CURRENCY: peso
ORGANISATIONS: UN, OAS

The country stretches over 30 degrees of latitude from the thick sub-tropical forests of the north through the immense flat grass plains of the pampas to the cool desert plateaux of Patagonia in the south. The economy of Argentina was long dominated by the produce of the rich soils of the pampas, beef and grain. Agricultural products account for over 60% of export revenue with grain crops pre-dominating, although the late 1980s saw a decline due to competition and falling world grain prices. Beef exports, the mainstay of the economy from 1850, decreased by over 50% between 1970 and 1983, again due to strong competition from western Europe. Industry has also declined during the last decade. Shortages of raw materials and foreign aid debts have meant lower production, unemployment and a strong decline in domestic demand. The expansion of the oil and gas industry and the steady growth of coal, hydro-electricity and nuclear power, is providing a base for industrial growth but internal inflation has not yet allowed this expansion.

# ARMENIA

STATUS: Republic
AREA: 30,000 sq km (11,580 sq miles)
POPULATION: 3,300,000
CAPITAL: Yerevan
LANGUAGE: Armenian, Russian
RELIGION: Russian Orthodox, Armenian Apostolic
CURRENCY: rouble
ORGANISATIONS: CIS

Smallest of the 15 republics of the former USSR, Armenia is a rugged and landlocked country with hot, dry summers and severe winters. Arable land is limited but fertile. Extensive mountain pastures support cattle, sheep and goats. Industry is mainly concerned with machine-building, chemicals and textiles. Conflict with neighbouring Azerbaijan looks set to cast a cloud over the immediate future.

## ARUBA

STATUS: Self-governing Island of Netherlands Realm
AREA: 193 sq km (75 sq miles)
POPULATION: 62,500
CAPITAL: Oranjestad

## ASCENSION

STATUS: Island Dependency of St Helena
AREA: 88 sq km (34 sq miles)
POPULATION: 1,007
CAPITAL: Georgetown

# AUSTRALIA

STATUS: Federal Nation
AREA: 7,682,300 sq km (2,965,370 sq miles)
POPULATION: 17,086,197
ANNUAL NATURAL INCREASE: 1.5%
CAPITAL: Canberra
LANGUAGE: English
RELIGION: 75% Christian. Aboriginal beliefs. Jewish minority
CURRENCY: Australian dollar (AUD)
ORGANISATIONS: Comm, UN, ANZUS, Col. Plan, OECD

### AUSTRALIAN CAPITAL TERRITORY (CANBERRA)
STATUS: Federal Territory
AREA: 2,432 sq km (939 sq miles)
POPULATION: 284,985
CAPITAL: Canberra

### NEW SOUTH WALES
STATUS: State
AREA: 801,430 sq km (309,350 sq miles)
POPULATION: 5,827,373
CAPITAL: Sydney

### NORTHERN TERRITORY
STATUS: Territory
AREA: 1,346,200 sq km (519,635 sq miles)
POPULATION: 157,304
CAPITAL: Darwin

### QUEENSLAND
STATUS: State
AREA: 1,727,000 sq km (666,620 sq miles)
POPULATION: 2,906,838
CAPITAL: Brisbane

### SOUTH AUSTRALIA
STATUS: State
AREA: 984,380 sq km (79,970 sq miles)
POPULATION: 1,439,157
CAPITAL: Adelaide

### TASMANIA
STATUS: State
AREA: 68,330 sq km (26,375 sq miles)
POPULATION: 456,663
CAPITAL: Hobart

### VICTORIA
STATUS: State
AREA: 227,600 sq km (87,855 sq miles)
POPULATION: 4,379,981
CAPITAL: Melbourne

## WESTERN AUSTRALIA

STATUS: State
AREA: 2,525,500 sq km (974,845 sq miles)
POPULATION: 1,633,896
CAPITAL: Perth

Australia is both a continent and a country and is the sixth largest country in terms of area. The centre and the west, over 50% of the land area, are desert and scrub with less than 25 cm (10 in) of rain. Only in the sub-tropical north and the eastern highlands does rainfall exceed 100 cm (39 in) annually. The majority of the population live in cities concentrated along the south-east coast. Australia is rich in both agricultural and natural resources. Wool, wheat, meat, sugar and dairy products account for over 40% of export revenue despite the immense growth in mineral exploitation. The country has vast reserves of coal, oil, natural gas, nickel, iron ore, bauxite and uranium ores. Gold, silver, lead, zinc and copper ores are also exploited. In 1989 minerals accounted for about 42% of export revenue. Recent high deficits in balance of trade have been caused by fluctuations in world demand, competition from the E.C. and recent unfavourable climatic conditions affecting agricultural surpluses. Increasing trade with eastern Asia, and Japan in particular, has opened up new areas of commerce to counteract the sharp decline in Europe as a market.

## AUSTRALIAN ANTARCTIC TERRITORY

STATUS: Territory
AREA: 6,120,000 sq km (2,320,000 sq miles)
POPULATION: No permanent population

## AUSTRIA

STATUS: Federal Republic
AREA: 83,855 sq km (32,370 sq miles)
POPULATION: 7,761,700
ANNUAL NATURAL INCREASE: 0.1%
CAPITAL: Vienna (Wien)
LANGUAGE: German
RELIGION: 89% Roman Catholic, 6% Protestant
CURRENCY: schilling (ATS)
ORGANISATIONS: UN, Council of Europe, EFTA, OECD

Austria is an alpine, land-locked country in central Europe. The mountainous Alps which cover 75% of the land consist of a series of east-west ranges enclosing lowland basins. The climate is continental with cold winters and warm summers. About 25% of the country, in the north and north-east, is lower foreland or flat land containing most of Austria's fertile farmland. Half is arable and the remainder is mainly for root or fodder crops. Manufacturing and heavy industry, however, account for the majority of export revenue, particularly pig-iron, steel, chemicals and vehicles. Over 70% of the country's power is hydroelectric. Tourism and forestry are also important to the economy.

## AZERBAIJAN

STATUS: Republic
AREA: 87,000 sq km (33,580 sq miles)
POPULATION: 7,100,000
CAPITAL: Baku
LANGUAGE: Azeri (a Turkish dialect), Armenian, Russian
RELIGION: Muslim (Shia), Armenian Apostolic, Orthodox
CURRENCY: rouble
ORGANISATIONS: CIS

Azerbaijan gained independence on the break-up of the USSR in 1991. The country includes two autonomous regions: Nakhichevan, from which it is cut off by a strip of intervening Armenian territory, and Nagorny Karabakh. Long-standing tensions over the latter escalated into civil war in 1992. Azerbaijan benefits from a dry subtropical climate with mild winters and long, hot summers. Traditional customs have largely disappeared under the impact of modernisation and urbanisation. Originally based on petroleum extraction and oil refining, industrial development in Azerbaijan has been supplemented by manufacturing, engineering and chemicals. Arable land accounts for less than 10% of the total area, with raw cotton the leading product. Tobacco ranks as the second most valuable crop, followed by grapes. The challenge facing the economy of adaptation to post-communist market conditions is exacerbated by political uncertainty.

## BAHAMAS

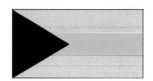

STATUS: Commonwealth State
AREA: 13,865 sq km (5,350 sq miles)
POPULATION: 254,685
ANNUAL NATURAL INCREASE: 1.9%
CAPITAL: Nassau
LANGUAGE: English
RELIGION: mainly Anglican Christian, Baptist and Roman Catholic
CURRENCY: Bahamian dollar (BSD)
ORGANISATIONS: Comm, UN, CARICOM, OAS

About 700 islands and over 2000 coral sand cays (reefs) constitute the sub-tropical Commonwealth of the Bahamas. The island group extends from the coast of Florida to Cuba and Haiti in the south. Only 29 islands are inhabited. Most of the 100cm (39in) of rainfall falls in the summer. The tourist industry is the main source of income and, although fluctuating through recession, still employs over 70% of the working population. Recent economic plans have concentrated on reducing imports by developing fishing and domestic agriculture. Other important sources of income are ship registration (the world's third largest open-registry fleet), income generated by offshore finance and banking, and export of rum, salt and cement.

## BAHRAIN

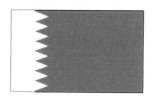

STATUS: State
AREA: 661 sq km (225 sq miles)
POPULATION: 503,000
ANNUAL NATURAL INCREASE: 4.3%
CAPITAL: Manama (Al Manamah)
LANGUAGE: Arabic, English
RELIGION: 60% Shia and 40% Sunni Muslim. Christian minority
CURRENCY: Bahraini dinar (BHD)
ORGANISATIONS: UN, Arab League

The sheikdom is a barren island in the Persian Gulf with less than 8cm (3in) rainfall. Summer temperatures average 32°C (89°F). Bahrain was the first country in the Arabian

peninsula to strike oil, in 1932. In 1985, oil accounted for 65% of revenue, but a decline in value of the product and lower production is now causing the government to diversify the economy with expansion of light and heavy industry and chemical plants, and the subsequent encouragement of trade and foreign investment.

## BANGLADESH

STATUS: Republic
AREA: 144,000 sq km (55,585 sq miles)
POPULATION: 109,291,000
ANNUAL NATURAL INCREASE: 2.8%
CAPITAL: Dhaka

LANGUAGE: Bengali (Bangla), Bihari, Hindi, English
RELIGION: 85% Muslim. Hindu, Buddhist and Christian minorities
CURRENCY: taka (BDT)
ORGANISATIONS: Comm, UN, Col. Plan

Bangladesh is one of the poorest and most densely populated countries of the world. Most of the territory of Bangladesh, except for bamboo-forested hills in the south-east, comprises the vast river systems of the Ganges and Brahmaputra which drain from the Himalayas into the Bay of Bengal, frequently changing course and flooding the flat delta plain. This land is, however, extremely fertile and attracts a high concentration of the population. The climate is tropical, and agriculture is dependent on monsoon rainfall. When the monsoon fails there is drought. 82% of the population of Bangladesh are farmers, the main crops being rice and jute. There are no extensive mineral deposits, although large reserves of natural gas under the Bay of Bengal are beginning to be exploited.

## BARBADOS

STATUS: Commonwealth State
AREA: 430 sq km (166 sq miles)
POPULATION: 257,082
ANNUAL NATURAL INCREASE: 0.3%
CAPITAL: Bridgetown
LANGUAGE: English
RELIGION: Anglican Christian majority. Methodist and Roman Catholic minorities
CURRENCY: Barbados dollar (BBD)
ORGANISATIONS: Comm, UN, CARICOM, OAS

The former British colony of Barbados in the Caribbean is the easternmost island of the Antilles chain. The gently rolling landscape of the island is lush and fertile, the temperature

ranging from 25°–28°C(77°–82°F) with 127–190cm(50–75in) rainfall per year. Sugar and its by-products, molasses and rum, form the mainstay of the economy. Tourism has become a growing industry in recent years.

## BELGIUM

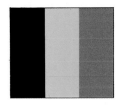

STATUS: Kingdom
AREA: 30,520 sq km (11,780 sq miles)
POPULATION: 9,845,000
ANNUAL NATURAL INCREASE: 0.0%
CAPITAL: Brussels (Bruxelles/Brussel)
LANGUAGE: French, Dutch (Flemish), German
RELIGION: Roman Catholic majority. Protestant, Jewish minorities
CURRENCY: Belgian franc (BEF)
ORGANISATIONS: UN, Council of Europe, EC, NATO, OECD, WEU

Belgium is situated between the hills of Northern France and the North European plain. Over two thirds of the country comprises the Flanders plain, a flat plateau covered by fertile wind-blown loess which extends from the North Sea coast down to the forested mountains of the Ardennes in the south, which rise to a height of 692m(2270ft). The climate is mild and temperate, although the country's proximity to the Atlantic means that low pressure fronts bring changeable weather and frequent rainfall (72–120cm or 28–47in per annum). Over half the country is intensively farmed – cereals (mainly wheat), root crops, vegetables and flax are the main crops. Extensive pastureland ensures that Belgium is self-sufficient in meat and dairy products. Belgium lacks mineral resources, except for coal, but its metal and engineering industries account for nearly one third of its exports. The Flanders region is famous for its textiles. Most of Belgium's trade passes through the North sea port of Antwerp, and an efficient communications network links the port with the rest of Europe.

## BELIZE

STATUS: Commonwealth State
AREA: 22,965 sq km (8,865 sq miles)
POPULATION: 188,000
ANNUAL NATURAL INCREASE: 2.8%
CAPITAL: Belmopan
LANGUAGE: English, Spanish, Maya
RELIGION: 60% Roman Catholic, 40% Protestant
CURRENCY: Belizean dollar (BZD)
ORGANISATIONS: Comm, UN, CARICOM, OAS

Bordering the Caribbean Sea, sub-tropical Belize is dominated by its dense forest cover. Principal crops for export are sugar-cane, fruit, rice, maize and timber products. Since

independence from Britain in 1973 the country has developed agriculture to lessen reliance on imported food products. Fish is a staple diet and also provides valuable foreign exchange.

## BELORUSSIA

STATUS: Republic
AREA: 208,000 sq km (80,290 sq miles)
POPULATION: 10,200,000
CAPITAL: Minsk
LANGUAGE: Belorussian, Russian
RELIGION: Roman Catholic, Uniate
CURRENCY: rouble
ORGANISATIONS: UN, CIS

Belorussia achieved independence in 1991. The country is mainly flat with forests covering more than one-third of the area. Swamps and marshlands cover large areas but, when drained, the soil is very fertile. The climate varies from maritime to continental with mild winters and high humidity. Grain, flax, potatoes and sugar beet are the main crops but livestock production accounts for more than half the value of agricultural output. Large areas of Belorussia are thinly populated; most people live in the central area. The republic is comparatively poor in mineral resources and suffered terrible devastation during the Second World War. Post-war industrialisation has been based on imported raw materials and semi-manufactured goods, concentrating on the production of trucks, tractors, agricultural machinery and other heavy engineering equipment. The capital, Minsk, serves as the administrative centre for the Commonwealth of Independent States, the successor organisation to the Soviet Union.

## BENIN

STATUS: Republic
AREA: 112,620 sq km (43,470 sq miles)
POPULATION: 188,000
ANNUAL NATURAL INCREASE: 3.2%
CAPITAL: Porto Novo
LANGUAGE: French, Fon, Adja
RELIGION: traditional beliefs majority, 15% Roman Catholic and 13% Muslim
CURRENCY: CFA franc (W Africa) (XOF)
ORGANISATIONS: UN, ECOWAS, OAU

Benin, formerly Dahomey, is a small strip of country descending from the wooded savannah hills of the north to the forested and cultivated lowlands fringing the Bight of Benin. The economy is dominated by agriculture, with palm oil, cotton, coffee, groundnuts and copra as main exports. The developing off-shore oil industry has proven reserves of over 20 million barrels.

## BERMUDA

STATUS: Self-governing UK Crown Colony
AREA: 54 sq km (21 sq miles)
POPULATION: 61,000
CAPITAL: Hamilton

---

# BHUTAN

STATUS: Kingdom
AREA: 46,620 sq km (17,995 sq miles)
POPULATION: 1,517,000
ANNUAL NATURAL INCREASE: 2.1%
CAPITAL: Thimphu
LANGUAGE: Dzongkha, Nepali, English
RELIGION: Mahayana Buddhist. Hindu minority
CURRENCY: ngultrum (BTN), Indian rupee (INR)
ORGANISATIONS: UN, Col. Plan

The country spreads across the Himalayan foothills between China and India east of Nepal. Rainfall is high at over 300cm (118in) per year but temperatures vary between extreme cold of the northern ranges to a July average of 27°C (81°F) in the southern forests. Long isolated, the economy of Bhutan is dominated by agriculture and small local industries. All manufactured goods are imported.

---

## BIOKO (FERNANDO PÓO)

STATUS: Island province of Equatorial Guinea
AREA: 2,034 sq km (785 sq miles)
POPULATION: 57,190
CAPITAL: Malabo

---

# BOLIVIA

STATUS: Republic
AREA: 1,098,575 sq km (424,050 sq miles)
POPULATION: 7,400,000
ANNUAL NATURAL INCREASE: 2.8%
CAPITAL: La Paz
LANGUAGE: Spanish, Quechua, Aymara
RELIGION: Roman Catholic majority
CURRENCY: boliviano (BOB)
ORGANISATIONS: UN, OAS

With an average life expectancy of 51 years, Bolivia is one of the world's poorest nations. Landlocked and isolated, the country stretches from the eastern Andes across high cool plateaux before dropping to the dense forest of the Amazon basin and the grasslands of the south-east. Development of the economy relies on the growth of exploitation of mineral resources as subsistence agriculture occupies the majority of the population. Crude oil, natural gas, tin, zinc and iron ore are the main mineral deposits.

---

## BONAIRE

STATUS: Self-governing Island of Netherlands Antilles
AREA: 288 sq km (111 sq miles)
POPULATION: 10,797
CAPITAL: Kralendijk

---

## BONIN ISLANDS (OGASAWARA-SHOTO)

STATUS: Islands of Japan
AREA: 104 sq km (40 sq miles)
POPULATION: 200

---

# BOTSWANA

STATUS: Republic
AREA: 582,000 sq km (224,652 sq miles)
POPULATION: 1,291,000
ANNUAL NATURAL INCREASE: 3.4%
CAPITAL: Gaborone
LANGUAGE: Setswana, English
RELIGION: traditional beliefs majority. Christian minority
CURRENCY: pula (BWP)
ORGANISATIONS: Comm, UN, OAU

The arid high plateau of Botswana, with its poor soils and low rainfall, supports little arable agriculture, but over 2.3 million cattle graze the dry grasslands. Diamonds, copper, nickel and gold are mined in the east and are the main mineral exports. The growth of light industries around the capital has stimulated trade with neighbouring countries.

---

## BOUGAINVILLE ISLAND

STATUS: Part of Papua New Guinea
AREA: 10,620 sq km (4,100 sq miles)
POPULATION: 159,100
CAPITAL: Arawa

---

# BRAZIL

STATUS: Federal Republic
AREA: 8,511,965 sq km (3,285,620 sq miles)
POPULATION: 155,600,000
ANNUAL NATURAL INCREASE: 2.2%
CAPITAL: Brasilia
LANGUAGE: Portuguese
RELIGION: 90% Roman Catholic. Protestant minority
CURRENCY: cruzeiro (BRC)
ORGANISATIONS: UN, OAS

Brazil is not only the largest country in South America but also has the fastest growing economy. Brazil is now an industrial power but with development limited to the heavily populated urban areas of the eastern coastal lowlands. The Amazon basin tropical rain forest covers roughly one third of the country; savannah grasslands of the centre west give way to light forest – now much cleared – of the eastern Brazilian Highlands, and the cool southern plateau of the south. This varied landscape is dominated by three river systems of the Amazon, São Francisco and Paraguay/Paraná. Economic variety reflects the changing landscape. In agricultural production Brazil is one of the world's leading exporters with coffee, soya beans, sugar, bananas, cocoa, tobacco, rice and cattle major commodities. Mineral resources, except for iron ore, at the moment do not play a significant role in the economy, but recent economic policies have concentrated on developing the industrial base – road and rail communications, on light and heavy industry and expansion of energy resources, particularly hydro-electric power harnessed from the great river systems.

---

# BRUNEI

STATUS: Sultanate
AREA: 5,765 sq km (2,225 sq miles)
POPULATION: 266,000
ANNUAL NATURAL INCREASE: 3.3%
CAPITAL: Bandar Seri Begawan
LANGUAGE: Malay, English, Chinese
RELIGION: 65% Sunni Muslim. Buddhist and Christian minorities
CURRENCY: Brunei dollar (BND)
ORGANISATIONS: Comm, UN, ASEAN

The Sultanate of Brunei is situated on the north-west coast of Borneo. Its tropical climate is hot and humid with annual rainfall ranging from 250cm(98in) on the thin coastal strip to

500cm(197in) in the mountainous interior. Oil, both on-shore and off-shore is the mainstay of the Brunei economy. Other exports include natural gas, which is transported to Japan, rubber and timber. Apart from oil, most other industries are local.

# BULGARIA

STATUS: Republic
AREA: 110,910 sq km (42,810 sq miles)
POPULATION: 9,011,000
ANNUAL NATURAL INCREASE: 0.2%
CAPITAL: Sofia (Sofiya)
LANGUAGE: Bulgarian, Turkish

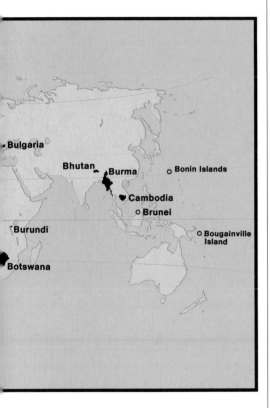

RELIGION: Eastern Orthodox majority, Muslim
CURRENCY: lev (BGL)
ORGANISATIONS: UN, OIEC

Bulgaria occupies the south-eastern portion of the Balkan peninsula and its landscape exhibits great variety, ranging from the fertile Danubian plain in the north and the mountainous central and southern parts with their high ranges, deep river gorges and extensive upland basins, to the Black Sea coastal region on the eastern fringe of the country. The climate is of the continental type with hot summers and cold winters. Bulgaria is not rich in natural resources but the Black Sea resorts contain much potential for development, as does the production and export of tobacco and wine. However, the communist regime has left the country with a disastrous ecological legacy. The political institutions of post-communist Bulgaria are still in a state of flux, and its society is undergoing a prolonged and painful crisis of transformation.

# BURKINA

STATUS: Republic
AREA: 274,122 sq km (105,811 sq miles)
POPULATION: 9,001,000
ANNUAL NATURAL INCREASE: 2.6%
CAPITAL: Ouagadougou
LANGUAGE: French, Moré (Mossi), Dyula
RELIGION: 60% animist, 30% Muslim,
10% Roman Catholic
CURRENCY: CFA franc, (W Africa) (XOF)
ORGANISATIONS: UN, ECOWAS, OAU

Situated on the southern edge of the Sahara, Burkina is a poor, landlocked country with thin soils supporting savannah grasslands. Frequent droughts, particularly in the north, seriously affect exports of cattle and cotton and the economy which is mainly subsistence agriculture. There is virtually no industry.

# BURMA

STATUS: Union of states and divisions
AREA: 678,030 sq km (261,720 sq miles)
POPULATION: 39,300,000
ANNUAL NATURAL INCREASE: 2.0%
CAPITAL: Rangoon (Yangon)
LANGUAGE: Burmese
RELIGION: 85% Buddhist. Animist, Muslim,
Hindu and Christian minorities
CURRENCY: kyat (BUK)
ORGANISATIONS: UN, Col. Plan

Much of Burma is covered by tropical rainforest divided by the central valley of the Irrawaddy, the Sittang and the Salween rivers. The western highlands are an extension of the Himalayas; hills to the east and south are a continuation of the Yunnan plateau of China. The economy is based on the export of the rice and forestry products. The irrigated central basin and the coastal region to the east of the Irrawaddy delta are the main rice-growing areas. Hardwoods, particularly teak, cover the highlands. There is potential for greater exploitation of tin, copper, oil and natural gas deposits. The small amount of industry concentrates on food processing.

# BURUNDI

STATUS: Republic
AREA: 27,835 sq km (10,745 sq miles)
POPULATION: 5,458,000
ANNUAL NATURAL INCREASE: 2.9%

CAPITAL: Bujumbura
LANGUAGE: French, Kirundi, Swahili
RELIGION: 60% Roman Catholic. Large animist
minority
CURRENCY: Burundi franc (BIF)
ORGANISATIONS: UN, OAU

This central African republic is one of the world's poorest nations. Manufacturing industry is almost non-existent and the population barely produce enough food for itself. Burundi is close to the equator but because of its altitude temperatures range between 17° and 23°C (63° and 74°F). The poverty has two basic causes — repeated droughts and slow recovery from tribal conflicts.

# CAMBODIA

STATUS: State
AREA: 181,000 sq km (69,865 sq miles)
POPULATION: 8,246,000
ANNUAL NATURAL INCREASE: 2.3%
CAPITAL: Phnom Penh
LANGUAGE: Khmer
RELIGION: Buddhist majority. Roman Catholic
and Muslim minorities
CURRENCY: riel (KHR)
ORGANISATIONS: UN, Col. Plan

Cambodia is a potentially rich country in S.E. Asia whose economy has been damaged since the 1970's by the aftermath of the Vietnam War. The central plain of the river Mekong covers over 70% of the country and provides ideal conditions for rice production and harvesting of fish. Over 50% of Cambodia is covered by monsoon rain forest.

# CAMEROON

STATUS: Republic
AREA: 475,500 sq km (183,545 sq miles)
POPULATION: 11,834,000
ANNUAL NATURAL INCREASE: 3.2%
CAPITAL: Yaoundé
LANGUAGE: English, French
RELIGION: 40% Christian, 39% traditional
beliefs, 21% Muslim
CURRENCY: CFA franc (C Africa) (XAF)
ORGANISATIONS: UN, OAU

Cameroon is situated on the coast of West Africa just north of the equator. Coastal lowlands rise to densely forested plateaux. Rainfall varies from over 1000 to only 50cm per year. The majority of the population are farmers with agricultural products accounting for over 80% of export revenue. Coffee and cocoa are the main cash crops. Mineral resources are underdeveloped but Cameroon already is one of Africa's major producers of bauxite, aluminium ore. Oil exploitation is playing an increasing role in the economy.

# CANADA

STATUS: Commonwealth Nation
AREA: 9,922,385 sq km (3,830,840 sq miles)
POPULATION: 26,800,000
ANNUAL NATURAL INCREASE: 1.0%
CAPITAL: Ottawa
LANGUAGE: English, French
RELIGION: 46% Roman Catholic, Protestant and Jewish minority
CURRENCY: Canadian dollar (CAD)
ORGANISATIONS: Comm, UN, Col. Plan, NATO, OECD, OAS, G7

## ALBERTA
STATUS: Province
AREA: 661,190 sq km (255,220 sq miles)
POPULATION: 2,468,000
CAPITAL: Edmonton

## BRITISH COLUMBIA
STATUS: Province
AREA: 948,595 sq km (366,160 sq miles)
POPULATION: 3,168,000
CAPITAL: Victoria

## MANITOBA
STATUS: Province
AREA: 650,090 sq km (250,935 sq miles)
POPULATION: 1,096,000
CAPITAL: Winnipeg

## NEW BRUNSWICK
STATUS: Province
AREA: 73,435 sq km (28,345 sq miles)
POPULATION: 723,000
CAPITAL: Fredericton

## NEWFOUNDLAND AND LABRADOR
STATUS: Province
AREA: 404,520 sq km (156,145 sq miles)
POPULATION: 573,000
CAPITAL: St. John's

## NORTHWEST TERRITORIES
STATUS: Territory
AREA: 3,379,685 sq km (1,304,560 sq miles)
POPULATION: 54,000
CAPITAL: Yellowknife

## NOVA SCOTIA
STATUS: Province
AREA: 55,490 sq km (21,420 sq miles)
POPULATION: 897,000
CAPITAL: Halifax

## ONTARIO
STATUS: Province
AREA: 1,068,630 sq km (412,490 sq miles)
POPULATION: 9,880,000
CAPITAL: Toronto

## PRINCE EDWARD ISLAND
STATUS: Province
AREA: 5,655 sq km (2,185 sq miles)
POPULATION: 132,000
CAPITAL: Charlottetown

## QUEBEC
STATUS: Province
AREA: 1,540,680 sq km (594,705 sq miles)
POPULATION: 6,779,000
CAPITAL: Quebec

## SASKATCHEWAN
STATUS: Province
AREA: 651,900 sq km (251,635 sq miles)
POPULATION: 1,005,000
CAPITAL: Regina

## YUKON TERRITORY
STATUS: Territory
AREA: 482,515 sq km (186,250 sq miles)
POPULATION: 27,000
CAPITAL: Whitehorse

Canada is the world's second largest country stretching from the great barren islands of the Arctic north to the vast grasslands of the central south, and from the Rocky Mountain chain of the west to the farmlands of the Great Lakes in the east. This huge area experiences great climatic differences but basically a continental climate prevails with extremes of heat and cold particularly in the central plains. The Arctic tundra of the far north provides summer grazing for caribou. Further south coniferous forests grow on the thin soils of the ancient shield landscape and on the extensive foothills of the Rocky Mountains. In contrast, the rich soils of the central prairies support grasslands and grain crops. The Great Lakes area provides fish, fruit, maize, root crops and dairy products; the prairies produce over 20% of the world's wheat; and the grasslands of Alberta support a thriving beef industry. Most minerals are mined and exploited in Canada with oil and natural gas, iron ore, bauxite, nickel, zinc, copper, gold and silver the major exports. The country's vast rivers provide huge amounts of hydro-electric power but most industry is confined to the Great Lakes and St Lawrence margins. The principal manufactured goods for export are steel products, motor vehicles, and paper for newsprint. Despite economic success, Canada still remains one of the world's most under-exploited countries so vast are the potential mineral resources and areas of land for agricultural development.

## CANARY ISLANDS
STATUS: Island Provinces of Spain
AREA: 7,275 sq km (2,810 sq miles)
POPULATION: 1,589,403
CAPITAL: Las Palmas (Gran Canaria) and Santa Cruz (Tenerife)

# CAPE VERDE

STATUS: Republic
AREA: 4,035 sq km (1,560 sq miles)
POPULATION: 370,000
ANNUAL NATURAL INCREASE: 2.5%
CAPITAL: Praia
LANGUAGE: Portuguese, Creole
RELIGION: 98% Roman Catholic
CURRENCY: Cape Verde escudo (CVE)
ORGANISATIONS: UN, ECOWAS, OAU

Independent since 1975, the ten inhabited volcanic islands of the republic are situated in the Atlantic 500km (310 miles) west of Senegal. Rainfall is low but irrigation encourages growth of sugar-cane, coconuts, fruit and maize. Fishing accounts for about 70% of export revenue. All consumer goods are imported and trading links continue to be maintained with Portugal.

## CAYMAN ISLANDS
STATUS: UK Dependent Territory
AREA: 259 sq km (100 sq miles)
POPULATION: 27,000
CAPITAL: George Town

# CENTRAL AFRICAN REPUBLIC

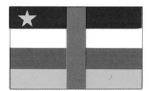

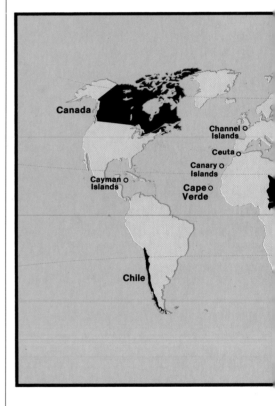

STATUS: Republic
AREA: 624,975 sq km (241,240 sq miles)
POPULATION: 3,039,000
ANNUAL NATURAL INCREASE: 2.7%
CAPITAL: Bangui
LANGUAGE: French, Sango (national)
RELIGION: Animist majority. 33% Christian. Muslim minority
CURRENCY: CFA franc (C Africa) (XAF)
ORGANISATIONS: UN, OAU

The republic is landlocked and remote from both east and west Africa. In size it rivals France, its former colonial power. It has a tropical climate with little variation in temperature. Savannah covers the rolling plateaux with rainforest in the south-east. To the north lies the Sahara Desert. Most farming is at subsistence level with a small amount of crops grown for export – cotton, coffee, timber and tobacco. Diamonds and uranium ore are the major mineral exports along with some small quantities of gold. Hardwood forests in the south-west provide timber for export.

## CEUTA
STATUS: Spanish External Province
AREA: 19.5 sq km (7.5 sq miles)
POPULATION: 68,970

## CHAD

STATUS: Republic
AREA: 1,284,000 sq km (495,625 sq miles)
POPULATION: 5,679,000
ANNUAL NATURAL INCREASE: 2.4%
CAPITAL: Ndjamena
LANGUAGE: French, Arabic, local languages

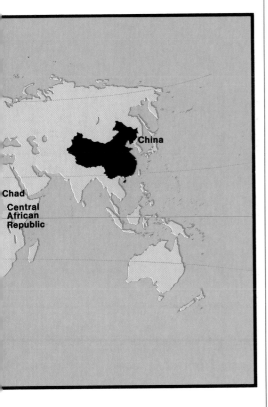

RELIGION: 50% Muslim, 45% animist,
5% Christian
CURRENCY: CFA franc (C Africa) (XAF)
ORGANISATIONS: UN, OAU

Chad, one of the world's poorest countries, is a vast state of central Africa stretching deep into the Sahara. The economy is based on agriculture but only the south, with 100 cm (39 in) of rainfall, can support crops for export – cotton, rice and groundnuts. Severe droughts, increasing desertification and border disputes have severely restricted development. Life expectancy at birth is still only 43 years. Salt is mined around Lake Chad where the majority of the population live.

## CHANNEL ISLANDS
STATUS: British Crown Dependency
AREA: 194 sq km (75 sq miles)
POPULATION: 138,668
CAPITAL: St Helier (Jersey),
St Peter Port (Guernsey)

# CHILE

STATUS: Republic
AREA: 751,625 sq km (290,125 sq miles)
POPULATION: 13,173,000
ANNUAL NATURAL INCREASE: 1.7%
CAPITAL: Santiago
LANGUAGE: Spanish
RELIGION: 85% Roman Catholic. Protestant
minority
CURRENCY: Chilean peso (CLP)
ORGANISATIONS: UN, OAS

Chile is a long thin country on the west coast of South America stretching throughout 38° degrees of latitude from the Atacama desert of the north to the ice deserts of Tierra del Fuego. Apart from a thin coastal strip of lowland, the country is dominated by the Andes mountains. The economy is based upon the abundance of mineral resources with copper (the world's largest reserve), iron ore, nitrates, coal, oil and gas all major exports. Most energy is provided by hydroelectric power. Light and heavy industries are based around Concepción and Santiago.

# CHINA

STATUS: People's Republic
AREA: 9,597,000 sq km (3,704,440 sq miles)
POPULATION: 1,088,870,000
ANNUAL NATURAL INCREASE: 1.3%
CAPITAL: Beijing (Peking)
LANGUAGE: Mandarin Chinese, regional
languages
RELIGION: Confucianist, Buddhist, Taoist. Small
Christian and Muslim minority
CURRENCY: Yuan Renminbi (CNY)
ORGANISATIONS: UN

## ANHUI (ANHWEI)
STATUS: Province
AREA: 139,900 sq km (54,000 sq miles)
POPULATION: 53,770,000
CAPITAL: Hefei

## BEIJING (PEKING)
STATUS: Municipality
AREA: 17,800 sq km (6,870 sq miles)
POPULATION: 10,819,407

## FUJIAN (FUKIEN)
STATUS: Province
AREA: 123,000 sq km (47,515 sq miles)
POPULATION: 28,450,000
CAPITAL: Fuzhou

## GANSU (KANSU)
STATUS: Province
AREA: 530,000 sq km (204,580 sq miles)
POPULATION: 21,360,000
CAPITAL: Lanzhou

## GUANGDONG
(KWANGTUNG)
STATUS: Province
AREA: 231,400 sq km (89,320 sq miles)
POPULATION: 59,280,000
CAPITAL: Guangzhou (Canton)

## GUANGXI-ZHUANG
(KWANGSI-CHUANG)
STATUS: Autonomous Region
AREA: 220,400 sq km (85,075 sq miles)
POPULATION: 40,880,000
CAPITAL: Nanning

## GUIZHOU (KWEICHOW)
STATUS: Province
AREA: 174,000 sq km (67,165 sq miles)
POPULATION: 31,270,000
CAPITAL: Guiyang

## HAINAN
STATUS: Province
AREA: 34,965 sq km (13,500 sq miles)
POPULATION: 6,280,000
CAPITAL: Haikou

## HEBEI (HOPEI)
STATUS: Province
AREA: 202,700 sq km (78,240 sq miles)
POPULATION: 57,950,000
CAPITAL: Shijiazhuang

## HEILONGJIANG
(HEILUNGKIANG)
STATUS: Province
AREA: 710,000 sq km (274,060 sq miles)
POPULATION: 34,660,000
CAPITAL: Harbin

## HENAN (HONAN)
STATUS: Province
AREA: 167,000 sq km (64,460 sq miles)
POPULATION: 80,940,000
CAPITAL: Zhengzhou

## HUBEI (HUPEH)
STATUS: Province
AREA: 187,500 sq km (72,375 sq miles)
POPULATION: 51,850,000
CAPITAL: Wuhan

## HUNAN (HUNAN)
STATUS: Province
AREA: 210,500 sq km (81,255 sq miles)
POPULATION: 58,900,000
CAPITAL: Changsha

## JIANGSU (KIANGSU)
STATUS: Province
AREA: 102,200 sq km (39,450 sq miles)
POPULATION: 64,380,000
CAPITAL: Nanjing (Nanking)

## JIANGXI (KIANGSI)
STATUS: Province
AREA: 164,800 sq km (63,615 sq miles)
POPULATION: 36,090,000
CAPITAL: Nanchang

## JILIN (KIRIN)
STATUS: Province
AREA: 290,000 sq km (111,940 sq miles)
POPULATION: 23,730,000
CAPITAL: Changchun

## LIAONING
STATUS: Province
AREA: 230,000 sq km (88,780 sq miles)
POPULATION: 38,200,000
CAPITAL: Shenyang

## NEI MONGOL (INNER MONGOLIA)
STATUS: Autonomous Region
AREA: 450,000 sq km (173,700 sq miles)
POPULATION: 20,940,000
CAPITAL: Hohhot

## NINGXIA HUI (NINGHSIA HUI)
STATUS: Autonomous Region
AREA: 170,000 sq km (65,620 sq miles)
POPULATION: 4,450,000
CAPITAL: Yinchuan

## QINGHAI (CHINGHAI)
STATUS: Province
AREA: 721,000 sq km (278,305 sq miles)
POPULATION: 4,340,000
CAPITAL: Xining

## SHAANXI (SHENSI)
STATUS: Province
AREA: 195,800 sq km (75,580 sq miles)
POPULATION: 31,350,000
CAPITAL: Xian

## SHANDONG (SHANTUNG)
STATUS: Province
AREA: 153,300 sq km (59,175 sq miles)
POPULATION: 80,610,000
CAPITAL: Jinan

## SHANGHAI
STATUS: Municipality
AREA: 5,800 sq km (2,240 sq miles)
POPULATION: 13,341,896

## SHANXI (SHANSI)
STATUS: Province
AREA: 157,100 sq km (60,640 sq miles)
POPULATION: 27,550,000
CAPITAL: Taiyuan

## SICHUAN (SZECHWAN)
STATUS: Province
AREA: 569,000 sq km (219,635 sq miles)
POPULATION: 105,760,000
CAPITAL: Chengdu

## TIANJIN (TIENTSIN)
STATUS: Municipality
AREA: 4,000 sq km (1,545 sq miles)
POPULATION: 8,785,402

## XINJIANG UYGUR (SINKIANG UIGHUR)
STATUS: Autonomous Region
AREA: 1,646,800 sq km (635,665 sq miles)
POPULATION: 14,260,000
CAPITAL: Urumqi

## XIZANG (TIBET)
STATUS: Autonomous Region
AREA: 1,221,600 sq km (471,540 sq miles)
POPULATION: 2,120,000
CAPITAL: Lhasa

## YUNNAN (YUNNAN)
STATUS: Province
AREA: 436,200 sq km (168,375 sq miles)
POPULATION: 35,940,000
CAPITAL: Kunming

## ZHEJIANG (CHEKIANG)
STATUS: Province
AREA: 101,800 sq km (39,295 sq miles)
POPULATION: 41,700,000
CAPITAL: Hangzhou

With population over one billion and vast mineral and agricultural resources China has made a tremendous effort during the late 1970's and 80's to erase the negative economic effects of the collectivisation policy implemented from 1955, and the cultural revolution of the late 1960's.

The land of China is one of the most diverse on Earth. The majority of the people live in the east where the economy is dictated by the great drainage basins of the Huang He and the Chang Jiang (Yangtze). Here, intensive irrigated agriculture produces one third of the world's rice as well as wheat, maize, sugar, soya beans and oil seeds. Pigs are reared and fish caught throughout China. The country is basically self-sufficient in cereals, livestock and fish.

Western and northern China are far less densely populated areas as cultivation is restricted to oases and sheltered valleys. In the south-west, the Tibetan plateau averages 4,900 m (16,000 ft) and supports scattered sheep herding. To the north are Sinkiang and the desert basins of Tarim and Dzungaria, and bordering Mongolia the vast dry Gobi desert. In the far north only in Manchuria does the rainfall allow extensive arable cultivation, mainly wheat, barley and maize.

The natural mineral resources of China are immense, varied and under-exploited. The Yunnan Plateau of the south-east is rich in tin, copper, and zinc; Manchuria possesses coal and iron ore; and oil is extracted from beneath the Yellow Sea. The main industrial centres are situated close to the natural resources and concentrate on the production of iron, steel, cement, light engineering and textile manufacturing. The economy is being built on this industrial base, with stable and adequate food production and increasing trade with the United States, Western Europe and Japan.

## CHRISTMAS ISLAND
STATUS: External Territory of Australia
AREA: 135 sq km (52 sq miles)
POPULATION: 2,000

## COCOS (KEELING) ISLANDS
STATUS: External Territory of Australia
AREA: 14 sq km (5 sq miles)
POPULATION: 616

# COLOMBIA

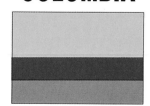

STATUS: Republic
AREA: 1,138,915 sq km (439,620 sq miles)
POPULATION: 32,987,000

ANNUAL NATURAL INCREASE: 2.1%
CAPITAL: Bogotá
LANGUAGE: Spanish, Indian languages
RELIGION: 95% Roman Catholic. Small Protestant and Jewish minorities
CURRENCY: Colombian peso (COP)
ORGANISATIONS: UN, OAS

Colombia is bounded in the north by the Caribbean Sea and in the west by the Pacific Ocean. The Andes chain runs from north to south through the country. The eastern part of the country consists of the headwaters of the Amazon and Orinoco basins. Two-thirds of Colombia is covered by tropical rainforest. The fertile river valleys in the uplands produce most of the famous Colombian coffee. Bananas, tobacco, cotton, sugar and rice are grown at lower altitudes. Coffee has always been the major export crop, but manufacturing industry and mining of coal, iron ore, copper and precious stones are becoming more dominant in the economy. Immense illegal quantities of cocaine are exported to the US and elsewhere.

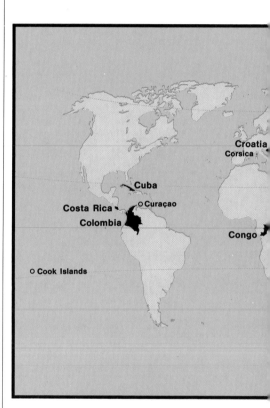

# COMOROS

STATUS: Federal Republic
AREA: 1,860 sq km (718 sq miles)
POPULATION: 551,000
ANNUAL NATURAL INCREASE: 3.7%
CAPITAL: Moroni
LANGUAGE: French, Arabic, Comoran
RELIGION: large Muslim majority. Christian minority
CURRENCY: Comoro franc (KMF)
ORGANISATIONS: UN, OAU

The Comoro Islands, comprising Moheli, Grand Comore, and Anjouan, are situated between Madagascar and the east African coast. In 1974, the island of Mayotte voted in referenda

to remain a French dependency. A cool, dry season alternates with hot, humid monsoon weather between November and April, and annual rainfall ranges from 100–114cm(40–45in). Mangoes, coconuts and bananas are grown around the coastal lowlands. The island's economy is based on the export of coffee, vanilla, copra, sisal, cacao and cloves. Timber and timber products are important to local development. There is no manufacturing.

---

# CONGO

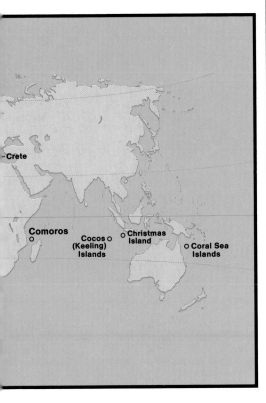

STATUS: People's Republic
AREA: 342,000 sq km (132,010 sq miles)
POPULATION: 2,271,000
ANNUAL NATURAL INCREASE: 3.4%
CAPITAL: Brazzaville
LANGUAGE: French, Kongo, Teke, Sanga
RELIGION: 50% traditional beliefs, 30% Roman Catholic. Small Protestant and Muslim minority
CURRENCY: CFA franc (C Africa) (XAF)
ORGANISATIONS: UN, OAU

The Congo, Africa's first communist state still has strong economic ties with the west, especially France, its former colonial ruler. Situated on the coast of West Africa, it contains over two-thirds swamp and forest, with wooded savannah on the highlands of the Batéké plateau near the Gabon border. Its climate is hot and humid with average rainfall of 122-128cm (48-50in). Over 60% of the population are employed in subsistence farming, the main crops being plantains, maize and cassava, while coffee, groundnuts and cocoa are all exported. Timber and timber products account for 60% of

all Congo's exports. Its mineral resources are considerable including industrial diamonds, gold, lead, zinc and extensive coastal oilfields. Manufacturing industry is concentrated in the major towns and is primarily food processing and textiles.

---

## COOK ISLANDS
STATUS: Self-governing Overseas Territory in free association with New Zealand
AREA: 233 sq km (90 sq miles)
POPULATION: 19,000
CAPITAL: Avarua

---

## CORAL SEA ISLANDS
STATUS: External Territory of Australia
AREA: 22 sq km (8.5 sq miles)
POPULATION: No permanent population

---

## CORSICA
STATUS: Island Region of France
AREA: 8,680 sq km (3,350 sq miles)
POPULATION: 246,000
CAPITAL: Ajaccio

---

# COSTA RICA

STATUS: Republic
AREA: 50,900 sq km (19,650 sq miles)
POPULATION: 2,994,000
ANNUAL NATURAL INCREASE: 2.3%
CAPITAL: San Jose
LANGUAGE: Spanish
RELIGION: 95% Roman Catholic
CURRENCY: Costa Rican colón (CRC)
ORGANISATIONS: UN, CACM, OAS

Costa Rica is a narrow country, situated between Nicaragua and Panama, with both a Pacific and a Caribbean coastline. The mountain chains that run the length of the country form the fertile uplands where coffee (one of the main crops and exports) and cattle flourish. Bananas are grown on the Pacific coast. Although gold, silver, iron ore and bauxite are mined, the principal industries are food processing and manufacture of textiles and chemicals, fertilizers and furniture.

---

## CRETE
STATUS: Island Region of Greece
AREA: 8,330 sq km (3,215 sq miles)
POPULATION: 501,082
CAPITAL: Iráklion

---

# CROATIA

STATUS: Republic
AREA: 56,540 sq km (21,825 sq miles)
POPULATION: 4,726,000
CAPITAL: Zagreb
LANGUAGE: Croat
RELIGION: Roman Catholic majority
CURRENCY: Croatian dinar

Croatia is an oddly-shaped country, which runs in a narrow strip along the Adriatic coast and extends inland in a broad curve. The fertile plains of central and eastern Croatia are intensively farmed and provide the country with surplus crops, meat and dairy products. The mountainous and barren littoral has been developed for tourism. Croatia used to be the most highly developed part of Yugoslavia, concentrating on electrical engineering, metalworking and machine-building, chemicals and rubber. All of this could mean future prosperity but the disruption of Croatia's trade with other parts of Yugoslavia and with the former Eastern Bloc has severely harmed the economy. The military conflict over the right to secession and for control of Serbian areas of settlement has caused further damage, with tourism all but collapsing in 1991.

---

# CUBA

STATUS: Republic
AREA: 114,525 sq km (44,205 sq miles)
POPULATION: 10,617,000
ANNUAL NATURAL INCREASE: 0.9%
CAPITAL: Havana (Habana)
LANGUAGE: Spanish
RELIGION: Roman Catholic majority
CURRENCY: Cuban peso (CUP)
ORGANISATIONS: UN, OIEC

Cuba, consisting of one large island and over fifteen hundred small ones, dominates the entrance to the Gulf of Mexico. It is a mixture of fertile plains, mountain ranges and gentle countryside with temperatures ranging from 22°-28°C (72°–82°F) and an average annual rainfall of 120cm (47in). Being the only communist state in the Americas, most of Cuba's trade relations are with the former USSR and Comecon countries. Sugar, tobacco and nickel are the main exports and the mining of manganese, chrome, copper and oil is expanding. Cuba has enough cattle and coffee for domestic use but many other food products are imported.

---

## CURAÇAO
STATUS: Self-governing Island of Netherlands Antilles
AREA: 444 sq km (171 sq miles)
POPULATION: 146,096
CAPITAL: Willemstad

# CYPRUS

STATUS: Republic
AREA: 9,250 sq km (3,570 sq miles)
POPULATION: 707,000
ANNUAL NATURAL INCREASE: 1.1%
CAPITAL: Nicosia
LANGUAGE: Greek, Turkish, English
RELIGION: Greek Orthodox majority, Muslim minority
CURRENCY: Cyprus pound (CYP), Turkish Lira (TL)
ORGANISATIONS: Comm, UN, Council of Europe

Cyprus is a prosperous Mediterranean island. The summers are very hot (38°C, 100°F) and dry, and the winters warm and wet. About two-thirds of the island is under cultivation and produces citrus fruit, potatoes, barley, wheat and olives. Sheep, goats and pigs are the principal livestock. The main exports are minerals (including copper and asbestos), fruit, wine and vegetables. Tourism is also an important source of foreign exchange, despite Turkish occupation of the north. Most industry consists of local manufacturing.

# CZECHOSLOVAKIA

STATUS: Federal Republic
AREA: 127,870 sq km (49,360 sq miles)
POPULATION: 15,678,000
ANNUAL NATURAL INCREASE: 0.3%
CAPITAL: Prague (Praha)
LANGUAGE: Czech, Slovak
RELIGION: 70% Roman Catholic, 8% Protestant
CURRENCY: koruna (CSK)
ORGANISATIONS: UN, OIEC, Council of Europe

At the heart of central Europe, Czechoslovakia is fringed by forested uplands in the west and the Carpathians to the east. Winters are cold and wet, while summers are hot and humid with frequent thundery showers. In spite of limited raw materials, Czechoslovakia has long been one of the more advanced European economies, a position which it managed to retain through the communist period. The country boasts a very productive and efficient agricultural sector as well as a comparatively healthy industrial base. Engineering is the largest branch of production, and Czechoslovakia used to be the most important supplier of machinery to the Eastern Bloc. It is also a significant exporter of armaments and explosives, but with the end of the Cold War and the collapse of communism, the country is now facing severe problems of adaptation. Moreover, the mounting tension between Czechs and Slovaks has been threatening to lead to a break-up of the country into two separate states.

# DENMARK

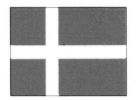

STATUS: Kingdom
AREA: 43,075 sq km (16,625 sq miles)
POPULATION: 5,140,000
ANNUAL NATURAL INCREASE: 0.0%
CAPITAL: Copenhagen (København)
LANGUAGE: Danish
RELIGION: 94% Lutheran. Roman Catholic minority
CURRENCY: Danish krone (DKK)
ORGANISATIONS: UN, Council of Europe, NATO, OECD, EC

Denmark, the smallest of the Scandinavian countries, acts as a bridge between Germany and Scandinavia. It consists of the Jutland Peninsula and over 400 islands of which only about one quarter are inhabited. The low-lying landscape was scarred by retreating glaciers leaving distinctive 'moraines' (accumulations of earth and stones carried by glaciers). The climate is mild, especially in the North Sea area, with rainfall all year round, mostly in the summer and autumn. Meat and dairy products – beef, butter, cheese, eggs, bacon and pork are exported but not in such great quantities as in the past. An extensive fishing industry is centred on the shallow lagoons which have formed along the indented western coastline. Recently the fishing industry has had problems with over-fishing and disputes over quotas. Over 30% of the total workforce are involved in industry, with manufactured goods being the main export. Denmark has few mineral resources.

# DJIBOUTI

STATUS: Republic
AREA: 23,000 sq km (8,800 sq miles)
POPULATION: 409,000
ANNUAL NATURAL INCREASE: 3.5%
CAPITAL: Djibouti
LANGUAGE: French, Somali, Dankali, Arabic
RELIGION: mainly Muslim. Roman Catholic minority
CURRENCY: Djibouti franc (DJF)
ORGANISATIONS: UN, Arab League, OAU

The former French colony of Djibouti, strategically situated at the mouth of the Red Sea, acts as a trade outlet for Ethiopia, as well as serving Red Sea shipping. Its climate is extremely hot and arid – average annual temperatures are 30°C(86°F) and the annual rainfall on the coast is as low as 38cm(15in), and there is consequently very little cultivation. Cattle, hides and skins are the main exports. The port of Djibouti is an important transit point for Red Sea trade.

# DOMINICA

STATUS: Commonwealth State
AREA: 751 sq km (290 sq miles)
POPULATION: 81,200
ANNUAL NATURAL INCREASE: 1.4%
CAPITAL: Roseau
LANGUAGE: English, French patois
RELIGION: 80% Roman Catholic
CURRENCY: East Caribbean dollar (XCD)
ORGANISATIONS: Comm, UN, CARICOM, OAS

Dominica is located in the Windward Islands of the east Caribbean between Martinique and Guadeloupe. Tropical rainforest covers the island which obtains foreign revenue from sugar cane, bananas, coconuts, soap, vegetables and citrus fruits. Tourism is the most rapidly expanding industry.

# DOMINICAN REPUBLIC

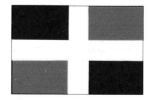

STATUS: Republic
AREA: 48,440 sq km (18,700 sq miles)
POPULATION: 7,170,000
ANNUAL NATURAL INCREASE: 2.3%
CAPITAL: Santo Domingo
LANGUAGE: Spanish
RELIGION: 90% Roman Catholic. Small Protestant and Jewish minority
CURRENCY: Dominican peso (DOP)
ORGANISATIONS: UN, OAS

The Caribbean island of Hispaniola is divided between Haiti and the Dominican Republic. The landscape is dominated by a series of mountain ranges, thickly covered with rain forest, reaching up to 3000m(9840ft). To the south there is a coastal plain where the capital, Santo Domingo, lies. The annual rainfall exceeds 100cm(40in). Agriculture forms the backbone of the economy – sugar, coffee, cocoa and tobacco are the staple crops. Minerals include bauxite, nickel, gold and silver.

# ECUADOR

STATUS: Republic
AREA: 461,475 sq km (178,130 sq miles)
POPULATION: 10,782,000

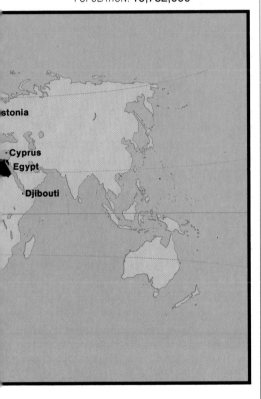

ANNUAL NATURAL INCREASE: 2.7%
CAPITAL: Quito
LANGUAGE: Spanish, Quechua, other Indian languages
RELIGION: 90% Roman Catholic
CURRENCY: sucre (ECS)
ORGANISATIONS: UN, OAS, OPEC

Ecuador falls into two distinctive geographical zones, the coastal lowlands which border the Pacific Ocean and inland, the Andean highlands. The highlands stretch about 400 km (250 miles) north–south, and here limited quantities of maize, wheat and barley are cultivated. Ecuador's main agricultural exports – bananas, coffee and cocoa, are all grown on the fertile coastal lowlands. The rapidly growing fishing industry, especially shrimps, is becoming more important. Large resources of crude oil have been found in the thickly-forested lowlands on the eastern border. Ecuador is now South America's second largest oil producer after Venezuela. Mineral reserves include silver, gold, copper and zinc.

# EGYPT

STATUS: Republic
AREA: 1,000,250 sq km (386,095 sq miles)
POPULATION: 53,153,000
ANNUAL NATURAL INCREASE: 2.6%
CAPITAL: Cairo (El Qâhira)
LANGUAGE: Arabic, Berber, Nubian, English, French
RELIGION: 80% Muslim (mainly Sunni), Coptic Christian minority
CURRENCY: Egyptian pound (EGP)
ORGANISATIONS: UN, Arab League, OAU

The focal point of Egypt, situated on the Mediterranean coast of north-east Africa, is the fertile, irrigated Nile Valley, sandwiched between two deserts. Egypt is virtually dependent on the River Nile for water as average rainfall varies between only 20cm (8 in) in the north and zero in the deserts. Cotton and Egyptian clover are the two most important crops, with increasing cultivation of cereals, fruits, rice, sugar cane and vegetables. Agriculture is concentrated around the Nile flood plain and delta. In spite of this, however, Egypt has to import over half the food it needs. Buffalo, cattle, sheep, goats and camels are the principal livestock. Tourism is an important source of revenue together with tolls from the Suez Canal. Major manufactures include cement, cotton goods, iron and steel, and processed foods. The main mineral deposits are phosphates, iron ore, salt, manganese and chromium.

# EL SALVADOR

STATUS: Republic
AREA: 21,395 sq km (8,260 sq miles)
POPULATION: 5,252,000
ANNUAL NATURAL INCREASE: 1.4%
CAPITAL: San Salvador
LANGUAGE: Spanish
RELIGION: 80% Roman Catholic
CURRENCY: El Salvador colón (SVC)
ORGANISATIONS: UN, CACM, OAS

Independent from Spain since 1821, El Salvador is a small, densely populated country on the Pacific coast of Central America. Most of the population live around the lakes in the central plain. Temperatures range from 24° to 26°C (75°–79°F) with an average, annual rainfall of 178cm (70 in). Coffee and cotton are important exports and the country is the main producer of balsam. Industry has expanded considerably with the production of textiles, shoes, cosmetics, cement, processed foods, chemicals and furniture. Mineral resources are negligible.

# EQUATORIAL GUINEA

STATUS: Republic
AREA: 28,050 sq km (10,825 sq miles)
POPULATION: 348,000
ANNUAL NATURAL INCREASE: 5.1%
CAPITAL: Malabo
LANGUAGE: Spanish, Fang, Bubi, other tribal languages
RELIGION: 96% Roman Catholic. 4% animist
CURRENCY: CFA franc (C Africa) (XAF)
ORGANISATIONS: UN, OAU

Independent from Spain since 1968, Equatorial Guinea is made up of two separate provinces – mainland Mbini with hot, wet climate and dense rain forest but little economic development, and the volcanic island of Bioko. Agriculture is the principal source of revenue. Cocoa and coffee from the island plantations are the main exports with wood products, fish and processed foods manufactured near the coast in Mbini.

# ESTONIA

STATUS: Republic
AREA: 45,100 sq km (17,413 sq miles)
POPULATION: 1,600,000
CAPITAL: Tallinn
LANGUAGE: Estonian, Russian
RELIGION: Lutheran, Roman Catholic and Orthodox minorities
CURRENCY: rouble, kroon (1992)
ORGANISATIONS: UN

With the mainland situated on the southern coast of the Gulf of Finland and encompassing a large number of islands, Estonia is the smallest and most northerly of the Baltic States. The generally flat or undulating landscape is characterised by extensive forests and many lakes. The country's mean altitude is only 49 m (160 ft) above sea level and nowhere exceeds 305 m (1000 ft). The climate is temperate. Estonia is poor in natural resources, the only deposits of importance being oil shale and phosphorite. The land is difficult to farm and agriculture, mainly livestock production, accounts for less than 20% of the gross national product. Industries include engineering and metalworking. Timber production, woodworking and textiles are also important. The economy is currently undergoing a profound transformation from central planning and state-ownership to a free market system based on private enterprise. Incorporated into the Soviet Union in 1940 Estonia, after a protracted struggle, was able to regain its independence in 1991.

# ETHIOPIA

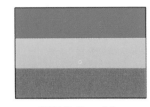

STATUS: Republic
AREA: 1,023,050 sq km (394,895 sq miles)
POPULATION: 50,774,000
ANNUAL NATURAL INCREASE: 2.9%
CAPITAL: Addis Ababa (Adis Abeba)
LANGUAGE: Amharic, English, Arabic
RELIGION: Ethiopian Orthodox, Muslim and animist
CURRENCY: birr (ETB)
ORGANISATIONS: UN, OAU

Situated on the Red Sea coast, the landscape of Ethiopia consists of heavily dissected plateaux and plains of arid desert. Rainfall in these latter areas is minimal and unreliable. Drought and starvation are an ever-present problem. Farming, in the high rural areas, accounts for 90% of export revenue with coffee as the principal crop and main export together with fruit and vegetables, oil-seeds, hides and skins. Gold and salt are mined on a small scale. The most important industries are cotton textiles, cement, canned foods, construction materials and leather goods. These are concentrated around the capital, and Asmara in the north. Difficulty of communication has hindered development. In recent years the economy has been devastated by droughts and civil wars.

## FAEROES
STATUS: Self-governing Island Region of Denmark
AREA: 1,399 sq km (540 sq miles)
POPULATION: 47,663
CAPITAL: Tórshavn

## FALKLAND ISLANDS
STATUS: UK Crown Colony
AREA: 12,175 sq km (4,700 sq miles)
POPULATION: 2,000
CAPITAL: (Port) Stanley

# FIJI

STATUS: Republic
AREA: 18,330 sq km (7,075 sq miles)
POPULATION: 765,000
ANNUAL NATURAL INCREASE: 1.8%
CAPITAL: Suva
LANGUAGE: Fijian, English, Hindi
RELIGION: 51% Methodist Christian, 40% Hindu, 8% Muslim
CURRENCY: Fiji dollar (FJD)
ORGANISATIONS: UN, Col. Plan

A country of some 320 tropical islands, of which over 100 are inhabited, the Republic of Fiji is located in the south central Pacific Ocean. Fiji's economy is geared to production of sugar-cane, coconut oil, bananas and rice. Main industries are sugar processing, gold-mining, copra processing and fish canning. Important livestock are cattle, goats, pigs and poultry.

# FINLAND

STATUS: Republic
AREA: 337,030 sq km (130,095 sq miles)
POPULATION: 4,986,000
ANNUAL NATURAL INCREASE: 0.4%
CAPITAL: Helsinki
LANGUAGE: Finnish, Swedish
RELIGION: 90% Evangelical Lutheran. Eastern Orthodox minority
CURRENCY: markka (Finnmark) (FIM)
ORGANISATIONS: UN, EFTA, OECD, Council of Europe

Finland is a flat land of lakes and forests. The soils are thin and poor on the ice-scarred granite plateau, but 80% of the country supports coniferous forest. Timber and timber products and dairy goods make up most of Finnish exports. Because of the harsh northern climate most of the population live in towns in the far south. Manufacturing industry has been developing rapidly in recent years.

# FRANCE

STATUS: Republic
AREA: 543,965 sq km (209,970 sq miles)
POPULATION: 56,556,000
ANNUAL NATURAL INCREASE: 0.4%
CAPITAL: Paris
LANGUAGE: French
RELIGION: 90% Roman Catholic. Protestant, Muslim and Jewish minorities
CURRENCY: French franc (FRF)
ORGANISATIONS: UN, Council of Europe, EC, OECD, WEU, NATO, G7

France encompasses a great variety of landscapes, a series of high plateaux, mountain ranges and lowland basins. The Pyrenees form the border with Spain in the south-west, and the Jura mountains form a border with Switzerland. The highest mountain range is the Alps, south of the Jura.

The highest plateau is the Massif Central which rises to 1886m(6188ft). The Vosges plateau borders the plain of Alsace, and the third major plateau, Armorica, occupies the Brittany peninsula.

The French climate is moderated by proximity to the Atlantic, and is generally mild. The south has a Mediterranean climate with hot dry summers, the rest of the country has rain all year round. Much of the French countryside is agricultural. France is self-sufficient in cereals, dairy products, meat, fruit and vegetables, and a leading exporter of wheat, barley and sugar-beet. Wine is also a major export. France has reserves of coal, oil and natural gas, and is one of the world's leading producers of iron ore. It has large steel-making and chemical refining industries. Its vehicle, aeronautical and armaments industries are among the world's most

important. Leading light industries are fashion, perfumes and luxury goods. Most of its heavy industry is concentrated in the major industrial zone of the north-east.

## FRANZ JOSEF LAND
STATUS: Islands of Russia
AREA: 16,575 sq km (6,400 sq miles)
POPULATION: No reliable figure available

## FRENCH GUIANA
STATUS: Overseas Department of France
AREA: 91,000 sq km (35,125 sq miles)
POPULATION: 93,540
CAPITAL: Cayenne

## FRENCH POLYNESIA
STATUS: Overseas Territory of France
AREA: 3,940 sq km (1,520 sq miles)
POPULATION: 188,814
CAPITAL: Papeete

## FRENCH SOUTHERN AND ANTARCTIC TERRITORIES
STATUS: Overseas Territory of France
AREA: 439,580 sq km (169,680 sq miles)
POPULATION: 180

# GABON

STATUS: Republic
AREA: 267,665 sq km (103,320 sq miles)
POPULATION: 1,172,000
ANNUAL NATURAL INCREASE: 3.7%
CAPITAL: Libreville
LANGUAGE: French, Bantu dialects, Fang
RELIGION: 60% Roman Catholic
CURRENCY: CFA franc (C Africa) (XAF)

Gabon, which lies on the equator, consists of the Ogooúe river basin covered with tropical rain forest. It is hot and wet all year with average annual temperatures of 25°C(77°F). It is one of the most prosperous states in Africa with valuable timber and mineral resources.

## GALAPAGOS ISLANDS

STATUS: Archipelago Province of Ecuador
AREA: 7,845 sq km (3,030 sq miles)
POPULATION: 7,954

# GAMBIA, THE

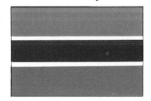

STATUS: Republic

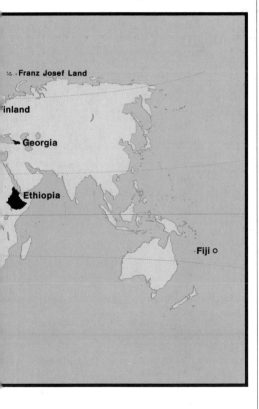

AREA: 10,690 sq km (4,125 sq miles)
POPULATION: 861,000
ANNUAL NATURAL INCREASE: 3.3%
CAPITAL: Banjul
LANGUAGE: English, Madinka, Fula, Wolof
RELIGION: 85% Muslim. Christian and
animist minorities
CURRENCY: dalasi (GMD)
ORGANISATIONS: Comm, UN, ECOWAS, OAU

The Gambia is the smallest country in Africa and, apart from its Atlantic coastline, is entirely surrounded by Senegal. It is 470km(292 miles) long, averages 24km(15 miles) wide and is divided by the Gambia river. The climate has two distinctive seasons. November to May is dry but July to October sees monsoon rainfall up to 130cm(51in). The temperatures average about 23°–27°C(73°–81°F) throughout the year. Groundnuts and subsidiary products are the mainstay of the economy but tourism is developing rapidly. The production of cotton, livestock, fish and rice is increasing to change the present economic reliance on groundnuts.

# GEORGIA

STATUS: Republic
AREA: 69,700 sq km (26,905 sq miles)
POPULATION: 5,400,000
CAPITAL: Tbilisi
LANGUAGE: Georgian, Armenian, Russian
RELIGION: Orthodox Christian
CURRENCY: rouble

Georgia, situated south of the Caucasus, is a mountainous country with forests covering one-third of its area. The climate ranges from sub-tropical on the shores of the Black Sea, to perpetual ice and snow on the Caucasian crests. Rich deposits of coal, petroleum and manganese, and considerable water-power resources, have led to industrialisation successfully concentrated on metallurgy and machine-building. With the exception of the fertile plain of Kolkhida, agricultural land is in short supply and difficult to work. This is partly compensated by the cultivation of labour-intensive and profitable crops such as tea, grapes, tobacco and citrus fruit. The question of regional autonomy for the Abkhaz, Adzhar and South Ossetian minorities has repeatedly led to violent ethnic conflict in recent years. The break-up of the Soviet Union brought independence for Georgia in 1991.

# GERMANY

STATUS: Federal Republic
AREA: 356,840 sq km (137,740 sq miles)
POPULATION: 78,500,000
ANNUAL NATURAL INCREASE: 0.2%
CAPITAL: Berlin
SEAT OF GOVERNMENT: Bonn, moving to Berlin
LANGUAGE: German
RELIGION: 45% Protestant (mostly Lutheran),
40% Roman Catholic
CURRENCY: Deutsch Mark (DEM)
ORGANISATIONS: UN, EC, NATO, OECD, WEU,
Council of Europe, G7

Geographically, Germany divides into three main areas: the Northern plain, stretching from the rivers Oder and Neisse in the east to the Dutch border; the central uplands with elevated plateaus intersected by river valleys and relieved by isolated mountains, gradually getting higher towards the south and rising to peaks of up to nearly 1500 m (5000 ft) in the Black Forest: finally the Bavarian Alps straddling the Austrian border. With the exception of the Danube, all German river systems run north and issue into the North or the Baltic Seas. The climate in Germany is predominantly continental with cold, wet winters and moderately warm summers. Only in the northwestern corner of the country does the weather become more oceanic in character. Germany as a whole has large stretches of very fertile farmland.

Politically, the division of Germany, a product of the post-1945 Cold War between the victorious Allies against Hitler, was rapidly overcome after the collapse of communism in Eastern Europe, and the unification of the two German states was effected in 1990. Economically, the legacy of 40 years of socialist rule in the East ensures that, in terms of both structure and performance, Germany will encompass two vastly different halves for a long time to come. Having lost its captive markets in what used to be the Soviet Bloc, the eastern economy then all but collapsed under the weight of superior western competition. The task of reconstruction is proving more difficult, more protracted and, most of all, more costly than expected. In the West, the Ruhr basin, historically the industrial heartland of Germany, with its emphasis on coal mining and iron and steel works, has long since been overtaken by more advanced industries elsewhere, notably in the Rhine-Maine area and further south in the regions around Stuttgart and Munich. The rapidly expanding services sector apart, the German economy is now dominated by the chemical, pharmaceutical, mechanical engineering, motor and high-tech industries. To lessen the country's dependence on oil imports, an ambitious nuclear energy programme has been adopted. Although poor in minerals and other raw materials with the exception of lignite and potash, Germany has managed to become one of the world's leading manufacturers and exporters of vehicles, machine tools, electrical and electronic products and of consumer goods of various description, in particular textiles. But the massive balance of trade surplus West Germany used to enjoy has now disappeared due to the sucking in of imports by, and the redistribution of output to, the newly acquired territories in the East.

# GHANA

STATUS: Republic
AREA: 238,305 sq km (91,985 sq miles)
POPULATION: 15,028,000
ANNUAL NATURAL INCREASE: 3.4%
CAPITAL: Accra
LANGUAGE: English, tribal languages
RELIGION: 42% Christian
CURRENCY: cedi (GHC)
ORGANISATIONS: Comm, UN, ECOWAS, OAU

Ghana, the West African state once known as the Gold Coast, gained independence from Britain in 1957. The landscape varies from tropical rain forest to dry scrubland, with the annual rainfall ranging from over 200cm(79in) to less than 100cm(40in). The temperature averages 27°C(81°F) all year. Cocoa is the principal crop and chief export but although most Ghanaians farm, there is also a thriving industrial base around Tema,where local bauxite is smelted into aluminium, the largest artificial harbour in Africa. Other exports include gold and diamonds and principal imports are fuel and manufactured goods.

## GIBRALTAR

STATUS: UK Crown Colony
AREA: 6.5 sq km (2.5 sq miles)
POPULATION: 30,689

# GREECE

STATUS: Republic
AREA: 131,985 sq km (50,945 sq miles)
POPULATION: 10,269,074
ANNUAL NATURAL INCREASE: 0.4%
CAPITAL: Athens (Athínai)
LANGUAGE: Greek
RELIGION: 97% Greek Orthodox
CURRENCY: drachma (GRD)
ORGANISATIONS: UN, Council of Europe, EC, NATO, OECD

Mainland Greece and the many islands are dominated by mountains and sea. The climate is predominantly Mediterranean with hot, dry summers and mild winters. Poor irrigation and drainage mean that much of the agriculture is localised but the main crop, olives, is exported and agricultural output generally is increasing. The surrounding seas are important, providing two-thirds of Greece's fish and supporting an active merchant fleet. Athens is the manufacturing base and at least one-quarter of the population live there. Greece is a very popular tourist destination which helps the craft industries in textiles, metals and ceramics and other local products.

## GREENLAND

STATUS: Self-governing Island Region of Denmark
AREA: 2,175,600 sq km (839,780 sq miles)
POPULATION: 55,558
CAPITAL: Godthåb (Nuuk)

# GRENADA

STATUS: Commonwealth State
AREA: 345 sq km (133 sq miles)
POPULATION: 99,205
ANNUAL NATURAL INCREASE: 0.8%
CAPITAL: St George's
LANGUAGE: English, French patois
RELIGION: Roman Catholic majority
CURRENCY: E. Caribbean dollar (XCD)
ORGANISATIONS: Comm, UN, CARICOM, OAS

The Caribbean island of Grenada is the southernmost of the Windward Islands. It is mountainous and thickly forested, with a settled warm climate (average temperature of 27°C or 81°F), which ensures that its tourist industry continues to expand. Bananas are the main export, although the island is also famous for its spices, especially nutmeg and cloves. Cocoa is also exported.

## GUADELOUPE

STATUS: Overseas Department of France
AREA: 1,780 sq km (687 sq miles)
POPULATION: 344,000
CAPITAL: Basse-Terre

## GUAM

STATUS: Unincorporated Territory of USA
AREA: 450 sq km (174 sq miles)
POPULATION: 132,726
CAPITAL: Agaña

# GUATEMALA

STATUS: Republic
AREA: 108,890 sq km (42,030 sq miles)
POPULATION: 9,197,000
ANNUAL NATURAL INCREASE: 2.9%
CAPITAL: Guatemala City
LANGUAGE: Spanish, Indian languages
RELIGION: 75% Roman Catholic, 25% Protestant
CURRENCY: quetzal (GTQ)
ORGANISATIONS: UN, CACM, OAS

The central American country of Guatemala has both a Pacific and a Caribbean coastline. The mountainous interior, with peaks reaching up to 4000m (13,120ft), covers two-thirds of the country; in addition there are coastal lowlands and a thickly forested mainland to the north known as the Petén. Agricultural products form the bulk of Guatemala's exports, notably coffee, sugar-cane and bananas. Mineral resources including nickel, antimony, lead, silver and, in the north, crude oil, are only just beginning to be exploited.

# GUINEA

STATUS: Republic
AREA: 245,855 sq km (94,900 sq miles)
POPULATION: 5,756,000
ANNUAL NATURAL INCREASE: 2.5%
CAPITAL: Conakry
LANGUAGE: French, Susu, Manika (Official languages: French and 8 others)
RELIGION: mainly Muslim, some animist, 1% Roman Catholic
CURRENCY: Guinea franc (GNF)
ORGANISATIONS: UN, ECOWAS, OAU

Guinea, a former French colony is situated on the West African coast. Its drowned coastline, lined with mangrove swamps contrasts strongly with its interior highlands containing the headwaters of the Gambia, Niger and Senegal rivers. Agriculture occupies 80% of the workforce, the main exports being coffee, bananas, pineapple and palm products. Guinea has some of the largest resources of bauxite (aluminium ore) in the world as well as gold and diamonds. Both bauxite and aluminium are exported.

# GUINEA-BISSAU

STATUS: Republic
AREA: 36,125 sq km (13,945 sq miles)
POPULATION: 965,000
ANNUAL NATURAL INCREASE: 1.9%
CAPITAL: Bissau
LANGUAGE: Portuguese, Crioulo, Guinean dialects
RELIGION: Animist and Muslim majorities. Roman Catholic minority
CURRENCY: Guinea-Bissau peso (GWP)
ORGANISATIONS: UN, ECOWAS, OAU

Guinea-Bissau, on the West African coast was once a centre for the Portuguese slave trade. The coast is swampy and lined with mangroves, and the interior consists of a low-lying plain densely covered with rain forest. The coast is

hot and humid with annual rainfall of 200–300cm (79–118in) a year, although the interior is cooler and drier. 80% of the country's exports comprise groundnuts, groundnut oil, palm kernels and palm oil. Fish, fish products and coconuts also make an important contribution to trade.

# GUYANA

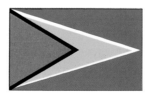

STATUS: Co-operative Republic
AREA: 214,970 sq km (82,980 sq miles)
POPULATION: 990,000
ANNUAL NATURAL INCREASE: 0.6%
CAPITAL: Georgetown
LANGUAGE: English, Hindi, Urdu, Amerindian dialects

RELIGION: mainly Christian, Muslim and Hindu
CURRENCY: Guyana dollar (GYD)
ORGANISATIONS: Comm, UN, CARICOM

The ex-British colony of Guyana borders both Venezuela and Brazil. Its Atlantic coast, the most densely-populated area, is flat and marshy, while towards the interior the landscape gradually rises to the Guiana Highlands – a region densely covered in rain forest. Sugar, molasses and rum, once Guyana's main exports, are now being outstripped by bauxite.

# HAITI

STATUS: Republic
AREA: 27,750 sq km (10,710 sq miles)
POPULATION: 6,486,000

ANNUAL NATURAL INCREASE: 1.8%
CAPITAL: Port-au-Prince
LANGUAGE: French, Creole (90%)
RELIGION: 80% Roman Catholic. Some Voodoo folk religion
CURRENCY: gourde (HTG)
ORGANISATIONS: UN, OAS

Haiti occupies the western part of the island of Hispaniola in the Caribbean. It is the poorest country in Central America. The country is mountainous with three main ranges, the highest reaching 2680m (8793 ft). Agriculture is restricted to the plains which divide the ranges. The climate is tropical. 90% of the workforce are farmers, and coffee is the main export. Light manufacturing industries are concentrated around the capital.

## HISPANIOLA
STATUS: Island of the West Indies comprising Haiti and Dominican Republic
AREA: 76,170 sq km (29,400 sq miles)
POPULATION: 12,154,000

## HOKKAIDO
STATUS: Island of Japan
AREA: 78,460 sq km (30,285 sq miles)
POPULATION: 5,671,000

# HONDURAS

STATUS: Republic
AREA: 112,085 sq km (43,265 sq miles)
POPULATION: 5,105,000
ANNUAL NATURAL INCREASE: 3.5%
CAPITAL: Tegucigalpa
LANGUAGE: Spanish, Indian dialects
RELIGION: large Roman Catholic majority
CURRENCY: lempira (HNL) or peso
ORGANISATIONS: UN, CACM, OAS

The Central American republic of Honduras is a poor, sparsely populated country which consists substantially of rugged mountains and high plateaux with, on the Caribbean coast, an area of hot and humid plains, densely covered with tropical vegetation. These low-lying plains are subject to high annual rainfall, an average of 250cm (98 in), and it is in this region that bananas and coffee, accounting for half the nation's exports, are grown. Other crops include sugar, rice, maize, beans and tobacco. Exploitation of lead, iron, tin and oil may lead, however, to a change in the traditional agriculture-based economy. Most industries are concerned with processing local products. Lead, silver and zinc are exported.

## HONG KONG
(INCLUDING KOWLOON AND THE NEW TERRITORIES)
STATUS: UK Dependent Territory
AREA: 1,067 sq km (412 sq miles)
POPULATION: 5,448,000

## HONSHU
STATUS: Main Island of Japan
AREA: 230,455 sq km (88,955 sq miles)
POPULATION: 98,352,000

# HUNGARY

STATUS: Republic
AREA: 93,030 sq km (35,910 sq miles)
POPULATION: 10,352,000
ANNUAL NATURAL INCREASE: –0.1%
CAPITAL: Budapest
LANGUAGE: Hungarian (Magyar)
RELIGION: 60% Roman Catholic, 20% Hungarian Reformed Church, Lutheran and Orthodox minorities
CURRENCY: forint (HUE)
ORGANISATIONS: UN, OIEC, Council of Europe

The undulating fertile plains of Hungary are bisected vertically by the Danube. Hungary is bordered by Czechoslovakia in the north, by Romania and Ukraine in the east, by Austria and Slovenia in the west, and by Croatia and Yugoslavia (Serbia) in the south. Winters in Hungary are severe, though in summer the enclosed plains can become very hot. Bauxite is Hungary's only substantial mineral resource, and less than 15% of the gross national product is now derived from agriculture. The massive drive for industrialisation has fundamentally transformed the structure of the economy in the period since 1945. Both capital and consumer goods industries were developed, and during the 1980s engineering accounted for more than half the total industrial output. After a series of more or less unsuccessful attempts to introduce market elements into what remained in essence a centrally planned and largely state-owned economy, the communist regime finally gave up in 1989/90. However, their democratically-elected successors have yet to prove that privatisation and free competition will eventually bring general prosperity as well as political stability to what is now a profoundly troubled society.

# ICELAND

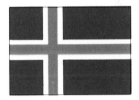

STATUS: Republic
AREA: 102,820 sq km (39,690 sq miles)
POPULATION: 255,000
ANNUAL NATURAL INCREASE: 1.1%
CAPITAL: Reykjavík
LANGUAGE: Icelandic
RELIGION: 93% Evangelical Lutheran
CURRENCY: Icelandic krona (ISK)
ORGANISATIONS: UN, Council of Europe, EFTA, NATO, OECD

The northernmost island in Europe, Iceland is 850km (530 miles) away from Scotland, its nearest neighbour. The landscape is entirely volcanic – compacted volcanic ash has been eroded by the wind and there are substantial ice sheets and lava fields as well as many still active volcanoes, geysers and hot springs. The climate is cold, with average summer temperatures of 9°–10°C(48°–50°F), and vegetation is sparse. An average of 950,000 tonnes of fish are landed each year and 95% of Iceland's exports consist of fish and fish products.

# INDIA

STATUS: Federal Republic
AREA: 3,166,830 sq km (1,222,395 sq miles)
POPULATION: 843,930,861
ANNUAL NATURAL INCREASE: 2.1%

CAPITAL: New Delhi
LANGUAGE: Hindi, English, regional languages
RELIGION: 83% Hindu, 11% Muslim
CURRENCY: Indian rupee (INR)
ORGANISATIONS: Comm, UN, Col. Plan

India has the world's second largest population. This vast country contains an extraordinary variety of landscapes, climates and resources. The Himalaya in the north is the world's highest mountain range with many peaks reaching over 6000 km (19,685 ft). The Himalayan foothills are covered with lush vegetation, water is in abundant supply (rainfall in Assam reaches 1,070 cm or 421 in a year) and the climate is hot, making this region a centre for tea cultivation. To the south lies the vast expanse of the Indo-Gangetic plain, 2500 km (1550 miles) east-west, divided by the Indus, Ganges and Brahmaputra rivers. This is one of the world's most fertile regions, although it is liable to flooding, and failure of monsoon rainfall (June to September) can result in severe drought. In the pre-monsoon season the heat becomes intense – average temperatures in New Delhi reach 38°C (100°F). Rice, wheat, cotton, jute, tobacco and sugar are the main crops. To the south lies the Deccan plateau. India's natural resources are immense – timber, coal, iron ore and nickel, and oil has been discovered in the Indian Ocean. There has been a rapid expansion of light industry and the manufacturing of consumer goods. Tourism is a valuable source of revenue. Nevertheless, 70% of the population live by subsistence farming. Main exports by value are precious stones and jewellery, engineering goods, clothing, leather goods, chemicals and cotton.

# INDONESIA

STATUS: Republic
AREA: 1,919,445 sq km (740,905 sq miles)
POPULATION: 179,321,641
ANNUAL NATURAL INCREASE: 2.1%
CAPITAL: Jakarta
LANGUAGE: Bahasa Indonesian, Dutch
RELIGION: 78% Muslim, 11% Christian, 11% Hindu and Buddhist
CURRENCY: rupiah (IDR)
ORGANISATIONS: UN, ASEAN, Col. Plan, OPEC

Indonesia consists of an arc of thousands of islands along the equator which includes Kalimantan (the central and southern parts of Borneo), Sumatra, Irian Jaya (the western part of New Guinea), Sulawesi and Java. Most of its people live along the coasts of the islands or in the river valleys. It is a Muslim nation and has the fourth largest population in the world. Most people live on Java, leaving parts of the other islands virtually uninhabited. The climate is tropical: hot, wet and subject to monsoons. Over three-quarters of the people live in villages and farm, but the crops produced are hardly enough for the increasing population and the fishing industry needs developing. Timber and oil production are becoming very important as sources of foreign exchange and there are also rich mineral deposits, as yet not fully exploited. Tourism is increasing.

# IRAN

STATUS: Republic
AREA: 1,648,000 sq km (636,130 sq miles)
POPULATION: 56,031,000
ANNUAL NATURAL INCREASE: 3.0%
CAPITAL: Tehran
LANGUAGE: Farsi, Kurdish, Arabic, Baluchi, Turkic
RELIGION: Shia Muslim majority. Sunni Muslim and Armenian Christian minorities
CURRENCY: Iranian rial (IRR)
ORGANISATIONS: UN, Col. Plan, OPEC

Iran is a large mountainous country situated between the Caspian Sea and the Persian Gulf. The climate is one of extremes with temperatures ranging from –20 to 55°C (–4 to 131°F) and rainfall varying from 200 cm (79 in) to almost zero. Iran is rich in oil and gas and the revenues have been used to improve communications and social conditions generally. The war with Iraq between 1980 and 1988 seriously restricted economic growth and particularly affected the Iranian oil industry in the Persian Gulf. Agricultural conditions are poor except around the Caspian Sea and wheat is the main crop though fruit (especially dates) and nuts are grown and exported. The main livestock is sheep and goats. Iran has substantial mineral deposits relatively underdeveloped.

# IRAQ

STATUS: Republic
AREA: 438,317 sq km (169,235 sq miles)
POPULATION: 18,920,000
ANNUAL NATURAL INCREASE: 3.6%
CAPITAL: Baghdad
LANGUAGE: Arabic, Kurdish, Turkoman
RELIGION: 50% Shia, 45% Sunni Muslim
CURRENCY: Iraqi dinar (IQD)
ORGANISATIONS: UN, Arab League, OPEC

Iraq is mostly marsh and mountain, but there are substantial areas of fertile land between the Tigris and the Euphrates. The two great rivers join and become the Shatt al-Arab which flows into the Persian Gulf. The climate is mainly arid with small and unreliable rainfall, less than 50 cm (20 in). Summers are very hot and winters cold. Iraq has a very short coastline making Basra the principal port with oil the major export. Light industry is situated around Baghdad, the capital, and there are major petro-chemical complexes around the Basra and Kirkuk oilfields. The war with Iran (1980-88) and the recent Gulf conflict (1991) have placed great strains on the economy with exports of oil and natural gas severely restricted. Iraq will take some time to recover from the damage caused to its infrastructure.

# IRELAND (EIRE)

STATUS: Republic
AREA: 68,895 sq km (26,595 sq miles)
POPULATION: 3,503,000
ANNUAL NATURAL INCREASE: 0.4%
CAPITAL: Dublin (Baile Atha Cliath)
LANGUAGE: Irish, English
RELIGION: 95% Roman Catholic, 5% Protestant
CURRENCY: punt or Irish pound (IEP)
ORGANISATIONS: UN, Council of Europe, EC, OECD

The Irish Republic forms 80% of the island of Ireland. It is a country where the cool, damp climate makes for rich pastureland, and livestock farming predominates. Meat and dairy produce is processed in the small market towns where there are also breweries and mills.

Large-scale manufacturing is centred round Dublin, the capital and main port. Ireland also possesses reserves of oil and natural gas, peat and deposits of lead and zinc.

# ISRAEL

STATUS: State
AREA: 20,770 sq km (8,015 sq miles)
POPULATION: 4,822,000
ANNUAL NATURAL INCREASE: 1.7%
CAPITAL: Jerusalem
LANGUAGE: Hebrew, Arabic, Yiddish
RELIGION: 85% Jewish, 13% Muslim
CURRENCY: shekel (ILS)
ORGANISATIONS: UN

This narrow country on the eastern Mediterranean littoral contains a varied landscape – a coastal plain bounded by foothills in the south and the Galilee Highlands in the north; a deep trough extending from the River Jordan to the Dead Sea, and the Negev, a desert region in the south extending to the Gulf of Aqaba. Economic development in Israel is the most advanced in the Middle East. Manufacturing, particularly diamond finishing and electronics, and mining are the most important industries although Israel also has a flourishing agricultural industry exporting fruit, flowers and vegetables to Western Europe.

# ITALY

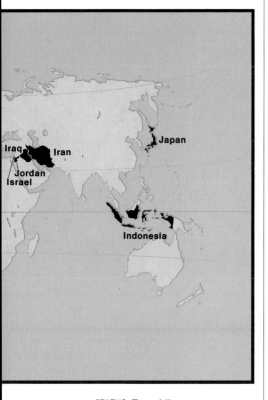

STATUS: Republic
AREA: 301,245 sq km (116,280 sq miles)
POPULATION: 57,690,000
ANNUAL NATURAL INCREASE: 0.2%
CAPITAL: Rome (Roma)
LANGUAGE: Italian, German, French
RELIGION: 90% Roman Catholic
CURRENCY: Italian lira (ITL)
ORGANISATIONS: UN, Council of Europe, EC
NATO, OECD, WEU, G7

Over 75% of the landscape of Italy is hill or mountain, with the north dominated by the flat plain of the River Po rising to the high Alps. Climate varies from hot summers and mild winters in the south and lowland areas, to mild summers and cold winters in the Alps. Agriculture flourishes with cereals, vegetables, olives and vines the principal crops. Italy is the world's largest wine producer. Cheese is also an important commodity. In spite of the lack of mineral and power resources textiles, manufacturing industry: cars, machine tools, textile machinery and engineering, mainly in the north, are

expanding rapidly and account for nearly 50% of the work force. This is increasing the imbalance between the north and south where the average income is far less per head, and where investment is lacking.

# IVORY COAST

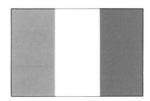

STATUS: Republic
AREA: 322,465 sq km (124,470 sq miles)
POPULATION: 11,998,000
ANNUAL NATURAL INCREASE: 4.0%
CAPITAL: Yamoussoukro
LANGUAGE: French, tribal languages
RELIGION: 65% traditional beliefs, 23% Muslim
12% Roman Catholic
CURRENCY: CFA franc (W Africa) (XOF)
ORGANISATIONS: UN, ECOWAS, OAU

Independent from the French since 1960, the Ivory Coast is divided between the low plains of the south and the plateaux of the north. The climate is tropical with rainfall all year round in the south. Much of the population is engaged in agriculture producing rice, cassava, maize, sorghum, plantains and yams. Exports include coffee, timber and cocoa. The main industrial area and leading port is centred on Abidjan. Important industries are food-processing, textiles and timber products.

# JAMAICA

STATUS: Commonwealth State
AREA: 11,425 sq km (4,410 sq miles)
POPULATION: 2,420,000
ANNUAL NATURAL INCREASE: 1.3%
CAPITAL: Kingston
LANGUAGE: English, local patois
RELIGION: Anglican Christian majority.
Rastafarian minority
CURRENCY: Jamaican dollar (JMD)
ORGANISATIONS: Comm, UN, CARICOM, OAS

Jamaica, part of the Greater Antilles chain of islands in the Caribbean is formed from the peaks of a submerged mountain range. The climate is tropical with an annual rainfall of over 500cm(197in) on the high ground. There is a plentiful supply of tropical fruits such as melons, bananas and guavas. Principal crops include sugar-cane, bananas and coffee. Jamaica is rich in bauxite which provides over half foreign-exchange earnings. Main manufacturing industries are food processing, textiles, cement and agricultural machinery.

# JAN MAYEN
STATUS: Island Territory of Norway
AREA: 380 sq km (147 sq miles)
POPULATION: No permanent population

# JAPAN

STATUS: Constituential monarchy
AREA: 369,700 sq km (142,705 sq miles)
POPULATION: 123,612,000
ANNUAL NATURAL INCREASE: 0.6%
CAPITAL: Tokyo
LANGUAGE: Japanese
RELIGION: Shintoist, Buddhist, Christian
minority
CURRENCY: yen (JPY)
ORGANISATIONS: UN, Col. Plan, OECD, G7

Japan consists of the main islands of Hokkaido, Honshu, Shikoku and Kyushu which stretch over 1,600km (995 miles). The land is mountainous and heavily forested with small, fertile patches and a climate ranging from harsh to tropical. The highest mountain is Mt Fuji 3,776m (12,388 ft). The archipelago is also subject to monsoons, earthquakes, typhoons and tidal waves. Very little of the available land is cultivable and although many of the farmers only work part-time Japan manages to produce enough rice for the growing population. Most food has to be imported but the Japanese also catch and eat a lot of fish. The Japanese fishing fleet is the largest in the world. Japan is a leading economic power and most of the population are involved in industry. Because of the importance of trade, industry has grown up round the major ports especially Yokohama and Osaka and Tokyo, the capital. The principal exports are electronic, electrical and optical equipment. To produce these goods Japan relies heavily on imported fuel and raw materials and is developing the country's nuclear power resources to reduce this dependence. Production of coal, oil and natural gas is also being increased.

# JORDAN

STATUS: Kingdom
AREA: 90,650 sq km (35,000 sq miles)
POPULATION: 3,170,000
ANNUAL NATURAL INCREASE: 3.7%
CAPITAL: Amman
LANGUAGE: Arabic
RELIGION: 90% Sunni Muslim, Christian and
Shia Muslim minorities
CURRENCY: Jordanian dinar (JOD)
ORGANISATIONS: UN, Arab League

Jordan is one of the few remaining kingdoms in the middle east. It is mostly desert, but has fertile pockets. Temperatures rise to 49°C(120°F) in the valleys but it is cooler and wetter in the east. Fruit and vegetables account for 20% of Jordan's exports and phosphate, the most valuable mineral, accounts for over 40% of export revenue. Amman is the manufacturing centre, processing bromide and potash from the Dead Sea. Other important industries are food processing and textiles.

# KAZAKHSTAN

STATUS: Republic
AREA: 2,717,300 sq km (1,048,880 sq miles)
POPULATION: 16,700,000
CAPITAL: Alma-Ata
LANGUAGE: Kazakh, Russian
RELIGION: mainly Muslim
CURRENCY: rouble
ORGANISATIONS: CIS

Stretching across central Asia, Kazakhstan is Russia's southern neighbour. Consisting of low-lands, hilly plains and plateaux, with a small mountainous area, the country has a continental climate with hot summers alternating with equally extreme winters. Exceptionally rich in raw materials, extractive industries have played a major role in the country's economy. Rapid industrialisation in recent years has focussed on iron and steel, cement, chemicals, fertilizers and consumer goods. Although three-quarters of all agricultural land is used for pasture, the nomadic ways of the Kazakh people have all but disappeared. Economic development during the Soviet period brought a massive influx of outside labour which swamped the indigenous population. The proportion of Kazakhs employed in the industrial sector has, until recently, been small, but with the move to the towns and better training, this balance is starting to be redressed. Since Kazakhstan's independence in 1991, its economic prospects appear favourable; but the Soviet legacy includes environmental problems, such as the ruthless exploitation of the Aral Sea for irrigation, which have to be faced.

# KENYA

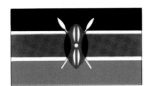

STATUS: Republic
AREA: 582,645 sq km (224,900 sq miles)
POPULATION: 24,032,000
ANNUAL NATURAL INCREASE: 3.8%
CAPITAL: Nairobi
LANGUAGE: Kiswahili, English, Kikuyu, Luo
RELIGION: traditional beliefs majority,
25% Christian, 6% Muslim
CURRENCY: Kenya shilling (KES)
ORGANISATIONS: Comm, UN, OAU

Kenya lies on the equator but as most of the country is on a high plateau the temperatures range from 10° to 27°C (50° to 81°F). Rainfall varies from 76 to 250cm (30 to 98in) depending on altitude. Poor soil and a dry climate mean that little of the land is under cultivation but exports are nonetheless dominated by farm products – coffee, tea, sisal and meat. Nairobi and Mombasa are the manufacturing centres. The tourist industry is growing. Electricity is generated from both geothermal sources and hydro-electric power stations on the Tana river.

# KIRGIZIA

STATUS: Republic
AREA: 198,500 sq km (76,620 sq miles)
POPULATION: 4,400,000
CAPITAL: Bishkek
LANGUAGE: Kirgizian, Russian
RELIGION: Muslim
CURRENCY: rouble
ORGANISATIONS: CIS

Located in the heart of Asia, Kirgizia is a mountainous country. Traditionally an agrarian-based economy, with stock raising prevalent, the country underwent rapid industrialisation during the Soviet period and is now a major producer of machinery and hydro-electric power. Coal, antimony and mercury are mined. The cultivation of cotton, sugar beet, tobacco and opium poppies is expanding and provides the basis for a growing processing industry. Independence came unexpectedly in 1991, although Kirgizia had long wanted to control its own affairs.

# KIRIBATI

STATUS: Republic
AREA: 717 sq km (277 sq miles)
POPULATION: 66,000
ANNUAL NATURAL INCREASE: 1.9%
CAPITAL: Bairiki (in Tarawa Atoll)
LANGUAGE: I-Kiribati, English
RELIGION: Christian majority
CURRENCY: Australian dollar (AUD)
ORGANISATIONS: Comm

Kiribati consists of sixteen Gilbert Islands, eight Phoenix Islands, three Line Islands and Ocean Island. These four groups are spread over 5 million sq km (1,930,000 sq miles) in the central and west Pacific. The temperature is a constant 27° to 32°C (80° to 90°F). The islanders grow coconut, breadfruit, bananas and babai (a coarse vegetable). Copra is the only major export. Main imports are machinery and manufactured goods.

# KOREA, NORTH

STATUS: Republic
AREA: 122,310 sq km (47,210 sq miles)
POPULATION: 21,773,000
ANNUAL NATURAL INCREASE: 1.2%
CAPITAL: Pyöngyang
LANGUAGE: Korean
RELIGION: mainly Buddhist, Confucianist, Daoist
and Chundo Kyo

CURRENCY: North Korean won (KPW)
ORGANISATIONS: UN, OIEC

High, rugged mountains and deep valleys typify North Korea. Climate is extreme with severe winters and warm, sunny summers. Cultivation is limited to the river valley plains where rice, millet, maize and wheat are the principal crops. North Korea is rich in minerals including iron ore, coal and copper and industrial development has been expanding. Further potential exists in the exploitation of the plentiful resources of hydro-electricity. Main exports are metal ores and metal products.

# KOREA, SOUTH

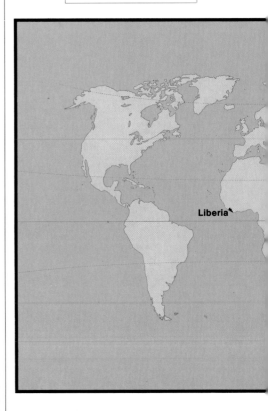

Liberia

STATUS: Republic
AREA: 98,445 sq km (38,000 sq miles)
POPULATION: 43,201,000
ANNUAL NATURAL INCREASE: 1.6%
CAPITAL: Seoul (Sŏul)
LANGUAGE: Korean
RELIGION: 26% Mahayana Buddhism,
22% Christian. Confucianist minority,
Daoism, Chundo Kyo
CURRENCY: won (KRW)
ORGANISATIONS: UN, Col. Plan

The terrain of South Korea is less rugged than the north and the climate is less extreme. The majority of the population live in the arable river valleys and along the coastal plain. Agriculture is very primitive, with rice the principal crop. Tungsten, coal and iron ore are the main mineral deposits. The country is a major industrial nation with iron and steel, chemicals, machinery, shipbuilding, vehicles and electronics dominating. South Korea builds more ships than any other nation except Japan. Oil and industrial materials have to be imported.

# KUWAIT

STATUS: State
AREA: 24,280 sq km (9,370 sq miles)
POPULATION: 1,000,000 (approx.)
ANNUAL NATURAL INCREASE: 4.3%
CAPITAL: Kuwait (Al Kuwayt)
LANGUAGE: Arabic, English
RELIGION: 95% Muslim, 5% Christian and Hindu
CURRENCY: Kuwaiti dinar (KWD)
ORGANISATIONS: UN, Arab League, OPEC

Situated at the mouth of the Gulf, Kuwait comprises low, undulating desert, with summer temperatures as high as 52°C (126°F). Annual rainfall fluctuates between 1 and 37 cm (½–15 in). Since the discovery of oil Kuwait has been

transformed into one of the world's wealthiest nations, exporting oil to Japan, France, The Netherlands and the UK since 1946. The natural gas fields have also been developed. Other industries include fishing (particularly shrimp), food processing, chemicals and building materials. In agriculture, the aim is to produce half the requirements of domestic vegetable consumption by expanding the irrigated area. The invasion and attempted annexation of Kuwait by Iraq in 1990-91 has had severe effects on the country's economy.

# LAOS

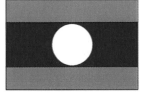

STATUS: Republic

AREA: 236,725 sq km (91,375 sq miles)
POPULATION: 4,139,000
ANNUAL NATURAL INCREASE: 2.7%
CAPITAL: Vientiane (Viangchan)
LANGUAGE: Lao, French, tribal languages
RELIGION: Buddhist majority, Christian and animist minorities
CURRENCY: kip (LAK)
ORGANISATIONS: UN, Col. Plan

Laos is a poor, landlocked country in Indo-China. Temperatures range from 15°C (59°F) in winter, to 32°C (90°F) before the rains, and 26°C (79°F) during the rainy season from May to October. Most of the sparse population are farmers growing small amounts of rice, maize, sweet potatoes and tobacco. The major exports are tin and teak, the latter floated down the Mekong river. Almost constant warfare since 1941 has hindered any possible industrial development. Main exports are timber products and coffee.

# LATVIA

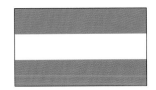

STATUS: Republic
AREA: 63,700 sq km (24,590 sq miles)
POPULATION: 2,700,000
CAPITAL: Riga
LANGUAGE: Latvian, Lithuanian, Russian
RELIGION: Lutheran, Roman Catholic and Orthodox minorities
CURRENCY: rouble (lat 1992)
ORGANISATIONS: UN

Latvia is situated on the shores of the Baltic Sea and the Gulf of Riga. Forests cover more than a third of the total territory, a second third being made up of meadows, swamps and wasteland. Farmland supports dairy and meat production and grain crops. The climate is oceanic: windy, cloudy and humid. The country possesses no mineral resources of any value. Industrial development has been sustained by a massive influx of Russian labour since Latvia's incorporation into the Soviet Union in 1940. Machine building and metal engineering are the chief manufacturing activities. Under the Soviets, Latvia was assigned the production of consumer durables such as refrigerators and motorcycles as well as ships, rolling stock and power generators. Environmental damage, commercial unprofitability and the collapse of communism necessitate fundamental reform. Latvia regained its independence in 1991.

# LEBANON

STATUS: Republic
AREA: 10,400 sq km (4,015 sq miles)
POPULATION: 2,701,000
ANNUAL NATURAL INCREASE: 2.1%
CAPITAL: Beirut (Beyrouth)
LANGUAGE: Arabic, French, English

RELIGION: 58% Shia and Sunni Muslim, 42% Roman Catholic and Maronite Christian
CURRENCY: Lebanese pound (LBP)
ORGANISATIONS: UN, Arab League

Physically, Lebanon can be divided into four main regions: a narrow coastal plain; a narrow, fertile, interior plateau; the west Lebanon and Anti-Lebanon mountains. The climate is of Mediterranean type with an annual rainfall ranging between 92cm (36in) on the coast and 230cm (91in) in the mountains. Trade and tourism have been severely affected by civil war since 1975. Agriculture accounts for nearly half the employed people. Cement, fertilisers, jewellery, sugar and tobacco products are all manufactured on a small scale.

# LESOTHO

STATUS: Kingdom
AREA: 30,345 sq km (11,715 sq miles)
POPULATION: 1,774,000
ANNUAL NATURAL INCREASE: 2.7%
CAPITAL: Maseru
LANGUAGE: Sesotho, English
RELIGION: 80% Christian
CURRENCY: loti (LSL), S African rand (ZAR)
ORGANISATIONS: Comm, UN, OAU

Lesotho, formerly Basutoland, is completely encircled by South Africa. This small country is rugged and mountainous, and southern Africa's highest mountain, Thabana Ntlenyana (3482m or 11,424ft) is to be found in the east Drakensberg. Because of the terrain, agriculture is limited to the lowlands and foothills. Sorghum, wheat, barley, maize, oats and legumes are the main crops. Cattle, sheep and goats graze on the highlands.

# LIBERIA

STATUS: Republic
AREA: 111,370 sq km (42,990 sq miles)
POPULATION: 2,607,000
ANNUAL NATURAL INCREASE: 3.1%
CAPITAL: Monrovia
LANGUAGE: English, tribal languages
RELIGION: Christian majority, 5% Muslim
CURRENCY: Liberian dollar (LRD)
ORGANISATIONS: UN, ECOWAS, OAU

The West African republic of Liberia is the only nation in Africa never to have been ruled by a foreign power. The hot and humid coastal plain with its savannah vegetation and mangrove swamps rises gently towards the Guinea Highlands, and the interior is densely covered by tropical rain forest. Rubber, formerly Liberia's main export has now been supplemented by iron, discovered in the Bomi Hills. Liberia has the world's largest merchant fleet of over 2,500 ships due to its flag of convenience tax regime.

# LIBYA

STATUS: Republic
AREA: 1,759,180 sq km (679,180 sq miles)
POPULATION: 4,545,000
ANNUAL NATURAL INCREASE: 4.2%
CAPITAL: Tripoli (Ţarābulus)
LANGUAGE: Arabic, Italian, English
RELIGION: Sunni Muslim
CURRENCY: Libyan dinar (LYD)
ORGANISATIONS: UN, Arab League, OAU, OPEC

Libya is situated on the lowlands of North Africa which rise southwards from the Mediterranean Sea. 95% of its territory is hot and dry desert or semi-desert with average rainfall of less than 13cm(5in). The coastal plains, however, have a moister Mediterranean climate with rainfall of 20–61cm(8–24in), and this is the most densely populated region. In these areas, a wide range of crops are cultivated including grapes, groundnuts, oranges, wheat and barley. Dates are grown in the desert oases. Only 30 years ago Libya was classed as one of the world's poorest nations but the exploitation of oil has transformed Libya's economy and now accounts for over 95% of its exports. Most imported goods come from Italy.

# LIECHTENSTEIN

STATUS: Principality
AREA: 160 sq km (62 sq miles)
POPULATION: 29,000
ANNUAL NATURAL INCREASE: 1.1%
CAPITAL: Vaduz
LANGUAGE: Alemannish, German
RELIGION: 87% Roman Catholic
CURRENCY: Franken (Swiss franc) (CHF)
ORGANISATIONS: UN, Council of Europe, EFTA

Situated in the central Alps between Switzerland and Austria, Liechtenstein is one of the smallest states in Europe. Its territory is divided into two zones – the flood plains of the Rhine to the north and Alpine mountain ranges to the south where cattle are reared. Liechtenstein's other main sources of revenue comprise light industry chiefly the manufacture of precision instruments, also textile production, food products and tourism.

# LITHUANIA

STATUS: Republic
AREA: 65,200 sq km (25,165 sq miles)
POPULATION: 3,700,000
CAPITAL: Vilnius
LANGUAGE: Lithuanian, Russian, Polish
RELIGION: mainly Roman Catholic
CURRENCY: rouble (lat to be introduced in 1992)
ORGANISATIONS: UN

Lying on the shores of the Baltic Sea, Lithuania is bounded by Latvia to the north, by Belorussia to the east and south, and in the southwest by Poland and the Kaliningrad (Königsberg) district, a territorial exclave belonging to Russia. The whole country consists of a low-lying plain, the climate being transitional between the oceanic type of western Europe and the continental conditions prevailing further east. After almost 50 years' involuntary incorporation into the Soviet Union, Lithuania led the renewed Baltic struggle for freedom, and in 1991 was able to win back its independence. However, the social and economic problems with which the country is beset defy an easy solution. The massive drive for industrialisation during the Soviet period has done enormous damage to the environment but failed to create competitive enterprises that can survive under market conditions. This has led to a dramatic fall in production in the recent past and to rising unemployment. Lithuania's agriculture, with its emphasis on meat and dairy products, still awaits decollectivisation.

# LUXEMBOURG

STATUS: Grand Duchy
AREA: 2,585 sq km (998 sq miles)
POPULATION: 378,000
ANNUAL NATURAL INCREASE: 0.4%
CAPITAL: Luxembourg
LANGUAGE: Letzeburgish, French, German
RELIGION: 95% Roman Catholic
CURRENCY: Luxembourg franc (LUF),
Belgian franc (BEF)
ORGANISATIONS: UN, Council of Europe, EC
NATO, OECD, WEU

The Grand Duchy of Luxembourg is strategically situated between France, Belgium and Germany. In the north the Oesling region is an extension of the Ardennes which are cut through by thickly forested river valleys. The Gutland to the south is an area of rolling lush pastureland. The climate is mild and temperate with rainfall ranging from 70–100cm(28–40in) a year. Just over half the land is arable, mainly cereals, dairy produce and potatoes, and wine is produced in the Moselle Valley. Iron ore is found in the south and is the basis of the thriving steel industry. Other major industries are textiles, chemicals, metal goods and pharmaceutical products.

## MACAU
STATUS: Overseas Territory of Portugal
AREA: 16 sq km (6 sq miles)
POPULATION: 479,000
CAPITAL: Macau

# MADAGASCAR

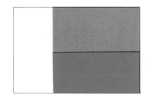

STATUS: Republic
AREA: 594,180 sq km (229,345 sq miles)
POPULATION: 11,197,000
ANNUAL NATURAL INCREASE: 2.8%
CAPITAL: Antananarivo
LANGUAGE: Malagasy, French, English
RELIGION: 57% animist, 40% Christian,
3% Muslim
CURRENCY: Malagasy franc (MGF)
ORGANISATIONS: UN, OAU

Madagascar is the world's fourth largest island, situated 400 km (250 miles) east of the Mozambique coast. The terrain consists largely of a high plateau reaching 1500m (4920ft), with

steppe and savannah vegetation and desert in the south. The mountains of the Tsaratanana Massif to the north reach up to 2876m (9435ft). Much of the hot humid east coast is covered by tropical rainforest – here rainfall reaches 150-200cm (59-79 in) per annum. Although farming is the occupation of about 85% of the population, only 3% of the land is cultivated. Coffee, rice and cassava are the main products. Much of Madagascar's plant and animal life is unique to the island. However, habitats are under increasing threat due to widespread deforestation, caused by the rapid development of forestry, and soil erosion.

## MADEIRA
STATUS: Self-governing Island Region
of Portugal
AREA: 796 sq km (307 sq miles)
POPULATION: 273,200
CAPITAL: Funchal

# MALAWI

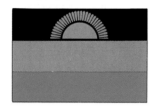

STATUS: Republic
AREA: 94,080 sq km (36,315 sq miles)
POPULATION: 8,289,000
ANNUAL NATURAL INCREASE: 3.4%
CAPITAL: Lilongwe
LANGUAGE: Chichewa, English
RELIGION: traditional beliefs majority,
10% Roman Catholic, 10% Protestant
CURRENCY: kwacha (MWK)
ORGANISATIONS: Comm, UN, OAU

Malawi is located at the southern end of the East African Rift Valley. The area around Lake Malawi is hot and humid with swampy vegeta-

tion, gradually supplemented by highlands to the west and south-east, where conditions are cooler. Malawi has an intensely rural economy – 96% of the population work on the land. Maize is the main subsistence crop, and tea, tobacco, sugar and groundnuts are the main exports. Malawi has deposits of both coal and bauxite, but they are under-exploited at present. Manufacturing industry concentrates on consumer goods and building and construction materials. All energy is produced by hydro-electric power.

# MALAYSIA

STATUS: Federation
AREA: 332,965 sq km (128,525 sq miles)

POPULATION: 17,861,000
ANNUAL NATURAL INCREASE: 2.6%
CAPITAL: Kuala Lumpur
LANGUAGE: Bahasa Malaysia, English
RELIGION: 53% Muslim, 25% Buddhist, Hindu,
Christian and animist minorities
CURRENCY: Malaysian dollar or ringgit (MYR)
ORGANISATIONS: Comm, UN, ASEAN, Col. Plan

## PENINSULAR MALAYSIA
STATUS: States
AREA: 131,585 sq km (50,790 sq miles)
POPULATION: 14,005,000

## SABAH
STATUS: State
AREA: 76,115 sq km (29,380 sq miles)
POPULATION: 1,342,631
CAPITAL: Kota Kinabalu

## SARAWAK
STATUS: State
AREA: 124,965 sq km (48,235 sq miles)
POPULATION: 1,550,000
CAPITAL: Kuching

The federation of Malaysia consists of two separate parts; West Malaysia is located on the Malay Peninsula, while East Malaysia consists of Sabah and Sarawak on the island of Borneo 700 km (435 miles) across the South China Sea. Despite this distance, both areas share a similar landscape, which is mountainous and covered with lush tropical rainforest. The climate is tropical, hot and humid all the year round, with annual average rainfall of 250 cm (98 in). Malaysia is one of the world's main tin producers, and also produces over 40% of the world's rubber, and is also a leading source of palm oil, bauxite and gold.

Chief exports by value are manufactured goods, rubber, crude oil, palm oil, timber and timber products and tin. Most industries are concerned with production and processing of local products – palm oil, furniture, food processing and petroleum products. Most of the population are engaged in agriculture for local needs but crops grown for export include pineapples, tobacco, cocoa and spices. Livestock is important to the home economy with pigs, cattle, goats, buffaloes and sheep predominant.

# MALDIVES

STATUS: Republic
AREA: 298 sq km (115 sq miles)
POPULATION: 214,139
ANNUAL NATURAL INCREASE: 3.4%
CAPITAL: Malé
LANGUAGE: Divehi
RELIGION: Sunni Muslim majority
CURRENCY: rufiyaa (MVR)
ORGANISATIONS: Comm, UN, Col. Plan

The Maldive Islands are listed as one of the world's poorest nations. They consist of a series of coral atolls stretching 885km(550 miles) across the Indian Ocean. Although there are 2000 islands, only about 215 are inhabited. The main island, Malé, is only 1½ miles long. Fishing is the main activity and fish and coconut fibre are both exported. Most staple foods have to be imported but coconuts, millet, cassava, yams and fruit are grown locally. Tourism is developing.

# MALI

STATUS: Republic
AREA: 1,240,140 sq km (478,695 sq miles)
POPULATION: 8,156,000
ANNUAL NATURAL INCREASE: 2.5%
CAPITAL: Bamako
LANGUAGE: French, native languages
RELIGION: 65% Muslim, 30% traditional beliefs
5% Christian
CURRENCY: CFA franc (W Africa) (XOF)
ORGANISATIONS: UN, ECOWAS, OAU

Mali is one of the world's most undeveloped countries. Over half the area is barren desert. South of Tombouctou the savannah-covered plains support a wide variety of wildlife. Most of the population live in the Niger valley and grow cotton, oil seeds and groundnuts. Fishing is important. Mali has few mineral resources. Recent droughts have taken their toll of livestock and agriculture. Main exports are cotton and livestock. There is no industry.

# MALTA

STATUS: Republic
AREA: 316 sq km (122 sq miles)
POPULATION: 356,000
ANNUAL NATURAL INCREASE: –0.6%
CAPITAL: Valletta
LANGUAGE: Maltese, English, Italian
RELIGION: Great majority Roman Catholic
CURRENCY: Maltese lira (MTL)
ORGANISATIONS: Comm, UN, Council of Europe

Malta lies about 96km(60 miles) south of Sicily, and consists of three islands; Malta, Gozo and Comino. Malta has a Mediterranean climate with mild winters, hot dry summers and an average rainfall of 51cm(20in). About 40% of the land is under cultivation with wheat, potatoes, tomatoes and vines the main crops. The large natural harbour at Valletta has made it a major transit port. Tourism is also an important source of revenue. Principal exports are machinery, beverages, tobacco, flowers, wine, leather goods and potatoes.

## MAN, ISLE OF
STATUS: British Crown Dependency
AREA: 572 sq km (221 sq miles)
POPULATION: 64,000
CAPITAL: Douglas

## MARIANA ISLANDS, NORTHERN
STATUS: Self-governing commonwealth territory of USA
AREA: 471 sq km (182 sq miles)
POPULATION: 20,591

## MARSHALL ISLANDS
STATUS: Self-governing State in Compact of Free Association with USA
AREA: 181 sq km (70 sq miles)
POPULATION: 40,609
CAPITAL: Majuro

## MARTINIQUE
STATUS: Overseas Department of France
AREA: 1,079 sq km (417 sq miles)
POPULATION: 359,000
CAPITAL: Fort-de-France

# MAURITANIA

STATUS: Republic
AREA: 1,030,700 sq km (397,850 sq miles)
POPULATION: 2,025,000
ANNUAL NATURAL INCREASE: 2.6%
CAPITAL: Nouakchott
LANGUAGE: Arabic, French
RELIGION: Muslim
CURRENCY: ouguiya (MRO)
ORGANISATIONS: UN, ECOWAS, Arab League, OAU

Situated on the west coast of Africa, Mauritania consists of savannah, steppes and desert with high temperatures, low rainfall and frequent droughts. There is very little arable farming except in the Senegal river valley where millet and dates are grown. Most Mauritanians raise cattle, sheep, goats or camels. The country has only one railway which is used to transport the chief export, iron ore, from the mines to the coast at Nouadhibou. Severe drought during the last decade decimated the livestock population and forced many nomadic tribesmen into the towns. Coastal fishing contributes nearly 50% of foreign earnings. Exports are almost exclusively confined to iron ore, copper and fish products.

# MAURITIUS

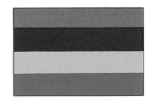

STATUS: Commonwealth State
AREA: 1,865 sq km (720 sq miles)
POPULATION: 1,075,000
ANNUAL NATURAL INCREASE: 1.0%
CAPITAL: Port Louis
LANGUAGE: English, French Creole, Hindi, Bhojpuri

RELIGION: 51% Hindu, 31% Christian 17% Muslim
CURRENCY: Mauritian rupee (MUR)
ORGANISATIONS: Comm, UN, OAU

Mauritius is a mountainous island in the Indian Ocean. It has a varied climate with temperatures ranging from 7° to 36°C(45° to 97°F) and annual rainfall of between 153 and 508cm(60 to 200in). Sugar-cane and its by-products are the mainstay of the economy and tourism is developing rapidly.

## MAYOTTE
STATUS: French 'Territorial Collectivity', claimed by Comoros
AREA: 376 sq km (145 sq miles)
POPULATION: 77,300
CAPITAL: Dzaoudzi

## MELILLA
STATUS: Spanish External Province
AREA: 12.5 sq km (4.8 sq miles)
POPULATION: 62,569

# MEXICO

STATUS: Federal Republic
AREA: 1,972,545 sq km (761,400 sq miles)
POPULATION: 86,154,000
ANNUAL NATURAL INCREASE: 2.2%
CAPITAL: Mexico City
LANGUAGE: Spanish
RELIGION: 96% Roman Catholic
CURRENCY: Mexican peso (MXP)
ORGANISATIONS: UN, OAS

The landscape of Mexico consists mainly of mountain ranges and dissected plateaux. The only extensive flat lands are in the Yucatan Peninsula. As much of the land is above 500 m (1640 ft) temperature and rainfall are modified by altitude and the landscape. The north is arid but the south is humid and tropical. The land requires irrigation to support agriculture. Maize and beans are grown for local consumption. The population has outstripped food production and many Mexicans have moved to the cities. Minerals, especially silver, uranium and gold, are the main source of Mexico's wealth but the mines are mostly foreign-owned and Mexico aims to lessen this dependence on foreign investment as the country develops. Oil, natural gas and coal all have considerable reserves and are gradually becoming more important. Main exports are crude oil and machinery, along with coffee and frozen shrimps. Tourism brings in important foreign revenue.

## MICRONESIA

STATUS: Self-governing Federation of States in Free Association with USA
AREA: 330 sq km (127 sq miles)
POPULATION: 109,000
CAPITAL: Kolonia

# MOLDAVIA

STATUS: Republic
AREA: 33,700 sq km (13,010 sq miles)
POPULATION: 4,400,000
CAPITAL: Kishinev
LANGUAGE: Romanian, Russian
RELIGION: Orthodox
CURRENCY: rouble
ORGANISATIONS: CIS

A country of hilly plains, Moldavia enjoys a warm and dry climate with relatively mild winters. Given its very fertile soil, arable farming dominates agricultural output with viticulture, fruit and vegetables especially important. Sunflower seeds are the main industrial crop; wheat and maize the chief grain crops. Tradi-

tionally, food processing has been the major industry but recently machine-building and engineering have been expanding. Although Moldavia has close ethnic, linguistic and historic ties with neighbouring Romania, any moves towards re-unification have been fiercely resisted by the Russian minority in the east.

# MONACO

STATUS: Principality
AREA: 1.6 sq km (0.6 sq miles)
POPULATION: 29,876
ANNUAL NATURAL INCREASE: 1.4%
CAPITAL: Monaco-ville
LANGUAGE: French, Monegasque, Italian, English

RELIGION: 90% Roman Catholic
CURRENCY: French franc (FRF)

The tiny Principality is the world's smallest independent state after the Vatican City. It occupies a thin strip of the French Mediterranean coast near the Italian border and is backed by the Maritime Alps. It comprises the towns of Monaco, la Condamine, Fontvieille and Monte Carlo. Most revenue comes from tourism, casinos and light industry. Land has been reclaimed from the sea to extend the area available for commercial development.

# MONGOLIA

STATUS: Republic
AREA: 1,565,000 sq km (604,090 sq miles)

POPULATION: 2,095,000
ANNUAL NATURAL INCREASE: 2.8%
CAPITAL: Ulan Bator (Ulaanbaatar)
LANGUAGE: Khalkha Mongolian
RELIGION: some Buddhist Lamaism
CURRENCY: tugrik (MNT)
ORGANISATIONS: UN, OIEC

Situated between China and the Russian Federation, Mongolia has one of the lowest population densities in the world. Much of the country consists of a high undulating plateau (1500 m or 4920 ft) covered with grassland. To the north, mountain ranges reaching 4231 m (13,881 ft) bridge the border with the Russian Federation, and to the south is the large expanse of the Gobi desert where rainfall averages only 10-13 cm (4-5 in) a year. The climate is very extreme with January temperatures falling to –34°C (–29°F). Mongolia is predominantly a farming economy, its main exports being cattle and horses, and wheat, barley, millet and oats are also grown. Its natural resources include some oil, coal, iron ore, gold, tin and copper.

## MONTSERRAT
STATUS: UK Crown Colony
AREA: 160 sq km (41 sq miles)
POPULATION: 13,000
CAPITAL: Plymouth

# MOROCCO

STATUS: Kingdom
AREA: 710,895 sq km (274,414 sq miles)
POPULATION: 25,061,000
ANNUAL NATURAL INCREASE: 2.7%
CAPITAL: Rabat
LANGUAGE: Arabic, French, Spanish, Berber
RELIGION: Muslim majority, Christian and Jewish minorities
CURRENCY: Moroccan dirham (MAD)
ORGANISATIONS: UN, Arab League

One third of Morocco, on the north-west coast of Africa, consists of the Atlas Mountains reaching 4165 m (13,665 ft). Between the Atlas and the Atlantic coastal strip is an area of high plateau bordered on the south by the Sahara. The north of the country has a Mediterranean climate and vegetable, and west-facing slopes of the Atlas have high annual rainfall and are thickly forested. Morocco has the world's largest phosphate deposits. The main crops are wheat and barley, and tourism is a major industry.

# MOZAMBIQUE

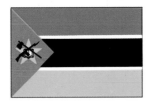

STATUS: Republic
AREA: 784,755 sq km (302,915 sq miles)
POPULATION: 15,656,000
ANNUAL NATURAL INCREASE: 2.7%
CAPITAL: Maputo
LANGUAGE: Portuguese, tribal languages
RELIGION: mainly traditional beliefs, 15% Christian, 15% Muslim
CURRENCY: metical (MZM)
ORGANISATIONS: UN, OAU

The ex-Portuguese colony of Mozambique consists of a large coastal plain, rising towards the interior to the plateaux and mountain ranges which border Malawi, Zambia and Zimbabwe. The highlands in the north reach 2436m (7992ft). The climate is tropical on the coastal plain, although high altitudes make it cooler inland. Over 90% of the population are subsistence farmers cultivating coconuts, cashews, cotton, maize and rice. Mozambique also acts as an entrepôt, handling exports from South Africa, and landlocked Zambia and Malawi. Coal is the main mineral deposit and there are large reserves. Other underexploited minerals are iron ore, bauxite and gold.

# NAMIBIA

STATUS: Republic
AREA: 824,295 sq km (318,180 sq miles)
POPULATION: 1,781,000
ANNUAL NATURAL INCREASE: 3.2%
CAPITAL: Windhoek
LANGUAGE: Afrikaans, German, English, regional languages
RELIGION: 90% Christian
CURRENCY: South African rand (ZAR)
ORGANISATIONS: Comm, UN, OAU

The south-west African country of Namibia is one of the driest in the world. The Namib desert on the coast has less than 5cm (2in) average rainfall a year, the Kalahari to the north-east 10-25cm (4-10in). The vegetation is sparse. Maize and sorghum are grown in the northern highlands and sheep are reared in the south. Namibia is, however, rich in mineral resources, with large deposits of diamonds, lead, tin and zinc, and the world's largest uranium mine. Once a trust territory under the auspices of the United Nations, Namibia achieved independence in 1990.

# NAURU

STATUS: Republic
AREA: 21 sq km (8 sq miles)
POPULATION: 10,000
ANNUAL NATURAL INCREASE: –0.3%
CAPITAL: Yaren
LANGUAGE: Nauruan, English
RELIGION: Nauruan Protestant majority
CURRENCY: Australian dollar (AUD)
ORGANISATIONS: Comm (special member)

Nauru is one of the smallest republics in the world. Its great wealth has been entirely derived from phosphate deposits. The flat coastal lowlands encircled by coral reefs rise gently to the central plateau where the phosphate is mined. Most phosphate is exported to Australasia and Japan. Deposits may soon be exhausted.

# NEPAL

STATUS: Kingdom
AREA: 141,415 sq km (54,585 sq miles)
POPULATION: 18,916,000
ANNUAL NATURAL INCREASE: 2.6%
CAPITAL: Kathmandu
LANGUAGE: Nepali, Maithir, Bhojpuri

RELIGION: 90% Hindu, 5% Buddhist,
3% Muslim
CURRENCY: Nepalese rupee (NPR)
ORGANISATIONS: UN, Col. Plan

Nepal is a Himalayan kingdom sandwiched between China and India. The climate changes sharply with altitude from the southern Tarai plain to the northern Himalayas. Central Kathmandu varies between 2°C(35°F) and 30°C(86°F). Most rain falls between June and October and can reach 250cm(100in). Agriculture concentrates on rice, maize and cattle, buffaloes, sheep and goats. The small amount of industry processes local products.

# NETHERLANDS

STATUS: Kingdom
AREA: 33,940 sq km (13,105 sq miles)
POPULATION: 15,010,000
ANNUAL NATURAL INCREASE: 0.5%
CAPITAL: Amsterdam (seat of Government:
The Hague)
LANGUAGE: Dutch
RELIGION: 40% Roman Catholic
30% Protestant. Jewish minority
CURRENCY: gulden (guilder) or florin (NLG)
ORGANISATIONS: UN, Council of Europe, EC,
NATO, OECD, WEU

The Netherlands is situated at the western edge of the North European plain. The country is exceptionally low-lying, and about 25% of its territory has been reclaimed from the sea. The wide coastal belt consists of flat marshland, mud-flats, sand-dunes and dykes. Further inland, the flat alluvial plain is drained by the Rhine, Maas and Ijssel. A complex network of dykes and canals prevents the area from flooding. To the south and east the land rises. Flat and exposed to strong winds, the Netherlands has mild winters and cool summers.

The Dutch are leading world producers of dairy goods and also cultivate crops such as wheat, barley, oats and potatoes. Lacking mineral resources, much of the industry of the Netherlands is dependent on natural gas. Most manufacturing industry has developed around Rotterdam. Here are oil refineries, steel-works and chemical and food processing plants.

## NETHERLANDS ANTILLES

STATUS: Self-governing part of Netherlands
Realm
AREA: 800 sq km (308 sq miles)
POPULATION: 192,866
CAPITAL: Willemstad

## NEW BRITAIN

STATUS: Island, part of
Papua New Guinea
AREA: 36,500 sq km (14,090 sq miles)
POPULATION: 268,400

## NEW CALEDONIA

STATUS: Overseas Territory of France
AREA: 19,105 sq km (7,375 sq miles)
POPULATION: 144,051
CAPITAL: Nouméa

## NEW GUINEA

STATUS: Island comprising Irian Jaya and
part of Papua New Guinea
AREA: 808,510 sq km (312,085 sq miles)
POPULATION: 3,763,300

# NEW ZEALAND

STATUS: Commonwealth Nation
AREA: 265,150 sq km (102,350 sq miles)
POPULATION: 3,390,000
ANNUAL NATURAL INCREASE: 0.8%
CAPITAL: Wellington
LANGUAGE: English, Maori
RELIGION: 35% Anglican Christian,
22% Presbyterian, 16% Roman Catholic
CURRENCY: New Zealand dollar (NZD)
ORGANISATIONS: Comm, UN, ANZUS, Col. Plan,
OECD

The two main islands that make up New Zealand lie in the South Pacific Ocean. The Southern Alps run the length of South Island with a narrow coastal strip in the west and a broader plain to the east. Stewart Island lies beyond the Foreaux Strait to the south. North Island is less mountainous. Most of the country enjoys a temperate climate. Nearly 20% of the land is forested and 50% pasture. New Zealand is one of the world's leading exporters of beef, mutton and wool. Most exploited minerals are for industrial use – clay, iron sand, limestone, sand and coal. Manufacturing industries and tourism are of increasing importance. New trading links are developing with countries bordering the Pacific.

# NICARAGUA

STATUS: Republic
AREA: 148,000 sq km (57,130 sq miles)
POPULATION: 3,871,000
ANNUAL NATURAL INCREASE: 3.4%
CAPITAL: Managua
LANGUAGE: Spanish
RELIGION: Roman Catholic
CURRENCY: cordoba-oro (NIO)
ORGANISATIONS: UN, CACM,
OAS

Nicaragua is the largest of the Central American republics south of Mexico situated between the Caribbean and the Pacific. Active volcanic mountains parallel the western coast. The south is dominated by Lakes Managua and Nicaragua. Climate is tropical with rains May to October. Agriculture is the main occupation with cotton, coffee, sugar-cane and fruit the main exports. Gold, silver and copper are mined.

# NIGER

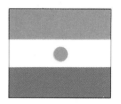

STATUS: Republic
AREA: 1,186,410 sq km (457,955 sq miles)
POPULATION: 7,732,000
ANNUAL NATURAL INCREASE: 3.5%
CAPITAL: Niamey
LANGUAGE: French, Hausa and other local
languages
RELIGION: 85% Muslim, 15% animist
CURRENCY: CFA franc (W Africa) (XOF)
ORGANISATIONS: UN, ECOWAS, OAU

Niger is a vast landlocked south Saharan republic with rainfall gradually decreasing from 56cm(22in) in the south to near zero in the north. Temperatures are above 35°C(95°F) for

much of the year. Most of the population are farmers particularly cattle, sheep and goat herders. Recent droughts have affected both cereals and livestock. Large deposits of uranium ore and phosphates are being exploited. The economy depends largely on foreign aid.

# NIGERIA

STATUS: Federal Republic
AREA: 923,850 sq km (356,605 sq miles)
POPULATION: 88,500,000
ANNUAL NATURAL INCREASE: 3.3%
CAPITAL: Abuja
LANGUAGE: English, Hausa, Yoruba,
Ibo

RELIGION: Muslim majority, 35% Christian, animist minority
CURRENCY: naira (NGN)
ORGANISATIONS: Comm, UN, ECOWAS, OAU, OPEC

The most populous nation in Africa, Nigeria is bounded to the north by the Sahara and to the west, east and south-east by tropical rain forest. The southern half of the country is dominated by the Niger and its tributaries, the north by the interior plateaux. Temperature averages 32°C(90°F) with high humidity. From a basic agricultural economy, Nigeria is slowly being transformed by oil discoveries in the Niger delta which account for 95% of exports.

## NIUE
STATUS: Self-governing Overseas Territory in Free Association with New Zealand
AREA: 259 sq km (100 sq miles)
POPULATION: 2,267
CAPITAL: Alofi

## NORFOLK ISLAND
STATUS: External Territory of Australia
AREA: 36 sq km (14 sq miles)
POPULATION: 1,977
CAPITAL: Kingston

# NORWAY

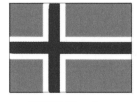

STATUS: Kingdom
AREA: 323,895 sq km (125,025 sq miles)
POPULATION: 4,242,000
ANNUAL NATURAL INCREASE: 0.3%
CAPITAL: Oslo

LANGUAGE: Norwegian (Bokmal and Nynorsk), Lappish
RELIGION: 92% Evangelical Lutheran Christian
CURRENCY: Norwegian krone (NOK)
ORGANISATIONS: UN, Council of Europe, EFTA, NATO, OECD

Norway is a mountainous country stretching from 58° to 72°N. The climate on the indented western coast is modified by the Gulf Stream with high rainfall and relatively mild winters with temperatures averaging −3.9°C(25°F) in January and 17°C(63°F) in July. Rainfall may be as high as 196cm(79in). Most settlements are scattered along the fjords, the coast and around Oslo in the south. Norway is rich in natural resources. Coal, petroleum, natural gas predominate in exports but are supplemented by forestry products and fishing. By value, the most important exports are crude oil and natural gas, food manufacturing and machinery. The advanced production of hydro-electric power has helped develop industry, particularly chemicals, metal products and paper.

# OMAN

STATUS: Sultanate
AREA: 271,950 sq km (104,970 sq miles)
POPULATION: 2,000,000
ANNUAL NATURAL INCREASE: 4.7%
CAPITAL: Muscat (Masqaṭ)
LANGUAGE: Arabic, English
RELIGION: 75% Ibadi Muslim, 25% Sunni Muslim
CURRENCY: rial Omani (OMR)
ORGANISATIONS: UN, Arab League

The Sultanate occupies the north-east coast of Arabia with a detached portion overlooking the Straits of Hormuz. The desert landscape consists of a coastal plain and low hills rising to plateau in the interior. The two fertile areas are the Batimah in the north and Dhofar in the south. The main crop is dates. Oil provides over 95% of export revenue.

# PAKISTAN

STATUS: Republic
AREA: 803,940 sq km (310,320 sq miles)
POPULATION: 112,050,000
ANNUAL NATURAL INCREASE: 3.2%
CAPITAL: Islamabad
LANGUAGE: Urdu, Punjabi, Sindhi, Pushtu, English
RELIGION: 90% Muslim
CURRENCY: Pakistani rupee (PKR)
ORGANISATIONS: Comm, UN, Col. Plan

The landscape and the economy of Pakistan are dominated by the river Indus and its tributaries which flow south flanked by the plateau of Baluchistan and the Sulaiman mountains to the west and the Thar desert to the east. The climate is dry and hot averaging 27°C(80°F). Rainfall reaches 90cm(36in) in the northern mountains. Over 50% of the population are engaged in agriculture which is confined to the irrigated areas near the great rivers. Main crops are wheat, cotton, maize, rice and sugarcane. There are many types of low-grade mineral deposits, such as coal and copper, but these are little developed. Main industries are food-processing and metals but these only contribute about 20% to the economy.

## PALAU
STATUS: UN Trustee Territory under US Administration
AREA: 497 sq km (192 sq miles)
POPULATION: 14,106
CAPITAL: Koror

# PANAMA

STATUS: Republic
AREA: 78,515 sq km (30,305 sq miles)
POPULATION: 2,315,000
ANNUAL NATURAL INCREASE: 2.2%
CAPITAL: Panama
LANGUAGE: Spanish, English
RELIGION: large Roman Catholic majority
CURRENCY: balboa (PAB), US dollar (USD)
ORGANISATIONS: UN, OAS

Panama is situated at the narrowest part of Central America and has both Pacific and Caribbean coastlines. The climate is tropical with little variation throughout the year – average temperature 27°C(80°F). The rainy season is from April to December. Panama probably has the world's largest copper reserves but these are hardly developed. Most foreign revenue is earned from the Panama Canal, and export of petroleum products.

# PAPUA NEW GUINEA

STATUS: Commonwealth Nation
AREA: 462,840 sq km (178,655 sq miles)
POPULATION: 3,699,000
ANNUAL NATURAL INCREASE: 2.4%
CAPITAL: Port Moresby
LANGUAGE: Pidgin English, English, native languages
RELIGION: Pantheist, Christian minority
CURRENCY: kina (PGK)
ORGANISATIONS: Comm, UN, Col. Plan

Papua New Guinea (the eastern half of New Guinea and neighbouring islands) is a mountainous country. It has an equatorial climate with temperatures of 21° to 32°C(70° to 90°F) and annual rainfall of over 200cm(79in). Copper is the major mineral deposit with large reserves on Bougainville, one of the neighbouring islands. Sugar and beef-cattle are developing areas of production. Major exports are copra, timber, coffee, rubber and tea.

# PARAGUAY

STATUS: Republic
AREA: 406,750 sq km (157,005 sq miles)
POPULATION: 4,277,000
ANNUAL NATURAL INCREASE: 3.2%
CAPITAL: Asunción
LANGUAGE: Spanish, Guarani
RELIGION: 90% Roman Catholic
CURRENCY: guarani (PYG)
ORGANISATIONS: UN, OAS

Paraguay is a landlocked country in South America with temperatures which average 15°C(59°F) all year. The country divides into lush, fertile plains and heavily forested plateau east of the River Paraguay and marshy scrubland (the Chaco) west of the river. Cassava, cotton, soyabeans and maize are the main crops but the rearing of livestock – cattle, horses, pigs and sheep – and food processing, dominate the export trade. The largest hydro-electric dam in the world is at Itaipú. This was constructed as a joint project with Brazil and will eventually have a capacity of 12.6 million kw.

# PERU

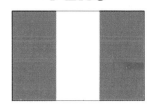

STATUS: Republic
AREA: 1,285,215 sq km (496,095 sq miles)
POPULATION: 22,332,000
ANNUAL NATURAL INCREASE: 2.2%
CAPITAL: Lima
LANGUAGE: Spanish, Quechua, Aymara
RELIGION: large Roman Catholic majority
CURRENCY: new sol (PEN)
ORGANISATIONS: UN, OAS

Peru divides into three geographical regions. The coastal region is very dry but fertile oases produce cotton, sugar, fruit and fodder crops. This is the most prosperous and heavily populated area which includes the industrial centres around Lima. In the ranges and plateaux of the Andes and the Amazon lowlands the soil is thin but the inhabitants depend on cultivation and grazing. Poor communications have hindered the development of Peru and there are great differences between rich and poor. Peru has rich mineral deposits of copper, lead, zinc and silver. There are oil reserves in the interior.

# PHILIPPINES

STATUS: Republic
AREA: 300,000 sq km (115,800 sq miles)
POPULATION: 62,868,000
ANNUAL NATURAL INCREASE: 2.4%
CAPITAL: Manila
LANGUAGE: Pilipino (Tagalog), English, Spanish, Cebuano
RELIGION: 90% Christian, 7% Muslim
CURRENCY: Philippine peso (PHP)
ORGANISATIONS: UN, ASEAN, Col. Plan

The Philippines consist of three main island groups, Luzon and its neighbours, the Visayas and Mindanao, including the Sulus. The archipelago is subject to earthquakes and typhoons. It has a monsoon climate and over 40% of the country is covered by rainforest. Fishing is important but small farms dominate the economy, producing rice and copra for domestic consumption and other coconut and sugar products for export. Forestry is becoming increasingly important. Main exports are textiles, fruit and electronic products. High unemployment and emigration are problems to be faced.

---

## PITCAIRN ISLAND
STATUS: UK Dependent Territory
AREA: 45 sq km (17.25 sq miles)
POPULATION: 59
CAPITAL: Adamstown

---

# POLAND

STATUS: Republic
AREA: 312,685 sq km (120,695 sq miles)
POPULATION: 38,180,000
ANNUAL NATURAL INCREASE: 0.8%
CAPITAL: Warsaw (Warszawa)
LANGUAGE: Polish
RELIGION: 90% Roman Catholic
CURRENCY: zloty (PLZ)
ORGANISATIONS: UN, OIEC

Poland occupies most of the southern coast of the Baltic Sea. Part of the North European Plain, the flat well-drained landscape rises gently towards the foothills of the Carpathians in the far south. The climate is continental with long severe winters. Average winter temperatures are below freezing point; rainfall averages between 52 and 73cm(21 and 29in). Both agriculture and natural resources play an important part in the economy and Poland is nearly self-sufficient in cereals sugar-beet and potatoes. There are large reserves of coal, copper, sulphur and natural gas. Major industries are ship-building in the north and production of metals and chemicals in the major mining centres in the south.

# PORTUGAL

STATUS: Republic
AREA: 91,630 sq km (35,370 sq miles)
POPULATION: 10,525,000
ANNUAL NATURAL INCREASE: 0.6%
CAPITAL: Lisbon (Lisboa)
LANGUAGE: Portuguese
RELIGION: large Roman Catholic majority
CURRENCY: escudo (PTE)
ORGANISATIONS: UN, Council of Europe, EC, NATO, OECD, WEU

Portugal occupies the western, Atlantic coast of the Iberian Peninsula. The Mediterranean climate is modified by westerly winds and the Gulf Stream. This is reflected in the lusher mixed

deciduous/coniferous forest in the northern mountains and the Mediterranean scrub in the far south. The hills along the coast rise to the interior plateaux. A quarter of the population are farmers growing vines, olives, wheat, maize and beans. Mineral deposits include coal, copper, kaolinite and uranium.

## PUERTO RICO
STATUS: Self-governing Commonwealth Territory of USA
AREA: 8,960 sq km (3,460 sq miles)
POPULATION: 3,599,000
CAPITAL: San Juan

# QATAR

STATUS: State
AREA: 11,435 sq km (4,415 sq miles)
POPULATION: 368,000

ANNUAL NATURAL INCREASE: 5.2%
CAPITAL: Doha (Ad Dawhah)
LANGUAGE: Arabic, English
RELIGION: Muslim
CURRENCY: Qatari Riyal (QAR)
ORGANISATIONS: UN, Arab League, OPEC

The country occupies all of the Qatar peninsula which reaches north from the north-east Arabian coast into the Persian Gulf. The land is flat and dry desert; the climate is hot and humid. July temperatures average 37°C (98°F) and annual rainfall averages 62mm (2.5in). Irrigation schemes are expanding production of fruit and vegetables for home consumption. The main source of revenue is from the exploitation of oil and gas reserves. The N.W. Dome oilfield contains 12% of known world gas reserves.

## RÉUNION
STATUS: Overseas Department of France
AREA: 2,510 sq km (969 sq miles)
POPULATION: 596,000
CAPITAL: Saint-Denis

## ROMANIA

STATUS: Republic
AREA: 237,500 sq km (91,675 sq miles)
POPULATION: 23,490,000
ANNUAL NATURAL INCREASE: 0.4%
CAPITAL: Bucharest (Bucuresti)
LANGUAGE: Romanian, Magyar
RELIGION: 65% Orthodox, 8% Roman Catholic, 3% Protestant
CURRENCY: leu (ROL)
ORGANISATIONS: UN, OIEC

The landscape of Romania is dominated by the great curve of the Carpathians. Lowlands to the west, east and south contain rich agricultural land. The climate in continental with variable rainfall, hot summers and cold winters. Forced industrialisation had taken the economy from one based on agriculture to one dependent on heavy industry, notably chemicals, metal processing and machine-building. Political and economic prospects for the future look bleak.

## RUSSIAN FEDERATION

STATUS: Federation
AREA: 17,078,005 sq km (6,592,110 sq miles)
POPULATION: 148,100,000
CAPITAL: Moscow (Moskva)
LANGUAGE: Russian
RELIGION: Russian Orthodox, Jewish and Muslim minorities
CURRENCY: rouble
ORGANISATIONS: UN, CIS

Covering much of eastern and north-eastern Europe and all of northern Asia, the Russian Federation (Russia) displays an enormous variety of landforms and climates. The Arctic deserts of the north give way to the wastes of the tundra and taiga which cover two-thirds of the country. In the far south, beyond the steppes some areas assume sub-tropical and semi-desert landscapes. Almost all of Russia's great rivers flow north. The majority of the population live west of the north–south spine of the Urals but in recent decades there has been a substantial migration eastwards to the Siberian basin in order to exploit its vast natural resources. Oil and gas pipelines link Siberia to refineries further west in Russia and elsewhere in Europe. Russia's extraordinary wealth of natural resources has been a key factor in the country's speedy industrialisation during the Soviet period. Heavy industry still plays a decisive role in the economy, while light and consumer industries have remained relatively backward and under developed. Agricultural land covers one-sixth of Russia's territory but there remains great potential for increase through drainage and clearance. By the mid-1980s the Soviet system was finally acknowledged to have reached an impasse, and the failure of the 'perestroika' programme for reform precipitated the disintegration of the Soviet Union, which finally broke up in 1991. The future is fraught with political and economic uncertainty.

## RWANDA

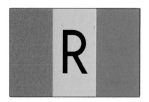

STATUS: Republic
AREA: 26,330 sq km (10,165 sq miles)
POPULATION: 7,181,000

ANNUAL NATURAL INCREASE: 3.3%
CAPITAL: Kigali
LANGUAGE: French, Kinyarwanda (Bantu), tribal languages
RELIGION: 50% animist, 50% Roman Catholic
CURRENCY: Rwanda franc (RWF)
ORGANISATIONS: UN, OAU

Small and isolated Rwanda supports a high density of population on the moist plateaux east of the Rift Valley. Agriculture is basically subsistence with coffee the major export. Few minerals have been discovered, and manufacturing is confined to food processing and construction materials.

## ST HELENA
STATUS: UK Dependent Territory
AREA: 122 sq km (47 sq miles)
POPULATION: 5,564
CAPITAL: Jamestown

## ST KITTS (ST CHRISTOPHER)-NEVIS

STATUS: Commonwealth State
AREA: 262 sq km (101 sq miles)
POPULATION: 44,000
ANNUAL NATURAL INCREASE: –0.9%
CAPITAL: Basseterre
LANGUAGE: English
RELIGION: Christian
CURRENCY: E. Caribbean dollar (XCD)
ORGANISATIONS: Comm, UN, CARICOM, OAS

St Kitts-Nevis, in the Leeward Islands, comprises two volcanic islands: St Christopher (St Kitts) and Nevis. The climate is tropical and humid with temperatures between 16°C and 33°C(61°F and 91°F) and an average annual rainfall of 140cm(55in). Main exports are sugar and molasses and cotton. Tourism is an important source of revenue.

## ST LUCIA

STATUS: Commonwealth State
AREA: 616 sq km (238 sq miles)
POPULATION: 146,600
ANNUAL NATURAL INCREASE: 2.0%
CAPITAL: Castries
LANGUAGE: English, French patois
RELIGION: 80% Roman Catholic
CURRENCY: E. Caribbean dollar (XCD)
ORGANISATIONS: Comm, UN, CARICOM, OAS

Independent since 1979 this small tropical Caribbean island in the Lesser Antilles grows coconuts, cocoa, citrus fruit and bananas. Most of the population are small farmers. Main industries are food and drink processing and all consumer goods are imported. There are no commercial mineral deposits. Tourism is a rapidly developing industry.

## ST PIERRE & MIQUELON

STATUS: Territorial Collectivity of France
AREA: 241 sq km (93 sq miles)
POPULATION: 6,392
CAPITAL: St Pierre

## ST VINCENT

STATUS: Commonwealth State
AREA: 389 sq km (150 sq miles)
POPULATION: 113,950
ANNUAL NATURAL INCREASE: 1.1%
CAPITAL: Kingstown
LANGUAGE: English
RELIGION: Christian
CURRENCY: E. Caribbean dollar (XCD)
ORGANISATIONS: Comm, UN, CARICOM, OAS

St Vincent in the Lesser Antilles comprises the main island and a chain of small islands called the Northern Grenadines. The climate is tropical. Most exports are foodstuffs: arrowroot, sweet potatoes, bananas, coconut products and yams. Some sugar-cane is grown for the production of rum and other drinks. Tourism is an expanding industry.

## SAN MARINO

STATUS: Republic
AREA: 61 sq km (24 sq miles)
POPULATION: 24,000
ANNUAL NATURAL INCREASE: 1.2%
CAPITAL: San Marino
LANGUAGE: Italian
RELIGION: Roman Catholic
CURRENCY: Italian lira (ITL),
San Marino coinage
ORGANISATIONS: Council of Europe

An independent state within Italy, San Marino straddles a limestone peak in the Apennines south of Rimini. The economy is centred around tourism and sale of postage stamps. Most of the population are farmers growing cereals, olives and vines and tending herds of sheep and goats. Wine and textiles are exported.

# SÃO TOMÉ AND PRINCÍPE

STATUS: Republic
AREA: 964 sq km (372 sq miles)
POPULATION: 115,600
ANNUAL NATURAL INCREASE: 3.0%
CAPITAL: São Tomé
LANGUAGE: Portuguese, Fang
RELIGION: Roman Catholic majority
CURRENCY: dobra (STD)
ORGANISATIONS: UN, OAU

Independent from Portugal since 1975, two large and several small islands make up this tiny state situated near the equator 200km(125 miles) off the west coast of Africa. The climate is tropical with temperatures averaging 25°C(77°F) and rainfall between 100 and 500cm (40 and 197in). Cocoa, coconuts and palm oil are the main crops grown on the rich volcanic soil. Other foods and consumer goods are imported.

## SARDINIA

STATUS: Island Region of Italy
AREA: 24,090 sq km (9,300 sq miles)
POPULATION: 1,651,218
CAPITAL: Cagliari

# SAUDI ARABIA

STATUS: Kingdom
AREA: 2,400,900 sq km (926,745 sq miles)
POPULATION: 12,000,000
ANNUAL NATURAL INCREASE: 5.1%
CAPITAL: Riyadh (Ar Riyād)
LANGUAGE: Arabic
RELIGION: Muslim (85% Sunni)
CURRENCY: Saudi riyal (SAR)
ORGANISATIONS: UN, Arab League, OPEC

Saudi Arabia occupies the heart of the vast arid Arabian Peninsula. There are no rivers which flow all year round. To the east, high mountains fringe the Red Sea but even here rainfall rarely exceeds 38cm (15in). Temperatures rise beyond 44°C (111°F) in the summer. The interior plateau slopes down gently eastwards to the Gulf and supports little vegetation. The south-east part of the country is well named as the 'Empty Quarter'; it is almost devoid of population. Only in the coastal strips and oases are cereals and date palms grown. Oil is the most important resource and export commodity and economic development is dependent on its revenue. Irrigation schemes and land reclamation projects are attempting to raise food production.

# SENEGAL

STATUS: Republic
AREA: 196,720 sq km (75,935 sq miles)
POPULATION: 7,327,000
ANNUAL NATURAL INCREASE: 3.0%
CAPITAL: Dakar
LANGUAGE: French, native languages
RELIGION: 90% Muslim (Sunni),
5% Roman Catholic
CURRENCY: CFA franc (W Africa) (XOF)
ORGANISATIONS: UN, ECOWAS, OAU

Senegal on the coast of West Africa, is a flat, dry country cut through by the Gambia, Casamance and Senegal rivers. Rainfall rarely ex-

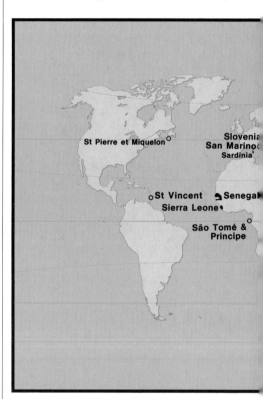

ceeds 58cm(23in) on the wetter coast. The interior savannah supports varied wildlife but little agriculture. Groundnuts, cotton and millet are the main crops, but frequent droughts have reduced their value as cash crops. Phosphate mining, ship-repairing and food processing are the major industries.

# SEYCHELLES

STATUS: Republic
AREA: 404 sq km (156 sq miles)
POPULATION: 67,000
ANNUAL NATURAL INCREASE: 0.9%
CAPITAL: Victoria
LANGUAGE: English, French, Creole

RELIGION: 90% Roman Catholic
CURRENCY: Seychelles rupee (SCR)
ORGANISATIONS: Comm, UN, OAU

This archipelago in the Indian Ocean comprises of over 100 granite or coral islands. Mahe, the largest, covers 155 sq km (60 sq miles) rising steeply to over 900 m (2953 ft). The coral islands rise only a few metres above sea level. Temperatures are a constant 24-29°C (75-84°F), and rainfall is in the range of 180-345 cm (71-135 in). Main exports are copra, coconuts and cinnamon. The staple food, rice, is imported although crops such as cassava, sweet potatoes, yams and sugar cane are grown for local consumption. Fishing is also important to the economy. Tourism has expanded greatly since the opening of the international airport in 1978.

### SHIKOKU
STATUS: Island Prefecture of Japan
AREA: 18,755 sq km (7,240 sq miles)
POPULATION: 4,224,000

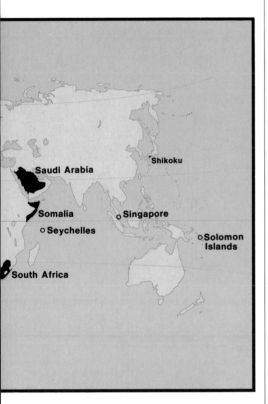

# SIERRA LEONE

STATUS: Republic
AREA: 72,325 sq km (27,920 sq miles)
POPULATION: 4,151,000
ANNUAL NATURAL INCREASE: 2.4%
CAPITAL: Freetown
LANGUAGE: English, (also Krio Temne, Mende)
RELIGION: animist majority. Muslim and Christian minorities
CURRENCY: leone (SLL)
ORGANISATIONS: Comm, UN, ECOWAS, OAU

A former British colony, the coastline of Sierra Leone is dominated by swamps broken only by the mountainous peninsula south of Freetown.

A wide coastal plain extends inland to the foothills of the interior plateaux and mountains. The land is not fertile due to the poor soils with most of the population farming at subsistence level. Mineral deposits include diamonds, iron ore and bauxite with manufacturing only developed around the capital. Oil-, rice- and timber-mills process these products for export.

# SINGAPORE

STATUS: Republic
AREA: 616 sq km (238 sq miles)
POPULATION: 3,002,800
ANNUAL NATURAL INCREASE: 1.2%
CAPITAL: Singapore
LANGUAGE: Malay, Chinese (Mandarin), Tamil, English
RELIGION: Daoist, Buddhist, Muslim, Christian and Hindu
CURRENCY: Singapore dollar (SGD)
ORGANISATIONS: Comm, UN, ASEAN, Col. Plan

Founded by Sir Stamford Raffles, the state of Singapore has been transformed from an island of mangrove swamps into one the world's major entrepreneurial centres. The island, connected to Peninsular Malaysia by a man-made causeway, has a hot, humid climate with 224cm(96in) of rain per year. With few natural resources, Singapore depends on manufacturing precision goods and electronic products along with financial services.

# SLOVENIA

STATUS: Republic
AREA: 20,250 sq km (7,815 sq miles)
POPULATION: 1,924,000
CAPITAL: Ljubljana
LANGUAGE: Slovenian
RELIGION: mainly Roman Catholic
CURRENCY: Slovenian dinar (Tolar)

The northernmost part of the former Yugoslav federation, Slovenia has always been one of the key gateways from the Balkans to central and western Europe. Much of the country is mountainous, its heartland and main centre of population being the Ljubljana basin. Extensive mountain pastures provide profitable dairy-farming, but the amount of cultivable land is restricted. There are large mercury mines in the northwest which, in recent decades, has also developed a broad range of light industries. Combined with tourism, this has given the country a well-balanced economy. After a brief military conflict Slovenia won its independence in 1991 which status has since been internationally recognised.

# SOLOMON ISLANDS

STATUS: Commonwealth Nation
AREA: 29,790 sq km (11,500 sq miles)
POPULATION: 321,000
ANNUAL NATURAL INCREASE: 3.5%
CAPITAL: Honiara
LANGUAGE: English, Pidgin English, native languages
RELIGION: 95% Christian
CURRENCY: Solomon Island dollar (SBD)
ORGANISATIONS: Comm, UN

Situated in the South Pacific Ocean the Solomon Islands consist of six main and many smaller islands. The mountainous large islands are covered by tropical rain forest reflecting the high temperatures and heavy rainfall. The main crops are coconuts, cocoa and rice, with copra, timber and palm oil being the main exports. This former British protectorate became independent in 1978. There are reserves of bauxite, phosphate and gold.

# SOMALIA

STATUS: Republic
AREA: 630,000 sq km (243,180 sq miles)
POPULATION: 7,497,000
ANNUAL NATURAL INCREASE: 3.0%
CAPITAL: Mogadishu (Muqdisho)
LANGUAGE: Somali, Arabic, English, Italian
RELIGION: Muslim. Roman Catholic minority
CURRENCY: Somali shilling (SOS)
ORGANISATIONS: UN, Arab League, OAU

Independent since 1960, Somalia, is a hot and arid country in north-east Africa. The semi-desert of the northern mountains contrasts with the plains of the south where the bush country is particularly rich in wildlife. Most of the population are nomadic, following herds of camels, sheep, goats and cattle. Little land is cultivated but cotton, maize, millet and sugarcane are grown. Bananas are a major export. Iron ore, gypsum and uranium deposits are found but none are yet exploited.

# SOUTH AFRICA

STATUS: Republic
AREA: 1,184,825 sq km (457,345 sq miles)
POPULATION: 35,282,000
ANNUAL NATURAL INCREASE: 2.4%
CAPITAL: Pretoria (administrative)
Cape Town (legislative)

LANGUAGE: Afrikaans, English, various African languages
RELIGION: mainly Christian, Hindu, Jewish and Muslim minorities
CURRENCY: rand (ZAR)
ORGANISATIONS: UN

## TRIBAL HOMELANDS

This includes the Bantu homelands and the South African homeland republics of Bophuthatswana, Ciskei, Transkei and Venda
POPULATION: 16,000,000 approx.

## CAPE PROVINCE

STATUS: Province
AREA: 656,640 sq km (253,465 sq miles)
POPULATION: 4,901,251

## NATAL

STATUS: Province
AREA: 86,965 sq km (33,570 sq miles)
POPULATION: 2,145,018

## ORANGE FREE STATE

STATUS: Province
AREA: 127,990 sq km (49,405 sq miles)
POPULATION: 1,863,327

## TRANSVAAL

STATUS: Province
AREA: 268,915 sq km (103,800 sq miles)
POPULATION: 7,532,179

The Republic of South Africa is the most highly developed country in Africa. Geographically, the interior consists of a plateau of over 900m(2955ft) drained by the Orange and Limpopo rivers. Surrounding the plateau is a pronounced escarpment below which the land descends by steps to the sea. Rainfall in most areas is less than 50cm(20in) becoming increasingly drier in the west. Agriculture is limited by poor soils but sheep and cattle are extensively grazed. Main crops are maize, wheat, sugar-cane, vegetables, cotton and vines. Wine is an important export commodity. South Africa abounds in minerals. Diamonds, gold, platinum, silver, uranium, copper, manganese and asbestos are mined and nearly 80% of the continent's coal reserves are in South Africa. Manufacturing and engineering is concentrated in southern Transvaal and around the ports. Most foreign revenue is earned through exports of minerals, metals, precious stones, textiles and chemicals and tobacco.

# SPAIN

STATUS: Kingdom
AREA: 504,880 sq km (194,885 sq miles)
POPULATION: 38,991,000
ANNUAL NATURAL INCREASE: 0.5%
CAPITAL: Madrid
LANGUAGE: Spanish (Castilian), Catalan, Basque, Galician
RELIGION: Roman Catholic
CURRENCY: Spanish peseta (ESP)
ORGANISATIONS: UN, Council of Europe, EC, NATO, OECD, WEU

Once a great colonial power, Spain occupies most of the Iberian Peninsula. Mountain ranges fringe the meseta, a vast plateau averaging 600m(1970ft). Climate is affected regionally by latitude and proximity to the Atlantic Ocean and Mediterranean Sea. Much of the land is covered by Mediterranean scrub but wheat, barley, maize, grapes and olives are cultivated. Main cash crops are cotton, olives, tobacco and citrus fruit. Textile manufacturing in the north-east and steel, chemicals, consumer goods and vehicle manufacturing in the towns and cities has proved a magnet for great numbers of the rural population. Other major industries are cement, fishing and forestry. Main minerals are coal, iron ore, uranium and zinc. Tourism is of vital importance to the economy.

---

# SRI LANKA

STATUS: Republic
AREA: 65,610 sq km (25,325 sq miles)
POPULATION: 16,993,000
ANNUAL NATURAL INCREASE: 1.5%
CAPITAL: Colombo
LANGUAGE: Sinhala, Tamil, English
RELIGION: 70% Buddhist, 15% Hindu. Roman Catholic and Muslim minorities
CURRENCY: Sri Lanka rupee (LKR)
ORGANISATIONS: Comm, UN, Col. Plan

Situated only 19km (12 miles) from mainland India, Sri Lanka (also called Ceylon) is an island of undulating coastal plain encircling the central highlands. The climate is divided accordingly between tropical on the coast and temperate in the hills. Annual rainfall averages only 100cm (39in) in the north and east while the south and west receive over 200cm (79in). Natural resources are limited but the rich agricultural land produces tea, rubber and coconuts. Gemstones (sapphire, ruby, beryl, topaz), graphite and salt are mined. The main industries are food processing, textiles, chemicals and rubber.

---

# SUDAN

STATUS: Republic
AREA: 2,505,815 sq km (967,245 sq miles)
POPULATION: 25,204,000
ANNUAL NATURAL INCREASE: 3.0%
CAPITAL: Khartoum
LANGUAGE: Arabic, tribal languages
RELIGION: Muslim (Sunni) 70%, animist and Christian
CURRENCY: Sudanese pound (SDP)
ORGANISATIONS: UN, Arab League, OAU

Sudan, in the upper Nile basin, is Africa's largest country. The land is mostly flat and infertile with a hot, arid climate. The White and Blue Niles are invaluable, serving not only to irrigate cultivated land but also as a potential source of hydro-electric power. Subsistence farming accounts for 80% of the Sudan's total production. Major exports include cotton, groundnuts, sugar cane, and sesame seed. The principal activity is nomadic herding with over 40 million cattle and sheep and 14 million goats.

# SURINAM

STATUS: Republic
AREA: 163,820 sq km (63,235 sq miles)
POPULATION: 422,000
ANNUAL NATURAL INCREASE: 2.5%
CAPITAL: Paramaribo

LANGUAGE: Dutch, English, Spanish, Surinamese (Sranang Tongo), Hindi and others
RELIGION: 45% Christian, 28% Hindu, 20% Muslim
CURRENCY: Surinam guilder (SRG)
ORGANISATIONS: UN, OAS

Independent from the Dutch since 1976, Surinam is a small state lying on the north-east coast in the tropics of South America. Physically, there are three main regions: a low-lying, marshy coastal strip; undulating savannah; densely forested highlands. Rice growing takes up 75% of all cultivated land. The introduction of cattle-raising for meat and dairy products is not yet complete. Bauxite accounts for 90% of Surinam's foreign earnings. Rice and timber products are also important. Timber resources are largely untapped.

---

## SVALBARD

STATUS: Archipelago Territory of Norway
AREA: 62,000 sq km (23,930 sq miles)
POPULATION: 3,942

# SWAZILAND

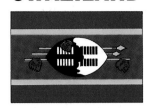

STATUS: Kingdom
AREA: 17,365 sq km (6,705 sq miles)
POPULATION: 768,000
ANNUAL NATURAL INCREASE: 3.4%
CAPITAL: Mbabane
LANGUAGE: English, SiSwati
RELIGION: 60% Christian, 40% traditional
beliefs
CURRENCY: lilangeni (SZL) S. African rand (ZAR)
ORGANISATIONS: Comm, UN, OAU

Landlocked Swaziland in southern Africa, is a sub-tropical, savannah country. It is divided into four main regions: the High, Middle and

Low Velds and the Lebombo Mountains. Rainfall is abundant promoting good pastureland for the many cattle and sheep. Major exports include sugar, meat, citrus fruits, textiles, wood products and asbestos.

# SWEDEN

STATUS: Kingdom
AREA: 449,790 sq km (173,620 sq miles)
POPULATION: 8,595,000
ANNUAL NATURAL INCREASE: 0.2%
CAPITAL: Stockholm
LANGUAGE: Swedish, Finnish, Lappish
RELIGION: 95% Evangelical Lutheran

CURRENCY: Swedish krona (SEK)
ORGANISATIONS: UN, Council of Europe, EFTA
OECD

Glacial debris, glacier-eroded valleys and thick glacial clay are all dominant features of Sweden. Physically, Sweden comprises four main regions: Norrland, the northern forested mountains; the Lake District of the centre south; the southern uplands of Jönköping; and the extremely fertile Scania plain of the far south. Summers are short and hot with long, cold winters. Annual rainfall varies between 200 cm (79 in) in the west and south-west, to 50 cm (20 in) in the east and south-east.

Over half the land area is forested resulting in a thriving timber industry, but manufacturing industry, particularly cars and trucks, metal products and machine tools, is becoming increasingly dominant. Mineral resources are also rich and plentiful – iron-ore production alone exceeds 17 million tons a year. There are also deposits of copper, lead and zinc.

# SWITZERLAND

STATUS: Federation
AREA: 41,285 sq km (15,935 sq miles)
POPULATION: 6,712,000
ANNUAL NATURAL INCREASE: 0.3%
CAPITAL: Bern (Berne)
LANGUAGE: German, French, Italian, Romansch
RELIGION: 44% Protestant, 48% Roman
Catholic. Jewish minority
CURRENCY: Swiss franc (CHF)
ORGANISATIONS: Council of Europe, EFTA, OECD

Switzerland is a mountainous, landlocked country in the Alps. Winters are very cold with heavy snowfall. Summers are mild with an average July temperature of 18°-19°C (64°-66°F). Rainfall is normally restricted to the summer months. Agriculture is based mainly on dairy farming. Major crops include hay, wheat, barley and potatoes. Industry plays a major role in Switzerland's economy, centred on metal engineering, watchmaking, food processing, textiles and chemicals. Switzerland's history of neutrality from armed conflict has made it an attractive location for the headquarters of several international organisations. The Swiss, on the whole, enjoy a high standard of living. Tourism is also an important source of income and employment. The financial services sector, especially banking, is also of great importance.

# SYRIA

STATUS: Republic
AREA: 185,680 sq km (71,675 sq miles)

POPULATION: 12,116,000
ANNUAL NATURAL INCREASE: 3.6%
CAPITAL: Damascus (Dimashq)
LANGUAGE: Arabic
RELIGION: 80% Sunni Muslim. Christian
minority
CURRENCY: Syrian pound (SYP)
ORGANISATIONS: UN, Arab League

Syria is situated at the heart of the Middle East bordered by Turkey, Iraq, Jordan, Israel and Lebanon. Its most fertile areas lie along the coastal strip on the Mediterranean Sea which supports the bulk of its population, and in the depressions and plateaux of the north-east which are cut through by the rivers Orontes and Euphrates. In the south the Anti-Lebanon range is bordered to the east by the Syrian desert. While the coast has a Mediterranean climate with dry hot summers and mild wet winters, the interior becomes increasingly hot and arid – average summer temperatures in the desert reach 43°C (109°F). Rainfall varies between 22 and 40 cm (9 and 16 in). Cotton is Syria's main export crop, and wheat and barley are also grown. Cattle, sheep and goats are the main livestock. Although traditionally an agriculturally-based economy, the country is rapidly becoming industrialised as oil, natural gas and phosphate resources are exploited. Salt and gypsum are mined, oil and oil products, food and textiles are also exported.

### TAHITI
STATUS: Main Island of French Polynesia
AREA: 1,042 sq km (402 sq miles)
POPULATION: 115,820

# TAIWAN

STATUS: Island Republic of China
AREA: 35,990 sq km (13,890 sq miles)
POPULATION: 19,700,000
ANNUAL NATURAL INCREASE: 1.5%
CAPITAL: Taipei
LANGUAGE: Mandarin Chinese
RELIGION: Buddhist majority. Muslim, Daoist
and Christian minorities
CURRENCY: New Taiwan dollar (TWD)

Taiwan is separated from mainland China by the Taiwan Strait (the former Formosa Channel) in which lie the Pescadores. Two-thirds of Taiwan is mountainous, the highest point attaining 3,950 m (12,959 ft). The flat to rolling coastal plain in the western part of the island accommodates the bulk of the population and the national commerce, industry and agriculture. Climate is tropical, marine, with persistent cloudy conditions. The monsoon rains fall in June to August, annual average 260 cm (102 in). Main crops are rice, tea, fruit, sugar cane and sweet potatoes. Industry is light and heavy, principal exports are textiles, electrical goods and services. Natural resources are limestone, marble, asbestos, copper and sulphur. Natural gas is extracted from the Strait.

# TAJIKISTAN

STATUS: Republic
AREA: 143,100 sq km (55,235 sq miles)
POPULATION: 5,200,000
CAPITAL: Dushanbe
LANGUAGE: Tajik, Uzbek, Russian
RELIGION: Muslim
CURRENCY: rouble
ORGANISATIONS: CIS

Situated in the mountainous heart of Asia, more than half the territory of Tajikistan lies above 3000 m (10,000 ft). The major settlement areas are related to the junction between mountain and steppe and to the principal rivers. The climate varies from continental to subtropical according to elevation and shelter. Extensive irrigation, without which agriculture would be severely limited, has made it possible for cotton growing to develop into the leading branch of agriculture, and on that basis textiles have become the largest industry in the country. Tajikistan is rich in mineral and fuel deposits, the exploitation of which became a major feature of economic development during the Soviet era. Preceding full independence in 1991 there was an upsurge of, sometimes violent, Tajik nationalism as a result of which many Russians and Uzbeks have left the country.

# TANZANIA

STATUS: Republic
AREA: 939,760 sq km (362,750 sq miles)
POPULATION: 25,635,000
ANNUAL NATURAL INCREASE: 3.5%
CAPITAL: Dodoma
LANGUAGE: Swahili, English
RELIGION: 40% Christian, 35% Muslim
CURRENCY: Tanzanian shilling (TZS)
ORGANISATIONS: Comm, UN, OAU

Much of this East African country consists of high interior plateaux covered by scrub and grassland, bordered to the north by the volcanic Kilimanjaro region, to the east by Lake Tanganyika, and by highlands to the south. Despite its proximity to the equator, the altitude of much of Tanzania means that temperatures are reduced, and only on the narrow coastal plain is the climate truly tropical. Average temperatures vary between 19° and 28°C (67° and 82°F), and rainfall 57 to 106 cm (23 to 43 in). Subsistence farming is the main way of life, although coffee, cotton, sisal, cashew nuts and tea are exported. Industry is limited, but gradually growing in importance, and involves textiles, food processing and tobacco. Tourism could be a future growth area.

# THAILAND

STATUS: Kingdom
AREA: 514,000 sq km (198,405 sq miles)
POPULATION: 54,532,000
ANNUAL NATURAL INCREASE: 1.9%
CAPITAL: Bangkok (Krung Thep)
LANGUAGE: Thai
RELIGION: Buddhist, 4% Muslim
CURRENCY: baht (THB)
ORGANISATIONS: UN, ASEAN, Col. Plan

Thailand consists of a flat undulating central plain, containing the Chao Phraye River, fringed by mountains and by a plateau in the north-east drained by the Mekong River. From May to October, monsoon rains are heavy with an annual average rainfall of 150 cm (59 in). The climate is tropical with temperatures reaching 36°C (97°F). Over 50% of the country is covered by dense rainforest. The central plain is well-served with irrigation canals which supply the paddy fields. Rice is the main export crop, although maize, beans, coconuts and groundnuts are also grown. Thailand is one of the world's largest producers of rubber and tin. A small-scale petrochemical industry has been developed.

# TOGO

STATUS: Republic
AREA: 56,785 sq km (21,920 sq miles)
POPULATION: 3,531,000
ANNUAL NATURAL INCREASE: 3.5%
CAPITAL: Lomé
LANGUAGE: French, Kabre, Ewe
RELIGION: 60% animist, 25% Christian 7.5% Muslim
CURRENCY: CFA franc (W Africa) (XOF)
ORGANISATIONS: UN, ECOWAS, OAU

Togo, formerly a German protectorate and French colony, is situated between Ghana and Benin in West Africa. A long narrow country, it has only 65 km (40 miles) of coast. The interior consists of mountains and high infertile tableland. The climate is tropical with an average temperature of 27°C (81°F). Most of Togo's farmers grow maize, cassava, yams, groundnuts and plantains, and the country is virtually self-sufficient in food-stuffs. Phosphates account for a half of export revenue. Cotton, cocoa and coffee are also exported.

## TOKELAU ISLANDS
STATUS: Overseas Territory of New Zealand
AREA: 10 sq km (4 sq miles)
POPULATION: 1,690

# TONGA

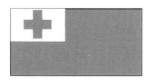

STATUS: Kingdom
AREA: 699 sq km (270 sq miles)
POPULATION: 95,000
ANNUAL NATURAL INCREASE: 0.4%
CAPITAL: Nuku'alofa
LANGUAGE: Tongan, English
RELIGION: Christian
CURRENCY: pa'anga (TOP)
ORGANISATIONS: Comm

Tonga consists of an archipelago of 169 islands in the Pacific 180km(112 miles) north of New Zealand. There are seven groups of islands, but the most important are Tongatapu, Ha'apai and Vava'u. All the islands are covered with dense tropical vegetation, and temperatures

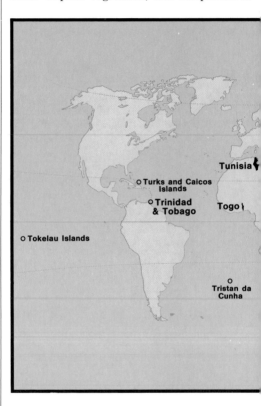

range from 11° to 29°C(52° to 84°F). Main exports are coconut products and bananas.

# TRINIDAD & TOBAGO

STATUS: Republic
AREA: 5,130 sq km (1,980 sq miles)
POPULATION: 1,234,388
ANNUAL NATURAL INCREASE: 1.7%
CAPITAL: Port of Spain
LANGUAGE: English
RELIGION: 60% Christian, 25% Hindu, 6% Muslim
CURRENCY: Trinidad & Tobago dollar (TTD)
ORGANISATIONS: Comm, UN, CARICOM, OAS

These Caribbean islands lie only 11 and 30km(7 and 19 miles) respectively from the Venezuelan coast. Both islands have mountainous interiors – the central range of Trinidad reaches 940m(3084ft) – and are densely covered with tropical rain forest. Sugar was once the mainstay of the economy but oil is now the leading source of revenue.

## TRISTAN DA CUNHA
STATUS: Dependency of St Helena
AREA: 98 sq km (38 sq miles)
POPULATION: 306

# TUNISIA

STATUS: Republic
AREA: 164,150 sq km (63,378 sq miles)
POPULATION: 8,180,000
ANNUAL NATURAL INCREASE: 2.5%
CAPITAL: Tunis
LANGUAGE: Arabic, French
RELIGION: Muslim
CURRENCY: Tunisian dinar (TND)
ORGANISATIONS: UN, Arab League, OAU

Tunisia is fringed to the north and west by the eastern end of the Atlas mountain range. Salt lakes are scattered throughout the central plains and to the south lies the Sahara. Average annual temperature ranges from 10° to 27°C (50° to 81°F) and while the coastal area has Mediterranean scrub, the interior is desert. The majority of the population live along the north-east coast. Wheat, barley, olives and citrus fruit are the main crops and oil, natural gas and sugar refining are the main industries. The tourist industry is expanding and is becoming increasingly important to the economy.

# TURKEY

STATUS: Republic
AREA: 779,450 sq km (300,870 sq miles)
POPULATION: 58,687,000
ANNUAL NATURAL INCREASE: 2.3%
CAPITAL: Ankara
LANGUAGE: Turkish, Kurdish
RELIGION: Sunni Muslim, Christian minority
CURRENCY: Turkish lira (TRL)
ORGANISATIONS: UN, Council of Europe, NATO, OECD

Turkey has always occupied a strategically important position linking Europe and Asia. The central Anatolian plateau is bordered to the north and south by mountain ranges which converge in the eastern Anatolian mountains crowned by Mt Ararat 5165m(16,945ft). The north, south and west coastlines are fringed by Mediterranean vegetation and have short, mild and wet winters and long, hot summers. The interior is arid with average rainfall less than 25cm(10in). The main crops are wheat and barley, but tobacco, olives, sugar-beet, tea and fruit are also grown, and sheep, goats and cattle are raised. Turkey is becoming increasingly industrialised and now leads the Middle East in the production of iron, steel, chrome, coal and lignite. Tourism is a rapidly growing industry.

# TURKMENISTAN

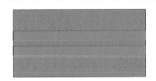

STATUS: Republic
AREA: 488,100 sq km (188,405 sq miles)
POPULATION: 3,600,000
CAPITAL: Ashkhabad
LANGUAGE: Turkmen, Russian
RELIGION: Muslim
CURRENCY: rouble
ORGANISATIONS: CIS

Situated in the far south of the former Soviet Union, Turkmenistan is a land of deserts and oases; only in the south do hills and mountains emerge. The continental climate is responsible for great fluctuations in temperature, both during the day and the year. Traditionally nomads, the Turkmen tribes under the Soviet regime, turned from pastoral farming to cotton-growing, made possible by extensive irrigation. Rich in minerals and chemicals, its industrial growth was forcibly developed by the Russians, resulting in ethnic-outsiders making up the majority of the urban population.

## TURKS & CAICOS ISLANDS
STATUS: UK Dependent Territory
AREA: 430 sq km (166 sq miles)
POPULATION: 11,696
CAPITAL: Cockburn Town

# TUVALU

STATUS: State
AREA: 24.6 sq km (9.5 sq miles)
POPULATION: 10,000
ANNUAL NATURAL INCREASE: 1.5%
CAPITAL: Funafuti
LANGUAGE: Tuvaluan, English
RELIGION: 98% Protestant
CURRENCY: Australian dollar (AUD), Tuvaluan coinage
ORGANISATIONS: Comm (special member)

Tuvalu consists of nine dispersed coral atolls, north of Fiji, in the Pacific Ocean. The climate is tropical; hot, with heavy annual rainfall (c.300cm or 118in). Fish is the staple food but coconuts and bread-fruit are cultivated.

# UGANDA

STATUS: Republic
AREA: 236,580 sq km (91,320 sq miles)
POPULATION: 18,795,000
ANNUAL NATURAL INCREASE: 3.2%
CAPITAL: Kampala
LANGUAGE: English, tribal languages
RELIGION: 60% Christian. Muslim minority
CURRENCY: Uganda shilling (UGX)
ORGANISATIONS: Comm, UN, OAU

Uganda is bordered to the west by the African Rift valley and to the east by Kenya. The central high plateau is savannah, while the area around Lake Victoria has been cleared for cultivation. To the west are mountain ranges reaching 5110m(16,765ft). The climate is warm (21°–24°C or 70°–75°F), and rainfall ranges from 75–150cm(30–59in). The main export crop is coffee. Lake Victoria has great supplies of freshwater fish.

# UKRAINE

STATUS: Republic
AREA: 603,700 sq km (233,030 sq miles)
POPULATION: 51,800,000
CAPITAL: Kiev
LANGUAGE: Ukrainian, Russian
RELIGION: Russian Orthodox, Uniate
CURRENCY: rouble (temporary coupon currency, new currency to be introduced in 1992)
ORGANISATIONS: UN, CIS

Ukraine consists mainly of level plains and mountainous border areas. The landscape is, however, diverse, with marshes, forests, wooded and treeless steppe. Deposits of 'black earth', among the most fertile soils, cover about 65% of Ukraine. Grain, potatoes, vegetables and fruits, industrial crops (notably sugar beets and sunflower seeds) and fodder crops are grown. Food processing is important to the economy, and southern regions are renowned for wines. Ukraine is rich in mineral resources, such as iron ore, coal and lignite, and has large reserves of petroleum and gas. Extensive mining, metal production, machine-building, engineering and chemicals dominate Ukraine industry, most of it is located in the Donets basin and the Dnepr lowland. These two regions account for four-fifths of the urban population. Natural wealth and advanced industrial development make Ukraine well-equipped for adaptation to free market conditions.

# UNITED ARAB EMIRATES (UAE)

STATUS: Federation of 7 emirates
AREA: 75,150 sq km (29,010 sq miles)
POPULATION: 1,600,000
ANNUAL NATURAL INCREASE: 4.6%
CAPITAL: Abu Dhabi
LANGUAGE: Arabic, English
RELIGION: Sunni Muslim
CURRENCY: UAE dirham (AED)
ORGANISATIONS: UN, Arab League, OPEC

## ABU DHABI
STATUS: Emirate
AREA: 64,750 sq km (24,995 sq miles)
POPULATION: 670,125

## ÁJMĀN
STATUS: Emirate
AREA: 260 sq km (100 sq miles)
POPULATION: 64,318

## DUBAI
STATUS: Emirate
AREA: 3,900 sq km (1,505 sq miles)
POPULATION: 419,104

## FUJAIRAH
STATUS: Emirate
AREA: 1,170 sq km (452 sq miles)
POPULATION: 54,425

## RAS AL-KHAIMAH
STATUS: Emirate
AREA: 1,690 sq km (652 sq miles)
POPULATION: 116,470

## SHARJAH
STATUS: Emirate
AREA: 2,600 sq km (1,005 sq miles)
POPULATION: 268,722

## UMM AL QAIWAIN
STATUS: Emirate
AREA: 780 sq km (300 sq miles)
POPULATION: 29,229

Seven emirates stretched along the south eastern shores of the Persian Gulf constitute this oil rich Arab state. Flat deserts cover most of the landscape rising to the Hajar mountains of the Musandam Peninsula. Summer temperatures reach 40°C(104°F) and winter rainfall 13cm(5in). Only the desert oases are fertile, producing fruit and vegetables. Trade is dominated by exports of oil and natural gas.

# UNITED KINGDOM OF GREAT BRITAIN & NORTHERN IRELAND (UK)

STATUS: Kingdom
AREA: 244,755 sq km (94,475 sq miles)
POPULATION: 55,514,500
ANNUAL NATURAL INCREASE: 0.2%
CAPITAL: London
LANGUAGE: English, Welsh, Gaelic
RELIGION: Protestant majority. Roman Catholic Jewish, Muslim and Hindu minorities
CURRENCY: Pound Sterling (GBP)
ORGANISATIONS: Comm, UN, Col. Plan, Council of Europe, NATO, OECD, WEU, EC, G7

## ENGLAND
STATUS: Constituent Country
AREA: 130,360 sq km (50,320 sq miles)
POPULATION: 46,170,300
CAPITAL: London

## NORTHERN IRELAND
STATUS: Constituent Region
AREA: 14,150 sq km (5,460 sq miles)
POPULATION: 1,589,000
CAPITAL: Belfast

## SCOTLAND
STATUS: Constituent Country
AREA: 78,750 sq km (30,400 sq miles)
POPULATION: 4,957,000
CAPITAL: Edinburgh

## WALES
STATUS: Principality
AREA: 20,760 sq km (8,015 sq miles)
POPULATION: 2,798,200
CAPITAL: Cardiff

The United Kingdom is part of the British Isles which are situated off the coast of north-west Europe separated from France by the English Channel and from Belgium, the Netherlands and Scandinavia by the North Sea. There are two main islands: the larger, Great Britain, comprises England, Scotland and Wales; the other, the island of Ireland separated from Britain by the Irish Sea, comprises Northern Ireland and the Irish Republic.

The Highland zone of Britain consists of ancient uplifted rocks which now form the mountainous dissected and glaciated areas of the Lake District in the north-west, and Wales, the Southern Uplands and Grampians of Scotland which rise to the highest point in the UK to

1344 m (4409 ft) at Ben Nevis. The latter are divided by the wide Central Lowland rift valley.

Central England is dominated by the Pennine mountain chain which stretches southwards from the Southern Uplands down the centre of England to the river Trent. The landscape of the south-west consists of the ancient uplifted granite domes of Dartmoor and Bodmin Moor.

Lowland Britain is a very contrasting landscape. Limestone and sandstone hills are separated by flat clay vales, east of a line joining the rivers Humber and Exe. Here is found both the richest agricultural land and the densest population.

The climate of the British Isles is mild, wet and variable. Summer temperatures average 13°–17°C (55°–63°F), and winter temperatures 5°–7°C (41°–45°F). Annual rainfall varies between 65 and 500 cm (26 and 200 in) with the highest in the central Lake District and the lowest on the coasts of East Anglia.

Although a tiny percentage of the nation's workforce are employed in agriculture, farm produce is important to both home and export

markets. 76% of the total UK land area is farmland. The main cereal crops are wheat, barley and oats. Potatoes, sugar-beet and green vegetable crops are widespread.

About 20% of the land is permanent pasture for raising of dairy and beef stock; and 28% of the land, mainly hill and mountain areas, is used for rough grazing of sheep. Pigs and poultry are widespread in both England and lowland Britain. The best fruit-growing areas are the south-east, especially Kent, and East Anglia and the central Vale of Evesham for apples, pears and soft fruit. Both forestry and fishing industries contribute to the economy.

The major mineral resources of the UK are coal, oil and natural gas. Coal output, mostly from the fields of South Wales, Central Scotland, North-East England, Yorkshire and the Midlands, goes towards the generation of electricity but oil and natural gas from the North Sea, and to a lesser extent nuclear power, are divided between the needs of industry and the consumer. Iron ore, once mined sufficiently to satisfy industry, is now imported to support the iron and steel manufacturing sector.

The UK produces a great range of industrial goods for home consumption and export. Heavy industry particularly the production of iron and steel is traditionally located close to fuel sources (coal) in South Wales, the North-East at Teesside and South Yorkshire. The majority of iron ore is imported. The main shipbuilding areas are Clydeside in western Scotland, Belfast in Northern Ireland and Tyneside in the North-East. Other heavy industrial goods, vehicles, engines and machinery are produced on Merseyside, Derby and Nottingham in the North Midlands, Birmingham in the West Midlands, Cardiff in South Wales, Clydeside and Belfast.

General and consumer good manufacturing is located in all heavy industrial areas but the London area, West Midlands and Lancashire and Merseyside predominate. Main products are food and drinks, chemicals, light engineering products, cotton and woollen textiles, electrical and electronic goods.

The UK is a trading nation. The balance of trade has changed during the last 30 years because of stronger economic, military and

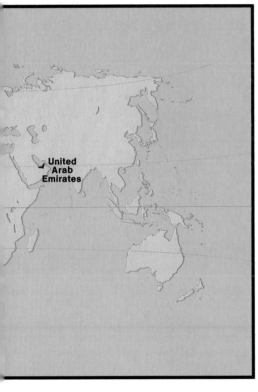

political ties within Europe – the EC and NATO – and consequently reduced trading links with former colonies particularly in Australasia. Major exports are cereals, meat, dairy products, beverages, tobacco products, textiles, metalliferous ores, petroleum and petroleum products, chemicals, pharmaceutical goods, plastics, leather goods, rubber, paper, iron and steel, other metal goods, engines and vehicles, machinery, electrical goods and transport equipment.

The UK has a highly developed transport network to move goods and services. Motorways, trunk roads and principal roads total over 50,000 km (31,070 miles). The railway network covers 16,730 km (10,395 miles) and now carries over 140 million tonnes of freight annually. The inland waterway system, once a major freight carrier, totals only 563 navigable kilometres (350 miles) but still carries over 4 million tonnes of goods annually.

# UNITED STATES OF AMERICA (USA)

STATUS: Federal Republic
AREA: 9,363,130 sq km (3,614,170 sq miles)
POPULATION: 248,709,873
ANNUAL NATURAL INCREASE: 1.0%
CAPITAL: Washington, DC
LANGUAGE: English, Spanish
RELIGION: Christian majority. Jewish minority
CURRENCY: US dollar (USD)
ORGANISATIONS: UN, ANZUS, Col. Plan, NATO OECD, OAS, G7

## ALABAMA
STATUS: State
AREA: 131,485 sq km (50,755 sq miles)
POPULATION: 3,984,000
CAPITAL: Montgomery

## ALASKA
STATUS: State
AREA: 1,478,450 sq km (570,680 sq miles)
POPULATION: 546,000
CAPITAL: Juneau

## ARIZONA
STATUS: State
AREA: 293,985 sq km (113,480 sq miles)
POPULATION: 3,619,000
CAPITAL: Phoenix

## ARKANSAS
STATUS: State
AREA: 134,880 sq km (52,065 sq miles)
POPULATION: 2,337,000
CAPITAL: Little Rock

## CALIFORNIA
STATUS: State
AREA: 404,815 sq km (156,260 sq miles)
POPULATION: 29,279,000
CAPITAL: Sacramento

## COLORADO
STATUS: State
AREA: 268,310 sq km (103,570 sq miles)
POPULATION: 3,272,000
CAPITAL: Denver

## CONNECTICUT
STATUS: State
AREA: 12,620 sq km (4,870 sq miles)
POPULATION: 3,227,000
CAPITAL: Hartford

## DELAWARE
STATUS: State
AREA: 5,005 sq km (1,930 sq miles)
POPULATION: 658,000
CAPITAL: Dover

## DISTRICT OF COLUMBIA
STATUS: Federal District
AREA: 163 sq km (63 sq miles)
POPULATION: 575,000
CAPITAL: Washington

## FLORIDA
STATUS: State
AREA: 140,255 sq km (54,140 sq miles)
POPULATION: 12,775,000
CAPITAL: Tallahassee

## GEORGIA
STATUS: State
AREA: 150,365 sq km (58,040 sq miles)
POPULATION: 6,387,000
CAPITAL: Atlanta

## HAWAII
STATUS: State
AREA: 16,640 sq km (6,425 sq miles)
POPULATION: 1,095,000
CAPITAL: Honolulu

## IDAHO
STATUS: State
AREA: 213,455 sq km (82,390 sq miles)
POPULATION: 1,004,000
CAPITAL: Boise

## ILLINOIS
STATUS: State
AREA: 144,120 sq km (55,630 sq miles)
POPULATION: 11,325,000
CAPITAL: Springfield

## INDIANA
STATUS: State
AREA: 93,065 sq km (35,925 sq miles)
POPULATION: 5,499,000
CAPITAL: Indianapolis

## IOWA
STATUS: State
AREA: 144,950 sq km (55,950 sq miles)
POPULATION: 2,767,000
CAPITAL: Des Moines

## KANSAS
STATUS: State
AREA: 211,805 sq km (81,755 sq miles)
POPULATION: 2,467,000
CAPITAL: Topeka

## KENTUCKY
STATUS: State
AREA: 102,740 sq km (39,660 sq miles)
POPULATION: 3,665,000
CAPITAL: Frankfort

## LOUISIANA
STATUS: State
AREA: 115,310 sq km (44,510 sq miles)
POPULATION: 4,181,000
CAPITAL: Baton Rouge

## MAINE
STATUS: State
AREA: 80,275 sq km (30,985 sq miles)
POPULATION: 1,218,000
CAPITAL: Augusta

## MARYLAND
STATUS: State
AREA: 25,480 sq km (9,835 sq miles)
POPULATION: 4,733,000
CAPITAL: Annapolis

## MASSACHUSETTS
STATUS: State
AREA: 20,265 sq km (7,820 sq miles)
POPULATION: 5,928,000
CAPITAL: Boston

## MICHIGAN
STATUS: State
AREA: 147,510 sq km (56,940 sq miles)
POPULATION: 9,179,000
CAPITAL: Lansing

## MINNESOTA
STATUS: State
AREA: 206,030 sq km (79,530 sq miles)
POPULATION: 4,359,000
CAPITAL: St Paul

## MISSISSIPPI
STATUS: State
AREA: 122,335 sq km (47,220 sq miles)
POPULATION: 2,535,000
CAPITAL: Jackson

## MISSOURI
STATUS: State
AREA: 178,565 sq km (68,925 sq miles)
POPULATION: 5,079,000
CAPITAL: Jefferson City

## MONTANA
STATUS: State
AREA: 376,555 sq km (145,350 sq miles)
POPULATION: 794,000
CAPITAL: Helena

## NEBRASKA
STATUS: State
AREA: 198,505 sq km (76,625 sq miles)
POPULATION: 1,573,000
CAPITAL: Lincoln

## NEVADA
STATUS: State
AREA: 284,625 sq km (109,865 sq miles)
POPULATION: 1,193,000
CAPITAL: Carson City

## NEW HAMPSHIRE
STATUS: State
AREA: 23,290 sq km (8,990 sq miles)
POPULATION: 1,103,000
CAPITAL: Concord

## NEW JERSEY
STATUS: State
AREA: 19,340 sq km (7,465 sq miles)
POPULATION: 7,617,000
CAPITAL: Trenton

## NEW MEXICO
STATUS: State
AREA: 314,255 sq km (121,300 sq miles)
POPULATION: 1,490,000
CAPITAL: Santa Fe

## NEW YORK
STATUS: State
AREA: 122,705 sq km (47,365 sq miles)
POPULATION: 17,627,000
CAPITAL: Albany

## NORTH CAROLINA
STATUS: State
AREA: 126,505 sq km (48,830 sq miles)
POPULATION: 6,553,000
CAPITAL: Raleigh

## NORTH DAKOTA
STATUS: State
AREA: 179,485 sq km (69,280 sq miles)
POPULATION: 634,000
CAPITAL: Bismarck

## OHIO
STATUS: State
AREA: 106,200 sq km (40,995 sq miles)
POPULATION: 10,778,000
CAPITAL: Columbus

## OKLAHOMA
STATUS: State
AREA: 177,815 sq km (68,635 sq miles)
POPULATION: 3,124,000
CAPITAL: Oklahoma City

## OREGON
STATUS: State
AREA: 249,115 sq km (96,160 sq miles)
POPULATION: 2,828,000
CAPITAL: Salem

## PENNSYLVANIA
STATUS: State
AREA: 116,260 sq km (44,875 sq miles)
POPULATION: 11,764,000
CAPITAL: Harrisburg

## RHODE ISLAND
STATUS: State
AREA: 2,730 sq km (1,055 sq miles)
POPULATION: 989,000
CAPITAL: Providence

## SOUTH CAROLINA
STATUS: State
AREA: 78,225 sq km (30,195 sq miles)
POPULATION: 3,272,000
CAPITAL: Columbia

## SOUTH DAKOTA
STATUS: State
AREA: 196,715 sq km (75,930 sq miles)
POPULATION: 693,000
CAPITAL: Pierre

## TENNESSEE
STATUS: State
AREA: 106,590 sq km (41,145 sq miles)
POPULATION: 4,822,000
CAPITAL: Nashville

## TEXAS
STATUS: State
AREA: 678,620 sq km (261,950 sq miles)
POPULATION: 16,825,000
CAPITAL: Austin

## UTAH
STATUS: State
AREA: 212,570 sq km (82,050 sq miles)
POPULATION: 1,711,000
CAPITAL: Salt Lake City

## VERMONT
STATUS: State
AREA: 24,900 sq km (9,612 sq miles)
POPULATION: 560,000
CAPITAL: Montpelier

## VIRGINIA
STATUS: State
AREA: 102,835 sq km (39,695 sq miles)
POPULATION: 6,128,000
CAPITAL: Richmond

## WASHINGTON
STATUS: State
AREA: 172,265 sq km (66,495 sq miles)
POPULATION: 4,827,000
CAPITAL: Olympia

## WEST VIRGINIA
STATUS: State
AREA: 62,470 sq km (24,115 sq miles)
POPULATION: 1,783,000
CAPITAL: Charleston

## WISCONSIN
STATUS: State
AREA: 140,965 sq km (54,415 sq miles)
POPULATION: 4,870,000
CAPITAL: Madison

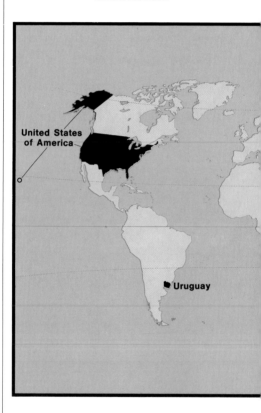

## WYOMING
STATUS: State
AREA: 251,200 sq km (96,965 sq miles)
POPULATION: 450,000
CAPITAL: Cheyenne

The United States of America is the world's third largest country after Canada and China, with the world's fourth largest population. The 19th and 20th centuries have brought 42 million immigrants to its shores, and the population of the USA now has the highest living standard of any country in the world. The large land area covers a huge spectrum of different landscapes, environments and climates. The eastern coast of New England where the European settlers first landed, is rocky, mountainous and richly wooded. South of New England is the Atlantic coastal plain, rising to the west towards the Appalachian mountain system. Beyond the Appalachians lie the central lowlands, a large undulating plain cut through by the Mississippi and Ohio rivers. Further west lie the Great Plains crossed by the Mis-

souri, Red and Arkansas rivers and rising gently towards the mighty Rockies, a spine of mountains running south from Alaska. The highest point is Mt. Whitney in California, at 4418 m (14,495 ft). Beyond the Rockies lies the Great Valley of California and the Pacific coast.

Climatic variety within this vast region is enormous, ranging from the Arctic conditions of Alaska to the desert of the south-west – winter temperatures in Alaska plummet to –28°C (–19°F), whereas in Florida they maintain a steady 19°C (66°F). In California the weather varies little, being constantly mild with a range of only 9°C (16°F), whereas in the central lowlands winters are severe and the summers very hot. The centre of the continent is dry, but both the north-west Pacific and the New England Atlantic coast are humid with heavy rainfall. Many areas of the USA fall prey to exceptional, often disastrous, weather conditions: the north-eastern seaboard is susceptible to heavy blizzards, the southern lowlands are vulnerable to spring thaw flooding and the Mississippi valley is prone to tornadoes.

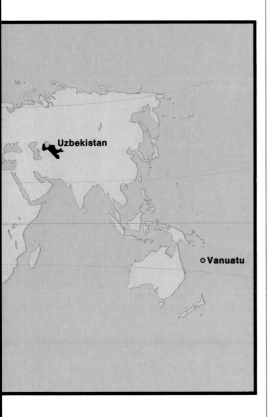

The natural vegetation of the USA reflects its climatic diversity. The north-west coast is rich in coniferous forest, especially Douglas fir, while the Appalachian mountain region is well endowed with hardwoods, notably maple and oak. In the arid south-west, vegetation is limited to desert scrub whereas the Gulf and South Atlantic coast are fringed with swampy wetlands. The central lowlands are endowed with rich black-earth soils (the agricultural heartland), gradually supplanted – towards the Rockies, by tall-grass prairie. The north-eastern states of Illinois, Iowa, Indiana and Nebraska form the so-called corn belt, whereas further west wheat supplements corn as the main crop. Spring wheat is grown in the northern states of North and South Dakota and Minnesota. The north-eastern corner of the USA is predominantly dairy country, and the states of the deep south are famous for their cotton, though cotton cultivation is declining. Rice is grown in Texas, California and Louisiana, and fruit and vegetables in Florida, Texas and California.

The USA consumes 25% of all the world's energy resources but is well endowed with energy reserves. There are substantial coal resources in Pennsylvania, the Appalachian region, the Dakotas and Wyoming, and oil and natural gas regions in Texas, Louisiana, Alaska, and off-shore, in the Gulf of Mexico. The vast resources of America's great rivers have been harnessed extensively for hydro-electric power. In the west, mineral deposits include copper, lead, zinc and silver, and there is iron ore around Lake Superior. Most specialist industrial minerals are imported. Diamonds, tin, chromite, nickel, asbestos, platinum, manganese, mercury, tungsten, cobalt, antimony and cadmium are not found in sufficient quantities for home demand. Main non-metallic minerals extracted within the USA are cement, clays, gypsum, lime, phosphate, salt, sand, gravel and sulphur.

About one fifth of the land area of the USA is covered by commercially usable coniferous and deciduous forest. Exploitation and re-planting are closely controlled. Atlantic and Pacific fishing, particularly around Alaska, is mainly carried out within the 200 mile fishery zone.

America's first industrialised area lies to the south of the Great Lakes, and has gradually extended south and west to form one of the largest industrial zones in the world. Chicago is the main steel-producing town, while Pennsylvania and Pittsburgh are famous for their steel and chemical industries. Manufacturing industries are more predominant towards the east of this zone.

Most of the fastest growing industrial areas are along the west coast. These stretch from Seattle and Portland in the north to San Francisco, Oakland and San Jose in central California and to Los Angeles, Anaheim, Santa Ana and San Diego in the south. The main industries are vehicle manufacture, armaments, machinery, electrical goods, electronics, textiles and clothing and entertainment.

# URUGUAY

STATUS: Republic
AREA: 186,925 sq km (72,155 sq miles)
POPULATION: 3,094,000
ANNUAL NATURAL INCREASE: 0.6%
CAPITAL: Montevideo
LANGUAGE: Spanish
RELIGION: Roman Catholic
CURRENCY: Uruguayan peso (UYP)
ORGANISATIONS: UN, OAS

Situated on the south-east coast of South America, Uruguay is the smallest country in South America. It consists of a narrow coastal plain with rolling hills inland. Maximum elevation is around 200 m (656 ft). The temperate climate and adequate rainfall provide good argicultural potential but most of the land is given over to the grazing of sheep and cattle. The entire economy relies on the production of meat and wool. Most industry is devoted to food processing. 87% of the land area is farmed. There are few mineral resources.

# UZBEKISTAN

STATUS: Republic
AREA: 447,400 sq km (172,695 sq miles)
POPULATION: 20,300,000
CAPITAL: Tashkent
LANGUAGE: Uzbek, Russian
RELIGION: Muslim
CURRENCY: rouble
ORGANISATIONS: CIS

Established in 1924 as a constituent republic of the Soviet Union, Uzbekistan became an independent state in 1991. The majority of the country consists of flat, sun-baked lowlands with mountains in the south and east. The climate is markedly continental and very dry with an abundance of sunshine and mild, short winters. The southern mountains are of great economic importance providing ample supplies of water for hydro-electric plants and irrigation schemes. The mountain regions also contain substantial reserves of natural gas, oil, coal, iron and other metals. With its fertile soils (when irrigated) and good pastures Uzbekistan is well situated for cattle raising and for producing cotton. Uzbekistan is the largest producer of machines and heavy equipment in central Asia, and has been specialising mainly in machinery for cotton cultivation and harvesting, machines for irrigation projects, for road-building and textile processing. During the Soviet period the urban employment market became increasingly dominated by Russians and other outsiders. The gradual emergence of better educated and better trained Uzbeks has generated fiercely nationalist sentiments. The country's future development will be severely hampered by the damage done to the natural environment under communism.

# VANUATU

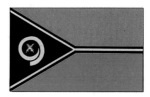

STATUS: Republic
AREA: 14,765 sq km (5,700 sq miles)
POPULATION: 147,000
ANNUAL NATURAL INCREASE: 2.9%
CAPITAL: Port Vila
LANGUAGE: Bislama (national), English, French, many Melanesian languages
RELIGION: Christian
CURRENCY: Vatu (VUV)
ORGANISATIONS: Comm, UN

Vanuatu is a chain of densely forested, mountainous, volcanic islands in the South Pacific. Climate is tropical and cyclonic. Copra, cocoa and coffee are grown mainly for export. Fish, pigs and sheep are important for home consumption as well as yam, taro, manioc and bananas. Manganese is the only mineral.

# VATICAN CITY

STATUS: Ecclesiastical State
AREA: 0.44 sq km (0.17 sq miles)
POPULATION: 766
LANGUAGE: Italian, Latin
RELIGION: Roman Catholic
CURRENCY: Italian lira (ITL), Papal coinage

The headquarters of the Roman Catholic church, the Vatican in Rome is the world's smallest independent state. The papal residence since the 5th century AD, it is the destination for pilgrims and tourists from all over the world. Most income is derived from voluntary contributions and interest on investments. The only industries are those connected with the Church.

# VENEZUELA

STATUS: Republic
AREA: 912,045 sq km (352,050 sq miles)
POPULATION: 19,735,000
ANNUAL NATURAL INCREASE: 2.8%
CAPITAL: Caracas
LANGUAGE: Spanish
RELIGION: Roman Catholic
CURRENCY: bolivar (VEB)
ORGANISATIONS: UN, OAS, OPEC

Venezuela, one of the richest countries of Latin America, is divided into four topographic regions: the continuation of the Andes in the west; the humid lowlands around Lake Maracaibo in the north; the savannah-covered central plains (llanos), and the extension of the Guiana Highlands covering almost half the country. The climate varies between tropical in the south to warm temperate along the northern coasts. The majority of the population live along the north coast. The economy is built around oil production in the Maracaibo region; over three-quarters of export revenue comes from oil. Bauxite and iron ore are also important. The majority of employment is provided by industrial and manufacturing developments.

# VIETNAM

STATUS: Republic
AREA: 329,566 sq km (127,246 sq miles)

POPULATION: 66,200,000
ANNUAL NATURAL INCREASE: 2.3%
CAPITAL: Hanoi
LANGUAGE: Vietnamese, French, Chinese
RELIGION: Buddhist
CURRENCY: dong (VND)
ORGANISATIONS: UN, OIEC

A long narrow country in South-East Asia, Vietnam has a mountainous backbone and two extensive river deltas: the Song Hong (Red River) in the north and the Mekong in the south. Monsoons bring 150cm (59in) of rain every year and rainforest covers most of the central mountainous areas. Rice is grown extensively throughout the north along with coffee and rubber in other parts of the country. Vietnam possesses a wide range of minerals including coal, lignite, anthracite, iron ore and tin. Industry is expanding rapidly, but decades of warfare and internal strife have impeded development.

## VIRGIN ISLANDS (UK)

STATUS: UK Dependent Territory
AREA: 153 sq km (59 sq miles)
POPULATION: 13,000
CAPITAL: Road Town

## VIRGIN ISLANDS (USA)

STATUS: External Territory of USA
AREA: 345 sq km (133 sq miles)
POPULATION: 117,000
CAPITAL: Charlotte Amalie

## WALLIS & FUTUNA ISLANDS

STATUS: Self-governing Overseas Territory
of France
AREA: 274 sq km (106 sq miles)
POPULATION: 15,400
CAPITAL: Mata-Utu

# WESTERN SAMOA

STATUS: Commonwealth State
AREA: 2,840 sq km (1,095 sq miles)
POPULATION: 170,000
ANNUAL NATURAL INCREASE: 0.3%
CAPITAL: Apia
LANGUAGE: English, Samoan
RELIGION: local beliefs
CURRENCY: talà (dollar) (WST)
ORGANISATIONS: Comm, UN

Nine volcanic tropical islands constitute this south Pacific state, of which only four are populated – Savaii, Upolu, Manono and Apolima. Annual rainfall is often 250cm(100in) per year. Temperatures average 26°C(79°F) for most months. Main exports are copra, timber, taro, cocoa and fruit. The only industries are food processing and timber products. Main imports are food products, consumer goods, machinery and animals.

## WRANGEL ISLAND

STATUS: Island Territory of Russia
AREA: 7,250 sq km (2,800 sq miles)
POPULATION: No permanent population

# YEMEN

STATUS: Republic
AREA: 477,530 sq km (184,325 sq miles)
POPULATION: 12,000,000
ANNUAL NATURAL INCREASE: 3.0%
CAPITAL: San'a
LANGUAGE: Arabic
RELIGION: Sunni and Shia Muslim

CURRENCY: Yemeni rial (YER)
ORGANISATIONS: UN, Arab League

The Yemen Arab Republic and the People's Democratic Republic of Yemen were unified in 1990 to form a single state with its capital at San'a. Situated in the southern part of the Arabian peninsula the country comprises several contrasting physical landscapes. The north is mainly mountainous and relatively wet with rainfall reaching 89cm (35in) in inland areas which helps to irrigate the cereals, cotton, fruits and vegetables which are grown on the mountain sides and along the coast. The south coast stretches for 1100km (685 miles) from the mouth of the Red Sea to Oman. The narrow southern coastal plain fringes the wide irrigated Hadhramaut valley in which are grown sorghum, millet, wheat and barley. To the north of the Hadhramaut lies the uninhabitated Arabian Desert. The majority of the people live in the west of the country where the climate is more suited to agriculture. A large proportion of the population are farmers and nomadic herders; the main livestock are sheep,

goats, cattle and poultry. The only commercial mineral being exploited is salt and the discovery of oil in the Marib area in 1984 and the beginning of exports in 1986 are making a vital contribution to the economy. Industrial output is mainly confined to small-scale manufacturing. A small amount of cotton and fish are exported; food and live animals are imported.

# YUGOSLAVIA

STATUS: Federation
AREA: 255,805 sq km (98,740 sq miles)
POPULATION: 23,898,000

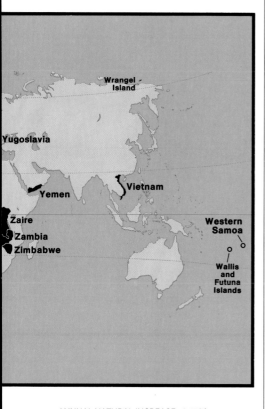

ANNUAL NATURAL INCREASE: 0.7%
CAPITAL: Belgrade (Beograd)
LANGUAGE: Serbian, Albanian, Macedonian, Slovene, Hungarian
RELIGION: 40% Orthodox Christian, 30% Roman Catholic, 10% Muslim
CURRENCY: dinar (YUN)
ORGANISATIONS: UN

## BOSNIA & HERCEGOVINA

AREA: 51,130 sq km (19,735 sq miles)
POPULATION: 4,795,000
ETHNIC COMPOSITION: 44% Muslim, 31% Serbian, 18% Croatian

## MACEDONIA

AREA: 25,715 sq km (9,925 sq miles)
POPULATION: 2,193,000
ETHNIC COMPOSITION: 70% Macedonian, 20% Albanian, 5% Turkish

## MONTENEGRO

AREA: 13,810 sq km (5,330 sq miles)
POPULATION: 664,000
ETHNIC COMPOSITION: 70% Montenegrin, 13% Muslim, 8% Albanian

## SERBIA

AREA: 88,360 sq km (34,105 sq miles)
POPULATION: 9,815,000
ETHNIC COMPOSITION: 70% Serbian, 15% Albanian, 5% Hungarian

The Yugoslav state, as first created in 1918 and reconstituted as a federation after 1945, had long been suffering from ethnic conflict and tensions between its component republics. It finally disintegrated in 1991 when, in the face of fierce opposition from the Serbian-dominated centre, Slovenia and Croatia managed to break away. Bosnia & Hercegovina and Macedonia have also declared their independence but have not yet gained international recognition. Yugoslavia may therefore be reduced to Montenegro and Serbia which are committed to staying together. On the other hand, Serbia has laid claim to various territories outside its present boundaries, which are wholly or partly inhabited by Serbs. Internally, it has abolished the autonomous status previously enjoyed by the provinces of Kosovo, with its overwhelmingly Albanian population, and Vojvodina which has a large proportion of ethnic Hungarians. The secession of the more advanced northern republics has dealt a very severe blow to the Yugoslav economy, as the majority of industrial installations are situated in this area, and the costly military campaign to stop secession, has wrought further havoc, with the currency becoming all but worthless in the process. Future potential revenue from tourism along the Adriatic coast has now been lost to Slovenia and Croatia. So whatever the outcome of the political crisis, the economic future of what is left of Yugoslavia looks bleak.

# ZAIRE

STATUS: Republic
AREA: 2,345,410 sq km (905,330 sq miles)
POPULATION: 35,562,000
ANNUAL NATURAL INCREASE: 3.1%
CAPITAL: Kinshasa
LANGUAGE: French, Kiswahili, Tshiluba, Kikongo, Lingala
RELIGION: traditional beliefs, 48% Roman Catholic, 13% Protestant
CURRENCY: zaïre (ZRZ)
ORGANISATIONS: UN, OAU

Zaire, formerly the Belgian Congo, is Africa's third largest country after Sudan and Algeria and is dominated by the drainage basin of the Zaire River. Tropical rainforest covers most of the basin. The climate is very variable but basically equatorial with high temperatures and high rainfall. Soils are poor with the majority of the population engaged in shifting agriculture. Cassava, cocoa, coffee, cotton, millet, rubber and sugar-cane are grown. 60% of

exports are minerals – copper, cobalt, diamonds, gold, manganese, uranium and zinc, with copper being the most important and accounting for 40% of total foreign exchange earnings. The country is the world's largest source of cobalt. Zaire has abundant wildlife and tourism is becoming important.

# ZAMBIA

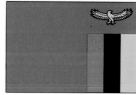

STATUS: Republic
AREA: 752,615 sq km (290,510 sq miles)
POPULATION: 7,818,447
ANNUAL NATURAL INCREASE: 3.7%
CAPITAL: Lusaka
LANGUAGE: English, African languages
RELIGION: 70% Christian, animist minority
CURRENCY: kwacha (ZMK)
ORGANISATIONS: Comm, UN, OAU

Mineral-rich Zambia, situated in the interior of south-central Africa, consists mainly of high rolling plateaux. Altitude moderates the potentially tropical climate so that the summer temperature averages only 13°-27°C (55°-81°F). The north receives over 125cm (49in) of rain per annum, the south, less. Most of the country is grassland with some forest in the north. Farming is mainly at subsistence level. Copper is still the mainstay of the country's economy although reserves are fast running out. Lead, zinc, cobalt and tobacco are also exported. Wildlife is diverse and abundant and contributes to expanding tourism.

# ZIMBABWE

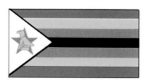

STATUS: Republic
AREA: 390,310 sq km (150,660 sq miles)
POPULATION: 9,369,000
ANNUAL NATURAL INCREASE: 3.6%
CAPITAL: Harare
LANGUAGE: English, Chishona, Sindebele
RELIGION: traditional beliefs, 20% Christian
CURRENCY: Zimbabwe dollar (ZWD)
ORGANISATIONS: Comm, UN, OAU

Landlocked Zimbabwe (formerly Rhodesia) consists of rolling plateaux (the high veld) 1,200-1,500m (3940-4920ft) and the low veld (the valleys of the Zambezi and Limpopo rivers). Altitude moderates the tropical climate of the high veld to temperate with low humidity. Mineral deposits include chrome, nickel, platinum and coal with gold and asbestos especially important. Maize is the most important crop as it is the staple food of a large proportion of the population. Tobacco, tea, sugar-cane and fruit are also grown. Manufacturing industry is slowly developing and now provides a wide range of consumer products.

## North and Central America
**25 349 000**
**9 785 000**

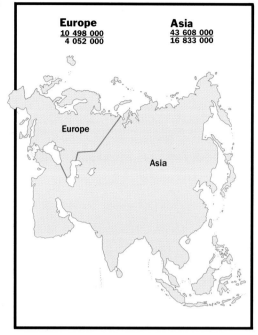

## CONTINENTS

land area ⬜ = **1 000 000** sq kms / **386 000** sq miles

### Europe
**10 498 000**
**4 052 000**

### Asia
**43 608 000**
**16 833 000**

Europe

Asia

## Africa
**30 335 000**
**11 709 000**

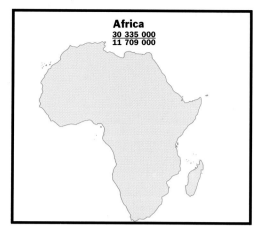

## South America
**17 611 000**
**6 798 000**

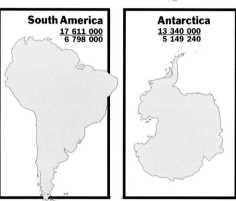

## Antarctica
**13 340 000**
**5 149 240**

## Australasia
**8 923 000**
**3 444 278**

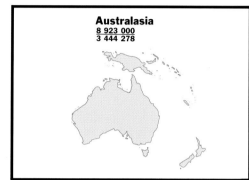

## METROPOLITAN AREAS

| Population | City | Country |
|---|---|---|
| 2,168,000 | **Abidjan** | *Ivory Coast* |
| 1,891,000 | **Addis Ababa** | *Ethiopia* |
| 3,646,000 | **Ahmadabad** | *India* |
| 3,684,000 | **Alexandria** | *Egypt* |
| 3,033,000 | **Algiers** | *Algeria* |
| 1,151,300 | **Alma-Ata** | *Kazakhstan* |
| 1,062,000 | **Amsterdam** | *Netherlands* |
| 3,022,236 | **Ankara** | *Turkey* |
| 2,517,080 | **Anshan** | *China* |
| 3,097,000 | **Athens** | *Greece* |
| 2,737,000 | **Atlanta** | *USA* |
| 864,700 | **Auckland** | *New Zealand* |
| 4,044,000 | **Baghdad** | *Iraq* |
| 1,780,000 | **Baku** | *Azerbaijan* |
| 2,342,000 | **Baltimore** | *USA* |
| 4,993,000 | **Bangalore** | *India* |
| 5,832,843 | **Bangkok** | *Thailand* |
| 1,677,699 | **Barcelona** | *Spain* |
| 10,819,407 | **Beijing (Peking)** | *China* |
| 1,500,000 | **Beirut** | *Lebanon* |
| 1,575,000 | **Belgrade** | *Yugoslavia* |
| 3,615,234 | **Belo Horizonte** | *Brazil* |
| 3,400,000 | **Berlin** | *Germany* |
| 2,310,900 | **Birmingham** | *UK* |
| 4,851,000 | **Bogotá** | *Colombia* |
| 11,169,000 | **Bombay** | *India* |
| 2,845,000 | **Boston** | *USA* |
| 1,803,478 | **Brasília** | *Brazil* |
| 970,501 | **Brussels** | *Belgium* |
| 2,194,000 | **Bucharest** | *Romania* |
| 2,115,000 | **Budapest** | *Hungary* |
| 12,604,018 | **Buenos Aires** | *Argentina* |
| 13,300,000 | **Cairo** | *Egypt* |
| 11,835,000 | **Calcutta** | *India* |
| 310,000 | **Canberra** | *Australia* |
| 2,310,000 | **Cape Town** | *South Africa* |
| 4,092,000 | **Caracas** | *Venezuela* |
| 3,213,000 | **Casablanca** | *Morocco* |
| 2,214,000 | **Changchun** | *China* |
| 1,362,000 | **Changsha** | *China* |
| 1,143,000 | **Chelyabinsk** | *Russian Federation* |
| 3,004,000 | **Chengdu** | *China* |
| 6,216,000 | **Chicago** | *USA* |
| 3,151,000 | **Chongqing** | *China* |
| 1,337,114 | **Copenhagen** | *Denmark* |
| 2,543,000 | **Dalian** | *China* |
| 3,766,000 | **Dallas – Fort Worth** | *USA* |
| 2,049,000 | **Damascus** | *Syria* |
| 1,657,000 | **Dar-es-Salaam** | *Tanzania* |
| 8,766,000 | **Delhi** | *India* |
| 4,352,000 | **Detroit** | *USA* |
| 6,646,000 | **Dhaka** | *Bangladesh* |
| 926,000 | **Dublin** | *Republic of Ireland* |
| 2,745,000 | **Essen – Dortmund** | *Germany* |
| 1,420,000 | **Fushun** | *China* |
| 373,000 | **Geneva** | *Switzerland* |
| 2,846,720 | **Guadalajara** | *Mexico* |
| 3,671,000 | **Guangzhou (Canton)** | *China* |
| 1,600,000 | **Hamburg** | *Germany* |
| 1,412,000 | **Hangzhou** | *China* |
| 1,088,862 | **Hanoi** | *Vietnam* |
| 2,966,000 | **Harbin** | *China* |
| 2,099,000 | **Havana** | *Cuba* |
| 5,448,000 | **Hong Kong** | *UK colony* |
| 3,247,000 | **Houston** | *USA* |
| 3,535,000 | **Hyderabad** | *India* |
| 6,665,000 | **Istanbul** | *Turkey* |
| 9,253,000 | **Jakarta** | *Indonesia* |
| 508,000 | **Jerusalem** | *Israel* |
| 1,327,000 | **Jilin** | *China* |
| 2,415,000 | **Jinan** | *China* |
| 1,714,000 | **Johannesburg** | *South Africa* |
| 2,000,000 | **Kābul** | *Afghanistan* |
| 7,702,000 | **Karachi** | *Pakistan* |
| 1,947,000 | **Khartoum** | *Sudan* |
| 2,624,000 | **Kiev** | *Ukraine* |
| 3,505,000 | **Kinshasa** | *Zaire* |
| 1,711,000 | **Kuala Lumpur** | *Malaysia* |
| 4,100,000 | **Lagos** | *Nigeria* |
| 4,092,000 | **Lahore** | *Pakistan* |
| 1,566,000 | **Lanzhou** | *China* |
| 6,404,500 | **Lima** | *Peru* |
| 1,603,000 | **Lisbon** | *Portugal* |
| 9,092,024 | **London** | *UK* |
| 10,845,000 | **Los Angeles** | *USA* |
| 5,702,000 | **Madras** | *India* |
| 2,991,223 | **Madrid** | *Spain* |
| 2,590,500 | **Manchester** | *UK* |
| 8,475,000 | **Manila – Quezon City** | *Philippines* |
| 1,585,000 | **Medellín** | *Colombia* |
| 3,081,000 | **Melbourne** | *Australia* |
| 18,748,000 | **Mexico City** | *Mexico* |
| 1,814,000 | **Miami** | *USA* |
| 2,388,000 | **Minneapolis – St Paul** | *USA* |
| 1,637,000 | **Minsk** | *Belorussia* |
| 2,521,697 | **Monterrey** | *Mexico* |
| 1,197,000 | **Montevideo** | *Uruguay* |
| 3,084,100 | **Montréal** | *Canada* |
| 9,000,000 | **Moscow** | *Russian Federation* |
| 1,631,000 | **Munich** | *Germany* |
| 2,160,000 | **Nagoya** | *Japan* |
| 1,503,000 | **Nairobi** | *Kenya* |
| 1,415,000 | **Nanchang** | *China* |
| 2,265,000 | **Nanjing** | *China* |
| 16,198,000 | **New York** | *USA* |
| 1,436,000 | **Novosibirsk** | *Russian Federation* |
| 1,115,000 | **Odessa** | *Ukraine* |
| 8,520,000 | **Osaka-Kobe** | *Japan* |
| 458,364 | **Oslo** | *Norway* |
| 885,300 | **Ottawa** | *Canada* |
| 9,060,000 | **Paris** | *France* |
| 4,920,000 | **Philadelphia** | *USA* |
| 2,030,000 | **Phoenix** | *USA* |
| 2,094,000 | **Pittsburg** | *USA* |
| 2,906,472 | **Pôrto Alegre** | *Brazil* |
| 1,294,000 | **Prague** | *Czechoslovakia* |
| 3,875,000 | **Pusan** | *South Korea* |
| 2,230,000 | **Pyôngyang** | *North Korea* |
| 622,000 | **Quebec** | *Canada* |
| 2,010,000 | **Qingdao** | *China* |
| 1,281,849 | **Quito** | *Ecuador* |
| 3,295,000 | **Rangoon** | *Burma* |
| 2,814,795 | **Recife** | *Brazil* |
| 915,000 | **Riga** | *Latvia* |
| 11,205,567 | **Rio de Janeiro** | *Brazil* |
| 1,975,000 | **Riyadh** | *Saudi Arabia* |
| 3,051,000 | **Rome** | *Italy* |
| 1,385,000 | **Sacramento** | *USA* |
| 3,237,000 | **Saigon (Ho Chi Minh)** | *Vietnam* |
| 2,424,878 | **Salvador** | *Brazil* |
| 2,370,000 | **San Diego** | *USA* |
| 5,028,000 | **San Francisco** | *USA* |
| 1,390,000 | **San Juan** | *Puerto Rico* |
| 4,734,000 | **Santiago** | *Chile* |
| 2,203,000 | **Santo Domingo** | *Dominican Republic* |
| 17,112,712 | **São Paulo** | *Brazil* |
| 10,979,000 | **Seoul** | *South Korea* |
| 13,341,896 | **Shanghai** | *China* |
| 4,763,000 | **Shenyang** | *China* |
| 2,723,000 | **Singapore** | *Singapore* |
| 1,190,000 | **Sofia** | *Bulgaria* |
| 2,467,000 | **St Louis** | *USA* |
| 5,035,000 | **St Petersburg** (formerly Leningrad) | *Russian Federation* |
| 1,662,000 | **Stockholm** | *Sweden* |
| 2,383,000 | **Surabaya** | *Indonesia* |
| 3,657,000 | **Sydney** | *Australia* |
| 2,518,000 | **Taegu** | *South Korea* |
| 2,961,000 | **Taipei** | *Taiwan* |
| 2,199,000 | **Taiyuan** | *China* |
| 482,000 | **Tallinn** | *Estonia* |
| 2,100,000 | **Tashkent** | *Uzbekistan* |
| 1,264,000 | **Tbilisi** | *Georgia* |
| 6,773,000 | **Tehran** | *Iran* |
| 1,029,700 | **Tel Aviv** | *Israel* |
| 8,785,402 | **Tianjin** | *China* |
| 11,935,700 | **Tokyo** | *Japan* |
| 3,822,400 | **Toronto** | *Canada* |
| 2,062,000 | **Tripoli** | *Libya* |
| 1,586,600 | **Vancouver** | *Canada* |
| 1,531,000 | **Vienna** | *Austria* |
| 582,000 | **Vilnius** | *Lithuania* |
| 1,655,100 | **Warsaw** | *Poland* |
| 3,734,000 | **Washington DC** | *USA* |
| 325,700 | **Wellington** | *New Zealand* |
| 648,500 | **Winnipeg** | *Canada* |
| 3,921,000 | **Wuhan** | *China* |
| 2,859,000 | **Xian** | *China* |
| 1,300,000 | **Yerevan** | *Armenia* |
| 1,174,512 | **Zagreb** | *Croatia* |
| 2,400,000 | **Zibo** | *China* |

## MOUNTAIN HEIGHTS

| metres | feet | | |
|---|---|---|---|
| 8,848 | 29,028 | **Everest (Qomolangma Feng)** | *China–Nepal* |
| 8,611 | 28,250 | **K2 (Qogir Feng) (Godwin Austen)** | *India–China* |
| 8,598 | 28,170 | **Kangchenjunga** | *India–Nepal* |
| 8,481 | 27,824 | **Makalu** | *China–Nepal* |
| 8,217 | 26,958 | **Cho Oyu** | *China–Nepal* |
| 8,167 | 26,795 | **Dhaulagiri** | *Nepal* |
| 8,156 | 26,758 | **Manaslu** | *Nepal* |
| 8,126 | 26,660 | **Nanga Parbat** | *India* |
| 8,078 | 26,502 | **Annapurna** | *Nepal* |
| 8,088 | 26,470 | **Gasherbrum** | *India–China* |
| 8,027 | 26,335 | **Xixabangma Feng (Gosainthan)** | *China* |
| 7,885 | 25,869 | **Distaghil Sar** | *Kashmir, India* |
| 7,820 | 25,656 | **Masherbrum** | *India* |
| 7,817 | 25,646 | **Nanda Devi** | *India* |
| 7,788 | 25,550 | **Rakaposhi** | *India* |
| 7,756 | 25,446 | **Kamet** | *China–India* |
| 7,756 | 25,447 | **Namjagbarwa Feng** | *China* |
| 7,728 | 25,355 | **Gurla Mandhata** | *China* |
| 7,723 | 25,338 | **Muztag** | *China* |
| 7,719 | 25,325 | **Kongur Shan (Kungur)** | |
| 7,690 | 25,230 | **Tirich Mir** | *Pakistan* |
| 7,556 | 24,790 | **Gongga Shan** | *China* |
| 7,546 | 24,757 | **Muztagata** | *China* |
| 7,495 | 24,590 | **Pik Kommunizma** | *Tajikistan* |
| 7,439 | 24,406 | **Pik Pobedy (Tomur Feng)** | *Kirgizia–China* |
| 7,313 | 23,993 | **Chomo Lhari** | *Bhutan–Tibet* |
| 7,134 | 23,406 | **Pik Lenina** | *Kirgizia* |
| 6,960 | 22,834 | **Aconcagua** | *Argentina* |
| 6,908 | 22,664 | **Ojos del Salado** | *Argentina–Chile* |
| 6,872 | 22,546 | **Bonete** | *Argentina* |
| 6,800 | 22,310 | **Tupungato** | *Argentina–Chile* |
| 6,770 | 22,211 | **Mercedario** | *Argentina* |
| 6.768 | 22,205 | **Huascarán** | *Peru* |
| 6,723 | 22,057 | **Llullaillaco** | *Argentina–Chile* |
| 6,714 | 22,027 | **Kangrinboqê Feng (Kailas)** | *Tibet, China* |
| 6,634 | 21,765 | **Yerupaja** | *Peru* |
| 6,542 | 21,463 | **Sajama** | *Bolivia* |
| 6,485 | 21,276 | **Illampu** | *Bolivia* |
| 6,425 | 21,079 | **Coropuna** | *Peru* |
| 6,402 | 21,004 | **Illimani** | *Bolivia* |
| 6,310 | 20,702 | **Chimborazo** | *Ecuador* |
| 6,194 | 20,320 | **McKinley** | *USA* |
| 6,050 | 19,849 | **Logan** | *Canada* |
| 5,896 | 19,344 | **Cotopaxi** | *Ecuador* |
| 5,895 | 19,340 | **Kilimanjaro** | *Tanzania* |
| 5,800 | 19,023 | **Sa. Nevada de Sta. Marta (Cristobal Colon)** | *Columbia* |
| 5,775 | 18,947 | **Bolivar** | *Venezuela* |
| 5,699 | 18,697 | **Citlaltépetl (Orizaba)** | *Mexico* |
| 5,642 | 18,510 | **El'brus** | *Russian Federation* |
| 5,601 | 18,376 | **Damāvand** | *Iran* |
| 5,489 | 18,008 | **Mt St. Elias** | *Canada* |
| 5,227 | 17,149 | **Mt Lucania** | *Canada* |
| 5,200 | 17,058 | **Kenya (Kirinyaga)** | *Kenya* |
| 5,165 | 16,945 | **Ararat (Büyük Ağri Daği)** | *Turkey* |
| 5,140 | 16,860 | **Vinson Massif** | *Antarctica* |
| 5,110 | 16,763 | **Stanley (Margherita)** | *Uganda–Zaire* |
| 5,029 | 16,499 | **Jaya (Carstensz)** | *Indonesia* |
| 5,005 | 16,421 | **Mt Bona** | *USA* |
| 4,949 | 16,237 | **Sandford** | *USA* |
| 4,936 | 16,194 | **Mt Blackburn** | *Canada* |
| 4,808 | 15,774 | **Mont Blanc** | *France–Italy* |
| 4,750 | 15,584 | **Klyuchevskaya Sopka** | *Russian Federation* |
| 4,634 | 15,203 | **Monte Rosa (Dufour)** | *Italy–Switzerland* |
| 4,620 | 15,157 | **Ras Dashen** | *Ethiopia* |
| 4,565 | 14,979 | **Meru** | *Tanzania* |
| 4,545 | 14,910 | **Dom (Mischabel group)** | *Switzerland* |
| 4,528 | 14,855 | **Kirkpatrick** | *Antarctica* |
| 4,508 | 14,790 | **Wilhelm** | *Papua, New Guinea* |
| 4,507 | 14,786 | **Karisimbi** | *Rwanda–Zaire* |
| 4,477 | 14,688 | **Matterhorn** | *Italy–Switzerland* |
| 4,418 | 14,495 | **Whitney** | *USA* |
| 4,398 | 14,431 | **Elbert** | *USA* |
| 4,392 | 14,410 | **Rainier** | *USA* |
| 4,351 | 14,275 | **Markham** | *Antarctica* |
| 4,321 | 14,178 | **Elgon** | *Kenya–Uganda* |
| 4,307 | 14,131 | **Batu** | *Ethiopia* |
| 4,169 | 13,677 | **Mauna Loa** | *USA, Hawaii* |
| 4,165 | 13,644 | **Toubkal** | *Morocco* |
| 4,095 | 13,435 | **Cameroon (Caméroun)** | *Cameroon* |
| 4,094 | 13,431 | **Kinabalu** | *Malaysia* |
| 3,794 | 12,447 | **Erebus** | *Antarctica* |
| 3,776 | 12,388 | **Fuji** | *Japan* |
| 3,764 | 12,349 | **Cook** | *New Zealand* |
| 3,718 | 12,198 | **Teide** | *Canary Is* |
| 3,482 | 11,424 | **Thabana Ntlenyana** | *Lesotho* |
| 3,482 | 11,424 | **Mulhacén** | *Spain* |
| 3,415 | 11,204 | **Emi Koussi** | *Chad* |
| 3,323 | 10,902 | **Etna** | *Italy, Sicily* |
| 2,743 | 9,000 | **Mt Balbi** | *Bougainville, Papua, New Guinea* |
| 2,655 | 8,708 | **Gerlachovsky stit (Tatra)** | *Czechoslovakia* |
| 2,230 | 7,316 | **Kosciusko** | *Australia* |

## ISLANDS

**land area** □ = 10 000 sq kms / 3 860 sq miles

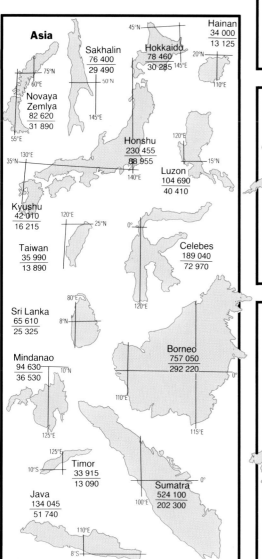

### Asia

Hainan 34 000 / 13 125
Sakhalin 76 400 / 29 490
Hokkaido 78 460 / 30 285
Novaya Zemlya 82 620 / 31 890
Honshu 230 455 / 88 955
Luzon 104 690 / 40 410
Kyushu 42 010 / 16 215
Taiwan 35 990 / 13 890
Celebes 189 040 / 72 970
Sri Lanka 65 610 / 25 325
Borneo 757 050 / 292 220
Mindanao 94 630 / 36 530
Timor 33 915 / 13 090
Sumatra 524 100 / 202 300
Java 134 045 / 51 740

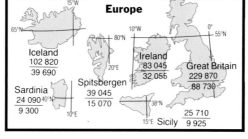

### Europe

Iceland 102 820 / 39 690
Ireland 83 045 / 32 055
Great Britain 229 870 / 88 730
Sardinia 24 090 / 9 300
Spitsbergen 39 045 / 15 070
Sicily 25 710 / 9 925

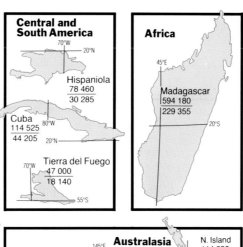

### Central and South America

Hispaniola 78 460 / 30 285
Cuba 114 525 / 44 205
Tierra del Fuego 47 000 / 18 140

### Africa

Madagascar 594 180 / 229 355

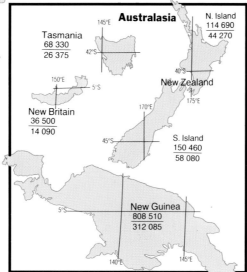

### Australasia

Tasmania 68 330 / 26 375
N. Island 114 690 / 44 270
New Zealand
New Britain 36 500 / 14 090
S. Island 150 460 / 58 080
New Guinea 808 510 / 312 085

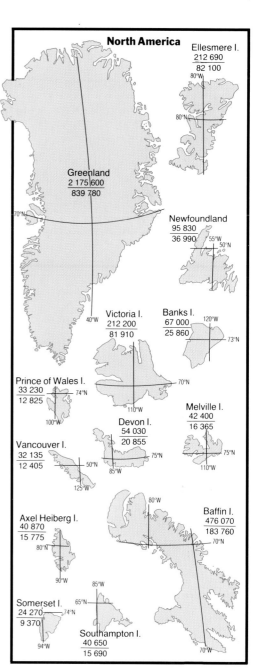

### North America

Ellesmere I. 212 690 / 82 100
Greenland 2 175 600 / 839 780
Newfoundland 95 830 / 36 990
Victoria I. 212 200 / 81 910
Banks I. 67 000 / 25 860
Prince of Wales I. 33 230 / 12 825
Melville I. 42 400 / 16 365
Devon I. 54 030 / 20 855
Vancouver I. 32 135 / 12 405
Axel Heiberg I. 40 870 / 15 775
Baffin I. 476 070 / 183 760
Somerset I. 24 270 / 9 370
Southampton I. 40 650 / 15 690

## OCEANS AND SEAS

water area ▢ = $\dfrac{1\,000\,000 \text{ sq km}}{386\,000 \text{ sq miles}}$

## OCEAN FACTS AND FIGURES

The area of the Earth covered by sea is estimated to be 361,740,000 sq km (139,670,000 sq miles), or 70.92% of the total surface. The mean depth is estimated to be 3554 m (11,660 ft), and the volume of the oceans to be 1,285,600,000 cu. km (308,400,000 cu. miles).

## INDIAN OCEAN

Mainly confined to the southern hemisphere, and at its greatest breadth (Tasmania to Cape Agulhas) 9600 km. Average depth is 4000 m; greatest depth is the Amirante Trench (9000 m).

## ATLANTIC OCEAN

Commonly divided into North Atlantic (36,000,000 sq km) and South Atlantic (26,000,000 sq km). The greatest breadth in the North is 7200 km (Morocco to Florida) and in the South 9600 km (Guinea to Brazil). Average depth is 3600 m; the greatest depths are the Puerto Rico Trench 9220 m, S. Sandwich Trench 8264 m, and Romansh Trench 7728 m.

## PACIFIC OCEAN

Covers nearly 40% of the world's total sea area, and is the largest of the oceans. The greatest breadth (E/W) is 16,000 km and the greatest length (N/S) 11,000 km. Average depth is 4200 m; also the deepest ocean. Generally the west is deeper than the east and the north deeper than the south. Greatest depths occur near island groups and include Mindanao Trench 11,524 m, Mariana Trench 11,022 m, Tonga Trench 10,882 m, Kuril-Kamchatka Trench 10,542 m, Philippine Trench 10,497 m, and Kermadec Trench 10,047 m.

| Comparisons (where applicable) | greatest distance N/S (km) | greatest distance E/W (km) | maximum depth (m) |
|---|---|---|---|
| Indian Ocean | — | 9600 | 9000 |
| Atlantic Ocean | — | 9600 | 9220 |
| Pacific Ocean | 11,000 | 16,000 | 11,524 |
| Arctic Ocean | — | — | 5450 |
| Mediterranean Sea | 960 | 3700 | 4846 |
| S. China Sea | 2100 | 1750 | 5514 |
| Bering Sea | 1800 | 2100 | 5121 |
| Caribbean Sea | 1600 | 2000 | 7100 |
| Gulf of Mexico | 1200 | 1700 | 4377 |
| Sea of Okhotsk | 2200 | 1400 | 3475 |
| E. China Sea | 1100 | 750 | 2999 |
| Yellow Sea | 800 | 1000 | 91 |
| Hudson Bay | 1250 | 1050 | 259 |
| Sea of Japan | 1500 | 1100 | 3743 |
| North Sea | 1200 | 550 | 661 |
| Red Sea | 1932 | 360 | 2246 |
| Black Sea | 600 | 1100 | 2245 |
| Baltic Sea | 1500 | 650 | 460 |

## EARTH'S SURFACE WATERS

| | |
|---|---|
| Total volume | c.1400 million cu. km |
| Oceans and seas | 1370 million cu. km |
| Ice | 24 million cu. km |
| Interstitial water (in rocks and sediments) | 4 million cu. km |
| Lakes and rivers | 230 thousand cu. km |
| Atmosphere (vapour) | c.140 thousand cu. km |

*to convert metric to imperial measurements:*
1 m = 3.281 feet
1 km = 0.621 miles
1 sq km = 0.386 sq miles

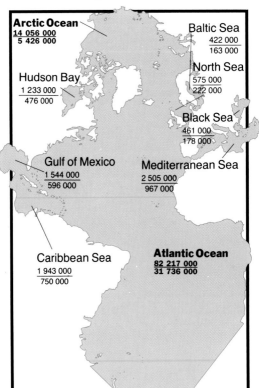

Red Sea
438 000
169 000

**Indian Ocean**
73 481 000
28 364 000

**Arctic Ocean**
14 056 000
5 426 000

Baltic Sea
422 000
163 000

Hudson Bay
1 233 000
476 000

North Sea
575 000
222 000

Black Sea
461 000
178 000

Gulf of Mexico
1 544 000
596 000

Mediterranean Sea
2 505 000
967 000

Caribbean Sea
1 943 000
750 000

**Atlantic Ocean**
82 217 000
31 736 000

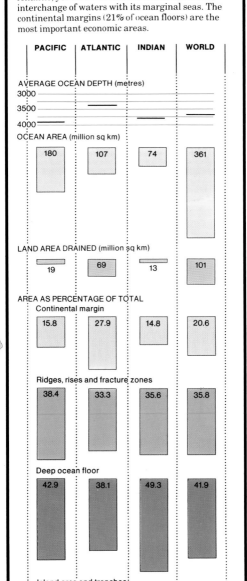

## FEATURES OF THE OCEAN BASIN

The majority of land drainage occurs in the Atlantic, yet this is the most saline ocean due to interchange of waters with its marginal seas. The continental margins (21% of ocean floors) are the most important economic areas.

| | PACIFIC | ATLANTIC | INDIAN | WORLD |
|---|---|---|---|---|
| **AVERAGE OCEAN DEPTH (metres)** | | | | |
| **OCEAN AREA (million sq km)** | 180 | 107 | 74 | 361 |
| **LAND AREA DRAINED (million sq km)** | 19 | 69 | 13 | 101 |
| **AREA AS PERCENTAGE OF TOTAL** | | | | |
| Continental margin | 15.8 | 27.9 | 14.8 | 20.6 |
| Ridges, rises and fracture zones | 38.4 | 33.3 | 35.6 | 35.8 |
| Deep ocean floor | 42.9 | 38.1 | 49.3 | 41.9 |
| Island arcs and trenches | 2.9 | 0.7 | 0.3 | 1.7 |

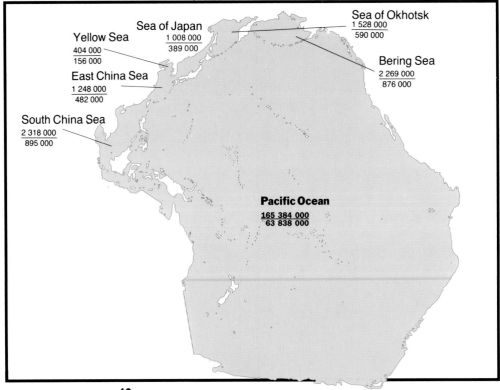

Sea of Japan
1 008 000
389 000

Sea of Okhotsk
1 528 000
590 000

Yellow Sea
404 000
156 000

Bering Sea
2 269 000
876 000

East China Sea
1 248 000
482 000

South China Sea
2 318 000
895 000

**Pacific Ocean**
165 384 000
63 838 000

# RIVER LENGTHS

| km | miles | | |
|---|---|---|---|
| 6,695 | 4,160 | **Nile** | *Africa* |
| 6,515 | 4,050 | **Amazon** | *South America* |
| 6,380 | 3,965 | **Yangtze (Chang Jiang)** | *Asia* |
| 6,019 | 3,740 | **Mississippi-Missouri** *North America* | |
| 5,570 | 3,460 | **Ob'-Irtysh** | *Asia* |
| 5,550 | 3,450 | **Yenisei-Angara** | *Asia* |
| 5,464 | 3,395 | **Yellow River (Huang He)** *Asia* | |
| 4,667 | 2,900 | **Congo (Zaire)** | *Africa* |
| 4,500 | 2,800 | **Paraná** | *South America* |
| 4,440 | 2,775 | **Irtysh** | *Asia* |
| 4,425 | 2,750 | **Mekong** | *Asia* |
| 4,416 | 2,744 | **Amur** | *Asia* |
| 4,400 | 2,730 | **Lena** | *Asia* |
| 4,250 | 2,640 | **Mackenzie** | *North America* |
| 4,090 | 2,556 | **Yenisei** | *Asia* |
| 4,030 | 2,505 | **Niger** | *Africa* |
| 3,969 | 2,466 | **Missouri** | *North America* |
| 3,779 | 2,348 | **Mississippi** | *North America* |
| 3,750 | 2,330 | **Murray-Darling** | *Australasia* |
| 3,688 | 2,290 | **Volga** | *Europe* |
| 3,218 | 2,011 | **Purus** | *South America* |
| 3,200 | 1,990 | **Madeira** | *South America* |
| 3,185 | 1,980 | **Yukon** | *North America* |
| 3,180 | 1,975 | **Indus** | *Asia* |
| 3,078 | 1,913 | **Syrdar'ya** | *Asia* |
| 3,060 | 1,901 | **Salween** | *Asia* |
| 3,058 | 1,900 | **St Lawrence** | *North America* |
| 2,900 | 1,800 | **São Francisco** *South America* | |
| 2,870 | 1,785 | **Rio Grande** | *North America* |
| 2,850 | 1,770 | **Danube** | *Europe* |
| 2,840 | 1,765 | **Brahmaputra** | *Asia* |
| 2,815 | 1,750 | **Euphrates** | *Asia* |
| 2,750 | 1,710 | **Pará-Tocantins** *South America* | |
| 2,750 | 1,718 | **Tarim** | *Asia* |
| 2,650 | 1,650 | **Zambezi** | *Africa* |
| 2,620 | 1,630 | **Amudar'ya** | *Asia* |
| 2,620 | 1,630 | **Araguaia** | *South America* |
| 2,600 | 1,615 | **Paraguay** | *South America* |
| 2,570 | 1,600 | **Nelson-Saskatchewan** *North America* | |

| | | | |
|---|---|---|---|
| 2,534 | 1,575 | **Ural** | *Asia* |
| 2,513 | 1,562 | **Kolyma** | *Asia* |
| 2,510 | 1,560 | **Ganges (Ganga)** | *Asia* |
| 2,500 | 1,555 | **Orinoco** | *South America* |
| 2,490 | 1,550 | **Shabeelle** | *Africa* |
| 2,490 | 1,550 | **Pilcomayo** | *South America* |
| 2,348 | 1,459 | **Arkansas** | *North America* |
| 2,333 | 1,450 | **Colorado** | *North America* |
| 2,285 | 1,420 | **Dneper** | *Europe* |
| 2,250 | 1,400 | **Columbia** | *North America* |
| 2,150 | 1,335 | **Irrawaddy** | *Asia* |
| 2,129 | 1,323 | **Pearl River (Xi Jiang)** | *Asia* |
| 2,032 | 1,270 | **Kama** | *Europe* |
| 2,000 | 1,240 | **Negro** | *South America* |
| 1,923 | 1,195 | **Peace** | *North America* |
| 1,899 | 1,186 | **Tigris** | *Asia* |
| 1,870 | 1,162 | **Don** | *Europe* |
| 1,860 | 1,155 | **Orange** | *Africa* |
| 1,809 | 1,124 | **Pechora** | *Europe* |
| 1,800 | 1,125 | **Okavango** | *Africa* |
| 1,609 | 1,000 | **Marañón** | *South America* |
| 1,609 | 1,095 | **Uruguay** | *South America* |
| 1,600 | 1,000 | **Volta** | *Africa* |
| 1,600 | 1,000 | **Limpopo** | *Africa* |
| 1,550 | 963 | **Magdalena** *South America* | |
| 1,515 | 946 | **Kura** | *Asia* |
| 1,480 | 925 | **Oka** | *Europe* |
| 1,480 | 925 | **Belaya** | *Europe* |
| 1,445 | 903 | **Godavari** | *Asia* |
| 1,430 | 893 | **Senegal** | *Africa* |
| 1,410 | 876 | **Dnester** | *Europe* |
| 1,400 | 875 | **Chari** | *Africa* |
| 1,368 | 850 | **Fraser** | *North America* |
| 1,320 | 820 | **Rhine** | *Europe* |
| 1,314 | 821 | **Vyatka** | *Europe* |
| 1,183 | 735 | **Donets** | *Europe* |
| 1,159 | 720 | **Elbe** | *Europe* |
| 1,151 | 719 | **Kizilirmak** | *Asia* |

| | | | |
|---|---|---|---|
| 1,130 | 706 | **Desna** | *Europe* |
| 1,094 | 680 | **Gambia** | *Africa* |
| 1,080 | 675 | **Yellowstone** | *North America* |
| 1,049 | 652 | **Tennessee** | *North America* |
| 1,024 | 640 | **Zelenga** | *Asia* |
| 1,020 | 637 | **Duena** | *Europe* |
| 1,014 | 630 | **Vistula (Wisła)** | *Europe* |
| 1,012 | 629 | **Loire** | *Europe* |
| 1,006 | 625 | **Tagus (Tejo)** | *Europe* |
| 977 | 607 | **Tisza** | *Europe* |
| 925 | 575 | **Meuse (Maas)** | *Europe* |
| 909 | 565 | **Oder** | *Europe* |
| 761 | 473 | **Seine** | *Europe* |
| 354 | 220 | **Severn** | *Europe* |
| 346 | 215 | **Thames** | *Europe* |
| 300 | 186 | **Trent** | *Europe* |

## DRAINAGE BASINS

| sq km | sq miles | | |
|---|---|---|---|
| 7,050,000 | 2,721,000 | **Amazon** | *South America* |
| 3,700,000 | 1,428,000 | **Congo** | *Africa* |
| 3,250,000 | 1,255,000 | **Mississippi-Missouri** *North America* | |
| 3,100,000 | 1,197,000 | **Paraná** | *South America* |
| 2,700,000 | 1,042,000 | **Yenisei** | *Asia* |
| 2,430,000 | 938,000 | **Ob'** | *Asia* |
| 2,420,000 | 934,000 | **Lena** | *Asia* |
| 1,900,000 | 733,400 | **Nile** | *Africa* |
| 1,840,000 | 710,000 | **Amur** | *Asia* |
| 1,765,000 | 681,000 | **Mackenzie** | *North America* |
| 1,730,000 | 668,000 | **Ganges-Brahmaputra** *Asia* | |
| 1,380,000 | 533,000 | **Volga** | *Europe* |
| 1,330,000 | 513,000 | **Zambezi** | *Africa* |
| 1,200,000 | 463,000 | **Niger** | *Africa* |
| 1,175,000 | 454,000 | **Yangtze** | *Asia* |
| 1,020,000 | 394,000 | **Orange** | *Africa* |
| 980,000 | 378,000 | **Yellow River** | *Asia* |
| 960,000 | 371,000 | **Indus** | *Asia* |
| 945,000 | 365,000 | **Orinoco** | *South America* |
| 910,000 | 351,000 | **Murray-Darling** *Australasia* | |
| 855,000 | 330,000 | **Yukon** | *North America* |
| 815,000 | 315,000 | **Danube** | *Europe* |
| 810,000 | 313,000 | **Mekong** | *Asia* |
| 225,000 | 86,900 | **Rhine** | *Europe* |

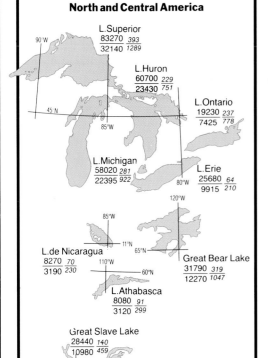

**North and Central America**

L.Superior 83270 *393* / 32140 *1289*

L.Huron 60700 *229* / 23430 *751*

L.Ontario 19230 *237* / 7425 *778*

L.Michigan 58020 *281* / 22395 *922*

L.Erie 25680 *64* / 9915 *210*

L.de Nicaragua 8270 *70* / 3190 *230*

Great Bear Lake 31790 *319* / 12270 *1047*

L.Athabasca 8080 *91* / 3120 *299*

Great Slave Lake 28440 *140* / 10980 *459*

Nettilling Lake 5250 / 2030

L.Winnipeg 24510 *21* / 9460 *69*

Reindeer Lake 6390 / 2470

## INLAND WATERS

water surface area ☐ = $\dfrac{1\ 000\ \text{sq km}}{386\ \text{sq miles}}$

deepest point $\dfrac{229\ \text{metres}}{751\ \text{feet}}$

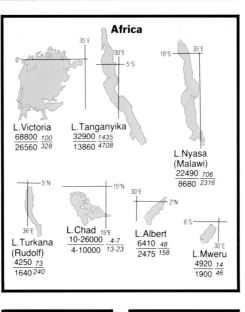

**Africa**

L.Victoria 68800 *100* / 26560 *328*

L.Tanganyika 32900 *1435* / 13860 *4708*

L.Nyasa (Malawi) 22490 *706* / 8680 *2316*

L.Turkana (Rudolf) 4250 *73* / 1640 *240*

L.Chad 10-26000 *4-7* / 4-10000 *13-23*

L.Albert 6410 *48* / 2475 *158*

L.Mweru 4920 *14* / 1900 *46*

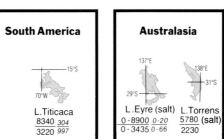

**South America**

L.Titicaca 8340 *304* / 3220 *997*

**Australasia**

L.Eyre (salt) 0-8900 *0-20* / 0-3435 *0-66*

L.Torrens 5780 (salt) / 2230

**Europe**

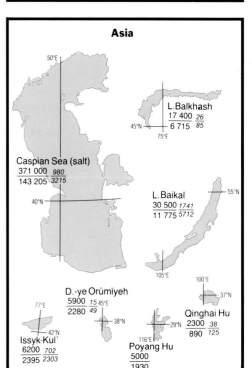

L.Onega 9600 *124* / 3705 *407*

L.Vänern 5580 *98* / 2155 *322*

L.Ladoga 18390 *230* / 7100 *755*

**Asia**

Caspian Sea (salt) 371 000 *980* / 143 205 *3215*

L.Balkhash 17 400 *26* / 6 715 *85*

L.Baikal 30 500 *1741* / 11 775 *5712*

D.-ye Orūmiyeh 5900 *15* / 2280 *49*

Issyk-Kul' 6200 *702* / 2395 *2303*

Qinghai Hu 2300 *38* / 890 *125*

Poyang Hu 5000 / 1930

S        I        B        E        R

Kotuy

Lena

Laptev
Sea

Honshu

Sakhalin

Kolyma

New Siberian
Islands

ARCTIC

Hokkaido

Sea of Okhotsk

East
Siberian
Sea

OCEAN

Kuril Islands

Kamchatka

Anadyr

Wrangel
Island

Chukchi
Sea

Beaufort
Sea

Melvil
Island

Bering

Chukotskiy
Peninsula

Bering Strait

Point Barrow

Banks
Island

Sea

Brooks Range

Yukon

Aleutian Islands

Alaska Range
Mount
McKinley

Victor

Mackenzie Mountains

Mackenzie

Great
Bear
Lake

Aleutian Range

Kodiak Island

Gulf
of
Alaska

Coast Mountains

R       O       C       K       Y

Great
Slave Lake

NORTH

Lake
Athabasca

Midway Islands

Peace

Athabasca

PACIFIC

Queen
Charlotte
Islands

Fraser

Saskatchewan

Hawaiian Islands

Vancouver
Island

Mount Rainier
Mount St Helens

M
o
u
n
t
a
i
n
s

Columbia

OCEAN

Cascade Range

Snake

Coast Ranges

Sierra Nevada

Great Salt
Lake

Colorado

Mount
Whitney

Gulf of California

Lower California

Sierra Madre Occidental

8

Lower California

Gulf of California

Sierra Madre Occidental

Rio Grande

Sierra Madre Oriental

MISSISSIPPI

Florida

GULF
OF
MEXICO

W
C u

GREA

Gulf of Campeche

Popocatépetl ▲

Yucatan

Gulf
of
Honduras

Islas Revillagigedo

Sierra Madre del Sur

Lake
Nicaragua

Clipperton
Island

Isthmus of

Gulf
of
Panama

PACIFIC

Isla del Coco

Isla de Malpelo

Cotopax

Galapagos Islands

Chimborazo ▲

OCEAN

NORTH

ATLANTIC

OCEAN

BAHAMAS

Sargasso
Sea

WEST INDIES

Hispaniola

Jamaica

GREATER ANTILLES

Puerto
Rico

CARIBBEAN

SEA

LESSER ANTILLES

Gulf
of
Darien

Lake
Maracaibo

Trinidad

Cordillera Occidental

Cauca

Magdalena

Cordillera Oriental

LLANOS

Orinoco

Guiana Highlands

Roraima▲

Panama

Branco

Japurá

Negro

Putumayo

Amazon

Amazon

Mouths
of the
Amazon

Marañón

Ucayali

Jurúa

Purus

Madeira

Tapajós

Xingu

Tocantins

Huascarán

Madre de Dios

Araguaia

Tocantins

Parnaíba

São Francisco

ANDES

MATO

GROSSO

Lake
Titicaca

Ancohuma

Brazilian Highlands

Lake
Poopó

GRAN CHACO

Salar
de Uyuni

Paraguay

Paraná

Atacama Desert

Pilcomayo

Galapagos Islands

Gran Chaco

Pilcomayo

Bermejo

Paraguay

Paraná

Uruguay

Salado

Plate

A
N
D
E
S

P a m p a s

San Félix   San Ambrosio

Aconcagua

Juan Fernández

Colorado

Negro

S O U T H

P
a
t
a
g
o
n
i
a

Chico

Chubut

Deseado

Falkland
Islands

Sala y Gomez

Tierra del
Fuego

Easter Island

Cape Horn

Drake   Passage

Elephant Island

P A C I F I C

South
Shetland
Islands

King
George I.

Ducie Island

Graham Land

Palmer Land

ANTARCTIC PENINSULA

Henderson Island

Pitcairn Island

Peter I Island

Bellingshausen
Sea

O C E A N

Ronn

Rapa

Ellsworth
Land

Amundsen
Sea

Lesser
Antarctica

A N T

Marie  Byrd
Land

Rockefeller
Plateau

Ross

Ross
Ice
Shelf

Sea

TRANSAN

MOUNTAINS

Mount Erebus

Scott Island

Oates
Land

Chatham
Islands

Balleny Islands

Bounty
Islands

Antipodes

New
Zealand

Campbell Island

INDIA

St Helena

S O U T H

Tristan da Cunha

Gough Island

Cunene

South Georgia

Kalahari
Desert

Orange River

South
Sandwich
Islands

Cape
of
Good Hope

A T L A N T I C

South Orkney
Islands

Limpopo

Bouvet Island

Madagascar

Weddell

Sea

Prince Edward
Islands

Lazarev
Sea

O C E A N

Limit of permanent pack ice

Ice Shelf

Queen Maud Land

A R C T I C A

Enderby Land

Greater Antarctica

Îles Crozet

SOUTH POLE

Îles Kerguelen

Macdonald Islands
Heard Island

St Paul
Amsterdam Island

George V
Land

Wilkes Land

O C E A N

Azores

Strait of Gibraltar

Chott Melrhir

El Jerid

Mediterra

Gulf of Sirte

Madeira

ATLAS MOUNTAINS

Libyan

Canary Islands

NORTH

ATLANTIC

OCEAN

Hoggar

Tibesti

S    A    H    A    R    A

Lac Faguibine

Senegal

Niger

S    A    H    E    L

Jebel Marra

Cape Verde Islands

Cape Verde

Lake Chad

Gambia

Lake Volta

Benue

Adamawa Highlands

Ubangi

Uele

Grain Coast

Slave Coast

Bight of Benin

Sanaga

Ivory Coast

Gold Coast

Mouths of the Niger

Zaire

St Paul Rocks

Gulf of Guinea

Bioko

Príncipe

São Tomé

Lac Mai-Ndombe

Pagalu

Kasai

Congo

Ascension

Cuango

S    O    U    T    H

Bie Plateau

Cubango

Okavango

Cunene

St Helena

Etosha Pan

Okavango

A    T    L    A    N    T    I    C

Lake Ngami

Walvis Bay

Kalahar

Desert

SOUTH AMERICA

O    C    E    A    N

Namib Desert

Orange River

Great Karoo

Cape of Good Hope

NORTH POLE .

ARCTIC

Ellesmere Island

Hudson Bay

Baffin Island

Greenland

Greenland Sea

Svalbard

Davis Strait

Bear Island

LABRADOR

Jan Mayen

Denmark Strait

Norwegian

Cape Farewell

Iceland

Sea

NORTH

Faeroe Islands

Shetland

S C A N D I

Orkney

Lake Vänern

Rockall

British Isles

Grampians

North

Lake Vättern

Ba

ATLANTIC

Irish Sea

Sea

Elbe

Oder

Severn

Thames

Rhine

N O R

Ne

English Channel

Seine

Danu

Loire

OCEAN

Bay of Biscay

Massif Central

Mt. Blanc

A L P S

Po

Adriatic

Dinar

Azores

Garonne

Cantabrian Mts

Pyrenees

Rhône

Apennines

Se

Ebro

Corsica

Tagus

Balearic Islands

Sardinia

Guadalquivir

M E D I T E R

Strait of Gibraltar

Sicily

Madeira

Malta

A T L A S   M O U N T A I N S

Chott Melrhir

Canary Islands

El Jerid

OCEAN

Severnaya
Zemlya

Limit of permanent pack ice

Franz
Josef
Land

Spitsbergen

*Kara
Sea*

Novaya
Zemlya

*Barents
Sea*

North Cape

White
Sea

Gulf of Bothnia

Pechora

EUROPEAN PLAIN

Severnaya Dvina

Lake
Onega

Lake
Ladoga

Gulf of Finland

tic Sea

EUROPE

Dvina

Vistula

Central
Russian

Uplands

Volga

URAL MOUNTAINS

CENTRAL SIBERIAN PLATEAU

Lena

Nizhnyaya Tunguska

Lena

Yenisey

WEST SIBERIAN PLAINS

Ob'

Ob'

Irtysh

Angara

Lake
Baikal

KIRGHIZ STEPPE

Lake
Balkhash

CARPATHIANS

Hungarian Plain

Tisza

Dniester

Dnieper

Don

Sea of Azov

Danube

Balkan Mountains

Rhodope

Alps

Pindus

Thrace

Bosporus

Dardanelles

Aegean
Sea

Sea of
Marmara

ASIA MINOR

Tuz
Gölü

Kizil Irmak

TAURUS

Crete

Cyprus

*Black Sea*

Caucasus

Volga

Ural

Caspian Sea

Aral
Sea

Kyzylkum

Syrdar'ya

Amudar'ya

Karakumy

Araxes

Lake
Van

Lake
Urmia

Elbruz Mts.

Daryācheh-ye-Namak

Zagros Mountains

**Plateau
of
Iran**

Mesopotamia

Tigris

Euphrates

Syrian Desert

Jordan

Dead Sea

Persian
Gulf

Gulf
of
Oman

ANEAN SEA

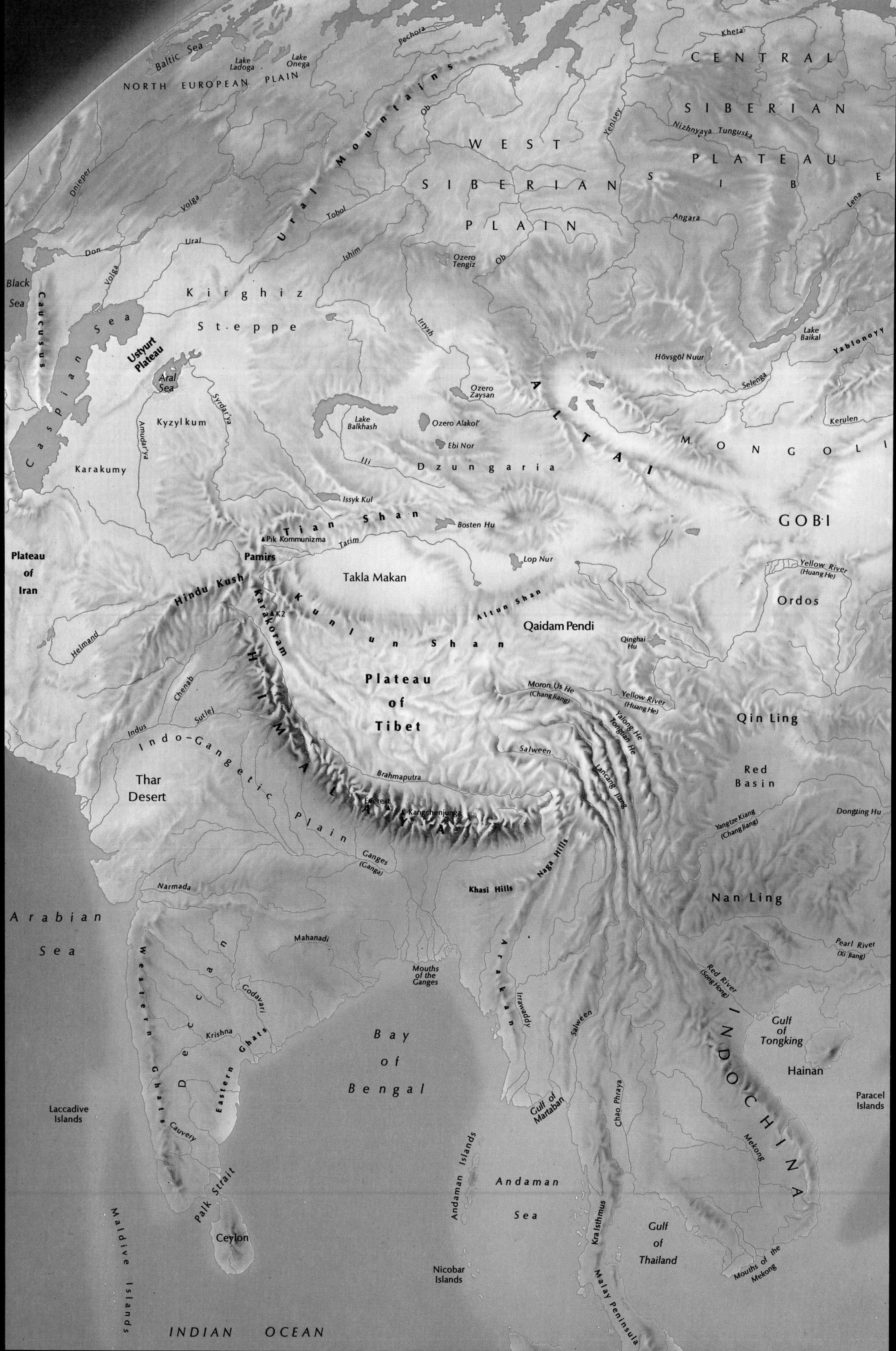

Baltic Sea

Lake Ladoga

Lake Onega

Pechora

Kheta

NORTH EUROPEAN PLAIN

CENTRAL

SIBERIAN

PLATEAU

Dnieper

Ural Mountains

Ob

WEST

SIBERIAN

Nizhnyaya Tunguska

Volga

Tobol

SIBERIAN

S

I

B

E

Don

Ural

Ishim

PLAIN

Yenisey

Angara

Lena

Volga

Ozero Tengiz

Ob

Black Sea

Caucusus

Caspian Sea

Ustyurt Plateau

Kirghiz

Steppe

Irtysh

Ozero Zaysan

ALTAI

Hövsgöl Nuur

Lake Baikal

Yablonoyy

Selenga

Kerulen

Aral Sea

Syrdar'ya

Lake Balkhash

Ozero Alakol'

MONGOLI

Amudar'ya

Kyzylkum

Ili

Ebi Nor

Dzungaria

GOBI

Karakumy

Issyk Kul

Tian Shan

Shan

Bosten Hu

Plateau of Iran

Pik Kommunizma

Pamirs

Tarim

Lop Nur

Yellow River (Huang He)

Hindu Kush

Karakoram

K2

Kunlun Shan

Takla Makan

Altun Shan

Qaidam Pendi

Ordos

Qinghai Hu

Qin Ling

Helmand

HIMALAYA

Plateau

of

Tibet

Moron Us He (Chang Jiang)

Yellow River (Huang He)

Yalong He

Tongtian He

Chenab

Indus

Sutlej

Indo-Gangetic

Plain

Salween

Lancang Jiang

Red Basin

Thar Desert

Brahmaputra

Everest

Kangchenjunga

Yangtze Kiang (Chang Jiang)

Dongting Hu

Ganges (Ganga)

Naga Hills

Narmada

Khasi Hills

Nan Ling

Arabian

Sea

Mahanadi

Arakan

Pearl River (Xi Jiang)

Western Ghats

Godavari

Mouths of the Ganges

Red River (Song Hong)

Gulf of Tongking

Krishna

Eastern Ghats

Bay

of

Bengal

Irrawaddy

INDOCHINA

Hainan

Deccan

Salween

Chao Phraya

Mekong

Paracel Islands

Laccadive Islands

Cauvery

Palk Strait

Gulf of Martaban

Andaman Islands

Andaman

Sea

Kra Isthmus

Gulf

of

Thailand

Mouths of the Mekong

Maldive Islands

Ceylon

Nicobar Islands

Malay Peninsula

INDIAN OCEAN

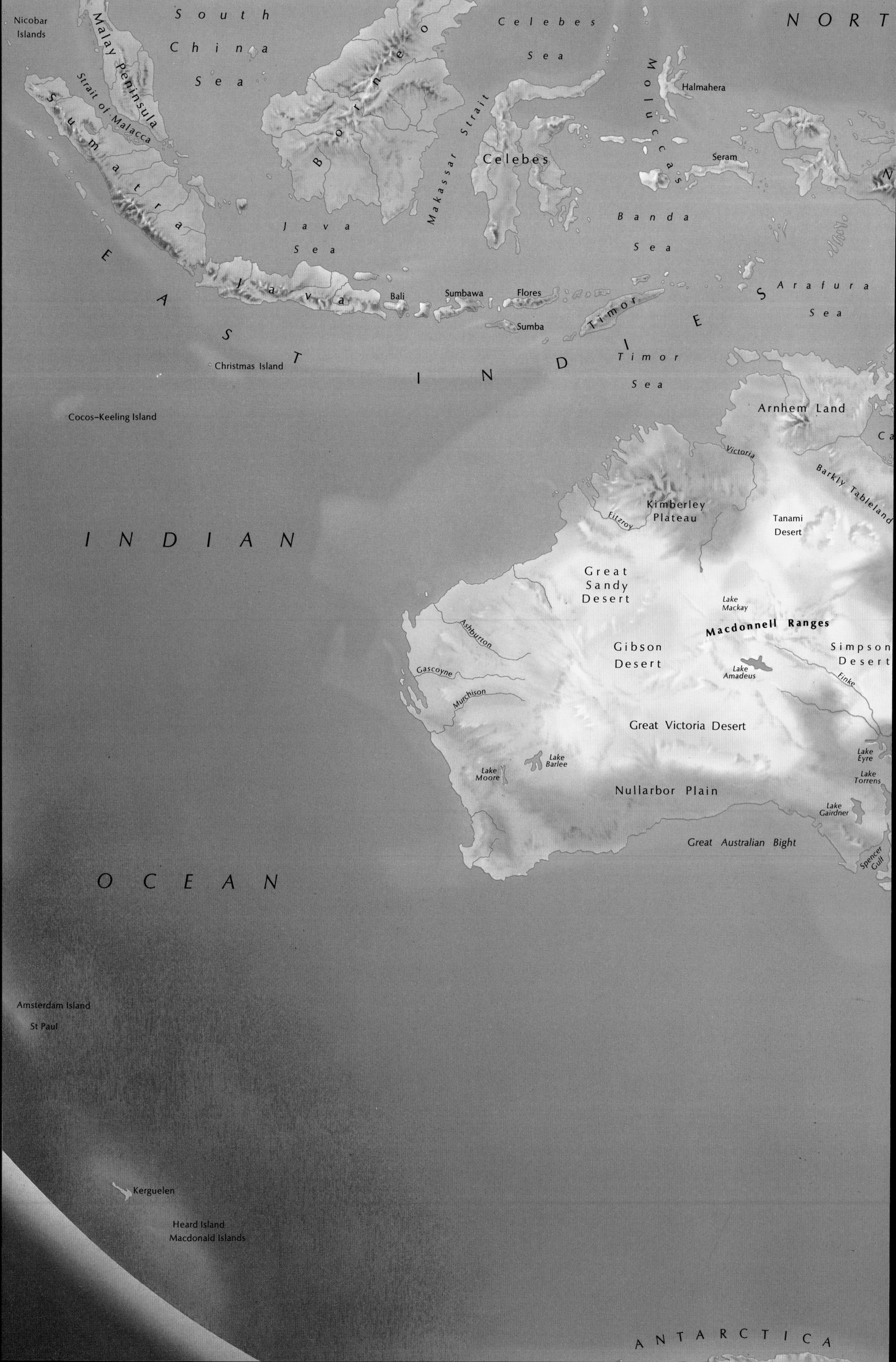

Nicobar
Islands

South
China
Sea

*Malay Peninsula*

Strait of Malacca

C e l e b e s
Sea

*Borneo*

N O R T

*Molucca s*

Halmahera

*S u m a t r a*

*B o r n e o*

Makassar Strait

Celebes

Seram

*J a v a*
Sea

*E*

Bali

Sumbawa

Flores

*Timor*

*B a n d a*
Sea

*A r a f u r a*
Sea

N

*A*

*J a v a*

Sumba

*Timor*

Christmas Island

*S*

*T*

*T i m o r*
Sea

Ca

Cocos–Keeling Island

*I*

*N*

*D*

*I*

*E*

*S*

Arnhem Land

*Victoria*

I N D I A N

*Fitzroy*

Kimberley
Plateau

Tanami
Desert

Barkly Tableland

Great
Sandy
Desert

*Lake
Mackay*

*Ashburton*

**Macdonnell Ranges**

Gibson
Desert

*Lake
Amadeus*

S i m p s o n
D e s e r t

*Gascoyne*

*Finke*

*Murchison*

Great Victoria Desert

Lake
Eyre

Lake
*Barlee*

Lake
*Moore*

Lake
Torrens

Nullarbor Plain

Lake
*Gairdner*

Great Australian Bight

*Spencer
Gulf*

O C E A N

Amsterdam Island

St Paul

Kerguelen

Heard Island
Macdonald Islands

A N T A R C T I C A

H PACIFIC OCEAN MICRONESIA SOUTH

Marshall Islands

MELANESIA

Admiralty Islands

ew Guinea

New Ireland

Bismarck Sea

New Britain

Bougainville

Solomon Islands

Nauru

Banaba

Kiribati

POLYNESIA

Tokelau Islands

Tuvalu

PACIFIC

Santa Cruz Islands

Torres Strait

Great Dividing Range

Coral

Cape York Peninsula

Great Barrier Reef

Sea

Vanuatu

Samoan Islands

Fiji

Tahiti

Gulf of rpentaria

Flinders

Georgina

Diamantina

Cooper Creek

New Caledonia

Tonga

OCEAN

Fraser Island

Warrego

Culgoa

Barwon

Darling

Lake Frome

Murray

Lachlan

Murrumbidgee

Murray

Murray

Mount Kosciusko

Australian Alps

Tasman

Norfolk Island

Lord Howe Island

Kermadec Islands

King Island

Bass Strait

Flinders Island

Sea

New Zealand

Cook Strait

Tasmania

Chatham Islands

Foveaux Strait

Stewart Island

Bounty Islands

Antipodes Islands

Auckland Islands

Campbell Island

Macquarie Island

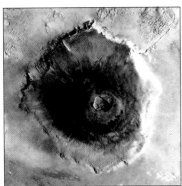

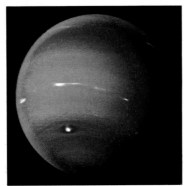

*Far left* The Caloris basin of Mercury is the largest impact feature on the planet.

*Left* Radar mapping of Venus has provided this computer-generated image of the volcano, Maat Mons.

*Top right* Io (left) and Europa are clearly visible as they cross the face of Jupiter.

*Far left* Olympus Mons on Mars is the largest known volcano in the solar system. It is 550km across at the base and more than 26km high.

*Right* The rings of Saturn lie in the equatorial plane and consist of countless ice-covered particles, perhaps up to several metres across.

*Left* Voyager 2 produced this false-colour image of Neptune in August 1989. A planet-wide haze (red) and white clouds are visible.

*Left* This image of Uranus in false-colour was taken from 9.1 million km by Voyager 2. The atmosphere is deep, cold and remarkably clear, but the false colours enhance the polar region. Here, the suggestion is that a brownish haze of smog is concentrated over the pole.

Current theory suggests that the solar system condensed from a primitive solar nebula of gas and dust during an interval of a few tens of millions of years about 4600 million years ago. Gravity caused this nebula to contract, drawing most of its mass into the centre. Turbulence gave the original cloud a tendency to rotate faster and faster, forcing the remainder of the cloud into a disc shape.

The centre of the cloud heated up as it compressed, and so eventually became hot enough for the Sun to begin to shine, through nuclear energy released at its core. Meanwhile the surrounding disc of cloud cooled, allowing material to condense into solid form. Particles stuck together as they collided and progressively larger bodies were built up. These swept up most of the debris to form the planets, which now orbit the Sun.

## EARTHLIKE PLANETS

**Mercury** is the nearest planet to the Sun, spinning three times for every two orbits around the Sun. It has an exceptionally large metallic core which may be responsible for Mercury's weak magnetic field. Mercury is an airless world subject to vast extremes of temperature, from $-180°C$ ($-292°F$) at night to $430°C$ ($806°F$) near the middle of its long day. The Mariner 10 space probe, during the mid-1970s, revealed the surface to be dominated by heavily cratered areas.

**Venus** has a dense atmosphere with a surface pressure 90 times that of the Earth. Made up of 96% carbon dioxide, the lower layers are rich in sulphur dioxide while sulphuric acid droplets populate the higher clouds. The clouds maintain a mean surface temperature of about $480°C$ ($896°F$). The hidden surface has been mapped by radar from orbiting probes and shows a rugged surface with some volcanoes, possibly still active.

**Mars** has a thin atmosphere of about 96% carbon dioxide mixed with other minor gasses. The polar caps consist of semi-permanent water-ice and solid carbon dioxide. Day and night surface temperatures vary between about $-120°C$ ($-184°F$) and $-20°C$ ($-4°F$). Mars has two small satellites, Phobos and Deimos, each less than about 25km (15.5 miles) across, probably captured asteroids.

Mars also shows evidence of erosional processes. The effect of winds is seen in the form of the deposition of sand dunes. Dust storms frequently obscure the surface. The large channels, such as the 5000km (3107 miles) long Valles Marineris, may have been cut by flowing water. Water is abundant in the polar caps and may be widespread, held in as permafrost.

## GAS GIANTS

**Jupiter** has at least 16 satellites and a debris ring system about 50,000km (31,070 miles) above the cloud tops. The outer atmosphere is all that can be directly observed of the planet itself. It is mostly hydrogen with lesser amounts of helium, ammonia, methane and water vapour. Jupiter's rapid rotation causes it to be flattened towards the poles. This rotation and heat flow from the interior cause complex weather patterns. Where cloud systems interact vast storms can occur in the form of vortices. Some last only a few days, but the most persistent of these, the Great Red Spot, has been present since it was first detected in the 17th century.

**Saturn** is the least dense of the planets. It has a stormy atmosphere situated above a 30,000km (18,640 miles) layer of liquid hydrogen and helium distorted by rotation.

The rings of Saturn are thought to be mostly made of icy debris, from 10m (33 ft) down to a few microns in size, derived from the break-up of a satellite. The rings are less than 1km thick.

**Uranus**, consisting mainly of hydrogen, was little known until Voyager 2 flew by it in 1986. The probe discovered ten new satellites and provided images of the planet's eleven icy rings of debris.

**Neptune** was visited by Voyager 2 in 1989. Six new satellites were discovered, one larger than Nereid, the smaller of the two known satellites. Triton, the largest satellite, was found to be smaller than previous estimates. The turbulent atmosphere is a mixture of hydrogen, helium and methane.

**Pluto** is now 4500 million km from the Sun, closer than Neptune until 1999, but its eccentric orbit will take it to 7500 million km by 2113. A tenuous atmosphere has been found above a surface of frozen methane. Charon, the satellite, is half Pluto's diameter.

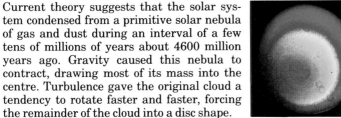

| | SUN | MERCURY | VENUS | EARTH | (MOON) | MARS | JUPITER | SATURN | URANUS | NEPTUNE | PLUTO |
|---|---|---|---|---|---|---|---|---|---|---|---|
| Mass (Earth = 1) | 333 400 | 0.055 | 0.815 | 1 (5.97 10²⁴kg) | 0.012 | 0.107 | 317.8 | 95.2 | 14.5 | 17.2 | 0.003 |
| Volume (Earth = 1) | 1 306 000 | 0.06 | 0.88 | 1 | 0.020 | 0.150 | 1 323 | 752 | 64 | 54 | 0.007 |
| Density (water = 1) | 1.41 | 5.43 | 5.24 | 5.52 | 3.34 | 3.94 | 1.33 | 0.70 | 1.30 | 1.64 | 2.0 |
| Equatorial diameter (km) | 1 392 000 | 4878 | 12 104 | 12 756 | 3 476 | 6 794 | 142 800 | 120 000 | 52 000 | 48 400 | 2 302 |
| Polar flattening | 0 | 0 | 0 | 0.003 | 0 | 0.005 | 0.065 | 0.108 | 0.060 | 0.021 | 0 |
| 'Surface' gravity (Earth = 1) | 27.9 | 0.37 | 0.88 | 1 | 0.16 | 0.38 | 2.69 | 1.19 | 0.93 | 1.22 | 0.05 |
| Number of satellites greater than 100 km diameter | — | 0 | 0 | 1 | — | 0 | 7 | 13 | 7 | 6 | 1 |
| Total number of satellites | — | 0 | 0 | 1 | — | 2 | 16 | 17 | 15 | 8 | 1 |
| Period of rotation (in Earth days) | 25.38 | 58.65 | −243 (retrograde) | 23hr 56m 4 secs | 27.32 | 1.03 | 0.414 | 0.426 | −0.74 (retrograde) | 0.67 | −6.39 (retrograde) |
| Length of year (in Earth days and years) | — | 88 days | 224.7 days | 365.26 days | — | 687 days | 11.86 years | 29.46 years | 84.01 years | 164.8 years | 247.7 years |
| Distance from Sun (mean) Mkm | — | 57.9 | 108.9 | 149.6 | — | 227.9 | 778.3 | 1 427 | 2870 | 4 497 | 5 900 |

## EARTH STRUCTURE

Internally, the Earth may be divided broadly into crust, mantle and core (*see right*).

The crust is a thin shell constituting only 0.2% of the mass of the Earth. The continental crust varies in thickness from 20 to 90km (12 to 56 miles) and is less dense than ocean crust. Two-thirds of the continents are overlain by sedimentary rocks of average thickness less than 2km (1.2 miles). Ocean crust is on average 7km (4.4 miles) thick. It is composed of igneous rocks, basalts and gabbros.

Crust and mantle are separated by the Mohorovičić Discontinuity (Moho). The mantle differs from the crust. It is largely igneous. The upper mantle extends to 350km (218 miles). The lower mantle has a more uniform composition. A sharp discontinuity defines the meeting of mantle and core. The inability of the outer core to transmit seismic waves suggests it is liquid. It is probably of metallic iron with other elements – sulphur, silicon, oxygen, potassium and hydrogen have all been suggested. The inner core is solid and probably of nickel-iron. Temperature at the core-mantle boundary is about 3700°C (5430°F) and 4000°–4500°C (7230°–8130°F) in the inner core.

## THE ATMOSPHERE

The ancient atmosphere lacked free oxygen. Plant life added oxygen to the atmosphere and transferred carbon dioxide to the crustal rocks and the hydrosphere. The composition of air today at 79% nitrogen and 20% oxygen remains stable by the same mechanism.

Solar energy is distributed around the Earth by the atmosphere. Most of the weather and climate processes occur in the troposphere at the lowest level. The atmosphere also shields the Earth. Ozone exists to the extent of 2 parts per million and is at its maximum at 30km (19 miles). It is the only gas which absorbs ultra-violet radiation. Water-vapour and $CO_2$ keep out infra-red radiation.

Above 80km (50 miles) nitrogen and oxygen tend to separate into atoms which become ionized (an ion is an atom lacking one or more of its electrons). The ionosphere is a zone of ionized belts which reflect radio waves back to Earth. These electrification belts change their position dependent on light and darkness and external factors.

Beyond the ionosphere, the magnetosphere extends to outer space. Ionized particles form a plasma (a fourth state of matter, ie. other than solid, liquid, gas) held in by the Earth's magnetic field.

## ORIGIN AND DEVELOPMENT OF LIFE

Primitive life-forms (blue-green algae) are found in rocks as old as 3500Ma (million years) and, although it cannot yet be proved, the origin of life on Earth probably dates back to about 4000Ma. It seems likely that the oxygen levels in the atmosphere increased only slowly at first, probably to about 1% of the present amount by 2000Ma. As the atmospheric oxygen built up so the protective ozone layer developed to allow organisms to live in shallower waters. More highly developed photosynthesising organisms led to the development of oxygen breathing animals. The first traces of multicellular life occur about 1000Ma; by 700Ma complex animals, such as jellyfish, worms and primitive molluscs, had developed.

Organisms developed hard parts that allowed their preservation as abundant fossils at about 570Ma. This coincided with a

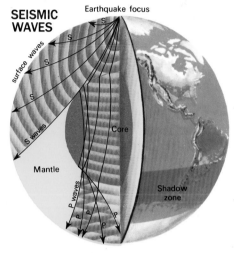

### THE EARTH'S SHELLS

Lithosphere
continental crust
oceanic crust
Moho
depth (km) 350
transition zone
upper mantle
900
seismic discontinuities
lower mantle
2900
core-mantle discontinuity
outer core
4700
5150
transition zone
inner core
6370

### SEISMIC WAVES

Earthquake focus
surface waves
S waves
P waves
Mantle
Core
Shadow zone

*Above* In an earthquake the shock generates vibrations, or seismic waves, which radiate in all directions from the focus. Surface waves travel close to the surface of the Earth. They cause most damage in the ground and most damage to structures.

Other waves known as body waves pass through the body of the Earth. Primary (P) waves are compressional. They are able to travel through solids and fluids and cause the particles of the Earth to vibrate in the direction of travel. Secondary (S) waves are transverse, or shear, waves. They can only pass through solids.

period of explosive evolution of marine life. Fishes appeared about 475Ma and by 400Ma land plants had developed. Between 340 and 305Ma dense vegetation covered the land, amphibians emerged from the sea, and by about 250Ma had given rise to reptiles and the first mammals. These expanded hugely about 65Ma.

## EARTHQUAKES

Earthquakes are the manifestation of a slippage at a geological fault. The majority occur at tectonic plate boundaries. The interior of a plate tends to be stable and less subject to earthquakes. When plates slide past each other strain energy is suddenly released. Even though the amount of movement is very small the energy released is colossal. It is transferred in shock waves.

Most earthquakes originate at not very great depths – 5km (3 miles) or so. Some, however, may be as deep as 700km (435 miles). The precise cause of these very deep earthquakes is not known. The point from which the earthquake is generated is the focus and the point on the surface immediately above the focus is the epicentre.

The Richter Scale is used to define the magnitude of earthquakes. In the Scale each unit is ten times the intensity of the next lower on the scale. The intensity is recorded by seismographs. There is no upper limit but the greatest magnitude yet recorded is 8.9.

## VOLCANOES

Almost all the world's active volcanoes, numbering 500–600 are located at convergent plate boundaries. Those are the volcanoes which give spectacular demonstrations of volcanic activity. Yet far greater volcanic activity continues unnoticed and without cessation at mid-ocean ridges where magma from the upper mantle is quietly being extruded on to the ocean floor to create new crustal material.

Chemical composition of magmas and the amount of gas they contain determine the nature of a volcanic eruption. Gas-charged basalts produce cinder cones. Violent eruptions usually occur when large clouds of lava come into contact with water to produce fine-grained ash. When andesites are charged with gas they erupt with explosive violence.

Nuées ardentes (burning clouds) are extremely destructive. They are produced by magmas which erupt explosively sending molten lava fragments and gas at great speeds down the mountain sides.

In spite of the destructiveness of many volcanoes people still live in their vicinity because of the fertile volcanic soils. Geothermal energy in regions of volcanic activity is another source of attraction.

## GRAVITY AND MAGNETISM

The Earth is spheroidal in form because it is a rotating body. Were it not so it would take the form of a sphere. The shape is determined by the mass of the Earth and its rate of rotation. Centrifugal force acting outwards reduces the pull of gravity acting inwards so that gravity at the equator is less than at the poles. Uneven distribution of matter within the Earth distorts the shape taken up by the mean sea-level surface (the geoid). Today the belief is that electric currents generated in the semi-molten outer core are responsible for the magnetic field. The Earth's magnetic poles have experienced a number of reversals, the north pole becoming the south and vice-versa.

### ROCK AND HYDROLOGICAL CYCLES

*Right* In the most familiar cycle rain falls onto the land, drains to the sea, evaporates, condenses into cloud and is precipitated onto the land again. Water is also released and recirculated. In the rock cycle rocks are weathered and eroded, forming sediments which are compacted into rocks that are eventually exposed and then weathered again.

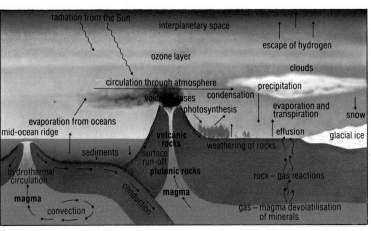

radiation from the Sun
interplanetary space
escape of hydrogen
ozone layer
clouds
circulation through atmosphere
precipitation
condensation
evaporation and transpiration
snow
photosynthesis
evaporation from oceans
effusion
glacial ice
mid-ocean ridge
volcanic rocks
weathering of rocks
sediments
surface run-off
hydrothermal circulation
plutonic rocks
rock – gas reactions
magma
conduction
magma
convection
gas – magma devolatilisation of minerals

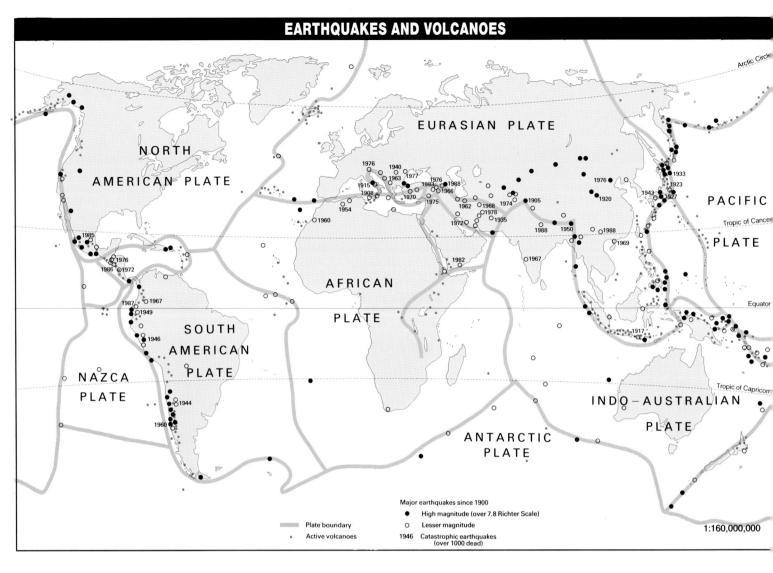

# EARTHQUAKES AND VOLCANOES

EURASIAN PLATE

NORTH AMERICAN PLATE

PACIFIC PLATE

AFRICAN PLATE

SOUTH AMERICAN PLATE

NAZCA PLATE

INDO–AUSTRALIAN PLATE

ANTARCTIC PLATE

Arctic Circle

Tropic of Cancer

Equator

Tropic of Capricorn

Major earthquakes since 1900

● High magnitude (over 7.8 Richter Scale)

○ Lesser magnitude

▨ Plate boundary

· Active volcanoes

1946 Catastrophic earthquakes (over 1000 dead)

1:160,000,000

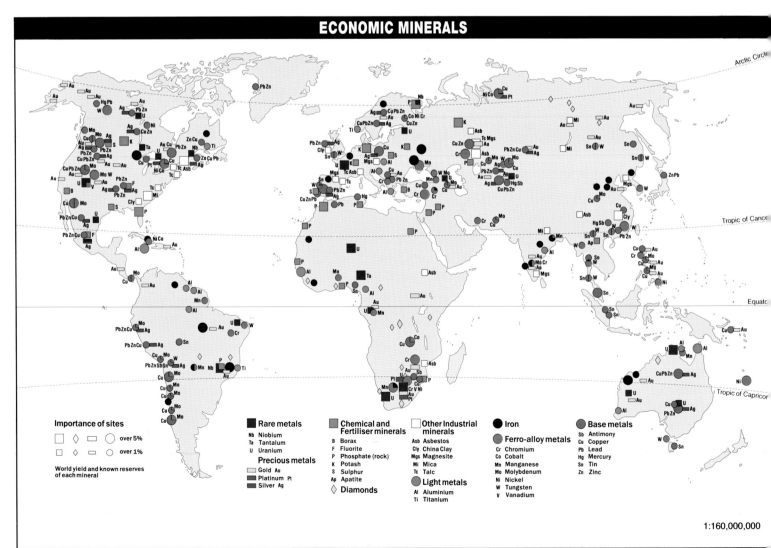

# ECONOMIC MINERALS

NORTH AMERICA

Arctic Circle

Tropic of Cancer

Equator

Tropic of Capricorn

**Importance of sites**

□ ◇ ▭ ○ over 5%

▫ ◇ ▭ ○ over 1%

World yield and known reserves of each mineral

■ **Rare metals**
Nb Niobium
Ta Tantalum
U Uranium

**Precious metals**
Gold Au
Platinum Pt
Silver Ag

■ **Chemical and Fertiliser minerals**
B Borax
F Fluorite
P Phosphate (rock)
K Potash
S Sulphur
Ap Apatite
◇ **Diamonds**

□ **Other Industrial minerals**
Asb Asbestos
Cly China Clay
Mgs Magnesite
Mi Mica
Tc Talc
● **Light metals**
Al Aluminium
Ti Titanium

● **Iron**

● **Ferro-alloy metals**
Cr Chromium
Co Cobalt
Mn Manganese
Mo Molybdenum
Ni Nickel
W Tungsten
V Vanadium

● **Base metals**
Sb Antimony
Cu Copper
Pb Lead
Hg Mercury
Sn Tin
Zn Zinc

1:160,000,000

64

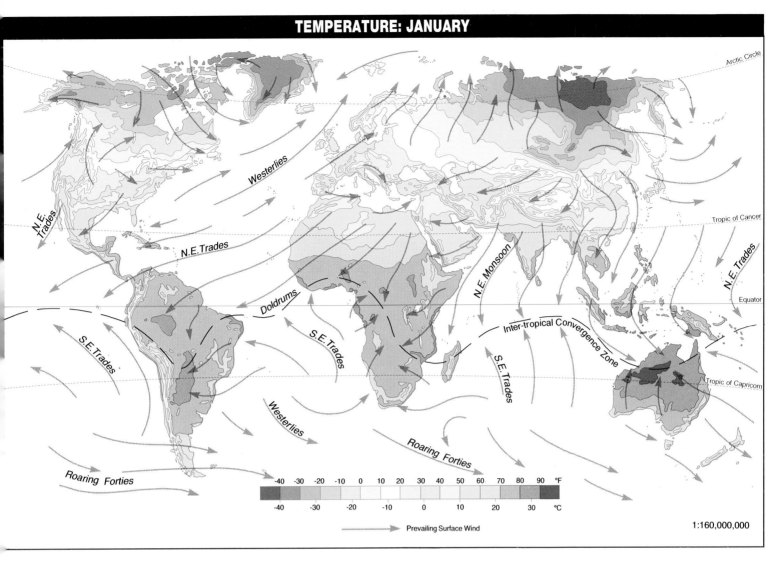

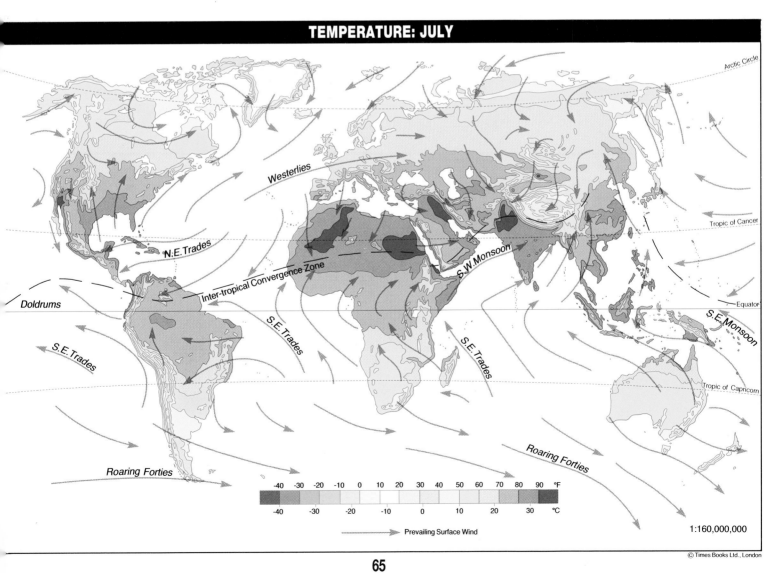

© Times Books Ltd., London

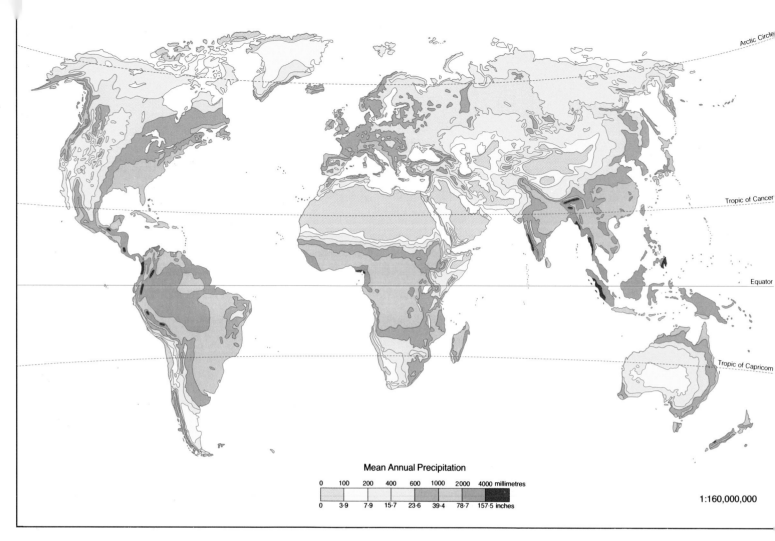

Mean Annual Precipitation

| 0 | 100 | 200 | 400 | 600 | 1000 | 2000 | 4000 millimetres |
|---|---|---|---|---|---|---|---|
| 0 | 3·9 | 7·9 | 15·7 | 23·6 | 39·4 | 78·7 | 157·5 inches |

1:160,000,000

# NATURAL VEGETATION

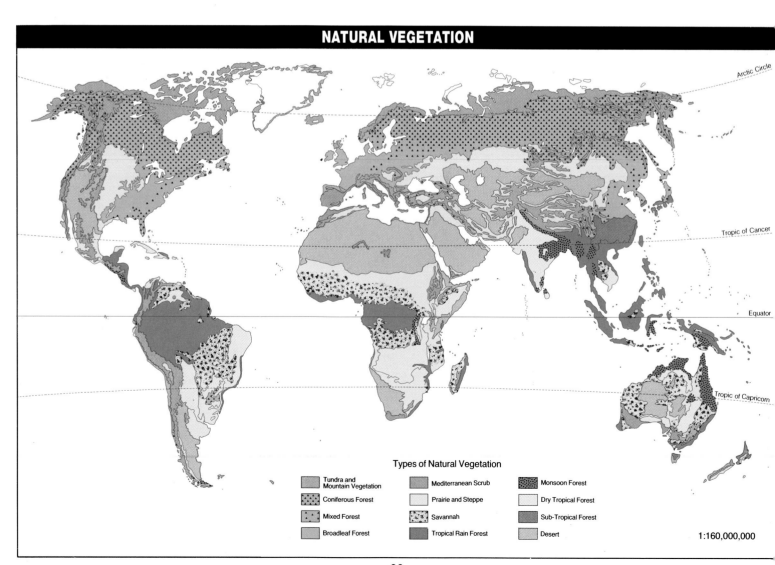

Types of Natural Vegetation

| | | |
|---|---|---|
| Tundra and Mountain Vegetation | Mediterranean Scrub | Monsoon Forest |
| Coniferous Forest | Prairie and Steppe | Dry Tropical Forest |
| Mixed Forest | Savannah | Sub-Tropical Forest |
| Broadleaf Forest | Tropical Rain Forest | Desert |

1:160,000,000

# POPULATION DENSITY

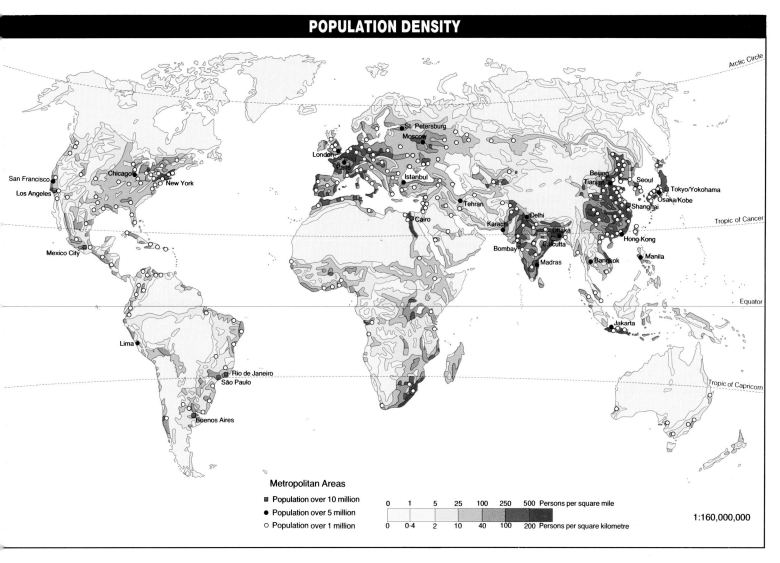

Metropolitan Areas

■ Population over 10 million
● Population over 5 million
○ Population over 1 million

| 0 | 1 | 5 | 25 | 100 | 250 | 500 | Persons per square mile |
| 0 | 0.4 | 2 | 10 | 40 | 100 | 200 | Persons per square kilometre |

1:160,000,000

# POPULATION CHANGE

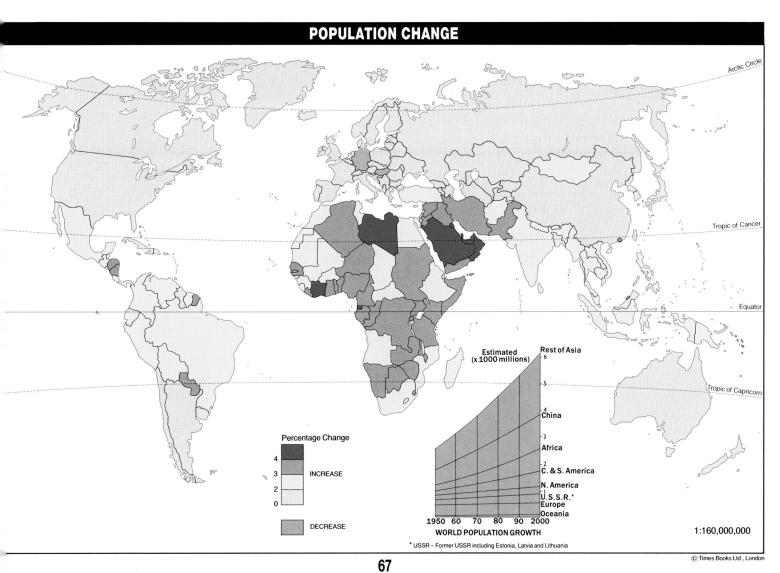

Percentage Change

4
3   INCREASE
2
0

DECREASE

Estimated
(x 1000 millions)

Rest of Asia
China
Africa
C. & S. America
N. America
U.S.S.R.*
Europe
Oceania

1950  60  70  80  90  2000
WORLD POPULATION GROWTH

1:160,000,000

* USSR – Former USSR including Estonia, Latvia and Lithuania

© Times Books Ltd., London

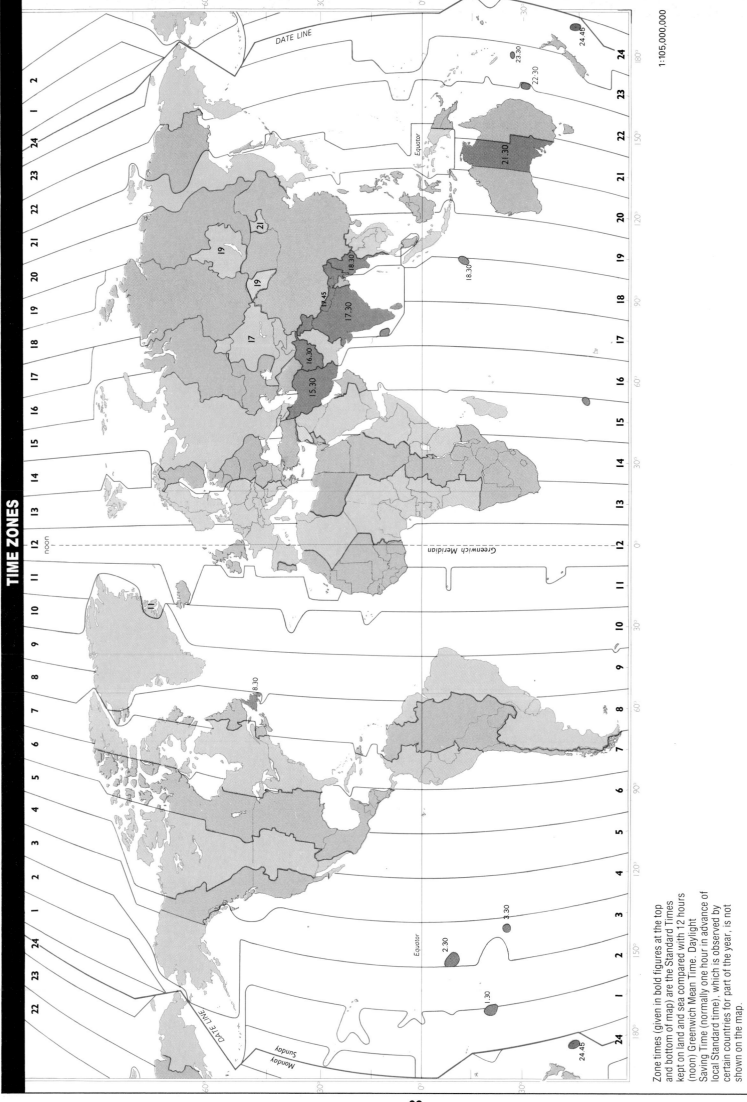

# TIME ZONES

DATE LINE

noon

Greenwich Meridian

Equator

DATE LINE

Monday
Sunday

1:105,000,000

Zone times (given in bold figures at the top
and bottom of map) are the Standard Times
kept on land and sea compared with 12 hours
(noon) Greenwich Mean Time. Daylight
Saving Time (normally one hour in advance of
local Standard time), which is observed by
certain countries for part of the year, is not
shown on the map.

68

This page explains the main symbols, lettering style and height/depth colours used on the reference maps on pages 2 to 76. The scale of each map is indicated at the foot of each page. Abbreviations used on the maps appear at the beginning of the index.

## BOUNDARIES

| | |
|---|---|
| ▪▪▪▪▪▪▪ | International |
| ▬ ▬ ▬ ▬ | International under Dispute |
| ▪ ▪ ▪ ▪ ▪ ▪ | Cease Fire Line |
| ▬▬▬▬▬ | Autonomous or State |
| ▬▬▬▬▬ | Administrative |
| ▬ ▬ ▬ ▬ | Maritime (National) |
| ▬ ▬ ▬ ▬ ▬ | International Date Line |

## COMMUNICATIONS

| | |
|---|---|
| ━━━━━ | Motorway/Express Highway |
| ▬▬▬▬▬ | Under Construction |
| ━━━━ | Major Highway |
| ─────── | Other Roads |
| ─ ─ ─ ─ | Under Construction |
| ▪ ▪ ▪ ▪ ▪ | Track |
| →▬▬▬← | Road Tunnel |
| ─ ─ ─ ─ | Car Ferry |
| ━━━▪━━ | Main Railway |
| ─────── | Other Railway |
| ─ ─ ─ ─ | Under Construction |
| →─ ─ ─← | Rail Tunnel |
| ─ ─ ─ ─ | Rail Ferry |
| ┼─┼─┼─┼ | Canal |
| ⊕ | International Airport |
| ✈ | Other Airport |

## LAKE FEATURES

| | |
|---|---|
| | Freshwater |
| | Saltwater |
| | Seasonal |
| | Salt Pan |

## LANDSCAPE FEATURES

| | |
|---|---|
| | Glacier, Ice Cap |
| | Marsh, Swamp |
| | Sand Desert, Dunes |

## OTHER FEATURES

| | |
|---|---|
| | River |
| | Seasonal River |
| ≍ | Pass, Gorge |
| | Dam, Barrage |
| | Waterfall, Rapid |
| →─ ─ ─← | Aqueduct |
| | Reef |
| ▲4231 | Summit, Peak |
| .217 | Spot Height, Depth |
| ⌣ | Well |
| △ | Oil Field |
| ▲ | Gas Field |
|  Gas/Oil | Oil/Natural Gas Pipeline |
|  Gemsbok Nat. Pk | National Park |
| ∴UR | Historic Site |

## LETTERING STYLES

| | |
|---|---|
| **CANADA** | Independent Nation |
| **FLORIDA** | State, Province or Autonomous Region |
| Gibraltar (U.K.) | Sovereignty of Dependent Territory |
| Lothian | Administrative Area |
| *LANGUEDOC* | Historic Region |
| *Loire* *Vosges* | Physical Feature or Physical Region |

## TOWNS AND CITIES

*Square symbols denote capital cities. Each settlement is given a symbol according to its relative importance, with type size to match.*

| | | | |
|---|---|---|---|
| ■ | ● | **New York** | Major City |
| ■ | ● | **Montréal** | City |
| □ | ○ | Ottawa | Small City |
| ▪ | ● | Québec | Large Town |
| □ | ○ | St John's | Town |
| □ | ○ | Yorkton | Small Town |
| □ | ○ | Jasper | Village |
| | | | Built-up-area |

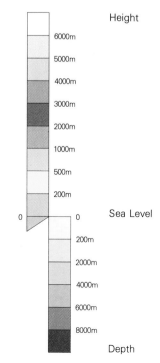

Height

6000m
5000m
4000m
3000m
2000m
1000m
500m
200m

0    0    Sea Level

200m
2000m
4000m
6000m
8000m

Depth

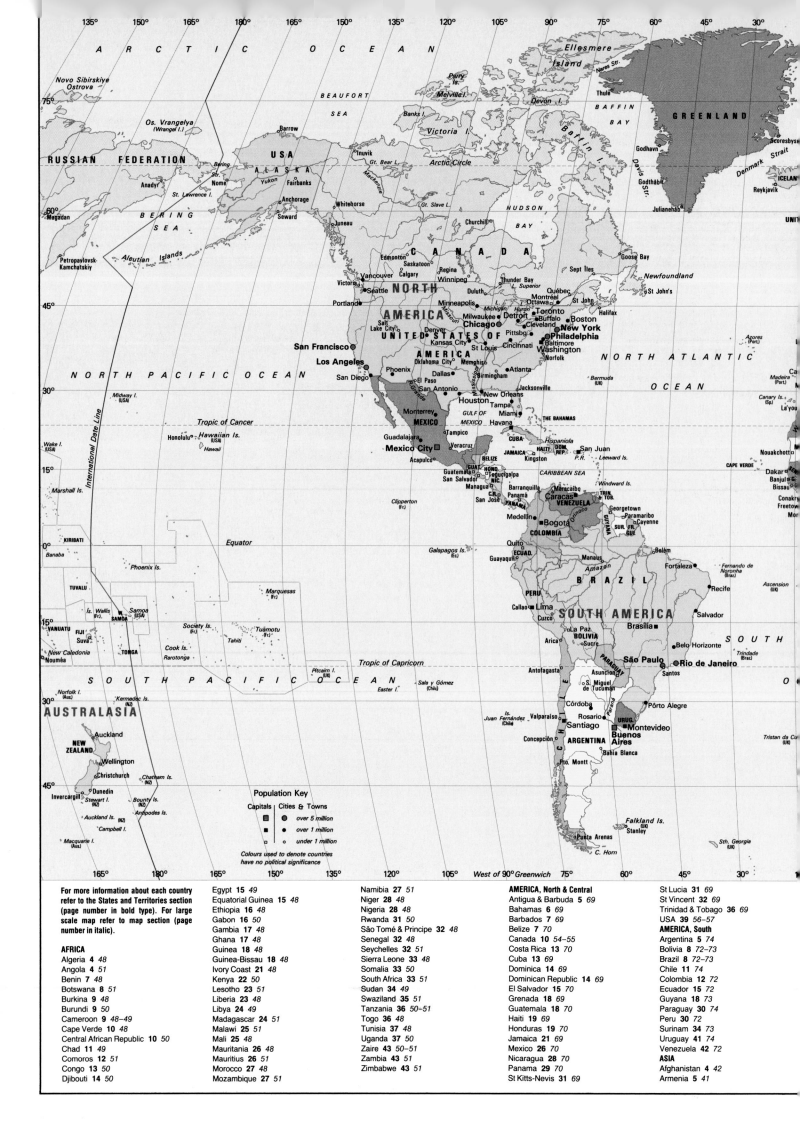

1:70 000 000
(45° N & S)

Meridian of 0° Greenwich    East of 90° Greenwich

Azerbaijan **6** *41*
Bahrain **6** *41*
Bangladesh **6** *43*
Bhutan **8** *43*
Brunei **8** *27*
Burma **9** *30*
Cambodia **9** *30*
China **11** *31*
Georgia **17** *21*
India **19** *42–44*
Indonesia **20** *27*
Iran **20** *41*
Iraq **20** *40–41*
Israel **20** *45*
Japan **21** *28–29*
Jordan **21** *40*
Kazakhstan **22** *24*
Kirgizia **22** *24*
North Korea **22** *28*
South Korea **22** *28*

Kuwait **23** *41*
Laos **23** *30*
Lebanon **23** *45*
Malaysia **25** *30*
Maldives **25** *44*
Mongolia **27** *26*
Nepal **27** *43*
Oman **29** *38*
Pakistan **29** *42*
Philippines **30** *27*
Qatar **30** *41*
Russian Federation **31** *24–25*
Saudi Arabia **32** *40–41*
Singapore **33** *30*
Sri Lanka **34** *44*
Syria **35** *40*
Taiwan **35** *31*
Tajikistan **36** *39*
Thailand **36** *30*
Turkey **37** *40*

Turkmenistan **37** *38*
UAE **38** *41*
Uzbekistan **41** *38*
Vietnam **42** *30*
Yemen **42** *38*
**AUSTRALASIA**
Australia **5** *32–34*
Fiji **16** *33*
Kiribati **22** *33*
Nauru **27** *33*
New Zealand **28** *35*
Papua New Guinea **29** *32*
Solomon Islands **33** *33*
Tonga **36** *33*
Tuvalu **37** *33*
Vanuatu **41** *33*
Western Samoa **42** *33*
**EUROPE**
Albania **4** *17*
Andorra **4** *15*

Austria **6** *18*
Belgium **7** *13*
Belorussia **7** *19*
Bulgaria **9** *17*
Croatia **13** *16*
Cyprus **14** *45*
Czechoslovakia **14** *18–19*
Denmark **14** *11*
Estonia **15** *20*
Finland **16** *12*
France **16** *14*
Germany **17** *18*
Greece **18** *17*
Hungary **19** *18–19*
Iceland **19** *5*
Ireland **20** *9*
Italy **21** *16*
Latvia **23** *19*
Liechtenstein **24** *16*
Lithuania **24** *19*

Luxembourg **24** *13*
Malta **25** *16*
Moldavia **26** *19*
Monaco **26** *14*
Netherlands **28** *13*
Norway **29** *12*
Poland **30** *18–19*
Portugal **30** *15*
Romania **31** *17*
Russian Federation **31** *20–21*
San Marino **32** *16*
Slovenia **33** *16*
Spain **34** *15*
Sweden **35** *12*
Switzerland **35** *16*
UK **38** *6–9*
Ukraine **37** *21*
Vatican City **42**
Yugoslavia **43** *16–17*

1:15M

OCEAN

Barents
Sea

White
Sea

H  30  J  40  K  50  L  70  60  M  70  ②  N  80  50

O.Kolguyev

Vorkuta

③

Ob'

Irtysh
Irtysh

Tavda

Murmansk

Apatity

Pechora

Ukhta

Omsk

Gällivare

Severodvinsk
Arkhangel'sk

Syktyvkar

Ishim

Ob'

Luleå
Oulu

Kotlas

Sev. Dvina

Kamskoye
Vdkhr.

Yekaterinburg

Umeå
Vaasa  Kuopio
Jyväskylä

Petrozavodsk  Lake
Onega

Kirov

Perm'

Magnitogorsk

Chelyabinsk

FINLAND

Pori  Tampere

Lake
Ladoga

Vologda

Kazan'

Ufa

Kama

50

Turku  Helsinki
Åland

Vyborg

Rybinskoye
Vdkhr.

Cherepovets

Kuybyshevskoye
Vdkhr.

St Petersburg
(Leningrad)

Yaroslavl'

Nizhniy
Novgorod

Volga

Tol'yatti
Samara

Gulf of Finland

Tallinn

ESTONIA

Pskov

Tver

Zagorsk

RUSSIAN  FEDERATION

Volga

Sea

Riga  LATVIA

Daugava

Moscow

Tula

Ural

KAZAKHSTAN

Daugavpils

Orsha

④

Aral Sea
(Aral'skoye More)

LITHUANIA

Nemunas

RUS. FED.
Kaliningrad  Kaunas

Vilnius

Minsk

Smolensk

Saratov

Vologradskoye
Vdkhr.

UZBEKISTAN

Grodno

BELORUSSIA

Voronezh

Warsaw
Warszawa

Brest

Kursk

Volgograd

Gur'yev

Łódź

Kiev

Dnepr

Khar'kov

Don

Volga

Astrakhan'

Cracow  L'vov

Kremenchugskoye
Vdkhr.

Tsimlyanskoye
Vdkhr.

KIA

UKRAINE

Dnepropetrovsk

Rog

Donetsk

Rostov

Shevchenko

CASPIAN

Zaporozh'ye
Mariupol'

MOLDAVIA  Kishinev
(Chişinău)

Kakhovskoye
Vdkhr.

Makhachkala

SEA

Budapest  Oradea

Odessa

Cluj  Tirgu Mureş

Kerch'

Krasnodar

Vladikavkaz

40

Szeged  Arad

TURKMENISTAN

ROMANIA

Galaţi

ARY

Timişoara

Sevastopol'

Belgrade
(Beograd)

Bucharest
Bucureşti

Constanţa

BLACK  SEA

GEORGIA  Tbilisi

Baku

SLAVIA

Niš  Pleven

Dunav  (Danube)

Varna

Batumi

AZERBAIJAN

ARMENIA  Yerevan

Sofiya

Burgas

Samsun

AZER.

Skopje

BULGARIA

Plovdiv  Edirne

Trabzon

Tabriz

ALBANIA

Tiranë

Istanbul
Üsküdar

Ankara

Erzurum

⑤

Tehrān

Thessaloniki

Bursa

IRAN

GREECE  Lárisa

Eskişehir

TURKEY

Firat

Mosul

Pátrai

Izmir

Denzil

Antalya

Adana

Halab

Esfahan

Athens
(Athína)  Cyclades

Kalámai

Khaniá  Crete

Dodecanese

SYRIA

Himş

Baghdād

Tigris

IRAQ

CYPRUS

Nicosia

LEBANON  Beirut
J  Damascus

Euphrates

K  Basra
Abadan

The
Gulf

20  30  40  50

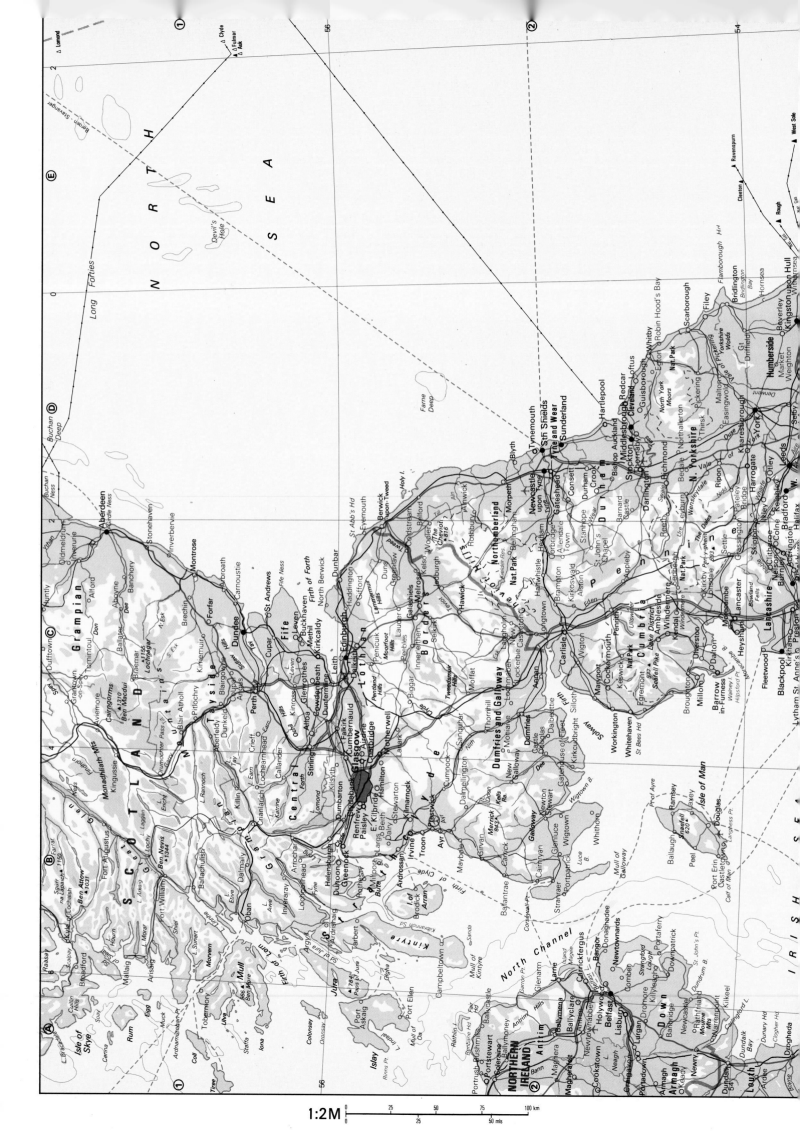

1:2M

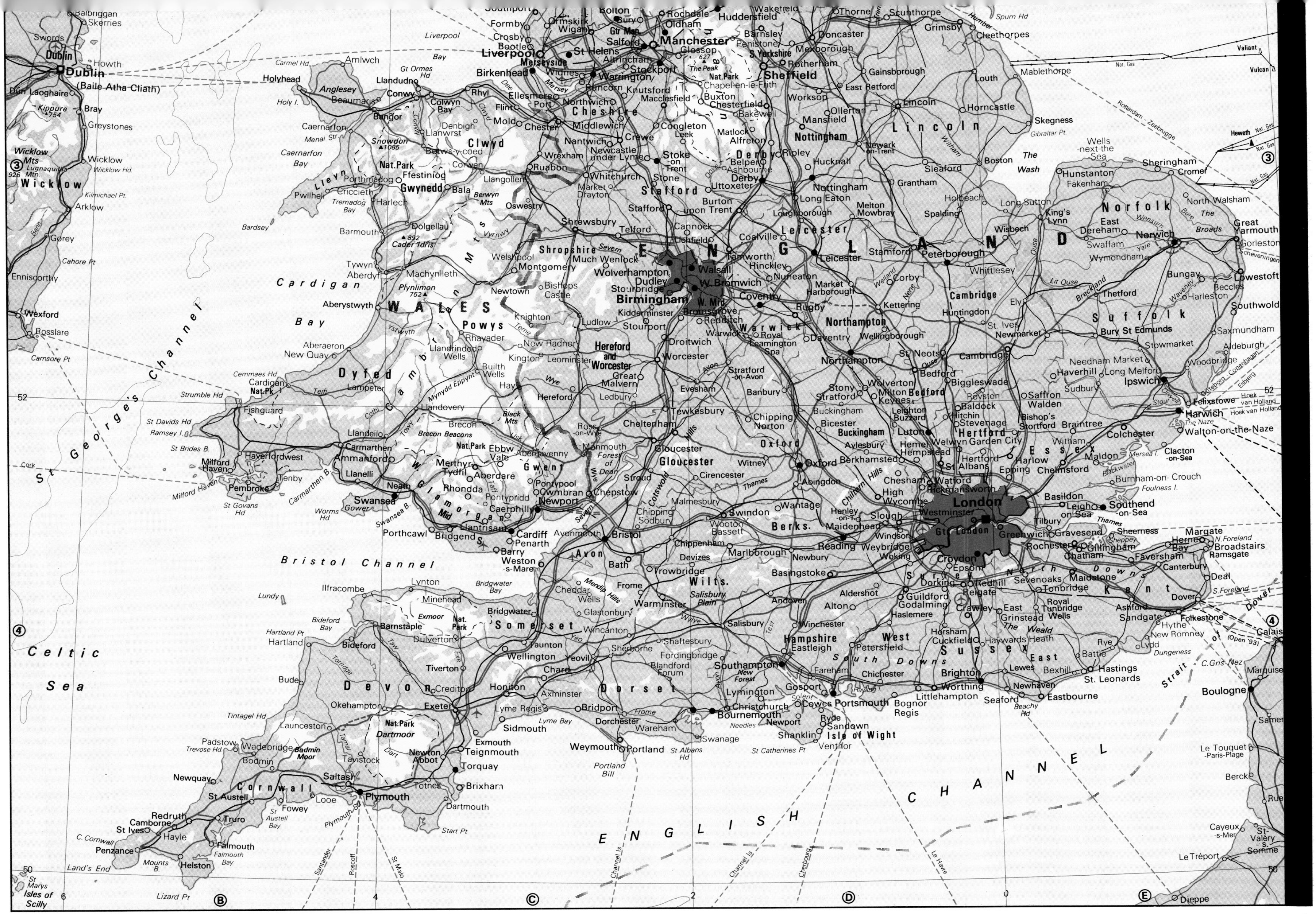
ENGLAND
WALES
ENGLISH CHANNEL
Bristol Channel
St George's Channel
Celtic Sea
Cardigan Bay
Liverpool Bay
The Wash
Strait of Dover
London
Gtr London
Westminster
Birmingham
Manchester
Liverpool
Sheffield
Dublin
(Baile Atha Cliath)
Bristol
Cardiff
Swansea
Newport
Plymouth
Exeter
Southampton
Portsmouth
Bournemouth
Brighton
Dover
Norwich
Ipswich
Cambridge
Oxford
Nottingham
Leicester
Coventry
Stoke -on Trent
Derby
Lincoln
Peterborough
Northampton
Gloucester
Worcester
Hereford
Shrewsbury
Chester
Reading
Swindon
Salisbury
Bath
Taunton
Torquay
Truro
Penzance
Land's End
Lizard Pt
Isles of Scilly
Boulogne
Calais
Dieppe
Le Tréport
Le Touquet -Paris-Plage
Norfolk
Suffolk
Essex
Kent
Sussex
Surrey
Hampshire
Dorset
Devon
Cornwall
Somerset
Wilts.
Berks.
Oxford
Gloucester
Hereford and Worcester
Warwick
Northampton
Leicester
Lincoln
Nottingham
Cheshire
Stafford
Shropshire
Clwyd
Gwynedd
Powys
Dyfed
Gwent
Mid Glamorgan
W. Glamorgan
Avon
Wicklow
Isle of Wight
Anglesey
Lleyn
Snowdon ▲1085
Cader Idris ▲892
Plynlimon 752
Cambrian Mts
Brecon Beacons
Black Mts
Exmoor
Dartmoor
Bodmin Moor
Mendip Hills
Cotswold Hills
Chiltern Hills
North Downs
South Downs
The Weald
Salisbury Plain
New Forest
The Broads
The Peak
Nat. Park
Thames
Severn
Wye
Ouse
Trent
Rotterdam - Zeebrugge
Hoek van Holland
Esbjerg
Göteborg Copenhagen
Cherbourg
Le Havre
St Malo
Roscoff
Santander
Channel Is
(Open '93)
50
52
0
2
4
6
B
C
D
E
3
4

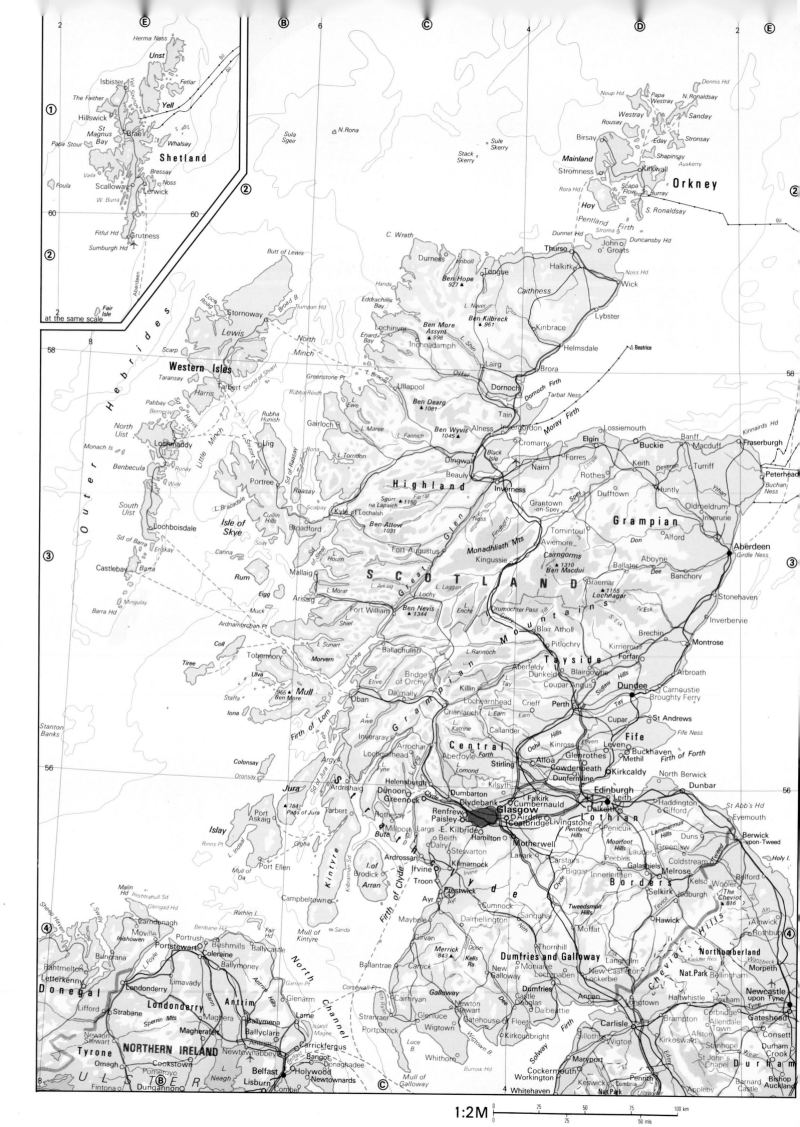

1:2M

25    50    75    100 km

25    50 mls

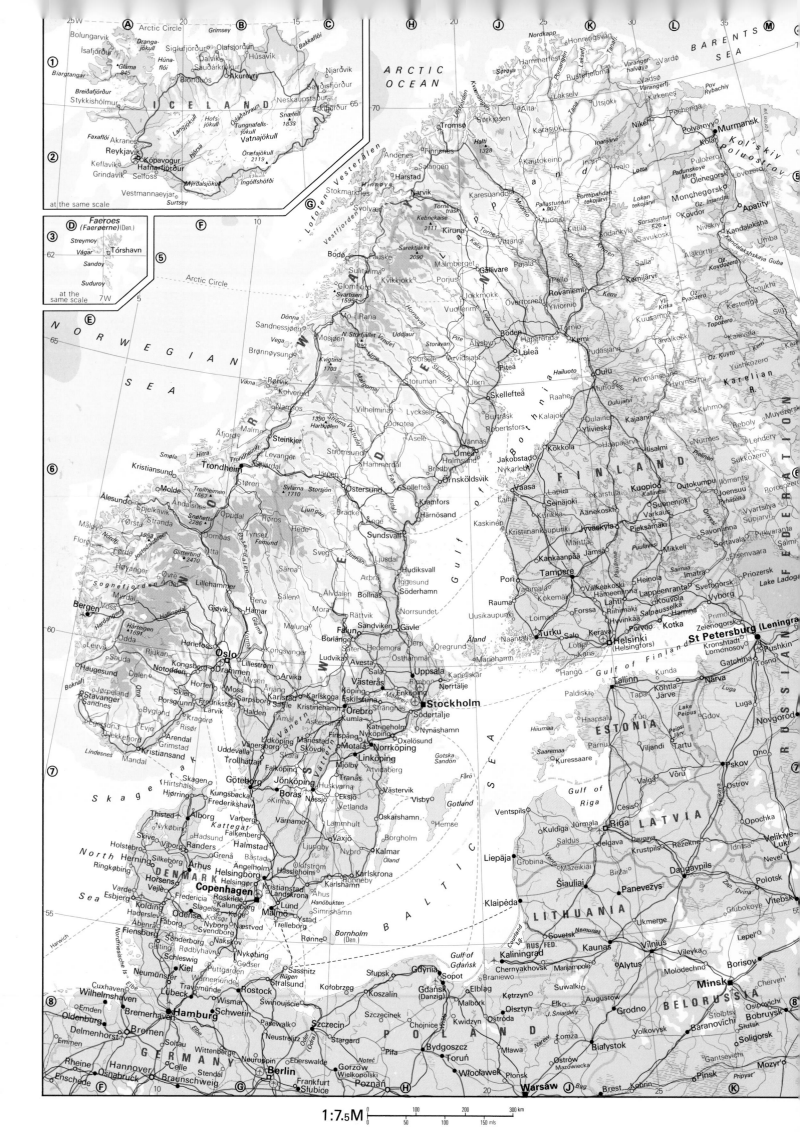

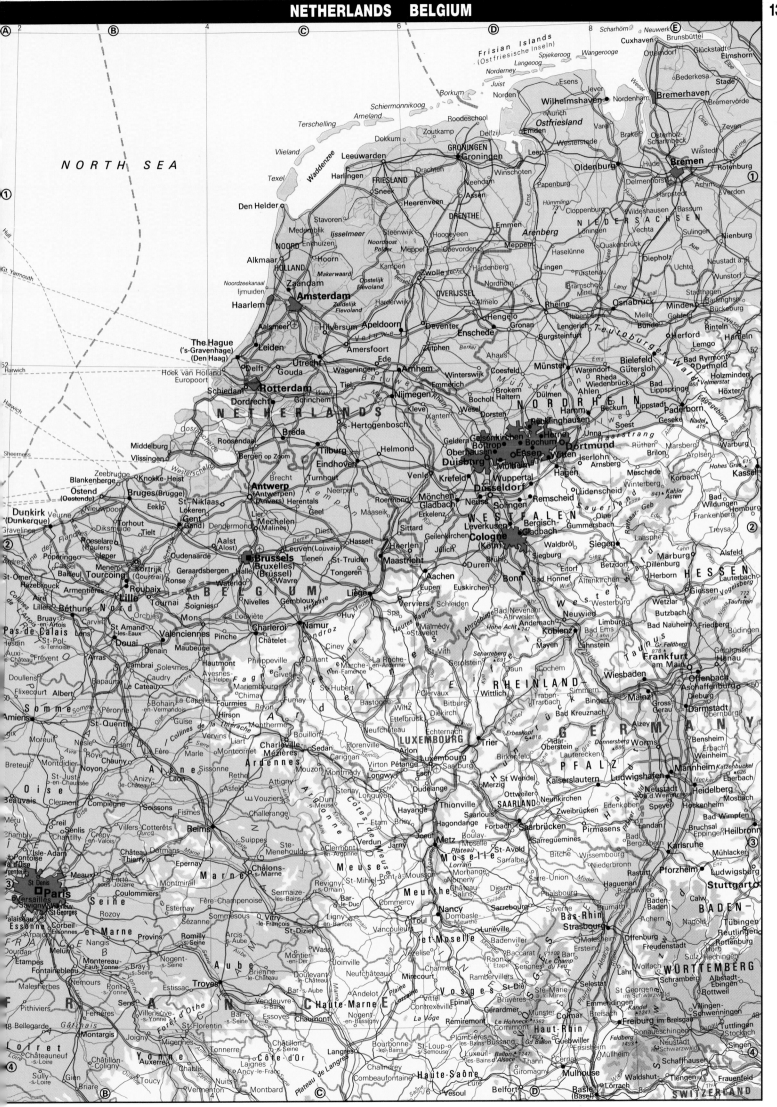

1:2.5M

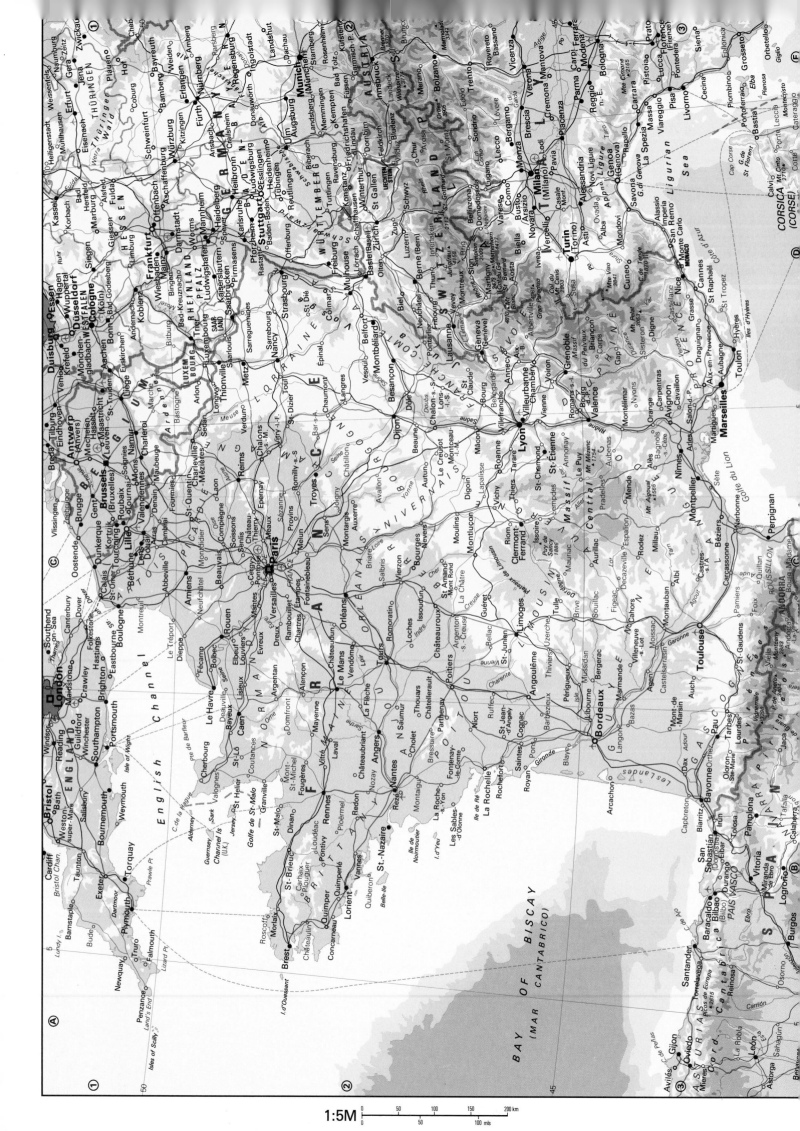

1:5M

0    50    100    150    200 km
0        50        100 mls

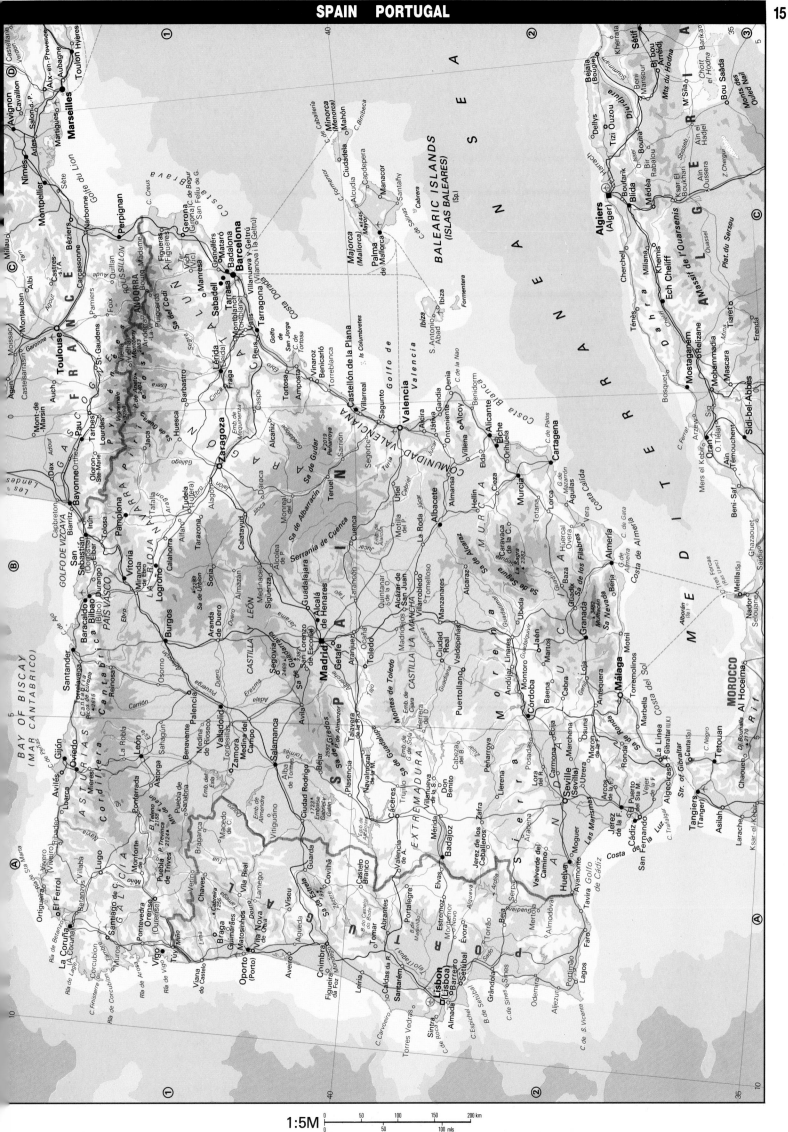

1:5M

0  50  100  150  200 km

0  50  100 mls

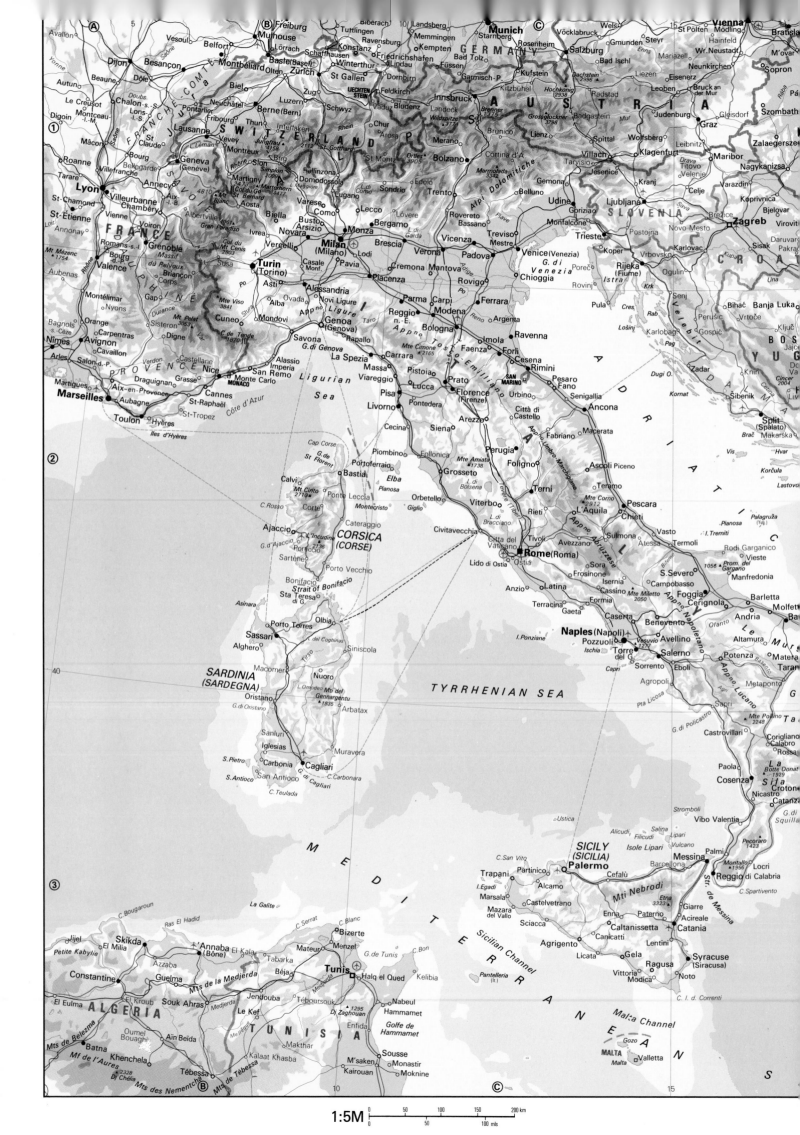

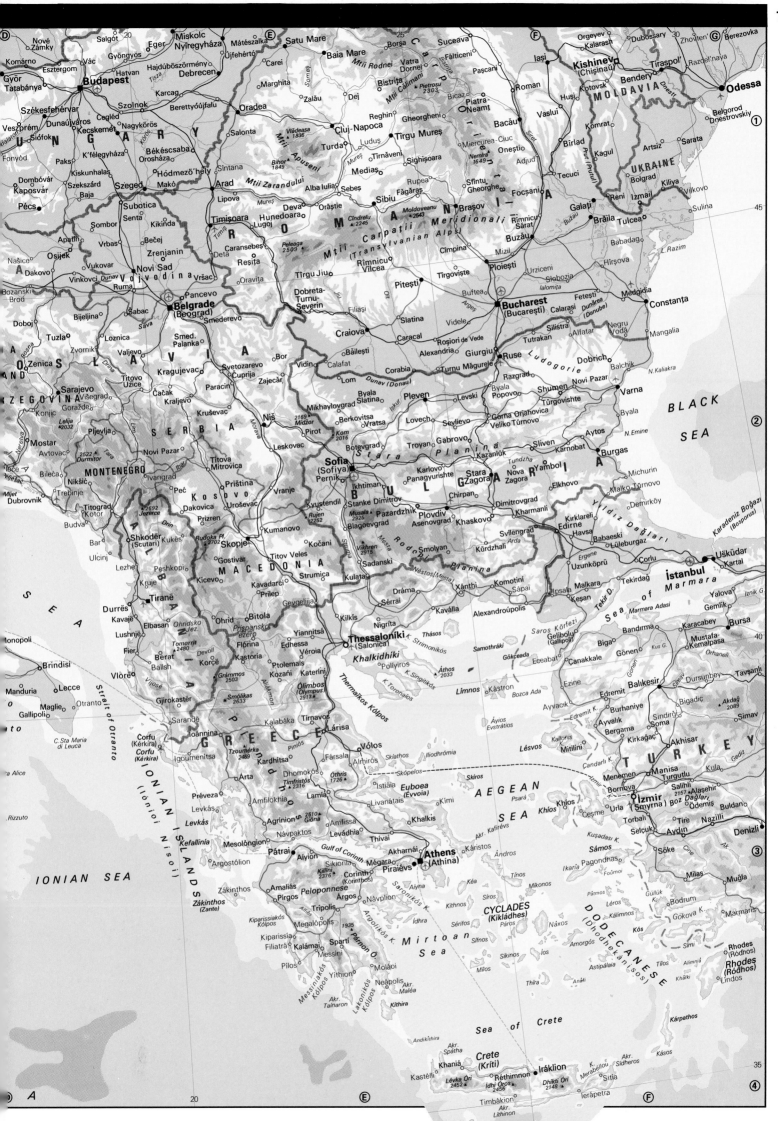

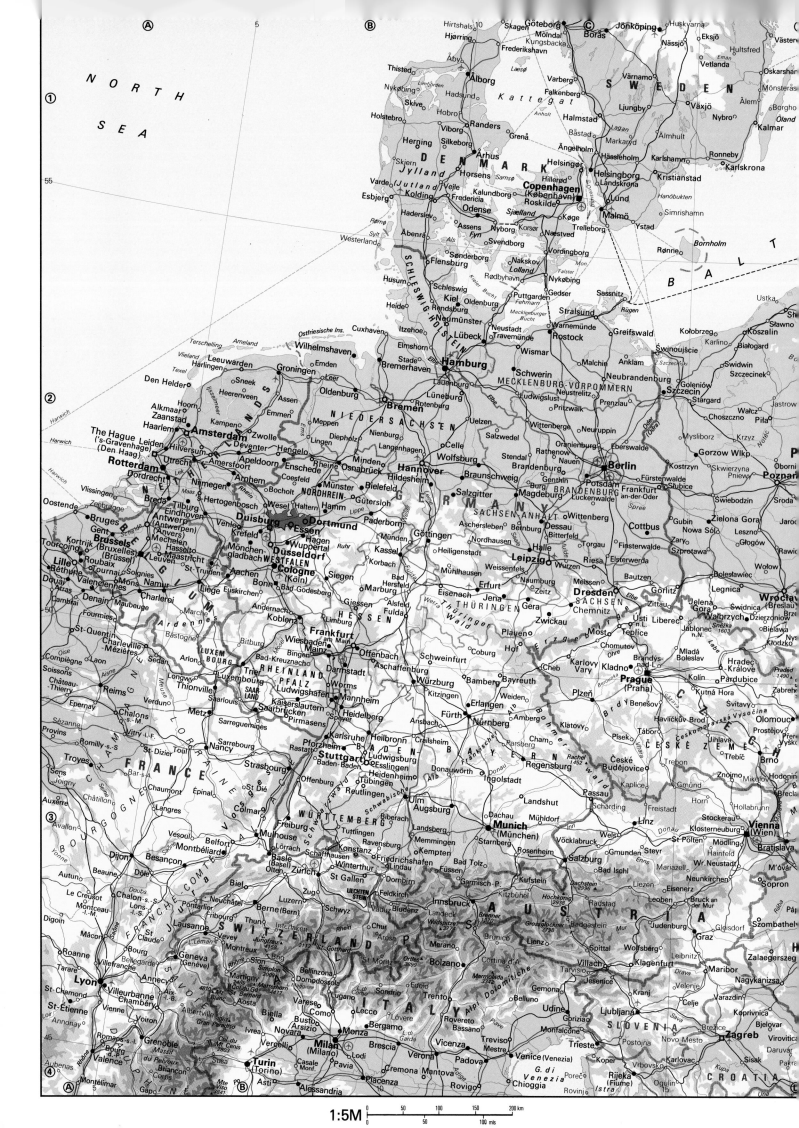

1:5M

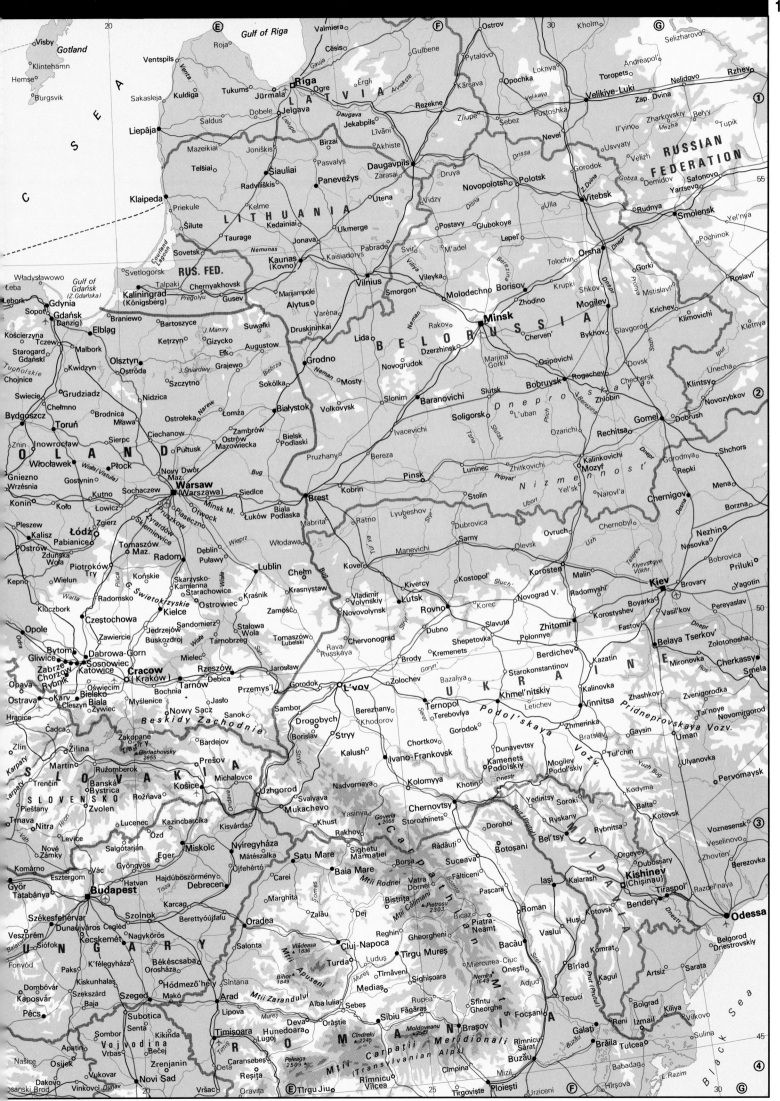

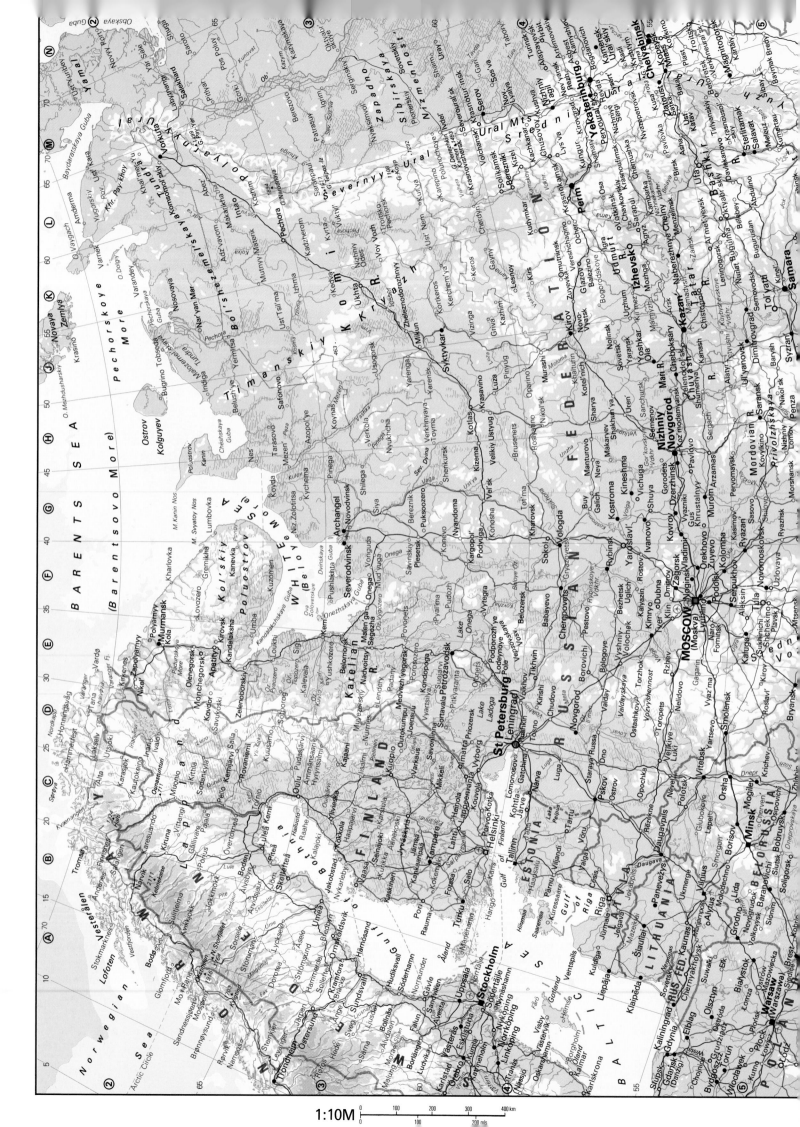

1:10M

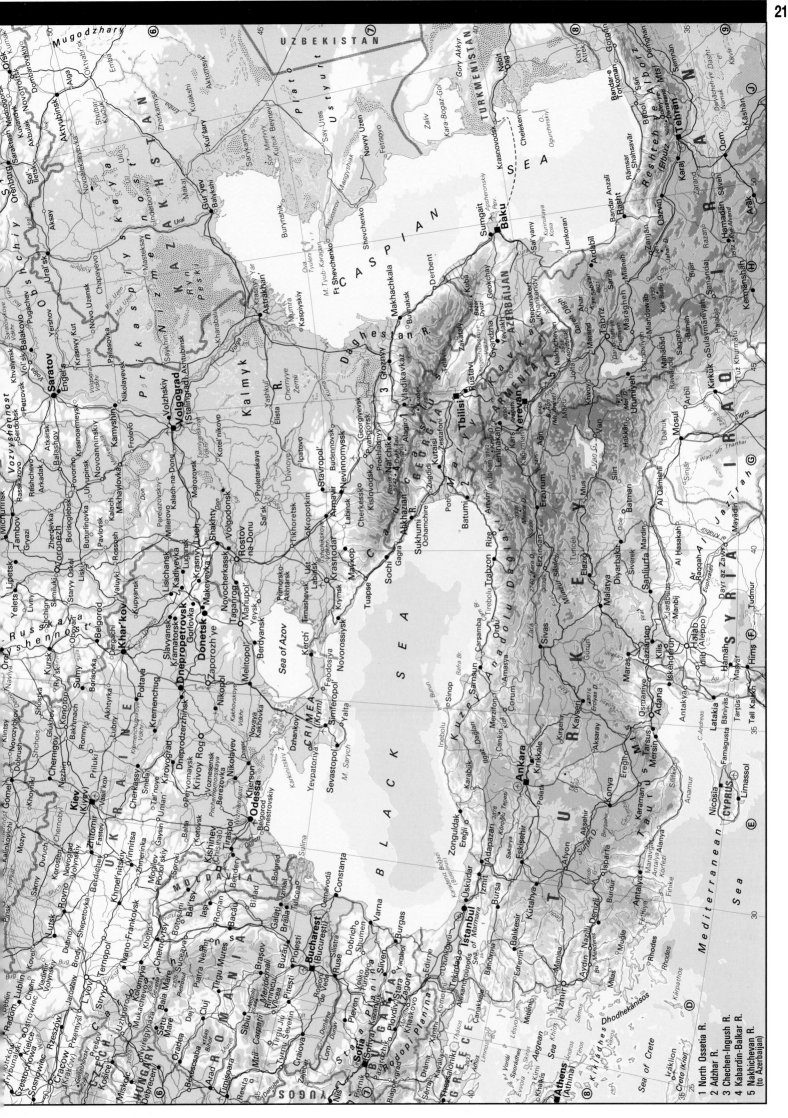

1 North Ossetia R.
2 Adzhar R.
3 Chechen-Ingush R.
4 Kabardin-Balkar R.
5 Nakhichevan (to Azerbaijan)

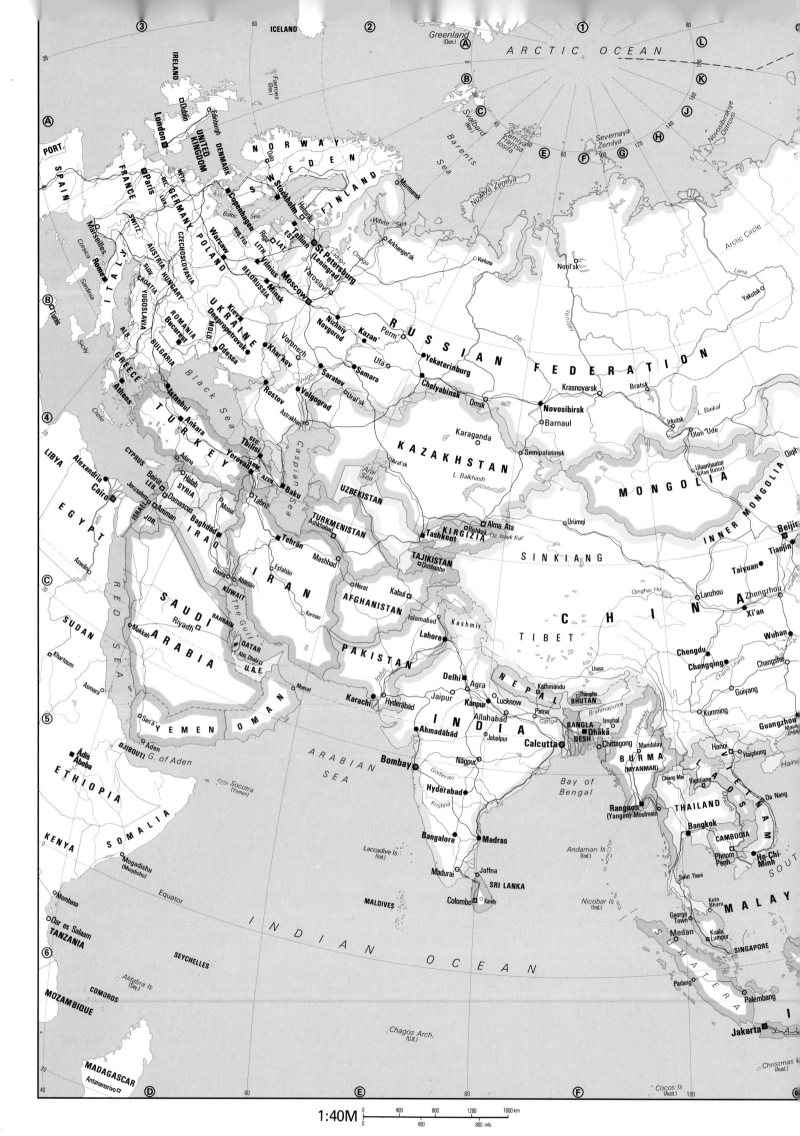

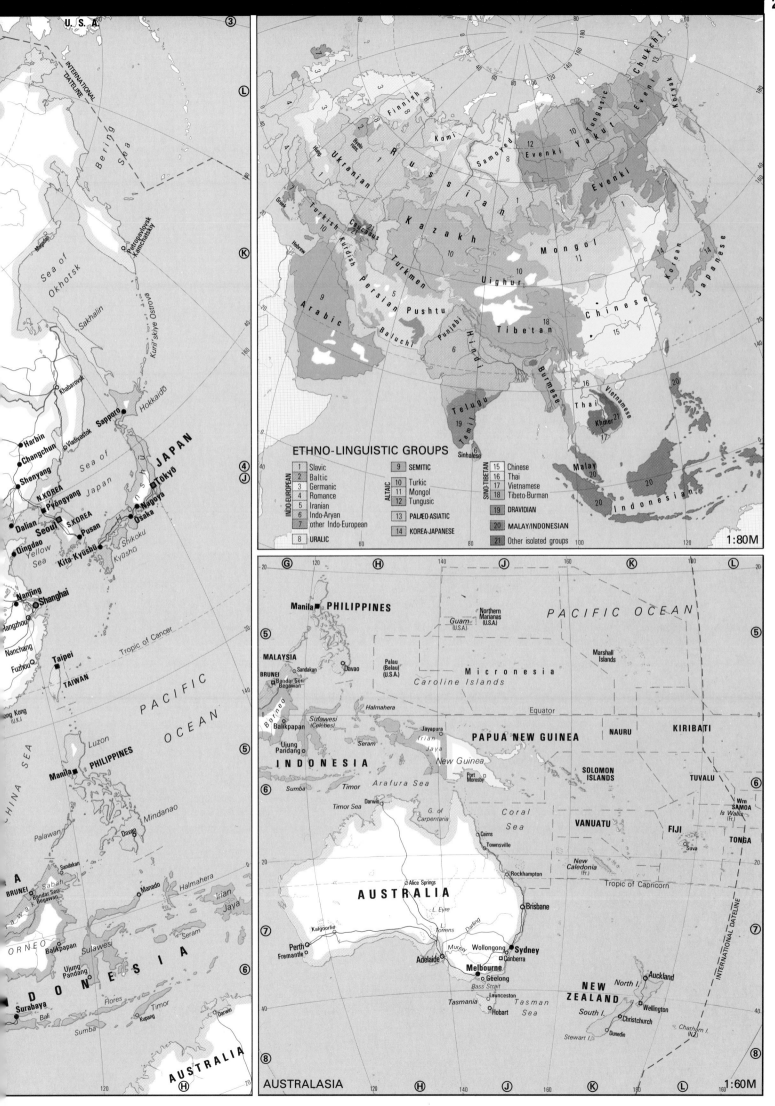

U.S.A.

INTERNATIONAL DATELINE

Bering Sea

Sea of Okhotsk

Magadan

Petropavlovsk-Kamchatskiy

Sakhalin

Kuril'skiye Ostrová

Khabarovsk

Harbin

Changchun

Shenyang

Vladivostok

Hokkaidō

Sapporo

**JAPAN**

N.KOREA

P'yŏngyang

Dalian

Seoul

S.KOREA

Pusan

Sea of Japan

Tokyo

Nagoya

Osaka

Shikoku

Kyūshū

Kita-Kyūshū

Qingdao

Yellow Sea

Nanjing

Shanghai

Yangzhou

Nanchang

Fuzhou

Taipei

**TAIWAN**

Tropic of Cancer

Hong Kong (U.K.)

CHINA SEA

Luzon

**PACIFIC OCEAN**

Manila

**PHILIPPINES**

Mindanao

Palawan

Davao

Sandakan

Saba

BRUNEI

Bandar Seri Begawan

Manado

Halmahera

Irian Jaya

ORNEO

Balikpapan

Sulawesi

Ujung Pandang

Seram

NDONESIA

Surabaya

Flores

Timor

Bali

Sumba

Kupang

Darwin

**AUSTRALIA**

## ETHNO-LINGUISTIC GROUPS

Finnish

Komi

Samoyed

Evenki

Yakut

Tungusic

Chukchi

Koryak

Evenki

Ukranian

R u s s i a n

Greek

Turkish

Caucasus

Turkmen

Kurdish

Persian

Pushtu

Baluchi

Arabic

Hebrew

Kazakh

Mongol

Uighur

Tibetan

Chinese

Korean

Japanese

Punjabi

Hindi

Telugu

Tamil

Sinhalese

Burmese

Thai

Vietnamese

Khmer

Malay

I n d o n e s i a n

| | | | | | | |
|---|---|---|---|---|---|---|
| INDO-EUROPEAN | 1 | Slavic | | 9 | SEMITIC | |
| | 2 | Baltic | ALTAIC | 10 | Turkic | |
| | 3 | Germanic | | 11 | Mongol | |
| | 4 | Romance | | 12 | Tungusic | |
| | 5 | Iranian | | 13 | PALÆO-ASIATIC | |
| | 6 | Indo-Aryan | | 14 | KOREA-JAPANESE | |
| | 7 | other Indo-European | | | | |
| | 8 | URALIC | | | | |

| SINO-TIBETAN | 15 | Chinese |
|---|---|---|
| | 16 | Thai |
| | 17 | Vietnamese |
| | 18 | Tibeto-Burman |
| | 19 | DRAVIDIAN |
| | 20 | MALAY/INDONESIAN |
| | 21 | Other isolated groups |

1:80M

**PACIFIC OCEAN**

Manila ■ **PHILIPPINES**

Guam (U.S.A.)

Northern Marianas (U.S.A.)

Marshall Islands

**MALAYSIA**

Davao

Palau (Belau) (U.S.A.)

M i c r o n e s i a

BRUNEI

Sandakan

Bandar Seri Begawan

Borneo

Halmahera

Caroline Islands

Balikpapan

Sulawesi (Celebes)

Equator

Ujung Pandang

Seram

Irian Jaya

Jayapura

**PAPUA NEW GUINEA**

New Guinea

**NAURU**

**KIRIBATI**

**SOLOMON ISLANDS**

**TUVALU**

**INDONESIA**

Sumba

Timor

Arafura Sea

Port Moresby

Wrn SAMOA Is Wallis (Fr.)

Timor Sea

Darwin

G. of Carpentaria

Coral Sea

**VANUATU**

**FIJI**

Suva

**TONGA**

Cairns

Townsville

New Caledonia (Fr.)

Tropic of Capricorn

Alice Springs

Rockhampton

**AUSTRALIA**

Brisbane

L. Eyre

Kalgoorlie

L. Torrens

Murray

Darling

Perth

Fremantle

Wollongong

**Sydney**

Adelaide

Canberra

**Melbourne**

Geelong

Bass Strait

Launceston

Tasmania

Hobart

Tasman Sea

North I.

**NEW ZEALAND**

South I.

Auckland

Wellington

Christchurch

Dunedin

Stewart I.

Chatham I. (N.Z.)

INTERNATIONAL DATELINE

AUSTRALASIA

1:60M

OCEAN
SEVERNAYA ZEMLYA
(NORTH LAND)
Ostrov Komsomolets
Ostrov Bol'shevik
Ostrov Oktyabrskoy Revolyutsii
Mys Chelyushin
Proliv Vilkitskogo
NOVOSIBIRSKYE OSTROVA
(NEW SIBERIAN ISLANDS)
Ostrov Kotel'nyy
Ostrov Faddeyevskiy
O.Novaya Sibir
LAPTEV SEA
EAST SIBERIAN SEA
CHUKCHI SEA
Wrangel I.
Proliv Longa
Bering Str.
BERING SEA
Chukotskiy Poluostrov
Chukotskiy Khrebet
Anadyrskiy Zaliv
Anadyrskoye Ploskogor'ye
Kolymskoye Nagor'ye
Koryakskoye Nagor'ye
Anadyr'
Bilibino
Pevek
Cherskiy
Markovo
Gory Byrranga
Poluostrov Taymyr
Nordvik
Khatanga
Tiksi
Yanskiy Zaliv
Polyarnyy
Chokurdakh
Deputatskiy
Khrebet Cherskogo
Verkhoyanskiy Khrebet
Khrebet Orulgan
YAKUT R.
Yakutsk
Vilyuysk
Mirnyy
Olekminsk
Aldan
Aldanskoye Nagor'ye
Dzhugdzhur
Stanovoy Khrebet
Magadan
Okhotsk
Ayan
Zaliv Shelikhova
KAMCHATKA
Sredinnyy Khrebet
Petropavlovsk-Kamchatskiy
Ust'Kamchatsk
Komandorskiye Ostrova
SEA OF OKHOTSK
SAKHALIN
Yuzhno-Sakhalinsk
Kuril Islands
(Kuril'skiye Ostrova)
Tatarskiy Proliv
Nikolayevsk-na-Amure
Komsomol'sk-na-Amure
Sikhote Alin'
Khabarovsk
Birobidzhan
Blagoveshchensk
Vladivostok
Nakhodka
Ussuriysk
HOKKAIDO
Sapporo
Hakodate
Wakkanai
Asahikawa
SEA OF JAPAN
JAPAN
HONSHU
Aomori
Morioka
Sendai
Akita
Niigata
Tokyo
Yokohama
Nagoya
Kyoto
Osaka
Kobe
Hiroshima
SHIKOKU
KYUSHU
Fukuoka
Kita-Kyushu
Nagasaki
Kagoshima
NORTH KOREA
SOUTH KOREA
P'yongyang
Seoul
Pusan
Taegu
Ch'ongjin
Hamhung
Wonsan
Korea Bay
YELLOW SEA
Bo Hai
MANCHURIA
Harbin
Changchun
Shenyang
Jilin
Qiqihar
Dalian
Beijing
(Peking)
Tianjin
(Tientsin)
Jinan
Qingdao
Taiyuan
Shijiazhuang
Baotou
Hohhot
Datong
Zhangjiakou
INNER MONGOLIA
GOBI
MONGOLIA
Ulaanbaatar
Erdenet
Darhan
Choybalsan
Hailar
Manzhouli
Da Hinggan Ling
Xiao Hinggan Ling
Yablonovyy Khrebet
Chita
Ulan Ude
Irkutsk
Ozero Baykal
Angarsk
Bratsk
Krasnoyarsk
Kansk
Achinsk
Abakan
Kyzyl
Tuva
Sayan
Altai
Gory Putorana
Noril'sk
Sredne Sibirskoye Ploskogor'ye
SIBERIA
FEDERATION
Tunguska
Lena
Yenisey
Vanavara
Kirensk
Lensk
Bodaybo
Tynda
Skovorodino
Zeya
Ordos
Yinchuan
Lanzhou
Hami
Yumen
Qilian Shan
Altun Shan
GREAT WALL
Lianyungang
Xuzhou

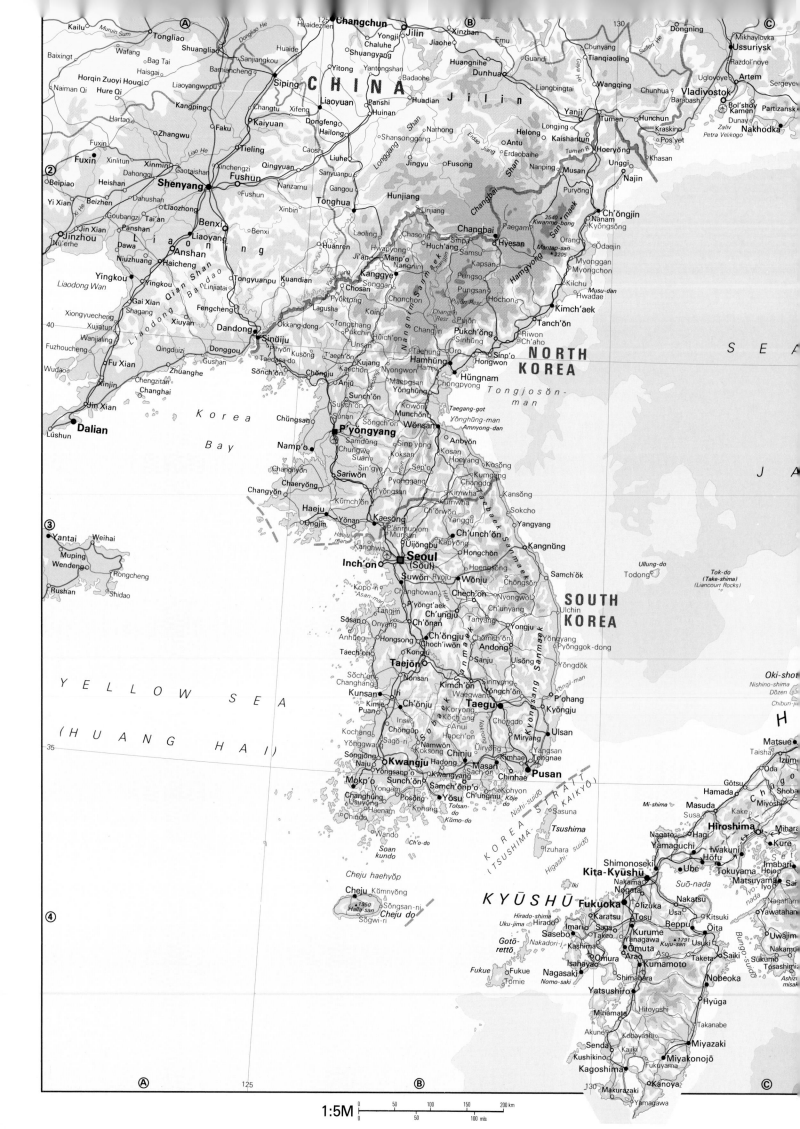

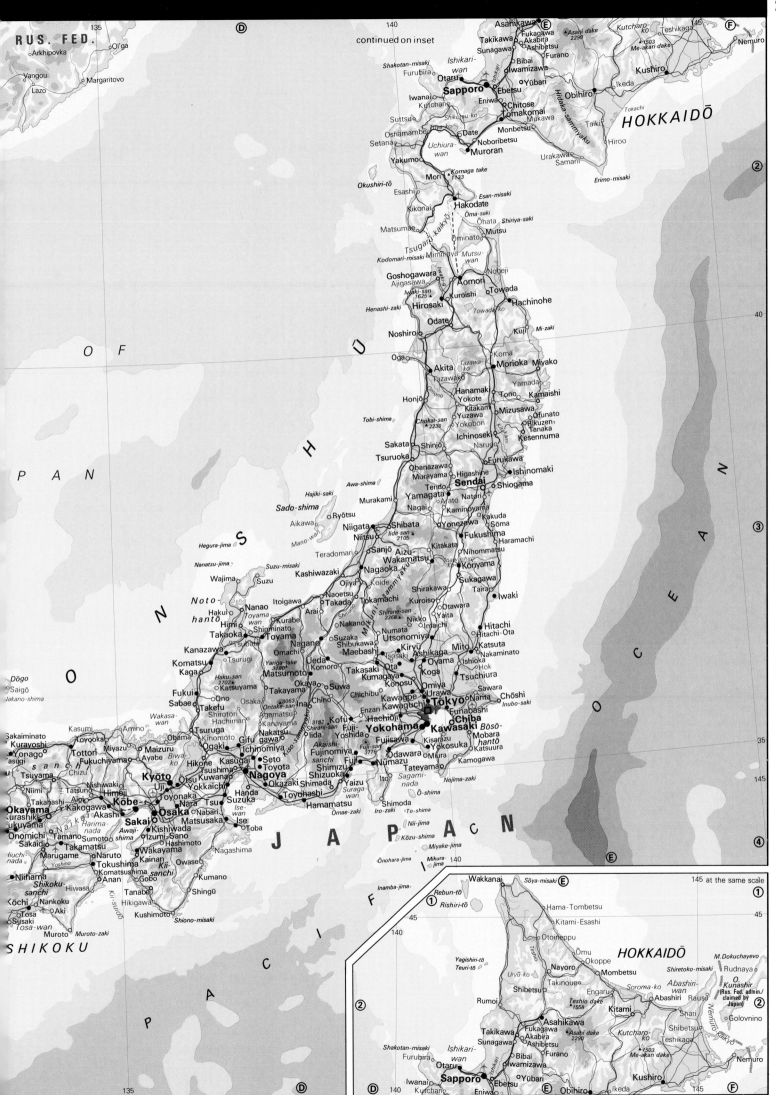

RUS. FED.

Arkhipovka
Vangou
Lazo
Margaritovo
Ol'ga

**HOKKAIDŌ**

Nemuro
Kutcharo-ko
Teshikaga
Me-akan dake
Asahi dake
2290
Asahikawa
Takikawa
Sunagawa
Fukagawa
Akabira
Ashibetsu
Furano
Bibai
Iwamizawa
Yūbari
Obihiro
Ikeda
Kushiro
Hiroo
Samani
Erimo-misaki
Urakawa
Hidaka sammyaku
Taiki
Mukawa
Tokachi
Otaru
**Sapporo**
Ebetsu
Eniwa
Chitose
Tomakomai
Noboribetsu
Muroran
Date
Monbetsu
Oshamambe
Setana
Yakumo
Mori
Komaga take 1133
Okushiri-tō
Esashi
Esan-misaki
Hakodate
Kikonai
Ōma-saki
Ōhata
Shiriya-saki
Matsumae
Mutsu
Tsugaru-kaikyō
Kodomari-misaki
Ominato
Minmaya
Mutsu-wan
Noheji
Goshogawara
Ajigasawa
Aomori
Towada
Hachinohe
Henashi-zaki
Iwaki-san 1625
Kuroishi
Hirosaki
Towada-ko
Kuji
Mi-zaki
Noshiro
Odate
Oga
Koma
Morioka
Miyako
Akita
Tazawa-ko
Hanamaki
Yamada
Honjō
Yokote
Tono
Kamaishi
Chokai-san 2230
Kitakami
Yuzawa
Mizusawa
Ōfunato
Tobi-shima
Yokobori
Tanaka
Rikuzen-
Sakata
Shinjō
Ichinoseki
Narudo
Kesennuma
Tsuruoka
Obanazawa
Furukawa
Murayama
Higashine
Ishinomaki
Awa-shima
Tendo
**Sendai**
Shiogama
Murakami
Yamagata
Arato
Natori
Nagai
Kaminoyama
Kakuda
Sōma
Sado-shima
Aikawa
Ryōtsu
Yonezawa
Haramachi
Mano-wan
Niigata
Shibata
Fukushima
Niitsu
Iide san 2105
Kitakata
Nihommatsu
Sanjō
Aizu Wakamatsu
Kōriyama
Hegura-jima
Teradomari
Nagaoka
Ojiya
Koide
Sukagawa
Shirakawa
Nanatsu-jima
Kashiwazaki
Tokamachi
Kuroiso
Tairo
Iwaki
Wajima
Naoetsu
Takada
Nakano
Numata
Nikko
Yaita
Suzu
Itoigawa
Arai
Suzuka
Shibukawa
Imaichi
Hitachi
Suzu-misaki
Nanao
Kurabe
Nagano
Maebashi
Kiryū
Utsonomiya
Hitachi-Ota
Noto-hantō
Himi
Toyama
Omachi
Ueda
Komoro
Ashikaga
Oyama
Mito
Katsuta
Hakui
Takaoka
Toyama-wan
Shinminato
Yariga-take 3180
Matsumoto
Takasaki
Ota
Koga
Nakaminato
Kanazawa
Tsubata
Kaga
Tsurugi
Suzaka
Okaya
Suwa
Konosu
Ishioka
Komatsu
Haku-san 2702
Katsuyama
Takayama
Chino
Chichibu
Kawagoe
Omiya
Tsuchiura
Fukui
Ono
Shirotori
Hachiman
Ontake-san 3063
Ina
Kanayama
Kawaguchi
Urawa
Sawara
Sabae
Takefu
Agematsu
Shirane-san 2368
Enzan
Hachiōji
**Tōkyō**
Narita
Chōshi
Tsuruga
Kinomoto
Gifu
Nakatsu-gawa
Iida
Kōfu
Kawasaki
Funabashi
Inubo-saki
Obama
Ichinomiya
Fuji-Yoshida
**Chiba**
Wakasa-wan
Ogaki
Kasugai
Koso sammyaku
**Yokohama**
Bōsō-hantō
Kasumi
Toyooka
Maizuru
Ayabe
Hikone
Seto
Toyota
Akaishi-sanchi
Fujinomiya
Fuji
Fujisawa
Kisarazu
Mobara
Kurayoshi
Miyazu
Fukuchiyama
Ōtsu Kuwana
Okazaki
Shimada
Fuji-san 3776
Numazu
Yokosuka
Katsuura
Yonago
Tottori
Chizu
Biwa-ko
Yokkaichi
Shimizu
Odawara
Miura
Tsuyama
Nishiwaki
Nara
Suzuka
Shizuoka
Ito
Kamogawa
Niimi
Takahashi
Aigi
Himeji
Toyonaka
Nabari
Matsusaka
Toyohashi
Yaizu
Sagami-nada
Tateyama
Nojima-zaki
Takasago
Akashi
Osaka
Kishiwada
Ise
Hamamatsu
Ōmae-zaki
Okayama
Kakogawa
**Kōbe**
**Sakai**
Ise-wan
Shimoda
Kurashiki
Nishiwaki
Izumi-Sano
Toba
Shimizu
Iro-zaki
To-shima
Onomichi
Tamano
Sumoto
Hashimoto
Ō-shima
Sakaidō
Harima-nada
Awaji-shima
Wakayama
Kainan
Marugame
Naruto
Tokushima
Kii-sanchi
Niihama
Komatsushima
Gobo
Tanabe
Yoshino
Anan
Kumano
Ōnohara-jima
Mikura-jima
Kōchi
Aki
Hiwasa
Shingū
Kushimoto
Shiono-misaki
Shikoku-sanchi
Tosa-wan
Tosa
Susaki
Muroto
Muroto-zaki

**SHIKOKU**

Dōgo
Saigō
Jakano-shima

Nii-jima
Kōzu-shima
Miyake-jima
Inamba-jima

**JAPAN**

**PACIFIC OCEAN**

O F   J A P A N

S E A   O F   J A P A N

continued on inset

Shakotan-misaki
Furubira
Ishikari-wan

Nii-jima
Kōzu-shima

at the same scale

Wakkanai
Sōya-misaki
Rebun-tō
Rishiri-tō
Hama-Tombetsu
Kitami-Esashi
**HOKKAIDŌ**
Ōmu
Okoppe
Mombetsu
Yagishiri-tō
Teuri-tō
Nayoro
Shiretoko-misaki
M. Dokuchayevo
Rudnaya
Uryū-ko
Takinoue
Soroma-ko
Abashiri-wan
Abashiri
O. Kunashir (Rus. Fed. admin./claimed by Japan)
Rumoi
Teshio dake 1558
Engaru
Kitami
Rausu
Shari
Shibetsu
Golovnino
Nemuro-kaikyō
Takikawa
Asahikawa
Sunagawa
Fukagawa
Akabira
Ashibetsu
Asahi dake 2290
Furano
Kutcharo-ko
Teshikaga
Bibai
Iwamizawa
Me-akan dake 1503
Otaru
Yūbari
Shibetsu
Iwanai
**Sapporo**
Ebetsu
Eniwa
Obihiro
Ikeda
Kushiro
Nemuro
Kutchan

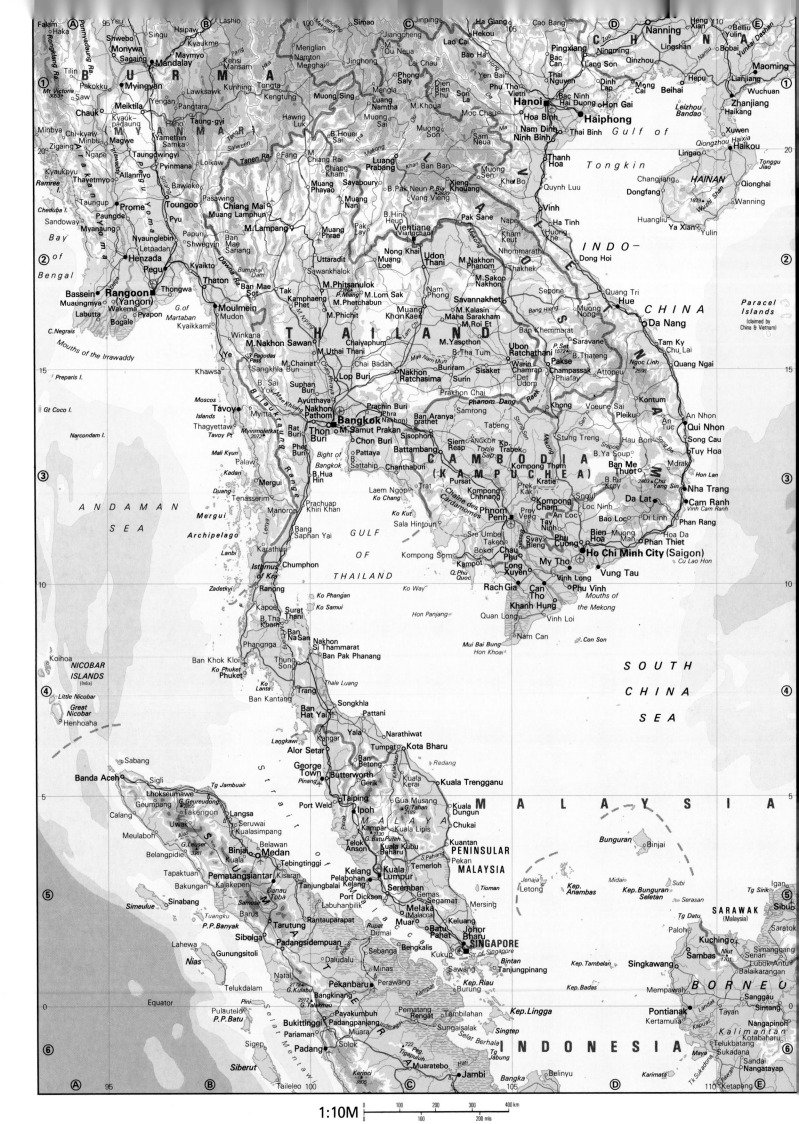

1:10M

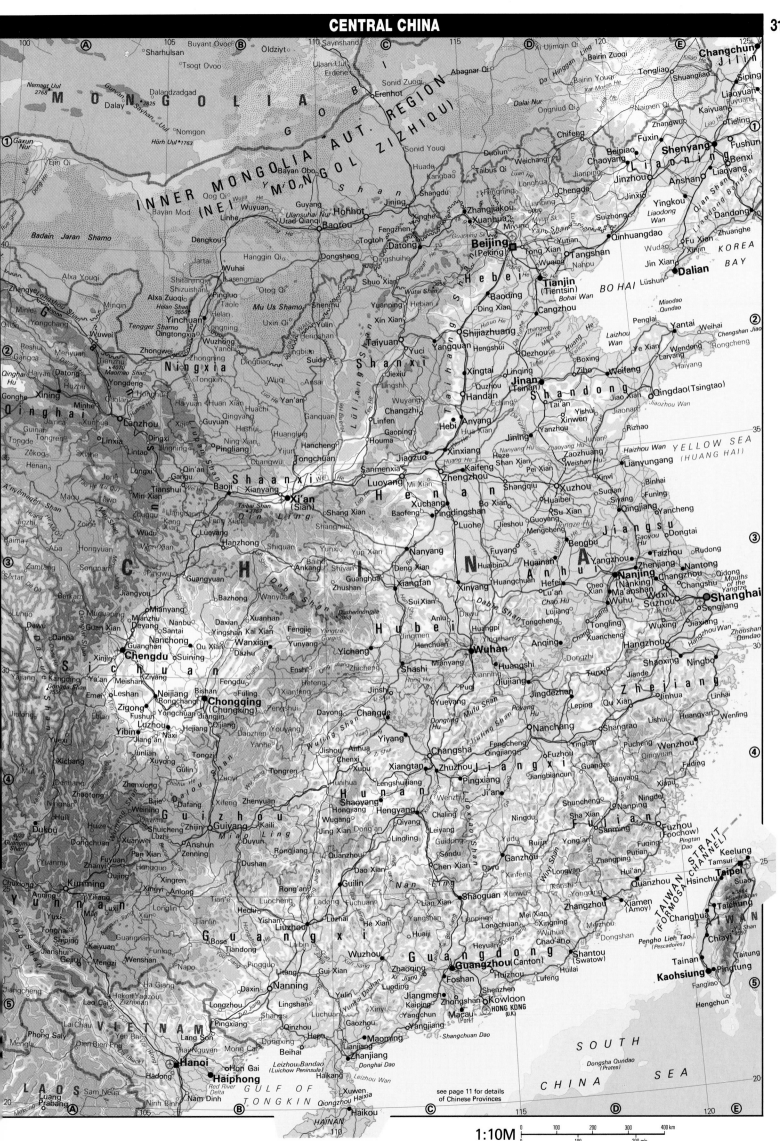

1:10M

see page 11 for details of Chinese Provinces

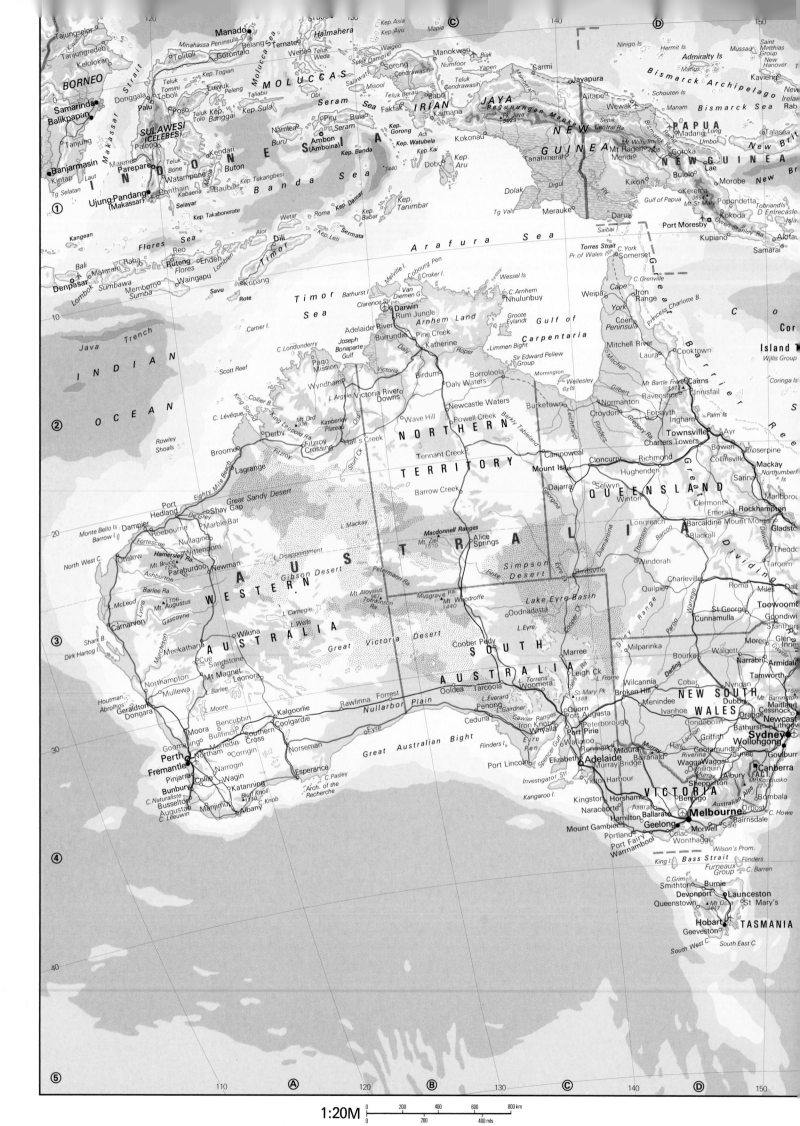

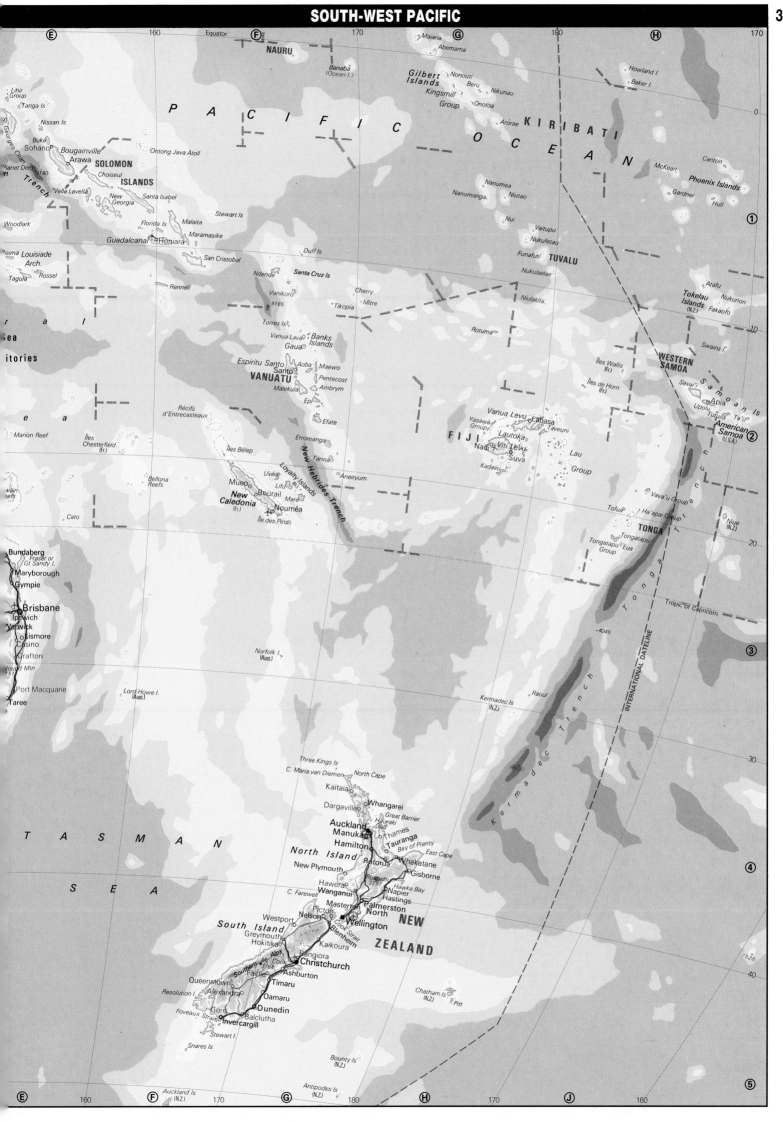

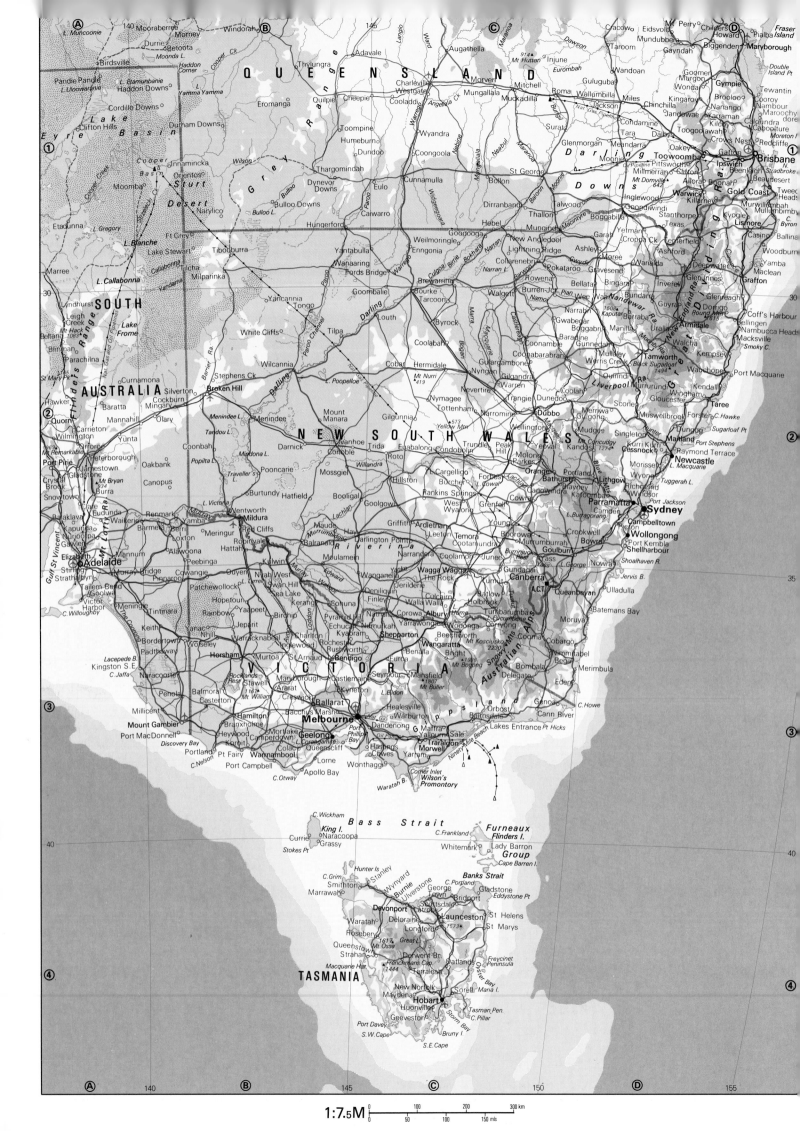

1:5M

0    50    100    150    200 km
0         50        100 mls

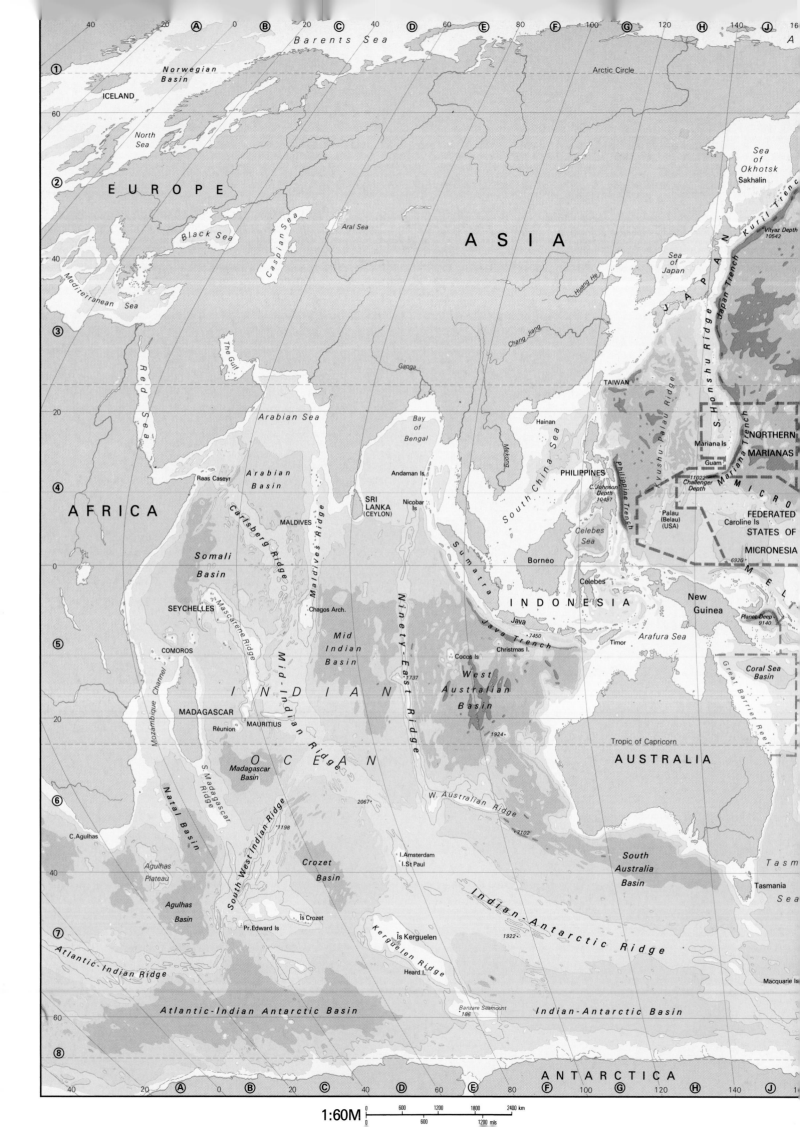

Barents Sea

① Norwegian
Basin

Arctic Circle

ICELAND

60

North
Sea

EUROPE

② Black Sea

Caspian Sea

Aral Sea

ASIA

Sea
of
Okhotsk
Sakhalin

40

Mediterranean  Sea

Huang He

Sea
of
Japan

Vityaz Depth
10542

③ The Gulf

Chang Jiang

Ganga

TAIWAN

Kuril Trench

Japan Trench

Arabian Sea

Bay
of
Bengal

Hainan

S. Honshu Ridge

20

Red Sea

Arabian
Basin

Andaman Is.

PHILIPPINES

South China Sea

Kyushu-Palau Ridge

Philippine Trench

Mariana Trench

Mariana Is

NORTHERN

MARIANAS

④ AFRICA

Raas Caseyr

Carlsberg Ridge

MALDIVES

SRI
LANKA
(CEYLON)

Nicobar
Is.

Maldives Ridge

C.Johnson
Depth
10497

Guam
11022
Challenger
Depth

MICRO

Palau
(Belau) (USA)

Caroline Is

FEDERATED
STATES OF

MICRONESIA

0 Somali
Basin

SEYCHELLES

Mascarene Ridge

Chagos Arch.

Celebes
Sea

Borneo

Celebes

INDONESIA

New
Guinea

6920

MEL

Planet Deep
9140

⑤ COMOROS

Mid
Indian
Basin

Ninety-East Ridge

Sumatra

Java

Java Trench

7450

Timor

Christmas I.

Arafura Sea

Coral Sea
Basin

Mozambique Channel

MADAGASCAR

INDIAN

Cocos Is

West
Australian
Basin

Great Barrier Reef

20 Réunion

MAURITIUS

S.Madagascar Ridge

Madagascar
Basin

OCEAN

1737

1924

Tropic of Capricorn

AUSTRALIA

Tas

⑥ C.Agulhas

Natal Basin

Mid-Indian Ridge

2067

W. Australian Ridge

7102

South
Australia
Basin

Tasmania
Sea

Agulhas
Plateau

South West Indian Ridge

Crozet
Basin

I.Amsterdam
I.St Paul

Indian-Antarctic Ridge

40

⑦ Agulhas
Basin

Pr.Edward Is

Ìs Crozet

Ìs Kerguelen

Kerguelen Ridge

1922

Tasmania

Macquarie Is

Atlantic-Indian Ridge

Heard I.

1198

⑧ Atlantic-Indian Antarctic Basin

Banzare Seamount
186

Indian-Antarctic Basin

60

ANTARCTICA

1:60M    0    600    1200    1800    2400 km
         0    600         1200 mls

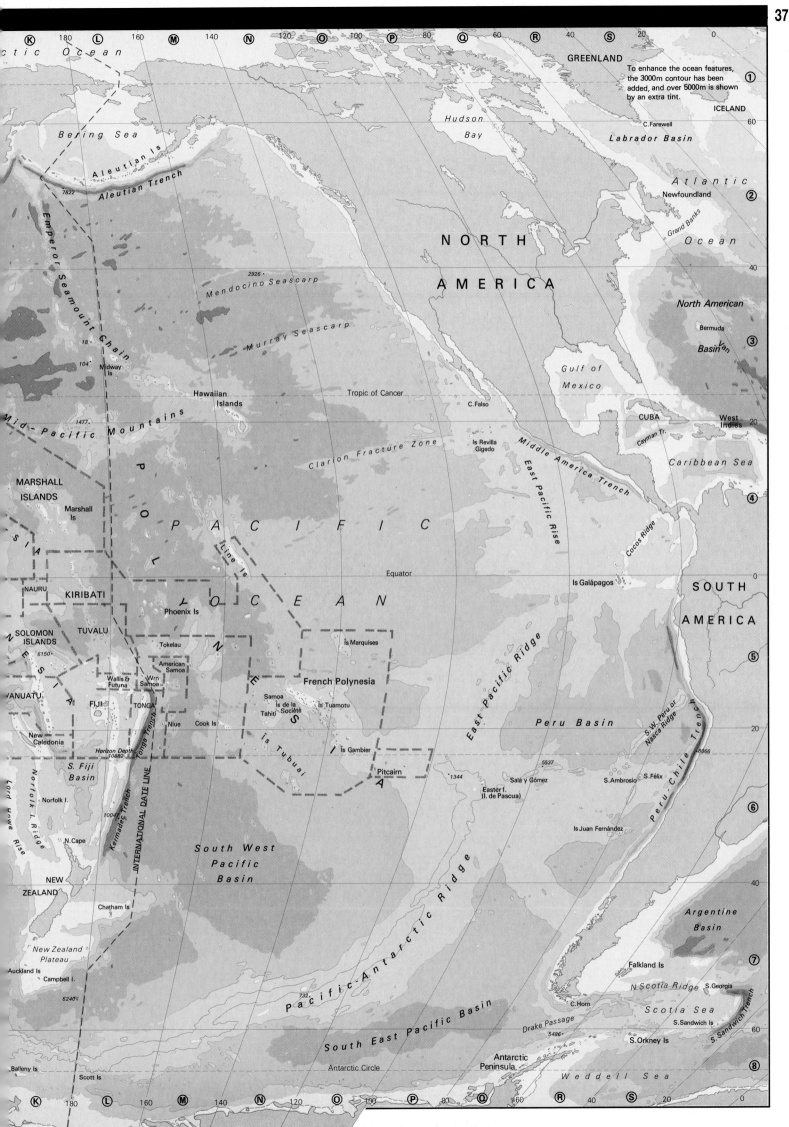

To enhance the ocean features, the 3000m contour has been added, and over 5000m is shown by an extra tint.

**GREENLAND**

ICELAND

C. Farewell

*Atlantic*

Newfoundland

**NORTH**

**AMERICA**

Hudson Bay

*Labrador Basin*

*Ocean*

Grand Banks

North American

Bermuda

*Basin*

Van

*Arctic Ocean*

*Bering Sea*

Aleutian Is

*Aleutian Trench*

7822

*Emperor Seamount Chain*

18

104

Midway Is

*Mid-Pacific Mountains*

1477

Mendocino Seascarp

2926

Murray Seascarp

Hawaiian Islands

Tropic of Cancer

C. Falso

*Gulf of Mexico*

CUBA

Cayman Tr.

West Indies

*Caribbean Sea*

Clarion Fracture Zone

Is Revilla Gigedo

*Middle America Trench*

*East Pacific Rise*

Cocos Ridge

Is Galápagos

**SOUTH**

**AMERICA**

**MARSHALL ISLANDS**

Marshall Is

NAURU

**KIRIBATI**

Phoenix Is

**TUVALU**

Tokelau

American Samoa

Wallis & Futuna

Wrn Samoa

**SOLOMON ISLANDS**

6150

**VANUATU**

**FIJI**

**TONGA**

Niue

Cook Is

New Caledonia

*P A C I F I C*

*O C E A N*

*P O L Y N E S I A*

*M E L A N E S I A*

Line Is

Îs Marquises

French Polynesia

Samoa

Îs de la Société

Tahiti

Îs Tuamotu

Îs Tubuai

Îs Gambier

Pitcairn

1344

Equator

*East Pacific Ridge*

*Peru Basin*

5537

Sala y Gómez

Easter I. (I. de Pascua)

S. Ambrosio

S. Félix

*S.W. Peru or Nasca Ridge*

8066

*Peru-Chile Trench*

Is Juan Fernández

Horizon Depth 10882

*Kermadec Trench*

*Tonga Trench*

New Caledonia

*S. Fiji Basin*

Norfolk I.

10047

*Norfolk I. Ridge*

N. Cape

*Lord Howe Rise*

**NEW ZEALAND**

Chatham Is

*New Zealand Plateau*

Auckland Is

Campbell I.

6240

*INTERNATIONAL DATE LINE*

*South West Pacific Basin*

*Pacific-Antarctic Ridge*

732

*South East Pacific Basin*

Balleny Is

Scott Is

Antarctic Circle

Antarctic Peninsula

*Argentine Basin*

Falkland Is

N. Scotia Ridge

S. Georgia

C. Horn

*Scotia Sea*

S. Sandwich Is

*S. Sandwich Trench*

S. Orkney Is

Drake Passage

5486

*Weddell Sea*

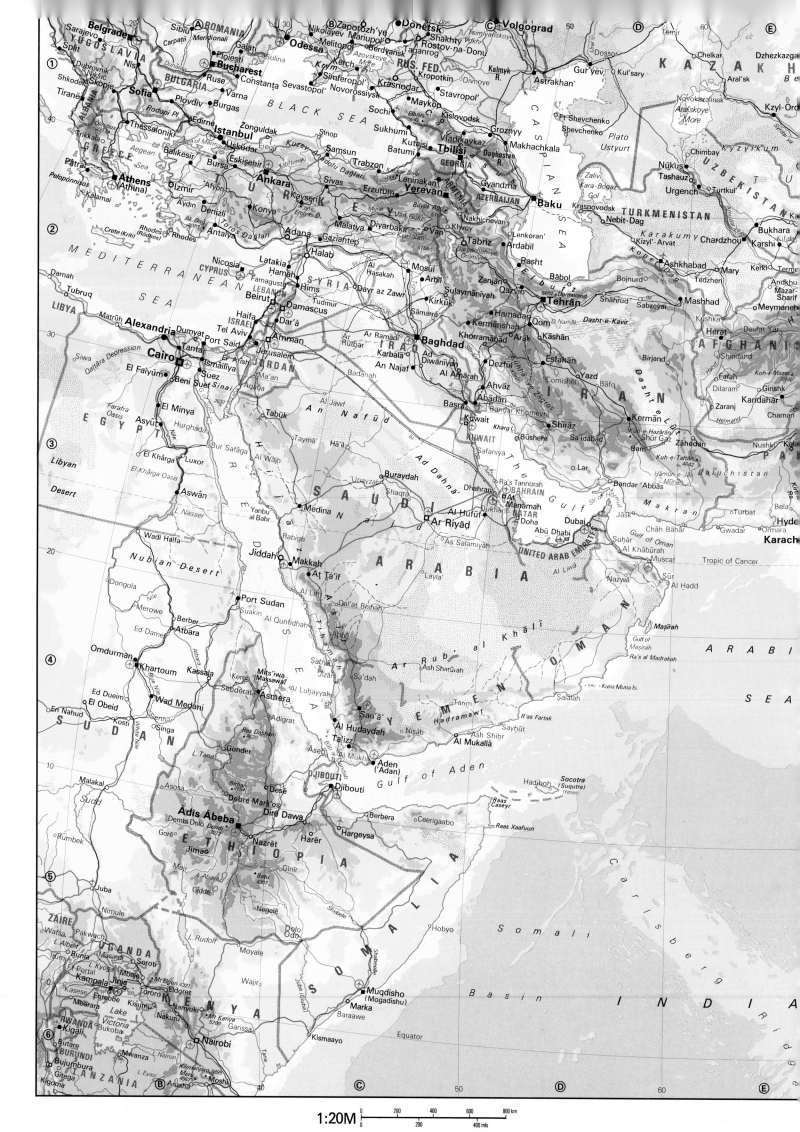

1:20M

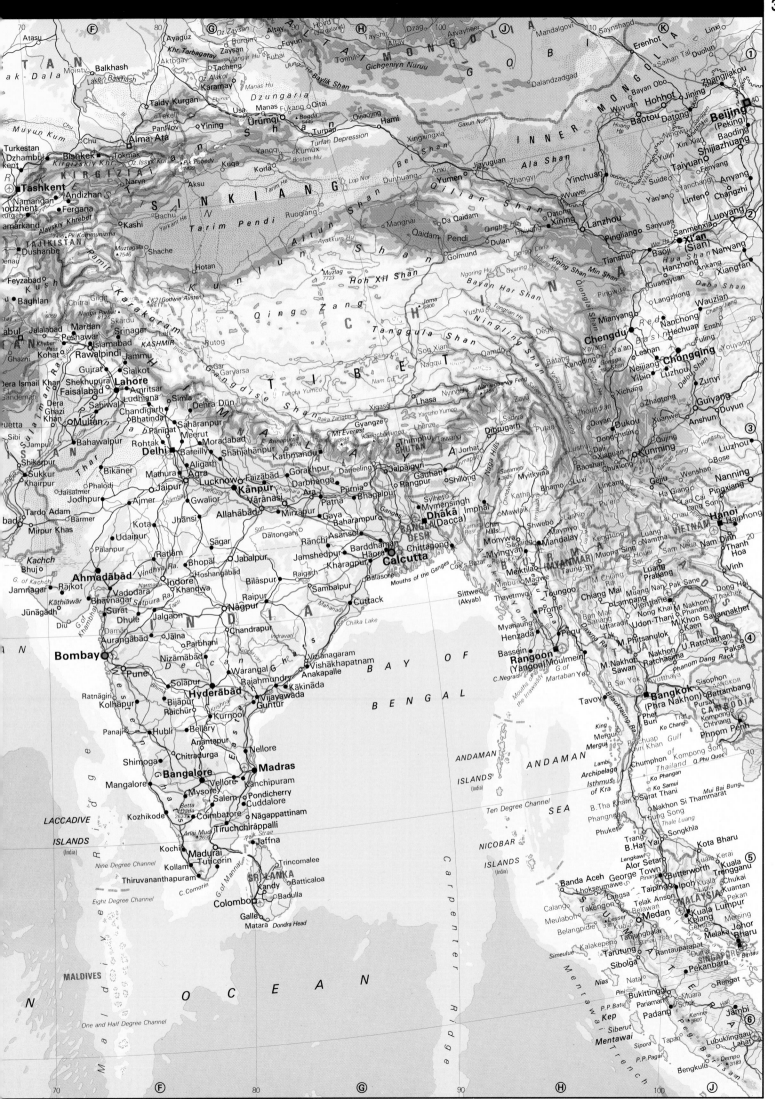

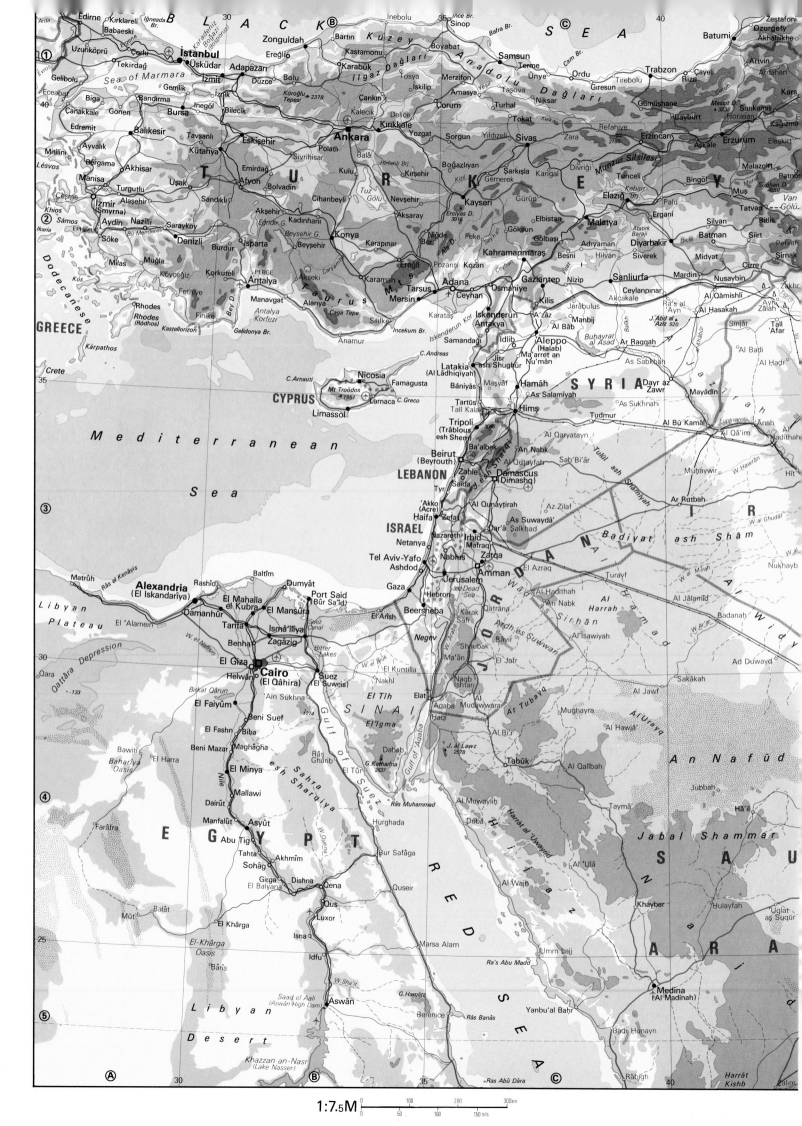

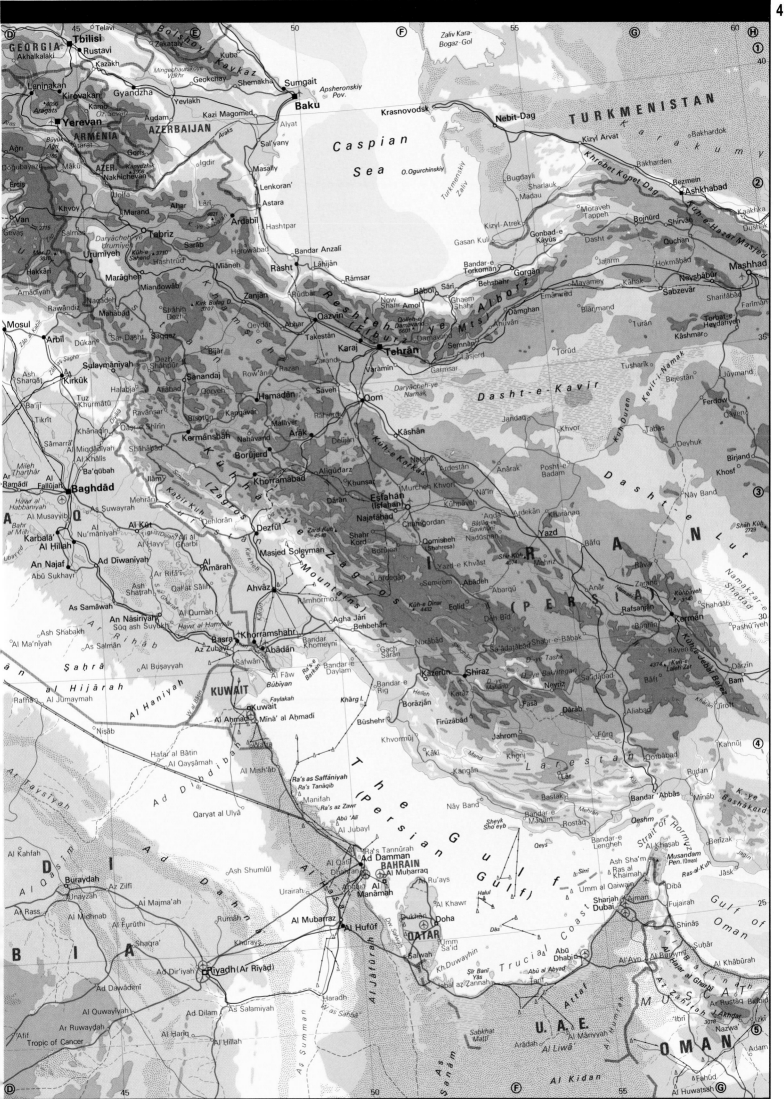

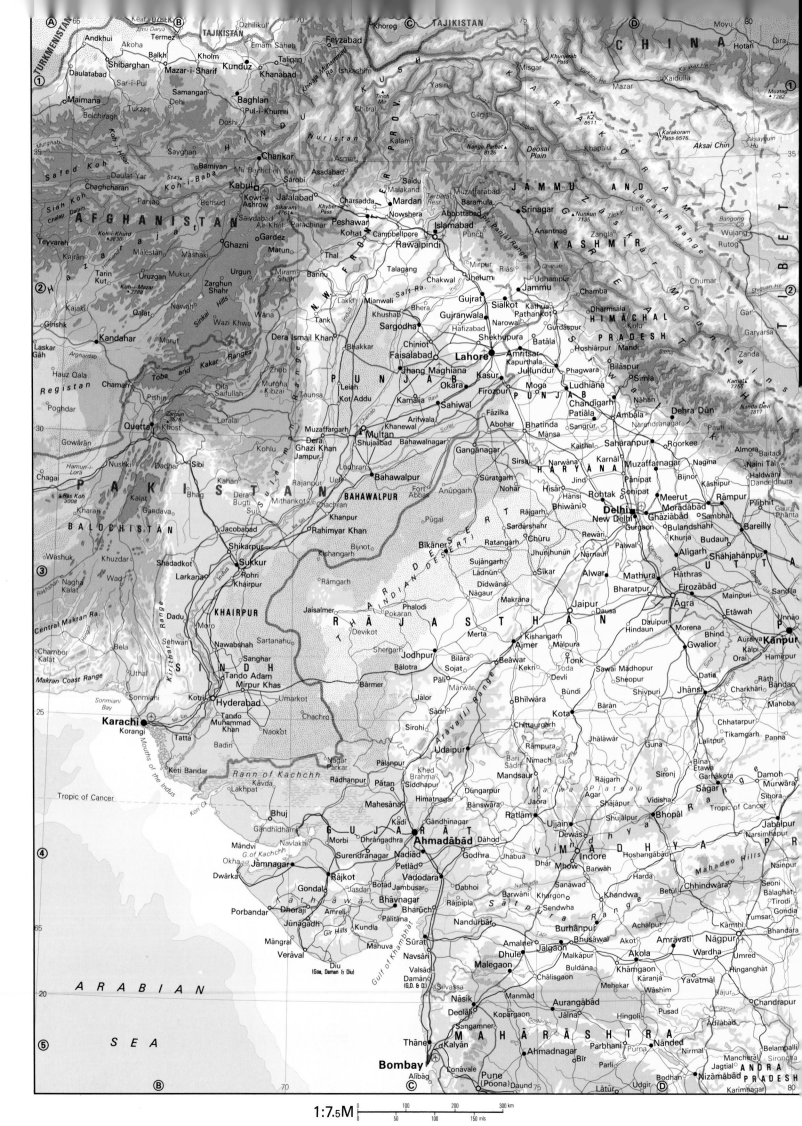

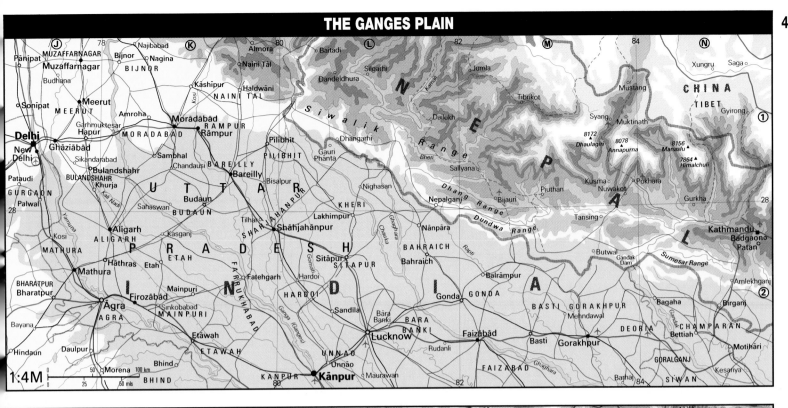

1:4M

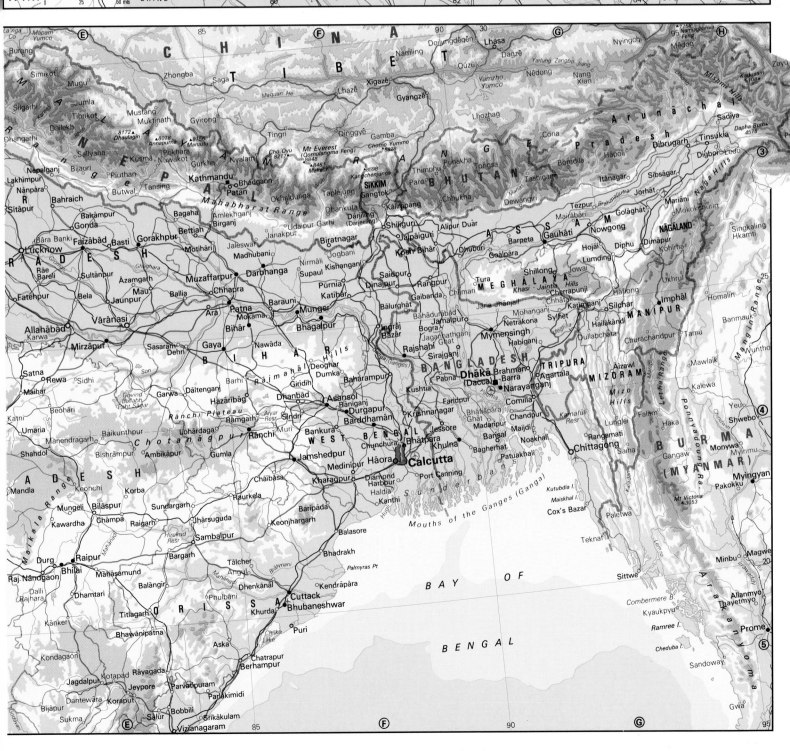

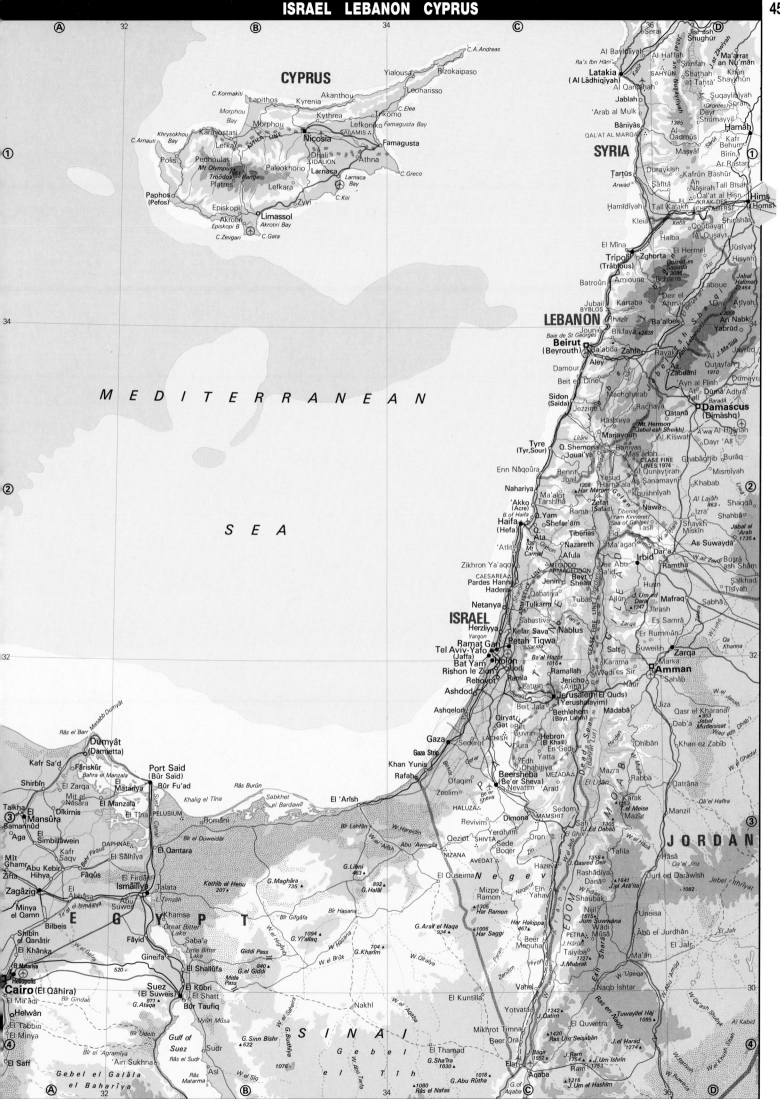

## CYPRUS

C.A.Andreas
Yialousa
Rizokaipaso
C.Kormakiti
Lapithos
Akanthou
Kyrenia
C.Elea
Trikomo
Leonarisso
Morphou
Bay
Morphou
Lefkoniko
Kythrea
Famagusta Bay
SALAMIS
Khrysokhou
Bay
Karavostasi
Lefka
ATTILA LINE
Niçosia
Famagusta
C.Arnauti
Polis
Pedhoulas
Dhali
IDALION
Athna
Paleokhorio
Larnaca
Troödos
Mt Olympus
1951
Range
Lefkara
Larnaca
Bay
Platres
Episkopi
Zyyi
C.Greco
Paphos
(Pefos)
Akrotiri
Limassol
C.Kiti
Episkopi B
Akrotiri Bay
C.Zevgari
C.Gata

## MEDITERRANEAN

## SEA

## SYRIA

Al Bayluliyah
Jisr ash Shughur
Serai
Ra's Ibn Hani'
Al Haffah
Taz Zawiyah
Ma'arrat
an Nu'man
Latakia
( Al Ladhiqiyah )
Silnfah
Shathah
Khan
Shaykhun
Al Qardahah
SAHYUN
Suqaylibiyah
Jablah
'Arab al Mulk
(Orontes) 'Asi
Dayr
Shumayyil
Baniyas
1385
Al Qadmus
Hamah
QAL'AT AL MARQAB
Kafr
Behum
Tartus
Duraykish
Masyaf
Birin
Ar Rastan
Arwad
Safita
An Nasirah Tall Bisah
Qal'at al Hisn
(KRAK-DES
CHEVALIERS)
Hims
(Homs)
Hamidiyah
Tall Kalakh
Shinshar
El Mina
Kleia
Kebir
Qoubayat
Al Qusayr
Tripoli
(Trablous)
Zghorta
Halba
El Hermel
Jusiyah
Hisyah
Batroun
Amioune
Bcharre
Cornet es
Saouda 3086
Jabal
Halimah
J.el
Ahmar
2464
Jubail
BYBLOS
Rhazir
Kartaba
Laboue
Dayr 'Atiyah

## LEBANON

Jounié
Bikfaya 2828
Ba'albek
2659
An Nabk
Yabrud
Beirut
(Beyrouth)
Ba'abda
Zahle
Rayak
Al J.Ma'lula
Jayrud
Baie de St Georges
Aley
Az
Zabdani
1910
Al Ma'arrat
Damour
Beit ed Dine
Machgharab
Ayn al Fijah
At Tall
Duma 'Adhra
Damascus
(Dimashq)
Sidon
(Saida)
Jezzine
Rachaya
Qatana
Jusi
Ji
Mt Hermon
(Jebel esh Sheikh)
A'waj Al Hijanah
Dayr 'Ali
Tyre
(Tyr,Sour)
Q.Shemona
Marjayoun
Baniyas
Mas'adah
Al Kiswah
Jouai'ya
Litani
CEASE FIRE
LINES 1974
Shaykh
Miskin
Enn Naqoura
Bennt
Jbail
1208
Al Qunaytirah
Ghabaghib
Buraq
Nahariya
Ma'alot
Har Meron
1208
Hama'ala
As Sanamayn
Mismiyah
Ma'alot
Tarshiha
1172
Jubeil
Nawa
Khushniyah
Al Lajah
'Akko
(Acre)
Q.Yam
Rama
Zefat
Safad
863
Izra'
Shahba
Haifa
(Hefa)
Q.Ata
Shefar'am
Tiberias
(Tabariya)
(Yam Kinneret
Sea of Galilee)
Tasil
Nawa
B.of Haifa
'Atlit
Mt
Carmel
Nazareth
Ma'agan
Jabal al
'Arab
1735
Zikhron Ya'aqov
Afula
Fiq
W. al Ehreir
As Suwayda
MEGIDDO
ARMAGEDDON
Deir Abu
Sa'id
Irbid
CAESAREA
Beyt
Shean
Husn
Pardes Hanna
Jenin
Ramtha
ash Sham
Hadera
Qabatiya
Ajlun
1247
Um ed
Dara
Mafraq
Sabha'
Netanya
Tulkarm
Tubas
Jarash
Es Samra
Sabstiya
Er Rumman
Qa
Khanna

## ISRAEL

Herzliyya
Kefar Sava
Nablus
Zarqa
Yarqon
Petah Tiqwa
Ba'al Hazor
Salt
Suweileh
Ramat Gan
Sarida
1016
Karama
Amman
Tel Aviv-Yafo
(Jaffa)
Holon
Lod
Wadi es Sir
Sahab
Bat Yam
Rishon le Zion
Ramallah
Jericho
(Ariha)
Naur
Marka
Rehovot
Ramla
Latrun
Madaba
Ashdod
Jerusalem(El Quds)
(Yerushalayim)
Jiza
Qasr el Kharana
Qiryat
Gat
Beit Jala
Bethlehem
(Bayt Lahm)
963
Dab'a
Wad edh Dhab
Ashqelon
Bet
Guvrin
Hebron
(El Khalil)
En Gedi
Jebel
Mudeisisat
Gaza
Sederot
Dura
Yatta
Mazra
Rabba
Gaza Strip
LACHISH
'Edh
Dhahiriya
Qatrana
Khan Yunis
Beersheba
(Be'er Sheva)
MEZADA
Karak
1253
Rafah
Ofaqim
Nevatim
Arad
T.el Meise
Mazar
Manzil
Zeelim
Be'er
Sheva
Sedom
Safi
El 'Arish
HALUZA
Revivim
Dimona
MAMSHIT
Khan ez Zabib
Romani
PELUSIUM
Bir Lahfan
W. Hareidin
Qeziot
Yeroham
1305
J.Ed Dabab
Dhiban
W. el Ghor
Bir el Duweidar
Abu 'Awergila
SHIVTA
Oron
Safi
Qatrana

## JORDAN

El Qantara
El Salhiya
Bir Hasana
NIZANA
Sede
Boqer
Zin
Tafila
Qa'el Jinz
El Firdan
Talata
AVEDAT
Hazeva
Rashadiya
Dana
1641
Jurf ed Darawish
Ismailiye
G.Libni
463
892
El Queseima
Negev
Negarot
J. Qasred Deir
1082
Khamsa
G.Maghara
735
G.Halal
Mizpe
Ramon
Ein
Yahav
1356
Zagazig
El Abbasa
G.Yi'allaq
1094
W.Hasana
G.Kharim
1305
Har Ramon
Nijil
Jum Suwwana
El Jafr
Bir Gifgafa
704
W.Qiraya
Har Saggi
PETRA
Musa
Fayid
G.Araif el Naqa
934
1006
Har Saggi
Beer
Menuha
Taiyiba
J.Mubrak
Great Bitter
Lake
Saba'a
Bir Hasana
840
G.el Giddi
Zenifim
J.Harun
1727
Abu el Jurdhan
Gineifa
Little Bitter
Lake
Giddi Pass
W. el Bruk
Hiyon
Ma'an
El Shallufa
520
W. el Aqaba
Nakhl
Mitla Pass
Vahel
Naqb Ishtar
Uneisa
Suez
(El Suweis)
El Kubri
1076
W. el Sderat
El Kuntilla
Yotvata
1242
J.Qatim
Abu el Jurdhan
El Jafr
Bur Taufiq
871
G.Ataqa
Uyun Musa
Mikhrot Timna
Beer Ora
J.el Harad
1274
Ras en Naqb
El Quweira
Gebel el Galala
el Bahariya
Ras
Matarma
G.Sinn Bishr
622
G.Buthiya
1420
Ras Um Seisaban
J.el Hashm
Elat
J.Baqir
1592
J.Um Ishrin
1754
1215
J.Um al Hashim
W.el Siq
1080
Aqaba
1216
J.Ram
Ram
1030
G.Sha'ira
1018
G.Abu Rutha
1080
Ras en Nafas
G. of Aqaba

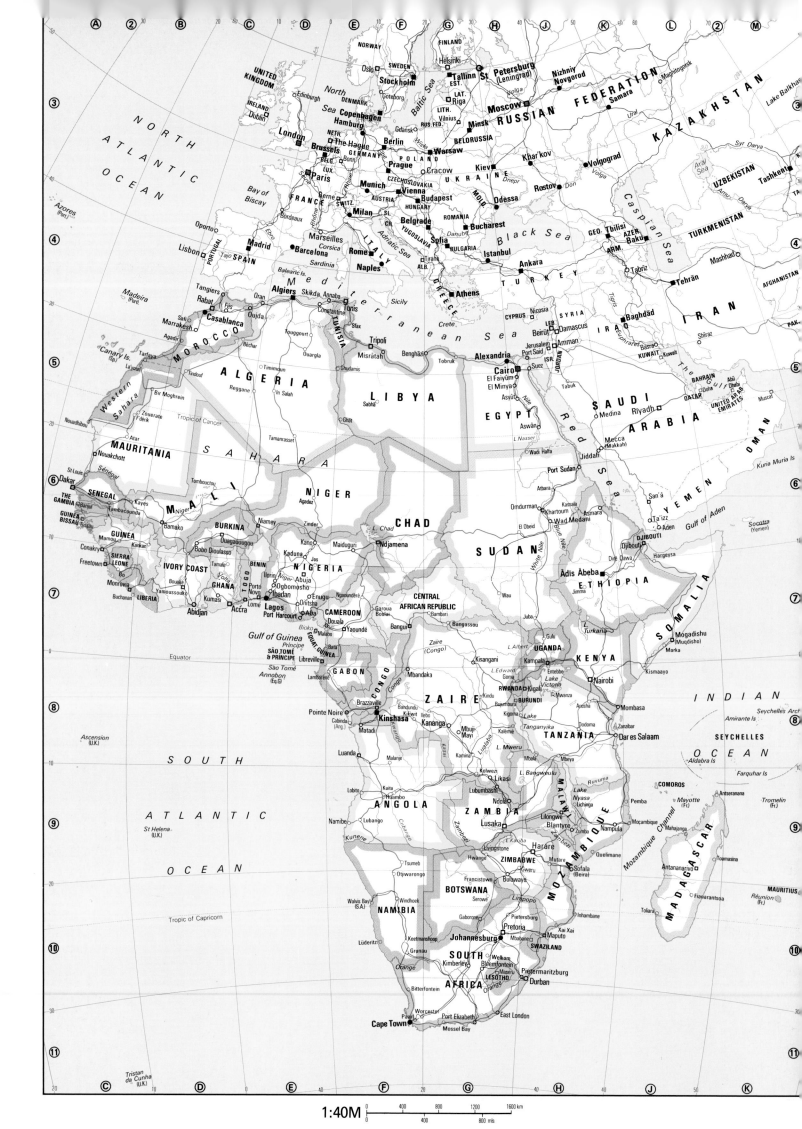

1:7.5M

| 0 | 100 | 200 | 300 km |
| 0 | 50 | 100 | 150 mls |

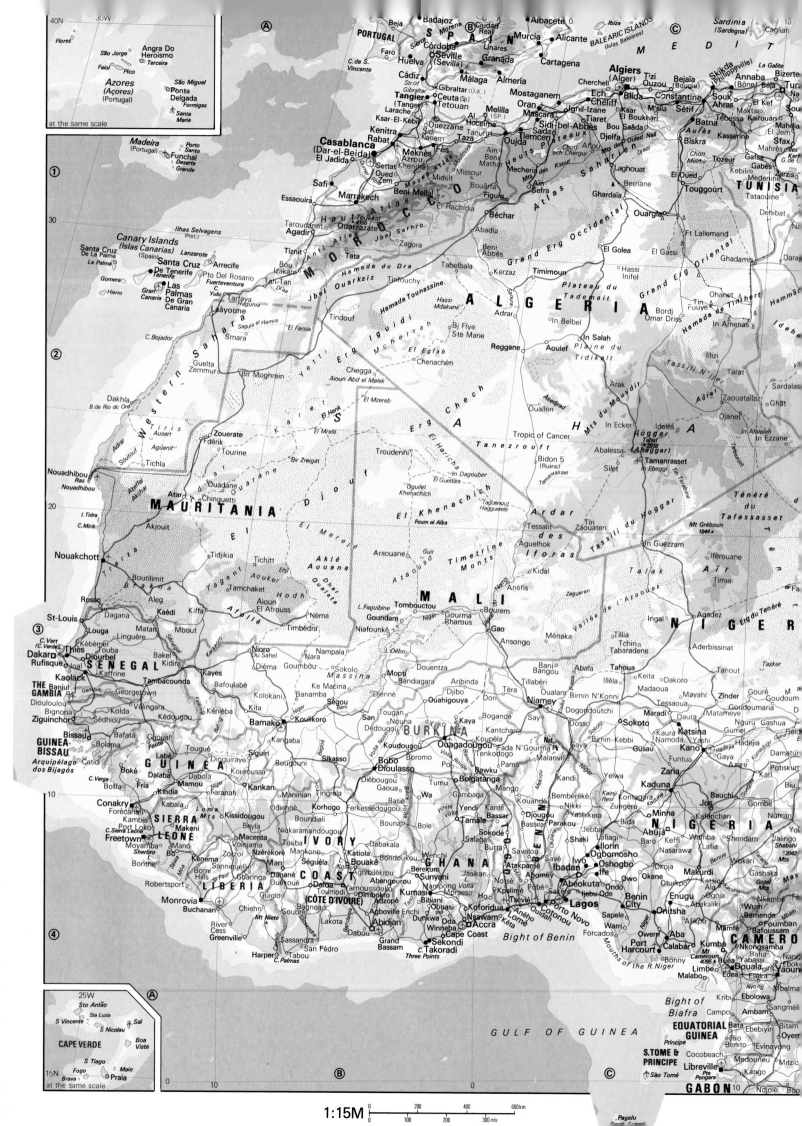

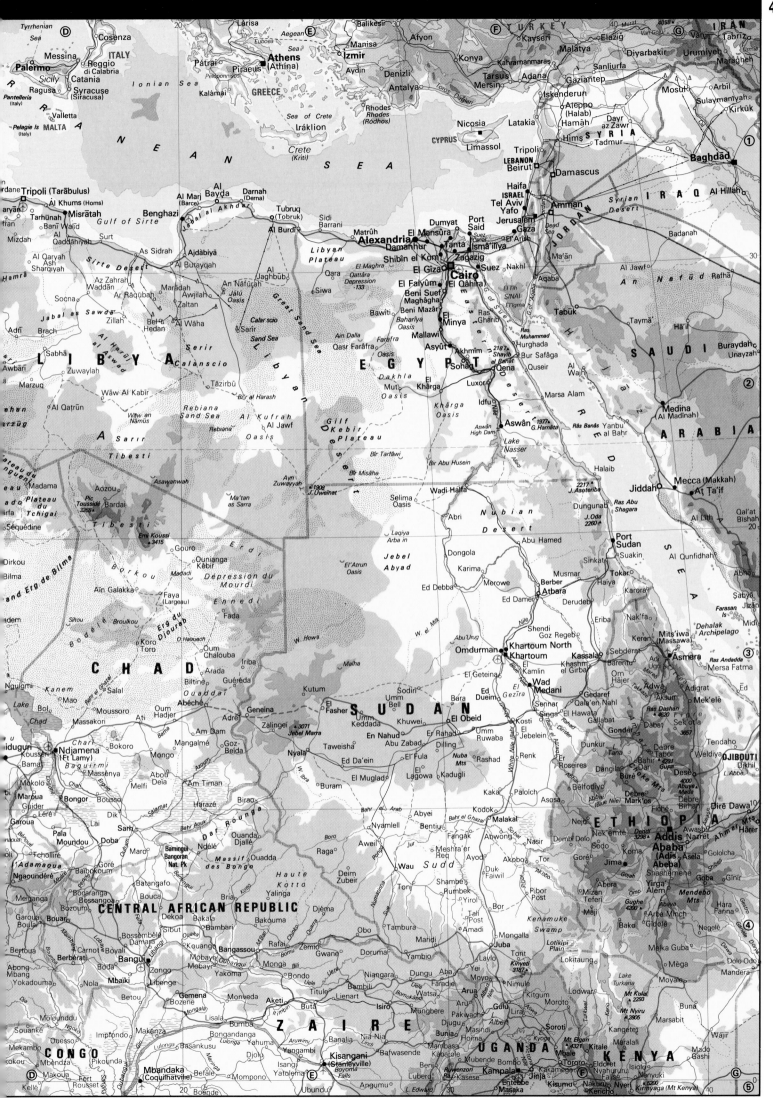

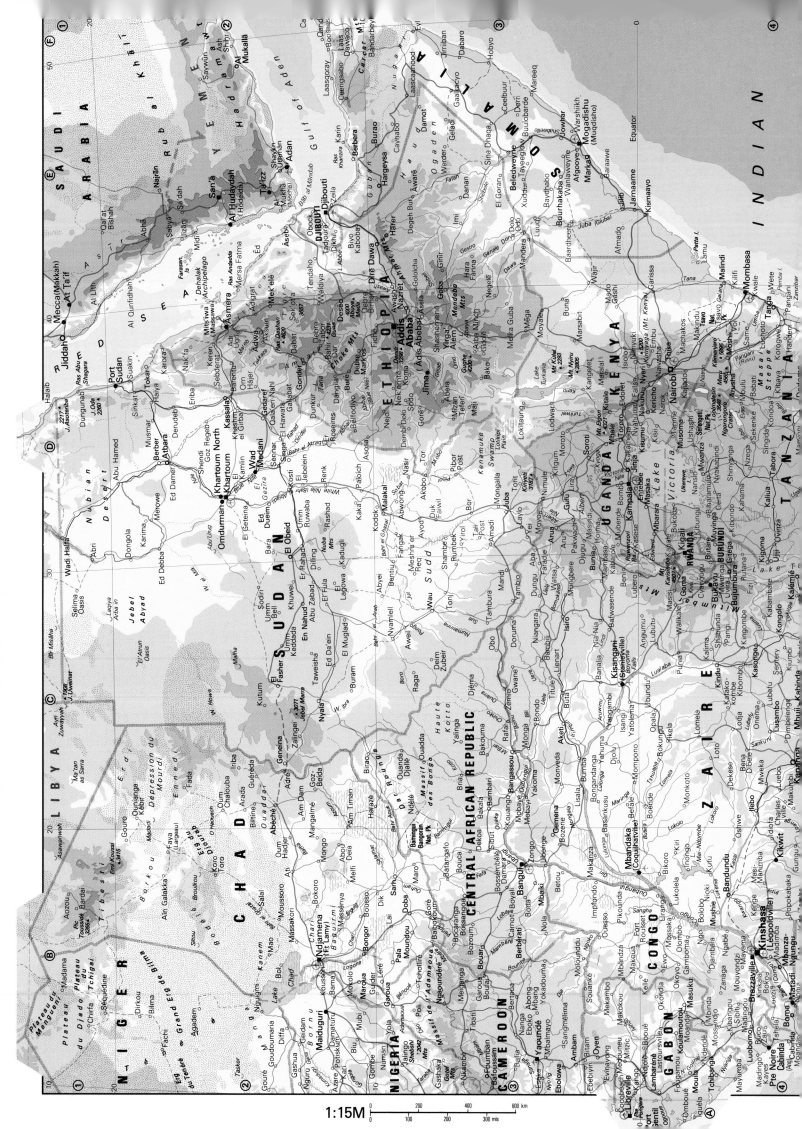

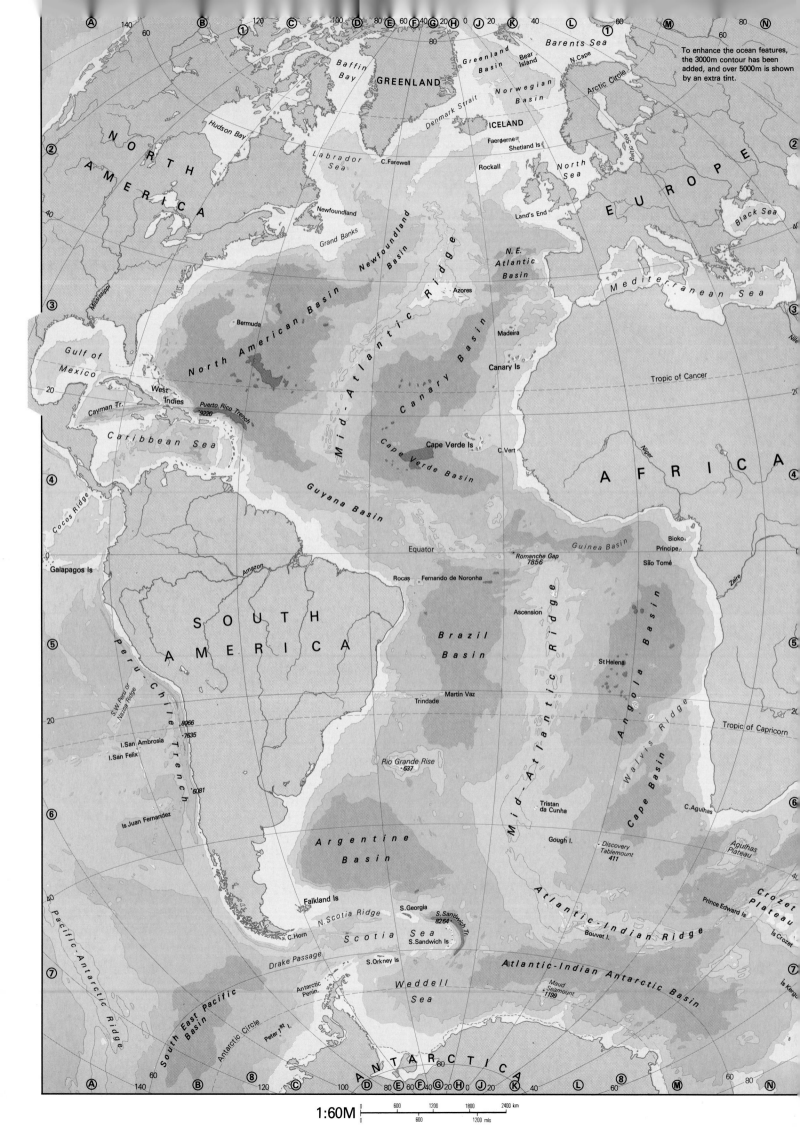

To enhance the ocean features, the 3000m contour has been added, and over 5000m is shown by an extra tint.

A 140 60 B 120 C 100 D 80 E 60 F 40 G H 0 J 20 K 40 L 60 M 80 N

1 120 100 80 60 40 20 0 20 40 60 1

Baffin Bay
GREENLAND
Greenland Basin
Bear Island
N.Cape
Barents Sea

Hudson Bay
Denmark Strait
Norwegian Basin
Arctic Circle

2 NORTH
Labrador Sea
C.Farewell
ICELAND
Faerøerne
Shetland Is
Rockall
North Sea
Baltic Sea
EUROPE 2

AMERICA
Newfoundland
Grand Banks
Newfoundland Basin
Land's End
Black Sea

N.E. Atlantic Basin
Mediterranean Sea

3 Mississippi
Bermuda
North American Basin
Mid-Atlantic Ridge
Azores
Canary Basin
Madeira
Nile 3

Gulf of Mexico
Tropic of Cancer

20 West Indies
Cayman Tr.
Puerto Rico Trench 9220
Canary Is
C.Vert
20

Caribbean Sea
Cape Verde Is
Cape Verde Basin

4 Cocos Ridge
Guyana Basin
Guinea Basin
Bioko
Príncipe
AFRICA 4

Galapagos Is
Equator
Romanche Gap 7856
São Tomé
Zaïre

0 Amazon
Rocas
Fernando de Noronha
0

SOUTH
Ascension

5 Peru-Chile Trench
S.W.Peru or Nazca Ridge
AMERICA
Brazil Basin
Mid-Atlantic Ridge
St Helena
Angola Basin
Walvis Ridge 5

20 8066
7635
Martin Vaz
Trindade
Tropic of Capricorn
20

I.San Ambrosia
I.San Felix
6081
Rio Grande Rise 637
Cape Basin
C.Agulhas

6 Is Juan Fernandez
Argentine Basin
Tristan da Cunha
Gough I.
Discovery Tablemount 411
Agulhas Plateau
Crozet Plateau 6

Falkland Is
S.Georgia
S.Sandwich Tr. 8264
Prince Edward Is
Is Crozet

N.Scotia Ridge
Atlantic-Indian Ridge
Bouvet I.

7 Pacific-Antarctic Ridge
C.Horn
Scotia Sea
S.Sandwich Is
Atlantic-Indian Antarctic Basin
Is Kergu 7

Drake Passage
S.Orkney Is
Weddell Sea
Maud Seamount 1139

South East Pacific Basin
Antarctic Penin.
Peter 1st I.
Antarctic Circle

8 A 140 B 120 C 100 D 80 E 60 F 40 G 20 H 0 J 20 K 40 L 60 M N 8

ANTARCTICA
80

1:60M
0 600 1200 1800 2400 km
0 600 1200 mils

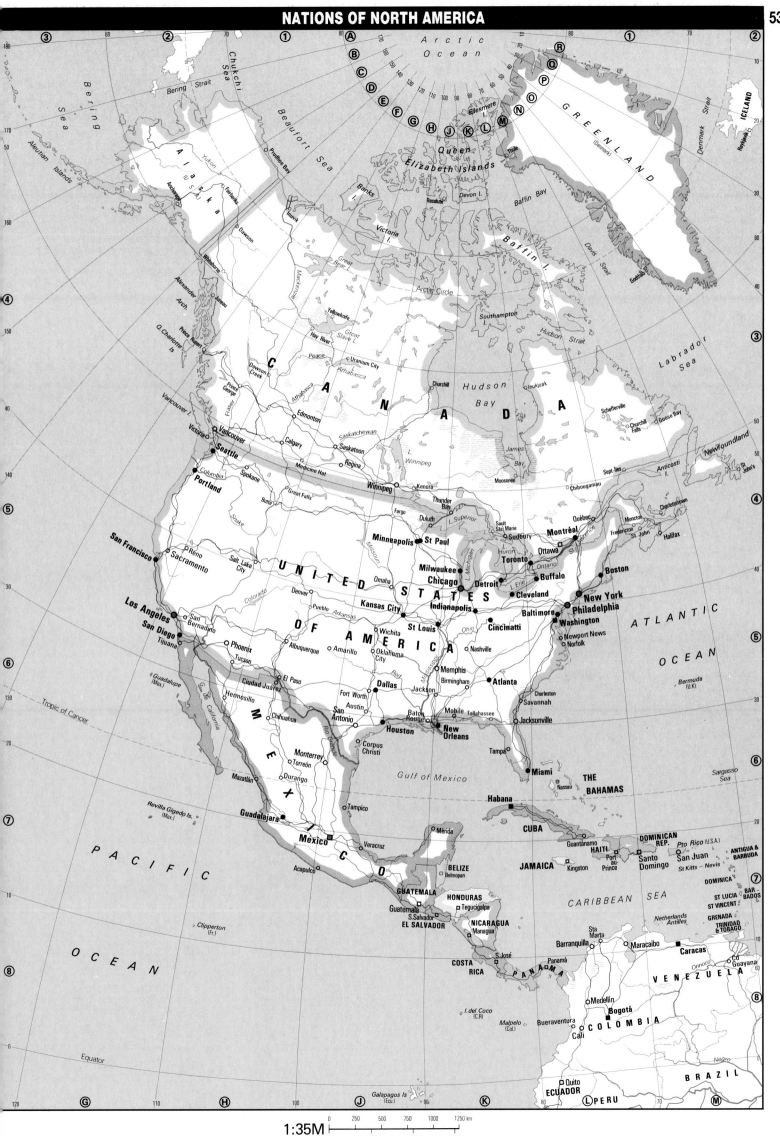

1:35M

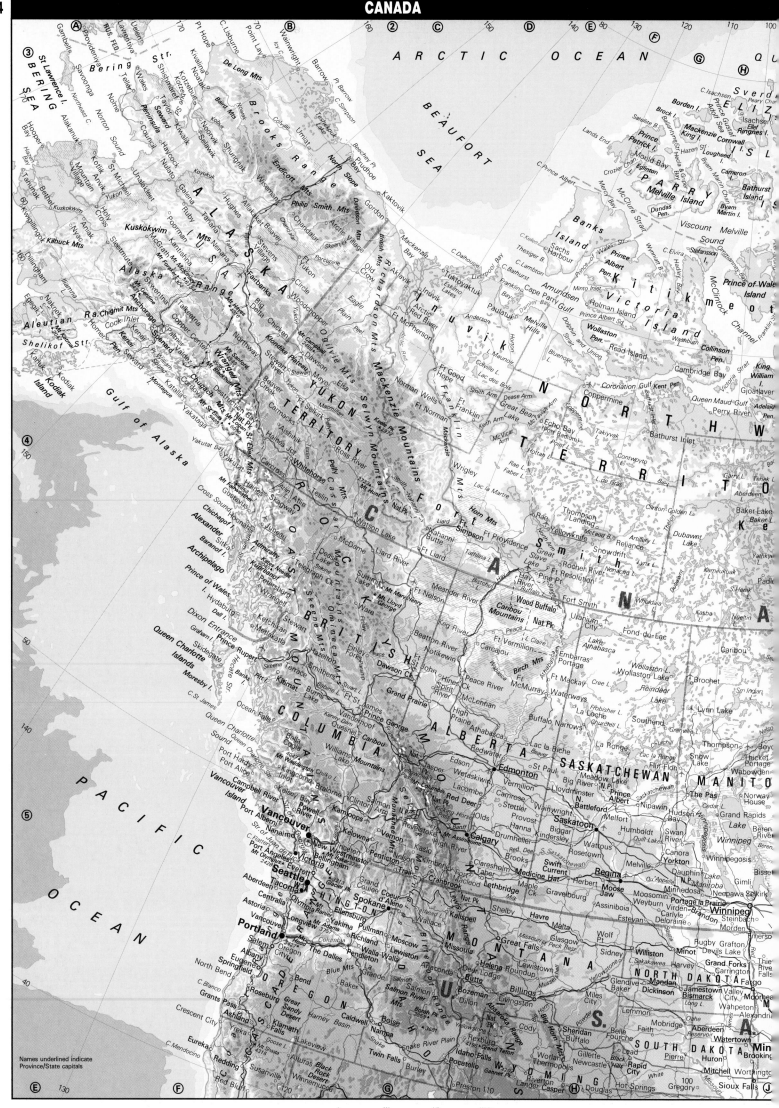

Names underlined indicate
Province/State capitals

1:15M

GREENLAND (Denmark)

ICELAND
Reykjavik

BAFFIN BAY

DAVIS STRAIT

DENMARK STRAIT

Arctic Circle

Ellesmere Island
Devon Island
Somerset Island
Baffin Island
Baffin Icecap
Foxe Basin
Foxe Peninsula
Foxe Channel
Southampton Island
Cumberland Peninsula
Cumberland Sound
Hall Peninsula
Frobisher Bay
Meta Incognito Pen.

Lancaster Sound
Prince Charles I.
Nettilling Lake
Amadjuak Lake

HUDSON STRAIT

Labrador Sea

NEWFOUNDLAND

HUDSON BAY

Ungava Bay
Kuujjuaq
Labrador

Churchill
Inukjuak
King George Is
Belcher Is.
Akimiski I.

James Bay

Rés. de La Grande 2
Rés. de La Grande 3
Rés. de La Grande 4

QUEBEC

Schefferville
Labrador City
Wabush
Churchill Falls
Goose Bay
Nain
Hopedale
Makkovik
Rigolet
Cartwright

Newfoundland
St John's
Gander
Corner Brook
Port aux Basques
Gulf of Saint Lawrence
Cape Breton I.

ONTARIO

Chibougamau
Baie-Comeau
Sept-Iles
Gaspé
I. d'Anticosti

NOVA SCOTIA
PRINCE EDWARD I.
Charlottetown
Sydney
Halifax
Dartmouth
Truro
New Glasgow

NEW BRUNSWICK
Fredericton
Saint John
Moncton

LAKE SUPERIOR
Thunder Bay
Sault Ste Marie
Sudbury

LAKE HURON
LAKE MICHIGAN

MICHIGAN
WISCONSIN
MINNESOTA

St Paul
Milwaukee
Madison
Detroit
Windsor
Toronto
Hamilton
Buffalo
London

Québec
Trois Rivieres
Montreal
Ottawa
Hull

MAINE
NEW HAMPSHIRE
VERMONT
MASS.
CONN.

Boston
Providence
Hartford
Worcester
Springfield
Albany
Syracuse
Rochester
New York

L. Ontario
L. Erie

ATLANTIC OCEAN

Labrador Sea

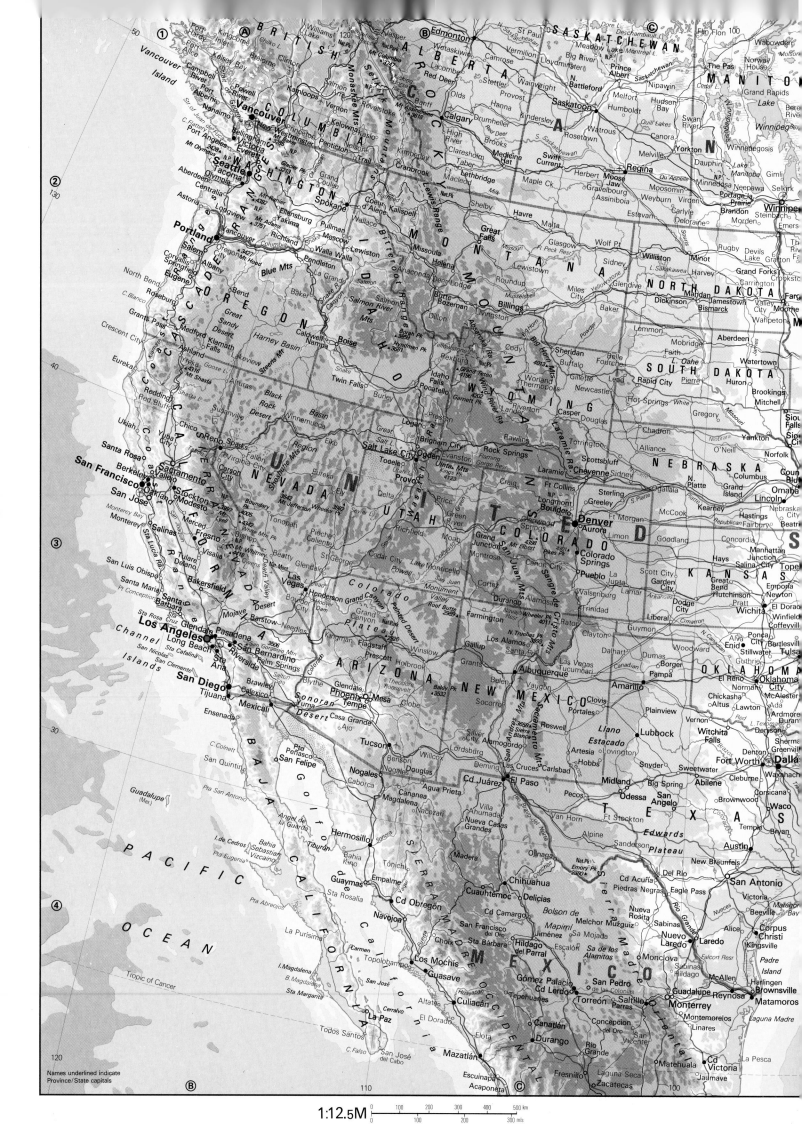

1:12.5M

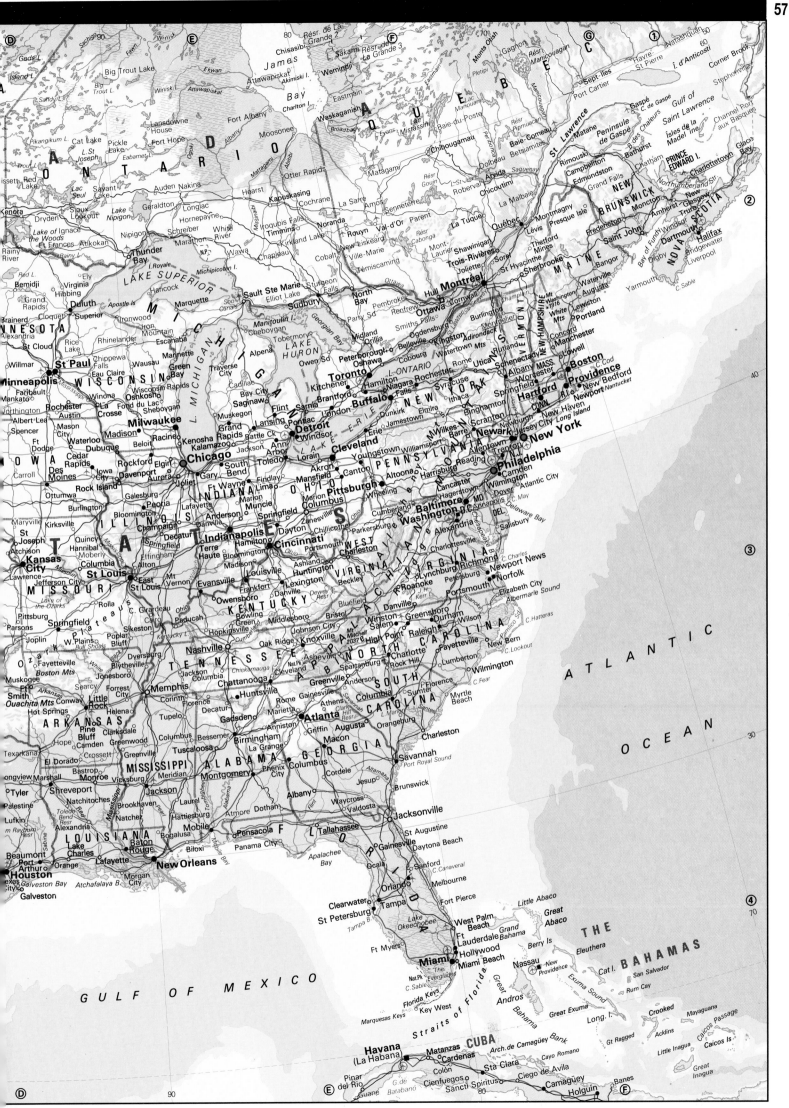

1:5M

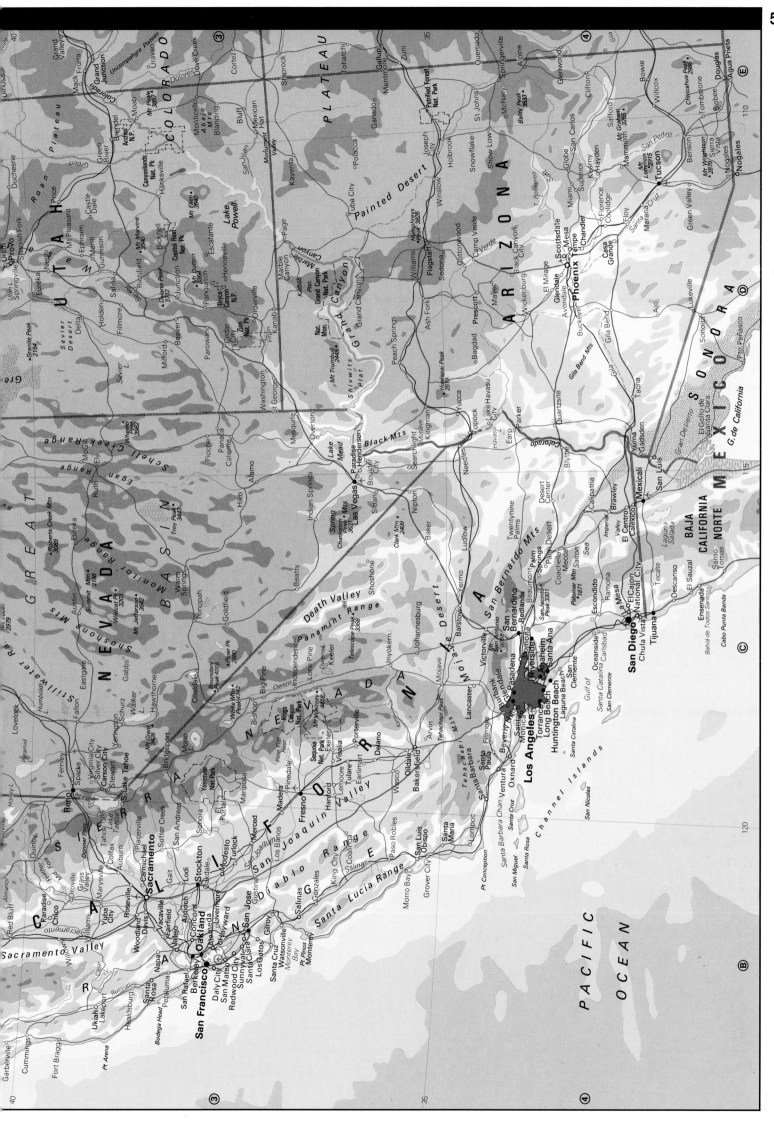

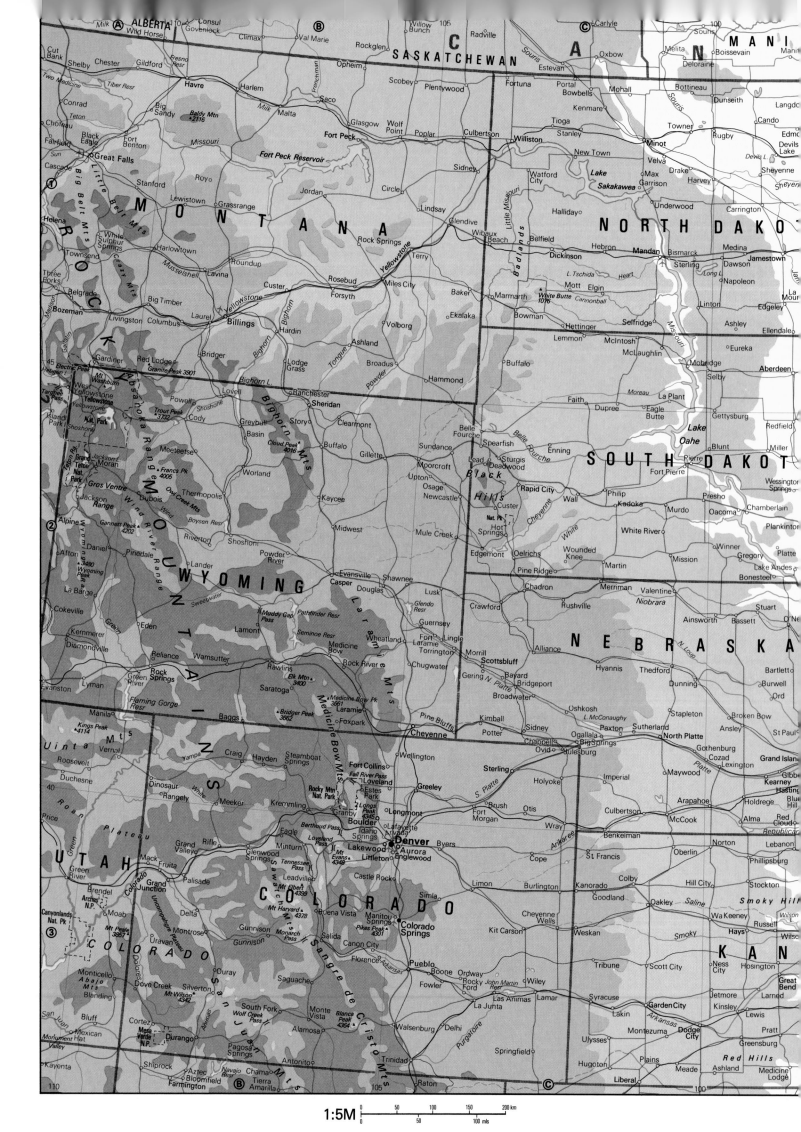

1:5M

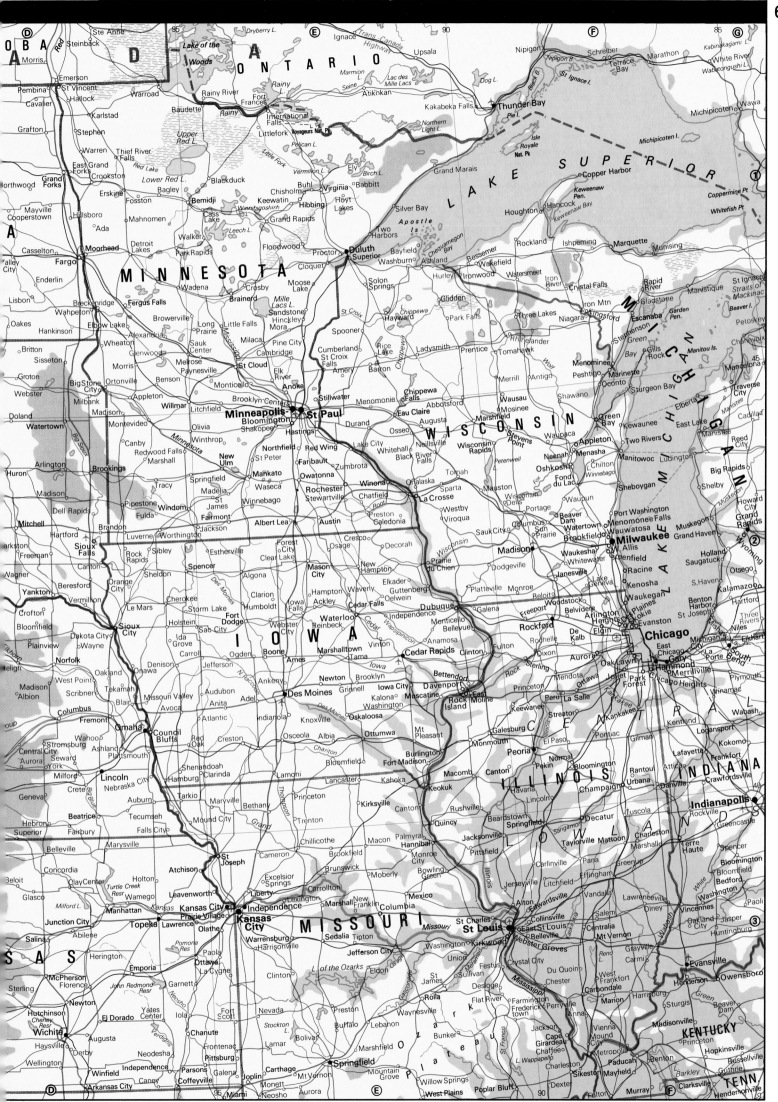

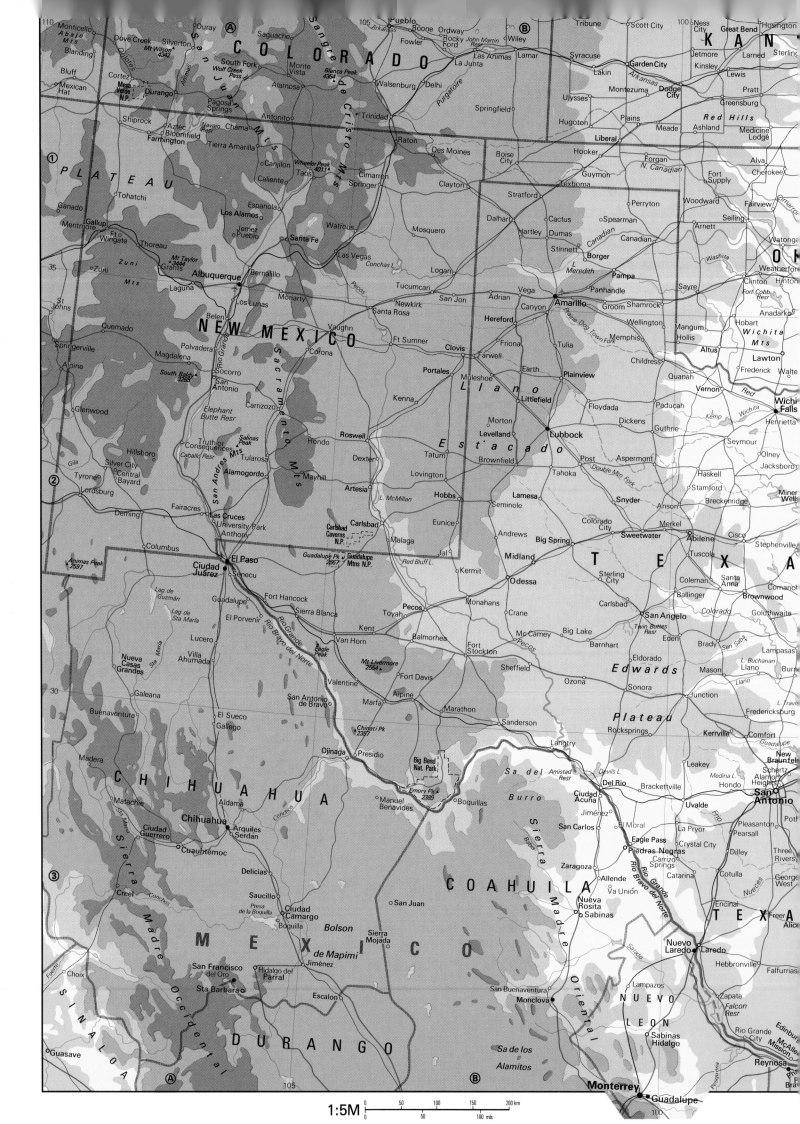

1:5M

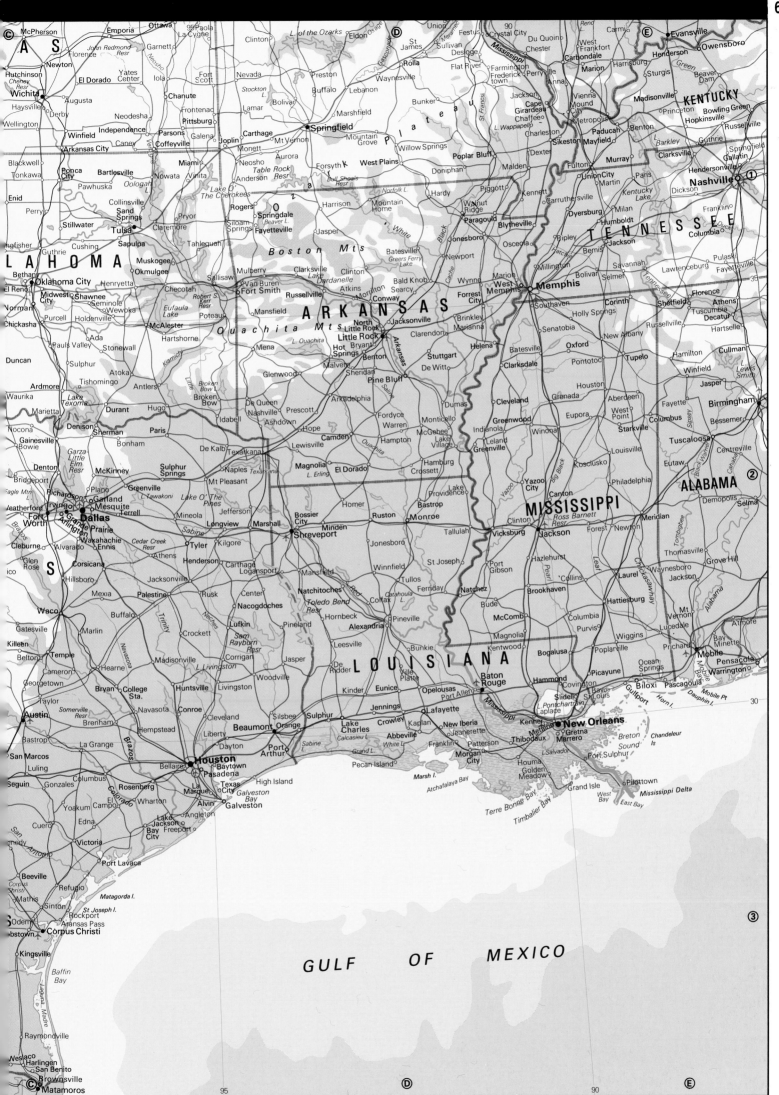

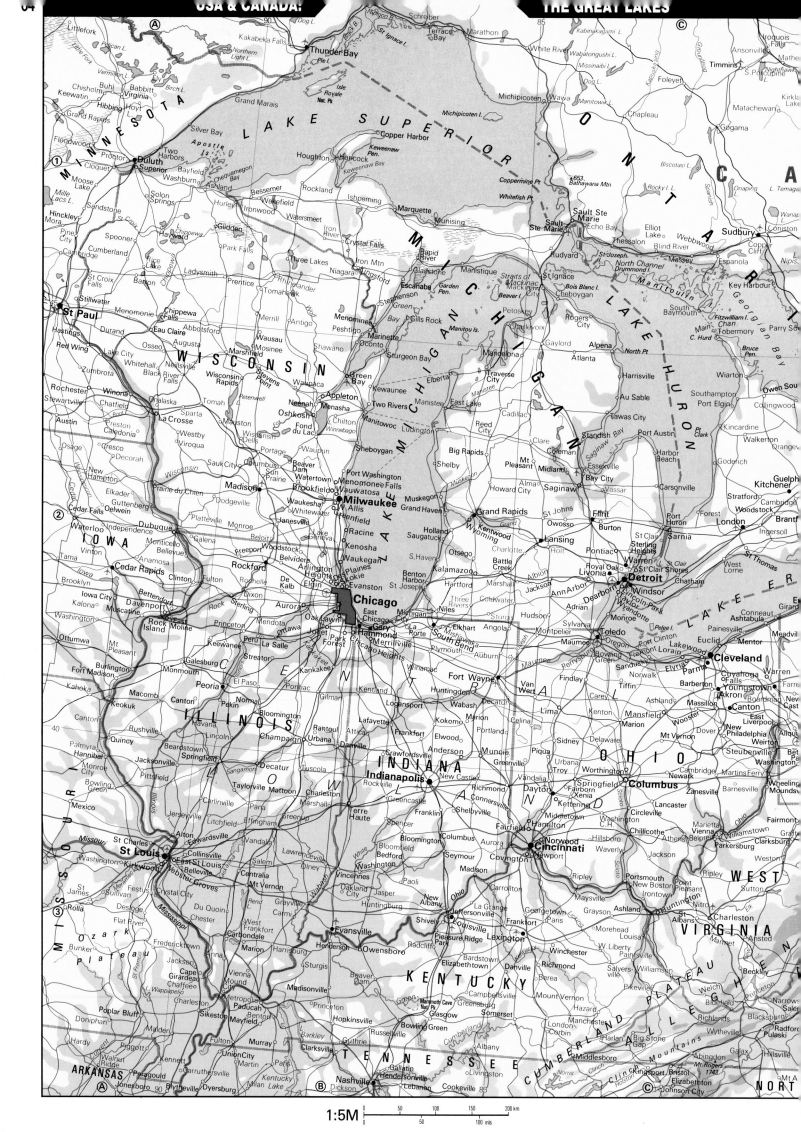

1:5M

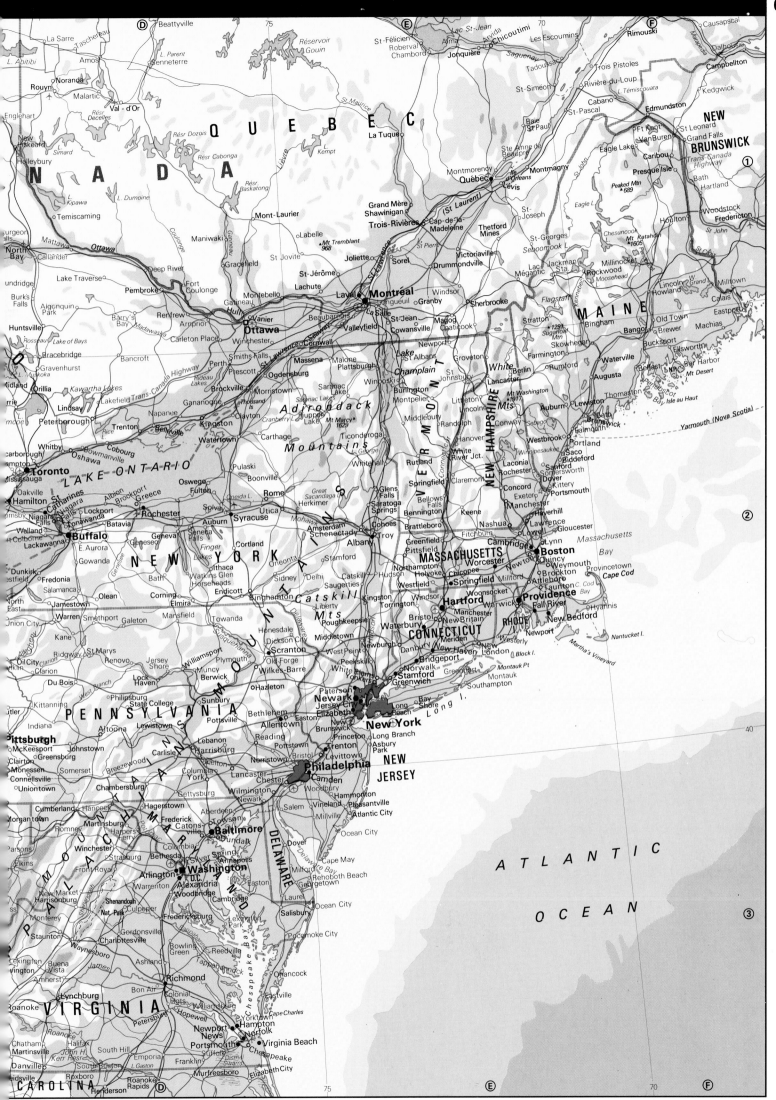

# CALIFORNIA HAWAII

1:2.5M

1:5M

USA, HAWAII

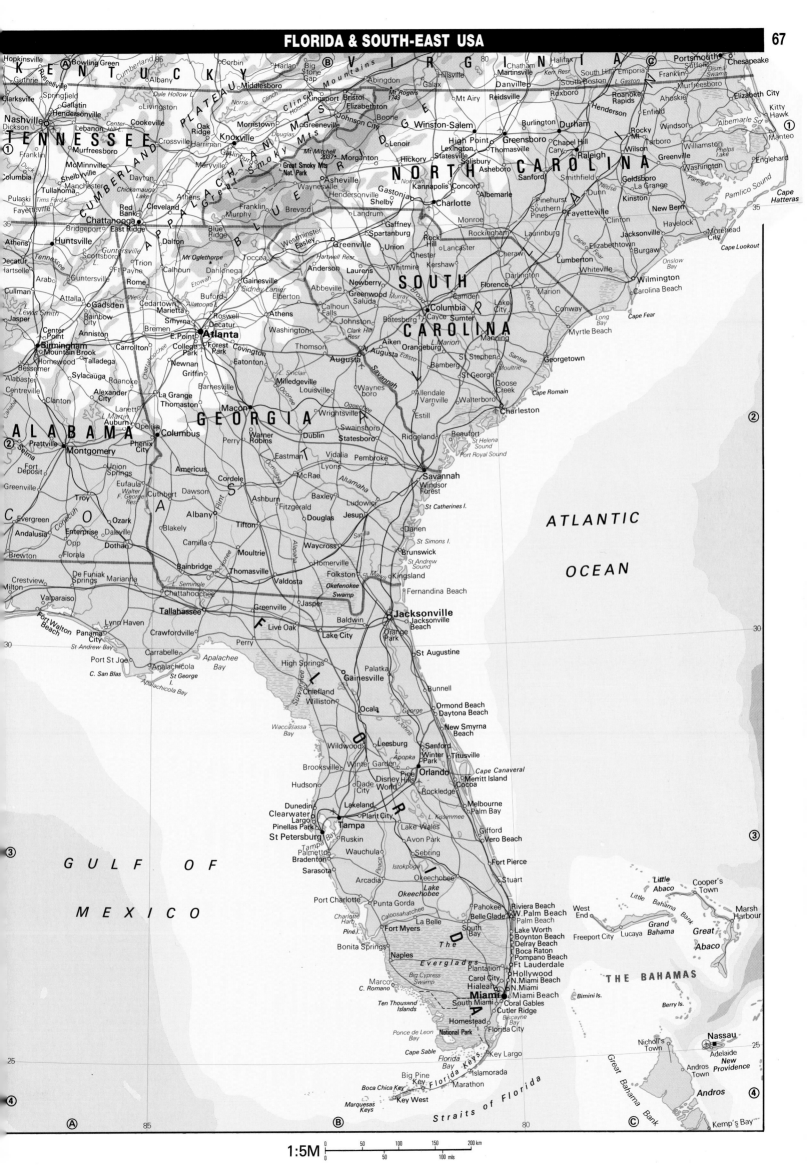

ATLANTIC OCEAN

**States / Regions:** NEW HAMPSHIRE, VERMONT, MASSACHUSETTS, RHODE ISLAND, CONNECTICUT, NEW YORK, PENNSYLVANIA, NEW JERSEY, DELAWARE, MARYLAND, VIRGINIA, W. VIRGINIA

**Major cities:** Boston, Providence, Hartford, Springfield, New York, Newark, Jersey City, Elizabeth, Paterson, Philadelphia, Camden, Trenton, Baltimore, Washington D.C., Arlington, Alexandria, Buffalo, Rochester, Syracuse, Utica, Albany, Schenectady, Troy, Scranton, Wilkes-Barre, Worcester, Cambridge, Quincy, Brockton, New Bedford, Fall River, Bridgeport, New Haven, Waterbury, Stamford, Harrisburg, Lancaster, Reading, Allentown, Bethlehem

**Water features:** Lake Ontario, Cape Cod, Cape Cod Bay, Massachusetts Bay, Long Island, Long Island Sound, Martha's Vineyard, Nantucket, Nantucket Island, Nantucket Sound, Block Island, Rhode Island Sd, Delaware Bay, Chesapeake Bay, Great South Bay, Raritan Bay, Hudson R, Delaware R, Susquehanna R, Connecticut R, Finger Lakes, Cayuga L, Seneca L, Lake George, Great Egg Harbor

Cape May

1:2.5M

0   25   50   75   100 km
0   25   50 mls

**TRINIDAD**

Galera Pt, Matura Bay, Matelot, Mt Aripo Range, St Joseph, Pt Radix, Upper Manzanilla, Galeota Pt, Grand Bay, Arima, Tunapuna, Northern Range, Princes Town, Port of Spain, San Juan, Chaguanas, San Fernando, Guayaguayare, Rio Claro, Debé, Sipana, Moruga, Point Fortin, Fullarton, Gulf of Paria

1:2.5 M

**DOMINICA** 1:2.5 M
C. Melville, Marigot, Anse Diablotin, Rosalie, Portsmouth, Roseau

**BARBADOS** 1:2.5 M
North Pt, Speightstown, Bridgetown, Holetown, Ragged Pt, South Pt, Blackman's

**TOBAGO** 1:2.5 M
Charlotteville, Speyside, Moriah, Crown Pt, Scarborough, Canaan

**ST LUCIA** 1:2.5 M
C. Melville, Gros Islet, Cap Pt, Castries, Dennery, Vieux Fort, C. Moule à Chique, Soufrière

**ST VINCENT** 1:2.5 M
Porter Pt, Georgetown, Barrouallie, Kingstown, Johnston Pt

**GRENADA** 1:2.5 M
Bedford Pt, Sauteurs, Grenville, Mt St Catherine, St George's, Pt Salines, Prickly Pt

**JAMAICA** 1:2.5 M
St Ann's Bay, Falmouth, Annotto Bay, Pt Antonio, The Blue Mtn Pk, Montego Bay, Wakefield, Cambridge, Mt Denham, The Cockpit Country, Moneague, Spanish Town, Kingston, Port Royal, Dry Harbour Mts, Ocho Rios, Chapelton, May Pen, Salt River, Portland Pt, Mandeville, Southfield, Savanna la Mar, Black River, S. Negril Point

**Windward Islands**
Guadeloupe (Fr.), Pointe-à-Pitre, Basse Terre, Marie Galante (Fr.), Montserrat (U.K.), ANTIGUA & BARBUDA, Barbuda, Martinique (Fr.), Fort-de-France, DOMINICA, Roseau, ST LUCIA, Castries, Kingstown, ST VINCENT, The Grenadines, GRENADA, St George's, BARBADOS, Bridgetown

**LESSER ANTILLES**

**LEEWARD ISLANDS**
Virgin Is (U.S.A. & U.K.), Anguilla (U.K.), St Martin (Fr. & Neth.), ST KITTS & NEVIS, St Croix (U.S.A.), Los Testigos, I. Blanquilla (Ven.), Isla Margarita

**PUERTO RICO** (U.S.A.)
San Juan, Arecibo, Caguas, Aguadilla, Cabo de Punta, Mayagüez, Ponce

**PUERTO RICO TRENCH**

**MONA PASSAGE**

**DOMINICAN REPUBLIC**
Puerto Plata, Santiago, S. Francisco, Monte Cristi, Samaná, Miches, Santo Domingo, La Romana, La Vega, Cordillera Central, I. Saona, C. Beata, I. Beata, Barahona

**HAITI**
Port-de-Paix, Cap-Haïtien, I. de la Gonâve, Port-au-Prince, La Tortue, Jacmel, Les Cayes, Massif de la Hotte, Anse d'Hainault

**Windward Passage**

**THE BAHAMAS**
Marsh Harbour, Great Abaco, Grand Bahama, Freeport, Nicholl's Town, New Providence, Nassau, Kemps Bay, Andros, Cat I., Eleuthera, Dunmore Town, Governor's Harbour, Great Exuma, San Salvador, Rum Cay, Long I., Crooked I., Acklins, Mayaguana, Great Inagua, Little Inagua, Matthew Town, Turks Is. (U.K.), Caicos Is. (U.K.), Deadman's Cay

**CUBA**
Havana, Guanabacoa, Matanzas, Güines, Pinar del Río, S. Antonio, Cienfuegos, Santa Clara, Nueva Gerona, I. de la Juventud (I. de Pinos), Sagua la Grande, Esmeralda, Morón, Sta Cruz del Sur, Victoria de las Tunas, Camagüey, Nuevitas, Banes, Holguín, Manzanillo, Palma Soriano, Bayamo, Santiago de Cuba, Guantánamo, Baracoa, Sagua de Tánamo, Cayman Islands (U.K.), Grand Cayman, Cayman Brac, Little Cayman

**CARIBBEAN SEA**

**CAYMAN TRENCH**

**VENEZUELA**
Caracas, Maracay, Valencia, Puerto Cabello, La Guaira, Maiquetía, Maracaibo, Coro, Barcelona, Cumaná, Carúpano, Güiria, Pto la Cruz, El Tigre, Ciudad Bolívar, Cd Guayana, Barinas, Barquisimeto, Trujillo, Valera, Mérida, San Fernando, Calabozo, Acarigua, Guanare, El Baúl, San Cristóbal, Orinoco, Lago de Maracaibo, Pen. de Paraguaná, G. de Venezuela, Islas los Roques (Ven.), Bonaire (Neth.), Curaçao (Neth.), Aruba (Neth.), Willemstad, Oranjestad

**COLOMBIA**
Barranquilla, Cartagena, Sta Marta, Ciénaga, Riohacha, Valledupar, Soledad, Sincelejo, Montería, Sabanalarga, El Banco, Gulf of Darién, Pen. de la Guajira

**TRINIDAD AND TOBAGO**
Scarborough, Port of Spain, San Fernando, Güiria

**FLORIDA**
Miami, Palm Beach, L. Worth, Delray Beach, Pompano Beach, Ft Lauderdale, Hollywood, Belle Glade, Naples, Key West, Marquesas Keys, Florida Keys, The Everglades, Straits of Florida, Florida Bay, Tropic of Cancer

**CENTRAL AMERICA**
PANAMA, Panama, Colón, La Chorrera, David, Pto Armuelles, Panama Canal, HONDURAS, NICARAGUA, COSTA RICA, San José, Alajuela, Heredia, Cartago, Limón, Bluefields, Puerto Cabezas, Cabo Gracias á Dios, San Juan del Norte, Rio Grande, Prinzapolca, Bonanza, Waspán, Caratasca, Brus Laguna, Swan Is. (Hond.), I. de Providencia (Col.), I. de San Andrés (Col.), I. del Maíz (Nic. & U.S.A.), Pedro Cays (Jam.), Serrana Bank

**ATLANTIC OCEAN**

1:10M
0 100 200 300 400 km
0 100 200 mls

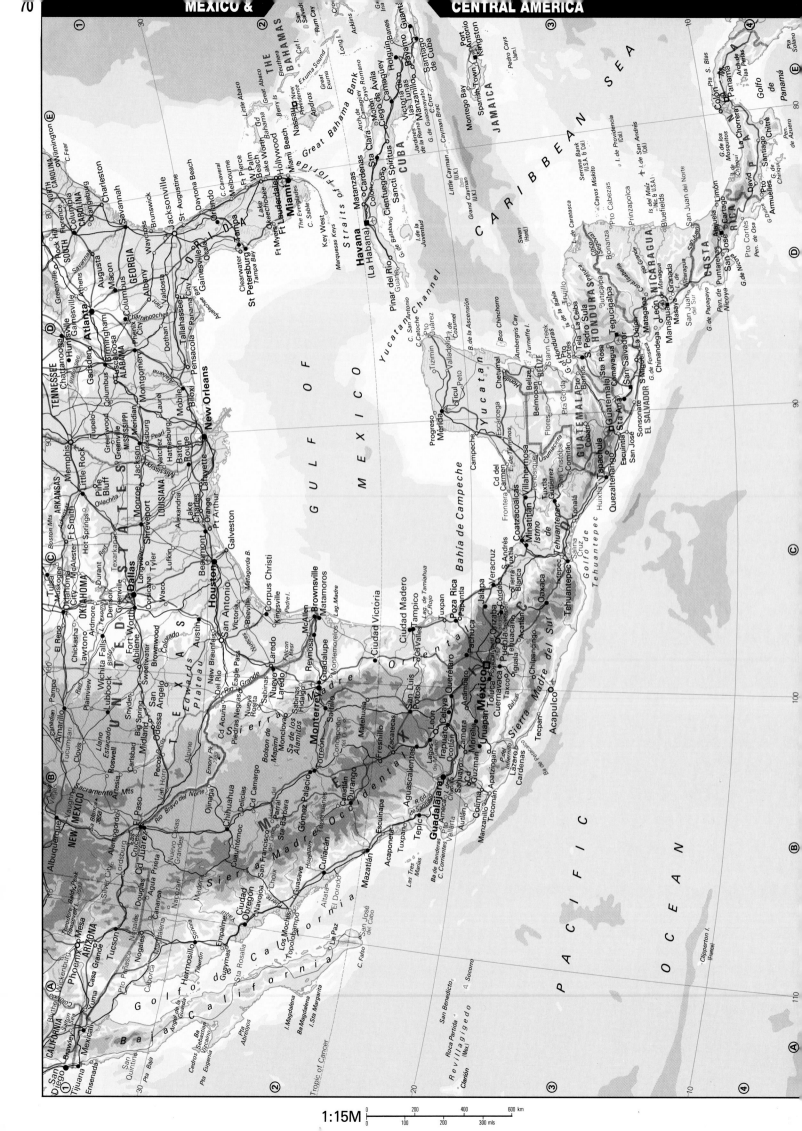

1:35M

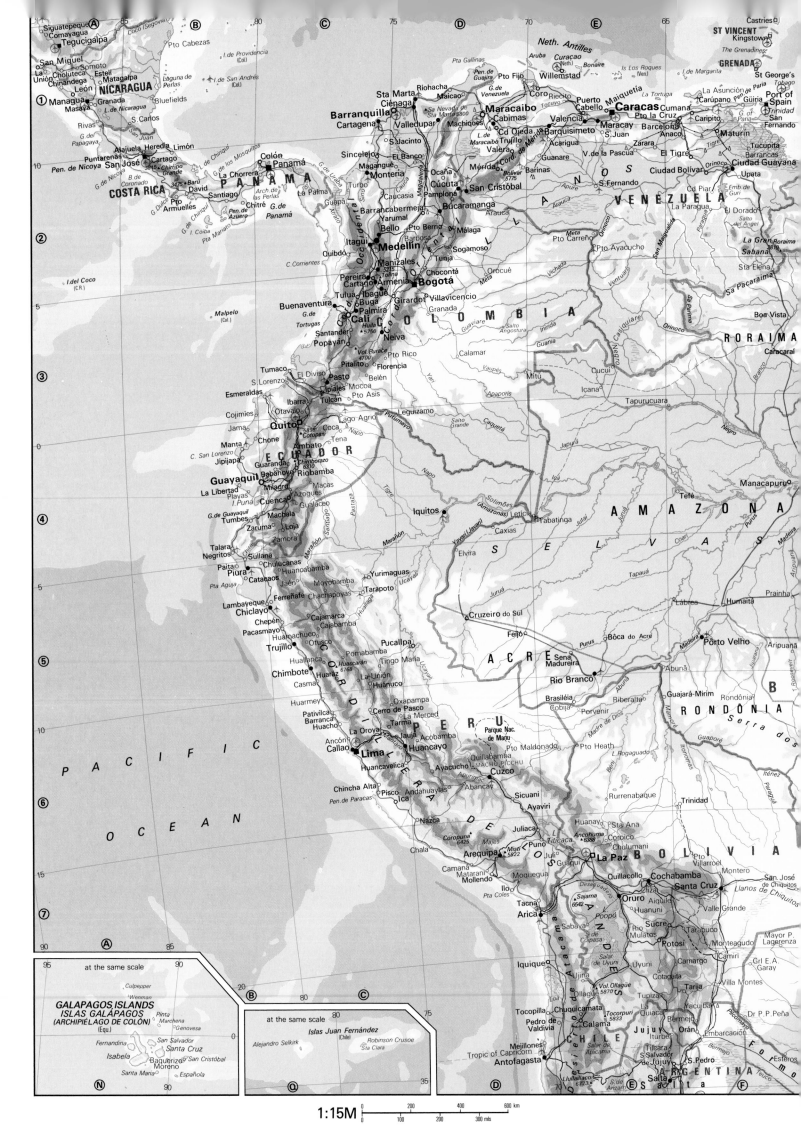

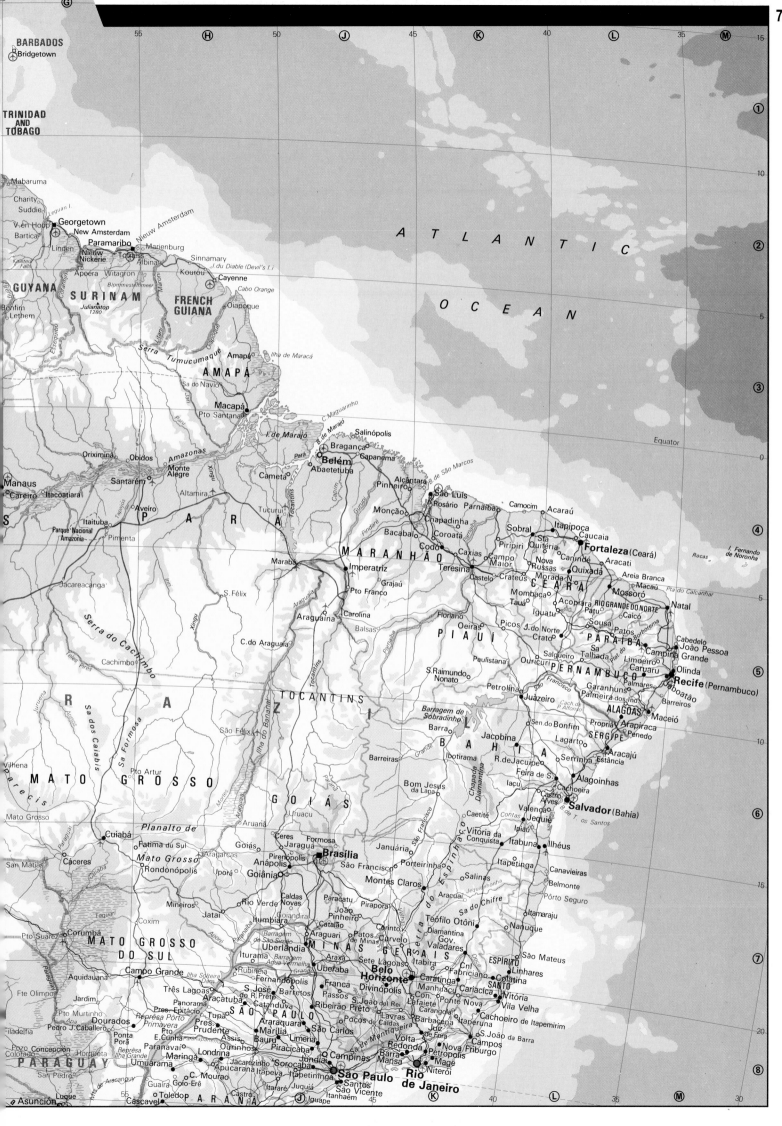

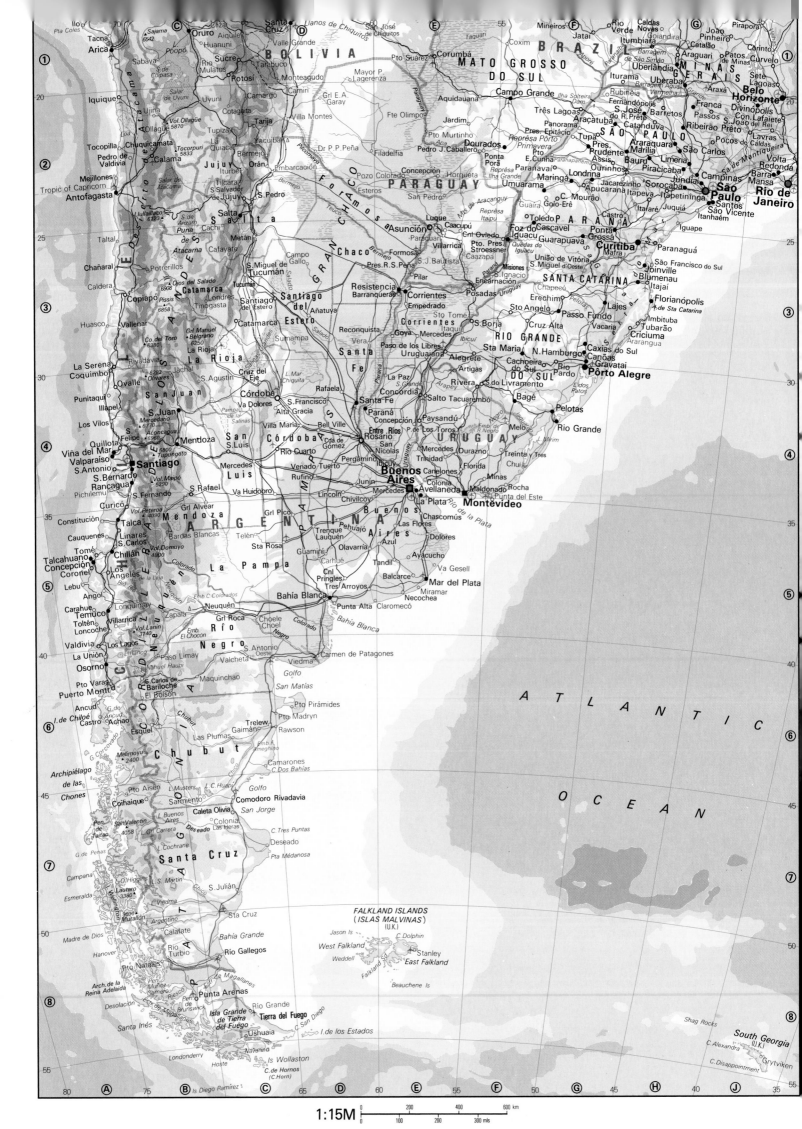

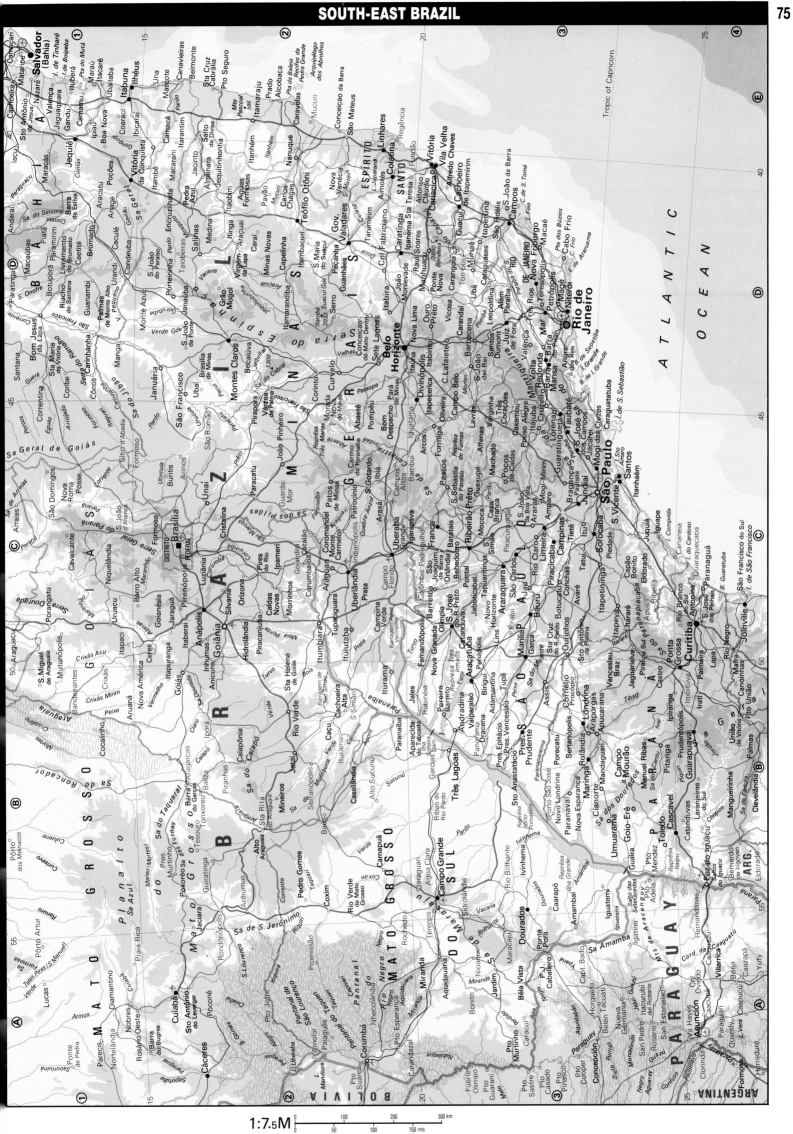

1:7.5M

0    100    200    300 km
0   50   100   150 mls

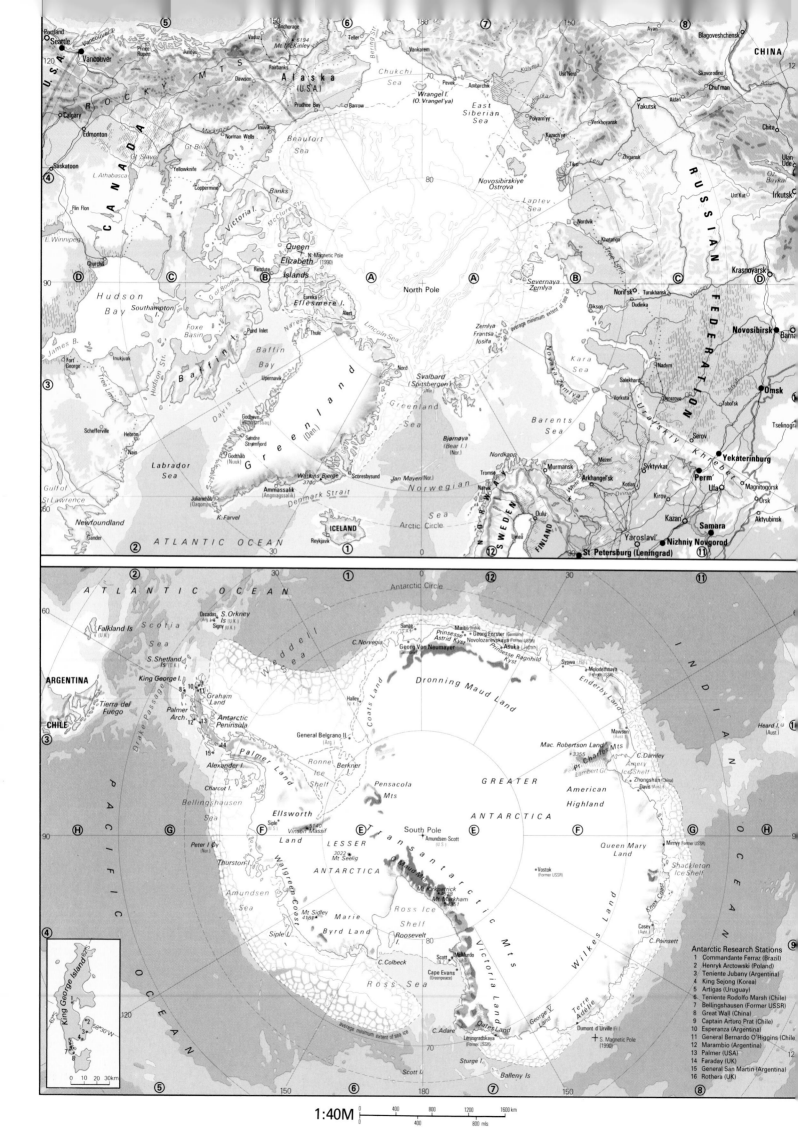

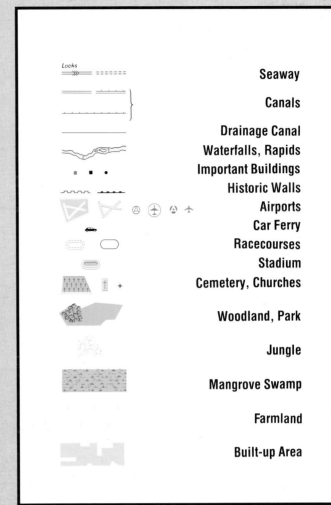

International Boundary
State Boundary
Department Boundary
City Limits
Borough, District Boundary
Military Zones
Armistice, Ceasefire Line
Demilitarised Zone
Main Railways
Other Railways
Projected Railways
Underground Railway
Aerial Cableway, Funicular
Metro Stations
Special Highway
Main Road
Secondary Road
Other Road, Street
Track
Road Tunnel
Bridge, Flyover

Seaway
Canals
Drainage Canal
Waterfalls, Rapids
Important Buildings
Historic Walls
Airports
Car Ferry
Racecourses
Stadium
Cemetery, Churches
Woodland, Park
Jungle
Mangrove Swamp
Farmland
Built-up Area

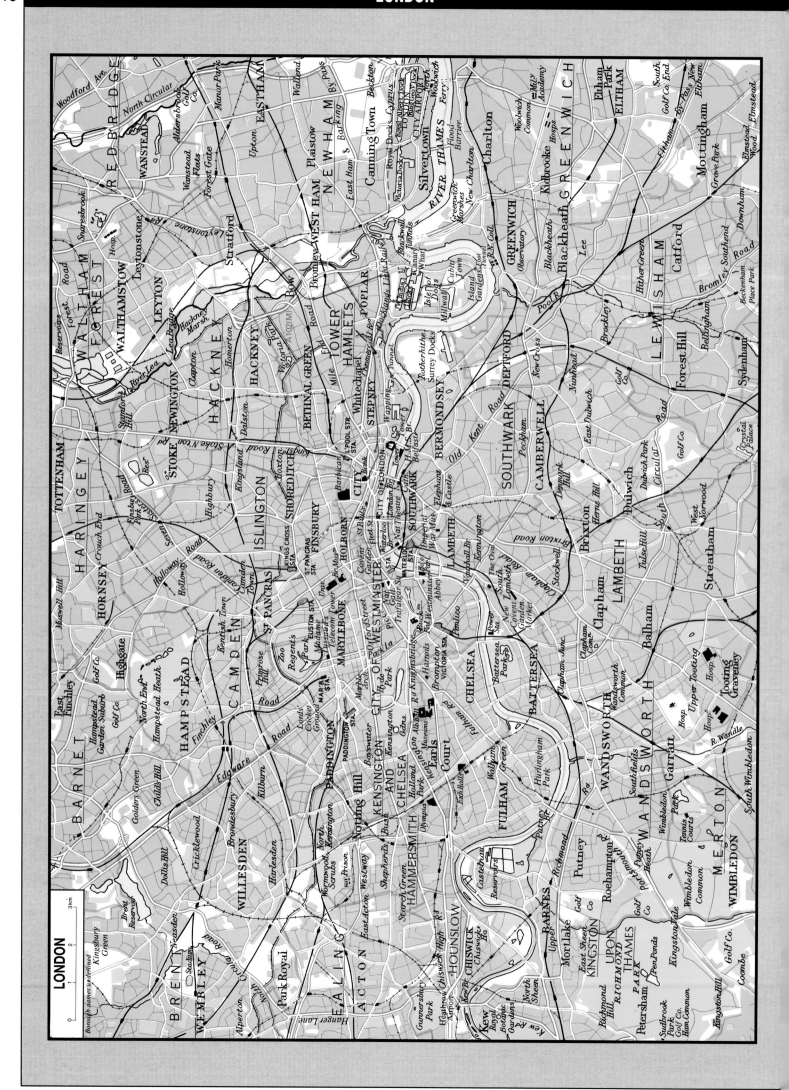

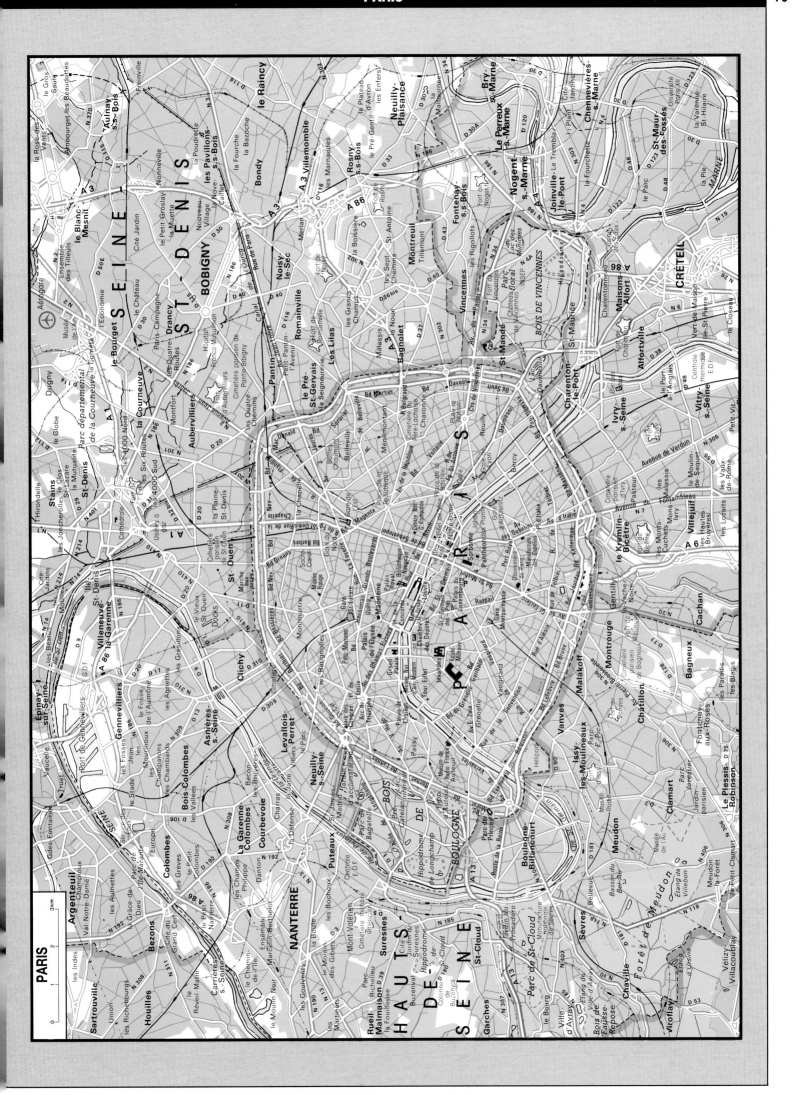

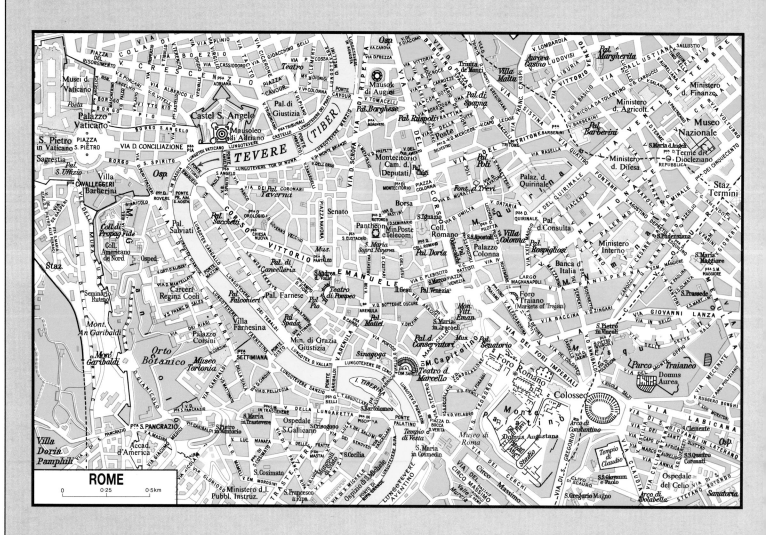

**ROME**

0    0·25    0·5km

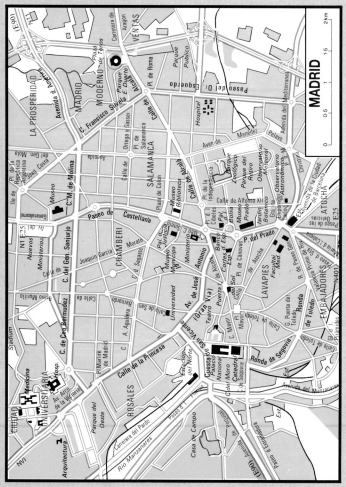

**MADRID**

2km

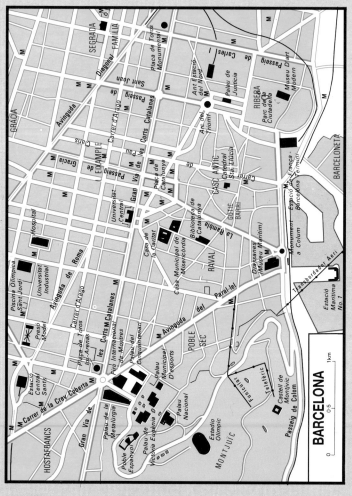

**BARCELONA**

1km

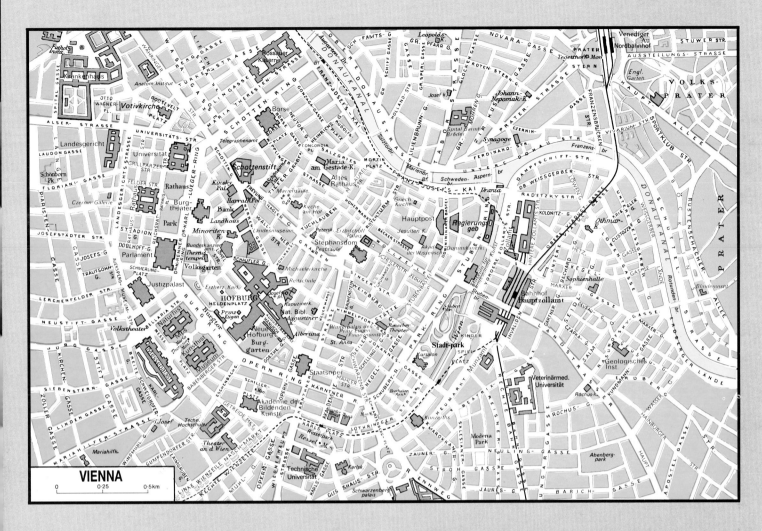

VIENNA

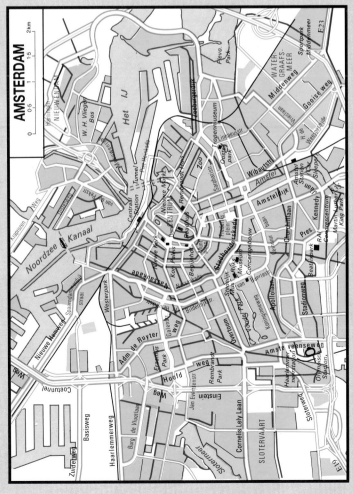

AMSTERDAM

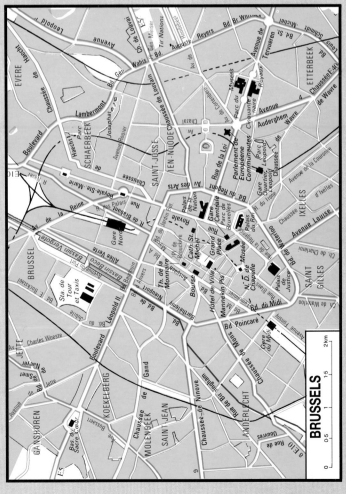

BRUSSELS

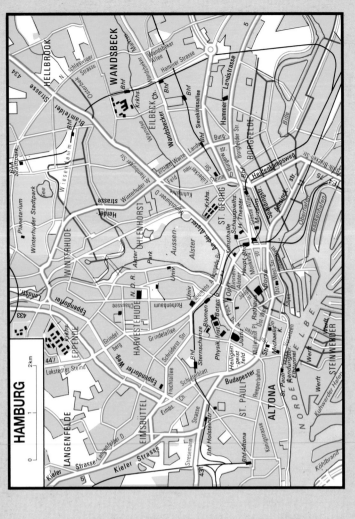

HAMBURG

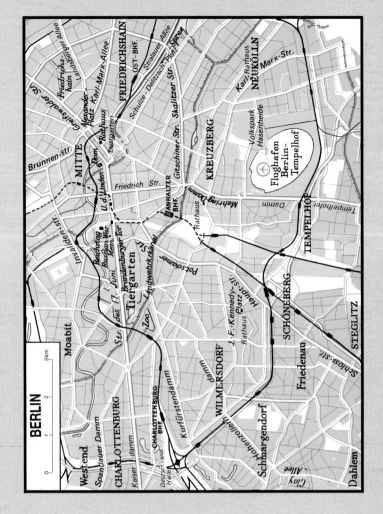

BERLIN

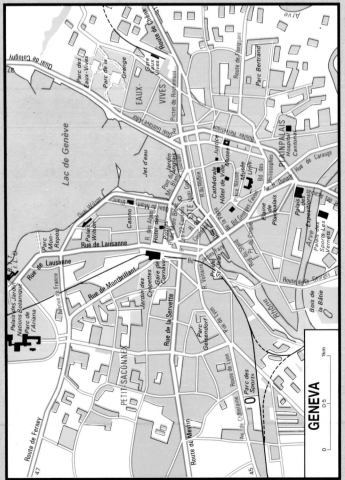

GENEVA

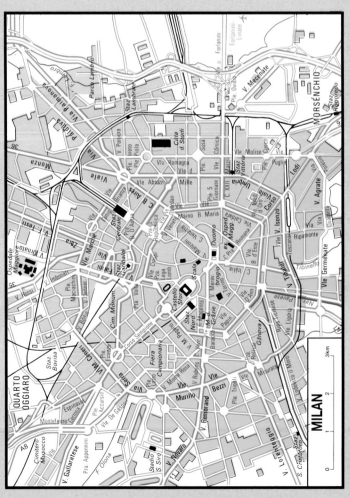

MILAN

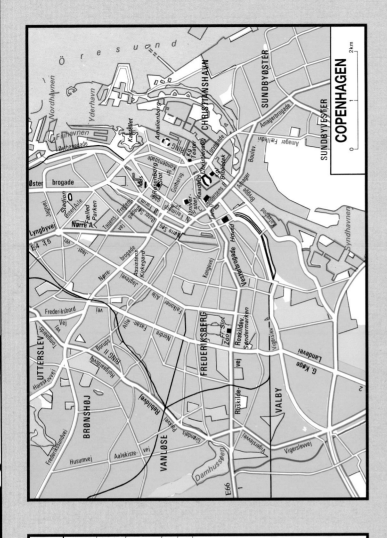

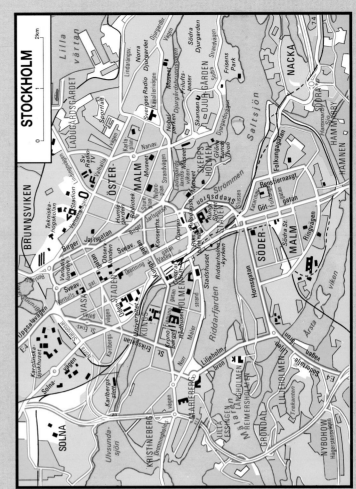

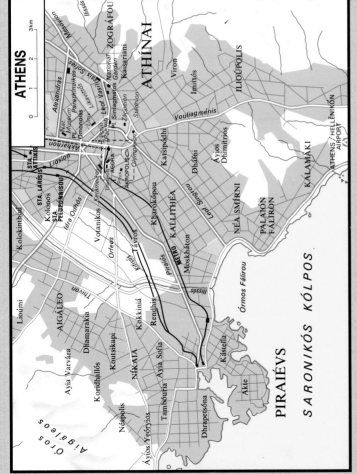

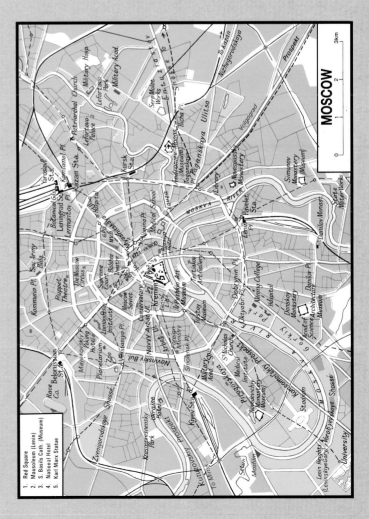

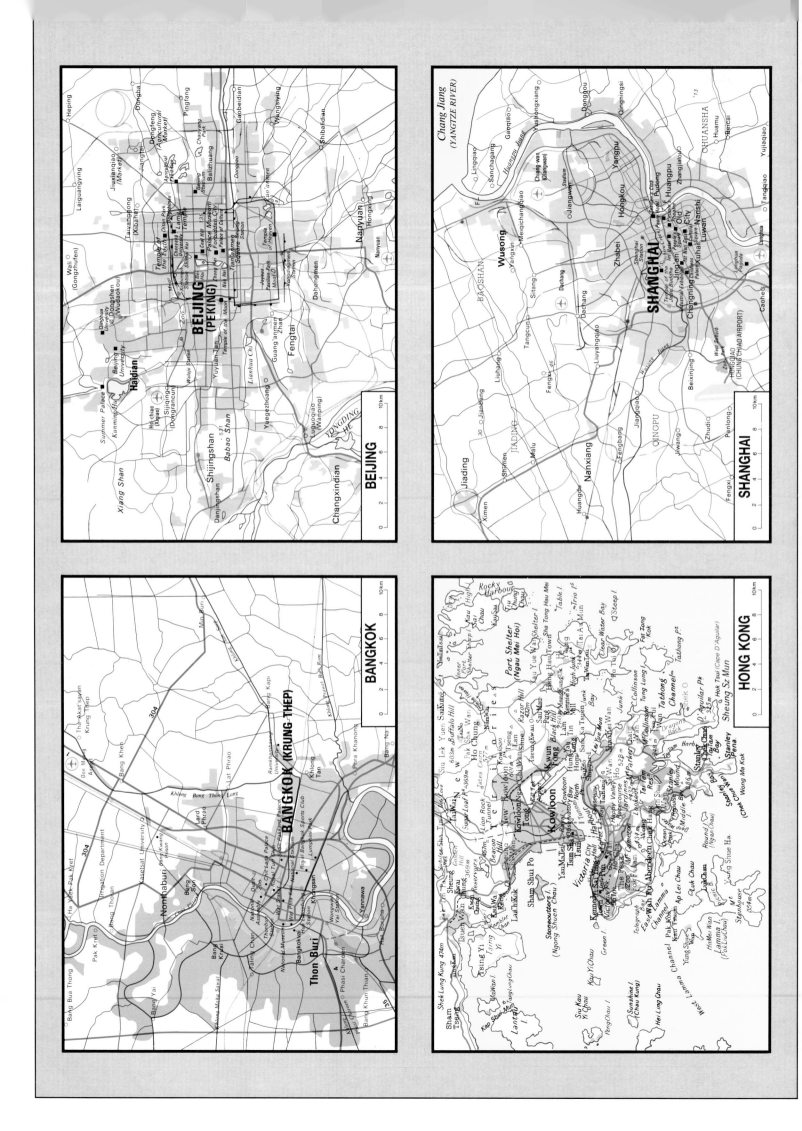

TOKYO

0   2   4   6   8   10km

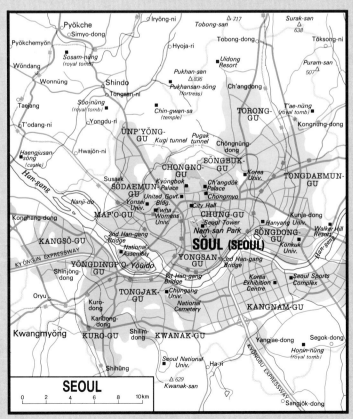

SEOUL

0   2   4   6   8   10km

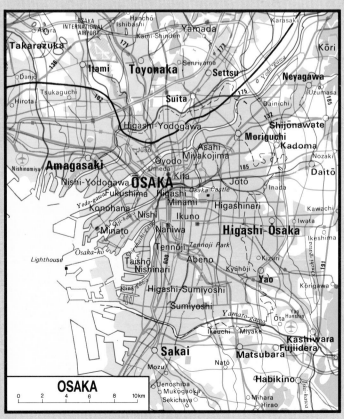

OSAKA

0   2   4   6   8   10km

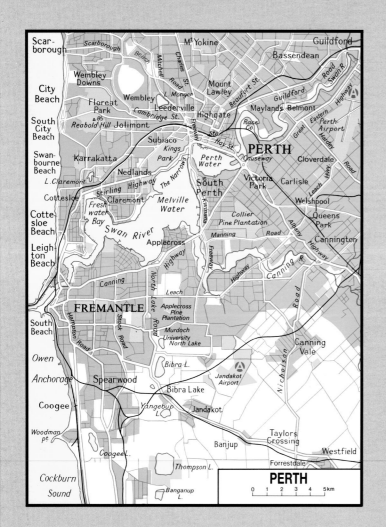

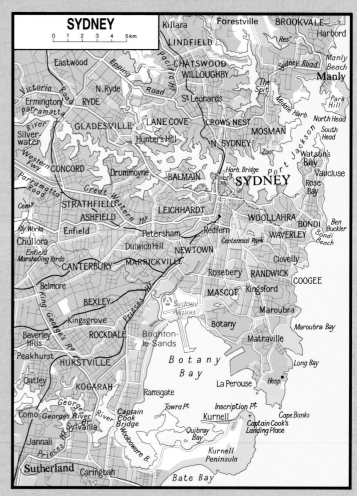

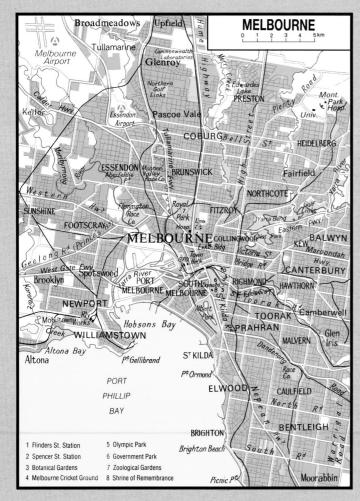

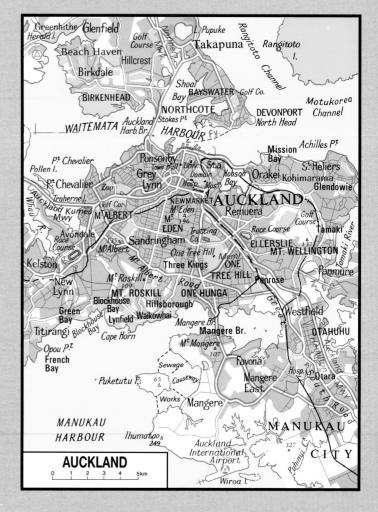

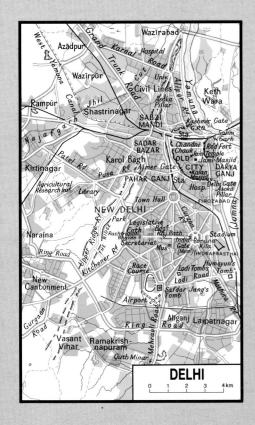

## DELHI

0 1 2 3 4km

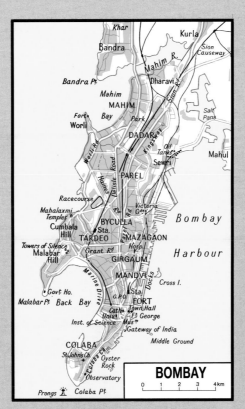

## BOMBAY

0 1 2 3 4km

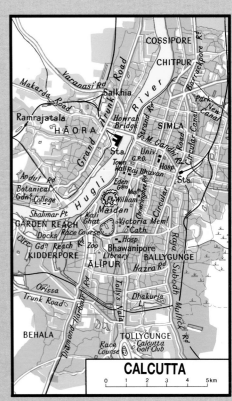

## CALCUTTA

0 1 2 3 4 5km

## SINGAPORE

0 1 2 3 4 5km

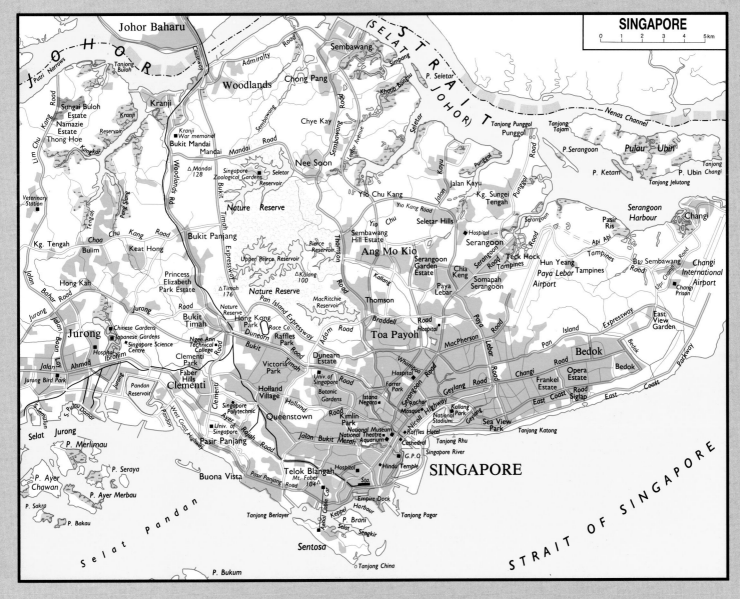

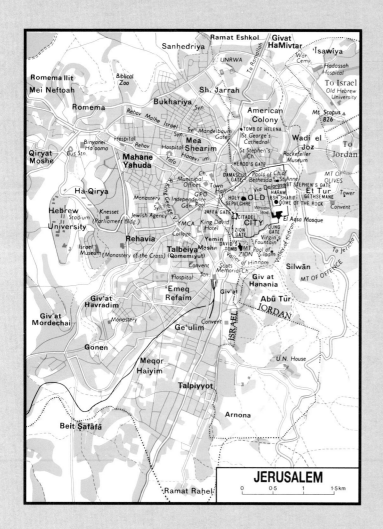

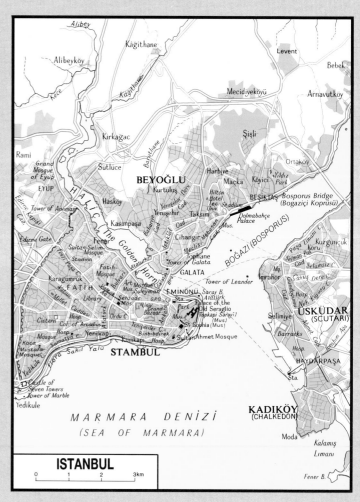

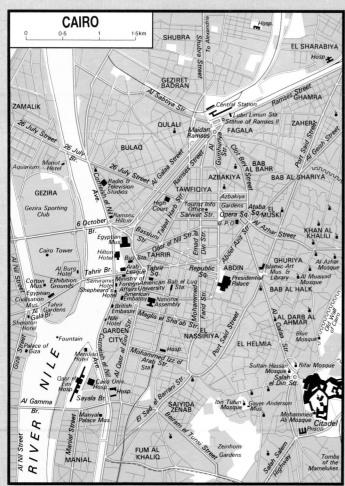

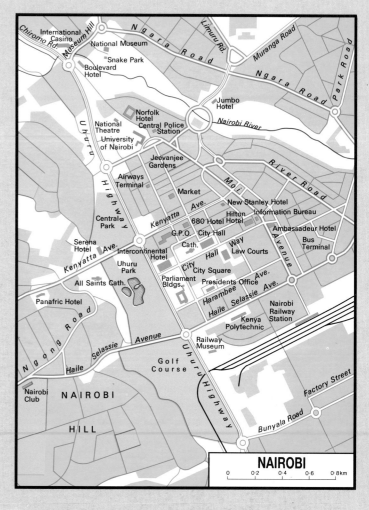

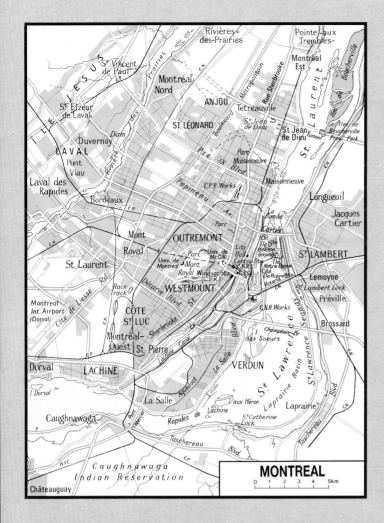

**MONTREAL**

0 1 2 3 4 5km

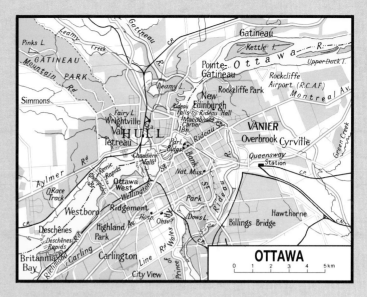

**OTTAWA**

0 1 2 3 4 5km

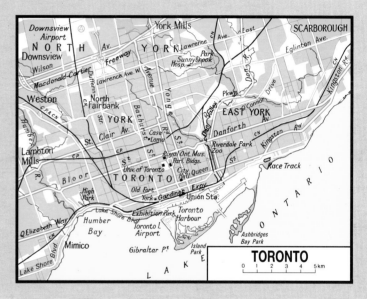

**TORONTO**

0 1 2 3 4 5km

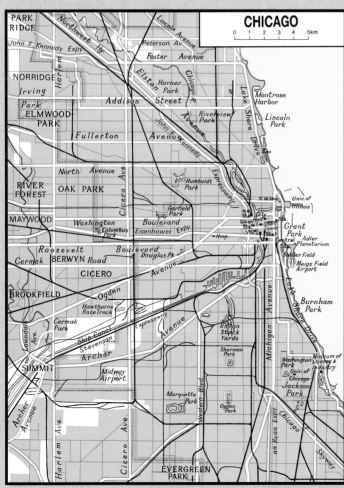

**CHICAGO**

0 1 2 3 4 5km

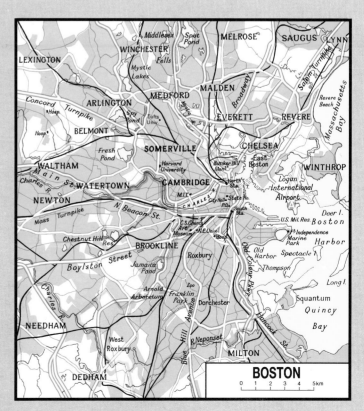

**BOSTON**

0 1 2 3 4 5km

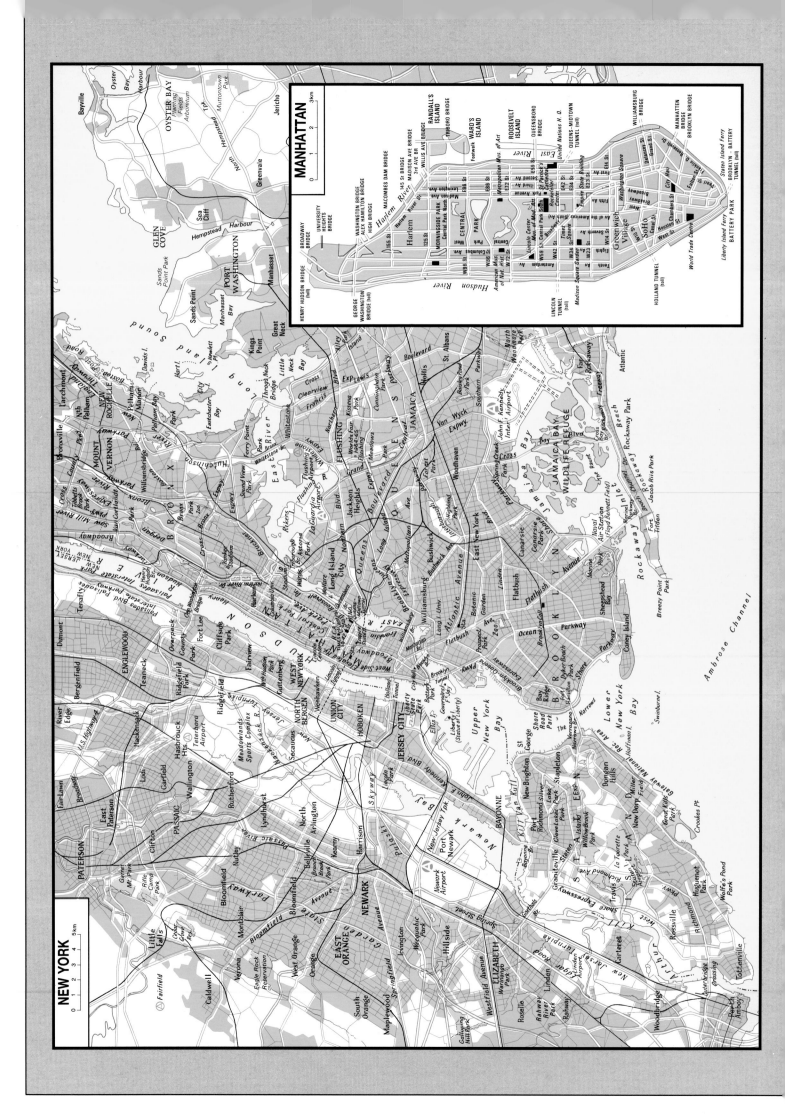

**MANHATTAN**

0  1  2  3km

BROADWAY BRIDGE
HENRY HUDSON BRIDGE (toll)
UNIVERSITY HEIGHTS BRIDGE
WASHINGTON BRIDGE
ALEX HAMILTON BRIDGE
HIGH BRIDGE
GEORGE WASHINGTON BRIDGE (toll)
MACOMBES DAM BRIDGE
145 St BRIDGE
MADISON AVE BRIDGE
3rd AVE BR
WILLIS AVE BRIDGE
RANDALL'S ISLAND
TRIBORO BRIDGE
WARD'S ISLAND
Footwork
ROOSEVELT ISLAND
QUEENSBORO BRIDGE
WILLIAMSBURG BRIDGE
MANHATTEN BRIDGE
BROOKLYN BRIDGE

Harlem River
East River
Hudson River

Harlem
Central Park North
MORNINGSIDE PARK
CENTRAL PARK
Metropolitan Mus. of Art
United Nations H.Q.
QUEENS-MIDTOWN TUNNEL (toll)

Washington Square
Greenwich Village
SoHo
Battery Park

LINCOLN TUNNEL (toll)
HOLLAND TUNNEL (toll)

Liberty Island Ferry
Staten Island Ferry
BROOKLYN-BATTERY TUNNEL (toll)

World Trade Centre

**NEW YORK**

0  1  2  3  4  5km

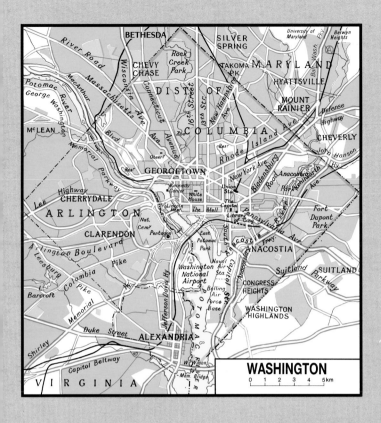

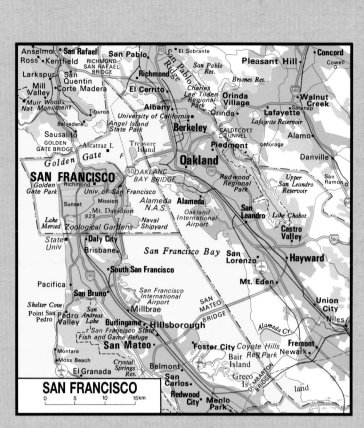

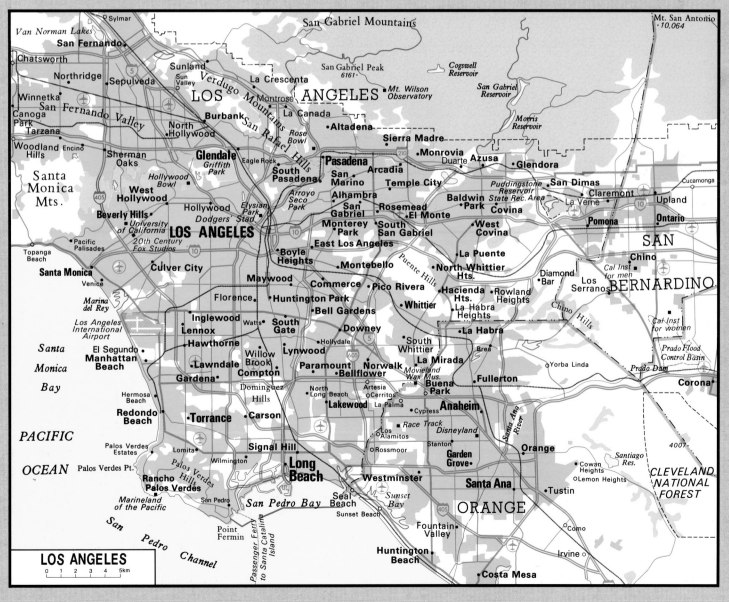

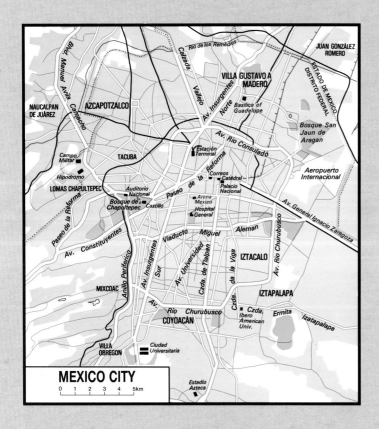

## MEXICO CITY

0 1 2 3 4 5km

## SAO PAULO

0 1 2 3 4 5km

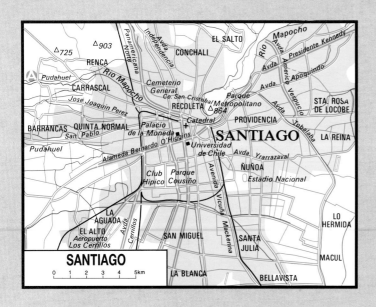

## SANTIAGO

0 1 2 3 4 5km

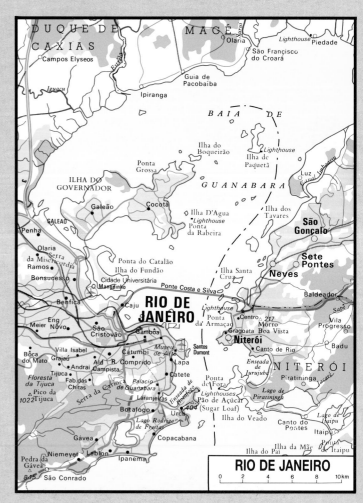

## RIO DE JANEIRO

0 2 4 6 8 10km

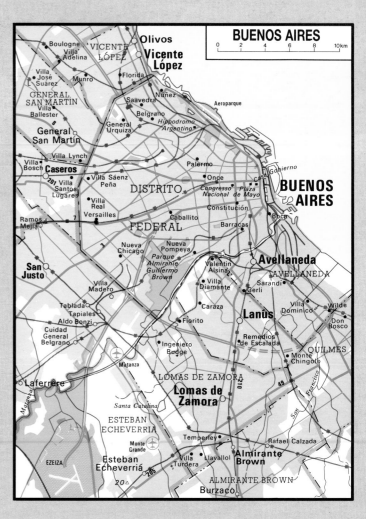

## BUENOS AIRES

0 2 4 6 8 10km

The roman alphabet is used world-wide. Yet the sounds of Latin from which it was inherited were far too few to allow the alphabet to be applied unaltered to the languages of the world. As a result numerous modifications have been made by adding supplementary letters, by changing the original letters or by adding accents or other diacritical signs.

This brief guide is intended to give no more than an indication of the English language equivalents of the more important letters, or combinations of letters in the various alphabets used in the Atlas. An English word is added in brackets to illustrate the sound intended.

## FRENCH
There are four nasal vowels:
am an aen em en aon      ā
aim ain en eim ein im in    ē
om on                 ō
um un                ēũ
ā ē ō ēũ are like a in hart; e in met; o in corn; oo in book pronounced nasally.
au, eau = o (no); é = ay (lay); è, ê, = e (met); oi oî = wa (wand)
c + a = k; c + e or i = ç = s (sit)
·ch = sh (fresh); g + a, o or u = g (got)
g + e or i = j = zh*; gn = ni (onion)
gu = g (got); gü = gw (iguana)
ll = l or y; qu = k; th = t
u = between e in few and oo in too

## SPANISH
c + a, o or u = k; c + e or i = th (thin) or s (sit)
ch = ch (cheese); g + a, o or u = g (got)
g + e or i = kh*; gu + a, o or u = gw (iguana)
gu + e or i = g (got); j = kh*; ñ = ny (canyon);
ll = y (yes)
qu + a, o or u = kw (quick); qu + e or i = k (kite)
y = y (yes); z = th (thin) or z depending on dialect

## ITALIAN
c + a, o or u = k; c + e or i = ch (cheese)
ch = k
g + a, o or u = g (got); g + e or i = j (jet)
gh = g (got); gli = lli (million)
qu = kw (quick); z = ts or dz

## ROMANIAN
ă = a in relative
â = i in ravine
c + a, o or u = k
c + e or i = ch (cheese); ch = k
g + a, o or u = g (got); g + e or i = j (jet)
ş = sh (fresh); ţ = ts (sits)

## PORTUGUESE
ã, ãe = French ē
õa, õe = French ō
c + a, o or u = k; c + e or i = s
ç = s; ch = sh (fresh)
ih = lli (million)
x = sh (fresh); z = z but = zh when final

## GERMAN
ä = e (met); au = ow (down)
äu = oy (boy); c = ts (sits)
ch = kh*; ei, ey = eye (= y in why)
eu = oy (boy); g = g (got)
ie = ie (retrieve); j = y (yes)
ö = oo (book); s = z but s when final
sch = sh (fresh); sp, st = shp, sht
ü = French u; v = f; w = v; z = ts (sits)

## DUTCH
aa ee are long vowels
c + e or i or z = s, otherwise k
ij = eye (= y in why)

## SCANDINAVIAN
å = aw (law); ä = e (met)
ø = oo (book); øj = oy (boy)
j = y (yes)

## ICELANDIC
ð = dh = th (then)
hv = kw; ll = tl; p = th

## FINNISH
ay = eye (= y in why)
j = y; y = French u; w = v

## HUNGARIAN
a = aw (law); cs = ch (cheese); ccs = chch;
gy = d + y (dew)
j = y; ny = ny (canyon)
s = sh (fresh); ss = shsh
sz = s (sit); ty = t + y (yes)
zs = zh*
ai = e (met); av = au or av
dh = th (then); th = th (thin)
kh = kh*; oi = i (ravine)
ou = oo (too)

## TURKISH
c = j (jet); ç = ch (cheese)
ö = oo (book); ş = sh
ü = French u
ı and i = i (ravine)

## RUSSIAN
ay = a + y (yes)
e = e or ye
ë = yaw; ëy = yoy
ch = ch (cheese); sh = sh (fresh)
sh ch = sh ch (fresh cheese)
ts = ts (sits)
ya = ya (yam); z = z (zoo)
zh = zh (measure)
' = sound of y (yes)
" = silent

## OTHER SLAVONIC

| §S-C | Pol | Cz | |
|---|---|---|---|
| c | c | c | = ts (sits) |
| | ć | | = ts + y (yes) |
| č | cz | č | = ch (cheese) |
| ć | | | = t + y (yes) |
| đ | | ď | = d + y (yes) |
| | | ě | = e (mother) |
| h | ch | ch | = kh* |
| j | j | j | = y (yes) |
| | ł | | = w (wood) |
| nj | ń | ň | = ny (canyon) |
| | | ř | = rzh* |
| š | sz | š | = sh (fresh) |
| | | ť | = t + y (yes) |
| ž | ż, rz, ź | ž | = zh* |

## ARABIC
long vowels have a macron (bar), ā
dh = th (then)
h = h (hat); j = (jet)
gh = French r, pronounce as g (got)
kh = kh* q = g (got)
' and ' are best treated as glottal stops
ḍ ḥ ṣ ṭ ẓ = d, h, s, t, z
Note: 1. in Egypt and Sudan g = g (got)
        2. in NW Africa Dj = j (jet)
                   ou = w (wadi)

## FARSI (IRAN)
Can be read as Arabic above. Stress is on the last syllable.

## SOMALI
long vowels are aa, ee, ii, oo, uu
c is silent = glottal stop
dh = th (then)
g = g (got); q = k (kite)
sh = sh (fresh); w = w (wadi)
x = kh*

## MALAY – INDONESIAN
As English except
c = ch (cheese)

## CHINESE (PINYIN)
q = ch (church); c = ts (sits)
x = hs = h + s

*zh = s in measure;
*kh = ch in Scottish loch
    = German ch in achtung

§S-C = Serbo-Croat
**Pol** = Polish
**Cz** = Czech

**ABLATION**   The loss of water from ice and snow surfaces, by melting and run-off, calving of icebergs, evaporation and snow-blowing.

**ABRASION**   The wearing down or away of rocks by friction.

**ABSOLUTE HUMIDITY**   The amount of water vapour in a specified amount of air, frequently expressed as grams of water vapour per kilogram of dry air containing the vapour.

**ABYSSAL**   Usually applied to the very deep parts of the oceans, over 3km below the surface.

**ACCRETION**   The growth of objects by collection of additional material, usually of smaller size. Ice particles in the atmosphere can grow by this process.

**ACID PRECIPITATION**   Rain and snow with a pH of less than 5.6.

**ADVECTION**   Movement of a property in air and water by their motion. Usually applied to horizontal rather than vertical motion.

**AEOLIAN**   Related to winds. Thus aeolian geomorphology is concerned with the processes whereby wind removes, distributes and deposits materials of the earth's surface.

**AGGLOMERATE**   A rock made of small pieces of lava that have been fused by heat.

**AGGRADATION**   The building up of a land surface by deposition of material by wind, water or ice.

**AGGREGATE**   A loose collection of rock fragments.

**ALLUVIAL PLAIN**   A plain, usually at low altitude, made of alluvium.

**ANTICYCLONE**   An extensive region of relatively high atmospheric pressure, usually a few thousand kilometres across, in which the low level winds spiral outwards, clockwise in the northern hemisphere and anticlockwise in the southern hemisphere.

**ARCHIPELAGO**   A sea or lake containing numerous islands, such as the area between Sumatra and the Philippines.

**ARTESIAN WELL**   A well which taps water held under pressure in rocks below the surface. The pressure results in a well water level higher than the highest part of the water-bearing rocks.

**ATOLL**   A coral reef surrounding a lagoon found in the tropical oceans.

**AURORA BOREALIS** (Northern Lights)   Flashing lights in the atmosphere some 400km above polar regions caused by solar particles being trapped in the earth's magnetic field.

**AVALANCHE**   The sudden and rapid movement of ice, snow, earth and rock down a slope.

**AZIMUTH**   Horizontal angle between two directions.

**B**

**BADLANDS**   Highly dissected landscapes, usually associated with poorly consolidated materials and sparse vegetation cover.

**BAR**   A usually sandy feature, lying parallel to the coast and frequently underwater.

**BARCHAN**   A crescentic sand dune whose horns point in the direction of dune movement.

**BAROGRAPH**   An instrument for recording atmospheric pressure. The output is a graph of pressure changes through time.

**BAROMETER**   An instrument for measuring atmospheric pressure. The reading is either by measuring the height of a column of mercury or by the compression or expansion of a series of vacuum chambers.

**BARRIER REEF**   A coral reef characterized by the presence of a lagoon or body of water between it and the associated coastline.

**BASALT**   A fine-grained and dark coloured igneous rock.

**BASE LEVEL**   The lower limit to the operation of erosional processes generating on land – usually defined with reference to the role of running water. Sea level is the most general form of base level.

**BASIN**   An area of land encompassing the water flow into any specific river channel – hence usually known as a drainage basin.

**BATHOLITH**   A large mass of intrusive igneous rock.

**BATHYMETRY**   Measurement of water depth.

**BAUXITE**   The main ore of aluminium.

**BEACH**   A coastal accumulation of various types of sediment, usually sands and pebbles.

**BEAUFORT SCALE**   A scale of wind speed devised by Admiral Sir Francis Beaufort based on effects of winds on ships. Later modified to include land-based phenomena.

**BENCH MARK**   A reference point used in the measurement of land height in topographic surveying.

**BENTHIC**   Relating to plants, animals and other organisms that inhabit the floors of lakes, seas and oceans.

**BERGSCHRUND**   The crevasse existing at the head of a glacier because of the movement of glacier ice away from the rock wall.

**BIGHT**   A bend in a coast forming an open bay, or the bay itself.

**BIOMASS**   The mass of biological material present per plant or animal, per community or per unit area.

**BIOME**   A mixed community of plants and animals occupying a large area of continental size.

**BIOSPHERE**   The zone at the interface of the earth's surface, ocean and atmosphere where life is found.

**BIOTA**   The entire collection of species or organisms, plants and animals found in a given region.

**BISE**   A cold, dry northerly to north-easterly wind occurring in the mountains of Central Europe in winter.

**BLACK EARTH**   A black soil rich in humus, found extensively in temperate grasslands such as the Russian Steppes.

**BLOW HOLE**   Vertical shaft leading from a sea cave to the surface. Air and water are frequently forced through it by advancing seas.

**BORE**   A large solitary wave which moves up funnel-shaped rivers and estuaries.

**BOREAL**   A descriptive term, usually of climate and forest, to characterize conditions in middle to high latitudes.

**BOURNE**   A river channel on chalk terrain that flows after heavy rain.

**BUTTE**   A small, flat-topped and often steep-sided hill standing isolated on a flat plain. *(see picture below)*

**C**

**CALDERA**   A depression, usually several kilometres across.

**CALVING**   The breaking away of a mass of ice from a floating glacier or ice shelf to form an iceberg.

**CANYON**   A steep sided valley, usually found in semi-arid and arid areas.

**CAPE**   An area of land jutting out into water, frequently as a peninsula or promontory.

**CARDINAL POINTS**   The four principal compass points, north, east, south and west.

**CATARACT**   A large waterfall over a precipice.

**CHINOOK**   A warm, dry wind that blows down the eastern slopes of the Rocky Mountains of North America.

*Above* Butte, Monument Valley, Arizona USA. This type of flat-topped, steep sided hill is characteristic of the arid plateau region of the western United States.

**CIRQUE OR CORRIE**   A hollow, open downstream but bounded upstream by a curved, steep headwall, with a gently sloping floor. Found in areas that have been glaciated.

**CLIMATE**   The long-term atmospheric characteristics of a specified area.

**CLOUD**   A collection of a vast number of small water droplets or ice crystals or both in the atmosphere.

**COL**   A pass or saddle between two mountain peaks.

**COLD FRONT**   A zone of strong horizontal temperature gradient in the atmosphere moving such that, for the surface observer, cold air replaces warm.

**CONDENSATION**   The process of formation of liquid water from water vapour.

**CONFLUENCE**   The 'coming together' of material

flows, most usually used in fluids such as the atmosphere and oceans.

**CONGLOMERATE** A rock which comprises or contains rounded pebbles more than about 2mm in diameter.

**CONTINENTAL DRIFT** The movement of continents relative to each other. (See *Plate Tectonics*)

**CONTINENTAL SHELF** A portion of the continental crust below sea level that slopes gently seaward forming an extension of the adjacent coastal plain separated from the deep ocean by the steeply sloping continental slope.

**CONTINENTAL SLOPE** Lies on the seaward edge of the continental shelf and slopes steeply to the ocean floor.

**CONTOUR** A line on a map that joins points of equal height or equal depth.

**CONVECTION CURRENT** A current resulting from convection which is a mode of mass transport within a fluid (especially heat) resulting in movement and mixing of properties of that fluid.

**CONVERGENCE** The opposite of divergence which is the outflowing mass of fluid. Hence convergence is the inflowing of such mass.

**CORAL REEF** Large structures fringing islands and coastlines consisting mostly of corals and algae.

**CORDILLERA** A system of mountain ranges consisting of a number of more or less parallel chains of mountain peaks – such as in the Rocky Mountains.

**CRATER** A depression at the top of a volcano where a vent carrying lava and gasses reaches the surface.

**CRATON** A continental area that has experienced little internal deformation in the last 600 million years.

**CREVASSE** A deep fissure in the surface of a body of ice.

**CYCLONE** A region of relatively low atmospheric pressure about 2000 km across around which air rotates anticlockwise in the northern hemisphere and clockwise in the southern.

## D

**DATUM LEVEL** Something (such as a fixed point or assumed value) used as a basis for calculating or measuring. Frequently a height of ground relative to which other heights are assessed.

**DECLINATION** Angular distance north or south from the equator measured along a line of longitude.

**DECIDUOUS FOREST** Forest in which the trees shed their leaves at a particular time, season or growth stage. The most common manifestation is the shedding in winter.

**DEFLATION** The process whereby the wind removes fine materials from the surface of a beach or desert.

**DEGRADATION** The lowering and often flattening of a land surface by erosion.

**DELTA** Accumulations of sediment deposited at the mouths of rivers. The Nile and Mississippi deltas are two famous examples.

**DENUDATION** The laying bare of underlying rocks or strata by the removal of overlying material.

**DEPOSITION** The laying down of material, which, in geomorphological terms, was previously carried by wind, liquid water or ice.

**DEPRESSION** See *cyclone*

**DESALINIZATION** To take out the salt content of a material. Usually applied to the extraction of salt from sea water to give fresh water.

**DESERT** An area in which vegetation cover is sparse or absent and precipitation is low in amount. Deserts can be hot or cold.

**DISCHARGE** The volume of flow of fluid in a given time period.

**DISSECTED PLATEAU** A relatively flat, high level area of land which has been cut by streams.

**DIURNAL** Occurring everyday or having a daily cycle.

**DIVERGENCE** A spreading of material. Frequently found in high pressure areas (anticyclones) in the atmosphere where air spirals outwards from the centre.

**DOLDRUMS** A zone of light, variable winds and low atmospheric pressure near or slightly north of the equator.

**DRAINAGE** The flow of material (usually a fluid) over the earth's surface due to the force of gravity. Most familiarly seen as rivers.

**DRIFT ICE** Ice bodies drifting in ocean currents.

**DROUGHT** Dryness caused by lack of precipitation, most easily seen in the hot, dry desert areas of the world.

**DROWNED VALLEY** A valley which has been filled with water due to a rise of sea level relative to the level with which the river mouth was previously in accord.

**DRUMLIN** A depositional landform, usually made of glacially-derived material, which has been streamlined by the passage of overlying ice.

**DRY VALLEY** A valley which is seldom, if ever, occupied by a stream channel.

**DUNE** An accumulation of sand deposited and shaped by wind.

**DUST** Solid particles carried in suspension by the atmosphere.

**DYKE** A sheet-like intrusion of igneous rock, usually oriented vertically, which cuts across the structural planes of the host rocks.

## E

**EARTH PILLAR** A pinnacle of soil or other unconsolidated material that is protected from erosion by the presence of a stone at the top.

**EARTHQUAKE** A series of shocks and tremors resulting from the sudden release of pressure along active faults and in areas of volcanic activity.

**EBB TIDE** Tide receding to or at its lowest point.

**ECLIPSE, LUNAR** The total or partial obscuring of the Moon by the Earth lying on a line between the Moon and the Sun.

**ECLIPSE, SOLAR** The total or partial obscuring of the Sun by the Moon lying on a line between the Sun and the Earth.

**ECOLOGY** A branch of science that studies the relations of plants and animals with each other and with their non-living environment.

**ECOSYSTEM** An entity within which ecological relations operate.

**EPICENTRE** The point on the earth's surface which lies directly above the focus of an earthquake.

**EQUINOX** The time of year when the sun is directly overhead at noon at the equator.

**ERG** A sand desert.

**EROSION** The group of processes whereby debris is loosened or dissolved and removed from any part of the earth's surface.

**ERRATIC** A rock that has been carried to its present location by a glacier.

**ESCARPMENT** A linear land form with one steep side (scarp slope) and one less steep side (dip slope).

**ESKER** A sinuous ridge of coarse gravel which has been deposited by a meltwater stream normally flowing underneath a glacier.

**ESTUARY** The sections of a river which flow into the sea and are influenced by tidal currents.

**EVAPORATION** The diffusion of water vapour into the atmosphere from freely exposed water surfaces.

**EXFOLIATION** The weathering of a rock by the peeling off of surface layers.

## F

**FATHOM** A unit of length equal to six feet, most usually used in measuring depth of water.

**FAULT** A crack or fissure in rock, resulting from tectonic movement.

**FAUNA** Animals or animal life of an area.

**FEN** A low lying area partially covered by water which is characterized by accumulations of peat.

**FJORD** A glacially eroded valley whose floor is occupied by the sea.

**FIRTH** A sea inlet, particularly in Scotland.

**FLORA** Plants or plant life in an area.

**FLUVIOGLACIAL** The activity of rivers which are fed by water melted from glaciers.

**FOG** An accumulation of water droplets or ice crystals in the atmosphere such that visibility is reduced to 1km or less.

**FÖHN WIND** A strong, gusty, warm, down-slope wind which occurs on the lee side of a mountain range.

**FOLD** A bend in rock strata resulting from movement of the crustal rocks.

**FOOD CHAIN** The transfer of food from one type of organism to another in a sequence.

**FORD** A shallow part of a river that allows easy crossing.

**FRACTURE** The splitting of material into parts: usually concerned with geological materials.

**FRAZIL ICE** Fine spikes of ice in suspension in water, usually associated with the freezing of sea water.

**FRONT** A transition zone between air of different density, temperature and humidity.

**FROST** A situation resulting from air temperatures falling to 0°C – either in the air (air frost) or at the ground (ground frost).

**FUMAROLE** A small, volcanic vent through which hot gasses are emitted.

# G

**GABBRO** A basic igneous rock, usually coarse grained and dark grey to black in colour.

**GEEST** Ancient alluvial sediments which still cover the land surfaces on which they were originally deposited.

**GEODESY** The determination of the size and shape of the earth by survey and calculation.

**GEOID** The shape of the earth at mean sea level.

**GEOLOGY** Science that deals with the nature and origin of the earth's rocks and sediments.

**GEOMORPHOLOGY** Science that deals with the nature and origin of landforms of the earth's surface.

**GEOSYNCLINE** A very large depression, tens or hundreds of kilometres across and up to ten kilometres deep, the floor of which is built up by sedimentation.

**GEYSER** A spring of geothermally heated water that erupts intermittently due to pressures beneath the surface. Old Faithful in Yellowstone National Park, USA, is the most famous example.

**GLACIATION** The incursion of ice into (or over) a landscape resulting in a whole suite of glacial processes operating thereupon.

**GLACIER** A large body of ice, in a valley or covering a much larger area. The largest are found in polar regions.

**GLEN** Valley. Term especially used in Scotland.

**GNEISS** A coarse-grained igneous rock that has been metamorphosed.

**GONDWANALAND** A large continent which it is thought was split very early in geological time to form parts of Africa, Australia, Antarctica, South America and India.

**GORGE** A deep and narrow section of a river valley, usually with very steep sides.

**GRAVEL** Loose, rounded fragments of rock.

**GREAT CIRCLE** A circle formed on the surface of the earth by the intersection of a plane through the centre of the earth with the surface. Lines of longitude and the Equator are great circles.

**GROUND FROST** See *frost*

**GROUND WATER** All water (gaseous, liquid or solid) lying below the earth's surface and not chemically combined with the minerals present.

**GROYNE** A man-made barrier running across a beach and into the sea; constructed to reduce erosion of the beach by longshore currents.

**GULF** A part of the sea that is partly or almost completely enclosed by land.

**GULLY** A linear depression worn in the earth by running water after rains.

**GUYOT** A flat-topped mountain on the sea floor which does not reach the sea surface.

**GYRE** Large circulations of water in the world's oceans, involving the major currents.

# H

**HAFF** A coastal lagoon separated from the open seas by a sand spit.

**HAIL** Solid precipitation which falls as ice particles from cumulonimbus clouds. Contrasts markedly with snow.

**HEMISPHERE** Half of the earth, usually thought of in terms of its surface. The most familiar are the northern and southern hemispheres, bounded by the Equator.

**HORIZON** Apparent junction of earth and sky.

**HORSE LATITUDE** The latitude belts over the oceans at latitudes of 30–35° where winds are predominantly calm or light and weather is often hot and dry.

**HOT SPOT** A small area of the earth's crust where an unusually high heat flow is associated with volcanic activity.

**HOT SPRING** An emission of hot water at the land surface.

**HURRICANE** A severe cyclone occurring in the tropics, characterized by high wind speeds and heavy precipitation.

**HYDROLOGICAL CYCLE** The continuous movement of all forms of water (vapour, liquid and solid) on, in and above the earth.

**HYDROSPHERE** The earth's water – saline, fresh, gaseous, liquid and solid.

**HYGROMETER** A device for measuring the relative humidity of the atmosphere.

**HYPSOGRAPHIC CURVE** A generalized profile of the earth and ocean floors which represents the proportions of the area of the surface at various altitudes above or below a datum.

# I

**ICEBERG** A large floating mass of ice detached from a glacier, usually tens of metres deep and can be several kilometres across.

**ICE-CAP** A dome-shaped glacier with a generally outward flow of ice.

**ICE FLOE** A piece of floating ice which is not attached to the land and is usually 2–3 metres thick.

**ICE SHELF** A floating sheet of ice attached to an embayment in the coast.

**IGNEOUS ROCK** Rock formed when molten material solidifies, either within the earth's crust or at the surface.

**INSELBERG** A large, residual hill which overlooks a surrounding eroded plain.

**INSOLATION** The amount of solar radiation received over a specified area and a specified time.

**INTERNATIONAL DATE LINE** An arbitary line, roughly along the 180° longitude line, east and west of which the date differs by one day.

**INVERSION (temperature)**
An increase of temperature with height.

**IRRIGATION** The supply of water to land by artificial means. Usually to improve agricultural productivity.

**ISLAND ARC** A chain of islands with an arcuate plan form. The islands are usually volcanic in origin.

**ISOBAR** A line drawn on diagrams joining equal values of atmospheric pressure. A particular kind of isopleth.

**ISOPLETH** A line drawn on diagrams joining equal values of the plotted element.

**ISOSTASY** The condition of balance between the rigid crustal elements of the earth's surface and the underlying, denser and more mobile material.

*Above* Limestone towers in the world's most spectacular karst region – Li River near Guilin, Guangxi Province, China. The towers are the result of erosional processes.

**ISTHMUS** A narrow strip of land which connects two islands or two large land masses.

# J

**JOINT** A fracture or crack in a rock.

**JUNGLE** An area of land overgrown with dense vegetation, usually in the tropics.

# K

**KAME** An irregular mound of stratified sediment deposited by, in association with stagnant ice.

**KARST** Limestone areas which have distinctive landforms such as caves, sinks and frequently a lack of surface water. *(see picture above)*

**KELP** A mass of large brown seaweeds.

**KETTLE HOLE** An enclosed depression resulting from the melting of buried ice.

**KNOT**   A measure of speed – one nautical mile per hour (1.15 mi hr$^{-1}$; 0.85 km hr$^{-1}$).

**KOPJE**   A small hill or rock outcrop; term used particularly in South Africa.

**KRILL**   Small marine animals, resembling shrimps.

**LACCOLITH**   A mass of intrusive rock, usually with a horizontal base and causing the doming of overlying strata.

**LAGOON**   A shallow pool separated from a larger body of water by a bar or reef.

**LANDSAT**   An unmanned satellite that carries sensors to record the resources of the earth.

**LANDSLIDE**   The movement downward under the influence of gravity of a mass of rock debris.

**LATERITE**   A red clay formed by the weathering of rock that consists especially of compounds of iron and aluminium.

**LAURASIA**   The northern part of Pangaea, a super-continent thought to have been broken up by continental drift.

**LAVA**   Molten rock material that emerges from volcanoes and volcanic fissures.

**LEACHING**   The downward movement of water through soil resulting in the removal of water-soluble materials from upper layers and their accumulation in lower layers.

**LEEWARD**   To the lee (downwind, downstream) of an obstacle lying in a flow.

**LEVEE**   A broad, long ridge running parallel and adjacent to a river on its flood-plain.

**LIGNITE**   A brownish black coal in which the texture of the original wood is distinct.

**LITHOSPHERE**   The earth's crust and a portion of the upper mantle that together comprise a layer of strength relative to the more easily deformable layer below.

**LITTORAL**   A coastal region.

**LLANOS**   An open grassy plain in S. America.

**LOAM**   A crumbly soil consisting of a mixture of clay, silt and sand.

**LOCH**   A lake or narrow sea inlet in Scotland.

**LOESS**   Unconsolidated and frequently unstratified material deposited after transport by wind.

**LONGSHORE CURRENT**   A current that runs along a coast. It may result in longshore drift, the transport of beach material along the coast.

**LOW**   See *cyclone*

**LUNAR MONTH**   The period of time between two successive new moons, being about 29½ days.

**MAGMA**   Fused, molten rock material beneath the earth's crust from which igneous rocks are formed.

**MAGNETIC ANOMALIES**   Areas with local surface variations in the earth's magnetic field relative to large-scale values.

**MAGNETIC FIELD**   The field of force exerted by the earth by virtue of its being like a giant magnet. Its most familiar manifestation is in the behaviour of a compass.

**MAGNETIC REVERSAL**   The reversal of the earth's magnetic field, such that a north-seeking compass points toward the South Pole. Such reversals have occurred in geological time.

**MANTLE**   The zone within the earth's interior extending from 25 to 70km below the surface to a depth of 2900km.

**MAP PROJECTION**   A mathematical device for representing a portion of all of the earth's curved surface on a flat surface.

**MAP SCALE**   A measure of the ratio of distances represented on a map to their true value.

**MAQUIS**   Scrub vegetation of evergreen shrubs characteristic of the western Mediterranean.

**MARL**   A fine grained mixture of clay and silt with a high proportion of calcium carbonate.

**MASSIF**   A large mountainous area, often quite distinct, containing several individual substantial mountains.

**MEANDER**   A sinuously winding portion of a river channel; also applied to similar forms within larger flows, such as the atmosphere and oceans.

**MEAN SEA LEVEL**   The level of the sea determined from a mean of the tidal ranges over periods of several months to several years.

**METAMORPHIC ROCKS**   Rocks in which their composition, structure and texture have been significantly altered by the action of heat and pressure greater than that produced normally by burial.

**METEOROLOGY**   The study of the workings of the atmosphere.

**MILLIBAR**   A unit of pressure, most widely used in meteorology. The average pressure exerted by the atmosphere on the surface of the earth is just over 1013 millibars.

**MISTRAL**   A cold, dry, north or northwest wind affecting the Rhone Valley.

**MONSOON**   A wind regime with marked seasonal reversal in direction, most famously found in the Indian sub-continent.

**MORAINE**   A landform resulting from the deposition of till by glaciers, taking on several

distinctive forms depending upon the location and mode of deposition.

**NADIR**   A point that is vertically below the observer.

**NASA**   National Aeronautics and Space Administration (USA).

**NEAP TIDE**   A tide of minimum height occurring at the first and third quarter of the moon.

**NÉVÉ**   Snow that is being compacted into ice, as found in the birth place of glaciers.

**NUNATAK**   A mountain completely surrounded by an ice cap or ice sheet.

**OASIS**   An area within a desert region where there is sufficient water to sustain animal and plant life throughout the year.

**OCEAN BASIN**   A large depression in the ocean floor analogous to basins on land.

**OCEANIC CRUST**   The portion of the earth's surface crust comprising largely sima (silica-magnesia rich rocks) about 5km thick. Underlies most of the world's oceans.

**OCEAN RIDGE**   A ridge in the ocean floor, sometimes 150 to 1500 km wide and hundreds of metres high.

**OCCLUSION**   The coming together of warm and cold fronts in cyclones in the latest stages of its evolution.

**OROGENESIS**   The formation of mountains, such as the Andes and Rocky Mountains. The mechanism is still uncertain but is probably related to plate tectonics.

**OUTWASH PLAIN**   Stratified material deposited by glacio-fluvial waters beyond the ice margin.

**OXBOW LAKE**   A lake, usually curved in plan, occupying an abandoned section of meandering river.

**PACK ICE**   Ice formed on sea surface when water temperatures fall to about −2°C and floating free under the influence of currents and wind.

**PAMPAS**   An extensive, generally grass-covered plain of temperate South America east of the Andes.

**PANGAEA**   The name given to a postulated continental landmass which split up to produce most of the present northern hemisphere continents.

**PASS**   A narrow passage over relatively low ground in a mountain range.

**PEDIMENT**   A smooth, erosional land surface typically sloping from the foot of a high-land area to a local base level.

**PELAGIC**   The part of an aquatic system that excludes its margins and substrate; it is essentially the main part of the water body.

**PENEPLAIN**   The supposed end land form resulting from erosional processes wearing down an initially uplifted block.

**PENUMBRA**   A region of partial darkness in a shadow surrounding the region of total darkness (umbra), such as seen in an eclipse.

**PERIHELION** The point in its orbit about the sun that a planet is closest to the sun.

**PIEDMONT GLACIER** A glacier which spreads out into a lobe as it flows onto a lowland.

**PILLOW LAVA** Lava that has solidified, probably under water, in rounded masses.

**PLACER DEPOSIT** A sediment, such as in the bed of a stream, which contains particles of valuable minerals.

**PLAIN** Extensive area of level or rolling treeless country.

**PLANKTON** Small freshwater and marine organisms that tend to move with water currents and comprise the food of larger and higher order organisms.

**PLATE TECTONICS** A theory which holds that the earth's surface is divided into several major rigid plates which are in motion with respect to each other and the underlying mantle. Continental drift results from plate motion and earthquakes, volcanoes and mountain-building tend to occur at the plate boundaries.

**PLUTONIC ROCK** Rock material that has formed at depth where cooling and crystallization have occurred slowly.

**POLAR WANDERING** The movements of the North and South Poles throughout geological time relative to the positions of the continents.

**POLDER** A low lying area of land that has been reclaimed from the sea or a lake by artificial means and is kept free of water by pumping.

**PRECIPITATION** The deposition of water from the atmosphere in liquid and solid form. Rain, snow, hail and dew are the most familiar forms.

**PRAIRIE** An extensive area of level or rolling, almost treeless grassland in North America.

**PRESSURE GRADIENT** The change per unit distance of pressure, perhaps most frequently met in atmospheric studies. The cause of winds.

## Q

**QUARTZ** A crystalline mineral consisting of silicon dioxide that is a major constituent of many rocks.

**QUICKSAND** Water-saturated sand that is semi-liquid and cannot bear the weight of heavy objects.

## R

**RADAR** A device that transmits radio waves and locates objects in the vicinity by analysis of the waves reflected back from them (radio detection and ranging).

**RADIATION** The transmission of energy in the form of electromagnetic waves and requiring no intervening medium.

**RAIN SHADOW** An area experiencing relatively low rainfall because of its position on the leeward side of a hill.

**RAISED BEACH** An emerged shoreline represented by stranded marine deposits and wave cut platforms, usually backed by former cliffs.

**RANGE** An open region over which livestock may roam and feed, particularly in North America.

**RAVINE** A narrow, steep sided valley usually formed by running water.

**REEF** A rocky construction found at or near sea-level; coral reefs are perhaps the most familiar type.

**RELATIVE HUMIDITY** The amount of water vapour in an air sample relative to the amount the sample could hold if it were saturated at the same temperature; expressed as a percentage.

**REMOTE SENSING** The observation and measurement of an object without touching it.

**RHUMB LINE** An imaginary line on the surface of the earth which makes equal oblique angles with all lines of longitude so that it forms a spiral coiling round the poles but never reaching them. This would be the course sailed by a ship following a single compass direction.

**RIA** An inlet of the sea formed by the flooding of river valleys by rising sea or sinking land. Contrast to fjords which are drowned glacial valleys.

**RIFT VALLEY** A valley formed when the area between two parallel faults sinks.

**RIVER TERRACE** A step like land form in the flood plain of rivers due to the river incising further into the plain and leaving remnants of its former flood plain at levels higher than the present level of the river channel.

**ROARING FORTIES** The area between 40° and 50°S, so called because of the high speeds of the winds occurring there. Sometimes applied to the winds themselves.

**RUN-OFF** The section of the hydrological cycle connecting precipitation to channel flow.

## S

**SALINITY** The presence of salts in the waters and soils of arid, semi-arid and coastal areas.

**SALT-MARSH** Vegetated mud-flats found commonly on many low-lying coasts in a wide range of temperate environments.

**SANDBANK** A large deposit of sand, usually in a river or coastal waters.

**SANDSTORM** A wind storm driving clouds of sand, most usually in hot, dry deserts.

**SAVANNAH** A grassland region of the tropics and sub-tropics.

**SCHIST** Medium to coarse-grained crystalline metamorphic rock.

**SEA-FLOOR SPREADING** The phenomenon when tectonic plates move apart.

**SEAMOUNT** A mountain or other area of high relief on the sea-floor which does not reach the surface.

**SEASAT** A satellite especially designed to sense remotely wind and sea conditions on the oceans.

**SEDIMENTARY ROCK** Rock composed of the fragments of older rocks which have been eroded and the debris deposited by wind and water, often as distinct strata.

**SEISMIC WAVE** Wave resulting from the movements of materials in earthquakes.

**SEISMOLOGY** Science that deals with earthquakes and other vibrations of the earth.

**SHALE** A compacted sedimentary rock, usually with fine-grained particles.

**SHALLOW-FOCUS EARTHQUAKE** An earthquake with a focus (or centre) at a shallow level relative to the earth's surface.

**SIAL** The part of the earth's crust with a composition dominated by minerals rich in silicon and aluminium.

**SIDEREAL DAY** A period of complete rotation of the earth on its axis, about 23 hours 56 minutes.

**SILL** A tabular sheet of igneous rock injected along the bedding planes of sedimentary and volcanic formations.

**SILT** An unconsolidated material of small particles ranging in size from about 2 to 60 micrometres.

**SIMA** The part of the earth's crust with a composition dominated by minerals rich in silicon and magnesium.

**SOIL CREEP** The slow movement downslope of soil, usually resulting in thinning of soils on the upper reaches and accumulations on the lower.

**SOLIFLUCTION** The slow movement downslope of water saturated, seasonally thawed materials.

**SOLSTICE** The days of maximum declination of the sun measured relative to the equator. When

*Above* On May 18 1980, Mt St Helens demonstrated a plinian eruption (a kind first described by Pliny the Elder). The apparent smoke cloud is pulverised ash.

the midday sun is overhead at 23½°N it gives the longest day in the northern hemisphere and the shortest day in the southern. The reverse applies when the sun is overhead at 23½°S.

**SPIT** Usually linear deposits of beach material attached at one end to land and free at the other.

**SPRING TIDE** A tide of greater than average range occurring at or around the times of the new and full moon.

**SQUALL** A sudden, violent wind, often associated with rain or hail; frequently occurs under cumulonimbus clouds.

**STALACTITE** A deposit of calcium carbonate, rather like an icicle, hanging from the roof of a cave.

**STALAGMITE** A deposit of calcium carbonate growing up from the floor of a cave due to the constant drip of water from the roof.

**STANDARD TIME** The officially established time, with reference to Greenwich Mean Time, of a region or country.

**STEPPE** Mid-latitude grasslands with few trees, most typically found in USSR.

**STORM SURGE** Changes in sea level caused by extreme weather events, notably the winds in storms.

**STRAIT** A narrow passage joining two large bodies of water.

**STRIAE** Scratches of a rock surface due to the passage over it of another rock of equal or greater hardness.

**SUBDUCTION ZONE** An area where the rocks comprising the sea floor are forced beneath continental rocks at a plate margin to be reincorporated in the magma beneath the earth's crust.

**SUBSEQUENT RIVER** A stream which follows a course determined by the structure of the local bedrock.

**SUBSIDENCE** Usually applied to the sinking of air in the atmosphere or the downward movement of the earth's surface.

**SUBSOIL** The layer of weathered material that underlies the surface soil.

**SUDD** Floating vegetable matter that forms obstructive masses in the upper White Nile.

**SUNSPOT** Relatively dark regions on the disk of the sun with surface temperature of about 4500K compared to the more normal 6000K of the rest of the surface.

**SURGE** A sudden excess over the normal value, usually of a flow of material (soil, ice, water).

**SWELL** A long, perturbation (usually wavelike) of a water surface that continues beyond its cause (eg a strong wind).

 **T**

**TAIGA** The most northerly coniferous forest of cold temperature regions found in Canada, Alaska and Eurasia.

**TECTONIC** Concerned with the broad structures of the earth's rocks and the processes of faulting, folding and warping that form them.

**TETHYS OCEAN** An ocean formed in the Palaeozoic Era which extended from what is now the Mediterranean Sea eastwards as far as South-east Asia.

**THERMOCLINE** A layer of water or a lake or sea that separates an upper, warmer, oxygen-rich zone from a lower, colder, oxygen-poor zone and in which temperature decreases by 1°C for every metre of increased depth.

**THRUST FAULT** A low-angle reverse fault.

**THUNDERSTORM** A cloud in which thunder and lightning occur, usually associated with heavy precipitation and strong winds.

**TIDAL BORE** A large solitary wave that moves up funnel-shaped rivers and estuaries with the rising tide, especially spring tides.

**TIDAL CURRENT** The periodic horizontal motions of the sea, generated by the gravitational attraction of the moon and sun, typically of $1ms^{-1}$ on continental shelves.

**TIDE** The regular movements of the seas due to the gravitational attraction of the moon and sun, most easily observed as changes in coastal sea levels.

**TOPOGRAPHY** The configuration of a land surface, including its relief and the position of its natural and man-made features.

**TOR** An exposure of bedrock usually as blocks and boulders, forming an abrupt, steep sided culmination of a more gentle rise to the summits of hills. Famous tors exist on Dartmoor.

**TORNADO** A violent, localized rotating storm with winds of $100ms^{-1}$ circulating round a funnel cloud some 100m in diameter. Frequent in mid-western USA.

**TRADE WIND** Winds with an easterly component which blow from the subtropic high pressure areas around 30° toward the equator.

**TROPICAL CYCLONE** *See hurricane*

**TROPOSPHERE** The portion of the earth's atmosphere between the earth's surface and a height about 15–20km. This layer contains virtually all the world's weather. Mean temperatures decrease and mean wind speeds increase with height in the troposphere.

**TSUNAMI** Sea-surface waves caused by submarine earthquakes and volcanic activity. Popularly called tidal waves.

**TURBULENCE** Chaotic and apparently random fluctuations in fluid flow, familiarly seen in the behaviour of smoke, either from a cigarette, a chimney or a volcano.

**TUNDRA** Extensive, level, treeless and marshy regions lying polewards of the taiga.

**TYPHOON** A term used in the Far East to describe tropical cyclones or hurricanes.

 **U**

**UMBRA** A region of total shadow, especially in an eclipse.

**UPWELLING** The upward movement of deeper water towards the sea surface.

 **V**

**VARVE** A sediment bed deposited in a body of water within the course of one year.

**VOE** An inlet or narrow bay of the Orkney or Shetland Islands.

**VOLCANIC ASH** Ash emitted from a volcano.

**VOLCANO** An opening through which magma, molten rock ash or volatiles erupts onto the earth's surface. Also used to describe the landform produced by the erupted material. *(see picture below left)*

 **W**

**WADI** An ephemeral river channel in deserts.

**WARM FRONT** An atmospheric front whereby, as it passes over an individual on the ground, warm air replaces cold.

**WATERFALL** A vertical or very steep descent of water in a stream.

**WATERSHED** A boundary dividing and separating the areas drained by different rivers.

**WATERSPOUT** A funnel-shaped, rotating cloud that forms occasionally over water when the atmosphere is very unstable. Akin to tornadoes which occur over land.

**WATER TABLE** The level below which the ground is wholly and permanently saturated with water.

**WAVE HEIGHT** The vertical extent of a wave.

**WAVE LENGTH** The horizontal extent of a wave, most easily seen as the distance along the direction of wave movement between crests or troughs.

**WAVE PERIOD** The time taken for a complete cycle of the oscillation occurring within a wave.

**WAVE VELOCITY** The velocity of a wave form, best seen by concentrating on one part of the wave such as its crest or trough.

**WEATHERING** The alteration by physical, chemical and biological processes of rocks and sediments in the top metres of the earth's crust. So called because this material is exposed to the effects of atmospheric and atmospherically related conditions.

**WEATHER ROUTEING** Choosing a route for a ship or aeroplane to minimise the deleterious effects of weather.

**WESTERLIES** Winds with a westerly component occurring between latitudes of about 35° and 60°. The whole regime forms a 'vortex' around each of the poles and forms a major element in world climate.

**WHIRLWIND** A general term to describe rotating winds of scales up to that of a tornado, usually a result of intense convection over small areas.

**WILLY-WILLY** Australasian term for a tropical cyclone or hurricane.

**WINDSHEAR** The variation of speed or direction or both of wind over a distance.

**Y**

**YARDANG** A desert landform, usually but not always, of unconsolidated material, shaped by and lying roughly along the direction of the wind.

**Z**

**ZENITH** A point that is vertically above the observer: the opposite of nadir.

**ZOOPLANKTON** One of the three kinds of plankton, including mature representatives of many animal groups such as Protozoa and Crustacea.

| ABBREVIATIONS | FULL FORM | ENGLISH FORM |
|---|---|---|
| **A** | | |
| a.d. | an der | on the |
| Akr. | Ákra, Akrotírion | cape |
| Appno | Appennino | mountain range |
| Arch. | Archipelago | |
| | Archipiélago | archipelago |
| **B** | | |
| B. | 1. Bahía, Baía, Baie, Bay, Bucht, Bukhta, Bugt | bay |
| | 2. Ban | village |
| | 3. Barrage, | dam |
| | 4. Bir, Bîr, Bi'r | well |
| Bol. | Bol'sh, -oy | big |
| Br. | 1. Branch | branch |
| | 2. Bridge, Brücke | bridge |
| | 3. Burun | cape |
| Brj | Baraj, -i | dam |
| **C** | | |
| C. | Cabo, Cap, Cape | cape |
| Can. | Canal | canal |
| Cd | Ciudad | town |
| Chan. | Channel | channel |
| Ck | Creek | creek |
| Co., Cord. | Cordillera | mountain chain |
| **D** | | |
| D. | 1. Dağ, Dagh, Dağı, Dağları | mountain, range |
| | 2. Daryācheh | lake |
| Dj. | Djebel | mountain |
| Dr. | doctor | doctor |
| **E** | | |
| E. | East | east |
| Emb. | Embalse | reservoir |
| Escarp. | Escarpment | escarpment |
| Estr. | Estrecho | strait |
| **F** | | |
| F. | Firth | estuary |
| Fj. | Fjord, Fjörður | fjord |
| Ft | Fort | fort |
| **G** | | |
| G. | 1. Gebel | mountain |
| | 2. Göl, Gölü | lake |
| | 3. Golfe, Golfo, Gulf | Gulf |
| | 4. Gora, -gory | mountain, range |
| | 5. Gunung | mountain |
| Gd, Gde | Grand, Grande | grand |
| Geb. | Gebirge | mountain range |
| Gl. | Glacier | glacier |
| Grl | General | general |
| Gt, Gtr | Great, Groot, -e, Greater | greater |
| **H** | | |
| Har. | Harbour, Harbor | harbour |
| Hd | Head | head |
| **I** | | |
| I. | Ile, Ilha, Insel, Isla, Island, Isle Isola, | island |
| | Isole | islands |
| In. | 1. Inner | inner |
| | 2. Inlet | inlet |
| Is | Iles, Ilhas, Islands, Isles, Islas | islands |
| Isth. | Isthmus | isthmus |
| **J** | | |
| J. | Jabal, Jebel, | mountain |
| **K** | | |
| K. | 1. Kaap, Kap, Kapp | cape |
| | 2. Kūh(hā) | mountain(s) |
| | 3. Kólpos | gulf |
| Kep. | Kepulauan | islands |
| Khr. | Khrebet | mountain range |
| Kör. | Körfez, -i | gulf, bay |
| **L** | | |
| L. | Lac, Lago, Lagoa, Lake, Liman, Limni, Loch, Lough | lake |
| Lag. | Lagoon, Laguna, Lagune, Lagoa | lagoon |
| Ld. | Land | land |
| Lit. | Little | little |
| **M** | | |
| M. | 1. Muang | town |
| | 2. Mys | cape |
| m | metre, -s | metre(s) |
| Mal. | Malyy | small |
| Mf | Massif | mountain group |
| Mgne | Montagne(s) | mountain(s) |
| Mt | Mont, Mount | mountain |
| Mte | Monte | mountain |
| Mti | Monti | mountains, range |
| Mtn | Mountain | mountain |
| Mts | Monts, Mountains, Montañas, Montes | mountains |
| **N** | | |
| N. | 1. Neu-, Ny- | new |
| | 2. Noord, Nord, Norte, North, Norra, Nørre | north |
| | 3. Nos | cape |
| Nat. | National | national |
| Nat. Pk | National Park | national park |
| Ndr | Nieder | lower |
| N.E. | North East | north east |
| N.M. | National Monument | national monument |
| N.P. | National Park | national park |
| N.W. | North West | north west |
| **O** | | |
| O. | 1. Oost, Ost | east |
| | 2. Ostrov | island |
| Ø | -øy | island |
| Oz. | Ozero, Ozera | lake(s) |
| **P** | | |
| P. | 1. Pass, Passo | pass |
| | 2. Pic, Pico, Pizzo | peak |
| | 3. Pulau | island |
| Pass. | Passage | passage |
| Peg. | Pegunungan | mountains |
| Pen. | Peninsula, Penisola | peninsula |
| Pk | 1. Park | park |
| | 2. Peak, Pik | peak |
| Plat. | Plateau, Planalto | plateau |
| Pov | Poluostrov | peninsula |
| Pr. | Prince | prince |
| P.P. | Pulau-pulau | islands |
| Pres. | Presidente | president |
| Promy | Promontory | promontory |
| Pt | Point | point |
| Pta | 1. Ponta, Punta | point |
| | 2. Puerta | pass |
| Pte | Pointe | point |
| Pto | Porto, Puerto | port |
| **R** | | |
| R. | Rio, Río, River, Rivière | river |
| Ra. | Range | range |
| Rap. | Rapids | rapids |
| Res. | Reserve, Reservation | reserve, reservation |
| Resp. | Respublika | Republic |
| Resr | Reservoir | reservoir |
| **S** | | |
| S. | 1. Salar, Salina | salt marsh |
| | 2. San, São | saint |
| | 3. See | sea, lake |
| | 4. South, Sud | south |
| s. | sur | on |
| Sa | Serra, Sierra | mountain range |
| Sd | Sound, Sund | sound |
| S.E. | South East | south east |
| Sev. | Severo-, Severnaya, -nyy | north peak |
| Sp. | Spitze | saint |
| St | Saint | saint |
| Sta | Santa | saint |
| Ste | Sainte | saint |
| Sto | Santo | strait |
| Str. | Strait | south west |
| S.W. | South West | |
| **T** | | |
| T. | Tall, Tell | hill, mountain |
| Tg | Tanjung | cape |
| Tk | Teluk | bay |
| Tr. | Trench, Trough | trench, trough |
| **U** | | |
| U. | Uad | wadi |
| Ug | Ujung | cape |
| Upr | Upper | upper |
| **V** | | |
| V. | 1. Val, Valle | valley |
| | 2. Ville | town |
| Va | Villa | town |
| Vdkhr. | Vodokhranilishche | reservoir |
| Vol. | Volcán, Volcano, Vulkan | volcano |
| Vozv. | Vozvyshennost' | upland |
| **W** | | |
| W. | 1. Wadi | wadi |
| | 2. Water | water |
| | 3. Well | well |
| | 4. West | west |
| **Y** | | |
| Yuzh. | Yuzhno-, Yuzhnyy | south |
| **Z** | | |
| Z | 1. Zaliv | gulf, bay |
| | 2. Zatoka | |
| Zap. | Zapad-naya, Zapadno-, Zapadnyy | western |
| Zem. | Zemlya | country, land |

# Introduction to the index

In the index, the first number refers to the page, and the following letter and number to the section of the map in which the index entry can be found.
For example, 14C2 **Paris** means that Paris can be found on page 14 where column C and row 2 meet.

## Abbreviations used in the index

| | |
|---|---|
| *Arch* | Archipelago |
| *B* | Bay |
| *C* | Cape |
| *Chan* | Channel |
| *Gl* | Glacier |
| *I(s)* | Island(s) |
| *Lg* | Lagoon |
| *L* | Lake |
| *Mt(s)* | Mountain(s) |
| *P* | Pass |
| *Pass* | Passage |
| *Pen* | Peninsula |
| *Plat* | Plateau |
| *Pt* | Point |
| *Res* | Reservoir |
| *R* | River |
| *S* | Sea |
| *Sd* | Sound |
| *Str* | Strait |
| UAE | United Arab Emirates |
| UK | United Kingdom |
| USA | United States of America |
| *V* | Valley |

## A

18B2 **Aachen** Germany
13C1 **Aalsmeer** Netherlands
13C2 **Aalst** Belgium
12K6 **Äänekoski** Finland
31A3 **Aba** China
48C4 **Aba** Nigeria
50D3 **Aba** Zaïre
41E3 **Ābādān** Iran
41F3 **Ābādeh** Iran
48B1 **Abadla** Algeria
75C2 **Abaeté** Brazil
75C2 **Abaeté** *R* Brazil
73J4 **Abaetetuba** Brazil
31D1 **Abagnar Qi** China
59E3 **Abajo Mts** USA
48C4 **Abakaliki** Nigeria
25L4 **Abakan** Russian Federation
48C3 **Abala** Niger
48C2 **Abalessa** Algeria
72D6 **Abancay** Peru
41F3 **Abarqū** Iran
29E2 **Abashiri** Japan
29E2 **Abashiri-wan** *B* Japan
27H7 **Abau** Papua New Guinea
50D3 **Abaya, L** Ethiopia
50D2 **Abbai** *R* Ethiopia/Sudan
50E2 **Abbe, L** Djibouti/Ethiopia
14C1 **Abbeville** France
63D3 **Abbeville** Louisiana, USA
67B2 **Abbeville** S Carolina, USA
58B1 **Abbotsford** Canada
64A2 **Abbotsford** USA
42C2 **Abbottabad** Pakistan
40D2 **'Abd al 'Azīz, Jebel** *Mt* Syria
20J5 **Abdulino** Russian Federation
50C2 **Abéché** Chad
48B4 **Abengourou** Ivory Coast
18B1 **Åbenrå** Denmark
48C4 **Abeokuta** Nigeria
50D3 **Abera** Ethiopia
7B3 **Aberaeron** Wales
7C4 **Aberdare** Wales
66C2 **Aberdeen** California, USA
65D3 **Aberdeen** Maryland, USA
63E2 **Aberdeen** Mississippi, USA
47C3 **Aberdeen** South Africa
8D3 **Aberdeen** Scotland
56D2 **Aberdeen** S Dakota, USA
56A2 **Aberdeen** Washington, USA
54J3 **Aberdeen L** Canada
7B3 **Aberdyfi** Wales
8D3 **Aberfeldy** Scotland
8C3 **Aberfoyle** Scotland
7C4 **Abergavenny** Wales
7B3 **Aberystwyth** Wales
20L2 **Abez'** Russian Federation
50E2 **Abhā** Saudi Arabia
41E2 **Abhar** Iran
48B4 **Abidjan** Ivory Coast
61D3 **Abilene** Kansas, USA
62C2 **Abilene** Texas, USA
7D4 **Abingdon** England
64C3 **Abingdon** USA
55K4 **Abitibi** *R* Canada
55L5 **Abitibi,L** Canada
21G7 **Abkhazian Republic** Georgia
42C2 **Abohar** India
48C4 **Abomey** Benin
50B3 **Abong Mbang** Cameroon
50B2 **Abou Deïa** Chad
8D3 **Aboyne** Scotland
41E4 **Abqaiq** Saudi Arabia
15A2 **Abrantes** Portugal
70A2 **Abreojos, Punta** *Pt* Mexico
50D1 **'Abri** Sudan
32A3 **Abrolhos** *I* Australia
75E2 **Abrolhos, Arquipélago dos** *Is* Brazil
56B2 **Absaroka Range** *Mts* USA
41F5 **Abū al Abyaḍ** *I* UAE
41E4 **Abū 'Alī** *I* Saudi Arabia
45D3 **Abu 'Amūd, Wadi** Jordan
45C3 **Abu 'Aweigīla** *Well* Egypt
41F5 **Abū Dhabi** UAE
45C3 **Abū el Jurdhān** Jordan
50D2 **Abu Hamed** Sudan
48C4 **Abuja** Nigeria
45A3 **Abu Kebir Hihya** Egypt
72E5 **Abunã** Brazil
72E6 **Abunã** *R* Bolivia/Brazil
45C4 **Abu Rûtha, Gebel** *Mt* Egypt
41D3 **Abú Sukhayr** Iraq
45B3 **Abu Suweir** Egypt
45B4 **Abu Tarfa, Wadi** Egypt
35B2 **Abut Head** *C* New Zealand
40B4 **Abu Tig** Egypt
50D2 **Abu'Urug** *Well* Sudan
50D2 **Abuye Meda** *Mt* Ethiopia
50C2 **Abu Zabad** Sudan
50D3 **Abwong** Sudan
18B1 **Åby** Denmark
50C3 **Abyei** Sudan
65F2 **Acadia Nat Pk** USA
70B2 **Acámbaro** Mexico
69B5 **Acandí** Colombia
70B2 **Acaponeta** Mexico
70B3 **Acapulco** Mexico
73L4 **Acaraú** Brazil
72E2 **Acarigua** Venezuela
70C3 **Acatlán** Mexico
48B4 **Accra** Ghana
6C3 **Accrington** England
42D4 **Achalpur** India
74B6 **Achao** Chile
13E3 **Achern** Germany
9A3 **Achill Hd** *Pt* Irish Republic
10A3 **Achill I** Irish Republic
13E1 **Achim** Germany
25L4 **Achinsk** Russian Federation
16D3 **Acireale** Sicily, Italy
61E2 **Ackley** USA
69C2 **Acklins** *I* The Bahamas
72D6 **Acobamba** Peru
74B4 **Aconcagua** *Mt* Chile
73L5 **Acopiara** Brazil
**Açores** *Is* = **Azores**
**A Coruña = La Coruña**
**Acre = 'Akko**
72D5 **Acre** *State* Brazil
66C3 **Acton** USA
63C2 **Ada** USA
15B1 **Adaja** *R* Spain
41G5 **Adam** Oman
50D3 **Adama** Ethiopia
75B3 **Adamantina** Brazil
50B3 **Adamaoua** *Region* Cameroon/Nigeria
50B3 **Adamaoua, Massif de l'** *Mts* Cameroon
68D1 **Adams** USA
44B4 **Adam's Bridge** India/Sri Lanka
56A2 **Adams,Mt** USA
44C4 **Adam's Peak** *Mt* Sri Lanka
**'Adan = Aden**
21F8 **Adana** Turkey
21E7 **Adapazari** Turkey
76F7 **Adare,C** Antarctica
34B1 **Adavale** Australia
41E4 **Ad Dahnā'** *Region* Saudi Arabia
41F4 **Ad Damman** Saudi Arabia
41D5 **Ad Dawādimī** Saudi Arabia
41E4 **Ad Dibdibah** *Region* Saudi Arabia
41E5 **Ad Dilam** Saudi Arabia
41E5 **Ad Dir'iyah** Saudi Arabia
50D3 **Addis Ababa** Ethiopia
41D3 **Ad Dīwanīyah** Iraq
40D3 **Ad Duwayd** Saudi Arabia
61E2 **Adel** USA
32C4 **Adelaide** Australia
67C4 **Adelaide** Bahamas
76G3 **Adelaide** *Base* Antarctica
54J3 **Adelaide Pen** Canada
27G8 **Adelaide River** Australia
66D3 **Adelanto** USA
38C4 **Aden** Yemen
38C4 **Aden,G of** Somalia/Yemen
48C3 **Aderbissinat** Niger
45D2 **Adhrā'** Syria
27G7 **Adi** *I* Indonesia
16C1 **Adige** *R* Italy
50D2 **Adigrat** Ethiopia
42D5 **Adilābād** India
58B2 **Adin** USA
65E2 **Adirondack Mts** USA
50D2 **Adi Ugrī** Ethiopia
40C2 **Adiyaman** Turkey
17F1 **Adjud** Romania
54E4 **Admiralty I** USA
55K2 **Admiralty Inlet** *B* Canada
32D1 **Admiralty Is** Papua New Guinea
44B2 **Ādoni** India
14B3 **Adour** *R* France
48B2 **Adrar** Algeria
48C2 **Adrar** *Mts* Algeria
48A2 **Adrar** *Region* Mauritius
48A2 **Adrar Soutouf** *Region* Morocco
50C2 **Adré** Chad
49D2 **Adri** Libya
64C2 **Adrian** Michigan, USA
62B1 **Adrian** Texas, USA
16C2 **Adriatic S** Italy/Yugoslavia
50D2 **Adwa** Ethiopia
25P3 **Adycha** *R* Russian Federation
48B4 **Adzopé** Ivory Coast
20K2 **Adz'va** *R* Russian Federation
20K2 **Adz'vavom** Russian Federation
17E3 **Aegean Sea** Greece
38E2 **Afghanistan** *Republic* Asia
50E3 **Afgooye** Somalia
41D5 **'Afif** Saudi Arabia
48C4 **Afikpo** Nigeria
12G6 **Åfjord** Norway
48C1 **Aflou** Algeria
50E3 **Afmado** Somalia
48A3 **Afollé** *Region* Mauritius
68C1 **Afton** New York, USA
58D2 **Afton** Wyoming, USA
45C2 **Afula** Israel
21E8 **Afyon** Turkey
45A3 **Aga** Egypt
50B2 **Agadem** Niger
48C3 **Agadez** Niger
48B1 **Agadir** Morocco
42D4 **Agar** India
43G4 **Agartala** India
58B1 **Agassiz** Canada
48B4 **Agboville** Ivory Coast
40E1 **Agdam** Azerbaijan
29C3 **Agematsu** Japan
14C3 **Agen** France
41E3 **Agha Jārī** Iran
48B4 **Agnibilékrou** Ivory Coast
14C3 **Agout** *R* France
42D3 **Āgra** India
41D2 **Ağri** Turkey
16D2 **Agri** *R* Italy
16C3 **Agrigento** Sicily, Italy
26H5 **Agrihan** *I* Marianas
17E3 **Agrínion** Greece
16C2 **Agropoli** Italy
20J4 **Agryz** Russian Federation
55N3 **Agto** Greenland
75B3 **Agua Clara** Brazil
69D3 **Aguadilla** Puerto Rico
70B1 **Agua Prieta** Mexico
75A3 **Aguaray Guazú** Paraguay
70B2 **Aguascalientes** Mexico
75D2 **Aguas Formosas** Brazil
75C2 **Agua Vermelha, Barragem** Brazil
15A1 **Agueda** Portugal
48C3 **Aguelhok** Mali
48A2 **Agüenit** *Well* Morocco
15B2 **Águilas** Spain
72B5 **Aguja, Puerta** Peru
36C7 **Agulhas Basin** Indian Ocean
51C7 **Agulhas,C** South Africa
36C6 **Agulhas Plat** Indian Ocean
**Ahaggar = Hoggar**
21H8 **Ahar** Iran
13D1 **Ahaus** Germany
35B1 **Ahipara B** New Zealand
13D2 **Ahlen** Germany
42C4 **Ahmadābād** India
44A2 **Ahmadnagar** India
50E3 **Ahmar Mts** Ethiopia
67C1 **Ahoskie** USA
13D2 **Ahr** *R* Germany
13D2 **Ahrgebirge** *Mts* Germany
12G7 **Åhus** Sweden
41F2 **Āhuvān** Iran
41E3 **Ahvāz** Iran
69A4 **Aiajuela** Costa Rica
14C3 **Aigoual, Mount** France
29C3 **Aikawa** Japan
67B2 **Aiken** USA
31A5 **Ailao Shan** *Upland* China
75D2 **Aimorés** Brazil
16B3 **Aïn Beïda** Algeria
48B1 **Aïn Beni Mathar** Morocco
49E2 **Ain Dalla** *Well* Egypt
15C2 **Aïn el Hadjel** Algeria
50B2 **Aïn Galakka** Chad
15C2 **Aïn Oussera** Algeria
48B1 **Aïn Sefra** Algeria
40B4 **'Ain Sukhna** Egypt
60D2 **Ainsworth** USA
15B2 **Aïn Témouchent** Algeria
29B4 **Aioi** Japan
48B2 **Aïoun Abd el Malek** *Well* Mauritius
48B3 **Aïoun El Atrouss** Mauritius
72E7 **Aiquile** Bolivia
48C3 **Aïr** *Desert Region* Niger
8D4 **Airdrie** Scotland
13B2 **Aire** France
6D3 **Aire** *R* England
13C3 **Aire** *R* France
55L3 **Airforce I** Canada
54E3 **Aishihik** Canada
13B3 **Aisne** *Department* France
14C2 **Aisne** *R* France
27H7 **Aitape** Papua New Guinea
19F1 **Aiviekste** *R* Latvia
14D3 **Aix-en-Provence** France
14D2 **Aix-les-Bains** France
43F4 **Aiyar Res** India
17E3 **Aíyion** Greece
17E3 **Aíyna** *I* Greece
43G4 **Āizawl** India
51B6 **Aizeb** *R* Namibia
29D3 **Aizu-Wakamatsu** Japan
16B2 **Ajaccio** Corsica, Italy
16B2 **Ajaccio, G d'** Corsica, Italy
49E1 **Ajdābiyā** Libya
29E2 **Ajigasawa** Japan
45C2 **Ajlūn** Jordan
41G4 **Ajman** UAE
42C3 **Ajmer** India
59D4 **Ajo** USA
15B1 **Ajo, Cabo de** *C* Spain
17F3 **Ak** *R* Turkey
29D2 **Akabira** Japan
29C3 **Akaishi-sanchi** *Mts* Japan
44B2 **Akalkot** India
45B1 **Akanthou** Cyprus
35B2 **Akaroa** New Zealand
29B4 **Akashi** Japan
21K5 **Akbulak** Russian Federation
40C2 **Akçakale** Turkey
48A2 **Akchar** *Watercourse* Mauritius
50C3 **Aketi** Zaïre
41D1 **Akhalkalaki** Georgia
40D1 **Akhalsikhe** Georgia
17E3 **Akharnái** Greece
49E1 **Akhdar, Jabal al** *Mts* Libya
41G5 **Akhdar, Jebel** *Mt* Oman
40A2 **Akhisar** Turkey
19F1 **Akhiste** Latvia
49F2 **Akhmîm** Egypt
21H6 **Akhtubinsk** Russian Federation
21E5 **Akhtyrka** Ukraine
29B4 **Aki** Japan
55K4 **Akimiski I** Canada
29E3 **Akita** Japan
48A3 **Akjoujt** Mauritius
45C2 **'Akko** Israel
54E3 **Aklavik** Canada
48B3 **Aklé Aouana** *Desert Region* Mauritius
50D3 **Akobo** Ethiopia
50D3 **Akobo** *R* Ethiopia/Sudan
42B1 **Akoha** Afghanistan
42D4 **Akola** India
42D4 **Akot** India
55M3 **Akpatok I** Canada
17E3 **Ákra Kafirévs** *C* Greece
17E4 **Ákra Líthinon** *C* Greece
17E3 **Ákra Maléa** *C* Greece
12A2 **Akranes** Iceland
17F3 **Ákra Sídheros** *C* Greece
17E3 **Ákra Spátha** *C* Greece
17E3 **Ákra Taínaron** *C* Greece
57E2 **Akron** USA
45B1 **Akrotiri** Cyprus
45B1 **Akrotiri B** Cyprus
42D1 **Aksai Chin** *Mts* China
21E8 **Aksaray** Turkey
21J5 **Aksay** Kazakhstan
42D1 **Aksayquin Hu** *L* China
40B2 **Akşehir** Turkey
40B2 **Akseki** Turkey
25N4 **Aksenovo Zilovskoye** Russian Federation
26E1 **Aksha** Russian Federation
39G1 **Aksu** China
50D2 **Aksum** Ethiopia
24J5 **Aktogay** Kazakhstan
21K6 **Aktumsyk** Kazakhstan
21K5 **Aktyubinsk** Kazakhstan
12B1 **Akureyri** Iceland
**Akyab = Sittwe**
24K5 **Akzhal** Kazakhstan
63E2 **Alabama** *R* USA
57E3 **Alabama** *State* USA
67A2 **Alabaster** USA
40C2 **Ala Dağlari** *Mts* Turkey
21G7 **Alagir** Russian Federation
73L5 **Alagoas** *State* Brazil
73L6 **Alagoinhas** Brazil
15B1 **Alagón** Spain
41E4 **Al Ahmadi** Kuwait
70D3 **Alajuela** Costa Rica
54B3 **Alakanuk** USA
24K5 **Alakol, Ozero** *L* Kazakhstan/Russian Federation
12L5 **Alakurtti** Russian Federation
27H5 **Alamagan** *I* Pacific Ocean
41E3 **Al Amārah** Iraq
59B3 **Alameda** USA
59C3 **Alamo** USA
62A2 **Alamogordo** USA
62C3 **Alamo Heights** USA
62A1 **Alamosa** USA
12H6 **Åland** *I* Finland
21E8 **Alanya** Turkey
67B2 **Alapaha** *R* USA
42L4 **Alapayevsk** Russian Federation
15B2 **Alarcón, Embalse de** *Res* Spain
40A2 **Alaşehir** Turkey
26D3 **Ala Shan** *Mts* China
54C3 **Alaska** *State* USA
54D4 **Alaska,G of** USA
54C3 **Alaska Range** *Mts* USA
16B2 **Alassio** Italy
20H5 **Alatyr'** Russian Federation
34B2 **Alawoona** Australia
41G5 **Al'Ayn** UAE
39F2 **Alayskiy Khrebet** *Mts* Tajikistan
25R3 **Alazeya** *R* Russian Federation
14D3 **Alba** Italy
15B2 **Albacete** Spain
15A1 **Alba de Tormes** Spain
40D2 **Al Badi** Iraq
17E1 **Alba Iulia** Romania
17D2 **Albania** *Republic* Europe
32A4 **Albany** Australia
67B2 **Albany** Georgia, USA
64B3 **Albany** Kentucky, USA
65E2 **Albany** New York, USA
56A2 **Albany** Oregon, USA
55K4 **Albany** *R* Canada
15B1 **Albarracin, Sierra de** *Mts* Spain
41G5 **Al Bātinah** *Region* Oman
27H8 **Albatross B** Australia
49E1 **Al Bayda** Libya
45C1 **Al Baylūlīyah** Syria
67B1 **Albemarle** USA
67C1 **Albemarle Sd** USA
15B1 **Alberche** *R* Spain
13B2 **Albert** France
54G4 **Alberta** *Province* Canada
27H7 **Albert Edward** *Mt* Papua New Guinea
47C3 **Albertinia** South Africa
50D3 **Albert,L** Uganda/Zaïre
57D2 **Albert Lea** USA
50D3 **Albert Nile** *R* Uganda
58D1 **Alberton** USA
14D2 **Albertville** France
14C3 **Albi** France
61E2 **Albia** USA
73H2 **Albina** Surinam
64C2 **Albion** Michigan, USA
61D2 **Albion** Nebraska, USA
65D2 **Albion** New York, USA
40C4 **Al Bi'r** Saudi Arabia
15B2 **Alborán** *I* Spain
12G7 **Ålborg** Denmark
13E3 **Albstadt-Ebingen** Germany
40D3 **Al Bū Kamāl** Syria
56C3 **Albuquerque** USA
41G5 **Al Buraymī** Oman
49D1 **Al Burayqah** Libya
49E1 **Al Burdī** Libya
32D4 **Albury** Australia
41E3 **Al Buşayyah** Iraq
15B1 **Alcalá de Henares** Spain
16C3 **Alcamo** Sicily, Italy
15B1 **Alcañiz** Spain
73K4 **Alcântara** Brazil
15A2 **Alcántara, Embalse de** *Res* Spain
15B2 **Alcaraz** Spain

**Anicuns** **Asturias**

75C2 **Anicuns** Brazil
62A1 **Animas** *R* USA
62A2 **Animas Peak** *Mt* USA
61E2 **Anita** USA
26H2 **Aniva, Mys** *C* Russian Federation
13B3 **Anizy-le-Château** France
14B2 **Anjou** *Region* France
51E5 **Anjouan** *I* Comoros
51E5 **Anjozorobe** Madagascar
28B3 **Anju** N Korea
31B3 **Ankang** China
21E8 **Ankara** Turkey
51E5 **Ankaratra** *Mt* Madagascar
51E6 **Ankazoabo** Madagascar
51E5 **Ankazobe** Madagascar
61E2 **Ankeny** USA
18C2 **Anklam** Germany
30D3 **An Loc** Vietnam
31B4 **Anlong** China
31C3 **Anlu** China
64B3 **Anna** USA
16B3 **'Annaba** Algeria
40C3 **An Nabk** Saudi Arabia
40C3 **An Nabk** Syria
40D4 **An Nafūd** *Desert* Saudi Arabia
49E2 **An Nāfūrah** Libya
41D3 **An Najaf** Iraq
8D4 **Annan** Scotland
65D3 **Annapolis** USA
43E3 **Annapurna** *Mt* Nepal
64C2 **Ann Arbor** USA
45D1 **An Nāsirah** Syria
41E3 **An Nāsirīyah** Iraq
14D2 **Annecy** France
30D3 **An Nhon** Vietnam
31A5 **Anning** China
67A2 **Anniston** USA
48C4 **Annobon** *I* Equatorial Guinea
14C2 **Annonay** France
69J1 **Annotto Bay** Jamaica
31D3 **Anqing** China
31B2 **Ansai** China
18C3 **Ansbach** Germany
69C3 **Anse d'Hainault** Haiti
31E1 **Anshan** China
31B4 **Anshun** China
60D2 **Ansley** USA
62C2 **Anson** USA
27F8 **Anson B** Australia
48C3 **Ansongo** Mali
64C1 **Ansonville** Canada
64C3 **Ansted** USA
21F8 **Antakya** Turkey
51F5 **Antalaha** Madagascar
21E8 **Antalya** Turkey
21E8 **Antalya Körfezi** *B* Turkey
51E5 **Antananarivo** Madagascar
76G1 **Antarctic Circle** Antarctica
76G3 **Antarctic Pen** Antarctica
15B2 **Antequera** Spain
62A2 **Anthony** USA
48B1 **Anti-Atlas** *Mts* Morocco
55M5 **Anticosti, Ī. de** Canada
64B1 **Antigo** USA
69E3 **Antigua** *I* Caribbean Sea
**Anti Lebanon = Sharqi, Jebel esh**
59B3 **Antioch** USA
33G5 **Antipodes Is** New Zealand
63C2 **Antlers** USA
74B2 **Antofagasta** Chile
75C4 **Antonina** Brazil
62A1 **Antonito** USA
9C2 **Antrim** Northern Ireland
68E1 **Antrim** USA
9C2 **Antrim** *County* Northern Ireland
9C2 **Antrim Hills** Northern Ireland
51E5 **Antsirabe** Madagascar
51E5 **Antsirañana** Madagascar
51E5 **Antsohiny** Madagascar
28B2 **Antu** China
30D3 **An Tuc** Vietnam
13C2 **Antwerp** Belgium
**Antwerpen = Antwerp**
9C3 **An Uaimh** Irish Republic
28A3 **Anui** S Korea
42C3 **Anūpgarh** India
44C4 **Anuradhapura** Sri Lanka
**Anvers = Antwerp**
54B3 **Anvik** USA
25L5 **Anxi** China
31C2 **Anyang** China
31A3 **A'nyêmaqên Shan** *Mts* China
25S3 **Anyuysk** Russian Federation
24K4 **Anzhero-Sudzhensk** Russian Federation
16C2 **Anzio** Italy
33F2 **Aoba** *I* Vanuatu
29E2 **Aomori** Japan
16B1 **Aosta** Italy
48B3 **Aouker** *Desert Region* Mauritius
48C2 **Aoulef** Algeria
50B1 **Aozou** Chad
74E2 **Apa** *R* Brazil/Paraguay
57E4 **Apalachee B** USA
67B3 **Apalachicola** USA
67A3 **Apalachicola B** USA
72D3 **Apaporis** *R* Brazil/Colombia
75B3 **Aparecida do Taboado** Brazil
27F5 **Aparri** Philippines
17D1 **Apatin** Croatia
20E2 **Apatity** Russian Federation
70B3 **Apatzingan** Mexico
18B2 **Apeldoorn** Netherlands
33H2 **Apia** Western Samoa
75C3 **Apiai** Brazil
73G2 **Apoera** Surinam
34B3 **Apollo Bay** Australia
67B3 **Apopka,L** USA
73H7 **Aporé** *R* Brazil
64A1 **Apostle Is** USA
57E3 **Appalachian Mts** USA
16C2 **Appennino Abruzzese** *Mts* Italy
16B2 **Appennino Ligure** *Mts* Italy
16D2 **Appennino Lucano** *Mts* Italy
16D2 **Appennino Napoletano** *Mts* Italy
16C2 **Appennino Tosco-Emilliano** *Mts* Italy
16C2 **Appennino Umbro-Marchigiano** *Mts* Italy
6C2 **Appleby** England
61D1 **Appleton** Minnesota, USA
64B2 **Appleton** Wisconsin, USA
21J7 **Apsheronskiy Poluostrov** *Pen* Azerbaijan
74F2 **Apucarana** Brazil
72E2 **Apure** *R* Venezuela
72D6 **Apurimac** *R* Peru
40C4 **'Aqaba** Jordan
40B4 **'Aqaba,G of** Egypt/Saudi Arabia
45C4 **'Aqaba, Wadi el** Egypt
41F3 **'Aqdā** Iran
73G8 **Aqidauana** Brazil
75A3 **Aquidabán** *R* Paraguay
74E2 **Aquidauana** Brazil
75A2 **Aquidauana** *R* Brazil
43E3 **Ara** India
67A2 **Arab** USA
45C1 **'Arab al Mulk** Syria
45C3 **'Araba, Wadi** Israel
36E4 **Arabian Basin** Indian Ocean
38E4 **Arabian Sea** SW Asia
45D2 **'Arab, Jabal al** *Mt* Syria
73L6 **Aracajú** Brazil
75A3 **Aracanguy,Mts de** Paraguay
73L4 **Aracati** Brazil
75D1 **Aracatu** Brazil
73H8 **Araçatuba** Brazil
15A2 **Aracena** Spain
73K7 **Araçuaí** Brazil
45C3 **'Arad** Israel
21C6 **Arad** Romania
50C2 **Arada** Chad
41F5 **'Arādah** UAE
32C1 **Arafura S** Indonesia/Australia
73H7 **Aragarças** Brazil
21G7 **Aragats** *Mt* Armenia
15B1 **Aragon** *R* Spain
15B1 **Aragón** *Region* Spain
75C1 **Araguaçu** Brazil
73H6 **Araguaia** *R* Brazil
73J5 **Araguaína** Brazil
73J7 **Araguari** Brazil
75C2 **Araguari** *R* Brazil
29C3 **Arai** Japan
45C3 **Araif el Naqa, Gebel** *Mt* Egypt
48C2 **Arak** Algeria
41E3 **Arāk** Iran
30A2 **Arakan Yoma** *Mts* Burma
44B3 **Arakkonam** India
41E2 **Araks** *R* Azerbaijan/Iran
24G5 **Aral S** Kazakhstan
24H5 **Aral'sk** Kazakhstan
15B1 **Aranda de Duero** Spain
10B2 **Aran I** Irish Republic
10B3 **Aran Is** Irish Republic
15B1 **Aranjuez** Spain
47B1 **Aranos** Namibia
63C3 **Aransas Pass** USA
28B4 **Arao** Japan
48B3 **Araouane** Mali
60D2 **Arapahoe** USA
74E4 **Arapey** *R* Uruguay
73L5 **Arapiraca** Brazil
75B3 **Araporgas** Brazil
74G3 **Ararangua** Brazil
73J8 **Araraquara** Brazil
75C3 **Araras** Brazil
32D4 **Ararat** Australia
41D2 **Ararat** Armenia
**Ararat, Mt = Büyük Ağri Daği**
75D3 **Araruama, Lagoa de** Brazil
40D3 **Ar'ar, Wadi** *Watercourse* Saudi Arabia
41D1 **Aras** *R* Turkey
21H8 **Aras** *R* Azerbaijan/Iran
29D3 **Arato** Japan
72E2 **Arauca** *R* Venezuela
72D2 **Arauea** Colombia
42C3 **Arāvalli Range** *Mts* India
33E1 **Arawa** Papua New Guinea
73J7 **Araxá** Brazil
21G8 **Araxes** *R* Iran
50D3 **Arba Minch** Ethiopia
16B3 **Arbatax** Sardinia,
21G8 **Arbīl** Iraq
12H6 **Arbrå** Sweden
8D3 **Arbroath** Scotland
14B3 **Arcachon** France
68A1 **Arcade** USA
67B3 **Arcadia** USA
58B2 **Arcata** USA
66D1 **Arc Dome** *Mt* USA
20G3 **Archangel** Russian Federation
68C2 **Archbald** USA
59E3 **Arches Nat Pk** USA
13C3 **Arcis-sur-Aube** France
58D2 **Arco** USA
75C3 **Arcos** Brazil
15A2 **Arcos de la Frontera** Spain
55K2 **Arctic Bay** Canada
76C1 **Arctic Circle**
54E3 **Arctic Red** *R* Canada
54E3 **Arctic Red River** Canada
54D3 **Arctic Village** USA
76G2 **Arctowski** *Base* Antarctica
17F2 **Arda** *R* Bulgaria
21H8 **Ardabīl** Iran
21G7 **Ardahan** Turkey
12F6 **Årdal** Norway
48C2 **Ardar des Iforas** *Upland* Algeria/Mali
9C3 **Ardee** Irish Republic
41F3 **Ardekān** Iran
13C3 **Ardennes** *Department* France
18B2 **Ardennes** *Region* Belgium
41F3 **Ardestāh** Iran
40C3 **Ardh es Suwwan** *Desert Region* Jordan
15A2 **Ardila** *R* Portugal
34C2 **Ardlethan** Australia
56D3 **Ardmore** USA
8B3 **Ardnamurchan Pt** Scotland
13A2 **Ardres** France
8C3 **Ardrishaig** Scotland
8C4 **Ardrossan** Scotland
69D3 **Arecibo** Puerto Rico
73L4 **Areia Branca** Brazil
59B3 **Arena,Pt** USA
13D1 **Arenberg** *Region* Germany
12F7 **Arendal** Norway
72D7 **Arequipa** Peru
16C2 **Arezzo** Italy
16C2 **Argenta** Italy
14C2 **Argentan** France
13B3 **Argenteuil** France
71D7 **Argentina** *Republic* S America
52F7 **Argentine Basin** Atlantic Ocean
74B8 **Argentino, Lago** Argentina
14C2 **Argenton-sur-Creuse** France
17F2 **Argeş** *R* Romania
42B2 **Arghardab** *R* Afghanistan
17E3 **Argolikós Kólpos** *G* Greece
13C3 **Argonne** *Region* France
17E3 **Árgos** Greece
17E3 **Argostólion** Greece
66B3 **Arguello,Pt** USA
66D3 **Argus Range** *Mts* USA
32B2 **Argyle,L** Australia
8C3 **Argyll** Scotland
18C1 **Århus** Denmark
51C6 **Ariamsvlei** Namibia
48B3 **Aribinda** Burkina
74B1 **Arica** Chile
42C2 **Arifwala** Pakistan
**Arihā = Jericho**
60C3 **Arikaree** *R* USA
69L1 **Arima** Trinidad
75C2 **Arinos** Brazil
73G6 **Arinos** *R* Brazil
69L1 **Aripo,Mt** Trinidad
72F5 **Aripuanã** Brazil
72F5 **Aripuanã** *R* Brazil
8C3 **Arisaig** Scotland
45B3 **'Arîsh, Wadi el** *Watercourse* Egypt
56B3 **Arizona** *State* USA
12G7 **Årjäng** Sweden
25Q4 **Arka** Russian Federation
21G5 **Arkadak** Russian Federation
63D2 **Arkadelphia** USA
8C3 **Arkaig, L** Scotland
24H4 **Arkalyk** Kazakhstan
57D3 **Arkansas** *R* USA
57D3 **Arkansas** *State* USA
63C1 **Arkansas City** USA
29C2 **Arkhipovka** Russian Federation
25K2 **Arkipelag Nordenshelda** *Arch* Russian Federation
10B3 **Arklow** Irish Republic
15B1 **Arlanzón** *R* Spain
14C3 **Arles** France
61D2 **Arlington** S Dakota, USA
63C2 **Arlington** Texas, USA
65D3 **Arlington** Virginia, USA
58B1 **Arlington** Washington, USA
64B2 **Arlington Heights** USA
18B3 **Arlon** Belgium
**Armageddon = Megiddo**
9C2 **Armagh** Northern Ireland
9C2 **Armagh** *County* Northern Ireland
13B4 **Armançon** *R* France
21G7 **Armavir** Russian Federation
72C3 **Armenia** Colombia
21G7 **Armenia** *Republic* Europe
13B2 **Armentières** Belgium
32E4 **Armidale** Australia
55L3 **Arnaud** *R* Canada
40B2 **Arnauti** *C* Cyprus
62C1 **Arnett** USA
18B2 **Arnhem** Netherlands
32C2 **Arnhem,C** Australia
32C2 **Arnhem Land** Australia
66B1 **Arnold** USA
65D1 **Arnprior** Canada
13E2 **Arnsberg** Germany
47B2 **Aroab** Namibia
13E2 **Arolsen** Germany
33G1 **Arorae** *I* Kiribati
16B1 **Arosa** Switzerland
13B3 **Arpajon** France
75C1 **Arraias** Brazil
75C1 **Arraias, Serra de** *Mts* Brazil
41D3 **Ar Ramādī** Iraq
8C4 **Arran, I of** Scotland
40C2 **Ar Raqqah** Syria
49D2 **Ar Rāqūbah** Libya
14C1 **Arras** France
41D4 **Ar Rass** Saudi Arabia
45D1 **Ar Rastan** Syria
48A2 **Arrecife** Canary Islands
41E3 **Ar Rifā'ī** Iraq
41E3 **Ar Rihāb** *Desert Region* Iraq
**Ar Riyād = Riyadh**
8C3 **Arrochar** Scotland
75C1 **Arrojado** *R* Brazil
58C2 **Arrowrock Res** USA
35A2 **Arrowtown** New Zealand
66B3 **Arroyo Grande** USA
41F4 **Ar Ru'ays** Qatar
41G5 **Ar Rustāq** Oman
40D3 **Ar Rutbah** Iraq
41D5 **Ar Ruwayḍah** Saudi Arabia
44B3 **Arsikere** India
20H4 **Arsk** Russian Federation
17E3 **Árta** Greece
28C2 **Artem** Russian Federation
25L4 **Artemovsk** Russian Federation
25N4 **Artemovskiy** Russian Federation
56C3 **Artesia** USA
35B2 **Arthurs P** New Zealand
74E4 **Artigas** Uruguay
54H3 **Artillery L** Canada
14C1 **Artois** *Region* France
19F3 **Artsiz** Ukraine
76G2 **Arturo Prat** *Base* Antarctica
21G7 **Artvin** Turkey
50D3 **Aru** Zaïre
73H6 **Aruanã** Brazil
69C4 **Aruba** *I* Caribbean Sea
27G7 **Aru, Kepulauan** *Arch* Indonesia
43F3 **Arun** *R* Nepal
43G3 **Arunāchal Pradesh** *Union Territory* India
44B4 **Aruppukkottai** India
50D4 **Arusha** Tanzania
50C3 **Aruwimi** *R* Zaïre
60B3 **Arvada** USA
26D2 **Arvayheer** Mongolia
55L5 **Arvida** Canada
12H5 **Arvidsjaur** Sweden
12G7 **Arvika** Sweden
59C3 **Arvin** USA
45C1 **Arwad** *I* Syria
20G4 **Arzamas** Russian Federation
15B2 **Arzew** Algeria
42C2 **Asadabad** Afghanistan
29B4 **Asahi** *R* Japan
29E2 **Asahi dake** *Mt* Japan
29E2 **Asahikawa** Japan
28A3 **Asan-man** *B* S Korea
43F4 **Asansol** India
49D2 **Asawanwah** *Well* Libya
20L4 **Asbest** Russian Federation
47C2 **Asbestos Mts** South Africa
65E2 **Asbury Park** USA
52H5 **Ascension** *I* Atlantic Ocean
70D3 **Ascensión, B de la** Mexico
18B3 **Aschaffenburg** Germany
18C2 **Aschersleben** Germany
16C2 **Ascoli Piceno** Italy
50E2 **Āseb** Ethiopia
48C2 **Asedjrad** *Upland* Algeria
50D3 **Asela** Ethiopia
12H6 **Åsele** Sweden
17E2 **Asenovgrad** Bulgaria
13C3 **Asfeld** France
20K4 **Asha** Russian Federation
7D3 **Ashbourne** England
67B2 **Ashburn** USA
33G5 **Ashburton** New Zealand
32A3 **Ashburton** *R* Australia
40B3 **Ashdod** Israel
63D2 **Ashdown** USA
67A1 **Asheboro** USA
57E3 **Asheville** USA
34D1 **Ashford** Australia
7E4 **Ashford** England
59D3 **Ash Fork** USA
29D2 **Ashibetsu** Japan
29D3 **Ashikaga** Japan
28B4 **Ashizuri-misaki** *Pt* Japan
24G6 **Ashkhabad** Turkmenistan
62C1 **Ashland** Kansas, USA
57E3 **Ashland** Kentucky, USA
60B1 **Ashland** Montana, USA
61D2 **Ashland** Nebraska, USA
64C2 **Ashland** Ohio, USA
56A2 **Ashland** Oregon, USA
65D3 **Ashland** Virginia, USA
61E1 **Ashland** Wisconsin, USA
34C1 **Ashley** Australia
60D1 **Ashley** USA
68C2 **Ashokan Res** USA
45C3 **Ashqelon** Israel
41D3 **Ash Shabakh** Iraq
41G4 **Ash Sha'm** UAE
41D2 **Ash Sharqāt** Iraq
41E3 **Ash Shaṭrah** Iraq
38C4 **Ash Shiḥr** Yemen
41E4 **Ash Shumlūl** Saudi Arabia
64C2 **Ashtabula** USA
55M4 **Ashuanipi L** Canada
21F8 **Asi** *R* Syria
15A2 **Asilah** Morocco
16B2 **Asinara** *I* Sardinia, Italy
24K4 **Asino** Russian Federation
50E1 **Asīr** *Region* Saudi Arabia
43E5 **Aska** India
40D2 **Aşkale** Turkey
12G7 **Askersund** Sweden
45B4 **Asl** Egypt
42C1 **Asmar** Afghanistan
50D2 **Asmera** Ethiopia
28B4 **Aso** Japan
50D2 **Asosa** Ethiopia
50D1 **Asoteriba, Jebel** *Mt* Sudan
62B2 **Aspermont** USA
35A2 **Aspiring,Mt** New Zealand
40C2 **As Sabkhah** Syria
41E5 **As Salamīyah** Saudi Arabia
40C2 **As Salamīyah** Syria
41D3 **As Salmān** Iraq
43G3 **Assam** *State* India
41E3 **As Samāwah** Iraq
41F5 **Aş Şanām** *Region* Saudi Arabia
45D2 **Aş Şanamayn** Syria
18B2 **Assen** Netherlands
18C1 **Assens** Denmark
49D1 **As Sidrah** Libya
54H5 **Assiniboia** Canada
54G4 **Assiniboine,Mt** Canada
73H8 **Assis** Brazil
40C3 **As Sukhnah** Syria
41E5 **Aş Şummān** *Region* Saudi Arabia
51E4 **Assumption** *I* Seychelles
40C3 **As Suwaydā'** Syria
41D3 **Aş Şuwayrah** Iraq
41E2 **Astara** Azerbaijan
16B2 **Asti** Italy
17F3 **Astipálaia** *I* Greece
15A1 **Astorga** Spain
56A2 **Astoria** USA
21H6 **Astrakhan'** Russian Federation
15A1 **Asturias** *Region* Spain

Asuka Ban Aranyaprathet


76F12 **Asuka** *Base* Antarctica
74E3 **Asunción** Paraguay
26H5 **Asuncion** *I* Marianas
50D3 **Aswa** *R* Uganda
40B5 **Aswân** Egypt
49F2 **Aswân High Dam** Egypt
49F2 **Asyût** Egypt
74C2 **Atacama, Desierto de** *Desert* Chile
33H1 **Atafu** *I* Tokelau Islands
45C3 **Atā'ita, Jebel el** *Mt* Jordan
48C4 **Atakpamé** Togo
27F7 **Atambua** Indonesia
55N3 **Atangmik** Greenland
45B4 **Ataqa, Gebel** *Mt* Egypt
48A2 **Atar** Mauritius
40C2 **Atatirk Baraji** *Res* Turkey
66B3 **Atascadero** USA
24J5 **Atasu** Kazakhstan
50D2 **Atbara** Sudan
24H4 **Atbasar** Kazakhstan
57D4 **Atchafalaya B** USA
57D3 **Atchison** USA
68C3 **Atco** USA
16C2 **Atessa** Italy
13B2 **Ath** Belgium
54G4 **Athabasca** Canada
54G4 **Athabasca** *R* Canada
54H4 **Athabasca,L** Canada
67A2 **Athens** Alabama, USA
57E3 **Athens** Georgia, USA
17E3 **Athens** Greece
64C3 **Athens** Ohio, USA
68B2 **Athens** Pennsylvania, USA
67B1 **Athens** Tennessee, USA
63C2 **Athens** Texas, USA
**Athína = Athens**
10B3 **Athlone** Irish Republic
45B1 **Athna** Cyprus
68D1 **Athol** USA
17E2 **Áthos** *Mt* Greece
9C3 **Athy** Irish Republic
50B2 **Ati** Chad
55J5 **Atikoken** Canada
25R3 **Atka** Russian Federation
21G5 **Atkarsk** Russian Federation
63D1 **Atkins** USA
57E3 **Atlanta** Georgia, USA
64C2 **Atlanta** Michigan, USA
61D2 **Atlantic** USA
57F3 **Atlantic City** USA
68C2 **Atlantic Highlands** USA
52H8 **Atlantic-Indian Antarctic Basin** Atlantic Ocean
52H7 **Atlantic Indian Ridge** Atlantic Ocean
**Atlas Mts = Haut Atlas, Moyen Atlas**
48C1 **Atlas Saharien** *Mts* Algeria
54E4 **Atlin** Canada
54E4 **Atlin L** Canada
45C2 **'Atlit** Israel
57E3 **Atmore** USA
51E6 **Atofinandrahana** Madagascar
63C2 **Atoka** USA
72C2 **Atrato** *R* Colombia
41F5 **Attaf** *Region* UAE
50E1 **Aṭ Ṭā'if** Saudi Arabia
45D2 **At Tall** Syria
67A2 **Attalla** USA
55K4 **Attawapiskat** Canada
55K4 **Attawapiskat** *R* Canada
41D3 **At Taysīyah** *Desert Region* Saudi Arabia
64B2 **Attica** Indiana, USA
68A1 **Attica** New York, USA
13C3 **Attigny** France
45B1 **Attila Line** Cyprus
65E2 **Attleboro** Massachusetts, USA
30D3 **Attopeu** Laos
40C4 **At Tubayq** *Upland* Saudi Arabia
12H7 **Atvidaberg** Sweden
66B2 **Atwater** USA
14D3 **Aubagne** France
13C3 **Aube** *Department* France
13C3 **Aube** *R* France
14C3 **Aubenas** France
67A2 **Aubrun** Alabama, USA
59B3 **Auburn** California, USA
64B2 **Auburn** Indiana, USA
65E2 **Auburn** Maine, USA
61D2 **Auburn** Nebraska, USA
65D2 **Auburn** New York, USA
58B1 **Auburn** Washington, USA
14C3 **Auch** France
33G4 **Auckland** New Zealand
37K7 **Auckland Is** New Zealand
14C3 **Aude** *R* France
55K4 **Auden** Canada
61E2 **Audubon** USA
34C1 **Augathella** Australia
9C2 **Aughnacloy** Northern Ireland
47B2 **Aughrabies Falls** South Africa
18C3 **Augsburg** Germany
32A4 **Augusta** Australia
57E3 **Augusta** Georgia, USA
63C1 **Augusta** Kansas, USA
57G2 **Augusta** Maine, USA
58D1 **Augusta** Montana, USA
64A2 **Augusta** Wisconsin, USA
19E2 **Augustow** Poland
32A3 **Augustus,Mt** Australia
47B1 **Auob** *R* Namibia
42D3 **Auraiya** India
42D5 **Aurangābād** India
48C1 **Aurès** *Mts* Algeria
16B3 **Aurès, Mt de l'** Algeria
13D1 **Aurich** Germany
14C3 **Aurillac** France
56C3 **Aurora** Colorado, USA
64B2 **Aurora** Illinois, USA
64C3 **Aurora** Indiana, USA
63D1 **Aurora** Mississippi, USA
61D2 **Aurora** Nebraska, USA
47B2 **Aus** Namibia
64C2 **Au Sable** USA
48A2 **Ausert** *Well* Morocco
8D2 **Auskerry, I** Scotland
57D2 **Austin** Minnesota, USA
59C3 **Austin** Nevada, USA
68A2 **Austin** Pennsylvania, USA
56D3 **Austin** Texas, USA
32D4 **Australian Alps** *Mts* Australia
18C3 **Austria** *Federal Republic* Europe
70B3 **Autlán** Mexico
14C2 **Autun** France
14C2 **Auvergne** *Region* France
14C2 **Auxerre** France
13A2 **Auxi-le-Château** France
14C2 **Avallon** France
66C4 **Avalon** USA
55N5 **Avalon Pen** Canada
75C3 **Avaré** Brazil
13E1 **Ave** *R* Germany
45C3 **Avedat** *Hist Site* Israel
73G4 **Aveiro** Brazil
15A1 **Aveiro** Portugal
74E4 **Avellaneda** Argentina
16C2 **Avellino** Italy
66B3 **Avenal** USA
13B2 **Avesnes-sur-Helpe** France
12H6 **Avesta** Sweden
16C2 **Avezzano** Italy
8D3 **Aviemore** Scotland
35B2 **Aviemore,L** New Zealand
14C3 **Avignon** France
15B1 **Avila** Spain
15A1 **Avilés** Spain
61D2 **Avoca** Iowa, USA
68B1 **Avoca** New York, USA
34B3 **Avoca** *R* Australia
68B1 **Avon** USA
7C4 **Avon** *County* England
7D4 **Avon** *R* Dorset, England
7D3 **Avon** *R* Warwick, England
59D4 **Avondale** USA
7C4 **Avonmouth** Wales
67B3 **Avon Park** USA
13B3 **Avre** *R* France
17D2 **Avtovac** Bosnia & Herzegovina, Yugoslavia
45D2 **A'waj** *R* Syria
29D4 **Awaji-shima** *I* Japan
50E3 **Awarē** Ethiopia
35A2 **Awarua Pt** New Zealand
50E3 **Awash** Ethiopia
50E3 **Awash** *R* Ethiopia
29C3 **Awa-shima** *I* Japan
35B2 **Awatere** *R* New Zealand
49D2 **Awbārī** Libya
50C3 **Aweil** Sudan
8C3 **Awe, Loch** *L* Scotland
49E2 **Awjilah** Libya
55J1 **Axel Heiberg I** Canada
7C4 **Axminster** England
29C3 **Ayabe** Japan
74E5 **Ayacucho** Argentina
69C5 **Ayacucho** Colombia
72D6 **Ayacucho** Peru
24K5 **Ayaguz** Kazakhstan
39G2 **Ayakkum Hu** *L* China
15A2 **Ayamonte** Spain
25P4 **Ayan** Russian Federation
72D6 **Ayaviri** Peru
21D8 **Aydin** Turkey
17F3 **Áyios Evstrátios** *I* Greece
25N3 **Aykhal** Russian Federation
7D4 **Aylesbury** England
45D2 **'Ayn al Fījah** Syria
40D2 **Ayn Zālah** Iraq
49E2 **Ayn Zuwayyah** *Well* Libya
50D3 **Ayod** Sudan
32D2 **Ayr** Australia
8C4 **Ayr** Scotland
8C4 **Ayr** *R* Scotland
6B2 **Ayre,Pt of** Isle of Man, British Isles
17F2 **Aytos** Bulgaria
30C3 **Ayutthaya** Thailand
17F3 **Ayvacik** Turkey
17F3 **Ayvalik** Turkey
43E3 **Āzamgarh** India
48B3 **Azaouad** *Desert Region* Mali
48C3 **Azaouak, Vallée de l'** Niger
48D3 **Azare** Nigeria
40C2 **A'zāz** Syria
**Azbine = Aïr**
48A2 **Azeffal** *Watercourse* Mauritius
21H7 **Azerbaijan** *Republic* Europe
72C4 **Azogues** Ecuador
20H2 **Azopol'ye** Russian Federation
46B4 **Azores** *Is* Atlantic Ocean
50C2 **Azoum** *R* Chad
21F6 **Azov, Sof** Russian Federation/Ukraine
48B1 **Azrou** Morocco
62A1 **Aztec** USA
72B2 **Azuero,Pen de** Panama
74E5 **Azul** Argentina
75B1 **Azul, Serra** *Mts* Brazil
16B3 **Azzaba** Algeria
45D2 **Az-Zabdānī** Syria
41G5 **Az Ẓāhirah** *Mts* Oman
49D2 **Az Zahrah** Libya
40C3 **Az Zilaf** Syria
41D4 **Az Zilfī** Saudi Arabia
41E3 **Az Zubayr** Iraq


## B


45C2 **Ba'abda** Lebanon
40C3 **Ba'albek** Lebanon
45C3 **Ba'al Hazor** *Mt* Israel
50E3 **Baardheere** Somalia
17F2 **Babadag** Romania
40A1 **Babaeski** Turkey
72C4 **Babahoyo** Ecuador
50E2 **Bāb al Mandab** *Str* Djibouti/Yemen
32B1 **Babar, Kepulauan** *I* Indonesia
50D4 **Babati** Tanzania
20F4 **Babayevo** Russian Federation
61E1 **Babbitt** USA
64C2 **Baberton** USA
54F4 **Babine L** Canada
32C1 **Babo** Indonesia
41F2 **Bābol** Iran
27F5 **Babuyan Is** Philippines
73J4 **Bacabal** Brazil
27F7 **Bacan** *I* Indonesia
21D6 **Bacău** Romania
30D1 **Bac Can** Vietnam
13D3 **Baccarat** France
34B3 **Bacchus Marsh** Australia
39F2 **Bachu** China
54J3 **Back** *R* Canada
30D1 **Bac Ninh** Vietnam
27F5 **Bacolod** Philippines
6C3 **Bacup** England
44B3 **Badagara** India
31A1 **Badain Jaran Shamo** *Desert* China
15A2 **Badajoz** Spain
15C1 **Badalona** Spain
40D3 **Badanah** Saudi Arabia
28B2 **Badaohe** China
13E3 **Bad Bergzabern** Germany
13D2 **Bad Ems** Germany
18B3 **Baden-Baden** Germany
13D3 **Badenviller** France
18B3 **Baden-Württemberg** *State* Germany
18C3 **Badgastein** Austria
66C2 **Badger** USA
18B2 **Bad-Godesberg** Germany
18B2 **Bad Hersfeld** Germany
13D2 **Bad Honnef** Germany
42B4 **Badin** Pakistan
16C1 **Bad Ischl** Austria
40C3 **Badiyat ash Sham** *Desert Region* Iraq/Jordan
18B3 **Bad-Kreuznach** Germany
60C1 **Badlands** *Region* USA
13E2 **Bad Lippspringe** Germany
13E2 **Bad Nauheim** Germany
13D2 **Bad Nevenahr-Ahrweiler** Germany
40C5 **Badr Ḥunayn** Saudi Arabia
13E2 **Bad Ryrmont** Germany
18C3 **Bad Tolz** Germany
44C4 **Badulla** Sri Lanka
13E2 **Bad Wildungen** Germany
13E3 **Bad Wimpfen** Germany
15B2 **Baena** Spain
48A3 **Bafatá** Guinea-Bissau
55L2 **Baffin B** Canada/Greenland
63C3 **Baffin B** USA
55L2 **Baffin I** Canada
50B3 **Bafia** Cameroon
48A3 **Bafing** *R* Mali
48A3 **Bafoulabé** Mali
50B3 **Bafoussam** Cameroon
41G3 **Bāfq** Iran
21F7 **Bafra Burun** *Pt* Turkey
41G4 **Bāft** Iran
50C3 **Bafwasende** Zaïre
43E3 **Bagaha** India
44B2 **Bāgalkot** India
51D4 **Bagamoyo** Tanzania
59D4 **Bagdad** USA
74F4 **Bagé** Brazil
60B2 **Baggs** USA
41D3 **Baghdād** Iraq
43F4 **Bagherhat** Bangladesh
41G3 **Bāghīn** Iran
42B1 **Baghlan** Afghanistan
61D1 **Bagley** USA
48B4 **Bagnoa** Ivory Coast
14C3 **Bagnols-sur-Cèze** France
48B3 **Bagoé** *R* Mali
28A2 **Bag Tai** China
27F5 **Baguio** Philippines
43F3 **Bāhādurābād** Bangladesh
57F4 **Bahamas,The** *Is* Caribbean Sea
43F4 **Baharampur** India
40A4 **Bahariya Oasis** Egypt
42C3 **Bahawalnagar** Pakistan
42C3 **Bahawalpur** Pakistan
42C3 **Bahawalpur** *Division* Pakistan
**Bahia = Salvador**
73K6 **Bahia** *State* Brazil
74D5 **Bahía Blanca** Argentina
70D3 **Bahía, Islas de la** Honduras
56B4 **Bahia Kino** Mexico
74C6 **Bahias, Cabo dos** Argentina
50D2 **Bahir Dar** Ethiopia
45A3 **Bahra el Manzala** *L* Egypt
43E3 **Bahraich** India
38D3 **Bahrain** *Sheikhdom* Arabian Pen
41D3 **Bahr al Milh** *L* Iraq
50C3 **Bahr Aouk** *R* Chad/Central African Republic
**Bahrat Lut = Dead Sea**
**Bahr el Abiad = White Nile**
50C3 **Bahr el Arab** *Watercourse* Sudan
**Bahr el Azraq = Blue Nile**
50D3 **Bahr el Ghazal** *R* Sudan
50B2 **Bahr el Ghazal** *Watercourse* Chad
45A3 **Bahr Fâqûs** *R* Egypt
15A2 **Baia de Setúbal** *B* Portugal
51B5 **Baia dos Tigres** Angola
21C6 **Baia Mare** Romania
50B3 **Baïbokoum** Chad
26F2 **Baicheng** China
55M5 **Baie-Comeau** Canada
45C2 **Baie de St Georges** *B* Lebanon
55L4 **Baie-du-Poste** Canada
65E1 **Baie St Paul** Canada
55N5 **Baie-Verte** Canada
31B3 **Baihe** China
31C3 **Bai He** *R* China
41D3 **Ba'ījī** Iraq
25M4 **Baikal, L** Russian Federation
43E4 **Baikunthpur** India
**Baile Atha Cliath = Dublin**
17E2 **Băileşti** Romania
13B2 **Bailleul** France
31A3 **Baima** China
67B2 **Bainbridge** USA
54B3 **Baird Mts** USA
31D1 **Bairin Youqi** China
31D1 **Bairin Zuoqi** China
32D4 **Bairnsdale** Australia
43E3 **Baitadi** Nepal
28A2 **Baixingt** China
17D1 **Baja** Hungary
70A1 **Baja California** *Pen* Mexico
59C4 **Baja California Norte** *State* Mexico
70A2 **Baja, Punta** *Pt* Mexico
20K5 **Bakal** Russian Federation
50C3 **Bakala** Central African Republic
48A3 **Bakel** Senegal
59C3 **Baker** California, USA
56C2 **Baker** Montana, USA
56B2 **Baker** Oregon, USA
55J3 **Baker Foreland** *Pt* Canada
54J3 **Baker L** Canada
54J3 **Baker Lake** Canada
56A2 **Baker,Mt** USA
56B3 **Bakersfield** USA
7D3 **Bakewell** England
41G2 **Bakharden** Turkmenistan
41G2 **Bakhardok** Turkmenistan
21E5 **Bakhmach** Ukraine
12C1 **Bakkaflói** *B* Iceland
50D3 **Bako** Ethiopia
50C3 **Bakouma** Central African Republic
21H7 **Baku** Azerbaijan
40B2 **Bala** Turkey
7C3 **Bala** Wales
27E6 **Balabac** *I* Philippines
27E6 **Balabac Str** Malaysia/Philippines
43E4 **Bālaghāt** India
34A2 **Balaklava** Australia
21H5 **Balakovo** Russian Federation
43E4 **Balāngīr** India
21G5 **Balashov** Russian Federation
43F4 **Balasore** India
17D1 **Balaton** *L* Hungary
9C3 **Balbriggan** Irish Republic
74E5 **Balcarce** Argentina
17F2 **Balchik** Bulgaria
33F5 **Balclutha** New Zealand
63D1 **Bald Knob** USA
7D4 **Baldock** England
67B2 **Baldwin** USA
58E1 **Baldy Mt** USA
56C3 **Baldy Peak** *Mt* USA
15C2 **Balearic Is** Spain
75E2 **Baleia, Ponta da** *Pt* Brazil
55M4 **Baleine, Rivière de la** *R* Canada
27F5 **Baler** Philippines
20J4 **Balezino** Russian Federation
32A1 **Bali** *I* Indonesia
40A2 **Balikesir** Turkey
40C2 **Balīkh** *R* Syria/Turkey
27E7 **Balikpapan** Indonesia
75B2 **Baliza** Brazil
42B1 **Balkh** Afghanistan
24J5 **Balkhash** Kazakhstan
24J5 **Balkhash, L** Kazakhstan
8C3 **Ballachulish** Scotland
8C4 **Ballantrae** Scotland
54G2 **Ballantyne Str** Canada
44B3 **Ballāpur** India
32D4 **Ballarat** Australia
8D3 **Ballater** Scotland
6B2 **Ballaugh** England
76G7 **Balleny Is** Antarctica
43E3 **Ballia** India
34D1 **Ballina** Australia
10B3 **Ballina** Irish Republic
62C2 **Ballinger** USA
9A4 **Ballinskelligis B** Irish Republic
13D4 **Ballon d'Alsace** *Mt* France
17D2 **Ballsh** Albania
68D1 **Ballston Spa** USA
9C2 **Ballycastle** Northern Ireland
9D2 **Ballyclare** Northern Ireland
9C4 **Ballycotton B** Irish Republic
9B3 **Ballyhaunis** Northern Ireland
9C2 **Ballymena** Northern Ireland
9C2 **Ballymoney** Northern Ireland
9C2 **Ballynahinch** Northern Ireland
9B2 **Ballyshannon** Irish Republic
9C3 **Ballyteige B** Irish Republic
34B3 **Balmoral** Australia
62B2 **Balmorhea** USA
42B3 **Balochistān** *Region* Pakistan
51B5 **Balombo** Angola
34C1 **Balonn** *R* Australia
42C3 **Bālotra** India
43E3 **Balrāmpur** India
32D4 **Balranald** Australia
73J5 **Balsas** Brazil
70B3 **Balsas** *R* Mexico
21D6 **Balta** Ukraine
12H7 **Baltic S** N Europe
40B3 **Baltîm** Egypt
57F3 **Baltimore** USA
43F3 **Bālurghāt** India
21J6 **Balykshi** Kazakhstan
41G4 **Bam** Iran
50B2 **Bama** Nigeria
48B3 **Bamako** Mali
50C3 **Bambari** Central African Republic
67B2 **Bamberg** USA
18C3 **Bamberg** Germany
50C3 **Bambili** Zaïre
75C3 **Bambuí** Brazil
50B3 **Bamenda** Cameroon
28A2 **Bamiancheng** China
50B3 **Bamingui** *R* Central African Republic
50B3 **Bamingui Bangoran National Park** Central African Republic
42B2 **Bamiyan** Afghanistan
33F1 **Banaba** *I* Kiribati
50C3 **Banalia** Zaïre
48B3 **Banamba** Mali
44E4 **Bananga** Nicobar Is, Indian Ocean
30C3 **Ban Aranyaprathet** Thailand

**Ban Ban** **Belcher Chan**


30C2 **Ban Ban** Laos
30C4 **Ban Betong** Thailand
9C2 **Banbridge** Northern Ireland
7D3 **Banbury** England
8D3 **Banchory** Scotland
70D3 **Banco Chinchorro** *Is* Mexico
65D1 **Bancroft** Canada
43E3 **Bānda** India
27C6 **Banda Aceh** Indonesia
27G7 **Banda, Kepulauan** *Arch* Indonesia
48B4 **Bandama** *R* Ivory Coast
41G4 **Bandar 'Abbās** Iran
21H8 **Bandar Anzalī** Iran
41F4 **Bandar-e Daylam** Iran
41F4 **Bandar-e Lengheh** Iran
41F4 **Bandar-e Māqām** Iran
41F4 **Bandar-e Rig** Iran
21J8 **Bandar-e Torkoman** Iran
41E3 **Bandar Khomeynī** Iran
27E6 **Bandar Seri Begawan** Brunei
27F7 **Banda S**Indonesia
75D3 **Bandeira** *Mt* Brazil
75B1 **Bandeirantes** Brazil
70B2 **Banderas, B de** Mexico
48B3 **Bandiagara** Mali
21D7 **Bandirma** Turkey
47D1 **Bandolier Kop** South Africa
50B4 **Bandundu** Zaïre
27D7 **Bandung** Indonesia
21H8 **Baneh** Iran
70E2 **Banes** Cuba
8D3 **Banff** Scotland
54G4 **Banff** *R* Canada
44B3 **Bangalore** India
50C3 **Bangassou** Central African Republic
32B1 **Banggai, Kepulauan** *I* Indonesia
27E6 **Banggi** *I* Malaysia
30D2 **Bang Hieng** *R* Laos
27D7 **Bangka** *I* Indonesia
30C3 **Bangkok** Thailand
30C3 **Bangkok, Bight of** *B* Thailand
39G3 **Bangladesh** *Republic* Asia
42D2 **Bangong Co** *L* China
57G2 **Bangor** Maine, USA
9D2 **Bangor** Northern Ireland
68C2 **Bangor** Pennsylvania, USA
7B3 **Bangor** Wales
30B3 **Bang Saphan Yai** Thailand
50B3 **Bangui** Central African Republic
51D5 **Bangweulu, L** Zambia
30C4 **Ban Hat Yai** Thailand
30C2 **Ban Hin Heup** Laos
30C1 **Ban Houei Sai** Laos
30B3 **Ban Hua Hin** Thailand
48B3 **Bani** *R* Mali
48C3 **Bani Bangou** Niger
49D1 **Banī Walīd** Libya
40C2 **Bāniyās** Syria
16D2 **Banja Luka** Bosnia & Herzegovina, Yugoslavia
27E7 **Banjarmasin** Indonesia
48A3 **Banjul** The Gambia
30B4 **Ban Kantang** Thailand
30D2 **Ban Khemmarat** Laos
30B4 **Ban Khok Kloi** Thailand
27H8 **Banks I** Australia
54E4 **Banks I** British Columbia, Canada
54F2 **Banks I** Northwest Territories, Canada
33F2 **Banks Is** Vanuatu
58C1 **Banks L** USA
35B2 **Banks Pen** New Zealand
34C4 **Banks Str** Australia
43F4 **Bankura** India
30B2 **Ban Mae Sariang** Thailand
30B2 **Ban Mae Sot** Thailand
43H4 **Banmauk** Burma
30D3 **Ban Me Thuot** Vietnam
9C3 **Bann** *R* Irish Republic
9C2 **Bann** *R* Northern Ireland
30B4 **Ban Na San** Thailand
42C2 **Bannu** Pakistan
30C2 **Ban Pak Neun** Laos
30C4 **Ban Pak Phanang** Thailand
30D3 **Ban Pu Kroy** Cambodia
30B3 **Ban Sai Yok** Thailand
30C3 **Ban Sattahip** Thailand
19D3 **Banská Bystrica** Czechoslovakia
42C4 **Bānswāra** India
30B4 **Ban Tha Kham** Thailand
30D2 **Ban Thateng** Laos
30C2 **Ban Tha Tum** Thailand
10B3 **Bantry** Irish Republic
10A3 **Bantry** *B* Irish Republic
27C6 **Banyak, Kepulauan** *Is* Indonesia
30D3 **Ban Ya Soup** Vietnam
27E7 **Banyuwangi** Indonesia
36E7 **Banzare Seamount** Indian Ocean
31D2 **Baoding** China
31C3 **Baofeng** China
30C1 **Bao Ha** Vietnam
31B3 **Baoji** China
30D3 **Bao Loc** Vietnam
26C4 **Baoshan** China
31C1 **Baotou** China
44C2 **Bāpatla** India
13B2 **Bapaume** France
45C4 **Bāqir, Jebel** *Mt* Jordan
41D3 **Ba'qūbah** Iraq
17D2 **Bar** Montenegro, Yugoslavia
50D2 **Bara** Sudan
50E3 **Baraawe** Somalia
43E3 **Bāra Banki** India
28C2 **Barabash** Russian Federation
24J4 **Barabinsk** Kazakhstan/ Russian Federation
24J4 **Barabinskaya Step** *Steppe* Kazakhstan/ Russian Federation
15B1 **Baracaldo** Spain
69C2 **Baracoa** Cuba
45D2 **Baradá** *R* Syria
34C2 **Baradine** Australia
44A2 **Bārāmati** India
42C2 **Baramula** Pakistan
42D3 **Bārān** India
54E4 **Baranof I** USA
20D5 **Baranovichi** Belorussia
34A2 **Baratta** Australia
43F3 **Barauni** India
73K8 **Barbacena** Brazil
69F4 **Barbados** *I* Caribbean Sea
15C1 **Barbastro** Spain
47E2 **Barberton** South Africa
14B2 **Barbezieux** France
72D2 **Barbosa** Colombia
69E3 **Barbuda** *I* Caribbean Sea
32D3 **Barcaldine** Australia
**Barce = Al Marj**
16D3 **Barcellona** Sicily, Italy
15C1 **Barcelona** Spain
72F1 **Barcelona** Venezuela
32D3 **Barcoo** *R* Australia
50B1 **Bardai** Chad
74C5 **Bardas Blancas** Argentina
43F4 **Barddhamān** India
19E3 **Bardejov** Czechoslovakia
7B3 **Bardsey** *I* Wales
64B3 **Bardstown** USA
42D3 **Bareilly** India
**Barentsovo More** *S* = **Barents Sea**
24D2 **Barentsøya** *I* Svalbard
20F1 **Barents S** Russian Federation
50D2 **Barentu** Ethiopia
14B2 **Barfleur, Pointe de** France
43E4 **Bargarh** India
25M4 **Barguzin** Russian Federation
25N4 **Barguzin** *R* Russian Federation
65F2 **Bar Harbor** USA
43F4 **Barhi** India
16D2 **Bari** Italy
15D2 **Barika** Algeria
72D2 **Barinas** Venezuela
43F4 **Baripāda** India
40B5 **Bârîs** Egypt
42C4 **Bari Sādri** India
43G4 **Barisal** Bangladesh
27D7 **Barisan, Pegunungan** *Mts* Indonesia
27E7 **Barito** *R* Indonesia
49D2 **Barjuj** *Watercourse* Libya
31A3 **Barkam** China
64B3 **Barkley,L** USA
47D3 **Barkly East** South Africa
32C2 **Barkly Tableland** *Mts* Australia
13C3 **Bar-le-Duc** France
32A3 **Barlee,L** Australia
32A3 **Barlee Range** *Mts* Australia
16D2 **Barletta** Italy
42C3 **Bārmer** India
34B2 **Barmera** Australia
7B3 **Barmouth** Wales
6D2 **Barnard Castle** England
24K4 **Barnaul** Russian Federation
68C3 **Barnegat** USA
68C3 **Barnegat B** USA
68A2 **Barnesboro** USA
55L2 **Barnes Icecap** Canada
67B2 **Barnesville** Georgia, USA
64C3 **Barnesville** Ohio, USA
62B2 **Barnhart** USA
7D3 **Barnsley** England
7B4 **Barnstaple** England
48C4 **Baro** Nigeria
43G3 **Barpeta** India
72E1 **Barquisimeto** Venezuela
13D3 **Barr** France
73K6 **Barra** Brazil
8B3 **Barra** *I* Scotland
34D2 **Barraba** Australia
75D1 **Barra da Estiva** Brazil
75A2 **Barra do Bugres** Brazil
75B2 **Barra do Garças** Brazil
75D3 **Barra do Piraí** Brazil
51D6 **Barra Falsa, Punta de** *Pt* Mozambique
73K6 **Barragem de Sobradinho** *Res* Brazil
15A2 **Barragem do Castelo do Bode** *Res* Portugal
15A2 **Barragem do Maranhão** *Res* Portugal
8B3 **Barra Head** *Pt* Scotland
73K8 **Barra Mansa** Brazil
72C6 **Barranca** Peru
72D2 **Barrancabermeja** Colombia
72F2 **Barrancas** Venezuela
74E3 **Barranqueras** Argentina
72D1 **Barranquilla** Colombia
8B3 **Barra,Sound of** *Chan* Scotland
68D1 **Barre** USA
73J6 **Barreiras** Brazil
15A2 **Barreiro** Portugal
73L5 **Barreiros** Brazil
32D5 **Barren,C** Australia
73J8 **Barretos** Brazil
65D2 **Barrie** Canada
34B2 **Barrier Range** *Mts* Australia
32E4 **Barrington,Mt** Australia
75C2 **Barro Alto** Brazil
27G8 **Barroloola** Australia
64A1 **Barron** USA
69N2 **Barrouallie** St Vincent
54C2 **Barrow** USA
9C3 **Barrow** *R* Irish Republic
32C3 **Barrow Creek** Australia
32A3 **Barrow I** Australia
6C2 **Barrow-in-Furness** England
54C2 **Barrow,Pt** USA
55J2 **Barrow Str** Canada
7C4 **Barry** Wales
65D1 **Barry's Bay** Canada
68C2 **Barryville** USA
44B2 **Barsi** India
13E1 **Barsinghausen** Germany
56B3 **Barstow** USA
14C2 **Bar-sur-Aube** France
13C3 **Bar-sur-Seine** France
73G2 **Bartica** Guyana
40B1 **Bartin** Turkey
32D2 **Bartle Frere,Mt** Australia
56D3 **Bartlesville** USA
60D2 **Bartlett** USA
51D6 **Bartolomeu Dias** Mozambique
6D3 **Barton-upon-Humber** England
19E2 **Bartoszyce** Poland
72B2 **Barú** *Mt* Panama
42D4 **Barwāh** India
42C4 **Barwāni** India
34C1 **Barwon** *R* Australia
20H5 **Barysh** Russian Federation
66C1 **Basalt** USA
50B3 **Basankusu** Zaïre
**Basel = Basle**
16D2 **Basento** *R* Italy
26F4 **Bashi Chan** Philippines/ Taiwan
20J5 **Bashkir Republic** Russian Federation
27F6 **Basilan** Philippines
27F6 **Basilan** *I* Philippines
7E4 **Basildon** England
58E2 **Basin** USA
7D4 **Basingstoke** England
56B2 **Basin Region** USA
65D1 **Baskatong, Réservoir** Canada
16B1 **Basle** Switzerland
41E3 **Basra** Iraq
13D3 **Bas-Rhin** *Department* France
30D3 **Bassac** *R* Cambodia
16C1 **Bassano** Italy
48C4 **Bassar** Togo
51D6 **Bassas da India** *I* Mozambique Channel
30A2 **Bassein** Burma
69E3 **Basse Terre** Guadeloupe
60D2 **Bassett** USA
48C4 **Bassila** Benin
66C2 **Bass Lake** USA
32D5 **Bass Str** Australia
13E1 **Bassum** Germany
12G7 **Båstad** Sweden
41F4 **Bastak** Iran
43E3 **Basti** India
16B2 **Bastia** Corsica, Italy
18B3 **Bastogne** Belgium
63D2 **Bastrop** Louisiana, USA
63C2 **Bastrop** Texas, USA
48C4 **Bata** Equatorial Guinea
27F5 **Bataan Pen** Philippines
69A2 **Batabanó, G de** Cuba
27E7 **Batakan** Indonesia
42D2 **Batāla** India
26C3 **Batang** China
50B3 **Batangafo** Central African Republic
27F5 **Batangas** Philippines
26F4 **Batan Is** Philippines
75C3 **Batatais** Brazil
65D2 **Batavia** USA
34D3 **Batemans Bay** Australia
67B2 **Batesburg** USA
63D1 **Batesville** Arkansas, USA
63E2 **Batesville** Mississippi, USA
65F1 **Bath** Canada
7C4 **Bath** England
65F2 **Bath** Maine, USA
65D2 **Bath** New York, USA
50B2 **Batha** *R* Chad
64C1 **Bathawana Mt** Canada
32D4 **Bathurst** Australia
55M5 **Bathurst** Canada
54F2 **Bathurst,C** Canada
32C2 **Bathurst I** Australia
54H2 **Bathurst I** Canada
54H3 **Bathurst Inlet** *B* Canada
48B4 **Batié** Burkina
41E4 **Bāṭin, Wadi al** *Watercourse* Iraq
41F3 **Bāṭlāq-e-Gavkhūnī** *Salt Flat* Iran
34C3 **Batlow** Australia
40D2 **Batman** Turkey
16B3 **Batna** Algeria
57D3 **Baton Rouge** USA
45C1 **Batroûn** Lebanon
30C3 **Battambang** Cambodia
44C4 **Batticaloa** Sri Lanka
44E4 **Batti Malv** *I* Nicobar Is, Indian Ocean
7E4 **Battle** England
57E2 **Battle Creek** USA
55N4 **Battle Harbour** Canada
58C2 **Battle Mountain** USA
21G7 **Batumi** Georgia
30C5 **Batu Pahat** Malaysia
45C2 **Bat Yam** Israel
32B1 **Baubau** Indonesia
48C3 **Bauchi** Nigeria
61E1 **Baudette** USA
55N4 **Bauld,C** Canada
25N4 **Baunt** Russian Federation
73J8 **Bauru** Brazil
75B2 **Baús** Brazil
18C2 **Bautzen** Germany
27E7 **Bawean** *I* Indonesia
49E2 **Bawîti** Egypt
48B3 **Bawku** Ghana
30B2 **Bawlake** Burma
34A2 **Bawlen** Australia
67B2 **Baxley** USA
70E2 **Bayamo** Cuba
43J2 **Bayana** India
26D2 **Bayandzürh** Mongolia
26C3 **Bayan Har Shan** *Mts* China
31A1 **Bayan Mod** China
31B1 **Bayan Obo** China
60C2 **Bayard** Nebraska, USA
62A2 **Bayard** New Mexico, USA
25N2 **Bayasgalant** Mongolia
40D1 **Bayburt** Turkey
57E2 **Bay City** Michigan, USA
63C3 **Bay City** Texas, USA
20M2 **Baydaratskaya Guba** *B* Russian Federation
50E3 **Baydhabo** Somalia
18C3 **Bayern** *State* Germany
14B2 **Bayeux** France
64A1 **Bayfield** USA
40C3 **Bāyir** Jordan
**Baykal, Ozero** *L* = **Baikal, L**
26D1 **Baykalskiy Khrebet** *Mts* Russian Federation
25L3 **Baykit** Russian Federation
25L5 **Baylik Shan** *Mts* China/ Mongolia
20K5 **Baymak** Russian Federation
63E2 **Bay Minette** USA
14B3 **Bayonne** France
18C3 **Bayreuth** Germany
63E2 **Bay St Louis** USA
65E2 **Bay Shore** USA
65D1 **Bays,L of** Canada
26B2 **Baytik Shan** *Mts* China
**Bayt Lahm = Bethlehem**
63D3 **Baytown** USA
15B2 **Baza** Spain
19F3 **Bazaliya** Ukraine
21H7 **Bazar-Dyuzi** *Mt* Azerbaijan
51D6 **Bazaruto, Ilha** Mozambique
14B3 **Bazas** France
31B3 **Bazhong** China
45D1 **Bcharre** Lebanon
60C1 **Beach** USA
68C3 **Beach Haven** USA
7E4 **Beachy Head** England
68D2 **Beacon** USA
51E5 **Bealanana** Madagascar
58D2 **Bear** *R* USA
64A2 **Beardstown** USA
24C2 **Bear I** Barents Sea
58D2 **Bear L** USA
66B1 **Bear Valley** USA
69C3 **Beata, Cabo** *C* Dominican Republic
69C3 **Beata, Isla** Dominican Republic
56D2 **Beatrice** USA
8D2 **Beatrice** *Oilfield* N Sea
54F4 **Beatton River** Canada
56B3 **Beatty** USA
65D1 **Beattyville** Canada
74E8 **Beauchene Is** Falkland Islands
34D1 **Beaudesert** Australia
67B2 **Beaufort** USA
54D2 **Beaufort S** Canada/USA
47C3 **Beaufort West** South Africa
65E1 **Beauharnois** Canada
8C3 **Beauly** Scotland
7B3 **Beaumaris** Wales
59C4 **Beaumont** California, USA
57D3 **Beaumont** Texas, USA
14C2 **Beaune** France
14C2 **Beauvais** France
54D3 **Beaver** USA
59D3 **Beaver** Utah, USA
54G4 **Beaver** *R* Canada
54D3 **Beaver Creek** Canada
64B3 **Beaver Dam** Kentucky, USA
64B2 **Beaver Dam** Wisconsin, USA
58D1 **Beaverhead Mts** USA
64B1 **Beaver I** USA
63D1 **Beaver L** USA
42C3 **Beāwar** India
75C3 **Bebedouro** Brazil
7E3 **Beccles** England
17E1 **Bečej** Serbia, Yugoslavia
48B1 **Béchar** Algeria
57E3 **Beckley** USA
13E2 **Beckum** Germany
6D2 **Bedale** England
13E1 **Bederkesa** Germany
7D3 **Bedford** England
64B3 **Bedford** Indiana, USA
68A3 **Bedford** Pennsylvania, USA
7D3 **Bedford** *County* England
69M2 **Bedford Pt** Grenada
68B2 **Beech Creek** USA
54D2 **Beechey Pt** USA
34C3 **Beechworth** Australia
34D1 **Beenleigh** Australia
45C3 **Beer Menuha** Israel
45C4 **Beer Ora** Israel
40B3 **Beersheba** Israel
**Be'er Sheva = Beersheba**
45C3 **Be'er Sheva** *R* Israel
56D4 **Beeville** USA
50C3 **Befale** Zaïre
51E5 **Befandriana** Madagascar
34C3 **Bega** Australia
**Begicheva, Ostrov** *I* = **Bol'shoy Begichev, Ostrov**
15C1 **Begur, C de** Spain
41F3 **Behbehān** Iran
41F2 **Behshahr** Iran
42B2 **Behsud** Afghanistan
26F2 **Bei'an** China
31B5 **Beihai** China
31D2 **Beijing** China
30E1 **Beiliu** China
31B4 **Beipan Jiang** *R* China
31E1 **Beipiao** China
**Beira = Sofala**
40C3 **Beirut** Lebanon
26C2 **Bei Shan** *Mts* China
47E1 **Beitbridge** Zimbabwe
45C2 **Beit ed Dīne** Lebanon
8C4 **Beith** Scotland
45C3 **Beit Jala** Israel
28A2 **Beizhen** China
15A2 **Beja** Portugal
16B3 **Béja** Tunisia
15C2 **Bejaïa** Algeria
15A1 **Béjar** Spain
41G3 **Bejestān** Iran
19E3 **Békéscsaba** Hungary
51E6 **Bekily** Madagascar
43E3 **Bela** India
42B3 **Bela** Pakistan
68B3 **Bel Air** USA
44B2 **Belampalli** India
27F6 **Belang** Indonesia
27C6 **Belangpidie** Indonesia
**Belau = Palau**
75A3 **Bela Vista** Brazil/ Paraguay
47E2 **Bela Vista** Mozambique
27C6 **Belawan** Indonesia
20K4 **Belaya** *R* Russian Federation
19G3 **Belaya Tserkov'** Ukraine
55J2 **Belcher Chan** Canada

Bistrita Braunschweig

17F1 **Bistrita** *R* Romania
50B3 **Bitam** Gabon
18B3 **Bitburg** Germany
13D3 **Bitche** France
40D2 **Bitlis** Turkey
17E2 **Bitola** Macedonia, Yugoslavia
18C2 **Bitterfeld** Germany
47B3 **Bitterfontein** South Africa
40B3 **Bitter Lakes** Egypt
56B2 **Bitteroot Range** *Mts* USA
48D3 **Biu** Nigeria
29D3 **Biwa-ko** *L* Japan
50E2 **Biyo Kaboba** Ethiopia
24K4 **Biysk** Russian Federation
16B3 **Bizerte** Tunisia
16D1 **Bjelovar** Croatia
48B2 **Bj Flye Ste Marie** Algeria
**Bjørnøya** *I* = **Bear I**
63D1 **Black** *R* USA
32D3 **Blackall** Australia
64B1 **Black B** Canada
6C3 **Blackburn** England
54D3 **Blackburn, Mt** USA
59D4 **Black Canyon City** USA
61E1 **Blackduck** USA
58D1 **Black Eagle** USA
58D2 **Blackfoot** USA
58D1 **Blackfoot** *R* USA
9B3 **Black Hd** *Pt* Irish Republic
54H5 **Black Hills** USA
8C3 **Black Isle** *Pen* Scotland
69Q2 **Blackman's** Barbados
59D3 **Black Mts** USA
7C4 **Black Mts** Wales
47B1 **Black Nosob** *R* Namibia
6C3 **Blackpool** England
69H1 **Black River** Jamaica
64A2 **Black River Falls** USA
56B2 **Black Rock Desert** USA
21D7 **Black S** Asia/Europe
64C3 **Blacksburg** USA
34D2 **Black Sugarloaf** *Mt* Australia
48B4 **Black Volta** *R* W Africa
63E2 **Black Warrior** *R* USA
7E4 **Blackwater** *R* England
10B3 **Blackwater** *R* Irish Republic
63C1 **Blackwell** USA
17E2 **Blagoevgrad** Bulgaria
25O4 **Blagoveshchensk** Russian Federation
58D1 **Blaikiston,Mt** Canada
58B1 **Blaine** USA
61D2 **Blair** USA
8D3 **Blair Atholl** Scotland
8D3 **Blairgowrie** Scotland
67C2 **Blakely** USA
74D5 **Blanca, Bahía** *B* Argentina
62A1 **Blanca Peak** *Mt* USA
16B3 **Blanc, C** Tunisia
34A1 **Blanche** *L* Australia
16B1 **Blanc, Mont** *Mt* France/Italy
56A2 **Blanco,C** USA
55N4 **Blanc Sablon** Canada
7C4 **Blandford Forum** England
59E3 **Blanding** USA
13B2 **Blankenberge** Belgium
69E4 **Blanquilla, Isla** Venezuela
51D5 **Blantyre** Malawi
9A3 **Blasket Sd** Irish Republic
14B2 **Blaye** France
34C2 **Blayney** Australia
33G5 **Blenheim** New Zealand
15C2 **Blida** Algeria
64C1 **Blind River** Canada
34A2 **Blinman** Australia
65E2 **Block I** USA
68E2 **Block Island Sd** USA
47D2 **Bloemfontin** South Africa
47D2 **Bloemhof** South Africa
47D2 **Bloemhof Dam** *Res* South Africa
73G3 **Blommesteinmeer** *L* Surinam
12A1 **Blönduós** Iceland
64B3 **Bloomfield** Indiana, USA
61E2 **Bloomfield** Iowa, USA
61D2 **Bloomfield** Nebraska, USA
62A1 **Bloomfield** New Mexico, USA
64B2 **Bloomington** Illinois, USA
64B3 **Bloomington** Indiana, USA
61E2 **Bloomington** Minnesota, USA
68B2 **Bloomsburg** USA
68B2 **Blossburg** USA
55Q3 **Blosseville Kyst** *Mts* Greenland
47D1 **Blouberg** *Mt* South Africa
18B3 **Bludenz** Austria
57E3 **Bluefield** USA
72B1 **Bluefields** Nicaragua
60D2 **Blue Hill** USA
68A2 **Blue Knob** *Mt* USA
69J1 **Blue Mountain Peak** *Mt* Jamaica
68B2 **Blue Mt** USA
34D2 **Blue Mts** Australia
56A2 **Blue Mts** USA
69J1 **Blue Mts, The** Jamaica
50D2 **Blue Nile** *R* Sudan
54G3 **Bluenose L** Canada
67C2 **Blue Ridge** USA
57E3 **Blue Ridge Mts** USA
9C2 **Blue Stack** *Mt* Irish Republic
35A3 **Bluff** New Zealand
59E3 **Bluff** USA
32A4 **Bluff Knoll** *Mt* Australia
74G3 **Blumenau** Brazil
60D2 **Blunt** USA
58B2 **Bly** USA
6D2 **Blyth** England
56B3 **Blythe** USA
57E3 **Blytheville** USA
48A4 **Bo** Sierra Leone
27F5 **Boac** Philippines
75D1 **Boa Nova** Brazil
64C2 **Boardman** USA
72F3 **Boa Vista** Brazil
48A4 **Boa Vista** *I* Cape Verde
30E1 **Bobai** China
44C2 **Bobbili** India
48B3 **Bobo Dioulasso** Burkina
19G2 **Bobrovica** Ukraine
20D5 **Bobruysk** Belorussia
67B4 **Boca Chica Key** *I* USA
72E5 **Bôca do Acre** Brazil
75D2 **Bocaiúva** Brazil
50B3 **Bocaranga** Central African Republic
67B3 **Boca Raton** USA
19E3 **Bochnia** Poland
18B2 **Bocholt** Germany
13D2 **Bochum** Germany
51B5 **Bocoio** Angola
50B3 **Boda** Central African Republic
25N4 **Bodaybo** Russian Federation
59B3 **Bodega Head** *Pt* USA
50B2 **Bodélé** *Desert Region* Chad
12J5 **Boden** Sweden
9C3 **Boderg, L** Irish Republic
44B2 **Bodhan** India
44B3 **Bodināyakkanūr** India
7B4 **Bodmin** England
7B4 **Bodmin Moor** *Upland* England
12G5 **Bodø** Norway
17F3 **Bodrum** Turkey
50C4 **Boende** Zaïre
48A3 **Boffa** Guinea
30B2 **Bogale** Burma
63E2 **Bogalusa** USA
34C2 **Bogan** *R* Australia
48B3 **Bogande** Burkina
40C2 **Boğazliyan** Turkey
20L4 **Bogdanovich** Russian Federation
26B2 **Bogda Shan** *Mt* China
47B2 **Bogenfels** Namibia
34D1 **Boggabilla** Australia
34C2 **Boggabri** Australia
7D4 **Bognor Regis** England
34C3 **Bogong** *Mt* Australia
27D7 **Bogor** Indonesia
25Q4 **Bogorodskoye** Russian Federation
20J4 **Bogorodskoye** Russian Federation
72D3 **Bogotá** Colombia
25K4 **Bogotol** Russian Federation
43F4 **Bogra** Bangladesh
31D2 **Bo Hai** *B* China
13B3 **Bohain-en-Vermandois** France
31D2 **Bohai Wan** *B* China
18C3 **Bohmer-wald** *Upland* Germany
27F6 **Bohol** *I* Philippines
27F6 **Bohol S** Philippines
75E1 **Boipeba, Ilha de** Brazil
75B2 **Bois** *R* Brazil
64C1 **Bois Blanc I** USA
56B2 **Boise** USA
62B1 **Boise City** USA
54F3 **Bois, Lac des** Canada
60C1 **Boissevain** Canada
48A2 **Bojador,C** Morocco
27F5 **Bojeador, C** Philippines
41G2 **Bojnūrd** Iran
48A3 **Boké** Guinea
34C1 **Bokhara** *R* Australia
12F7 **Boknafjord** *Inlet* Norway
50B4 **Boko** Congo
30C3 **Bokor** Cambodia
50B2 **Bokoro** Chad
50C4 **Bokungu** Zaïre
50B2 **Bol** Chad
48A3 **Bolama** Guinea-Bissau
14C2 **Bolbec** France
48B4 **Bole** Ghana
18D2 **Bolesławiec** Poland
48B3 **Bolgatanga** Ghana
21D6 **Bolgrad** Ukraine
63D1 **Bolivar** Missouri, USA
63E1 **Bolivar** Tennessee, USA
72D2 **Bolívar** *Mt* Venezuela
72E7 **Bolivia** *Republic* S America
12H6 **Bollnäs** Sweden
34C1 **Bollon** Australia
50B4 **Bolobo** Zaïre
16C2 **Bologna** Italy
20E4 **Bologoye** Russian Federation
26G1 **Bolon'** Russian Federation
26G2 **Bolon', Oz** *L* Russian Federation
16C2 **Bolsena, L di** Italy
25M2 **Bol'shevik, Ostrov** *I* Russian Federation
20J2 **Bol'shezemel'skaya Tundra** *Plain* Russian Federation
25S3 **Bol'shoy Anyuy** *R* Russian Federation
25N2 **Bol'shoy Begichev, Ostrov** *I* Russian Federation
21H5 **Bol'shoy Irgiz** *R* Russian Federation
28C2 **Bol'shoy Kamen** Russian Federation
**Bol'shoy Kavkaz** *Mts* = **Caucasus**
25Q2 **Bol'shoy Lyakhovskiy, Ostrov** *I* Russian Federation
21H6 **Bol'shoy Uzen** *R* Kazakhstan
56C4 **Bolson de Mapimi** *Desert* Mexico
7C3 **Bolton** England
40B1 **Bolu** Turkey
12A1 **Bolungarvik** Iceland
9A4 **Bolus Hd** *Pt* Irish Republic
40B2 **Bolvadin** Turkey
16C1 **Bolzano** Italy
50B4 **Boma** Zaïre
32D4 **Bombala** Australia
44A2 **Bombay** India
51E5 **Bombetoka, Baie de** *B* Madagascar
50D3 **Bombo** Uganda
75C2 **Bom Despacho** Brazil
43G3 **Bomdila** India
48A4 **Bomi Hills** Liberia
73K6 **Bom Jesus da Lapa** Brazil
25O4 **Bomnak** Russian Federation
50C3 **Bomokāndi** *R* Zaïre
50C3 **Bomu** *R* Central African Republic/Zaïre
65D3 **Bon Air** USA
69D4 **Bonaire** *I* Caribbean Sea
70D3 **Bonanza** Nicaragua
55N5 **Bonavista** Canada
16C3 **Bon, C** Tunisia
50C3 **Bondo** Zaïre
48B4 **Bondoukou** Ivory Coast
**Bône** = **'Annaba**
60D2 **Bonesteel** USA
73G3 **Bonfim** Guyana
50C3 **Bongandanga** Zaïre
50C3 **Bongo, Massif des** *Upland* Central African Republic
50B2 **Bongor** Chad
63C2 **Bonham** USA
16B2 **Bonifacio** Corsica, France
16B2 **Bonifacio,Str of** *Chan* Corsica, France/ Sardinia, Italy
**Bonin Is** = **Ogasawara Gunto**
67B3 **Bonita Springs** USA
75A3 **Bonito** Brazil
18B2 **Bonn** Germany
58C1 **Bonners Ferry** USA
48C4 **Bonny** Nigeria
32A1 **Bonthain** Indonesia
48A4 **Bonthe** Sierra Leone
50E2 **Booaaso** Somalia
34B2 **Booligal** Australia
34D1 **Boonah** Australia
62B1 **Boone** Colorado, USA
61E2 **Boone** Iowa, USA
67B1 **Boone** North Carolina, USA
65D2 **Boonville** USA
34C2 **Boorowa** Australia
55J2 **Boothia,G of** Canada
55J2 **Boothia Pen** Canada
7C3 **Bootle** England
50B4 **Booué** Gabon
47C2 **Bophuthatswana** *Self governing homeland* South Africa
62B3 **Boquillas** Mexico
50D3 **Bor** Sudan
40B2 **Bor** Turkey
17E2 **Bor** Serbia, Yugoslavia
56B2 **Borah Peak** *Mt* USA
12G7 **Borås** Sweden
41F4 **Borāzjān** Iran
14B3 **Bordeaux** France
54G2 **Borden I** Canada
55K2 **Borden Pen** Canada
68C2 **Bordentown** USA
8D4 **Borders** *Region* Scotland
34B3 **Bordertown** Australia
15C2 **Bordj bou Arréidj** Algeria
48C2 **Bordj Omar Driss** Algeria
**Borgå** = **Porvoo**
55Q3 **Borgarnes** Iceland
56C3 **Borger** USA
12H7 **Borgholm** Sweden
19E3 **Borislav** Ukraine
21G5 **Borisoglebsk** Russian Federation
20D5 **Borisov** Belorussia
21F5 **Borisovka** Russian Federation
75A4 **Borja** Paraguay
50B2 **Borkou** *Desert Region* Chad
13D1 **Borkum** *I* Germany
12H6 **Borlänge** Sweden
27E6 **Borneo** *I* Indonesia/ Malaysia
12H7 **Bornholm** *I* Denmark
17F3 **Bornova** Turkey
48D3 **Bornu** *Region* Nigeria
50C3 **Boro** *R* Sudan
25P3 **Borogontsy** Russian Federation
48B3 **Boromo** Burkina
66D3 **Boron** USA
20E4 **Borovichi** Russian Federation
32C2 **Borroloola** Australia
17E1 **Borsa** Romania
41F3 **Borūjen** Iran
41E3 **Borūjerd** Iran
18D2 **Bory Tucholskie** *Region* Poland
19G2 **Borzna** Ukraine
25N4 **Borzya** Russian Federation
31B5 **Bose** China
47D2 **Boshof** South Africa
17D2 **Bosna** *R* Bosnia & Herzegovina, Yugoslavia
17D2 **Bosnia & Herzegovina** *Republic* Yugoslavia
29D3 **Bōsō-hantō** *B* Japan
**Bosporus** = **Karadeniz Boğazi**
15C2 **Bosquet** Algeria
50B3 **Bossangoa** Central African Republic
50B3 **Bossèmbélé** Central African Republic
63D2 **Bossier City** USA
24K5 **Bosten Hu** *L* China
7D3 **Boston** England
57F2 **Boston** USA
57D3 **Boston Mts** USA
42C4 **Botād** India
17E2 **Botevgrad** Bulgaria
47D2 **Bothaville** South Africa
20B3 **Bothnia,G of** Finland/ Sweden
51C6 **Botletli** *R* Botswana
21D6 **Botoşani** Romania
51C6 **Botswana** *Republic* Africa
16D3 **Botte Donato** *Mt* Italy
60C1 **Bottineau** USA
13D2 **Bottrop** Germany
75C3 **Botucatu** Brazil
75D1 **Botuporã** Brazil
55N5 **Botwood** Canada
48B4 **Bouaké** Ivory Coast
50B3 **Bouar** Central African Republic
48B1 **Bouârfa** Morocco
50B3 **Bouca** Central African Republic
15C2 **Boufarik** Algeria
33E1 **Bougainville** *I* Papua New Guinea
16B3 **Bougaroun, C** Algeria
**Bougie** = **Bejaïa**
48B3 **Bougouni** Mali
15A2 **Bouhalla, Djebel** *Mt* Morocco
13C3 **Bouillon** France
15C2 **Bouïra** Algeria
48B2 **Bou Izakarn** Morocco
13D3 **Boulay-Moselle** France
56C2 **Boulder** Colorado, USA
58D1 **Boulder** Montana, USA
56B3 **Boulder City** USA
66A2 **Boulder Creek** USA
14C1 **Boulogne** France
50B3 **Boumba** *R* Cameroon/ Central African Republic
48B4 **Bouna** Ivory Coast
56B3 **Boundary Peak** *Mt* USA
48B4 **Boundiali** Ivory Coast
58D2 **Bountiful** USA
33G5 **Bounty Is** New Zealand
33F3 **Bourail** New Caledonia
13C4 **Bourbonne-les-Bains** France
48B3 **Bourem** Mali
14D2 **Bourg** France
14D2 **Bourg de Péage** France
14C2 **Bourges** France
14C3 **Bourg-Madame** France
14C2 **Bourgogne** *Region* France
34C2 **Bourke** Australia
7D4 **Bournemouth** England
15C2 **Bou Saâda** Algeria
50B2 **Bousso** Chad
48A3 **Boutilimit** Mauritius
52J7 **Bouvet I** Atlantic Ocean
60C1 **Bowbells** USA
32D2 **Bowen** Australia
59E4 **Bowie** Arizona, USA
63C2 **Bowie** Texas, USA
6C3 **Bowland Fells** England
57E3 **Bowling Green** Kentucky, USA
63D1 **Bowling Green** Missouri, USA
64C2 **Bowling Green** Ohio, USA
65D3 **Bowling Green** Virginia, USA
60C1 **Bowman** USA
65D2 **Bowmanville** Canada
9C3 **Bowna, L** Irish Republic
34D2 **Bowral** Australia
31D3 **Bo Xian** China
31D2 **Boxing** China
40B1 **Boyabat** Turkey
50B3 **Boyali** Central African Republic
19G2 **Boyarka** Ukraine
54J4 **Boyd** Canada
68C2 **Boyertown** USA
10B3 **Boyle** Irish Republic
9C3 **Boyne** *R* Irish Republic
67B3 **Boynton Beach** USA
50C3 **Boyoma Falls** Zaïre
58E2 **Boysen Res** USA
17D1 **Bozanski Brod** Yugoslavia
17F3 **Bozca Ada** *I* Turkey
17F3 **Boz Dağlari** *Mts* Turkey
56B2 **Bozeman** USA
**Bozen** = **Bolzano**
50B3 **Bozene** Zaïre
50B3 **Bozoum** Central African Republic
16D2 **Brač** *I* Croatia
8B3 **Bracadale, Loch** *Inlet* Scotland
16C2 **Bracciano, L di** Italy
65D1 **Bracebridge** Canada
49D2 **Brach** Libya
12H6 **Bräcke** Sweden
62B3 **Brackettville** USA
67B3 **Bradenton** USA
6D3 **Bradford** England
68A2 **Bradford** USA
66B3 **Bradley** USA
62C2 **Brady** USA
8E1 **Brae** Scotland
8D3 **Braemar** Scotland
15A1 **Braga** Portugal
73J4 **Bragança** Brazil
15A1 **Bragança** Portugal
75C3 **Bragança Paulista** Brazil
43G4 **Brahman-Baria** Bangladesh
43F4 **Brāhmani** *R* India
43G3 **Brahmaputra** *R* Bangladesh/India
21D6 **Brăila** Romania
57D2 **Brainerd** USA
7E4 **Braintree** England
47C3 **Brak** *R* South Africa
47D1 **Brak** *R* South Africa
13E1 **Brake** Germany
48A3 **Brakna** *Region* Mauritius
54F4 **Bralorne** Canada
65D2 **Brampton** Canada
6C2 **Brampton** England
13D1 **Bramsche** Germany
72F3 **Branco** *R* Brazil
51B6 **Brandberg** *Mt* Namibia
18C2 **Brandenburg** Germany
18C2 **Brandenburg** *State* Germany
47D2 **Brandfort** South Africa
56D2 **Brandon** Canada
61D2 **Brandon** USA
47C3 **Brandvlei** South Africa
18C2 **Brandýs-nad-Laben** Czechoslovakia
19D2 **Braniewo** Poland
57E2 **Brantford** Canada
34B3 **Branxholme** Australia
55M5 **Bras d'Or Lakes** Canada
72E6 **Brasiléia** Brazil
73J7 **Brasília** Brazil
75D2 **Brasília de Minas** Brazil
17F1 **Braşov** Romania
18D3 **Bratislava** Czechoslovakia
25M4 **Bratsk** Russian Federation
19F3 **Bratslav** Ukraine
65E2 **Brattleboro** USA
18C2 **Braunschweig** Germany

Brava Caga Tepe


48A4 **Brava** *I* Cape Verde
56B3 **Brawley** USA
9C3 **Bray** Irish Republic
55L3 **Bray I** Canada
13B3 **Bray-sur-Seine** France
71E5 **Brazil** *Republic* S America
52G5 **Brazil Basin** Atlantic Ocean
56D3 **Brazos** *R* USA
50B4 **Brazzaville** Congo
18C3 **Brdy** *Upland* Czechoslovakia
35A3 **Breaksea Sd** New Zealand
35B1 **Bream B** New Zealand
8D3 **Brechin** Scotland
13C2 **Brecht** Belgium
61D1 **Breckenridge** Minnesota, USA
62C2 **Breckenridge** Texas, USA
7E3 **Breckland** England
18D3 **Břeclav** Czechoslovakia
7C4 **Brecon** Wales
7C4 **Brecon Beacons** *Mts* Wales
7B3 **Brecon Beacons Nat Pk** Wales
18A2 **Breda** Netherlands
47C3 **Bredasdorp** South Africa
12H6 **Bredbyn** Sweden
20K5 **Bredy** Russian Federation
47B3 **Breede** *R* South Africa
65D2 **Breezewood** USA
12A1 **Breiethafjörethur** *B* Iceland
13D3 **Breisach** Germany
67A2 **Bremen** USA
18B2 **Bremen** Germany
18B2 **Bremerhaven** Germany
58B1 **Bremerton** USA
13E1 **Bremervörde** Germany
59E3 **Brendel** USA
63C2 **Brenham** USA
18C3 **Brenner** *P* Austria/Italy
66B2 **Brentwood** USA
16C1 **Brescia** Italy
**Breslau = Wrocław**
8E1 **Bressay** *I* Scotland
14B2 **Bressuire** France
14B2 **Brest** France
19E2 **Brest** Belorussia
14B2 **Bretagne** *Region* France
13B3 **Breteuil** France
63E3 **Breton Sd** USA
68C2 **Breton Woods** USA
35B1 **Brett,C** New Zealand
67B1 **Brevard** USA
34C1 **Brewarrina** Australia
65F2 **Brewer** USA
68D2 **Brewster** New York, USA
58C1 **Brewster** Washington, USA
67A2 **Brewton** USA
47D2 **Breyten** South Africa
16D1 **Brežice** Slovenia
50C3 **Bria** Central African Republic
14D3 **Briançon** France
14C2 **Briare** France
7C4 **Bridgend** Wales
8C3 **Bridge of Orchy** Scotland
67A2 **Bridgeport** Alabama, USA
59C3 **Bridgeport** California, USA
65E2 **Bridgeport** Connecticut, USA
60C2 **Bridgeport** Nebraska, USA
63C2 **Bridgeport** Texas, USA
66C1 **Bridgeport Res** USA
58E1 **Bridger** USA
60B2 **Bridger Peak** USA
68C3 **Bridgeton** USA
69R3 **Bridgetown** Barbados
55M5 **Bridgewater** Canada
68E2 **Bridgewater** USA
7C4 **Bridgwater** England
7C4 **Bridgwater B** England
6D2 **Bridlington** England
6E3 **Bridlington Bay** England
34C4 **Bridport** Australia
7C4 **Bridport** England
13C3 **Brienne-le-Château** France
13C3 **Briey** France
16B1 **Brig** Switzerland
56B2 **Brigham City** USA
34C3 **Bright** Australia
7D4 **Brighton** England
75A3 **Brilhante** *R* Brazil
13E2 **Brilon** Germany
17D2 **Brindisi** Italy
63D2 **Brinkley** USA
33E3 **Brisbane** Australia
65E2 **Bristol** Connecticut, USA
7C4 **Bristol** England
65E2 **Bristol** Pennsylvania, USA
68E2 **Bristol** Rhode Island, USA
57E3 **Bristol** Tennessee, USA
64C3 **Bristol** USA
7B4 **Bristol Chan** England/Wales
54F4 **British Columbia** *Province* Canada
55K1 **British Empire Range** *Mts* Canada
54E3 **British Mts** Canada
47D2 **Brits** South Africa
47C3 **Britstown** South Africa
61D1 **Britton** USA
14C2 **Brive** France
7C4 **Brixham** England
18D3 **Brno** Czechoslovakia
67B2 **Broad** *R* USA
68C1 **Broadalbin** USA
55L4 **Broadback** *R* Canada
8B2 **Broad Bay** *Inlet* Scotland
8C3 **Broadford** Scotland
9B2 **Broad Haven, B** Irish Republic
7E4 **Broadstairs** England
60B1 **Broadus** USA
60C2 **Broadwater** USA
54H4 **Brochet** Canada
54G2 **Brock I** Canada
65D2 **Brockport** USA
68E1 **Brockton** USA
65D2 **Brockville** Canada
68A2 **Brockway** USA
55K2 **Brodeur Pen** Canada
8C4 **Brodick** Scotland
19D2 **Brodnica** Poland
21D5 **Brody** Ukraine
13D2 **Brokem Haltern** Germany
60D2 **Broken Bow** Nebraska, USA
63D2 **Broken Bow** Oklahoma, USA
63D2 **Broken Bow L** USA
32D4 **Broken Hill** Australia
7C3 **Bromsgrove** England
12G5 **Brønnøysund** Norway
68D2 **Bronx** *Borough* New York, USA
27E6 **Brooke's Pt** Philippines
61E3 **Brookfield** Missouri, USA
64B2 **Brookfield** Wisconsin, USA
57D3 **Brookhaven** USA
58B2 **Brookings** Oregon, USA
56D2 **Brookings** South Dakota, USA
68E1 **Brookline** USA
61E2 **Brooklyn** USA
68D2 **Brooklyn** *Borough* New York, USA
61E1 **Brooklyn Center** USA
54G4 **Brooks** Canada
54C3 **Brooks Range** *Mts* USA
67B3 **Brooksville** USA
34D1 **Brooloo** Australia
32B2 **Broome** Australia
8C3 **Broom, Loch** *Estuary* Scotland
8D2 **Brora** Scotland
58B2 **Brothers** USA
6C2 **Broughton** England
8D3 **Broughty Ferry** Scotland
50B2 **Broulkou** *Well* Chad
19G2 **Brovary** Ukraine
61E1 **Browerville** USA
62B2 **Brownfield** USA
56D4 **Brownsville** USA
56D3 **Brownwood** USA
27F8 **Browse I** Australia
13B2 **Bruay-en-Artois** France
32A3 **Bruce,Mt** Australia
64C1 **Bruce Pen** Canada
13E3 **Bruchsal** Germany
18D3 **Bruck an der Mur** Austria
**Bruges = Brugge**
13B2 **Brugge** Belgium
13D2 **Brühl** Germany
45B3 **Brûk, Wadi el** Egypt
75D1 **Brumado** Brazil
13D3 **Brumath** France
58C2 **Bruneau** USA
58C2 **Bruneau** *R* USA
27E6 **Brunei** *State* Borneo
16C1 **Brunico** Italy
35B2 **Brunner,L** New Zealand
13E1 **Brunsbüttel** Germany
57E3 **Brunswick** Georgia, USA
65F2 **Brunswick** Maine, USA
61E3 **Brunswick** Mississippi, USA
74B8 **Brunswick,Pen de** Chile
34C4 **Bruny I** Australia
20G3 **Brusenets** Russian Federation
60C2 **Brush** USA
69A3 **Brus Laguna** Honduras
**Brüssel = Brussels**
18A2 **Brussels** Belgium
**Bruxelles = Brussels**
13D3 **Bruyères** France
56D3 **Bryan** USA
34A2 **Bryan,Mt** Australia
20E5 **Bryansk** Russian Federation
63D2 **Bryant** USA
59D3 **Bryce Canyon Nat Pk** USA
18D2 **Brzeg** Poland
41E4 **Būbīyan** *I* Kuwait
50D4 **Bubu** *R* Tanzania
47E1 **Bubye** *R* Zimbabwe
72D2 **Bucaramanga** Colombia
8E3 **Buchan** *Oilfield* N Sea
48A4 **Buchanan** Liberia
62C2 **Buchanan,L** USA
8E3 **Buchan Deep** N Sea
55L2 **Buchan G** Canada
10C2 **Buchan Ness** *Pen* Scotland
55N5 **Buchans** Canada
17F2 **Bucharest** Romania
66B3 **Buchon,Pt** USA
13E1 **Bückeburg** Germany
59D4 **Buckeye** USA
8D3 **Buckhaven** Scotland
8D3 **Buckie** Scotland
7D3 **Buckingham** England
65F2 **Bucksport** USA
50B4 **Buco Zau** Congo
**București = Bucharest**
19D3 **Budapest** Hungary
42D3 **Budaun** India
7B4 **Bude** England
63D2 **Bude** USA
21G7 **Budennovsk** Russian Federation
43J1 **Budhana** India
45B4 **Budhîya, Gebel** Egypt
13E2 **Büdingen** Germany
17D2 **Budva** Montenegro, Yugoslavia
48C4 **Buéa** Cameroon
66B3 **Buellton** USA
72C3 **Buenaventura** Colombia
62A3 **Buenaventura** Mexico
60B3 **Buena Vista** Colorado, USA
65D3 **Buena Vista** Virginia, USA
66C3 **Buena Vista L** USA
74E4 **Buenos Aires** Argentina
74E5 **Buenos Aires** *State* Argentina
74B7 **Buenos Aires, Lago** Argentina
63D1 **Buffalo** Mississipi, USA
57F2 **Buffalo** New York, USA
60C1 **Buffalo** S Dakota, USA
63C2 **Buffalo** Texas, USA
56C2 **Buffalo** Wyoming, USA
47E2 **Buffalo** *R* South Africa
58C1 **Buffalo Hump** *Mt* USA
54G3 **Buffalo L** Canada
54H4 **Buffalo Narrows** Canada
67B2 **Buford** USA
17F2 **Buftea** Romania
19E2 **Bug** *R* Poland/Ukraine
72C3 **Buga** Colombia
41F2 **Bugdayli** Turkmenistan
20H2 **Bugrino** Russian Federation
20J5 **Bugulma** Russian Federation
20J5 **Buguruslan** Russian Federation
40C2 **Buḩayrat al Asad** *Res* Syria
58D2 **Buhl** Idaho, USA
61E1 **Buhl** Minnesota, USA
7C3 **Builth Wells** Wales
50C4 **Bujumbura** Burundi
33E1 **Buka** *I* Papua New Guinea
51C4 **Bukama** Zaïre
50C4 **Bukavu** Zaïre
38E2 **Bukhara** Uzbekistan
27D7 **Bukittinggi** Indonesia
50D4 **Bukoba** Tanzania
27G7 **Bula** Indonesia
27F5 **Bulan** Philippines
42D3 **Bulandshahr** India
51C6 **Bulawayo** Zimbabwe
17F3 **Buldan** Turkey
42D4 **Buldāna** India
26D2 **Bulgan** Mongolia
17E2 **Bulgaria** *Republic* Europe
35B2 **Buller** *R* New Zealand
34C3 **Buller,Mt** Australia
32A4 **Bullfinch** Australia
34B1 **Bulloo** *R* Australia
34B1 **Bulloo Downs** Australia
34B1 **Bulloo L** Australia
63D1 **Bull Shoals Res** USA
32D1 **Bulolo** Papua New Guinea
47D2 **Bultfontein** South Africa
27E6 **Bulu, Gunung** *Mt* Indonesia
50C3 **Bumba** Zaïre
21D8 **Bu Menderes** *R* Turkey
30B2 **Bumphal Dam** Thailand
50D3 **Buna** Kenya
32A4 **Bunbury** Australia
9C2 **Buncrana** Irish Republic
33E3 **Bundaberg** Australia
34D2 **Bundarra** Australia
13E1 **Bünde** Germany
42D3 **Būndi** India
7E3 **Bungay** England
34C1 **Bungil** *R* Australia
51B4 **Bungo** Angola
28B4 **Bungo-suidō** *Str* Japan
27D6 **Bunguran** *I* Indonesia
27D6 **Bunguran, Kepulauan** *I* Indonesia
50D3 **Bunia** Zaïre
63D1 **Bunker** USA
63D2 **Bunkie** USA
67B3 **Bunnell** USA
27E7 **Buntok** Indonesia
27F6 **Buol** Indonesia
50C2 **Buram** Sudan
43E2 **Burang** China
50E3 **Burao** Somalia
45D2 **Burāq** Syria
41D4 **Buraydah** Saudi Arabia
59C4 **Burbank** USA
34C2 **Burcher** Australia
21E8 **Burdur** Turkey
50D2 **Burē** Ethiopia
7E3 **Bure** *R* England
26G1 **Bureinskiy Khrebet** *Mts* Russian Federation
26F2 **Bureya** Russian Federation
45B3 **Bûr Fu'ad** Egypt
18C2 **Burg** Germany
17F2 **Burgas** Bulgaria
67C2 **Burgaw** USA
47D3 **Burgersdorp** South Africa
15B1 **Burgos** Spain
13D1 **Burgsteinfurt** Germany
19D1 **Burgsvik** Sweden
17F3 **Burhaniye** Turkey
42D4 **Burhānpur** India
30C2 **Buriram** Thailand
75C2 **Buritis** Brazil
32C2 **Burketown** Australia
48B3 **Burkina** *Republic* W Africa
65D1 **Burk's Falls** Canada
56B2 **Burley** USA
60C3 **Burlington** Colorado, USA
57D2 **Burlington** Iowa, USA
68C2 **Burlington** New Jersey, USA
67C1 **Burlington** North Carolina, USA
57F2 **Burlington** Vermont, USA
58B1 **Burlington** Washington, USA
39H3 **Burma** *Republic* Asia
62C2 **Burnet** USA
58B2 **Burney** USA
68B2 **Burnham** USA
7E4 **Burnham-on-Crouch** England
32D5 **Burnie** Australia
6C3 **Burnley** England
58C2 **Burns** USA
54F4 **Burns Lake** Canada
24K5 **Burqin** China
34A2 **Burra** Australia
34D2 **Burragorang,L** Australia
8D2 **Burray** *I* Scotland
34C2 **Burren Junction** Australia
34C2 **Burrinjuck Res** Australia
62B3 **Burro, Serranías del** *Mts* Mexico
8C4 **Burrow Head** *Pt* Scotland
27G8 **Burrundie** Australia
21D7 **Bursa** Turkey
40B4 **Bur Safâga** Egypt
**Bûr Saîd = Port Said**
45B4 **Bûr Taufiq** Egypt
64C2 **Burton** USA
7D3 **Burton upon Trent** England
12J6 **Burtrask** Sweden
34B2 **Burtundy** Australia
27F7 **Buru** *I* Indonesia
50C4 **Burundi** *Republic* Africa
60D2 **Burwell** USA
7C3 **Bury** England
25N4 **Buryat Republic** Russian Federation
21J6 **Burynshik** Kazakhstan
7E3 **Bury St Edmunds** England
28A3 **Bushan** China
41F4 **Būshehr** Iran
9C2 **Bushmills** Northern Ireland
50B4 **Busira** *R* Zaïre
19E2 **Buskozdroj** Poland
45D2 **Buşrá ash Shām** Syria
13D4 **Bussang** France
32A4 **Busselton** Australia
16B1 **Busto Arsizio** Italy
50C3 **Buta** Zaïre
50C4 **Butare** Rwanda
8C4 **Bute** *I* Scotland
26F2 **Butha Qi** China
65D2 **Butler** USA
32B1 **Buton** *I* Indonesia
48C4 **Butta** Togo
56B2 **Butte** USA
30C4 **Butterworth** Malaysia
47D3 **Butterworth** South Africa
10B2 **Butt of Lewis** *C* Scotland
55M3 **Button Is** Canada
66C3 **Buttonwillow** USA
27F6 **Butuan** Philippines
21G5 **Buturlinovka** Russian Federation
43E3 **Butwal** Nepal
13E2 **Butzbach** Germany
50E3 **Buulobarde** Somalia
50E3 **Buurhakaba** Somalia
7D3 **Buxton** England
20G4 **Buy** Russian Federation
31B1 **Buyant Ovoo** Mongolia
21H7 **Buynaksk** Russian Federation
25N5 **Buyr Nuur** *L* Mongolia
21G8 **Büyük Ağri Daği** *Mt* Turkey
40A2 **Büyük Menderes** *R* Turkey
17F1 **Buzău** Romania
17F1 **Buzău** *R* Romania
75D3 **Búzios, Ponta dos** *Pt* Brazil
20J5 **Buzuluk** Russian Federation
68E2 **Buzzards B** USA
17F2 **Byala** Bulgaria
17E2 **Byala Slatina** Bulgaria
54H2 **Byam Martin Channel** Canada
54H2 **Byam Martin I** Canada
45C1 **Byblos** *Hist site* Lebanon
19D2 **Bydgoszcz** Poland
60C3 **Byers** USA
12F7 **Bygland** Norway
19G2 **Bykhov** Belorussia
55L2 **Bylot I** Canada
34C2 **Byrock** Australia
66B2 **Byron** USA
34D1 **Byron** *C* Australia
25P3 **Bytantay** *R* Russian Federation
19D2 **Bytom** Poland


## C


74E3 **Caacupú** Paraguay
75A4 **Caaguazú** Paraguay
51B5 **Caála** Angola
75A4 **Caapucú** Paraguay
75B3 **Caarapó** Brazil
74E3 **Caazapá** Paraguay
15C1 **Caballería, Cabo de** *C* Spain
62A2 **Caballo Res** USA
27F5 **Cabanatuan** Philippines
65F1 **Cabano** Canada
73M5 **Cabedelo** Brazil
15A2 **Cabeza del Buey** Spain
72D1 **Cabimas** Venezuela
50B4 **Cabinda** Angola
50B4 **Cabinda** *Province* Angola
58C1 **Cabinet Mts** USA
75D3 **Cabo Frio** Brazil
55L5 **Cabonga,Réservoire** Canada
34D1 **Caboolture** Australia
51D5 **Cabora Bassa Dam** Mozambique
70A1 **Caborca** Mexico
55M5 **Cabot Str** Canada
15B2 **Cabra** Spain
75D2 **Cabral, Serra do** *Mts* Brazil
15A1 **Cabreira** *Mt* Portugal
15C2 **Cabrera** *I* Spain
15B2 **Cabriel** *R* Spain
17E2 **Čačak** Serbia, Yugoslavia
68A3 **Cacapon** *R* USA
73G7 **Cáceres** Brazil
15A2 **Cáceres** Spain
63D1 **Cache** *R* USA
66A1 **Cache Creek** *R* USA
58D2 **Cache Peak** *Mt* USA
74C3 **Cachi** Argentina
73G5 **Cachimbo** Brazil
73G5 **Cachimbo, Serra do** *Mts* Brazil
73L6 **Cachoeira** Brazil
75B2 **Cachoeira Alta** Brazil
73L5 **Cachoeira de Paulo Afonso** *Waterfall* Brazil
74F4 **Cachoeira do Sul** Brazil
73K8 **Cachoeiro de Itapemirim** Brazil
66C3 **Cachuma,L** USA
51B5 **Cacolo** Angola
51B5 **Caconda** Angola
62B1 **Cactus** USA
75B2 **Caçu** Brazil
75D1 **Caculé** Brazil
51B5 **Caculuvar** *R* Angola
19D3 **Čadca** Czechoslovakia
7C3 **Cader Idris** *Mt* Wales
57E2 **Cadillac** USA
15A2 **Cádiz** Spain
15A2 **Cádiz, Golfo de** *G* Spain
14B2 **Caen** France
7B3 **Caernarfon** Wales
7B3 **Caernarfon B** Wales
7C4 **Caerphilly** Wales
45C2 **Caesarea** *Hist Site* Israel
75D1 **Caetité** Brazil
74C3 **Cafayate** Argentina
40B2 **Caga Tepe** *Mt* Turkey

Cagayan de Oro Catanduanes

27F6 **Cagayan de Oro** Philippines
16B3 **Cagliari** Sardinia, Italy
16B3 **Cagliari, G di** Sardinia, Italy
69D3 **Caguas** Puerto Rico
67A2 **Cahaba** *R* USA
9C3 **Cahir** Irish Republic
9C3 **Cahore Pt** Irish Republic
14C3 **Cahors** France
51D5 **Caia** Mozambique
73G6 **Caiabis, Serra dos** *Mts* Brazil
51C5 **Caianda** Angola
75B2 **Caiapó** *R* Brazil
75B2 **Caiapônia** Brazil
75B2 **Caiapó, Serra do** *Mts* Brazil
73L5 **Caicó** Brazil
69C2 **Caicos Is** Caribbean Sea
57F4 **Caicos Pass** The Bahamas
8D3 **Cairngorms** *Mts* Scotland
8C4 **Cairnryan** Scotland
32D2 **Cairns** Australia
40B3 **Cairo** Egypt
57E3 **Cairo** USA
8D2 **Caithness** Scotland
34B1 **Caiwarro** Australia
72C5 **Cajabamba** Peru
72C5 **Cajamarca** Peru
48C4 **Calabar** Nigeria
69D5 **Calabozo** Venezuela
17E2 **Calafat** Romania
74B8 **Calafate** Argentina
15B1 **Calahorra** Spain
14C1 **Calais** France
65F1 **Calais** USA
74C2 **Calama** Chile
72D3 **Calamar** Colombia
27E5 **Calamian Group** *Is* Philippines
51B4 **Calandula** Angola
27C6 **Calang** Indonesia
49E2 **Calanscio Sand Sea** Libya
27F5 **Calapan** Philippines
17F2 **Calarasi** Romania
15B1 **Calatayud** Spain
66B2 **Calaveras Res** USA
63D3 **Calcasieu L** USA
43F4 **Calcutta** India
15A2 **Caldas da Rainha** Portugal
73J7 **Caldas Novas** Brazil
74B3 **Caldera** Chile
56B2 **Caldwell** USA
47B3 **Caledon** South Africa
47D3 **Caledon** *R* South Africa
64A2 **Caledonia** Minnesota, USA
68B1 **Caledonia** New York, USA
74C7 **Caleta Olivia** Argentina
56B3 **Calexico** USA
54G4 **Calgary** Canada
67B2 **Calhoun** USA
67B2 **Calhoun Falls** USA
72C3 **Cali** Colombia
66C3 **Caliente** California, USA
56B3 **Caliente** Nevada, USA
62A1 **Caliente** New Mexico, USA
56A3 **California** *State* USA
66C3 **California Aqueduct** USA
70A1 **California, G de** Mexico
44B3 **Calimera,Pt** India
59C4 **Calipatria** USA
47C3 **Calitzdorp** South Africa
34B1 **Callabonna** *R* Australia
34A1 **Callabonna,L** Australia
65D1 **Callander** Canada
8C3 **Callander** Scotland
72C6 **Callao** Peru
68C2 **Callicoon** USA
67B3 **Caloosahatchee** *R* USA
34D1 **Caloundra** Australia
16C3 **Caltanissetta** Sicily, Italy
51B4 **Caluango** Angola
51B5 **Calulo** Angola
51B5 **Caluquembe** Angola
50F2 **Caluula** Somalia
16B2 **Calvi** Corsica, France
47B3 **Calvinia** South Africa
13E3 **Calw** Germany
75E1 **Camacari** Brazil
70E2 **Camagüey** Cuba
70E2 **Camagüey,Arch de** *Is* Cuba
75E1 **Camamu** Brazil
72D7 **Camaná** Peru
75B2 **Camapuã** Brazil
72E8 **Camargo** Bolivia
66C3 **Camarillo** USA
74C6 **Camarones** Argentina
58B1 **Camas** USA
51B4 **Camaxilo** Angola
51B4 **Cambatela** Angola
30C3 **Cambodia** *Republic* SE Asia
7B4 **Camborne** England
14C1 **Cambrai** France
66B3 **Cambria** USA
7C3 **Cambrian Mts** Wales
64C2 **Cambridge** Canada
7E3 **Cambridge** England
69H1 **Cambridge** Jamaica
65D3 **Cambridge** Maryland, USA
65E2 **Cambridge** Massachussets, USA
61E1 **Cambridge** Minnesota, USA
35C1 **Cambridge** New Zealand
64C2 **Cambridge** Ohio, USA
7D3 **Cambridge** *County* England
54H3 **Cambridge Bay** Canada
27F8 **Cambridge G** Australia
21F7 **Cam Burun** *Pt* Turkey
57D3 **Camden** Arkansas, USA
34D2 **Camden** Australia
65E3 **Camden** New Jersey, USA
68C1 **Camden** New York, USA
67B2 **Camden** South Carolina, USA
61E3 **Cameron** Missouri, USA
63C2 **Cameron** Texas, USA
54H2 **Cameron I** Canada
35A3 **Cameron Mts** New Zealand
50B3 **Cameroon** *Federal Republic* Africa
48C4 **Cameroun, Mt** Cameroon
73J4 **Cametá** Brazil
67B2 **Camilla** USA
66B1 **Camino** USA
72F8 **Camiri** Bolivia
51C4 **Camissombo** Angola
73K4 **Camocim** Brazil
32C2 **Camooweal** Australia
44E4 **Camorta** *I* Nicobar Is, Indian Ocean
74A7 **Campana** *I* Chile
47C2 **Campbell** South Africa
35B2 **Campbell,C** New Zealand
37K7 **Campbell I** New Zealand
54E3 **Campbell,Mt** Canada
42C2 **Campbellpore** Pakistan
54F5 **Campbell River** Canada
64B3 **Campbellsville** USA
55M5 **Campbellton** Canada
34D2 **Campbelltown** Australia
8C4 **Campbeltown** Scotland
70C3 **Campeche** Mexico
70C2 **Campeche, B de** Mexico
34B3 **Camperdown** Australia
73L5 **Campina Grande** Brazil
73J8 **Campinas** Brazil
75C2 **Campina Verde** Brazil
66C2 **Camp Nelson** USA
48C4 **Campo** Cameroon
16C2 **Campobasso** Italy
75C3 **Campo Belo** Brazil
75C2 **Campo Florido** Brazil
74D3 **Campo Gallo** Argentina
74F2 **Campo Grande** Brazil
73K4 **Campo Maior** Brazil
74F2 **Campo Mourão** Brazil
75D3 **Campos** Brazil
75C2 **Campos Altos** Brazil
59D4 **Camp Verde** USA
30D3 **Cam Ranh** Vietnam
54G4 **Camrose** Canada
51B5 **Camucuio** Angola
69K1 **Canaan** Tobago
68D1 **Canaan** USA
51B5 **Canacupa** Angola
53F3 **Canada** *Dominion* N America
74D4 **Cañada de Gómez** Argentina
68C2 **Canadensis** USA
62B1 **Canadian** USA
56C3 **Canadian** *R* USA
21D7 **Çanakkale** Turkey
68B1 **Canandaigua** USA
68B1 **Canandaigua L** USA
70A1 **Cananea** Mexico
75C4 **Cananeia** Brazil
**Canarias, Islas = Canary Islands**
52G3 **Canary Basin** Atlantic Ocean
48A2 **Canary Is** *Atlantic Ocean*
75C3 **Canastra, Serra da** *Mts* Brazil
70B2 **Canatlán** Mexico
57E4 **Canaveral,C** USA
73L7 **Canavieiras** Brazil
32D4 **Canberra** Australia
58B2 **Canby** California, USA
61D2 **Canby** Minnesota, USA
17F3 **Çandarli Körfezi** *B* Turkey
68D2 **Candlewood,L** USA
60D1 **Cando** USA
68B1 **Candor** USA
74E4 **Canelones** Uruguay
63C1 **Caney** USA
51C5 **Cangamba** Angola
51C5 **Cangombe** Angola
31D2 **Cangzhou** China
55M4 **Caniapiscau** *R* Canada
55M4 **Caniapiscau, Réservoir** *Res* Canada
16C3 **Canicatti** Sicily, Italy
73L4 **Canindé** Brazil
68B1 **Canisteo** USA
68B1 **Canisteo** *R* USA
62A1 **Canjilon** USA
40B1 **Çankiri** Turkey
8B3 **Canna** *I* Scotland
44B3 **Cannanore** India
14D3 **Cannes** France
7C3 **Cannock** England
60C1 **Cannonball** *R* USA
34C3 **Cann River** Australia
74F3 **Canõas** England
75B4 **Canoinhas** Brazil
60B3 **Canon City** USA
34B2 **Canopus** Australia
54H4 **Canora** Canada
34C2 **Canowindra** Australia
15B1 **Cantabria** *Region* Spain
14A3 **Cantabrica, Cord** *Mts* Spain
7E4 **Canterbury** England
35B2 **Canterbury Bight** *B* New Zealand
35B2 **Canterbury Plains** New Zealand
30D4 **Can Tho** Vietnam
66D3 **Cantil** USA
**Canton = Guangzhou**
63E2 **Canton** Mississippi, USA
64A2 **Canton** Missouri, USA
57E2 **Canton** Ohio, USA
68B2 **Canton** Pensylvania, USA
61D2 **Canton** S Dakota, USA
33H1 **Canton** *I* Phoenix Islands
75B3 **Cantu, Serra do** *Mts* Brazil
62B2 **Canyon** USA
58C2 **Canyon City** USA
58D1 **Canyon Ferry L** USA
59E3 **Canyonlands Nat Pk** USA
58B2 **Canyonville** USA
51C4 **Canzar** Angola
30D1 **Cao Bang** Vietnam
28B2 **Caoshi** China
73J4 **Capanema** Brazil
75C3 **Capão Bonito** Brazil
75D3 **Caparaó, Serra do** *Mts* Brazil
14B3 **Capbreton** France
16B2 **Cap Corse** *C* Corsica, France
14B2 **Cap de la Hague** *C* France
65E1 **Cap-de-la-Madeleine** Canada
15C2 **Capdepera** Spain
34C4 **Cape Barren I** Australia
52J6 **Cape Basin** Atlantic Ocean
55N5 **Cape Breton I** Canada
**Cape, Cabo etc: see also individual cape names**
48B4 **Cape Coast** Ghana
65E2 **Cape Cod B** USA
55M3 **Cape Dyer** Canada
76F7 **Cape Evans** *Base* Antarctica
67C2 **Cape Fear** *R* USA
63E1 **Cape Girardeau** USA
74C8 **Cape Horn** Chile
36H4 **Cape Johnson Depth** Pacific Ocean
75D2 **Capelinha** Brazil
54B3 **Cape Lisburne** USA
51B5 **Capelongo** Angola
65E3 **Cape May** USA
54F5 **Cape Mendocino** USA
51B4 **Capenda Camulemba** Angola
54F2 **Cape Parry** Canada
47C3 **Cape Province** South Africa
47B3 **Cape Town** South Africa
52G4 **Cape Verde** *Is* Atlantic Ocean
52G4 **Cape Verde Basin** Atlantic Ocean
32D2 **Cape York Pen** Australia
69C3 **Cap-Haïtien** Haiti
73J4 **Capim** *R* Brazil
75A3 **Capitán Bado** Paraguay
59E3 **Capitol Reef Nat Pk** USA
75A2 **Capivari** *R* Brazil
9C3 **Cappoquin** Irish Republic
69P2 **Cap Pt** St Lucia
16C2 **Capri** *I* Italy
51C5 **Caprivi Strip** *Region* Namibia
72D4 **Caquetá** *R* Colombia
17E2 **Caracal** Romania
72F3 **Caracaraí** Brazil
72E1 **Caracas** Venezuela
75A3 **Caracol** Brazil
75C3 **Caraguatatuba** Brazil
74B5 **Carahue** Chile
75D2 **Caraí** Brazil
75D3 **Carandaí** Brazil
75A2 **Carandazal** Brazil
73K8 **Carangola** Brazil
17E1 **Caransebeş** Romania
69A3 **Caratasca** Honduras
70D3 **Caratasca, L de** *Lg* Honduras
75D2 **Caratinga** Brazil
15B2 **Caravaca de la Cruz** Spain
75E2 **Caravelas** Brazil
16B3 **Carbonara, C** Sardinia, Italy
64B3 **Carbondale** Illinois, USA
68C2 **Carbondale** Pennsylvania, USA
55N5 **Carbonear** Canada
16B3 **Carbonia** Sardinia, Italy
54G4 **Carcajou** Canada
50E2 **Carcar Mts** Somalia
14C3 **Carcassonne** France
54E3 **Carcross** Canada
30C3 **Cardamomes, Chaîne des** *Mts* Cambodia
70D2 **Cardenas** Cuba
7C4 **Cardiff** Wales
7B3 **Cardigan** Wales
7B3 **Cardigan B** Wales
75C4 **Cardoso, Ilha do** Brazil
17E1 **Carei** Romania
73G4 **Careiro** Brazil
64C2 **Carey** USA
14B2 **Carhaix-Plouguer** France
74D5 **Carhué** Argentina
73K8 **Cariacica** Brazil
71C2 **Caribbean S** Central America
54J4 **Caribou** Canada
65F1 **Caribou** USA
54G4 **Caribou Mts** Alberta, Canada
54F4 **Caribou Mts** British Columbia, Canada
13C3 **Carignan** France
75D1 **Carinhanha** Brazil
75D1 **Carinhanha** *R* Brazil
72F1 **Caripito** Venezuela
65D1 **Carleton Place** Canada
47D2 **Carletonville** South Africa
58C2 **Carlin** USA
9C2 **Carlingford, L** Northern Ireland
64B3 **Carlinville** USA
6C2 **Carlisle** England
65D2 **Carlisle** USA
75D2 **Carlos Chagas** Brazil
9C3 **Carlow** Irish Republic
9C3 **Carlow** *County* Irish Republic
59C4 **Carlsbad** California, USA
56C3 **Carlsbad** New Mexico, USA
62B2 **Carlsbad Caverns Nat Pk** USA
36E4 **Carlsberg Ridge** Indian Ocean
54H5 **Carlyle** Canada
54E3 **Carmacks** Canada
7B4 **Carmarthen** Wales
7B4 **Carmarthen B** Wales
66B2 **Carmel** California, USA
68D2 **Carmel** New York, USA
7B3 **Carmel Hd** *Pt* Wales
45C2 **Carmel,Mt** Israel
66B2 **Carmel Valley** USA
56B4 **Carmen** *I* Mexico
74D6 **Carmen de Patagones** Argentina
64B3 **Carmi** USA
59B3 **Carmichael** USA
75C2 **Carmo do Paranaiba** Brazil
15A2 **Carmona** Spain
75E2 **Carnacá** Brazil
32A3 **Carnarvon** Australia
47C3 **Carnarvon** South Africa
9C2 **Carndonagh** Irish Republic
32B3 **Carnegie,L** Australia
44E4 **Car Nicobar** *I* Nicobar Is, Indian Ocean
50B3 **Carnot** Central African Republic
8D3 **Carnoustie** Scotland
9C3 **Carnsore Pt** Irish Republic
67B3 **Carol City** USA
73J5 **Carolina** Brazil
47E2 **Carolina** South Africa
67C2 **Carolina Beach** USA
27H6 **Caroline Is** Pacific Ocean
19F3 **Carpathian Mts** Romania
21C6 **Carpathians** *Mts* EEurope
32C2 **Carpentaria,G of** Australia
39H5 **Carpenter Ridge** Indian Ocean
14D3 **Carpentras** France
16C2 **Carpi** Italy
66C3 **Carpinteria** USA
67B3 **Carrabelle** USA
16C2 **Carrara** Italy
10B3 **Carrauntoohill** *Mt* Irish Republic
8C4 **Carrick** Scotland
9D2 **Carrickfergus** Northern Ireland
9C3 **Carrickmacross** Irish Republic
9C3 **Carrick-on-Suir** Irish Republic
34A2 **Carrieton** Australia
54J5 **Carrington** USA
15B1 **Carrión** *R* Spain
62C3 **Carrizo Springs** USA
62A2 **Carrizozo** USA
57D2 **Carroll** USA
67A2 **Carrollton** Georgia, USA
64B3 **Carrollton** Kentucky, USA
61E3 **Carrollton** Missouri, USA
9B2 **Carrowmore,L** *Irish Republic*
63E1 **Carruthersville** USA
21F7 **Carşamba** Turkey
21E8 **Carşamba** *R* Turkey
56B3 **Carson City** USA
64C2 **Carsonville** USA
8D4 **Carstairs** Scotland
69B4 **Cartagena** Colombia
15B2 **Cartagena** Spain
72C3 **Cartago** Colombia
70D4 **Cartago** Costa Rica
66C2 **Cartago** USA
35C2 **Carterton** New Zealand
63D1 **Carthage** Missouri, USA
65D2 **Carthage** New York, USA
63D2 **Carthage** Texas, USA
32B2 **Cartier I** Timor Sea
55N4 **Cartwright** Canada
73L5 **Caruaru** Brazil
72F1 **Carúpano** Venezuela
13B2 **Carvin** France
15A2 **Carvoeiro, Cabo** *C* Portugal
67C1 **Cary** USA
48B1 **Casablanca** Morocco
75C3 **Casa Branca** Brazil
56B3 **Casa Grande** USA
16B1 **Casale Monferrato** Italy
58D1 **Cascade** USA
35A2 **Cascade Pt** New Zealand
56A2 **Cascade Range** *Mts* USA
58C2 **Cascade Res** USA
74F2 **Cascavel** Brazil
16C2 **Caserta** Italy
76G9 **Casey** *Base* Antarctica
9C3 **Cashel** Irish Republic
33E3 **Casino** Australia
72C5 **Casma** Peru
66B3 **Casmalia** USA
15C1 **Caspe** Spain
56C2 **Casper** USA
21H7 **Caspian S** Asia/Europe
65D3 **Cass** USA
51C5 **Cassamba** Angola
13B2 **Cassel** France
61D1 **Casselton** USA
54E3 **Cassiar Mts** Canada
75B2 **Cassilândia** Brazil
16C2 **Cassino** Italy
61E1 **Cass Lake** USA
66C3 **Castaic** USA
14D3 **Castellane** France
16C2 **Castello, Città di** Italy
15C1 **Castellón de la Plana** Spain
73K5 **Castelo** Brazil
15A2 **Castelo Branco** Portugal
14C3 **Castelsarrasin** France
16C3 **Castelvetrano** Sicily, Italy
34B3 **Casterton** Australia
15B2 **Castilla la Mancha** *Region* Spain
15B1 **Castilla y León** *Region* Spain
10B3 **Castlebar** Irish Republic
8B3 **Castlebay** Scotland
9C2 **Castleblayney** Irish Republic
59D3 **Castle Dale** USA
8D4 **Castle Douglas** Scotland
6D3 **Castleford** England
58C1 **Castlegar** Canada
34B3 **Castlemaine** Australia
66B3 **Castle Mt** USA
58D2 **Castle Peak** *Mt* USA
34C2 **Castlereagh** *R* Australia
60C3 **Castle Rock** USA
6B2 **Castletown** England
9B4 **Castletown Bere** Irish Republic
14C3 **Castres-sur-l'Agout** France
69P2 **Castries** St Lucia
74B6 **Castro** Argentina
74F2 **Castro** Brazil
73L6 **Castro Alves** Brazil
16D3 **Castrovillari** Italy
66B2 **Castroville** USA
35A2 **Caswell Sd** New Zealand
70E2 **Cat** *I* The Bahamas
72B5 **Catacaos** Peru
75D3 **Cataguases** Brazil
63D2 **Catahoula L** USA
75C2 **Catalão** Brazil
15C1 **Cataluña** *Region* Spain
74C3 **Catamarca** Argentina
74C3 **Catamarca** *State* Argentina
51D5 **Catandica** Mozambique
27F5 **Catanduanes** *I* Philippines

Dimāpur East Branch Delaware


43G3 **Dimāpur** India
**Dimashq = Damascus**
50C4 **Dimbelenge** Zaïre
48B4 **Dimbokro** Ivory Coast
17F2 **Dimitrovgrad** Bulgaria
20H5 **Dimitrovgrad** Russian Federation
45C3 **Dīmona** Israel
27F5 **Dinaget** *I* Philippines
43F3 **Dinajpur** India
14B2 **Dinan** France
13C2 **Dinant** Belgium
40B2 **Dinar** Turkey
50D2 **Dinder** *R* Sudan
44B3 **Dindigul** India
31B2 **Dingbian** China
43F3 **Dinggyê** China
10A3 **Dingle** Irish Republic
10A3 **Dingle B** Irish Republic
48A3 **Dinguiraye** Guinea
8C3 **Dingwall** Scotland
31A2 **Dingxi** China
31D2 **Ding Xian** China
30D1 **Dinh Lap** Vietnam
60B2 **Dinosaur** USA
66C2 **Dinuba** USA
48A3 **Diouloulou** Senegal
43G3 **Diphu** India
50E3 **Dirē Dawa** Ethiopia
32A3 **Dirk Hartog** *I* Australia
50B2 **Dirkou** Niger
34C1 **Dirranbandi** Australia
74J8 **Disappointment,C** South Georgia
58B1 **Disappointment,C** USA
32B3 **Disappointment,L** Australia
34B3 **Discovery B** Australia
27E5 **Discovery Reef** S China Sea
52J7 **Discovery Tablemount** Atlantic Ocean
40B4 **Dishna** Egypt
55N3 **Disko** *I* Greenland
55N3 **Disko Bugt** *B* Greenland
55N3 **Diskofjord** Greenland
65D3 **Dismal Swamp** USA
19F1 **Disna** *R* Belorussia
67B3 **Disney World** USA
75C2 **Distrito Federal** Brazil
42C4 **Diu** India
73K8 **Divinópolis** Brazil
21G6 **Divnoye** Russian Federation
40C2 **Divriği** Turkey
66B1 **Dixon** California, USA
64B2 **Dixon** Illinois, USA
58D1 **Dixon** Montana, USA
54E4 **Dixon Entrance** *Sd* Canada/USA
41E3 **Diyālā** *R* Iraq
21G8 **Diyarbakir** Turkey
41E3 **Diz** *R* Iran
50B3 **Dja** *R* Cameroon
50B1 **Djado,Plat du** Niger
50B4 **Djambala** Congo
48C2 **Djanet** Algeria
48C1 **Djedi** *Watercourse* Algeria
48C1 **Djelfa** Algeria
50C3 **Djéma** Central African Republic
48B3 **Djenné** Mali
48B3 **Djibo** Burkina
50E2 **Djibouti** Djibouti
50E2 **Djibouti** *Republic* EAfrica
50C3 **Djolu** Zaïre
48C4 **Djougou** Benin
50B2 **Djourab, Erg du** *Desert Region* Chad
50D3 **Djugu** Zaïre
12C2 **Djúpivogur** Iceland
15C2 **Djurdjura** *Mts* Algeria
25P2 **Dmitriya Lapteva, Proliv** *Str* Russian Federation
20F4 **Dmitrov** Russian Federation
21E6 **Dnepr** *R* Ukraine
21E6 **Dneprodzerzhinsk** Ukraine
21F6 **Dnepropetrovsk** Ukraine
20D5 **Dneprovskaya Nizmennost'** *Region* Belorussia
21C6 **Dnestr** *R* Ukraine
20E4 **Dno** Russian Federation
50B3 **Doba** Chad
19E1 **Dobele** Latvia
32C1 **Dobo** Indonesia
17D2 **Doboj** Bosnia & Herzegovina, Yugoslavia
17F2 **Dobrich** Bulgaria
21E5 **Dobrush** Belorussia
73K7 **Doce** *R* Brazil
74D2 **Doctor P P Peña** Paraguay
44B3 **Dod** India
44B3 **Doda Betta** *Mt* India
17F3 **Dodecanese** *Is* Greece
55C3 **Dodge City** USA
64A2 **Dodgeville** USA
50D4 **Dodoma** Tanzania
64B1 **Dog L** Canada
64C1 **Dog L** Canada
29B3 **Dōgo** *I* Japan
48C3 **Dogondoutchi** Niger
41D2 **Doğubayazit** Turkey
41F4 **Doha** Qatar
43G3 **Doilungdêqên** China
13D1 **Dokkum** Netherlands
29F2 **Dokuchayevo, Mys** *C* Russian Federation
32C1 **Dolak** *I* Indonesia
61D2 **Doland** USA
55L5 **Dolbeau** Canada
14D2 **Dôle** France
7C3 **Dolgellau** Wales
68C1 **Dolgeville** USA
20K2 **Dolgiy, Ostrov** *I* Russian Federation
50E3 **Dolo Odo** Ethiopia
74E5 **Dolores** Argentina
60B3 **Dolores** *R* USA
54G3 **Dolphin and Union Str** Canada
74E8 **Dolphin,C** Falkland Islands
27G7 **Dom** *Mt* Indonesia
21K5 **Dombarovskiy** Russian Federation
12F6 **Dombås** Norway
13D3 **Dombasle-sur-Meurthe** France
17D1 **Dombóvár** Hungary
14B2 **Domfront** France
69E3 **Dominica** *I* Caribbean Sea
69C3 **Dominican Republic** Caribbean Sea
55L3 **Dominion,C** Canada
55N4 **Domino** Canada
26E1 **Domna** Russian Federation
16B1 **Domodossola** Italy
74B5 **Domuyo, Vol** Argentina
34D1 **Domville,Mt** Australia
8D3 **Don** *R* Scotland
21G6 **Don** *R* Russian Federation
9C2 **Donaghadee** Northern Ireland
**Donau = Dunav** Bulgaria
18C3 **Donau** *R* Austria/Germany
13E4 **Donaueschingen** Germany
18C3 **Donauwörth** Germany
15A2 **Don Benito** Spain
7D3 **Doncaster** England
51B4 **Dondo** Angola
51D5 **Dondo** Mozambique
44C4 **Dondra Head** *C* Sri Lanka
10B3 **Donegal** Irish Republic
9C2 **Donegal** *County* Irish Republic
10B3 **Donegal B** Irish Republic
9C2 **Donegal Mts** Irish Republic
9B3 **Donegal Pt** Irish Republic
21F6 **Donetsk** Ukraine
31C4 **Dong'an** China
32A3 **Dongara** Australia
31A4 **Dongchuan** China
30D2 **Dongfang** China
28B2 **Dongfeng** China
32A1 **Donggala** Indonesia
26C3 **Donggi Cona** *L* China
28A3 **Donggou** China
31C5 **Donghai Dao** *I* China
31A1 **Dong He** *R* China
30D2 **Dong Hoi** Vietnam
31C5 **Dong Jiang** *R* China
28A2 **Dongliao He** *R* China
28C2 **Dongning** China
50D2 **Dongola** Sudan
31D5 **Dongshan** China
26E4 **Dongsha Qundao** *I* China
31C2 **Dongsheng** China
31E3 **Dongtai** China
31C4 **Dongting Hu** *L* China
31B5 **Dongxing** China
31D3 **Dongzhi** China
63D1 **Doniphan** USA
16D2 **Donji Vakuf** Bosnia & Herzegovina, Yugoslavia
12G5 **Dönna** *I* Norway
59B3 **Donner P** USA
13D3 **Donnersberg** *Mt* Germany
47D2 **Donnybrook** South Africa
**Donostia = San Sebatián**
66B2 **Don Pedro Res** USA
8C4 **Doon, Loch** *L* Scotland
31A3 **Do Qu** *R* China
14D2 **Dorbirn** Austria
7C4 **Dorchester** England
55L3 **Dorchester,C** Canada
14C2 **Dordogne** *R* France
18A2 **Dordrecht** Netherlands
47D3 **Dordrecht** South Africa
68D1 **Dorest Peak** *Mt* USA
48B3 **Dori** Burkina
47B3 **Doring** *R* South Africa
7D4 **Dorking** England
13B3 **Dormans** France
18B3 **Dornbirn** Austria
8C3 **Dornoch** Scotland
8D3 **Dornoch Firth** *Estuary* Scotland
12H6 **Dorotea** Sweden
34D2 **Dorrigo** Australia
58B2 **Dorris** USA
7C4 **Dorset** *County* England
55L3 **Dorset, Cape** Canada
13D2 **Dorsten** Germany
18B2 **Dortmund** Germany
50C3 **Doruma** Zaïre
25N4 **Dosatuy** Russian Federation
42B1 **Doshi** Afghanistan
66B2 **Dos Palos** USA
48C3 **Dosso** Niger
24G5 **Dossor** Kazakhstan
57E3 **Dothan** USA
14C1 **Douai** France
50A3 **Douala** Cameroon
34D1 **Double Island Pt** Australia
62B2 **Double Mountain Fork** *R* USA
66C3 **Double Mt** USA
14D2 **Doubs** *R* France
35A3 **Doubtful Sd** New Zealand
48B3 **Douentza** Mali
56C3 **Douglas** Arizona, USA
67B2 **Douglas** Georgia, USA
6B2 **Douglas** Isle of Man, British Isles
47C2 **Douglas** South Africa
56C2 **Douglas** Wyoming, USA
67B1 **Douglas L** USA
13C2 **Doulevant-le-Château** France
13B2 **Doullens** France
75B2 **Dourada, Serra** *Mts* Brazil
75C1 **Dourada, Serra** *Mts* Brazil
73H8 **Dourados** Brazil
75B3 **Dourados** *R* Brazil
75B3 **Dourados, Serra dos** *Mts* Brazil
13B3 **Dourdan** France
15A1 **Douro** *R* Portugal
7D3 **Dove** *R* England
62A1 **Dove Creek** USA
65D3 **Dover** Delaware, USA
7E4 **Dover** England
65E2 **Dover** New Hampshire, USA
68C2 **Dover** New Jersey, USA
64C2 **Dover** Ohio, USA
7E4 **Dover,Str of** England/France
19G2 **Dovsk** Belorussia
9C2 **Down** *County* Northern Ireland
68C3 **Downingtown** USA
9D2 **Downpatrick** Northern Ireland
68C1 **Downsville** USA
68C2 **Doylestown** USA
28B3 **Dōzen** *I* Japan
65D1 **Dozois, Réservoir** Canada
48A2 **Dr'aa** *Watercourse* Morocco
75B3 **Dracena** Brazil
13D1 **Drachten** Netherlands
68E1 **Dracut** USA
14D3 **Draguignan** France
60C1 **Drake** USA
51D6 **Drakensberg** *Mts* South Africa
47D2 **Drakensberg** *Mt* South Africa
52E7 **Drake Passage** Atlantic O/Pacific Ocean
17E2 **Dráma** Greece
12G7 **Drammen** Norway
12A1 **Drangajökull** *Ice cap* Iceland
16D1 **Drava** *R* Slovenia
13D1 **Drenthe** *Province* Netherlands
18C2 **Dresden** Germany
14C2 **Dreux** France
58C2 **Drewsey** USA
68A2 **Driftwood** USA
17E2 **Drin** *R* Albania
17D2 **Drina** *R* Bosnia & Herzegovina, Yugoslavia
19F1 **Drissa** *R* Belorussia
9C3 **Drogheda** Irish Republic
19E3 **Drogobych** Ukraine
9C3 **Droihead Nua** Irish Republic
7C3 **Droitwich** England
9C2 **Dromore** Northern Ireland
76F12 **Dronning Maud Land** *Region* Antarctica
54G4 **Drumheller** Canada
58D1 **Drummond** USA
64C1 **Drummond I** USA
65E1 **Drummondville** Canada
8C3 **Drumochter Pass** Scotland
19E2 **Druskininkai** Lithuania
25Q3 **Druzhina** Russian Federation
61E1 **Dryberry L** Canada
55J5 **Dryden** Canada
68B1 **Dryden** USA
69H1 **Dry Harbour Mts** Jamaica
30B3 **Duang** *I* Burma
40C4 **Dubā** Saudi Arabia
41G4 **Dubai** UAE
54H3 **Dubawnt** *R* Canada
54H3 **Dubawnt L** Canada
32D4 **Dubbo** Australia
9C3 **Dublin** Irish Republic
67B2 **Dublin** USA
9C3 **Dublin** *County* Irish Republic
20F4 **Dubna** Russian Federation
21D5 **Dubno** Ukraine
58D2 **Dubois** Idaho, USA
65D2 **Du Bois** USA
58E2 **Dubois** Wyoming, USA
19F3 **Dubossary** Moldavia
19F2 **Dubrovica** Ukraine
17D2 **Dubrovnik** Croatia
57D2 **Dubuque** USA
59D2 **Duchesne** USA
67A1 **Duck** *R* USA
66C3 **Ducor** USA
13D3 **Dudelange** Luxembourg
24K3 **Dudinka** Russian Federation
7C3 **Dudley** England
25L2 **Dudypta** *R* Russian Federation
48B4 **Duekoué** Ivory Coast
15B1 **Duero** *R* Spain
33F1 **Duff Is** Solomon Islands
8D3 **Dufftown** Scotland
16C2 **Dugi Otok** *I* Croatia
18B2 **Duisburg** Germany
47E1 **Duiwelskloof** South Africa
41E3 **Dūkan** Iraq
50D3 **Duk Faiwil** Sudan
41F4 **Dukhān** Qatar
31A4 **Dukou** China
26C3 **Dulan** China
70D4 **Dulce, Golfo** Costa Rica
43G4 **Dullabchara** India
13D2 **Dülmen** Germany
57D2 **Duluth** USA
7C4 **Dulverton** England
45D2 **Dūmā** Syria
27D6 **Dumai** Indonesia
56C3 **Dumas** USA
45D2 **Ḑumayr** Syria
8C4 **Dumbarton** Scotland
48B1 **Dumer Rbia** Morocco
8D4 **Dumfries** Scotland
8C4 **Dumfries and Galloway** *Region* Scotland
43F4 **Dumka** India
65D1 **Dumoine,L** Canada
76G8 **Dumont d'Urville** *Base* Antarctica
49F1 **Dumyat** Egypt
17F2 **Dunărea** *R* Romania
9C3 **Dunary Head** *Pt* Irish Republic
17E2 **Dunav** *R* Bulgaria
17D1 **Dunav** *R* Croatia/Serbia, Yugoslavia
28C2 **Dunay** Russian Federation
19F3 **Dunayevtsy** Ukraine
8D4 **Dunbar** Scotland
63C2 **Duncan** USA
68B2 **Duncannon** USA
44E3 **Duncan Pass** *Chan* Andaman Islands
8D2 **Duncansby Head** *Pt* Scotland
9C2 **Dundalk** Irish Republic
68B3 **Dundalk** USA
9C3 **Dundalk B** Irish Republic
55M2 **Dundas** Greenland
54G2 **Dundas Pen** Canada
27G8 **Dundas Str** Australia
47E2 **Dundee** South Africa
8D3 **Dundee** Scotland
68B1 **Dundee** USA
34B1 **Dundoo** Australia
9D2 **Dundrum B** Northern Ireland
43M2 **Dundwa Range** *Mts* Nepal
33G5 **Dunedin** New Zealand
67B3 **Dunedin** USA
34C2 **Dunedoo** Australia
8D3 **Dunfermline** Scotland
9C2 **Dungannon** Northern Ireland
42C4 **Dūngarpur** India
9C3 **Dungarvan** Irish Republic
7E4 **Dungeness** *Pen* England
34D2 **Dungog** Australia
50C3 **Dungu** Zaïre
50D1 **Dungunab** Sudan
28B2 **Dunhua** China
26C2 **Dunhuang** China
8D3 **Dunkeld** Scotland
**Dunkerque = Dunkirk**
13B2 **Dunkirk** France
57F2 **Dunkirk** USA
50D2 **Dunkur** Ethiopia
48B4 **Dunkwa** Ghana
10B3 **Dun Laoghaire** Irish Republic
9B4 **Dunmanus** Irish Republic
68C2 **Dunmore** USA
69B1 **Dunmore Town** The Bahamas
67C1 **Dunn** USA
8D2 **Dunnet Head** *Pt* Scotland
60C2 **Dunning** USA
8C4 **Dunoon** Scotland
8D4 **Duns** Scotland
60C1 **Dunseith** USA
58B2 **Dunsmuir** USA
35A2 **Dunstan Mts** New Zealand
13C3 **Dun-sur-Meuse** France
31D1 **Duolun** China
60C1 **Dupree** USA
64B3 **Du Quoin** USA
45C3 **Dura** Israel
14D3 **Durance** *R* France
64A2 **Durand** USA
70B2 **Durango** Mexico
15B1 **Durango** Spain
56C3 **Durango** USA
56D3 **Durant** USA
45D1 **Duraykīsh** Syria
74E4 **Durazno** Uruguay
47E2 **Durban** South Africa
13D2 **Duren** Germany
43E4 **Durg** India
43F4 **Durgapur** India
6D2 **Durham** England
57F3 **Durham** N Carolina, USA
68E1 **Durham** New Hampshire, USA
6D2 **Durham** *County* England
34B1 **Durham Downs** Australia
17D2 **Durmitor** *Mt* Montenegro, Yugoslavia
8C2 **Durness** Scotland
17D2 **Durrës** Albania
34B1 **Durrie** Australia
17F3 **Dursunbey** Turkey
35B2 **D'Urville I** New Zealand
41H2 **Dushak** Turkmenistan
31B4 **Dushan** China
39E2 **Dushanbe** Tajikistan
68B2 **Dushore** USA
35A3 **Dusky Sd** New Zealand
18B2 **Düsseldorf** Germany
59D3 **Dutton,Mt** USA
31B4 **Duyun** China
40B1 **Düzce** Turkey
20F2 **Dvinskaya Guba** *B* Russian Federation
42B4 **Dwārka** India
58C1 **Dworshak Res** USA
57E3 **Dyersburg** USA
7B3 **Dyfed** *County* Wales
21G7 **Dykh Tau** *Mt* Russian Federation
34B1 **Dynevor Downs** Australia
26C2 **Dzag** Mongolia
26E2 **Dzamīn Uūd** Mongolia
51E5 **Dzaoudzi** Mayotte, Indian Ocean
26C2 **Dzavhan Gol** *R* Mongolia
20G4 **Dzerzhinsk** Russian Federation
25O4 **Dzhalinda** Russian Federation
24J5 **Dzhambul** Kazakhstan
21E6 **Dzhankoy** Ukraine
24H5 **Dzhezkazgan** Kazakhstan
42B1 **Dzhilikul'** Tajikistan
25P4 **Dzhugdzhur, Khrebet** *Mts* Russian Federation
24J5 **Dzhungarskiy Alatau** *Mts* Kazakhstan
18D2 **Dzierzoniow** Poland
39G1 **Dzungaria Basin** China
25L5 **Dzüyl** Mongolia


## E


55K4 **Eabamet L** Canada
60B3 **Eagle** Colorado, USA
60C1 **Eagle Butte** USA
58B2 **Eagle L** California, USA
65F1 **Eagle L** Maine, USA
65F1 **Eagle Lake** USA
63C2 **Eagle Mountain L** USA
56C4 **Eagle Pass** USA
62A2 **Eagle Peak** *Mt* USA
54E3 **Eagle Plain** Canada
59C3 **Earlimart** USA
8D3 **Earn** *R* Scotland
8C3 **Earn, Loch** *L* Scotland
59D4 **Earp** USA
62B2 **Earth** USA
6D2 **Easingwold** England
67B2 **Easley** USA
65D2 **East Aurora** USA
63E2 **East B** USA
7E4 **Eastbourne** England
68C1 **East Branch Delaware** *R* USA

East C Erzgebirge


33G4 **East C** New Zealand
64B2 **East Chicago** USA
26F3 **East China Sea** China/ Japan
7E3 **East Dereham** England
37O6 **Easter I** Pacific Ocean
43E5 **Eastern Ghats** *Mts* India
74E8 **East Falkland** *Is* Falkland Islands
59C3 **Eastgate** USA
61D1 **East Grand Forks** USA
7D4 **East Grinstead** England
68D1 **Easthampton** USA
68D2 **East Hampton** USA
8C4 **East Kilbride** Scotland
64B2 **East Lake** USA
7D4 **Eastleigh** England
64C2 **East Liverpool** USA
47D3 **East London** South Africa
55L4 **Eastmain** Canada
55L4 **Eastmain** *R* Canada
67B2 **Eastman** USA
64A2 **East Moline** USA
65D3 **Easton** Maryland, USA
65D2 **Easton** Pennsylvania, USA
68C2 **East Orange** USA
37O5 **East Pacific Ridge** Pacific Ocean
37O4 **East Pacific Rise** Pacific Ocean
67B2 **East Point** USA
65F2 **Eastport** USA
7D3 **East Retford** England
67A1 **East Ridge** USA
57D3 **East St Louis** USA
25R2 **East Siberian S**Russian Federation
7E4 **East Sussex** *County* England
65D3 **Eastville** USA
66C1 **East Walker** *R* USA
67B2 **Eatonton** USA
61E2 **Eau Claire** USA
27H6 **Eauripik** *I* Pacific Ocean
7C4 **Ebbw Vale** Wales
50B3 **Ebebiyin** Equatorial Guinea
68A2 **Ebensburg** USA
13E3 **Eberbach** Germany
18C2 **Eberswalde** Germany
29D2 **Ebetsu** Japan
31A4 **Ebian** China
24K5 **Ebinur** *L* China
16D2 **Eboli** Italy
50B3 **Ebolowa** Cameroon
15B1 **Ebro** *R* Spain
40A1 **Eceabat** Turkey
15C2 **Ech Cheliff** Algeria
31D2 **Eching** China
58C1 **Echo** USA
54G3 **Echo Bay** Canada
13D3 **Echternach** Luxembourg
34B3 **Echuca** Australia
15A2 **Ecija** Spain
55K2 **Eclipse Sd** Canada
72C4 **Ecuador** *Republic* S America
50E2 **Ed** Ethiopia
8D2 **Eday** *I* Scotland
50C2 **Ed Da'ein** Sudan
50D2 **Ed Damer** Sudan
50D2 **Ed Debba** Sudan
8C2 **Eddrachillis B** Scotland
50D2 **Ed Dueim** Sudan
34C4 **Eddystone Pt** Australia
13C1 **Ede** Netherlands
50A3 **Edea** Cameroon
34C3 **Eden** Australia
62C2 **Eden** Texas, USA
58E2 **Eden** Wyoming, USA
6C2 **Eden** *R* England
47D2 **Edenburg** South Africa
35A3 **Edendale** New Zealand
9C3 **Edenderry** Irish Republic
13D3 **Edenkoben** Germany
13E2 **Eder** *R* Germany
60D1 **Edgeley** USA
55M3 **Edgell I** Canada
60C2 **Edgemont** USA
24D2 **Edgeøya** *I* Svalbard, Norway
68B3 **Edgewood** USA
45C3 **Edh Dhahiriya** Israel
17E2 **Edhessa** Greece
62C3 **Edinburg** USA
8D3 **Edinburgh** Scotland
21D7 **Edirne** Turkey
66C3 **Edison** USA
67B2 **Edisto** *R* USA
58B1 **Edmonds** USA
54G4 **Edmonton** Canada
60D1 **Edmore** USA
55M5 **Edmundston** Canada
63C3 **Edna** USA
16C1 **Edolo** Italy
45C3 **Edom** *Region* Jordan
21D8 **Edremit** Turkey
17F3 **Edremit Körfezi** *B* Turkey
26C2 **Edrengiyn Nuruu** *Mts* Mongolia
54G4 **Edson** Canada
34B3 **Edward** *R* Australia
50C4 **Edward,L** Uganda/Zaïre
66D3 **Edwards** USA
56C3 **Edwards Plat** USA
64B3 **Edwardsville** USA
13B2 **Eeklo** Belgium
33F2 **Efate** *I* Vanuatu
57E3 **Effingham** USA
16C3 **Egadi,I** Sicily, Italy
59D3 **Egan Range** *Mts* USA
55N3 **Egedesminde** Greenland
54C4 **Egegik** USA
19E3 **Eger** Hungary
12F7 **Egersund** Norway
13E2 **Eggegebirge** *Mts* Germany
68C3 **Egg Harbor City** USA
54G2 **Eglinton I** Canada
35B1 **Egmont,C** New Zealand
35B1 **Egmont,Mt** New Zealand
6C2 **Egremont** England
40B2 **Eğridir Gölü** *L* Turkey
6D2 **Egton** England
75C1 **Eguas** *R* Brazil
25U3 **Egvekinot** Russian Federation
49E2 **Egypt** *Republic* Africa
15B1 **Eibar** Spain
34D1 **Eidsvold** Australia
13D2 **Eifel** *Region* Germany
8B3 **Eigg** *I* Scotland
39F5 **Eight Degree Chan** Indian Ocean
32B2 **Eighty Mile Beach** Australia
34C3 **Eildon,L** Australia
18B2 **Eindhoven** Netherlands
45C3 **Ein Yahav** Israel
18C2 **Eisenach** Germany
18C3 **Eisenerz** Austria
13D2 **Eitorf** Germany
31A1 **Ejin qi** China
60C1 **Ekalaka** USA
35C2 **Eketahuna** New Zealand
24J4 **Ekibastuz** Kazakhstan
25P4 **Ekimchan** Russian Federation
12H7 **Eksjö** Sweden
57E1 **Ekwan** *R* Canada
45A3 **El Abbâsa** Egypt
40A3 **El'Alamein** Egypt
47D2 **Elands** *R* South Africa
47C3 **Elands Berg** *Mt* South Africa
40B3 **El'Arîsh** Egypt
40B4 **Elat** Israel
50C2 **El' Atrun Oasis** Sudan
21F8 **Elaziğ** Turkey
40C3 **El Azraq** Jordan
16C2 **Elba** *I* Italy
49F2 **El Balyana** Egypt
72D2 **El Banco** Colombia
17E2 **Elbasan** Albania
69D5 **El Baúl** Venezuela
18C2 **Elbe** *R* Germany
45D1 **El Beqa'a** *R* Lebanon
64B2 **Elberta** USA
56C3 **Elbert,Mt** USA
67B2 **Elberton** USA
14C2 **Elbeuf** France
40C2 **Elbistan** Turkey
19D2 **Elbląg** Poland
74B6 **El Bolsón** Argentina
61D1 **Elbow Lake** USA
21G7 **Elbrus** *Mt* Russian Federation
**Elburz Mts = Reshteh-ye Alborz**
59C4 **El Cajon** USA
63C3 **El Campo** USA
59C4 **El Centro** USA
15B2 **Elche** Spain
74C5 **El Chocón, Embalse** *Res* Argentina
15B2 **Elda** Spain
25P3 **El'dikan** Russian Federation
72C3 **El Diviso** Colombia
48B2 **El Djouf** *Desert Region* Mauritius
63D1 **Eldon** USA
75B4 **Eldorado** Argentina
57D3 **El Dorado** Arkansas, USA
75C3 **Eldorado** Brazil
56D3 **El Dorado** Kansas, USA
70B2 **El Dorado** Mexico
62B2 **Eldorado** Texas, USA
72F2 **El Dorado** Venezuela
50D3 **Eldoret** Kenya
68A2 **Eldred** USA
45C1 **Elea, C** Cyprus
66C1 **Eleanor,L** USA
58D2 **Electric Peak** *Mt* USA
48B2 **El Eglab** *Region* Algeria
62A2 **Elephant Butte Res** USA
40D2 **Eleşkirt** Turkey
16B3 **El Eulma** Algeria
57F4 **Eleuthera** *I* The Bahamas
40B4 **El Faiyûm** Egypt
48B2 **El Farsia** *Well* Morocco
50C2 **El Fasher** Sudan
40B4 **El Fashn** Egypt
15A1 **El Ferrol** Spain
45B3 **El Firdân** Egypt
50C2 **El Fula** Sudan
48C1 **El Gassi** Algeria
50D2 **El Geteina** Sudan
50D2 **El Gezîra** *Region* Sudan
45C3 **El Ghor** *V* Israel/Jordan
57E2 **Elgin** Illinois, USA
60C1 **Elgin** N Dakota, USA
8D3 **Elgin** Scotland
40B3 **El Gîza** Egypt
48C1 **El Golea** Algeria
59D4 **El Golfo de Santa Clara** Mexico
50D3 **Elgon,Mt** Kenya/Uganda
50E3 **El Goran** Ethiopia
48B2 **El Guettara** *Well* Mali
48B2 **El Hank** *Region* Mauritius
48B2 **El Haricha** *Desert Region* Mali
40A4 **El Harra** Egypt
15C2 **El Harrach** Algeria
50D2 **El Hawata** Sudan
40B4 **El'Igma** *Desert Region* Egypt
**Elisabethville = Lubumbashi**
12K6 **Elisenvaara** Russian Federation
**El Iskandarîya = Alexandria**
21G6 **Elista** Russian Federation
32C4 **Elizabeth** Australia
65E2 **Elizabeth** USA
47B2 **Elizabeth B** Namibia
57F3 **Elizabeth City** USA
68E2 **Elizabeth Is** USA
67B1 **Elizabethton** Tennessee, USA
64B3 **Elizabethtown** Kentucky, USA
67C2 **Elizabethtown** N Carolina, USA
68B2 **Elizabethtown** Pennsylvania, USA
48B1 **El Jadida** Morocco
40C3 **El Jafr** Jordan
45D3 **El Jafr** *L* Jordan
50D2 **El Jebelein** Sudan
48D1 **El Jem** Tunisia
19E2 **Ełk** Poland
68C3 **Elk** *R* Maryland/ Pennsylvania, USA
64C3 **Elk** *R* W Virginia, USA
61E2 **Elkader** USA
16B3 **El Kala** Algeria
50D2 **El Kamlin** Sudan
48C1 **El Kef** Tunisia
66B1 **Elk Grove** USA
**El Khalil = Hebron** Israel
45A3 **El Khânka** Egypt
40B4 **El Khârga** Egypt
40B4 **El-Khârga Oasis** Egypt
64B2 **Elkhart** USA
48B2 **El Khenachich** *Desert Region* Mali
61D2 **Elkhorn** *R* USA
17F2 **Elkhovo** Bulgaria
65D3 **Elkins** USA
68B2 **Elkland** USA
60B2 **Elk Mt** USA
58C1 **Elko** Canada
56B2 **Elko** USA
16B3 **El Kroub** Algeria
68C3 **Elkton** USA
45B3 **El Kûbri** Egypt
40B3 **El Kuntilla** Egypt
50C2 **El Lagowa** Sudan
54H2 **Ellef Ringnes I** Canada
60D1 **Ellendale** USA
59D3 **Ellen,Mt** USA
56A2 **Ellensburg** USA
68C2 **Ellenville** USA
55K2 **Ellesmere I** Canada
35B2 **Ellesmere,L** New Zealand
7C3 **Ellesmere Port** England
68B3 **Ellicott City** USA
47D3 **Elliot** South Africa
55K5 **Elliot Lake** Canada
58D2 **Ellis** USA
45C3 **El Lisān** *Pen* Jordan
47D1 **Ellisras** South Africa
65F2 **Ellsworth** USA
76F3 **Ellsworth Land** *Region* Antarctica
45A4 **El Ma'âdi** Egypt
49E1 **El Maghra** *L* Egypt
40B3 **El Mahalla el Kubra** Egypt
40B3 **El Mansûra** Egypt
45A3 **El Manzala** Egypt
45B3 **El Matarîya** Egypt
68C3 **Elmer** USA
48B3 **El Merejé** *Desert Region* Mali/Mauritius
16B3 **El Milia** Algeria
45C1 **El Mîna** Lebanon
40B4 **El Minya** Egypt
66B1 **Elmira** California, USA
57F2 **Elmira** New York, USA
59D4 **El Mirage** USA
62B3 **El Moral** Mexico
48B2 **El Mreiti** *Well* Mauritius
18B2 **Elmshorn** Germany
50C2 **El Muglad** Sudan
48B2 **El Mzereb** *Well* Mali
50D2 **El Obeid** Sudan
48C1 **El Oued** Algeria
59D4 **Eloy** USA
56C3 **El Paso** USA
59B3 **El Portal** USA
62A2 **El Porvenir** Mexico
15A2 **El Puerto del Sta Maria** Spain
**El Qâhira = Cairo**
45B3 **El Qantara** Egypt
**El Quds = Jerusalem**
45C3 **El Quseima** Egypt
45C4 **El Quwetra** Jordan
56D3 **El Reno** USA
54E3 **Elsa** Canada
45A4 **El Saff** Egypt
45B3 **El Sâlhîya** Egypt
70D3 **El Salvador** *Republic* Central America
59C4 **El Sauzal** Mexico
45B3 **El Shallûfa** Egypt
45B4 **El Shatt** Egypt
45A3 **El Simbillâwein** Egypt
66D4 **Elsinore L** USA
18C2 **Elsterwerde** Germany
62A3 **El Sueco** Mexico
**El Suweis = Suez**
45A4 **El Tabbin** Egypt
15A1 **El Teleno** *Mt* Spain
35B1 **Eltham** New Zealand
45C4 **El Thamad** Egypt
72F2 **El Tigre** Venezuela
40B4 **El Tîh** *Desert Region* Egypt
45B3 **El Tîna** Egypt
58C1 **Eltopia** USA
40B4 **El Tûr** Egypt
44C2 **Elūru** India
15A2 **Elvas** Portugal
72D5 **Elvira** Brazil
54H2 **Elvira,C** Canada
64B2 **Elwood** USA
7E3 **Ely** England
57D2 **Ely** Minnesota, USA
56B3 **Ely** Nevada, USA
64C2 **Elyria** USA
45A3 **El Zarqa** Egypt
41G2 **Emāmrūd** Iran
42B1 **Emām Sāheb** Afghanistan
18D1 **Eman** *R* Sweden
21K6 **Emba** Kazakhstan
21K6 **Emba** *R* Kazakhstan
**Embalse de Ricobayo = Esla, Embalse**
74D2 **Embarcación** Argentina
54G4 **Embarras Portage** Canada
50D4 **Embu** Kenya
18B2 **Emden** Germany
31A4 **Emei** China
32D3 **Emerald** Australia
54J5 **Emerson** Canada
58C2 **Emigrant P** USA
50B1 **Emi Koussi** *Mt* Chad
40B2 **Emirdağ** Turkey
68C2 **Emmaus** USA
18B2 **Emmen** Netherlands
13D3 **Emmendingen** Germany
13D2 **Emmerich** Germany
58C2 **Emmett** USA
68B3 **Emmitsburg** USA
56C4 **Emory Peak** *Mt* USA
70A2 **Empalme** Mexico
47E2 **Empangeni** South Africa
74E3 **Empedrado** Argentina
37K2 **Emperor Seamount Chain** Pacific Ocean
63C1 **Emporia** Kansas, USA
65D3 **Emporia** Virginia, USA
68A2 **Emporium** USA
18B2 **Ems** *R* Germany
28B2 **Emu** China
8C2 **Enard B** Scotland
74E3 **Encarnación** Paraguay
48B4 **Enchi** Ghana
62C3 **Encinal** USA
66D4 **Encinitas** USA
75D2 **Encruzilhada** Brazil
32B1 **Endeh** Indonesia
76G11 **Enderby Land** *Region* Antarctica
61D1 **Enderlin** USA
65D2 **Endicott** USA
54C3 **Endicott Mts** USA
16C3 **Enfida** Tunisia
67C1 **Enfield** USA
27F5 **Engaño, C** Philippines
29D2 **Engaru** Japan
45C3 **En Gedi** Israel
21H5 **Engel's** Russian Federation
27D7 **Enggano** *I* Indonesia
10C3 **England** UK
55N4 **Englee** Canada
67C1 **Englehard** USA
65D1 **Englehart** Canada
60C3 **Englewood** USA
10C3 **English Channel** England/ France
63C1 **Enid** USA
29D2 **Eniwa** Japan
48B3 **Enji** *Well* Mauritius
13C1 **Enkhuizen** Netherlands
12H7 **Enköping** Sweden
16C3 **Enna** Sicily, Italy
50C2 **En Nahud** Sudan
50C2 **Ennedi** *Desert Region* Chad
9C3 **Ennell, L** Irish Republic
34C1 **Enngonia** Australia
60C2 **Enning** USA
10B3 **Ennis** Irish Republic
58D1 **Ennis** Montana, USA
63C2 **Ennis** Texas, USA
9C3 **Enniscorthy** Irish Republic
9C2 **Enniskillen** Northern Ireland
45C2 **Enn Nâqoûra** Lebanon
18C3 **Enns** *R* Austria
12F8 **Enschede** Netherlands
70A1 **Ensenada** Mexico
31B3 **Enshi** China
13D4 **Ensisheim** France
50D4 **Entebbe** Uganda
67A2 **Enterprise** Alabama, USA
58C1 **Enterprise** Oregon, USA
74E4 **Entre Ríos** *State* Argentina
48C4 **Enugu** Nigeria
13E3 **Enz** *R* Germany
29C3 **Enzan** Japan
14C2 **Epernay** France
40A2 **Ephesus** Turkey
59D3 **Ephraim** USA
68B2 **Ephrata** Pennsylvania, USA
58C1 **Ephrata** Washington, USA
33F2 **Epi** *I* Vanuatu
14D2 **Épinal** France
45B1 **Episkopi** Cyprus
45B1 **Episkopi B** Cyprus
7E4 **Epping** England
13E3 **Eppingen** Germany
7D4 **Epsom** England
47B1 **Epukiro** Namibia
41F3 **Eqlid** Iran
46D7 **Equator**
48C4 **Equatorial Guinea** *Republic* W Africa
68D1 **Equinox Mt** USA
68C2 **Equinunk** USA
13E3 **Erbach** Germany
13D3 **Erbeskopf** *Mt* Germany
41D2 **Erciş** Turkey
21F8 **Erciyas Dağlari** *Mt* Turkey
28B2 **Erdaobaihe** China
28B2 **Erdao Jiang** *R* China
31C1 **Erdene** Mongolia
26D2 **Erdenet** Mongolia
50C2 **Erdi** *Desert Region* Chad
74F3 **Erechim** Brazil
40B1 **Ereğli** Turkey
40B2 **Ereğli** Turkey
26E2 **Erenhot** China
15B1 **Eresma** *R* Spain
13D2 **Erft** *R* Germany
18C2 **Erfurt** Germany
40C2 **Ergani** Turkey
48B2 **Erg Chech** *Desert Region* Algeria/Mali
48D3 **Erg du Ténéré** *Desert Region* Niger
40A1 **Ergene** *R* Turkey
48B2 **Erg Iguidi** *Region* Algeria/Mauritania
19F1 **Ērgli** Latvia
50B2 **Erguig** *R* Chad
25N4 **Ergun'** *R* China/Russian Federation
26E1 **Ergun** *R* China/Russian Federation
25O4 **Ergun Zuoqi** China
50D2 **Eriba** Sudan
8C2 **Eriboll, Loch** *Inlet* Scotland
8C3 **Ericht, Loch** *L* Scotland
57F2 **Erie** USA
57E2 **Erie,L** Canada/USA
29D2 **Erimo-misaki** *C* Japan
8B3 **Eriskay** *I* Scotland
50D2 **Eritrea** *Region* Ethiopia
13D2 **Erkelenz** Germany
18C3 **Erlangen** Germany
63D2 **Erling,L** USA
47D2 **Ermelo** South Africa
44B4 **Ernākulam** India
9C2 **Erne, L** Northern Ireland
44B3 **Erode** India
34B1 **Eromanga** Australia
47B1 **Erongoberg** *Mt* Namibia
48B1 **Er Rachidia** Morocco
50D2 **Er Rahad** Sudan
51D5 **Errego** Mozambique
10B2 **Errigal** *Mt* Irish Republic
10A3 **Erris Head** *Pt* Irish Republic
33F2 **Erromanga** *I* Vanuatu
50D2 **Er Roseires** Sudan
45C2 **Er Rummān** Jordan
61D1 **Erskine** USA
13D3 **Erstein** France
18C2 **Erzgebirge** *Upland* Germany

**Erzincan** **Forel,Mt**


21F8 **Erzincan** Turkey
21G8 **Erzurum** Turkey
29D2 **Esan-misaki** *C* Japan
29D2 **Esashi** Japan
18B1 **Esbjerg** Denmark
59D3 **Escalante** USA
56C4 **Escalón** Mexico
57E2 **Escanaba** USA
70C3 **Escárcega** Mexico
13C3 **Esch** Luxembourg
59C4 **Escondido** USA
70B2 **Escuinapa** Mexico
70C3 **Escuintla** Guatemala
50B3 **Eséka** Cameroon
13D1 **Esens** Germany
14C3 **Esera** *R* Spain
15C1 **Esera** *R* Spain
41F3 **Eşfahān** Iran
47E2 **Eshowe** South Africa
45C3 **Esh Sharā** *Upland* Jordan
8D4 **Esk** *R* Scotland
35C1 **Eskdale** New Zealand
12C1 **Eskifjördur** Iceland
12H7 **Eskilstuna** Sweden
54E3 **Eskimo Lakes** Canada
55J3 **Eskimo Point** Canada
21E8 **Eskişehir** Turkey
15A1 **Esla** *R* Spain
15A1 **Esla, Embalse del** *Res* Spain
69B2 **Esmeralda** Cuba
74A7 **Esmeralda** *I* Chile
72C3 **Esmeraldas** Ecuador
14C3 **Espalion** France
64C1 **Espanola** Canada
62A1 **Espanola** USA
32B4 **Esperance** Australia
76G2 **Esperanza** *Base* Antarctica
15A2 **Espichel, Cabo** *C* Portugal
75D2 **Espinhaço, Serra do** *Mts* Brazil
75D2 **Espírito Santo** *State* Brazil
33F2 **Espiritu Santo** *I* Vanuatu
51D6 **Espungabera** Mozambique
74B6 **Esquel** Argentina
58B1 **Esquimalt** Canada
45D2 **Es Samrā** Jordan
48B1 **Essaouira** Morocco
18B2 **Essen** Germany
73G3 **Essequibo** *R* Guyana
7E4 **Essex** *County* England
64C2 **Essexville** USA
18B3 **Esslingen** Germany
13B3 **Essonne** *Department* France
13C3 **Essoyes** France
74D8 **Estados, Isla de los** Argentina
73L6 **Estância** Brazil
47D2 **Estcourt** South Africa
72A1 **Esteí** Nicaragua
13B3 **Esternay** France
66B3 **Estero B** USA
74D2 **Esteros** Paraguay
60B2 **Estes Park** USA
54H5 **Estevan** Canada
61E2 **Estherville** USA
67B2 **Estill** USA
13B3 **Estissac** France
20C4 **Estonia** *Republic* Europe
66B3 **Estrella** *R* USA
15A2 **Estremoz** Portugal
19D3 **Esztergom** Hungary
34A1 **Etadunna** Australia
55L2 **Etah** Canada
43K2 **Etah** India
13C3 **Etam** France
14C2 **Étampes** France
34A1 **Etamunbanie,L** Australia
42D3 **Etāwah** India
50D3 **Ethiopia** *Republic* Africa
8C3 **Etive, Loch** *Inlet* Scotland
16C3 **Etna** *Vol* Sicily, Italy
51B5 **Etosha Nat Pk** Namibia
51B5 **Etosha Pan** *Salt L* Namibia
67B2 **Etowah** *R* USA
13C3 **Ettelbruck** Luxembourg
33H3 **Eua** *I* Tonga
34C2 **Euabalong** Australia
17E3 **Euboea** *I* Greece
64C2 **Euclid** USA
34C3 **Eucumbene,L** Australia
34A2 **Eudunda** Australia
63C1 **Eufala L** USA
67A2 **Eufaula** USA
56A2 **Eugene** USA
70A2 **Eugenia, Punta** *Pt* Mexico
34C1 **Eulo** Australia
63D2 **Eunice** Louisiana, USA
62B2 **Eunice** New Mexico, USA
13D2 **Eupen** Germany
40D3 **Euphrates** *R* Iraq/Syria
63E2 **Eupora** USA
14C2 **Eure** *R* France
58B2 **Eureka** California, USA
55K1 **Eureka** Canada
58C1 **Eureka** Montana, USA
56B3 **Eureka** Nevada, USA
60D1 **Eureka** S Dakota, USA
59D3 **Eureka** Utah, USA
55K2 **Eureka Sd** Canada
66D2 **Eureka V** USA
34C3 **Euroa** Australia
34C1 **Eurombah** *R* Australia
51E6 **Europa** *I* Mozambique Channel
13C2 **Europoort** Netherlands
18B2 **Euskirchen** Germany
63E2 **Eutaw** USA
55K1 **Evans,C** Canada
55L4 **Evans,L** Canada
60B3 **Evans,Mt** Colorado, USA
58D1 **Evans,Mt** Montana, USA
55K3 **Evans Str** Canada
64B2 **Evanston** Illinois, USA
56B2 **Evanston** Wyoming, USA
57E3 **Evansville** Indiana, USA
60B2 **Evansville** Wyoming, USA
47D2 **Evaton** South Africa
32C4 **Everard,L** Australia
39G3 **Everest,Mt** China/Nepal
68A2 **Everett** Pennsylvania, USA
56A2 **Everett** Washington, USA
68D1 **Everett,Mt** USA
57E4 **Everglades,The** *Swamp* USA
67A2 **Evergreen** USA
7D3 **Evesham** England
50B3 **Evinayong** Equatorial Guinea
12F7 **Evje** Norway
15A2 **Évora** Portugal
14C2 **Evreux** France
**Évvoia = Euboea**
8C3 **Ewe, Loch** *Inlet* Scotland
50B4 **Ewo** Congo
66C1 **Excelsior Mt** USA
66C1 **Excelsior Mts** USA
61E3 **Excelsior Springs** USA
7C4 **Exe** *R* England
59C3 **Exeter** California, USA
7C4 **Exeter** England
65E2 **Exeter** New Hampshire, USA
7C4 **Exmoor** England
7C4 **Exmouth** England
15A2 **Extremadura** *Region* Spain
70E2 **Exuma Sd** The Bahamas
50D4 **Eyasi, L** Tanzania
8D4 **Eyemouth** Scotland
50E3 **Eyl** Somalia
32B4 **Eyre** Australia
32C3 **Eyre Creek** *R* Australia
32C3 **Eyre,L** Australia
32C4 **Eyre Pen** Australia
17F3 **Ezine** Turkey

## F

54G3 **Faber L** Canada
12F7 **Fåborg** Denmark
16C2 **Fabriano** Italy
50B2 **Fachi** Niger
50C2 **Fada** Chad
48C3 **Fada N'Gourma** Burkina
25Q2 **Faddeyevskiy, Ostrov** *I* Russian Federation
16C2 **Faenza** Italy
55N3 **Færingehavn** Greenland
**Færøerne = Faeroes**
12D3 **Faeroes** *Is* N Atlantic Oc
50B3 **Fafa** *R* Central African Republic
50E3 **Fafan** *R* Ethiopia
17E1 **Făgăraş** Romania
13C2 **Fagnes** *Region* Belgium
48B3 **Faguibine,L** Mali
41G5 **Fahūd** Oman
48A1 **Faial** *I* Azores
62A2 **Fairacres** USA
54D3 **Fairbanks** USA
64C3 **Fairborn** USA
56D2 **Fairbury** USA
68B3 **Fairfax** USA
59B3 **Fairfield** California, USA
68D2 **Fairfield** Connecticut, USA
58D2 **Fairfield** Idaho, USA
58D1 **Fairfield** Montana, USA
64C3 **Fairfield** Ohio, USA
9C2 **Fair Head** *Pt* Northern Ireland
10C2 **Fair Isle** *I* Scotland
35B2 **Fairlie** New Zealand
61E2 **Fairmont** Minnesota, USA
64C3 **Fairmont** W Virginia, USA
68B1 **Fairport** USA
62C1 **Fairview** USA
54E4 **Fairweather,Mt** USA
27H6 **Fais** *I* Pacific Ocean
42C2 **Faisalabad** Pakistan
60C1 **Faith** USA
8E1 **Faither,The** *Pen* Scotland
33H1 **Fakaofo** *I* Tokelau Islands
7E3 **Fakenham** England
32C1 **Fakfak** Indonesia
28A2 **Faku** China
43G4 **Falam** Burma
70C2 **Falcon Res** Mexico/USA
48A3 **Falémé** *R* Mali/Senegal/Guinea
62C3 **Falfurrias** USA
12G7 **Falkenberg** Sweden
8D4 **Falkirk** Scotland
74D8 **Falkland Is** *Dependency* S Atlantic
74E8 **Falkland Sd** Falkland Islands
12G7 **Falköping** Sweden
66D4 **Fallbrook** USA
56B3 **Fallon** USA
65E2 **Fall River** USA
60B2 **Fall River P** USA
61D2 **Falls City** USA
7B4 **Falmouth** England
69H1 **Falmouth** Jamaica
65E2 **Falmouth** Maine, USA
68E2 **Falmouth** Massachusetts, USA
7B4 **Falmouth Bay** England
47B3 **False B** South Africa
70A2 **Falso,C** Mexico
18C2 **Falster** *I* Denmark
17F1 **Fălticeni** Romania
12H6 **Falun** Sweden
40B2 **Famagusta** Cyprus
45B1 **Famagusta B** Cyprus
13C2 **Famenne** *Region* Belgium
66C3 **Famoso** USA
30B2 **Fang** Thailand
50D3 **Fangak** Sudan
31E5 **Fangliao** Taiwan
8C3 **Fannich, L** Scotland
16C2 **Fano** Italy
45A3 **Fâqûs** Egypt
76G3 **Faraday** *Base* Antarctica
50C3 **Faradje** Zaïre
51E6 **Farafangana** Madagascar
49E2 **Farafra Oasis** Egypt
38E2 **Farah** Afghanistan
27H5 **Farallon de Medinilla** *I* Pacific Ocean
26H4 **Farallon de Pajaros** *I* Marianas
48A3 **Faranah** Guinea
50E2 **Farasan Is** Saudi Arabia
27H6 **Faraulep** *I* Pacific Ocean
55J5 **Farbault** USA
7D4 **Fareham** England
55O4 **Farewell,C** Greenland
33G5 **Farewell,C** New Zealand
35B2 **Farewell Spit** *Pt* New Zealand
56D2 **Fargo** USA
45C2 **Fari'a** *R* Israel
57D2 **Faribault** USA
43F4 **Faridpur** Bangladesh
41G2 **Farīmān** Iran
45A3 **Fâriskûr** Egypt
65E2 **Farmington** Maine, USA
63D1 **Farmington** Missouri, USA
68E1 **Farmington** New Hampshire, USA
56C3 **Farmington** New Mexico, USA
58D2 **Farmington** Utah, USA
66B2 **Farmington Res** USA
6D2 **Farne Deep** N Sea
15A2 **Faro** Portugal
12H7 **Fåró** *I* Sweden
46K9 **Farquhar Is** Indian Ocean
8C3 **Farrar** *R* Scotland
64C2 **Farrell** USA
43K2 **Farrukhabad** *District* India
17E3 **Fársala** Greece
75B4 **Fartura, Serra de** *Mts* Brazil
62B2 **Farwell** USA
41F4 **Fasā** Iran
21D5 **Fastov** Ukraine
43K2 **Fatehgarh** India
43E3 **Fatehpur** India
73H7 **Fatima du Sul** Brazil
58C1 **Fauquier** Canada
47D2 **Fauresmith** South Africa
12H5 **Fauske** Norway
7E4 **Faversham** England
55K4 **Fawn** *R* Canada
12H6 **Fax** *R* Sweden
12A2 **Faxaflói** *B* Iceland
50B2 **Faya** Chad
63E2 **Fayette** USA
57D3 **Fayetteville** Arkansas, USA
57F3 **Fayetteville** N Carolina, USA
67A1 **Fayetteville** Tennessee, USA
45B3 **Fâyid** Egypt
41E4 **Faylakah** *I* Kuwait
42C2 **Fāzilka** India
48A2 **Fdérik** Mauritius
57F3 **Fear,C** USA
66B1 **Feather** *R* USA
59B3 **Feather Middle Fork** *R* USA
14C2 **Fécamp** France
18C2 **Fehmarn** *I* Germany
75D3 **Feia, Lagoa** Brazil
72D5 **Feijó** Brazil
31C5 **Feilai Xai Bei Jiang** *R* China
35C2 **Feilding** New Zealand
51D5 **Feira** Zambia
73L6 **Feira de Santan** Brazil
40C2 **Feke** Turkey
13D4 **Feldberg** *Mt* Germany
18B3 **Feldkirch** Austria
10D3 **Felixstowe** England
12G6 **Femund** *L* Norway
28A2 **Fengcheng** China
31B4 **Fengdu** China
31B3 **Fengjie** China
31D1 **Fengning** China
31B3 **Feng Xian** China
31C1 **Fengzhen** China
31C2 **Fen He** *R* China
51E5 **Fenoarivo Atsinanana** Madagascar
21F7 **Feodosiya** Ukraine
41G3 **Ferdow** Iran
13B3 **Fère-Champenoise** France
39F1 **Fergana** Uzbekistan
61D1 **Fergus Falls** USA
48B4 **Ferkessedougou** Ivory Coast
9C2 **Fermanagh** *County* Northern Ireland
67B2 **Fernandina Beach** USA
73M4 **Fernando de Noronha, Isla** Brazil
75B3 **Fernandópolis** Brazil
**Fernando Poo** *I* **=Bioko**
58B1 **Ferndale** USA
58C1 **Fernie** Canada
59C3 **Fernley** USA
16C2 **Ferrara** Italy
15B2 **Ferrat, Cap** *C* Algeria
72C5 **Ferreñafe** Peru
63D2 **Ferriday** USA
13B3 **Ferrières** France
48B1 **Fès** Morocco
63D1 **Festus** USA
17F2 **Feteşti** Romania
9C3 **Fethard** Irish Republic
40A2 **Fethiye** Turkey
21J7 **Fetisovo** Kazakhstan
8E1 **Fetlar** *I* Scotland
55L4 **Feuilles, Rivière aux** *R* Canada
24J6 **Feyzabad** Afghanistan
7C3 **Ffestiniog** Wales
51E6 **Fianarantsoa** Madagascar
50D3 **Fichē** Ethiopia
47D2 **Ficksburg** South Africa
45C3 **Fidan, Wadi** Jordan
17D2 **Fier** Albania
8D3 **Fife** *Region* Scotland
8D3 **Fife Ness** *Pen* Scotland
14C3 **Figeac** France
15A1 **Figueira da Foz** Portugal
**Figueres = Figueras**
15C1 **Figueras** Spain
48B1 **Figuig** Morocco
33G2 **Fiji** *Is* Pacific Ocean
15B2 **Filabres, Sierra de los** *Mts* Spain
73G8 **Filadelfia** Paraguay
6D2 **Filey** England
17E2 **Filiaşi** Romania
17E3 **Filiatrá** Greece
16C3 **Filicudi** *I* Italy
59C4 **Fillmore** California, USA
59D3 **Fillmore** Utah, USA
8C3 **Findhorn** *R* Scotland
57E2 **Findlay** USA
65D2 **Finger Lakes** USA
51D5 **Fingoè** Mozambique
21E8 **Finike** Turkey
15A1 **Finisterre, Cabo** *C* Spain
32C3 **Finke** *R* Australia
20C3 **Finland** *Republic* N Europe
12J7 **Finland,G of** N Europe
54F4 **Finlay** *R* Canada
54F4 **Finlay Forks** Canada
34C3 **Finley** Australia
9C2 **Finn** *R* Irish Republic
12H5 **Finnsnes** Norway
27H7 **Finschhafen** Papua New Guinea
12H7 **Finspång** Sweden
18C2 **Finsterwalde** Germany
9C2 **Fintona** Northern Ireland
35A3 **Fiordland Nat Pk** New Zealand
45C2 **Fiq** Syria
21F8 **Firat** *R* Turkey
66B2 **Firebaugh** USA
**Firenze = Florence**
42D3 **Firozābād** India
42C2 **Firozpur** India
8C4 **Firth of Clyde** *Estuary* Scotland
8D3 **Firth of Forth** *Estuary* Scotland
8B3 **Firth of Lorn** *Estuary* Scotland
10C2 **Firth of Tay** *Estuary* Scotland
41F4 **Firūzābād** Iran
47B2 **Fish** *R* Namibia
47C3 **Fish** *R* South Africa
66C2 **Fish Camp** USA
68D2 **Fishers I** USA
55K3 **Fisher Str** Canada
7B4 **Fishguard** Wales
55N3 **Fiskenæsset** Greenland
13B3 **Fismes** France
65E2 **Fitchburg** USA
8E2 **Fitful Head** *Pt* Scotland
67B2 **Fitzgerald** USA
32B2 **Fitzroy** *R* Australia
32B2 **Fitzroy Crossing** Australia
64C1 **Fitzwilliam I** Canada
**Fiume = Rijeka**
50C4 **Fizi** Zaïre
47D3 **Flagstaff** South Africa
56B3 **Flagstaff** USA
65E1 **Flagstaff L** USA
6D2 **Flamborough Head** *C* England
56C2 **Flaming Gorge Res** USA
27G7 **Flamingo, Teluk** *B* Indonesia
13B2 **Flandres, Plaine des** Belgium/France
8B2 **Flannan Isles** Scotland
56B2 **Flathead L** USA
63D1 **Flat River** USA
27H8 **Flattery,C** Australia
56A2 **Flattery,C** USA
6C3 **Fleetwood** England
12F7 **Flekkefjord** Norway
26H4 **Fleming Deep** Pacific Ocean
68C2 **Flemington** USA
18B2 **Flensburg** Germany
32C4 **Flinders** *I* Australia
32D5 **Flinders** *I* Australia
32D2 **Flinders** *R* Australia
32C4 **Flinders Range** *Mts* Australia
54H4 **Flin Flon** Canada
57E2 **Flint** USA
7C3 **Flint** Wales
57E3 **Flint** *R* USA
13B2 **Flixecourt** France
64A1 **Floodwood** USA
67A2 **Florala** USA
57E3 **Florence** Alabama, USA
59D4 **Florence** Arizona, USA
60B3 **Florence** Colorado, USA
16C2 **Florence** Italy
63C1 **Florence** Kansas, USA
58B2 **Florence** Oregon, USA
57F3 **Florence** S Carolina, USA
66C2 **Florence L** USA
72C3 **Florencia** Colombia
74C6 **Florentine Ameghino, Embalse** *Res* Argentina
13C3 **Florenville** Belgium
70D3 **Flores** Guatemala
48A1 **Flores** *I* Azores
32B1 **Flores** *I* Indonesia
27E7 **Flores S** Indonesia
73K5 **Floriano** Brazil
74G3 **Florianópolis** Brazil
74E4 **Florida** Uruguay
70D2 **Florida** *State* USA
67B3 **Florida B** USA
67B3 **Florida City** USA
33E1 **Florida Is** Solomon Islands
57E4 **Florida Keys** *Is* USA
57E4 **Florida,Strs of** USA
17E2 **Flórina** Greece
12F6 **Florø** Norway
62B2 **Floydada** USA
32D1 **Fly** *R* Papua New Guinea
17F1 **Focşani** Romania
16D2 **Foggia** Italy
48A4 **Fogo** *I* Cape Verde
14C3 **Foix** France
64C1 **Foleyet** Canada
55L3 **Foley I** Canada
16C2 **Foligno** Italy
7E4 **Folkestone** England
67B2 **Folkston** USA
16C2 **Follonica** Italy
66B1 **Folsom** USA
68C1 **Fonda** USA
54H4 **Fond-du-Lac** Canada
57E2 **Fond du Lac** USA
70D3 **Fonseca, G de** Honduras
14C2 **Fontainbleau** France
14B2 **Fontenay-le-Comte** France
17D1 **Fonyód** Hungary
**Foochow = Fuzhou**
54C3 **Foraker, Mt** USA
13D3 **Forbach** France
34C2 **Forbes** Australia
48C4 **Forcados** Nigeria
66C3 **Ford City** USA
12F6 **Førde** Norway
7D4 **Fordingbridge** England
34C1 **Fords Bridge** Australia
63D2 **Fordyce** USA
48A4 **Forécariah** Guinea
55P3 **Forel,Mt** Greenland

**Foremost** **Gedaref**


58D1 **Foremost** Canada
64C2 **Forest** Canada
63E2 **Forest** USA
61E2 **Forest City** Iowa, USA
68C2 **Forest City** Pennsylvania, USA
7C4 **Forest of Dean** England
67B2 **Forest Park** USA
66A1 **Forestville** USA
13B3 **Forêt d'Othe** France
8D3 **Forfar** Scotland
62B1 **Forgan** USA
58B1 **Forks** USA
16C2 **Forli** Italy
7C3 **Formby** England
15C2 **Formentera** *I* Spain
15C1 **Formentor, Cabo** *C* Spain
16C2 **Formia** Italy
48A1 **Formigas** *I* Azores
**Formosa = Taiwan**
74E3 **Formosa** Argentina
73J7 **Formosa** Brazil
74D2 **Formosa** *State* Argentina
**Formosa Channel = Taiwan Str**
73G6 **Formosa, Serra** *Mts* Brazil
75C1 **Formoso** Brazil
75C1 **Formoso** *R* Brazil
8D3 **Forres** Scotland
32B4 **Forrest** Australia
57D3 **Forrest City** USA
32D2 **Forsayth** Australia
12J6 **Forssa** Finland
34D2 **Forster** Australia
63D1 **Forsyth** Missouri, USA
60B1 **Forsyth** Montana, USA
42C3 **Fort Abbas** Pakistan
55K4 **Fort Albany** Canada
73L4 **Fortaleza** Brazil
8C3 **Fort Augustus** Scotland
47D3 **Fort Beaufort** South Africa
58D1 **Fort Benton** USA
59B3 **Fort Bragg** USA
62C1 **Fort Cobb Res** USA
56C2 **Fort Collins** USA
65D1 **Fort Coulonge** Canada
62B2 **Fort Davis** USA
69E4 **Fort-de-France** Martinique
67A2 **Fort Deposit** USA
57D2 **Fort Dodge** USA
32A3 **Fortescue** *R* Australia
57D2 **Fort Frances** Canada
54F3 **Fort Franklin** Canada
54F3 **Fort Good Hope** Canada
34B1 **Fort Grey** Australia
8C3 **Forth** *R* Scotland
62A2 **Fort Hancock** USA
55K4 **Fort Hope** Canada
8F3 **Forties** *Oilfield* N Sea
65F1 **Fort Kent** USA
48C1 **Fort Lallemand** Algeria
**Fort Lamy = Ndjamena**
60C2 **Fort Laramie** USA
57E4 **Fort Lauderdale** USA
54F3 **Fort Liard** Canada
54G4 **Fort Mackay** Canada
54G5 **Fort Macleod** Canada
54G4 **Fort McMurray** Canada
54E3 **Fort McPherson** Canada
64A2 **Fort Madison** USA
56C2 **Fort Morgan** USA
57E4 **Fort Myers** USA
54F4 **Fort Nelson** Canada
54F3 **Fort Norman** Canada
67A2 **Fort Payne** USA
60B1 **Fort Peck** USA
56C2 **Fort Peck Res** USA
57E4 **Fort Pierce** USA
60C2 **Fort Pierre** USA
68C1 **Fort Plain** USA
54G3 **Fort Providence** Canada
54G3 **Fort Resolution** Canada
50B4 **Fort Rousset** Congo
54F4 **Fort St James** Canada
54F4 **Fort St John** Canada
63D1 **Fort Scott** USA
54E3 **Fort Selkirk** Canada
55K4 **Fort Severn** Canada
21J7 **Fort Shevchenko** Kazakhstan
54F3 **Fort Simpson** Canada
54G3 **Fort Smith** Canada
57D3 **Fort Smith** USA
54F3 **Fort Smith** *Region* Canada
56C3 **Fort Stockton** USA
62B2 **Fort Sumner** USA
62C1 **Fort Supply** USA
58B2 **Fortuna** California, USA
60C1 **Fortuna** N Dakota, USA
54G4 **Fort Vermilion** Canada
67A2 **Fort Walton Beach** USA
57E2 **Fort Wayne** USA
8C3 **Fort William** Scotland
62A1 **Fort Wingate** USA
56D3 **Fort Worth** USA
54D3 **Fort Yukon** USA
31C5 **Foshan** China
55K2 **Fosheim Pen** Canada
61D1 **Fosston** USA
50B4 **Fougamou** Gabon
14B2 **Fougères** France
8D1 **Foula** *I* Scotland
7E4 **Foulness I** England
35B2 **Foulwind,C** New Zealand
50B3 **Foumban** Cameroon
48B2 **Foum el Alba** *Region* Mali
14C1 **Fourmies** France
17F3 **Foúrnoi** *I* Greece
48A3 **Fouta Djallon** *Mts* Guinea
33F5 **Foveaux Str** New Zealand
7B4 **Fowey** England
62B1 **Fowler** USA
64B2 **Fox** *R* USA
55K3 **Foxe Basin** *G* Canada
55K3 **Foxe Chan** Canada
55L3 **Foxe Pen** Canada
60B2 **Foxpark** USA
35C2 **Foxton** New Zealand
10B2 **Foyle, Lough** *Estuary* Irish Republic/Northern Ireland
51B5 **Foz do Cuene** Angola
74F3 **Foz do Iguaçu** Brazil
68B2 **Frackville** USA
15C1 **Fraga** Spain
68E1 **Framingham** USA
73J8 **Franca** Brazil
14C2 **France** *Republic* Europe
14D2 **Franche Comté** *Region* France
47D1 **Francistown** Botswana
58E2 **Francs Peak** *Mt* USA
13E2 **Frankenberg** Germany
64B2 **Frankfort** Indiana, USA
57E3 **Frankfort** Kentucky, USA
68C1 **Frankfort** New York, USA
47D2 **Frankfort** South Africa
18B2 **Frankfurt am Main** Germany
18C2 **Frankfurt an-der-Oder** Germany
18C3 **Fränkischer Alb** *Upland* Germany
58D2 **Franklin** Idaho, USA
64B3 **Franklin** Indiana, USA
63D3 **Franklin** Louisiana, USA
68E1 **Franklin** Massachusetts, USA
67B1 **Franklin** N Carolina, USA
68E1 **Franklin** New Hampshire, USA
68C2 **Franklin** New Jersey, USA
65D2 **Franklin** Pennsylvania, USA
67A1 **Franklin** Tennessee, USA
65D3 **Franklin** Virginia, USA
54F2 **Franklin B** Canada
58C1 **Franklin D Roosevelt** *L* USA
54F3 **Franklin Mts** Canada
54J2 **Franklin Str** Canada
68A1 **Franklinville** USA
35B2 **Franz Josef Glacier** New Zealand
**Franz-Josef-Land = Zemlya Frantsa Josifa**
54F5 **Fraser** *R* Canada
47C3 **Fraserburg** South Africa
8D3 **Fraserburgh** Scotland
34D1 **Fraser I** Australia
68C3 **Frederica** USA
18B1 **Fredericia** Denmark
65D3 **Frederick** Maryland, USA
62C2 **Frederick** Oklahoma, USA
62C2 **Fredericksburg** Texas, USA
65D3 **Fredericksburg** Virginia, USA
64A3 **Fredericktown** USA
55M5 **Fredericton** Canada
55N3 **Frederikshåp** Greenland
12G7 **Frederikshavn** Denmark
65D2 **Fredonia** USA
12G7 **Fredrikstad** Norway
68C2 **Freehold** USA
66C1 **Freel Peak** *Mt* USA
61D2 **Freeman** USA
64B2 **Freeport** Illinois, USA
63C3 **Freeport** Texas, USA
69B1 **Freeport** The Bahamas
62C3 **Freer** USA
48A4 **Freetown** Sierra Leone
18B3 **Freiburg** Germany
13D3 **Freiburg im Breisgau** Germany
18C3 **Freistadt** Austria
32A4 **Fremantle** Australia
66B2 **Fremont** California, USA
61D2 **Fremont** Nebraska, USA
64C2 **Fremont** Ohio, USA
73H3 **French Guiana** *Dependency* S America
60B1 **Frenchman** *R* USA
34C4 **Frenchmans Cap** *Mt* Australia
37M5 **French Polynesia** *Is* Pacific Ocean
15C2 **Frenda** Algeria
70B2 **Fresnillo** Mexico
56B3 **Fresno** USA
66C2 **Fresno** *R* USA
58D1 **Fresno Res** USA
13E3 **Freudenstadt** Germany
13B2 **Frévent** France
34C4 **Freycinet Pen** Australia
48A3 **Fria** Guinea
66C2 **Friant** USA
66C2 **Friant Dam** USA
16B1 **Fribourg** Switzerland
13E2 **Friedberg** Germany
18B3 **Friedrichshafen** Germany
13C1 **Friesland** *Province* Netherlands
62C3 **Frio** *R* USA
75D3 **Frio, Cabo** *C* Brazil
62B2 **Friona** USA
55M3 **Frobisher B** Canada
55M3 **Frobisher Bay** Canada
54H4 **Frobisher L** Canada
21G6 **Frolovo** Russian Federation
7C4 **Frome** England
7C4 **Frome** *R* England
32C4 **Frome,L** Australia
63D1 **Frontenac** USA
70C3 **Frontera** Mexico
65D3 **Front Royal** USA
16C2 **Frosinone** Italy
60B3 **Fruita** USA
31C5 **Fuchuan** China
31E4 **Fuding** China
70B2 **Fuerte** *R* Mexico
75A3 **Fuerte Olimpo** Brazil
74E2 **Fuerte Olimpo** Paraguay
48A2 **Fuerteventura** *I* Canary Islands
31C2 **Fugu** China
26B2 **Fuhai** China
41G4 **Fujairah** UAE
29C3 **Fuji** Japan
31D4 **Fujian** *Province* China
26G2 **Fujin** China
29C3 **Fujinomiya** Japan
29D3 **Fuji-san** *Mt* Japan
29C3 **Fujisawa** Japan
29C3 **Fuji-Yoshida** Japan
29D2 **Fukagawa** Japan
24K5 **Fukang** China
29D3 **Fukuchiyama** Japan
28A4 **Fukue** Japan
28A4 **Fukue** *I* Japan
29D3 **Fukui** Japan
28C4 **Fukuoka** Japan
29E3 **Fukushima** Japan
29C4 **Fukuyama** Japan
61D2 **Fulda** USA
18B2 **Fulda** Germany
18B2 **Fulda** *R* Germany
31B4 **Fuling** China
69L1 **Fullarton** Trinidad
66D4 **Fullerton** USA
6F1 **Fulmar** *Oilfield* N Sea
64A2 **Fulton** Illinois, USA
64B3 **Fulton** Kentucky, USA
65D2 **Fulton** New York, USA
13C2 **Fumay** France
29D3 **Funabashi** Japan
33G1 **Funafuti** *I* Tuvalu
48A1 **Funchal** Madeira
75D2 **Fundão** Brazil
55M5 **Fundy,B of** Canada
51D6 **Funhalouro** Mozambique
31B5 **Funing** China
31D3 **Funing** China
48C3 **Funtua** Nigeria
31D4 **Fuqing** China
51D5 **Furancungo** Mozambique
29D2 **Furano** Japan
41G4 **Fūrg** Iran
75B2 **Furnas, Serra das** *Mts* Brazil
32D5 **Furneaux Group** *Is* Australia
13D1 **Fürstenau** Germany
18C2 **Fürstenwalde** Germany
18C3 **Fürth** Germany
29D2 **Furubira** Japan
29E3 **Furukawa** Japan
55K3 **Fury and Hecla Str** Canada
28A2 **Fushun** China
31A4 **Fushun** Sichuan, China
28B2 **Fusong** China
18C3 **Füssen** Germany
31E2 **Fu Xian** China
31E1 **Fuxin** China
31D3 **Fuyang** China
31E1 **Fuyuan** Liaoning, China
31A4 **Fuyuan** Yunnan, China
26B2 **Fuyun** China
31D4 **Fuzhou** China
28A3 **Fuzhoucheng** China
18C1 **Fyn** *I* Denmark
8C3 **Fyne, Loch** *Inlet* Scotland

## G

50E3 **Gaalkacyo** Somalia
59C3 **Gabbs** USA
66C1 **Gabbs Valley Range** *Mts* USA
51B5 **Gabela** Angola
48D1 **Gabès, G de** Tunisia
66B2 **Gabilan Range** *Mts* USA
50B4 **Gabon** *Republic* Africa
47D1 **Gaborone** Botswana
15A1 **Gabriel y Galán, Embalse** *Res* Spain
17F2 **Gabrovo** Bulgaria
41F3 **Gach Sārān** Iran
44B2 **Gadag** India
67A2 **Gadsden** Alabama, USA
59D4 **Gadsden** Arizona, USA
16C2 **Gaeta** Italy
27H6 **Gaferut** *I* Pacific Ocean
67B1 **Gaffney** USA
45A3 **Gafra, Wadi el** Egypt
48C1 **Gafsa** Tunisia
20E4 **Gagarin** Russian Federation
55M4 **Gagnon** Canada
21G7 **Gagra** Georgia
43F3 **Gaibanda** Bangladesh
74C6 **Gaimán** Argentina
67B3 **Gainesville** Florida, USA
67B2 **Gainesville** Georgia, USA
63C2 **Gainesville** Texas, USA
7D3 **Gainsborough** England
32C4 **Gairdner, L** Australia
8C3 **Gairloch** Scotland
68B3 **Gaithersburg** USA
28A2 **Gai Xian** China
44B2 **Gajendragarh** India
31D4 **Ga Jiang** *R* China
47C2 **Gakarosa** *Mt* South Africa
50D4 **Galana** *R* Kenya
72N **Galapagos Is** Pacific Ocean
**Gálápagos, Islas = Galapagos Islands**
8D4 **Galashiels** Scotland
17F1 **Galaţi** Romania
64C3 **Galax** USA
62A2 **Galeana** Mexico
54C3 **Galena** Alaska, USA
64A2 **Galena** Illinois, USA
63D1 **Galena** Kansas, USA
69L1 **Galeota Pt** Trinidad
69L1 **Galera Pt** Trinidad
64A2 **Galesburg** USA
68B2 **Galeton** USA
20G4 **Galich** Russian Federation
15A1 **Galicia** *Region* Spain
**Galilee,S of = Tiberias,L**
69J1 **Galina Pt** Jamaica
50D2 **Gallabat** Sudan
67A1 **Gallatin** USA
58D1 **Gallatin** *R* USA
44C4 **Galle** Sri Lanka
62A3 **Gallego** Mexico
15B1 **Gállego** *R* Spain
72D1 **Gallinas, Puerta** Colombia
**Gallipolī = Gelibolu**
17D2 **Gallipoli** Italy
20C2 **Gällivare** Sweden
8C4 **Galloway** *District* Scotland
8C4 **Galloway,Mull of** *C* Scotland
62A1 **Gallup** USA
66B1 **Galt** USA
9B3 **Galty Mts** Irish Republic
70C2 **Galveston** USA
57D4 **Galveston B** USA
10B3 **Galway** Irish Republic
10B3 **Galway B** Irish Republic
43F3 **Gamba** China
48B3 **Gambaga** Ghana
54A3 **Gambell** USA
48A3 **Gambia** *R* Senegal/The Gambia
48A3 **Gambia,The** *Republic* Africa
37N6 **Gambier, Îles** Pacific Ocean
50B4 **Gamboma** Congo
51B5 **Gambos** Angola
44C4 **Gampola** Sri Lanka
59E3 **Ganado** USA
50E3 **Ganale Dorya** *R* Ethiopia
65D2 **Gananoque** Canada
**Gand = Gent**
51B5 **Ganda** Angola
51C4 **Gandajika** Zaïre
43N2 **Gandak** *R* India/Nepal
43M2 **Gandak Dam** Nepal
42B3 **Gandava** Pakistan
55N5 **Gander** Canada
42B4 **Gāndhīdhām** India
42C4 **Gāndhīnagar** India
42D4 **Gāndhi Sāgar** *L* India
15B2 **Gandia** Spain
75E1 **Gandu** Brazil
**Ganga** *R* **=Ganges**
42C3 **Gangānagar** India
43G4 **Gangaw** Burma
31A2 **Gangca** China
39G2 **Gangdise Shan** *Mts* China
22F4 **Ganges** *R* India
43F4 **Ganges, Mouths of the** Bangladesh/India
28B2 **Gangou** China
43F3 **Gangtok** India
31B3 **Gangu** China
58E2 **Gannett Peak** *Mt* USA
31B2 **Ganquan** China
12K8 **Gantsevichi** Belorussia
31D4 **Ganzhou** China
48C3 **Gao** Mali
31A2 **Gaolan** China
31C2 **Gaoping** China
48B3 **Gaoua** Burkina
48A3 **Gaoual** Guinea
31D3 **Gaoyou Hu** *L* China
31C5 **Gaozhou** China
14D3 **Gap** France
42D2 **Gar** China
9C3 **Gara,L** Irish Republic
34C1 **Garah** Australia
73L5 **Garanhuns** Brazil
59B2 **Garberville** USA
75C3 **Garça** Brazil
15A2 **Garcia de Sola, Embalse de** *Res* Spain
75B3 **Garcias** Brazil
16C1 **Garda, L di** Italy
62B1 **Garden City** USA
64B1 **Garden Pen** USA
42B2 **Gardez** Afghanistan
58D1 **Gardiner** USA
68D2 **Gardiners I** USA
68E1 **Gardner** USA
33H1 **Gardner** *I* Phoenix Islands
66C1 **Gardnerville** USA
16D2 **Gargano, Monte** *Mt* Italy
16D2 **Gargano, Prom. del** Italy
42D4 **Garhākota** India
43K1 **Garhmuktesar** India
20L4 **Gari** Russian Federation
47B3 **Garies** South Africa
50D4 **Garissa** Kenya
63C2 **Garland** USA
18C3 **Garmisch-Partenkirchen** Germany
41F2 **Garmsar** Iran
63C1 **Garnett** USA
56B2 **Garnett Peak** *Mt* USA
14C3 **Garonne** *R* France
49D4 **Garoua** Cameroon
49D4 **Garoua Boulai** Cameroon
60C1 **Garrison** USA
9D2 **Garron** *Pt* Northern Ireland
8C3 **Garry** *R* Scotland
54H3 **Garry L** Canada
43E4 **Garwa** India
64B2 **Gary** USA
39G2 **Garyarsa** China
63C2 **Garza-Little Elm** *Res* USA
41F2 **Gasan Kuli** Turkmenistan
14B3 **Gascogne** *Region* France
63D1 **Gasconade** *R* USA
32A3 **Gascoyne** *R* Australia
50B3 **Gashaka** Nigeria
48D3 **Gashua** Nigeria
57G2 **Gaspé** Canada
57G2 **Gaspé,C de** Canada
57G2 **Gaspé, Peninsule de** Canada
67B1 **Gastonia** USA
67C1 **Gaston,L** USA
45B1 **Gata, C** Cyprus
15B2 **Gata, Cabo de** *C* Spain
20D4 **Gatchina** Russian Federation
8C4 **Gatehouse of Fleet** Scotland
6D2 **Gateshead** England
63C2 **Gatesville** USA
13B3 **Gâtinais** *Region* France
65D1 **Gatineau** Canada
65D1 **Gatineau** *R* Canada
67B1 **Gatlinburg** USA
34D1 **Gatton** Australia
33F2 **Gaua** *I* Vanuatu
43G3 **Gauhāti** India
19E1 **Gauja** *R* Latvia
43E3 **Gauri Phanta** India
17E4 **Gávdhos** *I* Greece
75D1 **Gavião** *R* Brazil
66B3 **Gaviota** USA
12H6 **Gävle** Sweden
32C4 **Gawler Ranges** *Mts* Australia
31A1 **Gaxun Nur** *L* China
43E4 **Gaya** India
48C3 **Gaya** Niger
48C3 **Gaya** Nigeria
28B2 **Gaya He** *R* China
64C1 **Gaylord** USA
34D1 **Gayndah** Australia
20J3 **Gayny** Russian Federation
19F3 **Gaysin** Ukraine
40B3 **Gaza** Israel
40C2 **Gaziantep** Turkey
48B4 **Gbaringa** Liberia
48D1 **Gbbès** Tunisia
19D2 **Gdańsk** Poland
19D2 **Gdańsk,G of** Poland
12K7 **Gdov** Russian Federation
19D2 **Gdynia** Poland
45A4 **Gebel el Galâla el Baharîya** *Desert* Egypt
50D2 **Gedaref** Sudan

Gediz Gran Desierto


17F3 **Gediz** *R* Turkey
18C2 **Gedser** Denmark
13C2 **Geel** Belgium
34B3 **Geelong** Australia
34C4 **Geeveston** Australia
48D3 **Geidam** Nigeria
13D2 **Geilenkirchen** Germany
50D4 **Geita** Tanzania
31A5 **Gejiu** China
16C3 **Gela** Italy
50E3 **Geladī** Ethiopia
13D2 **Geldern** Germany
17F2 **Gelibolu** Turkey
40B2 **Gelidonya Burun** Turkey
13E2 **Gelnhausen** Germany
13D2 **Gelsenkirchen** Germany
12F8 **Gelting** Germany
30C5 **Gemas** Malaysia
13C2 **Gembloux** Belgium
50B3 **Gemena** Zaïre
40C2 **Gemerek** Turkey
40A1 **Gemlik** Turkey
16C1 **Gemona** Italy
47C2 **Gemsbok Nat Pk** Botswana
50C2 **Geneina** Sudan
74C5 **General Alvear** Argentina
76F2 **General Belgrano** *Base* Antarctica
76G2 **General Bernardo O'Higgins** *Base* Antarctica
74B7 **General Carrera, Lago** Chile
74D2 **General Eugenio A Garay** Paraguay
66C2 **General Grant Grove Section** *Region* USA
74C3 **General Manuel Belgrano** *Mt* Argentina
74D5 **General Pico** Argentina
74C5 **General Roca** Argentina
27F6 **General Santos** Philippines
65D2 **Genesee** *R* USA
65D2 **Geneseo** USA
61D2 **Geneva** Nebraska, USA
68B1 **Geneva** New York, USA
16B1 **Geneva** Switzerland
**Geneva,L of = Léman, L**
**Genève = Geneva**
15B2 **Genil** *R* Spain
16B2 **Gennargentu, Monti del** *Mt* Sardinia, Italy
34C3 **Genoa** Australia
16B2 **Genoa** Italy
**Genova = Genoa**
16B2 **Genova, G di** Italy
13B2 **Gent** Belgium
27D7 **Genteng** Indonesia
18C2 **Genthin** Germany
21H7 **Geokchay** Azerbaijan
47C3 **George** South Africa
55M4 **George** *R* Canada
34C2 **George,L** Australia
67B3 **George,L** Florida, USA
65E2 **George,L** New York, USA
35A2 **George Sd** New Zealand
34C4 **George Town** Australia
66B1 **Georgetown** California, USA
65D3 **Georgetown** Delaware, USA
73G2 **Georgetown** Guyana
64C3 **Georgetown** Kentucky, USA
30C4 **George Town** Malaysia
69N2 **Georgetown** St Vincent
67C2 **Georgetown** S Carolina, USA
63C2 **Georgetown** Texas, USA
48A3 **Georgetown** The Gambia
76G8 **George V Land** *Region* Antarctica
62C3 **George West** USA
21G7 **Georgia** *Republic* Europe
76F12 **Georg Forster** *Base* Antarctica
67B2 **Georgia** *State* USA
64C1 **Georgian B** Canada
54F5 **Georgia, Str of** Canada
32C3 **Georgina** *R* Australia
21F5 **Georgiu-Dezh** Russian Federation
21G7 **Georgiyevsk** Russian Federation
76F1 **Georg von Neumayer** *Base* Antarctica
18C2 **Gera** Germany
13B2 **Geraardsbergen** Belgium
75C1 **Geral de Goiás, Serra** *Mts* Brazil
35B2 **Geraldine** New Zealand
75C2 **Geral do Paraná, Serra** *Mts* Brazil
32A3 **Geraldton** Australia
57E2 **Geraldton** Canada
75D2 **Geral, Serra** *Mts* Bahia, Brazil
75B4 **Geral, Serra** *Mts* Paraná, Brazil
45C3 **Gerar** *R* Israel
13D3 **Gérardmer** France
54C3 **Gerdine,Mt** USA
30C4 **Gerik** Malaysia
60C2 **Gering** USA
21C6 **Gerlachovsky** *Mt* Poland
47D2 **Germiston** South Africa
13D2 **Gerolstein** Germany
15C1 **Gerona** Spain
13E2 **Geseke** Germany
50E3 **Gestro** *R* Ethiopia
15B1 **Getafe** Spain
68B3 **Gettysburg** Pennsylvania, USA
60D1 **Gettysburg** S Dakota, USA
41D2 **Gevaş** Turkey
17E2 **Gevgeliija** Macedonia, Yugoslavia
45D2 **Ghabāghib** Syria
45D3 **Ghadaf, Wadi el** Jordan
48C1 **Ghadamis** Libya
41F2 **Ghaem Shahr** Iran
43E3 **Ghāghara** *R* India
48B4 **Ghana** *Republic* Africa
47C1 **Ghanzi** Botswana
48C1 **Ghardaïa** Algeria
49D1 **Gharyān** Libya
49D2 **Ghāt** Libya
15B2 **Ghazaouet** Algeria
42D3 **Ghāziābād** India
42B2 **Ghazni** Afghanistan
17F1 **Gheorgheni** Romania
40D3 **Ghudāf, Wadi al** *Watercourse* Iraq
16D3 **Giarre** Sicily, Italy
60D2 **Gibbon** USA
47B2 **Gibeon** Namibia
15A2 **Gibraltar** *Colony* SW Europe
7E7 **Gibraltar** *Pt* England
15A2 **Gibraltar,Str of** Africa/Spain
32B3 **Gibson Desert** Australia
58B1 **Gibsons** Canada
44B2 **Giddalūr** India
45B3 **Giddi, Gebel el** *Mt* Egypt
45B3 **Giddi Pass** Egypt
50D3 **Gīdolē** Ethiopia
13B4 **Gien** France
18B2 **Giessen** Germany
8D4 **Gifford** Scotland
67B3 **Gifford** USA
29D3 **Gifu** Japan
8C4 **Gigha** *I* Scotland
16C2 **Giglio** *I* Italy
15A1 **Gijón** Spain
59D4 **Gila** *R* USA
59D4 **Gila Bend** USA
59D4 **Gila Bend Mts** USA
32D2 **Gilbert** *R* Australia
33G1 **Gilbert Is** Pacific Ocean
58D1 **Gildford** USA
51D5 **Gilé** Mozambique
45C2 **Gilead** *Region* Jordan
49E2 **Gilf Kebir Plat** Egypt
34C2 **Gilgandra** Australia
42C1 **Gilgit** Pakistan
42C1 **Gilgit** *R* Pakistan
34C2 **Gilgunnia** Australia
55J4 **Gillam** Canada
60B2 **Gillette** USA
7E4 **Gillingham** England
64B1 **Gills Rock** USA
64B2 **Gilman** USA
66B2 **Gilroy** USA
69P2 **Gimie, Mont** St Lucia
45B3 **Gineifa** Egypt
47E2 **Gingindlovu** South Africa
50E3 **Gīnīr** Ethiopia
17E3 **Gióna** *Mt* Greece
34C3 **Gippsland** *Mts* Australia
64C2 **Girard** USA
72D3 **Girardot** Colombia
8D3 **Girdle Ness** *Pen* Scotland
40C1 **Giresun** Turkey
40B4 **Girga** Egypt
42C4 **Gīr Hills** India
50B3 **Giri** *R* Zaïre
43F4 **Girīdīh** India
42A2 **Girishk** Afghanistan
13D4 **Giromagny** France
**Girona = Gerona**
14B2 **Gironde** *R* France
8C4 **Girvan** Scotland
35C1 **Gisborne** New Zealand
50C4 **Gitega** Burundi
**Giuba,R = Juba,R**
17F2 **Giurgiu** Romania
13C2 **Givet** France
25S3 **Gizhiga** Russian Federation
19E2 **Gizycko** Poland
17E2 **Gjirokastër** Albania
54J3 **Gjoatlaven** Canada
12G6 **Gjøvik** Norway
55M5 **Glace Bay** Canada
58B1 **Glacier Peak** *Mt* USA
55K2 **Glacier Str** Canada
32E3 **Gladstone** Queensland, Australia
34A2 **Gladstone** S Australia, Australia
34C4 **Gladstone** Tasmania, Australia
64B1 **Gladstone** USA
12A1 **Gláma** *Mt* Iceland
12G6 **Glåma** *R* Norway
13D3 **Glan** *R* Germany
61D3 **Glasco** USA
64B3 **Glasgow** Kentucky, USA
60B1 **Glasgow** Montana, USA
8C4 **Glasgow** Scotland
68C3 **Glassboro** USA
66C2 **Glass Mt** USA
7C4 **Glastonbury** England
20J4 **Glazov** Russian Federation
18D3 **Gleisdorf** Austria
35C1 **Glen Afton** New Zealand
9D2 **Glenarm** Northern Ireland
68B3 **Glen Burnie** USA
47E2 **Glencoe** South Africa
59D4 **Glendale** Arizona, USA
66C3 **Glendale** California, USA
60C1 **Glendive** USA
60C2 **Glendo Res** USA
9C2 **Glengad Hd** *Pt* Irish Republic
34D1 **Glen Innes** Australia
8C4 **Glenluce** Scotland
34C1 **Glenmorgan** Australia
34D2 **Glenreagh** Australia
68B3 **Glen Rock** USA
63C2 **Glen Rose** USA
8D3 **Glenrothes** Scotland
68D1 **Glens Falls** USA
63D2 **Glenwood** Arkansas, USA
61D1 **Glenwood** Minnesota, USA
62A2 **Glenwood** New Mexico, USA
60B3 **Glenwood Springs** USA
64A1 **Glidden** USA
12F6 **Glittertind** *Mt* Norway
19D2 **Gliwice** Poland
59D4 **Globe** USA
18D2 **Głogów** Poland
12G5 **Glomfjord** Norway
51E5 **Glorieuses, Isles** Madagascar
7C3 **Glossop** England
34D2 **Gloucester** Australia
7C4 **Gloucester** England
68E1 **Gloucester** USA
7C4 **Gloucester** *County* England
68C1 **Gloversville** USA
19F1 **Glubokoye** Belorussia
13E1 **Glückstadt** Germany
21E5 **Glukhov** Ukraine
18D3 **Gmünd** Austria
18C3 **Gmunden** Austria
19D2 **Gniezno** Poland
44A2 **Goa, Daman and Diu** *Union Territory* India
47B2 **Goageb** Namibia
43G3 **Goālpāra** India
50D3 **Goba** Ethiopia
47B1 **Gobabis** Namibia
31B1 **Gobi** *Desert* China/Mongolia
29C4 **Gobo** Japan
19G1 **Gobza** *R* Russian Federation
47B1 **Gochas** Namibia
7D4 **Godalming** England
44C2 **Godāvari** *R* India
66C2 **Goddard,Mt** USA
64C2 **Goderich** Canada
55N3 **Godhavn** Greenland
42C4 **Godhra** India
57D1 **Gods L** Canada
55N3 **Godthåb** Greenland
**Godwin Austen** *Mt* **=K2**
68E1 **Goffstown** USA
64C1 **Gogama** Canada
13E1 **Gohfeld** Germany
75C2 **Goiandira** Brazil
75C2 **Goianésia** Brazil
75C2 **Goiânia** Brazil
75B2 **Goiás** Brazil
73J6 **Goiás** *State* Brazil
75B3 **Goio-Erê** Brazil
50D3 **Gojab** *R* Ethiopia
17F2 **Gökçeada** *I* Turkey
17F3 **Gökova Körfezi** *B* Turkey
21F8 **Goksu** *R* Turkey
40C2 **Göksun** Turkey
43G3 **Golāghāt** India
9B2 **Gola, I** Irish Republic
40C2 **Gölbaşi** Turkey
24K2 **Gol'chikha** Russian Federation
58C2 **Golconda** USA
68B2 **Gold** USA
58B2 **Gold Beach** USA
34D1 **Gold Coast** Australia
35B2 **Golden B** New Zealand
58B1 **Goldendale** USA
66A2 **Golden Gate** *Chan* USA
63D3 **Golden Meadow** USA
59C3 **Goldfield** USA
66D2 **Gold Point** USA
67C1 **Goldsboro** USA
62C2 **Goldthwaite** USA
18C2 **Goleniów** Poland
66C3 **Goleta** USA
26C3 **Golmud** China
50E3 **Gololcha** Ethiopia
29F2 **Golovnino** Russian Federation
50C4 **Goma** Zaïre
43L2 **Gomati** India
48D3 **Gombe** Nigeria
19G2 **Gomel** Belorussia
48A2 **Gomera** *I* Canary Islands
70B2 **Gómez Palacio** Mexico
25O4 **Gonam** *R* Russian Federation
69C3 **Gonâve, Isla de la** Cuba
41G2 **Gonbad-e Kāvūs** Iran
43E3 **Gonda** India
42C4 **Gondal** India
50D2 **Gonder** Ethiopia
43E4 **Gondia** India
40A1 **Gönen** Turkey
17F3 **Gonen** *R* Turkey
31A4 **Gongga Shan** *Mt* China
31A2 **Gonghe** China
75D1 **Gongogi** *R* Brazil
48D3 **Gongola** *R* Nigeria
66B2 **Gonzales** California, USA
63C3 **Gonzales** Texas, USA
47B3 **Good Hope,C of** South Africa
58D2 **Gooding** USA
60C3 **Goodland** USA
34C1 **Goodooga** *R* Australia
7D3 **Goole** England
34C2 **Goolgowi** Australia
34A3 **Goolwa** Australia
32A4 **Goomalling** Australia
34C2 **Goombalie** Australia
34D1 **Goomeri** Australia
34D1 **Goondiwindi** Australia
55N4 **Goose Bay** Canada
67C2 **Goose Creek** USA
58B2 **Goose L** USA
44B2 **Gooty** India
32D1 **Goraka** Papua New Guinea
43E3 **Gorakhpur** India
20K3 **Gora Koyp** *Mt* Russian Federation
25M4 **Gora Munku Sardyk** *Mt* Mongolia/Russian Federation
20K3 **Gora Narodnaya** *Mt* Russian Federation
20L2 **Gora Pay-Yer** *Mt* Russian Federation
20K3 **Gora Telpos-Iz** *Mt*
17D2 **Goražde** Bosnia & Herzegovina, Yugoslavia
54D2 **Gordon** USA
65D3 **Gordonsville** USA
50B3 **Goré** Chad
50D3 **Gorē** Ethiopia
35A3 **Gore** New Zealand
25P4 **Gore Topko** *Mt* Russian Federation
9C3 **Gorey** Irish Republic
41F2 **Gorgān** Iran
13C2 **Gorinchem** Netherlands
41E2 **Goris** Armenia
16C1 **Gorizia** Italy
19G2 **Gorki** Belorussia
20M2 **Gorki** Russian Federation
20G4 **Gor'kovskoye Vodokhranilishche** *Res* Russian Federation
7E3 **Gorleston** England
18C2 **Görlitz** Germany
21F6 **Gorlovka** Ukraine
66C3 **Gorman** USA
17F2 **Gorna Orjahovica** Bulgaria
26B1 **Gorno-Altaysk** Russian Federation
26H2 **Gornozavodsk** Russian Federation
20K3 **Goro Denezhkin Kamen'** *Mt* Russian Federation
20G4 **Gorodets** Russian Federation
19G2 **Gorodnya** Ukraine
19F1 **Gorodok** Belorussia
19E3 **Gorodok** Ukraine
19F3 **Gorodok** Ukraine
27H7 **Goroka** Papua New Guinea
51D5 **Gorongosa** Mozambique
27F6 **Gorontalo** Indonesia
20L4 **Goro Yurma** *Mt* Russian Federation
75D2 **Gorutuba** *R* Brazil
25M4 **Goryachinsk** Russian Federation
21J7 **Gory Akkyr** *Upland* Turkmenistan
25L2 **Gory Byrranga** *Mts* Russian Federation
19F3 **Goryn'** *R* Ukraine
25L3 **Gory Putorana** *Mts* Russian Federation
19E2 **Góry Świetokrzyskie** *Upland* Poland
12H8 **Gorzów Wielkopolski** Poland
66C2 **Goshen** USA
29E2 **Goshogawara** Japan
16D2 **Gospić** Croatia
7D4 **Gosport** England
17E2 **Gostivar** Macedonia Yugoslavia
19D2 **Gostynin** Poland
12G7 **Göteborg** Sweden
50B3 **Gotel Mts** Nigeria
60C2 **Gothenburg** USA
12H7 **Gotland** *I* Sweden
28B4 **Gotō-rettō** *Is* Japan
12H7 **Gotska Sandön** *I* Sweden
28C4 **Gōtsu** Japan
18B2 **Göttingen** Germany
28A2 **Goubangzi** China
13C2 **Gouda** Netherlands
50B2 **Goudoumaria** Niger
52H7 **Gough I** Atlantic Ocean
55L5 **Gouin, Réservoire** Canada
34C2 **Goulburn** Australia
48B3 **Goumbou** Mali
48B3 **Goundam** Mali
50B2 **Gouré** Niger
48B3 **Gourma Rharous** Mali
50B2 **Gouro** Chad
58E1 **Govenlock** Canada
27G8 **Gove Pen** Australia
21C6 **Goverla** *Mt* Ukraine
75D2 **Governador Valadares** Brazil
43E4 **Govind Ballabh Paht Sāgar** *L* India
42B3 **Gowārān** Afghanistan
7B4 **Gower** Wales
74E3 **Goya** Argentina
50C2 **Goz-Beïda** Chad
16C3 **Gozo** *I* Malta
50D2 **Goz Regeb** Sudan
47C3 **Graaff-Reinet** South Africa
65D1 **Gracefield** Canada
69A4 **Gracias à Dios, Cabo** Honduras
34D1 **Grafton** Australia
61D1 **Grafton** N Dakota, USA
64C3 **Grafton** W Virginia, USA
54E4 **Graham I** Canada
59E4 **Graham,Mt** USA
47D3 **Grahamstown** South Africa
73J5 **Grajaú** Brazil
19E2 **Grajewo** Poland
17E2 **Grámmos** *Mt* Albania/Greece
8C3 **Grampian** *Mts* Scotland
8D3 **Grampian** *Region* Scotland
72D3 **Granada** Colombia
72A1 **Granada** Nicaragua
15B2 **Granada** Spain
65E1 **Granby** Canada
60B2 **Granby** USA
48A2 **Gran Canaria** *I* Canary Islands
74D3 **Gran Chaco** *Region* Argentina
64B2 **Grand** *R* Michigan, USA
61E2 **Grand** *R* Missouri, USA
69Q2 **Grand B** Dominica
57F4 **Grand Bahama** *I* The Bahamas
13D4 **Grand Ballon** *Mt* France
55N5 **Grand Bank** Canada
52F2 **Grand Banks** Atlantic Ocean
48B4 **Grand Bassam** Ivory Coast
59D3 **Grand Canyon** USA
59D3 **Grand Canyon Nat Pk** USA
69A3 **Grand Cayman** *I* Cayman Is, Caribbean Sea
58C1 **Grand Coulee** USA
73K6 **Grande** *R* Bahia, Brazil
75C2 **Grande** *R* Minas Gerais/São Paulo, Brazil
55L4 **Grande 2, Rēservoir de la** Canada
55L4 **Grande 3, Rēservoir de la** Canada
55L4 **Grande 4, Rēservoir de la** Canada
74C8 **Grande, Bahía** *B* Argentina
51E5 **Grande Comore** *I* Comoros
75D3 **Grande, Ilha** Brazil
63C2 **Grande Prairie** USA
50B2 **Grand Erg de Bilma** *Desert Region* Niger
48C1 **Grand Erg Occidental** *Desert* Algeria
48C2 **Grand Erg Oriental** *Desert* Algeria
55L4 **Grande Rivière de la Baleine** *R* Canada
58C1 **Grande Ronde** *R* USA
59D4 **Gran Desierto** USA

63D2 Jacksonville Arkansas, USA
67B2 Jacksonville Florida, USA
64A3 Jacksonville Illinois, USA
67C2 Jacksonville N Carolina, USA
63C2 Jacksonville Texas, USA
67B2 Jacksonville Beach USA
69C3 Jacmel Haiti
42B3 Jacobabad Pakistan
73K6 Jacobina Brazil
Jadotville = Likasi
72C5 Jaén Peru
15B2 Jaén Spain
Jaffa = Tel Aviv-Yafo
34A3 Jaffa,C Australia
44B4 Jaffna Sri Lanka
68D1 Jaffrey USA
43F4 Jagannathganj Ghat Bangladesh
44C2 Jagdalpur India
41G4 Jagin R Iran
44B2 Jagtial India
75E1 Jaguaquara Brazil
74F4 Jaguarão R Brazil/ Uruguay
75C3 Jaguariaiva Brazil
21H8 Jahan Dāgh Mt Iran
41F4 Jahrom Iran
31A2 Jainca China
42D3 Jaipur India
42C3 Jaisalmer India
41G2 Jajarm Iran
16D2 Jajce Bosnia & Herzegovina, Yugoslavia
27D7 Jakarta Indonesia
55N3 Jakobshavn Greenland
12J6 Jakobstad Finland
62B2 Jal USA
42C2 Jalalabad Afghanistan
70C3 Jalapa Mexico
75B3 Jales Brazil
43F3 Jaleswar Nepal
42D4 Jalgaon India
48D4 Jalingo Nigeria
42D5 Jālna India
15B1 Jalón R Spain
49E2 Jalo Oasis Libya
42C3 Jālor India
43F3 Jalpāiguri India
49E2 Jālu Oasis Libya
72B4 Jama Ecuador
50E3 Jamaame Somalia
69B3 Jamaica I Caribbean Sea
69B3 Jamaica Chan Haiti/ Jamaica
43F4 Jamalpur Bangladesh
27D7 Jambi Indonesia
42C4 Jambusar India
60D1 James R N Dakota, USA
65D3 James R Virginia, USA
55K4 James B Canada
34A2 Jamestown Australia
60D1 Jamestown N Dakota, USA
65D2 Jamestown New York, USA
68E2 Jamestown Rhode Island, USA
47D3 Jamestown South Africa
54J5 Jamestown USA
44B2 Jamkhandi India
42C2 Jammu India
42D2 Jammu and Kashmīr State India
42B4 Jāmnagar India
42C3 Jampur Pakistan
20C3 Jämsä Finland
43F4 Jamshedpur India
45D3 Janab, Wadi el Jordan
43F3 Janakpur Nepal
75D2 Janaúba Brazil
41F3 Jandaq Iran
34D1 Jandowae Australia
64B2 Janesville USA
76B1 Jan Mayen I Norwegian Sea
75D2 Januária Brazil
42D4 Jaora India
26G3 Japan, Sof Japan
36J3 Japan Trench Pacific Ocean
72E4 Japurá R Brazil
40C2 Jarābulus Syria
75C2 Jaraguá Brazil
75B3 Jaraguari Brazil
15B1 Jarama R Spain
45C2 Jarash Jordan
75A3 Jardim Brazil
69B2 Jardines de la Reina Is Cuba
Jargalant = Hovd
73H3 Jari R Brazil
43G3 Jaria Jhānjail Bangladesh
13C3 Jarny France
18D2 Jarocin Poland
19E2 Jarosław Poland
12G6 Järpen Sweden
31B2 Jartai China
42C4 Jasdan India
48C4 Jasikan Ghana
41G4 Jāsk Iran

19E3 Jasło Poland
74D8 Jason Is Falkland Islands
63E2 Jasper Alabama, USA
63D1 Jasper Arkansas, USA
54G4 Jasper Canada
67B2 Jasper Florida, USA
64B3 Jasper Indiana, USA
63D2 Jasper Texas, USA
18D2 Jastrowie Poland
75B2 Jataí Brazil
15B2 Játiva Spain
75C3 Jaú Brazil
72C6 Jauja Peru
43E3 Jaunpur India
44B3 Javadi Hills India
27D7 Java,I Indonesia
Javari R = Yavari
27D7 Java SIndonesia
32A2 Java Trench Indonesia
Jawa = Java
27G7 Jaya, Pk Indonesia
27H7 Jayapura Indonesia
45D2 Jayrūd Syria
63D3 Jeanerette USA
48C4 Jebba Nigeria
50C2 Jebel Abyad Desert Region Sudan
Jebel esh Sheikh = Hermon, Mt
8D4 Jedburgh Scotland
Jedda = Jiddah
19E2 Jędrzejów Poland
61E2 Jefferson Iowa, USA
63D2 Jefferson Texas, USA
58D1 Jefferson R USA
57D3 Jefferson City USA
56B3 Jefferson,Mt USA
64B3 Jeffersonville USA
45C3 Jeib, Wadi el Israel/ Jordan
75A3 Jejui-Guazú R Paraguay
20D4 Jekabpils Latvia
18D2 Jelena Gora Poland
20C4 Jelgava Latvia
27E7 Jember Indonesia
62A1 Jemez Pueblo USA
18C2 Jena Germany
16B3 Jendouba Tunisia
45C2 Jenin Israel
63D2 Jennings USA
55O3 Jensen Nunatakker Mt Greenland
55K3 Jens Munk I Canada
34B3 Jeparit Australia
73L6 Jequié Brazil
75D2 Jequitaí R Brazil
75D2 Jequitinhonha Brazil
73K7 Jequitinhonha R Brazil
48D1 Jerba, I de Tunisia
15A2 Jerez de la Frontera Spain
15A2 Jerez de los Caballeros Spain
45C3 Jericho Israel
34C3 Jerilderie Australia
58D2 Jerome USA
14B2 Jersey I Channel Islands
57F2 Jersey City USA
65D2 Jersey Shore USA
64A3 Jerseyville USA
40C3 Jerusalem Israel
34D3 Jervis B Australia
16C1 Jesenice Slovenia
18D2 Jeseniky Upland Czechoslovakia
43F4 Jessore Bangladesh
57E3 Jesup USA
62C1 Jetmore USA
13D1 Jever Germany
68E2 Jewett City USA
44C2 Jeypore India
17D2 Jezerce Mt Albania
19E2 Jezioro Mamry L Poland
19E2 Jezioro Śniardwy L Poland
45C2 Jezzine Lebanon
42C4 Jhābua India
42D4 Jhālāwār India
42C2 Jhang Maghiana Pakistan
42D3 Jhānsi India
43E4 Jhārsuguda India
42C2 Jhelum Pakistan
42C2 Jhelum R Pakistan
42D3 Jhunjhunūn India
31B3 Jialing Jiang R China
26G2 Jiamusi China
28B2 Ji'an China
31C4 Ji'an Jiangxi, China
31D4 Jiande China
31B4 Jiang'an China
31D4 Jiangbiancun China
31A5 Jiangcheng China
31C5 Jiangmen China
31D3 Jiangsu Province China
31C4 Jiangxi Province China
31A3 Jiangyou China
31D1 Jianping China
31A5 Jianshui China
31D4 Jian Xi R China
31D4 Jianyang China
28B2 Jiaohe China
31E2 Jiaonan China
31E2 Jiao Xian China
31E2 Jiaozhou Wan B China

31C2 Jiaozuo China
31E3 Jiaxiang China
26C3 Jiayuguan China
75C2 Jibāo, Serra do Mts Brazil
50D1 Jiddah Saudi Arabia
31D3 Jieshou China
31C2 Jiexiu China
31A3 Jigzhi China
18D3 Jihlava Czechoslovakia
16B3 Jijel Algeria
50E3 Jilib Somalia
28B2 Jilin China
28B2 Jilin Province China
15B1 Jiloca R Spain
50D3 Jima Ethiopia
62B3 Jiménez Coahuila, Mexico
31D2 Jinan China
42D3 Jind India
31B2 Jingbian China
31D4 Jingdezhen China
30C1 Jinghong China
31C3 Jingmen China
31B2 Jingning China
31B4 Jing Xian China
28B2 Jingyu China
31D4 Jinhua China
31C1 Jining Inner Mongolia, China
31D2 Jining Shandong, China
50D3 Jinja Uganda
30C1 Jinping China
31A4 Jinsha Jiang R China
31C4 Jinshi China
31E1 Jinxi China
28A2 Jin Xian China
31E1 Jinzhou China
72F5 Jiparaná R Brazil
72B4 Jipijapa Ecuador
41G4 Jīroft Iran
50E3 Jirriiban Somalia
31B4 Jishou China
40C2 Jisr ash Shughūr Syria
17E2 Jiu R Romania
31D4 Jiujiang China
31C4 Jiuling Shan Hills China
31A4 Jiulong China
31D4 Jiulong Jiang R China
26G2 Jixi China
45C3 Jiza Jordan
50E2 Jīzān Saudi Arabia
48A3 Joal Senegal
75D2 João Monlevade Brazil
73M5 João Pessoa Brazil
73J7 João Pinheiro Brazil
42C3 Jodhpur India
12K6 Joensuu Finland
13C3 Joeuf France
43F3 Jogbani India
44A3 Jog Falls India
47D2 Johannesburg South Africa
59C3 Johannesburg USA
55L2 Johan Pen Canada
58C2 John Day USA
58B1 John Day R USA
57F3 John H Kerr L USA
65D3 John H. Kerr Res USA
62B1 John Martin Res USA
8D2 John o'Groats Scotland
63C1 John Redmond Res USA
68A2 Johnsonburg USA
68C1 Johnson City New York, USA
67B1 Johnson City Tennessee, USA
67B2 Johnston USA
69N2 Johnston Pt St Vincent
68C1 Johnstown New York, USA
65D2 Johnstown Pennsylvania, USA
30C5 Johor Bharu Malaysia
14C2 Joigny France
74G3 Joinville Brazil
13C3 Joinville France
20J5 Jok R Russian Federation
12H5 Jokkmokk Sweden
21H8 Jolfa Iran
57E2 Joliet USA
55L5 Joliette Canada
27F6 Jolo Philippines
27F6 Jolo I Philippines
39H2 Joma Mt China
19E1 Jonava Lithuania
31A3 Joně China
57D3 Jonesboro Arkansas, USA
63D2 Jonesboro Louisiana, USA
55K2 Jones Sd Canada
19E1 Joniškis Lithuania
12G7 Jönköping Sweden
65E1 Jonquière Canada
57D3 Joplin USA
60B1 Jordan Montana, USA
68B1 Jordan New York, USA
40C3 Jordan Kingdom SW Asia
45C2 Jordan R Israel
58C2 Jordan Valley USA
75B4 Jordão R Brazil
43G3 Jorhāt India

20C2 Jörn Sweden
12F7 Jørpeland Norway
48C3 Jos Nigeria
32B2 Joseph Bonaparte G Australia
59D3 Joseph City USA
55M4 Joseph, Lac Canada
24B3 Jotunheimen Mt Norway
45C2 Jouai'ya Lebanon
45C2 Jounié Lebanon
43G3 Jowai India
50E3 Jowhar Somalia
54F5 Juan de Fuca,Str of Canada/USA
51E5 Juan de Nova I Mozambique Channel
72Q Juan Fernández, Islas Pacific Ocean
73K5 Juàzeiro Brazil
73L5 Juàzeiro do Norte Brazil
50D3 Juba Sudan
50E3 Juba R Somalia
45C1 Jubail Lebanon
76G2 Jubany Base Antarctica
40D4 Jubbah Saudi Arabia
15B2 Júcar R Spain
18C3 Judenburg Austria
13D1 Juist I Germany
73K8 Juiz de Fora Brazil
74C2 Jujuy State Argentina
60C2 Julesburg USA
72E7 Juli Peru
72D7 Juliaca Peru
73G3 Julianatop Mt Surinam
55O3 Julianehåb Greenland
13D2 Jülich Germany
42D2 Jullundur India
43E3 Jumla Nepal
45C3 Jum Suwwāna Mt Jordan
42C4 Jūnāgadh India
31D2 Junan China
62C2 Junction Texas, USA
59D3 Junction Utah, USA
56D3 Junction City USA
74G2 Jundiaí Brazil
54E4 Juneau USA
32D4 Junee Australia
66C2 June Lake USA
16B1 Jungfrau Mt Switzerland
68B2 Juniata R USA
74D4 Junín Argentina
66B2 Junipero Serra Peak Mt USA
31A4 Junlian China
75D2 Juparaná, Lagoa Brazil
74G2 Juquiá Brazil
50C3 Jur R Sudan
8C4 Jura I Scotland
14D2 Jura Mts France
8C3 Jura,Sound of Chan Scotland
45C3 Jurf ed Darāwīsh Jordan
24K4 Jurga Russian Federation
20C4 Jūrmala Latvia
72E4 Juruá R Brazil
73G6 Juruena R Brazil
45D1 Jūsiyah Syria
72E4 Jutaí R Brazil
70D3 Juticalpa Honduras
Jutland Pen = Jylland
69A2 Juventud, Isla de la Cuba
41G3 Jūymand Iran
18B1 Jylland Pen Denmark
12K6 Jyväskylä Finland

## K

39F2 K2 Mt China/India
41G2 Kaakhka Turkmenistan
47E2 Kaapmuiden South Africa
27F7 Kabaena Indonesia
32B1 Kabaena I Indonesia
48A4 Kabala Sierra Leone
50D4 Kabale Uganda
50C4 Kabalo Zaïre
50C4 Kabambare Zaïre
50D3 Kabarole Uganda
64C1 Kabinakagami L Canada
50C4 Kabinda Zaïre
45C1 Kabīr R Syria
41E3 Kabir Kuh Mts Iran
51C5 Kabompo Zambia
51C5 Kabompo R Zambia
51C4 Kabongo Zaïre
42B2 Kabul Afghanistan
42B4 Kachchh,G of India
20K4 Kachkanar Russian Federation
25M4 Kachug Russian Federation
30B3 Kadan I Burma
42C4 Kadi India
40B2 Kadinhani Turkey
44B3 Kadiri India
21F6 Kadiyevka Ukraine
60C2 Kadoka USA
51C5 Kadoma Zimbabwe
50C3 Kadugli Sudan
48C3 Kaduna Nigeria
48C3 Kaduna R Nigeria
44B3 Kadūr India
43H3 Kadusam Mt China

20K3 Kadzherom Russian Federation
28A3 Kaechon N Korea
48A3 Kaédi Mauritius
66E5 Kaena Pt Hawaiian Islands
28B3 Kaesong N Korea
48C4 Kafanchan Nigeria
48A3 Kaffrine Senegal
45D1 Kafr Behum Syria
45A3 Kafr Sa'd Egypt
45A3 Kafr Saqv Egypt
45D1 Kafrūn Bashūr Syria
51C5 Kafue Zambia
51C5 Kafue R Zambia
51C5 Kafue Nat Pk Zambia
29D3 Kaga Japan
24H6 Kagan Uzbekistan
21G7 Kağizman Turkey
19F3 Kagul Moldavia
41G2 Kāhak Iran
50D4 Kahama Tanzania
42B3 Kahan Pakistan
51B4 Kahemba Zaïre
13E2 Kahler Asten Mt Germany
41G4 Kahnūj Iran
64A2 Kahoka USA
66E5 Kahoolawe I Hawaiian Islands
40C2 Kahramanmaraş Turkey
66E5 Kahuku Pt Hawaiian Islands
66E5 Kahului Hawaiian Islands
35B2 Kaiapoi New Zealand
59D3 Kaibab Plat USA
73G2 Kaieteur Falls Guyana
31C3 Kaifeng China
27G7 Kai, Kepulauan Arch Indonesia
35B1 Kaikohe New Zealand
33G5 Kaikoura New Zealand
35B2 Kaikoura Pen New Zealand
35B2 Kaikoura Range Mts New Zealand
31B4 Kaili China
28A2 Kailu China
66E5 Kailua Hawaii
66E5 Kailua Oahu, Hawaiian Islands
27G7 Kaimana Indonesia
35C1 Kaimenawa Mts New Zealand
29C4 Kainan Japan
48C3 Kainji Res Nigeria
35B1 Kaipara Harbour B New Zealand
31C5 Kaiping China
16C3 Kairouan Tunisia
66C2 Kaiser Peak Mt USA
14D2 Kaiserslautern Germany
28B2 Kaishantun China
19E2 Kaisiadorys Lithuania
35B1 Kaitaia New Zealand
35A3 Kaitangata New Zealand
42D3 Kaithal India
66E5 Kaiwi Chan Hawaiian Islands
31B3 Kai Xian China
28A2 Kaiyuan Liaoning, China
31A5 Kaiyuan Yunnan, China
12K6 Kajaani Finland
42B2 Kajaki Afghanistan
50D4 Kajiado Kenya
42B2 Kajrān Afghanistan
50D2 Kaka Sudan
64B1 Kakabeka Falls Canada
50D3 Kakamega Kenya
28B4 Kake Japan
21E6 Kakhovskoye Vodokhranilishche Res Ukraine
41F4 Kāki Iran
44C2 Kākināda India
29B4 Kakogawa Japan
54D2 Kaktovik USA
29D3 Kakuda Japan
16B3 Kalaat Khasba Tunisia
17E3 Kalabáka Greece
51C5 Kalabo Zambia
21G5 Kalach Russian Federation
21G6 Kalach-na-Donu Russian Federation
43G4 Kaladan R Burma/India
66E5 Ka Lae C Hawaiian Islands
51C6 Kalahari Desert Botswana
47C2 Kalahari Gemsbok Nat Pk South Africa
20C3 Kalajoki Finland
25N4 Kalakan Russian Federation
27C6 Kalakepen Indonesia
42C1 Kalam Pakistan
17E3 Kalámai Greece
57E2 Kalamazoo USA
66E5 Kalapana Hawaiian Islands
19F3 Kalarash Moldavia
42B3 Kalat Pakistan

Kent Kohyon


7E4 Kent County England
64B2 Kentland USA
64C2 Kenton USA
54H3 Kent Pen Canada
64C3 Kentucky R USA
57E3 Kentucky State USA
57E3 Kentucky L USA
63D2 Kentwood Louisiana, USA
64B2 Kentwood Michigan, USA
50D3 Kenya Republic Africa
50D4 Kenya,Mt Kenya
64A2 Keokuk USA
43E4 Keonchi India
43F4 Keonjhargarh India
19D2 Kepno Poland
44B3 Kerala State India
34B3 Kerang Australia
12K6 Kerava Finland
21F6 Kerch' Ukraine
20J3 Kerchem'ya Russian Federation
32D1 Kerema Papua New Guinea
58C1 Keremeos Canada
50D2 Keren Ethiopia
36E7 Kerguelen Is Indian Ocean
36E7 Kerguelen Ridge Indian Ocean
50D4 Kericho Kenya
27D7 Kerinci Mt Indonesia
50D3 Kerio R Kenya
48D1 Kerkenna, Îles Tunisia
38E2 Kerki Turkmenistan
Kérkira = Corfu
33H3 Kermadec Is Pacific Ocean
33H4 Kermadec Trench Pacific Ocean
41G3 Kermān Iran
66B2 Kerman USA
41E3 Kermānshāh Iran
62B2 Kermit USA
59C3 Kern R USA
66C3 Kernville USA
20J3 Keros Russian Federation
62C2 Kerrville USA
9B3 Kerry Hd Irish Republic
67B2 Kershaw USA
25N5 Kerulen R Mongolia
48B2 Kerzaz Algeria
17F2 Keşan Turkey
43N2 Kesariya India
29E3 Kesennuma Japan
21G7 Kesir Dağlari Mt Turkey
12L5 Kesten'ga Russian Federation
6C2 Keswick England
48C4 Kéta Ghana
27E7 Ketapang Indonesia
54E4 Ketchikan USA
42B4 Keti Bandar Pakistan
19E2 Kętrzyn Poland
7D3 Kettering England
64C3 Kettering USA
58C1 Kettle R Canada
66C2 Kettleman City USA
58C1 Kettle River Range Mts USA
55L3 Kettlestone B Canada
68B1 Keuka L USA
41G3 Kevir-i-Namak Salt Flat Iran
64B2 Kewaunee USA
64B1 Keweenaw B USA
64B1 Keweenaw Pen USA
64C1 Key Harbour Canada
67B3 Key Largo USA
57E4 Key West USA
25M4 Kezhma Russian Federation
45D2 Khabab Syria
26G2 Khabarovsk Russian Federation
21G8 Khabūr, al R Syria
42B3 Khairpur Pakistan
42B3 Khairpur Division Pakistan
47C1 Khakhea Botswana
45B3 Khalig el Tîna B Egypt
38D4 Khalīj Maşīrah G Oman
17F3 Khálki I Greece
17E2 Khalkidhikí Pen Greece
17E3 Khalkís Greece
20L2 Khal'mer-Yu Russian Federation
20H4 Khalturin Russian Federation
42C4 Khambhāt,G of India
42D4 Khāmgaon India
30C2 Kham Keut Laos
44C2 Khammam India
45B3 Khamsa Egypt
41E2 Khamseh Mts Iran
30C2 Khan R Laos
42B1 Khanabad Afghanistan
41E3 Khānaqīn Iraq
42D4 Khandwa India
42C2 Khanewal Pakistan
45D3 Khan ez Zabīb Jordan
30D4 Khanh Hung Vietnam
17E3 Khaniá Greece
26G2 Khanka, Ozero L China/ Russian Federation
Khankendy = Stepanakert
42C3 Khanpur Pakistan
45D1 Khān Shaykhūn Syria
24H3 Khanty-Mansiysk Russian Federation
45C3 Khan Yunis Israel
42D1 Khapalu India
26E2 Khapcheranga Russian Federation
21H6 Kharabali Russian Federation
43F4 Kharagpur India
42B3 Kharan Pakistan
41G4 Khārān R Iran
41F3 Kharānaq Iran
41F4 Khārg I Iran
49F2 Khârga Oasis Egypt
42D4 Khargon India
45B3 Kharîm, Gebel Mt Egypt
21F6 Khar'kov Ukraine
20F2 Kharlovka Russian Federation
17F2 Kharmanli Bulgaria
20G4 Kharovsk Russian Federation
50D2 Khartoum Sudan
50D2 Khartoum North Sudan
28C2 Khasan Russian Federation
50D2 Khashm el Girba Sudan
43G3 Khasi-Jaintia Hills India
17F2 Khaskovo Bulgaria
25M2 Khatanga Russian Federation
25N2 Khatangskiy Zaliv Estuary Russian Federation
25T3 Khatyrka Russian Federation
30B3 Khawsa Burma
40C4 Khaybar Saudi Arabia
40B5 Khazzan an-Nasr L Egypt
30C2 Khe Bo Vietnam
42C4 Khed Brahma India
15C2 Khemis Algeria
16B3 Khenchela Algeria
48B1 Khenifra Morocco
43L1 Kheri District India
15D2 Kherrata Algeria
21E6 Kherson Ukraine
25N4 Khilok Russian Federation
17F3 Khíos Greece
17F3 Khíos I Greece
21D6 Khmel'nitskiy Ukraine
19E3 Khodorov Ukraine
39E1 Khodzhent Tajikistan
42B1 Kholm Afghanistan
19G1 Kholm Russian Federation
47B1 Khomas Hochland Mts Namibia
30D3 Khong Laos
41F4 Khonj Iran
26G2 Khor Russian Federation
41F5 Khōr Duwayhin B UAE
42C1 Khorog Tajikistan
41E3 Khorramābad Iran
41E3 Khorramshahr Iran
41G3 Khosf Iran
42B2 Khost Pakistan
21D6 Khotin Ukraine
21D5 Khoyniki Belorussia
41G2 Khrebet Kopet Dag Mts Iran/Turkmenistan
20L2 Khrebet Pay-khoy Mts Russian Federation
45B1 Khrysokhou B Cyprus
20L3 Khulga R Russian Federation
43F4 Khulna Bangladesh
42D1 Khunjerāb P China/India
41F3 Khunsar Iran
41E4 Khurays Saudi Arabia
43F4 Khurda India
42D3 Khurja India
42C2 Khushab Pakistan
45C2 Khushnīyah Syria
45D4 Khush Shah, Wadi el Jordan
19E3 Khust Ukraine
50C2 Khuwei Sudan
42B3 Khuzdar Pakistan
21H5 Khvalynsk Russian Federation
41G3 Khvor Iran
41F4 Khvormūj Iran
21G8 Khvoy Iran
42C1 Khwaja Muhammad Ra Mts Afghanistan
42C2 Khyber P Afghanistan/ Pakistan
51C4 Kiambi Zaïre
63C2 Kiamichi R USA
50B4 Kibangou Congo
50D4 Kibaya Tanzania
50C4 Kibombo Zaïre
50D4 Kibondo Tanzania
50D4 Kibungu Rwanda
17E2 Kicevo Macedonia, Yugoslavia
54G4 Kicking Horse P Canada
48C3 Kidal Mali
7C3 Kidderminster England
48A3 Kidira Senegal
35C1 Kidnappers,C New Zealand
18C2 Kiel Germany
19E2 Kielce Poland
6C2 Kielder Res England
18C2 Kieler Bucht B Germany
21E5 Kiev Ukraine
38E2 Kifab Uzbekistan
48A3 Kiffa Mauritius
50D4 Kigali Rwanda
50C4 Kigoma Tanzania
66E5 Kiholo Hawaiian Islands
29C4 Kii-sanchi Mts Japan
29C4 Kii-suidō Str Japan
25R4 Kikhchik Russian Federation
17E1 Kikinda Serbia, Yugoslavia
Kikládhes = Cyclades
32D1 Kikon Papua New Guinea
29D2 Kikonai Japan
27H7 Kikori Papua New Guinea
50B4 Kikwit Zaïre
66E5 Kilauea Crater Vol Hawaiian Islands
8C4 Kilbrannan Sd Scotland
54C3 Kilbuck Mts USA
28B2 Kilchu N Korea
34D1 Kilcoy Australia
9C3 Kildare Irish Republic
9C3 Kildare County Irish Republic
63D2 Kilgore USA
50E4 Kilifi Kenya
50D4 Kilimanjaro Mt Tanzania
51D4 Kilindoni Tanzania
40C2 Kilis Turkey
19F3 Kiliya Ukraine
9D2 Kilkeel Northern Ireland
9C3 Kilkenny Irish Republic
9C3 Kilkenny County Irish Republic
17E2 Kilkís Greece
34D1 Killarney Australia
10B3 Killarney Irish Republic
63C2 Killeen USA
8C3 Killin Scotland
17E3 Killíni Mt Greece
9B3 Killorglin Irish Republic
9D2 Killyleagh Northern Ireland
8C4 Kilmarnock Scotland
20J4 Kil'mez Russian Federation
9C3 Kilmichael Pt Irish Republic
51D4 Kilosa Tanzania
10B3 Kilrush Irish Republic
8C4 Kilsyth Scotland
51C4 Kilwa Zaïre
51D4 Kilwa Kisiwani Tanzania
51D4 Kilwa Kivinje Tanzania
60C2 Kimball USA
54G5 Kimberley Canada
47C2 Kimberley South Africa
32B2 Kimberley Plat Australia
28B2 Kimch'aek N Korea
28B3 Kimch'ōn S Korea
28A3 Kimhae S Korea
17E3 Kími Greece
28A3 Kimje S Korea
20F4 Kimry Russian Federation
28A3 Kimwha N Korea
27E6 Kinabalu Mt Malaysia
8D2 Kinbrace Scotland
64C2 Kincardine Canada
63D2 Kinder USA
48A3 Kindia Guinea
50C4 Kindu Zaïre
20J5 Kinel' Russian Federation
20G4 Kineshma Russian Federation
34D1 Kingaroy Australia
59B3 King City USA
54F4 Kingcome Inlet Canada
63C1 Kingfisher USA
76H4 King George I Antarctica
55L4 King George Is Canada
32D5 King I Australia
32B2 King Leopold Range Mts Australia
56B3 Kingman USA
50C4 Kingombe Zaïre
66C2 Kingsburg USA
59C3 Kings Canyon Nat Pk USA
32B2 King Sd Australia
64B1 Kingsford USA
67B2 Kingsland USA
7E3 King's Lynn England
33G1 Kingsmill Group Is Kiribati
68D2 Kings Park USA
56B2 Kings Peak Mt USA
67B1 Kingsport USA
32C4 Kingston Australia
55L5 Kingston Canada
70E3 Kingston Jamaica
65E2 Kingston New York, USA
35A3 Kingston New Zealand
68C2 Kingston Pennsylvania, USA
69N2 Kingstown St Vincent
56D4 Kingsville USA
7C3 Kington England
8C3 Kingussie Scotland
54J3 King William I Canada
47D3 King William's Town South Africa
50B4 Kinkala Congo
12G7 Kinna Sweden
8D3 Kinnairds Head Pt Scotland
29C3 Kinomoto Japan
8D3 Kinross Scotland
50B4 Kinshasa Zaïre
62C1 Kinsley USA
67C1 Kinston USA
27E7 Kintap Indonesia
8C4 Kintyre Pen Scotland
50D3 Kinyeti Mt Sudan
17E3 Kiparissía Greece
17E3 Kiparissiakós Kólpos G Greece
65D1 Kipawa,L Canada
51D4 Kipili Tanzania
9C3 Kippure Mt Irish Republic
51C5 Kipushi Zaïre
25M4 Kirensk Russian Federation
24J5 Kirgizia Republic Asia
39F1 Kirgizskiy Khrebet Mts Kirgizia
50B4 Kiri Zaïre
33G1 Kiribati Is, Republic Pacific Ocean
21E8 Kirikkale Turkey
40B2 Kirikkale Turkey
20E4 Kirishi Russian Federation
42B3 Kirithar Range Mts Pakistan
17F3 Kirkağaç Turkey
21H8 Kirk Bulāg Dāgh Mt Iran
6C2 Kirkby England
8D3 Kirkcaldy Scotland
8C4 Kirkcudbright Scotland
12K5 Kirkenes Norway
6C3 Kirkham England
55K5 Kirkland Lake Canada
40A1 Kirklareli Turkey
6C2 Kirkoswald England
76E7 Kirkpatrick,Mt Antarctica
57D2 Kirksville USA
41D2 Kirkūk Iraq
8D2 Kirkwall Scotland
47D3 Kirkwood South Africa
61E3 Kirkwood USA
20E5 Kirov Russian Federation
20H4 Kirov Russian Federation
41D1 Kirovakan Armenia
20K4 Kirovgrad Russian Federation
21E6 Kirovograd Ukraine
20E2 Kirovsk Russian Federation
25R4 Kirovskiy Kamchatka, Russian Federation
8D3 Kirriemuir Scotland
20J4 Kirs Russian Federation
40B2 Kirşehir Turkey
18C2 Kiruna Sweden
29C3 Kiryū Japan
50C3 Kisangani Zaïre
29C3 Kisarazu Japan
43F3 Kishanganj India
42C3 Kishangarh India
19F3 Kishinev Moldavia
29C4 Kishiwada Japan
50D4 Kisii Kenya
51D4 Kisiju Tanzania
17D1 Kiskunfélegyháza Hungary
19D3 Kiskunhalas Hungary
21G7 Kislovodsk Russian Federation
50E4 Kismaayo Somalia
29C3 Kiso-sammyaku Mts Japan
48B4 Kissidougou Guinea
67B3 Kissimmee,L USA
50D4 Kisumu Kenya
19E3 Kisvárda Hungary
48B3 Kita Mali
24H6 Kitab Uzbekistan
29D3 Kitakami Japan
29D3 Kitakami R Japan
29D3 Kitakata Japan
28C4 Kita-Kyūshū Japan
50D3 Kitale Kenya
26H4 Kitalo I Japan
29E2 Kitami Japan
29D2 Kitami-Esashi Japan
60C3 Kit Carson USA
55K5 Kitchener Canada
50D3 Kitgum Uganda
17E3 Kíthira I Greece
17E3 Kíthnos I Greece
45B1 Kiti, C Cyprus
54G2 Kitikmeot Region Canada
54F4 Kitimat Canada
12K5 Kitinen R Finland
28B4 Kitsuki Japan
65D2 Kittanning USA
65E2 Kittery USA
12J5 Kittilä Finland
67C1 Kitty Hawk USA
51D4 Kitunda Tanzania
51C5 Kitwe Zambia
18C3 Kitzbühel Austria
18C3 Kitzingen Germany
50C4 Kiumbi Zaïre
54B3 Kivalina USA
19F2 Kivercy Ukraine
50C4 Kivu,L Rwanda/Zaïre
54B3 Kiwalik USA
Kiyev = Kiev
19G2 Kiyevskoye Vodokhranilishche Res Ukraine
20K4 Kizel Russian Federation
20G3 Kizema Russian Federation
40C2 Kizil R Turkey
38D2 Kizyl'-Arvat Turkmenistan
21J8 Kizyl-Atrek Turkmenistan
18C2 Kladno Czechoslovakia
18C3 Klagenfurt Austria
20C4 Klaipēda Lithuania
58B2 Klamath R USA
56A2 Klamath Falls USA
58B2 Klamath Mts USA
18C3 Klatovy Czechoslovakia
45C1 Kleiat Lebanon
47B2 Kleinsee South Africa
47D2 Klerksdorp South Africa
19G2 Kletnya Russian Federation
13D2 Kleve Germany
19G2 Klimovichi Belorussia
20F4 Klin Russian Federation
19D1 Klintehamn Sweden
21E5 Klintsy Russian Federation
47C3 Klipplaat South Africa
16D2 Ključ Bosnia & Herzegovina, Yugoslavia
18D2 Kłodzko Poland
54D3 Klondike Plat Canada/ USA
18D3 Klosterneuburg Austria
19D2 Kluczbork Poland
6D2 Knaresborough England
7C3 Knighton Wales
16D2 Knin Croatia
32A4 Knob,C Australia
9B3 Knockmealdown Mts Irish Republic
13B2 Knokke-Heist Belgium
76G9 Knox Coast Antarctica
61E2 Knoxville Iowa, USA
57E3 Knoxville Tennessee, USA
55Q3 Knud Rasmussens Land Region Greenland
7C3 Knutsford England
47C3 Knysna South Africa
55O3 Kobberminebugt B Greenland
29D4 Kōbe Japan
København = Copenhagen
18B2 Koblenz Germany
19E2 Kobrin Belorussia
27G7 Kobroör I Indonesia
54B3 Kobuk R USA
17E2 Kočani Macedonia, Yugoslavia
28B3 Kochang S Korea
28B3 Koch'ang S Korea
30C3 Ko Chang I Thailand
43F3 Koch Bihār India
55L3 Koch I Canada
44B4 Kochi India
29C4 Kōchi Japan
54C4 Kodiak USA
54C4 Kodiak I USA
44B3 Kodikkarai India
50D3 Kodok Sudan
29D2 Kodomari-misaki C Japan
19F3 Kodyma Ukraine
66D3 Koehn L USA
47B2 Koes Namibia
47D2 Koffiefontein South Africa
48B4 Koforidua Ghana
29D3 Kofu Japan
29C3 Koga Japan
12G7 Køge Denmark
42C2 Kohat Pakistan
42B2 Koh-i-Baba Mts Afghanistan
42B1 Koh-i-Hisar Mts Afghanistan
42B2 Koh-i-Khurd Mt Afghanistan
43G3 Kohīma India
42B2 Koh-i-Mazar Mt Afghanistan
42B3 Kohlu Pakistan
20D4 Kohtla Järve Estonia
28A4 Kohung S Korea
28A4 Kohyon S Korea

Koide Kutcharo-ko

29C3 **Koide** Japan
30A4 **Koihoa** Nicobar Is, India
28A2 **Koin** N Korea
28B4 **Koje Dŏ** *I* S Korea
29C2 **Ko-jima** *I* Japan
24H4 **Kokchetav** Kazakhstan
12J6 **Kokemäki** *L* Finland
12J6 **Kokkola** Finland
32D1 **Kokoda** Papua New Guinea
64B2 **Kokomo** USA
27G7 **Kokonau** Indonesia
26B2 **Kokpekty** Kazakhstan
28A3 **Koksan** N Korea
55M4 **Koksoak** *R* Canada
28A3 **Koksŏng** S Korea
47D3 **Kokstad** South Africa
30C3 **Ko Kut** *I* Thailand
20E2 **Kola** Russian Federation
27F7 **Kolaka** Indonesia
30B4 **Ko Lanta** *I* Thailand
44B3 **Kolār** India
44B3 **Kolār Gold Fields** India
48A3 **Kolda** Senegal
12F7 **Kolding** Denmark
20H2 **Kolguyev, Ostrov** *I* Russian Federation
44A2 **Kolhāpur** India
18D2 **Kolín** Czechoslovakia
44B4 **Kollam** India
**Köln = Cologne**
19D2 **Koło** Poland
66E5 **Koloa** Hawaiian Islands
18D2 **Kołobrzeg** Poland
48B3 **Kolokani** Mali
20F4 **Kolomna** Russian Federation
21D6 **Kolomyya** Ukraine
25R4 **Kolpakovskiy** Russian Federation
24K4 **Kolpashevo** Russian Federation
17F3 **Kólpos Merabéllou** *B* Greece
17E2 **Kólpos Singitikós** *G* Greece
17E2 **Kólpos Strimonikós** *G* Greece
17E2 **Kólpos Toronaíos** *G* Greece
20F2 **Kol'skiy Poluostrov** *Pen* Russian Federation
20K2 **Kolva** *R* Russian Federation
12G6 **Kolvereid** Norway
51C5 **Kolwezi** Zaïre
25R3 **Kolyma** *R* Russian Federation
25R3 **Kolymskaya Nizmennost'** *Lowland* Russian Federation
25S3 **Kolymskoye Nagor'ye** *Mts* Russian Federation
17E2 **Kom** *Mt* Bulgaria/Serbia, Yugoslavia
50D3 **Koma** Ethiopia
29D3 **Koma** Japan
48D3 **Komadugu Gana** *R* Nigeria
29D2 **Komaga take** *Mt* Japan
25S4 **Komandorskiye Ostrova** *Is* Russian Federation
19D3 **Komárno** Czechoslovakia
47E2 **Komati** *R* South Africa/ Swaziland
47E2 **Komati Poort** South Africa
29D3 **Komatsu** Japan
29B4 **Komatsushima** Japan
20J3 **Komi Republic** Russian Federation
26B1 **Kommunar** Russian Federation
27E7 **Komodo** *I* Indonesia
27G7 **Komoran** *I* Indonesia
29C3 **Komoro** Japan
17F2 **Komotiní** Greece
47C3 **Kompasberg** *Mt* South Africa
30D3 **Kompong Cham** Cambodia
30C3 **Kompong Chhnang** Cambodia
30C3 **Kompong Som** Cambodia
30D3 **Kompong Thom** Cambodia
30D3 **Kompong Trabek** Cambodia
19F3 **Komrat** Moldavia
47C3 **Komsberg** *Mts* South Africa
25L1 **Komsomolets, Ostrov** *I* Russian Federation
20L2 **Komsomol'skiy** Russian Federation
25P4 **Komsomol'sk na Amure** Russian Federation
24H4 **Konda** *R* Russian Federation
43E5 **Kondagaon** India
50D4 **Kondoa** Tanzania
20E3 **Kondopoga** Russian Federation
44B2 **Kondukūr** India
20F3 **Konevo** Russian Federation
55P3 **Kong Christian IX Land** *Region* Greenland
55O3 **Kong Frederik VI Kyst** *Region* Greenland
28A3 **Kongju** S Korea
24D2 **Kong Karls Land** *Is* Svalbard
50C4 **Kongolo** Zaïre
12F7 **Kongsberg** Norway
12G6 **Kongsvinger** Norway
**Königsberg = Kaliningrad**
19D2 **Konin** Poland
17D2 **Konjic** Bosnia & Herzegovina, Yugoslavia
20G3 **Konosha** Russian Federation
29C3 **Konosu** Japan
21E5 **Konotop** Ukraine
19E2 **Końskie** Poland
18B3 **Konstanz** Germany
48C3 **Kontagora** Nigeria
30D3 **Kontum** Vietnam
21E8 **Konya** Turkey
58C1 **Kootenay L** Canada
42C5 **Kopargaon** India
55R3 **Kópasker** Iceland
12A2 **Kópavogur** Iceland
16C1 **Koper** Slovenia
38D2 **Kopet Dag** *Mts* Iran/ Turkmenistan
20L4 **Kopeysk** Russian Federation
30C4 **Ko Phangan** *I* Thailand
30B4 **Ko Phuket** *I* Thailand
12H7 **Köping** Sweden
28A3 **Kopo-ri** S Korea
44B2 **Koppal** India
16D1 **Koprivnica** Croatia
42B4 **Korangi** Pakistan
44C2 **Koraput** India
43E4 **Korba** India
18B2 **Korbach** Germany
17E2 **Korçë** Albania
16D2 **Korčula** *I* Croatia
31E2 **Korea B** China/Korea
28B2 **Korea, North** *Republic* Asia
28B3 **Korea, South** *Republic* Asia
26F3 **Korea Strait** Japan/Korea
19F2 **Korec** Ukraine
25S3 **Korf** Russian Federation
40B1 **Körğlu Tepesi** *Mt* Turkey
48B4 **Korhogo** Ivory Coast
42B4 **Kori Creek** India
**Kórinthos = Corinth**
29E3 **Kōriyama** Japan
20L5 **Korkino** Russian Federation
25R3 **Korkodon** Russian Federation
25R3 **Korkodon** *R* Russian Federation
40B2 **Korkuteli** Turkey
39G1 **Korla** China
45B1 **Kormakiti, C** Cyprus
16D2 **Kornat** *I* Croatia
21E7 **Köroğlu Tepesi** *Mt* Turkey
50D4 **Korogwe** Tanzania
34B3 **Koroit** Australia
27G6 **Koror** Palau, Pacific Ocean
19E3 **Körös** *R* Hungary
21D5 **Korosten** Ukraine
19F2 **Korostyshev** Ukraine
50B2 **Koro Toro** Chad
26H2 **Korsakov** Russian Federation
12G7 **Korsør** Denmark
20J3 **Kortkeros** Russian Federation
18A2 **Kortrijk** Belgium
25S3 **Koryakskoye Nagor'ye** *Mts* Russian Federation
28A3 **Koryong** S Korea
17F3 **Kós** *I* Greece
30C4 **Ko Samui** *I* Thailand
28A3 **Kosan** N Korea
19D2 **Kościerzyna** Poland
63E2 **Kosciusko** USA
32D4 **Kosciusko** *Mt* Australia
43J2 **Kosi** India
43K1 **Kosi** *R* India
19E3 **Košice** Czechoslovakia
20J2 **Kosma** *R* Russian Federation
28B3 **Kosŏng** N Korea
17E2 **Kosovo** *Region* Serbia, Yugoslavia
48B4 **Kossou** *L* Ivory Coast
47D2 **Koster** South Africa
50D2 **Kosti** Sudan
19F2 **Kostopol'** Ukraine
20G4 **Kostroma** Russian Federation
18C2 **Kostrzyn** Poland
20K2 **Kos'yu** *R* Russian Federation
12H8 **Koszalin** Poland
42D3 **Kota** India
30C4 **Kota Bharu** Malaysia
42C2 **Kot Addu** Pakistan
27E6 **Kota Kinabalu** Malaysia
44C2 **Kotapad** India
20H4 **Kotel'nich** Russian Federation
21G6 **Kotel'nikovo** Russian Federation
25P2 **Kotel'nyy, Ostrov** *I* Russian Federation
12K6 **Kotka** Finland
20H3 **Kotlas** Russian Federation
54B3 **Kotlik** USA
17D2 **Kotor** Montenegro, Yugoslavia
21D6 **Kotovsk** Ukraine
42B3 **Kotri** Pakistan
44C2 **Kottagūdem** India
44B4 **Kottayam** India
50C3 **Kotto** *R* Central African Republic
44B3 **Kottūru** India
25L3 **Kotuy** *R* Russian Federation
54B3 **Kotzebue** USA
54B3 **Kotzebue Sd** USA
48C3 **Kouandé** Benin
50C3 **Kouango** Central African Republic
48B3 **Koudougou** Burkina
47C3 **Kougaberge** *Mts* South Africa
50B4 **Koulamoutou** Gabon
48B3 **Koulikoro** Mali
48B3 **Koupéla** Burkina
73H2 **Kourou** French Guiana
48B3 **Kouroussa** Guinea
50B2 **Kousséri** Cameroon
12K6 **Kouvola** Finland
12L5 **Kovdor** Russian Federation
12L5 **Kovdozero, Ozero** *L* Russian Federation
19E2 **Kovel** Ukraine
**Kovno = Kaunas**
20G4 **Kovrov** Russian Federation
20G5 **Kovylkino** Russian Federation
20F3 **Kovzha** *R* Russian Federation
30C4 **Ko Way** *I* Thailand
31C5 **Kowloon** Hong Kong
28A3 **Kowŏn** N Korea
42B2 **Kowt-e-Ashrow** Afghanistan
40A2 **Köycegğiz** Turkey
20G2 **Koyda** Russian Federation
44A2 **Koyna Res** India
20H3 **Koynas** Russian Federation
54C3 **Koyukuk** USA
40C2 **Kozan** Turkey
17E2 **Kozańi** Greece
44B3 **Kozhikode** India
20K2 **Kozhim** Russian Federation
20H4 **Koz'modemyansk** Russian Federation
29C4 **Kōzu-shima** *I* Japan
48C4 **Kpalimé** Togo
47D3 **Kraai** *R* South Africa
12F7 **Kragerø** Norway
17E2 **Kragujevac** Serbia, Yugoslavia
30B3 **Kra,Isthmus of** Burma/ Malaysia
45D1 **Krak des Chevaliers** *Hist Site* Syria
**Kraków = Cracow** Poland
17E2 **Kraljevo** Serbia, Yugoslavia
21F6 **Kramatorsk** Ukraine
12H6 **Kramfors** Sweden
16C1 **Kranj** Slovenia
20H3 **Krasavino** Russian Federation
20J1 **Krasino** Russian Federation
28C2 **Kraskino** Russian Federation
19E2 **Kraśnik** Poland
21H5 **Krasnoarmeysk** Russian Federation
21F6 **Krasnodar** Russian Federation
20K4 **Krasnokamsk** Russian Federation
20L4 **Krasnotur'insk** Russian Federation
20K4 **Krasnoufimsk** Russian Federation
20K5 **Krasnousol'skiy** Russian Federation
20K3 **Krasnovishersk** Russian Federation
21J7 **Krasnovodsk** Turkmenistan
25L4 **Krasnoyarsk** Russian Federation
19E2 **Krasnystaw** Poland
21H5 **Krasnyy Kut** Russian Federation
21F6 **Krasnyy Luch** Ukraine
21H6 **Krasnyy Yar** Russian Federation
30D3 **Kratie** Cambodia
55N2 **Kraulshavn** Greenland
18B2 **Krefeld** Germany
21E6 **Kremenchug** Ukraine
21E6 **Kremenchugskoye Vodokhranilische** *Res* Ukraine
19F2 **Kremenets** Ukraine
60B2 **Kremming** USA
48C4 **Kribi** Cameroon
20E5 **Krichev** Belorussia
44B2 **Krishna** *R* India
44B3 **Krishnagiri** India
43F4 **Krishnanagar** India
12F7 **Kristiansand** Norway
12G7 **Kristianstad** Sweden
24B3 **Kristiansund** Norway
12J6 **Kristiinankaupunki** Finland
12G7 **Kristinehamn** Sweden
**Kríti = Crete**
21E6 **Krivoy Rog** Ukraine
16C1 **Krk** *I* Croatia
47D1 **Krokodil** *R* South Africa
25S4 **Kronotskaya Sopka** *Mt* Russian Federation
25S4 **Kronotskiy, Mys** *C* Russian Federation
55P3 **Kronprins Frederik Bjerge** *Mts* Greenland
12K7 **Kronshtadt** Russian Federation
47D2 **Kroonstad** South Africa
21G6 **Kropotkin** Russian Federation
47E1 **Kruger Nat Pk** South Africa
47D2 **Krugersdorp** South Africa
17D2 **Kruje** Albania
**Krung Thep = Bangkok**
19F2 **Krupki** Belorussia
17E2 **Kruševac** Serbia, Yugoslavia
12K7 **Krustpils** Latvia
**Krym = Crimea**
21F7 **Krymsk** Russian Federation
18D2 **Krzyz** Poland
15C2 **Ksar El Boukhari** Algeria
15A2 **Ksar-el-Kebir** Morocco
48C1 **Ksour, Mts des** Algeria
27C6 **Kuala** Indonesia
30C5 **Kuala Dungun** Malaysia
30C4 **Kuala Kerai** Malaysia
30C5 **Kuala Kubu Baharu** Malaysia
30C5 **Kuala Lipis** Malaysia
30C5 **Kuala Lumpur** Malaysia
30C4 **Kuala Trengganu** Malaysia
27F6 **Kuandang** Indonesia
28A2 **Kuandian** China
30C5 **Kuantan** Malaysia
21H7 **Kuba** Azerbaijan
27H7 **Kubor** *Mt* Papua New Guinea
27E6 **Kuching** Malaysia
27E6 **Kudat** Malaysia
20J4 **Kudymkar** Russian Federation
18C3 **Kufstein** Austria
41G3 **Kuh Duren** *Upland* Iran
41F3 **Kūh-e Dinar** *Mt* Iran
41G2 **Kūh-e-Hazār Masjed** *Mts* Iran
41G4 **Kūh-e Jebāl Barez** *Mts* Iran
41F3 **Kūh-e Karkas** *Mts* Iran
41G4 **Kūh-e Laleh Zar** *Mt* Iran
41E2 **Kūh-e Sahand** *Mt* Iran
38E3 **Kuh-e-Taftān** *Mt* Iran
21H9 **Kūhhaye Alvand** *Mts* Iran
21H8 **Kūhhaye Sabalan** *Mts* Iran
41E3 **Kūhhā-ye Zāgros** *Mts* Iran
12K6 **Kuhmo** Finland
41F3 **Kūhpāyeh** Iran
41G3 **Kūhpāyeh** *Mt* Iran
41G4 **Kūh-ye Bashākerd** *Mts* Iran
41E2 **Kūh-ye Sabalan** *Mt* Iran
47B2 **Kuibis** Namibia
47B1 **Kuiseb** *R* Namibia
51B5 **Kuito** Angola
28A3 **Kujang** N Korea
29E2 **Kuji** Japan
28B4 **Kuju-san** *Mt* Japan
17E2 **Kukës** Albania
30C5 **Kukup** Malaysia
41G4 **Kūl** *R* Iran
17F3 **Kula** Turkey
21K6 **Kulakshi** Kazakhstan
50D3 **Kulal,Mt** Kenya
17E2 **Kulata** Bulgaria
20C4 **Kuldīga** Latvia
20G2 **Kulov** *R* Russian Federation
21J6 **Kul'sary** Kazakhstan
42D2 **Kulu** India
40B2 **Kulu** Turkey
24J4 **Kulunda** Russian Federation
34B2 **Kulwin** Australia
21H7 **Kuma** *R* Russian Federation
29C3 **Kumagaya** Japan
27E7 **Kumai** Indonesia
21L5 **Kumak** Russian Federation
28C4 **Kumamoto** Japan
29C4 **Kumano** Japan
17E2 **Kumanovo** Macedonia, Yugoslavia
48B4 **Kumasi** Ghana
48C4 **Kumba** Cameroon
44B3 **Kumbakonam** India
28A3 **Kŭmch'ŏn** N Korea
20K5 **Kumertau** Russian Federation
28A3 **Kumgang** N Korea
12H7 **Kumla** Sweden
28A4 **Kŭmnyŏng** S Korea
28A4 **Kŭmo-do** *I* S Korea
44A3 **Kumta** India
39G1 **Kumüx** China
28B3 **Kumwha** S Korea
42C2 **Kunar** *R* Afghanistan
29F2 **Kunashir, Ostrov** *I* Russian Federation
12K7 **Kunda** Estonia
42C4 **Kundla** India
42B1 **Kunduz** Afghanistan
**Kunene** *R* **= Cunene R**
12G7 **Kungsbacka** Sweden
20K4 **Kungur** Russian Federation
30B1 **Kunhing** Burma
39G2 **Kunlun Shan** *Mts* China
31A4 **Kunming** China
20M3 **Kunovat** *R* Russian Federation
28B3 **Kunsan** S Korea
12K6 **Kuopio** Finland
16D1 **Kupa** *R* Bosnia & Herzegovina, Yugoslavia/Croatia
32B2 **Kupang** Indonesia
32D2 **Kupiano** Papua New Guinea
54E4 **Kupreanof I** USA
21F6 **Kupyansk** Ukraine
39G1 **Kuqa** China
21H8 **Kura** *R* Azerbaijan
29C3 **Kurabe** Japan
29C4 **Kurashiki** Japan
29B3 **Kurayoshi** Japan
41E2 **Kurdistan** *Region* Iran
17F2 **Kŭrdzhali** Bulgaria
28C4 **Kure** Japan
20C4 **Kuressaare** Estonia
25L3 **Kureyka** *R* Russian Federation
24H4 **Kurgan** Russian Federation
12J6 **Kurikka** Finland
25Q5 **Kuril Is** Russian Federation
**Kuril'skiye Ostrova** *Is* **= Kuril Islands**
36J2 **Kuril Trench** Pacific Ocean
21H8 **Kurinskaya Kosa** *Sand Spit* Azerbaijan
44B2 **Kurnool** India
29D2 **Kuroishi** Japan
29D3 **Kuroiso** Japan
35B2 **Kurow** New Zealand
34D2 **Kurri Kurri** Australia
21F5 **Kursk** Russian Federation
26B2 **Kuruktag** *R* China
47C2 **Kuruman** South Africa
47C2 **Kuruman** *R* South Africa
28C4 **Kurume** Japan
44C3 **Kurunegala** Sri Lanka
24K5 **Kurunktag** *R* China
20K3 **Kur'ya** Russian Federation
20K4 **Kusa** Russian Federation
17F3 **Kuşadasi Körfezi** *B* Turkey
17F2 **Kus Golü** *L* Turkey
29D4 **Kushimoto** Japan
29E2 **Kushiro** Japan
38E2 **Kushka** Afghanistan
43F4 **Kushtia** Bangladesh
21J5 **Kushum** *R* Kazakhstan
20K4 **Kushva** Russian Federation
54B3 **Kuskokwim** *R* USA
54C3 **Kuskokwim Mts** USA
43E3 **Kusma** Nepal
28B3 **Kusŏng** N Korea
24H4 **Kustanay** Kazakhstan
27E7 **Kuta** *R* Indonesia
21D8 **Kütahya** Turkey
21G7 **Kutaisi** Georgia
29D2 **Kutchan** Japan
29E2 **Kutcharo-ko** *L* Japan

57E2 **Marion** Indiana, USA
57E2 **Marion** Ohio, USA
67C2 **Marion** S Carolina, USA
57E3 **Marion,L** USA
33E2 **Marion Reef** Australia
59C3 **Mariposa** USA
66B2 **Mariposa** Res USA
66B2 **Mariposa Res** USA
21D7 **Marista** *R* Bulgaria
21F6 **Mariupol'** Ukraine
45C2 **Marjayoun** Lebanon
19F2 **Marjina Gorki** Belorussia
45C3 **Marka** Jordan
50E3 **Marka** Somalia
18C1 **Markaryd** Sweden
7C3 **Market Drayton** England
7D3 **Market Harborough** England
6D3 **Market Weighton** England
76E7 **Markham,Mt** Antarctica
66C1 **Markleeville** USA
25T3 **Markovo** Russian Federation
68E1 **Marlboro** Massachusetts, USA
68D1 **Marlboro** New Hampshire, USA
32D3 **Marlborough** Australia
7D4 **Marlborough** England
13B3 **Marle** France
63C2 **Marlin** USA
68D1 **Marlow** USA
14C3 **Marmande** France
17F2 **Marmara Adasi** *I* Turkey
40A1 **Marmara,S of** Turkey
17F3 **Marmaris** Turkey
60C1 **Marmarth** USA
64C3 **Marmet** USA
61E1 **Marmion L** Canada
16C1 **Marmolada** *Mt* Italy
13C3 **Marne** *Department* France
13B3 **Marne** *R* France
50B3 **Maro** Chad
51E5 **Maroantsetra** Madagascar
51D5 **Marondera** Zimbabwe
73H3 **Maroni** *R* French Guiana
34D1 **Maroochydore** Australia
50B2 **Maroua** Cameroon
51E5 **Marovoay** Madagascar
57E4 **Marquesas Keys** *Is* USA
57E2 **Marquette** USA
37N5 **Marquises, Îles** Pacific Ocean
34C2 **Marra** *R* Australia
47E2 **Marracuene** Mozambique
50C2 **Marra, Jebel** *Mt* Sudan
48B1 **Marrakech** Morocco
32C3 **Marree** Australia
63D3 **Marrero** USA
51D5 **Marromeu** Mozambique
51D5 **Marrupa** Mozambique
40B4 **Marsa Alam** Egypt
50D3 **Marsabit** Kenya
16C3 **Marsala** Sicily, Italy
13E2 **Marsberg** Germany
14D3 **Marseilles** France
75D3 **Mar, Serra do** *Mts* Brazil
64B3 **Marshall** Illinois, USA
64C2 **Marshall** Michigan, USA
61D2 **Marshall** Minnesota, USA
61E3 **Marshall** Missouri, USA
57D3 **Marshall** Texas, USA
68B3 **Marshall** Virginia, USA
37K4 **Marshall Is** Pacific Ocean
61E2 **Marshalltown** USA
63D1 **Marshfield** Missouri, USA
64A2 **Marshfield** Wisconsin, USA
69B1 **Marsh Harbour** The Bahamas
63D3 **Marsh I** USA
30B2 **Martaban,G of** Burma
65E2 **Martha's Vineyard** *I* USA
14D2 **Martigny** Switzerland
14D3 **Martigues** France
19D3 **Martin** Czechoslovakia
60C2 **Martin** S Dakota, USA
63E1 **Martin** Tennessee, USA
35C2 **Martinborough** New Zealand
69E4 **Martinique** *I* Caribbean Sea
67A2 **Martin,L** USA
65D3 **Martinsburg** USA
64C2 **Martins Ferry** USA
65D3 **Martinsville** USA
52G6 **Martin Vaz** *I* Atlantic Ocean
35C2 **Marton** New Zealand
15B2 **Martos** Spain
54G3 **Martre, Lac la** Canada
42B2 **Maruf** Afghanistan
29B4 **Marugame** Japan
59D3 **Marvine,Mt** USA
42C3 **Mārwār** India
24H6 **Mary** Turkmenistan
33E3 **Maryborough** Queensland, Australia
34B3 **Maryborough** Victoria, Australia

54F4 **Mary Henry,Mt** Canada
57F3 **Maryland** *State* USA
6C2 **Maryport** England
59B3 **Marysville** California, USA
61D3 **Marysville** Kansas, USA
58B1 **Marysville** Washington, USA
57D2 **Maryville** Iowa, USA
61D2 **Maryville** Missouri, USA
67B1 **Maryville** Tennessee, USA
49D2 **Marzuq** Libya
45A3 **Masabb Dumyât** *C* Egypt
**Masada = Mezada**
45C2 **Mas'adah** Syria
50D4 **Masai Steppe** *Upland* Tanzania
50D4 **Masaka** Uganda
41E2 **Masally** Azerbaijan
28B3 **Masan** S Korea
51D5 **Masasi** Tanzania
70D3 **Masaya** Nicaragua
27F5 **Masbate** Philippines
27F5 **Masbate** *I* Philippines
15C2 **Mascara** Algeria
36D5 **Mascarene Ridge** Indian Ocean
75E2 **Mascote** Brazil
47D2 **Maseru** Lesotho
42B2 **Mashaki** Afghanistan
41G2 **Mashhad** Iran
50B4 **Masi-Manimba** Zaïre
50D3 **Masindi** Uganda
38D3 **Maşirah** *I* Oman
50C4 **Masisi** Zaïre
41E3 **Masjed Soleyman** Iran
51F5 **Masoala, C** Madagascar
66C1 **Mason** Nevada, USA
62C2 **Mason** Texas, USA
57D2 **Mason City** USA
**Masqat = Muscat**
16C2 **Massa** Italy
57F2 **Massachusetts** *State* USA
65E2 **Massachusetts B** USA
50B2 **Massakori** Chad
51D6 **Massangena** Mozambique
**Massawa = Mits'iwa**
65E2 **Massena** USA
50B2 **Massénya** Chad
64C1 **Massey** Canada
14C2 **Massif Central** *Mts* France
51E6 **Massif de l'Isalo** *Upland* Madagascar
51E5 **Massif du Tsaratanana** *Mts* Madagascar
64C2 **Massillon** USA
48B3 **Massina** *Region* Mali
51D6 **Massinga** Mozambique
47E1 **Massingir** Mozambique
21J6 **Masteksay** Kazakhstan
33G5 **Masterton** New Zealand
28C4 **Masuda** Japan
50B4 **Masuku** Gabon
40C2 **Maşyāf** Syria
64C1 **Matachewan** Canada
62A3 **Matachie** Mexico
50B4 **Matadi** Zaïre
72A1 **Matagalpa** Nicaragua
55L5 **Matagami** Canada
56D4 **Matagorda B** USA
63C3 **Matagorda I** USA
35C1 **Matakana I** New Zealand
51B5 **Matala** Angola
44C4 **Matale** Sri Lanka
48A3 **Matam** Senegal
48C3 **Matameye** Niger
70C2 **Matamoros** Mexico
49E2 **Ma'tan as Sarra** *Well* Libya
55M5 **Matane** Canada
70D2 **Matanzas** Cuba
65F1 **Matapedia** *R* Canada
44C4 **Matara** Sri Lanka
32A1 **Mataram** Indonesia
72D7 **Matarani** Peru
75E1 **Mataripe** Brazil
15C1 **Mataró** Spain
47D3 **Matatiele** South Africa
35A3 **Mataura** New Zealand
70B2 **Matehuala** Mexico
69L1 **Matelot** Trinidad
16D2 **Matera** Italy
19E3 **Mátészalka** Hungary
16B3 **Mateur** Tunisia
66C2 **Mather** USA
64C1 **Matheson** Canada
63C3 **Mathis** USA
42D3 **Mathura** India
7D3 **Matlock** England
73G6 **Mato Grosso** *State* Brazil
73G7 **Mato Grosso do Sul** *State* Brazil
47E2 **Matola** Mozambique
49E1 **Matrûh** Egypt
28C3 **Matsue** Japan
50C4 **Mbuji-Mayi** Zaïre
50D4 **Mbulu** Tanzania
48B2 **Mcherrah** *Region* Algeria
51D5 **Mchinji** Malawi
30D3 **Mdrak** Vietnam
62B1 **Meade** USA

56B3 **Mead,L** USA
54H4 **Meadow Lake** Canada
64C2 **Meadville** USA
29D2 **Me-akan dake** *Mt* Japan
55N4 **Mealy Mts** Canada
34C1 **Meandarra** Australia
54G4 **Meander River** Canada
9C3 **Meath** Irish Republic
14C2 **Meaux** France
50E1 **Mecca** Saudi Arabia
59C4 **Mecca** USA
68D1 **Mechanicville** USA
24G2 **Mechdusharskiy, O** *I* Russian Federation
18A2 **Mechelen** Belgium
48B1 **Mecheria** Algeria
18C2 **Meckenburg-Vorpommern** *State* Germany
18C2 **Mecklenburger Bucht** *B* Germany
51D5 **Meconta** Mozambique
51D5 **Mecuburi** Mozambique
51E5 **Mecufi** Mozambique
51D5 **Mecula** Mozambique
27C6 **Medan** Indonesia
74C7 **Médanosa, Puerta** *Pt* Argentina
15C2 **Médéa** Algeria
72C2 **Medellín** Colombia
13C1 **Medemblik** Netherlands
48D1 **Medenine** Tunisia
56A2 **Medford** USA
17F2 **Medgidia** Romania
17E1 **Mediaş** Romania
58C1 **Medical Lake** USA
60B2 **Medicine Bow** USA
60B2 **Medicine Bow Mts** USA
60B2 **Medicine Bow Peak** *Mt* USA
54G5 **Medicine Hat** Canada
62C1 **Medicine Lodge** USA
75D2 **Medina** Brazil
60D1 **Medina** N Dakota, USA
68A1 **Medina** New York, USA
40C5 **Medina** Saudi Arabia
15B1 **Medinaceli** Spain
15A1 **Medina del Campo** Spain
15A1 **Medina de Rioseco** Spain
62C3 **Medina L** USA
43F4 **Medinipur** India
46E4 **Mediterranean S** Europe
16B3 **Medjerda** *R* Algeria/Tunisia
16B3 **Medjerda, Mts de la** Algeria/Tunisia
21K5 **Mednogorsk** Russian Federation
25S4 **Mednyy, Ostrov** *I* Russian Federation
43H3 **Mêdog** China
50B3 **Medouneu** Gabon
21G5 **Medvedista** *R* Russian Federation
25S2 **Medvezh'i Ova** *Is* Russian Federation
20E3 **Medvezh'yegorsk** Russian Federation
32A3 **Meekatharra** Australia
60B2 **Meeker** USA
42D3 **Meerut** India
58E2 **Meeteetse** USA
50D3 **Mēga** Ethiopia
17E3 **Megalópolis** Greece
17E3 **Mégara** Greece
43G3 **Meghālaya** *State* India
43G4 **Meghna** *R* Bangladesh
45C2 **Megiddo** *Hist Site* Israel
42D4 **Mehekar** India
43M2 **Mehndawal** India
41F4 **Mehrān** *R* Iran
41F3 **Mehriz** Iran
75C2 **Meia Ponte** *R* Brazil
50B3 **Meiganga** Cameroon
30B1 **Meiktila** Burma
31A4 **Meishan** China
18C2 **Meissen** Germany
31D5 **Mei Xian** China
31D5 **Meizhou** China
72D8 **Mejillones** Chile
50B3 **Mekambo** Gabon
50D2 **Mek'elē** Ethiopia
48B1 **Meknès** Morocco
30D3 **Mekong** *R* Cambodia
30D4 **Mekong, Mouths of the** Vietnam
48C3 **Mekrou** *R* Benin
30C5 **Melaka** Malaysia
36J5 **Melanesia** *Region* Pacific Ocean
32D4 **Melbourne** Australia
57E4 **Melbourne** USA
56C4 **Melchor Muźguiz** Mexico
20K5 **Meleuz** Russian Federation
50B2 **Melfi** Chad
54H4 **Melfort** Canada
15B2 **Melilla** NW Africa
60C1 **Melita** Canada
21F6 **Melitopol'** Ukraine
50D3 **Melka Guba** Ethiopia
13E1 **Melle** Germany

16B3 **Mellégue** *R* Algeria/Tunisia
47E2 **Melmoth** South Africa
74F4 **Melo** Uruguay
75A3 **Melo** *R* Brazil
66B2 **Melones Res** USA
8D4 **Melrose** Scotland
61E1 **Melrose** USA
7D3 **Melton Mowbray** England
14C2 **Melun** France
54H4 **Melville** Canada
55M2 **Melville Bugt** *B* Greenland
69Q2 **Melville,C** Dominica
54F3 **Melville Hills** Canada
32C2 **Melville I** Australia
54G2 **Melville I** Canada
55N4 **Melville,L** Canada
55K3 **Melville Pen** Canada
51E5 **Memba** Mozambique
32A1 **Memboro** Indonesia
18C3 **Memmingen** Germany
57E3 **Memphis** Tennessee, USA
62B2 **Memphis** Texas, USA
63D2 **Mena** USA
19G2 **Mena** Ukraine
7B3 **Menai Str** Wales
48C3 **Ménaka** Mali
64B2 **Menasha** USA
27E7 **Mendawai** *R* Indonesia
14C3 **Mende** France
50D3 **Mendebo Mts** Ethiopia
32D1 **Mendi** Papua New Guinea
7C4 **Mendip Hills** *Upland* England
58B2 **Mendocino,C** USA
37M3 **Mendocino Seascarp** Pacific Ocean
66B2 **Mendota** California, USA
64B2 **Mendota** Illinois, USA
74C4 **Mendoza** Argentina
74C5 **Mendoza** *State* Argentina
17F3 **Menemen** Turkey
13B2 **Menen** Belgium
31D3 **Mengcheng** China
30B1 **Menghai** China
31A5 **Mengla** China
30B1 **Menglian** China
31A5 **Mengzi** China
32D4 **Menindee** Australia
34B2 **Menindee L** Australia
34A3 **Meningie** Australia
64B1 **Menominee** USA
64B2 **Menomonee Falls** USA
64A2 **Menomonie** USA
51B5 **Menongue** Angola
**Menorca** *I* **= Minorca**
27C7 **Mentawai, Kepulauan** *Is* Indonesia
62A1 **Mentmore** USA
27D7 **Mentok** Indonesia
64C2 **Mentor** USA
27E6 **Menyapa** *Mt* Indonesia
31A2 **Menyuan** China
16B3 **Menzel** Tunisia
20J4 **Menzelinsk** Russian Federation
13D1 **Meppel** Netherlands
18B2 **Meppen** Germany
15B1 **Mequinenza, Embalse de** *Res* Spain
63D1 **Meramec** *R* USA
16C1 **Merano** Italy
27E7 **Meratus, Pegunungan** *Mts* Indonesia
32D1 **Merauke** Indonesia
56A3 **Merced** USA
66B2 **Merced** *R* USA
74B4 **Mercedario** *Mt* Argentina
74E4 **Mercedes** Buenos Aires, Argentina
74E3 **Mercedes** Corrientes, Argentina
74C4 **Mercedes** San Luis, Argentina
74E4 **Mercedes** Uruguay
35C1 **Mercury B** New Zealand
35C1 **Mercury Is** New Zealand
54F2 **Mercy B** Canada
55M3 **Mercy,C** Canada
62B1 **Meredith,L** USA
30B3 **Mergui** Burma
30B3 **Mergui Arch** Burma
70D2 **Mérida** Mexico
15A2 **Mérida** Spain
72D2 **Mérida** Venezuela
72D2 **Mérida, Cordillera de** Venezuela
57E3 **Meridian** USA
34C3 **Merimbula** Australia
34B2 **Meringur** Australia
27G6 **Merir** *I* Pacific Ocean
62B2 **Merkel** USA
50D2 **Merowe** Sudan
32A4 **Merredin** Australia
8C4 **Merrick** *Mt* Scotland
64B1 **Merrill** USA
64B2 **Merrillville** USA
68E1 **Merrimack** *R* USA

Negombo Northallerton


44B4 **Negombo** Sri Lanka
30A2 **Negrais,C** Burma
72B4 **Negritos** Peru
72F4 **Negro** *R* Amazonas, Brazil
74D5 **Negro** *R* Argentina
75A2 **Negro** *R* Mato Grosso do Sul, Brazil
75A3 **Negro** *R* Paraguay
74F4 **Negro** *R* Brazil/Uruguay
15A2 **Negro, Cap** *C* Morocco
27F6 **Negros** *I* Philippines
17F2 **Negru Vodă** Romania
31B4 **Neijiang** China
64A2 **Neillsville** USA
**Nei Monggol Zizhiqu = Inner Mongolia Aut. Region**
72C3 **Neiva** Colombia
50D3 **Nejo** Ethiopia
50D3 **Nek'emte** Ethiopia
20E4 **Nelidovo** Russian Federation
61D2 **Neligh** USA
44B3 **Nellore** India
26G2 **Nel'ma** Russian Federation
54G5 **Nelson** Canada
6C3 **Nelson** England
35B2 **Nelson** New Zealand
34B3 **Nelson,C** Australia
47E2 **Nelspruit** South Africa
48B3 **Néma** Mauritius
31A1 **Nemagt Uul** *Mt* Mongolia
16B3 **Nementcha, Mts Des** Algeria
17F1 **Nemira** *Mt* Romania
13B3 **Nemours** France
19E1 **Nemunas** *R* Lithuania
29F2 **Nemuro** Japan
29F2 **Nemuro-kaikyō** *Str* Japan/Russian Federation
25O5 **Nen** *R* China
10B3 **Nenagh** Irish Republic
54D3 **Nenana** USA
7D3 **Nene** *R* England
26F2 **Nenjiang** China
63C1 **Neodesha** USA
63D1 **Neosho** USA
25M4 **Nepa** Russian Federation
39G3 **Nepal** *Kingdom* Asia
43E3 **Nepalganj** Nepal
59D3 **Nephi** USA
45C3 **Neqarot** *R* Israel
26E1 **Nerchinsk** Russian Federation
17D2 **Neretva** *R* Bosnia & Herzegovina, Yugoslavia/Croatia
27H5 **Nero Deep** Pacific Ocean
20G2 **Nes'** Russian Federation
12C1 **Neskaupstaður** Iceland
13B3 **Nesle** France
62C1 **Ness City** USA
8C3 **Ness, Loch** *L* Scotland
17E2 **Néstos** *R* Greece
45C2 **Netanya** Israel
68C2 **Netcong** USA
18B2 **Netherlands** *Kingdom* Europe
53M7 **Netherlands Antilles** *Is* Caribbean Sea
43G4 **Netrakona** Bangladesh
55L3 **Nettilling L** Canada
18C2 **Neubrandenburg** Germany
16B1 **Neuchâtel** Switzerland
13C3 **Neufchâteau** Belgium
13C3 **Neufchâteau** France
14C2 **Neufchâtel** France
18B2 **Neumünster** Germany
16D1 **Neunkirchen** Austria
13D3 **Neunkirchen** Germany
74C5 **Neuquén** Argentina
74C5 **Neuquén** *R* Argentina
74B5 **Neuquén** *State* Argentina
18C2 **Neuruppin** Germany
67C1 **Neuse** *R* USA
13D2 **Neuss** Germany
18C2 **Neustadt** Germany
13E3 **Neustadt an der Weinstrasse** Germany
13E1 **Neustadt a R** Germany
13E4 **Neustadt im Schwarzwald** Germany
18C2 **Neustrelitz** Germany
13E1 **Neuwerk** *I* Germany
13D2 **Neuwied** Germany
63D1 **Nevada** USA
56B3 **Nevada** *State* USA
15B2 **Nevada, Sierra** *Mts* Spain
45C3 **Nevatim** Israel
20D4 **Nevel'** Russian Federation
14C2 **Nevers** France
34C2 **Nevertire** Australia
**Nevis = St Kitts-Nevis**
40B2 **Nevşehir** Turkey
20L4 **Nev'yansk** Russian Federation
64C3 **New** *R* USA
51D5 **Newala** Tanzania
64B3 **New Albany** Indiana, USA
63E2 **New Albany** Mississippi, USA
73G2 **New Amsterdam** Guyana
34C1 **New Angledool** Australia
65D3 **Newark** Delaware, USA
57F2 **Newark** New Jersey, USA
68B1 **Newark** New York, USA
64C2 **Newark** Ohio, USA
7D3 **Newark-upon-Trent** England
65E2 **New Bedford** USA
58B1 **Newberg** USA
67C1 **New Bern** USA
67B2 **Newberry** USA
47C3 **New Bethesda** South Africa
69B2 **New Bight** The Bahamas
64C3 **New Boston** USA
62C3 **New Braunfels** USA
68D2 **New Britain** USA
32E1 **New Britain** *I* Papua New Guinea
32E1 **New Britain Trench** Papua New Guinea
68C2 **New Brunswick** USA
55M5 **New Brunswick** *Province* Canada
68C2 **Newburgh** USA
7D4 **Newbury** England
68E1 **Newburyport** USA
33F3 **New Caledonia** *I* SW Pacific Ocean
68D2 **New Canaan** USA
34D2 **Newcastle** Australia
64B3 **New Castle** Indiana, USA
9D2 **Newcastle** Northern Ireland
64C2 **New Castle** Pennsylvania, USA
47D2 **Newcastle** South Africa
60C2 **Newcastle** Wyoming, USA
8D4 **New Castleton** Scotland
7C3 **Newcastle under Lyme** England
6D2 **Newcastle upon Tyne** England
32C2 **Newcastle Waters** Australia
66C3 **New Cuyama** USA
42D3 **New Delhi** India
34D2 **New England Range** *Mts* Australia
68A1 **Newfane** USA
7D4 **New Forest,The** England
55N5 **Newfoundland** *I* Canada
55M4 **Newfoundland** *Province* Canada
52F2 **Newfoundland Basin** Atlantic Ocean
61E3 **New Franklin** USA
8C4 **New Galloway** Scotland
33E1 **New Georgia** *I* Solomon Islands
55M5 **New Glasgow** Canada
32D1 **New Guinea** *I* SE Asia
66C3 **Newhall** USA
57F2 **New Hampshire** *State* USA
61E2 **New Hampton** USA
47E2 **New Hanover** South Africa
32E1 **New Hanover** *I* Papua New Guinea
7E4 **Newhaven** England
65E2 **New Haven** USA
33F3 **New Hebrides Trench** Pacific Ocean
63D2 **New Iberia** USA
32E1 **New Ireland** *I* Papua New Guinea
57F2 **New Jersey** *State* USA
62B2 **Newkirk** USA
55L5 **New Liskeard** Canada
68D2 **New London** USA
32A3 **Newman** Australia
66B2 **Newman** USA
7E3 **Newmarket** England
65D3 **New Market** USA
58C2 **New Meadows** USA
56C3 **New Mexico** *State* USA
68D2 **New Milford** Connecticut, USA
68C2 **New Milford** Pennsylvania, USA
67B2 **Newnan** USA
34C4 **New Norfolk** Australia
57D3 **New Orleans** USA
68C2 **New Paltz** USA
64C2 **New Philadelphia** USA
35B1 **New Plymouth** New Zealand
63D1 **Newport** Arkansas, USA
7D4 **Newport** England
64C3 **Newport** Kentucky, USA
68D1 **Newport** New Hampshire, USA
58B2 **Newport** Oregon, USA
68B2 **Newport** Pennsylvania, USA
65E2 **Newport** Rhode Island, USA
65E2 **Newport** Vermont, USA
7C4 **Newport** Wales
58C1 **Newport** Washington, USA
66D4 **Newport Beach** USA
57F3 **Newport News** USA
69B1 **New Providence** *I* The Bahamas
7B4 **Newquay** England
7B3 **New Quay** Wales
55L3 **New Quebec Crater** Canada
7C3 **New Radnor** Wales
7E4 **New Romney** England
9C3 **New Ross** Irish Republic
9C2 **Newry** Northern Ireland
**New Siberian Is = Novosibirskye Ostrova**
67B3 **New Smyrna Beach** USA
32D4 **New South Wales** *State* Australia
61E2 **Newton** Iowa, USA
63C1 **Newton** Kansas, USA
68E1 **Newton** Massachusetts, USA
63E2 **Newton** Mississippi, USA
68C2 **Newton** New Jersey, USA
9D2 **Newtonabbey** Northern Ireland
7C4 **Newton Abbot** England
9C2 **Newton Stewart** Northern Ireland
8C4 **Newton Stewart** Scotland
60C1 **New Town** USA
7C3 **Newtown** Wales
9D2 **Newtownards** Northern Ireland
61E2 **New Ulm** USA
68B2 **Newville** USA
54F5 **New Westminster** Canada
57F2 **New York** USA
57F2 **New York** *State* USA
33G5 **New Zealand** *Dominion* SWPacific Ocean
37K7 **New Zealand Plat** Pacific Ocean
20G4 **Neya** Russian Federation
41F4 **Neyrīz** Iran
41G2 **Neyshābūr** Iran
21E5 **Nezhin** Ukraine
50B4 **Ngabé** Congo
51C6 **Ngami, L** Botswana
49D4 **Ngaoundéré** Cameroon
30A1 **Ngape** Burma
35C1 **Ngaruawahia** New Zealand
35C1 **Ngaruroro** *R* New Zealand
35C1 **Ngauruhoe,Mt** New Zealand
50B4 **Ngo** Congo
30D2 **Ngoc Linh** *Mt* Vietnam
50B3 **Ngoko** *R* Cameroon/Central African Republic/Congo
26C3 **Ngoring Hu** *L* China
50D4 **Ngorongoro Crater** Tanzania
50B4 **N'Gounié** *R* Gabon
50B2 **Nguigmi** Niger
27G6 **Ngulu** *I* Pacific Ocean
48D3 **Nguru** Nigeria
30D3 **Nha Trang** Vietnam
75A2 **Nhecolândia** Brazil
34B3 **Nhill** Australia
47E2 **Nhlangano** Swaziland
30D2 **Nhommarath** Laos
32C2 **Nhulunbuy** Australia
48B3 **Niafounké** Mali
64B1 **Niagara** USA
65D2 **Niagara Falls** Canada
65D2 **Niagara Falls** USA
27E6 **Niah** Malaysia
48B4 **Niakaramandougou** Ivory Coast
48C3 **Niamey** Niger
50C3 **Niangara** Zaïre
50C3 **Nia Nia** Zaïre
27E6 **Niapa** *Mt* Indonesia
27C6 **Nias** *I* Indonesia
70D3 **Nicaragua** *Republic* Central America
70D3 **Nicaragua, L de** Nicaragua
16D3 **Nicastro** Italy
14D3 **Nice** France
69B1 **Nicholl's Town** The Bahamas
68C2 **Nicholson** USA
39H5 **Nicobar Is** India
45B1 **Nicosia** Cyprus
72A2 **Nicoya, Golfo de** Costa Rica
70D3 **Nicoya,Pen de** Costa Rica
6D2 **Nidd** *R* England
13E2 **Nidda** *R* Germany
19E2 **Nidzica** Poland
13D3 **Niederbronn** France
18B2 **Niedersachsen** *State* Germany
50C4 **Niemba** Zaïre
18B2 **Nienburg** Germany
13D2 **Niers** *R* Germany
48B4 **Niete,Mt** Liberia
73G2 **Nieuw Amsterdam** Surinam
73G2 **Nieuw Nickerie** Surinam
47B3 **Nieuwoudtville** South Africa
13B2 **Nieuwpoort** Belgium
40B2 **Niğde** Turkey
48B3 **Niger** *R* W Africa
48C3 **Niger** *Republic* Africa
48C4 **Nigeria** *Federal Republic* Africa
48C4 **Niger, Mouths of the** Nigeria
43L1 **Nighasan** India
64C1 **Nighthawk L** Canada
17E2 **Nigríta** Greece
29D3 **Nihommatsu** Japan
29D3 **Niigata** Japan
29C4 **Niihama** Japan
29C4 **Nii-jima** *I* Japan
29B4 **Niimi** Japan
29D3 **Niitsu** Japan
45C3 **Nijil** Jordan
18B2 **Nijmegen** Netherlands
20E2 **Nikel'** Russian Federation
48C4 **Nikki** Benin
29D3 **Nikko** Japan
21E6 **Nikolayev** Ukraine
21H6 **Nikolayevsk** Russian Federation
25Q4 **Nikolayevsk-na-Amure** Russian Federation
20H5 **Nikol'sk** Penza, Russian Federation
20H4 **Nikol'sk** Russian Federation
21E6 **Nikopol** Ukraine
40C1 **Niksar** Turkey
38A1 **Nikšić** Yugoslavia
17D2 **Nikšić** Montenegro, Yugoslavia
33G1 **Nikunau** *I* Kiribati
27F7 **Nila** *I* Indonesia
38B3 **Nile** *R* NE Africa
64B2 **Niles** USA
44B3 **Nilgiri Hills** India
42C4 **Nimach** India
14C3 **Nîmes** France
34C3 **Nimmitabel** Australia
50D3 **Nimule** Sudan
39F5 **Nine Degree Chan** Indian Ocean
36F5 **Ninety-East Ridge** Indian Ocean
34C3 **Ninety Mile Beach** Australia
31D4 **Ningde** China
31D4 **Ningdu** China
26C3 **Ningjing Shan** *Mts* China
30D1 **Ningming** China
31A4 **Ningnan** China
31B2 **Ningxia** *Province* China
31B2 **Ning Xian** China
31B5 **Ninh Binh** Vietnam
32D1 **Ninigo Is** Papua New Guinea
75A3 **Nioaque** Brazil
60C2 **Niobrara** *R* USA
50B4 **Nioki** Zaïre
48B3 **Nioro du Sahel** Mali
14B2 **Niort** France
54H4 **Nipawin** Canada
55K5 **Nipigon** Canada
64B1 **Nipigon B** Canada
55K5 **Nipigon,L** Canada
64C1 **Nipissing,L** Canada
66B3 **Nipomo** USA
59C3 **Nipton** USA
75C1 **Niquelândia** Brazil
44B2 **Nirmal** India
43F3 **Nirmāli** India
17E2 **Niš** Serbia, Yugoslavia
38C4 **Nişāb** Yemen
26H4 **Nishino-shima** *I* Japan
28C3 **Nishino-shima** *I* Japan
28A4 **Nishi-suidō** *Str* S Korea
29B4 **Nishiwaki** Japan
33E1 **Nissan Is** Papua New Guinea
55L4 **Nitchequon** Canada
73K8 **Niterói** Brazil
8D4 **Nith** *R* Scotland
19D3 **Nitra** Czechoslovakia
64C3 **Nitro** USA
33J2 **Niue** *I* Pacific Ocean
33G2 **Niulakita** *I* Tuvalu
27E6 **Niut** *Mt* Indonesia
33G1 **Niutao** *I* Tuvalu
28A2 **Niuzhuang** China
13C2 **Nivelles** Belgium
14C2 **Nivernais** *Region* France
12L5 **Nivskiy** Russian Federation
44B2 **Nizāmābād** India
45C3 **Nizana** *Hist Site* Israel
26C1 **Nizhneudinsk** Russian Federation
20K4 **Nizhniye Sergi** Russian Federation
20G5 **Nizhniy Lomov** Russian Federation
20G4 **Nizhiny Novgorod** Russian Federation
20J3 **Nizhniy Odes** Russian Federation
20K4 **Nizhniy Tagil** Russian Federation
25L3 **Nizhnyaya Tunguska** *R* Russian Federation
20G2 **Nizhnyaya Zolotitsa** Russian Federation
40C2 **Nizip** Turkey
12C1 **Njarðvík** Iceland
51C5 **Njoko** *R* Zambia
51D4 **Njombe** Tanzania
50B3 **Nkambé** Cameroon
51D5 **Nkhata Bay** Malawi
50B3 **Nkongsamba** Cameroon
48C3 **N'Konni** Niger
43G4 **Noakhali** Bangladesh
54B3 **Noatak** USA
54B3 **Noatak** *R* USA
28C4 **Nobeoka** Japan
29D2 **Noboribetsu** Japan
75A1 **Nobres** Brazil
63C2 **Nocona** USA
70A1 **Nogales** Sonora, Mexico
59D4 **Nogales** USA
28B4 **Nogata** Japan
13C3 **Nogent-en-Bassigny** France
13B3 **Nogent-sur-Seine** France
20F4 **Noginsk** Russian Federation
42C3 **Nohar** India
29D2 **Noheji** Japan
14B2 **Noirmoutier, Ile de** *I* France
47C1 **Nojane** Botswana
29C4 **Nojima-zaki** *C* Japan
50B3 **Nola** Central African Republic
20H4 **Nolinsk** Russian Federation
68E2 **Nomans Land** *I* USA
54B3 **Nome** USA
13D3 **Nomeny** France
31B1 **Nomgon** Mongolia
28A4 **Nomo-saki** *Pt* Japan
54H3 **Nonacho L** Canada
30C2 **Nong Khai** Thailand
47E2 **Nongoma** South Africa
33G1 **Nonouti** *I* Kiribati
28A3 **Nonsan** S Korea
13C1 **Noord Holland** *Province* Netherlands
47B2 **Noordoewer** Namibia
13C1 **Noordoost Polder** Netherlands
13C1 **Noordzeekanal** Netherlands
54B3 **Noorvik** USA
50B4 **Noqui** Angola
55L5 **Noranda** Canada
13B2 **Nord** *Department* France
24D2 **Nordaustlandet** *I* Svalbard
13D1 **Norden** Germany
13E1 **Nordenham** Germany
13D1 **Norderney** *I* Germany
12F6 **Nordfjord** *Inlet* Norway
12F8 **Nordfriesische** *Is* Germany
18C2 **Nordhausen** Germany
13D1 **Nordhorn** Germany
18B2 **Nordrhein Westfalen** *State* Germany
12J4 **Nordkapp** *C* Norway
55N3 **Nordre Strømfyord** *Fyord* Greenland
12G5 **Nord Storfjället** *Mt* Sweden
25N2 **Nordvik** Russian Federation
9C3 **Nore** *R* Irish Republic
61D2 **Norfolk** Nebraska, USA
65D3 **Norfolk** Virginia, USA
7E3 **Norfolk** *County* England
33F3 **Norfolk I** Pacific Ocean
37K6 **Norfolk I Ridge** Pacific Ocean
63D1 **Norfolk L** USA
25K3 **Noril'sk** Russian Federation
64B2 **Normal** USA
63C1 **Norman** USA
14B2 **Normandie** *Region* France
67B1 **Norman,L** USA
32D2 **Normanton** Australia
54F3 **Norman Wells** Canada
20B2 **Norra Storfjället** *Mt* Sweden
67B1 **Norris L** USA
65D2 **Norristown** USA
12H7 **Norrköping** Sweden
12H6 **Norrsundet** Sweden
12H7 **Norrtälje** Sweden
32B4 **Norseman** Australia
26F1 **Norsk** Russian Federation
75A1 **Nortelândia** Brazil
6D2 **Northallerton** England

**Northam** **Okmulgee**


32A4 **Northam** Australia
47D2 **Northam** South Africa
52E3 **North American Basin** Atlantic Ocean
32A3 **Northampton** Australia
7D3 **Northampton** England
65E2 **Northampton** USA
7D3 **Northampton** *County* England
44E3 **North Andaman** *I* Indian Ocean
54G3 **North Arm** *B* Canada
67B2 **North Augusta** USA
55M4 **North Aulatsivik** *I* Canada
54H4 **North Battleford** Canada
55L5 **North Bay** Canada
58B2 **North Bend** USA
8D3 **North Berwick** Scotland
68E1 **North Berwick** USA
55M5 **North,C** Canada
62B1 **North Canadian** *R* USA
57E3 **North Carolina** *State* USA
58B1 **North Cascades Nat Pk** USA
64C1 **North Chan** Canada
6B2 **North Chan** Ireland/ Scotland
56C2 **North Dakota** *State* USA
7E4 **North Downs** England
65D2 **North East** USA
52H2 **North East Atlantic Basin** Atlantic Ocean
54B3 **Northeast C** USA
10B3 **Northern Ireland** UK
61E1 **Northern Light L** Canada/ USA
27H5 **Northern Mariana Is** Pacific Ocean
69L1 **Northern Range** *Mts* Trinidad
32C2 **Northern Territory** Australia
8D3 **North Esk** *R* Scotland
68D1 **Northfield** Massachusetts, USA
61E2 **Northfield** Minnesota, USA
7E4 **North Foreland** England
35B1 **North I** New Zealand
28B3 **North Korea** *Republic* SE Asia
**North Land = Severnaya Zemlya**
63D2 **North Little Rock** USA
60C2 **North Loup** *R* USA
76B4 **North Magnetic Pole** Canada
67B3 **North Miami** USA
67B3 **North Miami Beach** USA
66C2 **North Palisade** *Mt* USA
60C2 **North Platte** USA
56C2 **North Platte** *R* USA
76A **North Pole** Arctic
69R3 **North Pt** Barbados
64C1 **North Pt** USA
61E2 **North Raccoon** *R* USA
10B2 **North Rona** *I* Scotland
8D2 **North Ronaldsay** *I* Scotland
52F7 **North Scotia Ridge** Atlantic Ocean
10D2 **North Sea** NW Europe
44E3 **North Sentinel** *I* Andaman Islands
54D3 **North Slope** *Region* USA
34D1 **North Stradbroke I** Australia
68B1 **North Syracuse** USA
35B1 **North Taranaki Bight** *B* New Zealand
68A1 **North Tonawanda** USA
56C3 **North Truchas Peak** *Mt* USA
8B3 **North Uist** *I* Scotland
6C2 **Northumberland** *County* England
32E3 **Northumberland Is** Australia
55M5 **Northumberland Str** Canada
58B1 **North Vancouver** Canada
68C1 **Northville** USA
7E3 **North Walsham** England
54D3 **Northway** USA
32A3 **North West C** Australia
42C2 **North West Frontier Province** Pakistan
55M4 **North West River** Canada
54G3 **North West Territories** Canada
61D1 **Northwood** USA
6D2 **North York Moors** England
6D2 **North Yorkshire** *County* England
60D3 **Norton** *R* USA
54B3 **Norton Sd** USA
76F1 **Norvegia,C** Antarctica
68D2 **Norwalk** Connecticut, USA
64C2 **Norwalk** Ohio, USA
12F6 **Norway** *Kingdom* Europe
54J4 **Norway House** Canada
55J2 **Norwegian B** Canada
52H1 **Norwegian Basin** Norwegian Sea
24B3 **Norwegian S** NW Europe
68D2 **Norwich** Connecticut, USA
7E3 **Norwich** England
68C1 **Norwich** New York, USA
68E1 **Norwood** Massachusetts, USA
64C3 **Norwood** Ohio, USA
17F2 **Nos Emine** *C* Bulgaria
29E2 **Noshiro** Japan
17F2 **Nos Kaliakra** *C* Bulgaria
47B1 **Nosob** *R* Namibia
20J2 **Nosovaya** Russian Federation
19G2 **Nosovka** Ukraine
8E1 **Noss** *I* Scotland
8D2 **Noss Head, Pt** Scotland
51E5 **Nosy Barren** *I* Madagascar
51E5 **Nosy Bé** *I* Madagascar
51F5 **Nosy Boraha** *I* Madagascar
51E6 **Nosy Varika** Madagascar
18D2 **Notéc** *R* Poland
54G4 **Notikewin** Canada
16D3 **Noto** Italy
12F7 **Notodden** Norway
29C3 **Noto-hantō** *Pen* Japan
55N5 **Notre Dame B** Canada
48C4 **Notsé** Togo
7D3 **Nottingham** England
7D3 **Nottingham** *County* England
55L3 **Nottingham** Canada
55L3 **Nottingham Island** Canada
48A2 **Nouadhibou** Mauritius
48A3 **Nouakchott** Mauritius
33F3 **Nouméa** New Caledonia
48B3 **Nouna** Burkina
8D2 **Noup Head, Pt** Scotland
47C3 **Noupoort** South Africa
55L3 **Nouvelle-France, Cap de** *C* Canada
75C2 **Nova América** Brazil
51B4 **Nova Caipemba** Angola
75B3 **Nova Esperança** Brazil
75D3 **Nova Friburgo** Brazil
51B5 **Nova Gaia** Angola
75C3 **Nova Granada** Brazil
75C3 **Nova Horizonte** Brazil
75D3 **Nova Lima** Brazil
**Nova Lisboa = Huambo**
75B3 **Nova Londrina** Brazil
51D6 **Nova Mambone** Mozambique
16B1 **Novara** Italy
75C1 **Nova Roma** Brazil
73K4 **Nova Russas** Brazil
55M5 **Nova Scotia** *Province* Canada
66A1 **Novato** USA
75D2 **Nova Venécia** Brazil
21E6 **Novaya Kakhovka** Ukraine
25R2 **Novaya Sibir, Ostrov** *I* Russian Federation
24G2 **Novaya Zemlya** *I* Russian Federation
17F2 **Nova Zagora** Bulgaria
17D1 **Nové Zámky** Czechoslovakia
20E4 **Novgorod** Russian Federation
16B2 **Novi Ligure** Italy
17F2 **Novi Pazar** Bulgaria
17E2 **Novi Pazar** Serbia, Yugoslavia
17D1 **Novi Sad** Serbia, Yugoslavia
21K5 **Novoalekseyevka** Kazakhstan
21G5 **Novoanninskiy** Russian Federation
21F6 **Novocherkassk** Russian Federation
20G3 **Novodvinsk** Russian Federation
21D5 **Novograd Volynskiy** Ukraine
19F2 **Novogrudok** Belorussia
74F3 **Novo Hamburgo** Brazil
24H5 **Novokazalinsk** Kazakhstan
24K4 **Novokuznetsk** Russian Federation
76F12 **Novolazarevskaya** *Base* Antarctica
16D1 **Novo Mesto** Slovenia
19G3 **Novomirgorod** Ukraine
20F5 **Novomoskovsk** Russian Federation
**Novo Redondo = Sumbe**
21F7 **Novorossiysk** Russian Federation
25M2 **Novorybnoye** Russian Federation
24K4 **Novosibirsk** Russian Federation
25P2 **Novosibirskye Ostrova** *Is* Russian Federation
21K5 **Novotroitsk** Russian Federation
21H5 **Novo Uzensk** Russian Federation
19E2 **Novovolynsk** Ukraine
20H4 **Novo Vyatsk** Russian Federation
21E5 **Novozybkov** Russian Federation
24J3 **Novvy Port** Russian Federation
19E2 **Novy Dwór Mazowiecki** Poland
20L4 **Novyy Lyalya** Russian Federation
20N2 **Novyy Port** Russian Federation
21J7 **Novyy Uzen** Kazakhstan
18D2 **Nowa Sól** Poland
63C1 **Nowata** USA
43G3 **Nowgong** India
34D2 **Nowra** Australia
41F2 **Now Shahr** Iran
42C2 **Nowshera** Pakistan
19E3 **Nowy Sącz** Poland
13B3 **Noyon** France
14B2 **Nozay** France
48B4 **Nsawam** Ghana
47E1 **Nuanetsi** Zimbabwe
50D2 **Nuba Mts** Sudan
50D1 **Nubian Desert** Sudan
56D4 **Nueces** *R* USA
54J3 **Nueltin L** Canada
28A2 **Nü'erhe** China
70B1 **Nueva Casas Grandes** Mexico
75A3 **Nueva Germania** Paraguay
69A2 **Nueva Gerona** Cuba
70B2 **Nueva Rosita** Mexico
69B2 **Nuevitas** Cuba
70B1 **Nuevo Casas Grandes** Mexico
70C2 **Nuevo Laredo** Mexico
50E3 **Nugaal** *Region* Somalia
55N2 **Nûgâtsiaq** Greenland
55N2 **Nûgussuaq** *I* Greenland
55N2 **Nûgussuaq** *Pen* Greenland
33G1 **Nui** *I* Tuvalu
31A5 **Nui Con Voi** *R* Vietnam
13C4 **Nuits** France
40D3 **Nukhayb** Iraq
33G1 **Nukufetau** *I* Tuvalu
33G1 **Nukulaelae** *I* Tuvalu
33H1 **Nukunon** *I* Tokelau Islands
24G5 **Nukus** Uzbekistan
54C3 **Nulato** USA
32B4 **Nullarbor Plain** Australia
48D4 **Numan** Nigeria
29C3 **Numata** Japan
50C3 **Numatinna** *R* Sudan
29D3 **Numazu** Japan
27G7 **Numfoor** *I* Indonesia
34C3 **Numurkah** Australia
68A1 **Nunda** USA
7D3 **Nuneaton** England
42D2 **Nunkun** *Mt* India
16B2 **Nuoro** Sicily, Italy
41F3 **Nurābād** Iran
34A2 **Nuriootpa** Australia
42C1 **Nuristan** *Region* Afghanistan
20J5 **Nurlat** Russian Federation
12K6 **Nurmes** Finland
18C3 **Nürnberg** Germany
34C2 **Nurri,Mt** Australia
40D2 **Nusaybin** Turkey
45D1 **Nuşayrīyah, Jabalan** *Mts* Syria
42B3 **Nushki** Pakistan
55M4 **Nutak** Canada
**Nuuk = Godthåb**
43E3 **Nuwakot** Nepal
44C4 **Nuwara-Eliya** Sri Lanka
47C3 **Nuweveldreeks** *Mts* South Africa
55L3 **Nuyukjuak** Canada
54C3 **Nyac** USA
68D2 **Nyack** USA
50D3 **Nyahururu Falls** Kenya
34B3 **Nyah West** Australia
26C3 **Nyainqentanglha Shan** *Mts* Tibet, China
50D4 **Nyakabindi** Tanzania
20L3 **Nyaksimvol'** Russian Federation
50C2 **Nyala** Sudan
43F3 **Nyalam** China
50C3 **Nyamlell** Sudan
51D6 **Nyanda** Zimbabwe
20G3 **Nyandoma** Russian Federation
50B4 **Nyanga** *R* Gabon
51D5 **Nyasa, L** Malawi/ Mozambique
30B2 **Nyaunglebin** Burma
20K4 **Nyazepetrovsk** Russian Federation
12G7 **Nyborg** Denmark
12H7 **Nybro** Sweden
24J3 **Nyda** Russian Federation
55M1 **Nyeboes Land** *Region* Canada
50D4 **Nyeri** Kenya
51D5 **Nyimba** Zambia
39H2 **Nyingchi** China
19E3 **Nyíregyháza** Hungary
50D3 **Nyiru,Mt** Kenya
12J6 **Nykarleby** Finland
12F7 **Nykøbing** Denmark
12G8 **Nykøbing** Denmark
12H7 **Nyköping** Sweden
47D1 **Nyl** *R* South Africa
47D1 **Nylstroom** South Africa
34C2 **Nymagee** Australia
12H7 **Nynäshamn** Sweden
34C2 **Nyngan** Australia
50B3 **Nyong** *R* Cameroon
28A3 **Nyongwol** S Korea
28A3 **Nyongwon** N Korea
14D3 **Nyons** France
18D2 **Nysa** Poland
58C2 **Nyssa** USA
20H3 **Nyukhcha** Russian Federation
26F1 **Nyukzha** *R* Russian Federation
25N3 **Nyurba** Russian Federation
50D4 **Nzega** Tanzania
48B4 **Nzérékoré** Guinea
51B4 **N'zeto** Angola


## O


60D2 **Oacoma** USA
60C2 **Oahe,L** *Res* USA
66E5 **Oahu** *I* Hawaiian Islands
34B2 **Oakbank** Australia
66B2 **Oakdale** USA
61D1 **Oakes** USA
34D1 **Oakey** Australia
59B3 **Oakland** California, USA
61D2 **Oakland** Nebraska, USA
58B2 **Oakland** Oregon, USA
64B3 **Oakland City** USA
64B2 **Oak Lawn** USA
66B2 **Oakley** California, USA
60C3 **Oakley** Kansas, USA
67B1 **Oak Ridge** USA
58B2 **Oakridge** USA
65D2 **Oakville** Canada
35B3 **Oamaru** New Zealand
66D2 **Oasis** California, USA
58D2 **Oasis** Nevada, USA
76F7 **Oates Land** *Region* Antarctica
34C4 **Oatlands** Australia
70C3 **Oaxaca** Mexico
24H3 **Ob'** *R* Russian Federation
29C3 **Obama** Japan
35A3 **Oban** New Zealand
8C3 **Oban** Scotland
29D3 **Obanazawa** Japan
13D2 **Oberhausen** Germany
60C3 **Oberlin** USA
13E3 **Obernburg** Germany
27F7 **Obi** *I* Indonesia
73G4 **Obidos** Brazil
29E2 **Obihiro** Japan
26G2 **Obluch'ye** Russian Federation
50C3 **Obo** Central African Republic
50E2 **Obock** Djibouti
18D2 **Oborniki** Poland
21F5 **Oboyan'** Russian Federation
58B2 **O'Brien** USA
21J5 **Obshchiy Syrt** *Mts* Russian Federation
24J3 **Obskaya Guba** *B* Russian Federation
48B4 **Obuasi** Ghana
67B3 **Ocala** USA
72D2 **Ocaña** Colombia
15B2 **Ocaña** Spain
65D3 **Ocean City** Maryland, USA
68C3 **Ocean City** New Jersey, USA
54F4 **Ocean Falls** Canada
**Ocean I = Banaba**
66B3 **Oceano** USA
66D4 **Oceanside** USA
63E2 **Ocean Springs** USA
20J4 **Ocher** Russian Federation
8D3 **Ochil Hills** Scotland
67B2 **Ochlockonee** *R* USA
69H1 **Ocho Rios** Jamaica
67B2 **Ocmulgee** *R* USA
67B2 **Oconee** *R* USA
64B2 **Oconto** USA
70B2 **Ocotlán** Mexico
48B4 **Oda** Ghana
28B3 **Oda** Japan
12B2 **Ódáðahraun** *Region* Iceland
28A2 **Ŏdaejin** N Korea
50D1 **Oda, Jebel** *Mt* Sudan
29E2 **Odate** Japan
29D3 **Odawara** Japan
12F6 **Odda** Norway
48C4 **Ode** Nigeria
63C3 **Odem** USA
15A2 **Odemira** Portugal
17F3 **Ödemiş** Turkey
47D2 **Odendaalsrus** South Africa
12G7 **Odense** Denmark
18C2 **Oder** *R* Germany/Poland
62B2 **Odessa** Texas, USA
21E6 **Odessa** Ukraine
58C1 **Odessa** Washington, USA
48B4 **Odienné** Ivory Coast
**Odra = Oder**
19D2 **Odra** *R* Poland
73K5 **Oeiras** Brazil
60C2 **Oelrichs** USA
61E2 **Oelwein** USA
16D2 **Ofanto** *R* Italy
45C3 **Ofaqim** Israel
9C3 **Offaly** *County* Irish Republic
13E2 **Offenbach** Germany
13D3 **Offenburg** Germany
29D3 **Ofunato** Japan
29D3 **Oga** Japan
50E3 **Ogaden** *Region* Ethiopia
29D3 **Ōgaki** Japan
60C2 **Ogallala** USA
26H4 **Ogasawara Gunto** *Is* Japan
48C4 **Ogbomosho** Nigeria
61E2 **Ogden** Iowa, USA
58D2 **Ogden** Utah, USA
65D2 **Ogdensburg** USA
67B2 **Ogeechee** *R* USA
54E3 **Ogilvie Mts** Canada
67B2 **Oglethorpe,Mt** USA
48C4 **Ogoja** Nigeria
19E1 **Ogre** Latvia
48B2 **Oguilet Khenachich** *Well* Mali
16D1 **Ogulin** Croatia
68E1 **Ogunquit** USA
21J8 **Ogurchinskiy, Ostrov** *I* Turkmenistan
35A3 **Ohai** New Zealand
35C1 **Ohakune** New Zealand
48C2 **Ohanet** Algeria
29D2 **Ōhata** Japan
35A2 **Ohau,L** New Zealand
74B7 **O'Higgins, Lago** Chile
64B3 **Ohio** *R* USA
57E2 **Ohio** *State* USA
13E2 **Ohm** *R* Germany
51B5 **Ohopoho** Namibia
18C2 **Ohre** *R* Czechoslovakia
17E2 **Ohrid** Macedonia, Yugoslavia
17E2 **Ohridsko Jezero** *L* Albania/Macedonia, Yugoslavia
35B1 **Ohura** New Zealand
73H3 **Oiapoque** French Guiana
65D2 **Oil City** USA
66C3 **Oildale** USA
13B3 **Oise** *Department* France
14C2 **Oise** *R* France
28C4 **Ōita** Japan
66C3 **Ojai** USA
70B2 **Ojinaga** Mexico
29C3 **Ojiya** Japan
74C3 **Ojos del Salado** *Mt* Argentina
20F5 **Oka** *R* Russian Federation
47B1 **Okahandja** Namibia
58C1 **Okanagan Falls** Canada
58C1 **Okanogan** USA
58C1 **Okanogan** *R* USA
58B1 **Okanogan Range** *Mts* Canada/USA
42C2 **Okara** Pakistan
47B1 **Okasise** Namibia
51B5 **Okavango** *R* Angola/ Namibia
51C5 **Okavango Delta** *Marsh* Botswana
29D3 **Okaya** Japan
29C4 **Okayama** Japan
29C4 **Okazaki** Japan
67B3 **Okeechobee** USA
67B3 **Okeechobee,L** USA
67B2 **Okefenokee Swamp** USA
48C4 **Okene** Nigeria
42B4 **Okha** India
43F3 **Okhaldunga** Nepal
25Q4 **Okhotsk** Russian Federation
25Q4 **Okhotsk, Sof** Russian Federation
26F4 **Okinawa** *I* Japan
26F4 **Okinawa gunto** *Arch* Japan
28C3 **Oki-shotō** *Is* Japan
28A2 **Okkang-dong** N Korea
56D3 **Oklahoma** *State* USA
63C1 **Oklahoma City** USA
63C1 **Okmulgee** USA

20G2 **Ponoy** *R* Russian Federation
14B2 **Pons** France
48A1 **Ponta Delgada** Azores
75B4 **Ponta Grossa** Brazil
75C3 **Pontal** Brazil
13C3 **Pont-à-Mousson** France
75A3 **Ponta Pora** Brazil
14D2 **Pontarlier** France
63D2 **Pontchartrain,L** USA
75A1 **Ponte de Pedra** Brazil
16C2 **Pontedera** Italy
7D3 **Pontefract** England
16B2 **Ponte Leccia** Corsica, France
15A1 **Pontevedra** Spain
64B2 **Pontiac** Illinois, USA
64C2 **Pontiac** Michigan, USA
27D7 **Pontianak** Indonesia
14B2 **Pontivy** France
13B3 **Pontoise** France
63E2 **Pontotoc** USA
13B3 **Pont-sur-Yonne** France
7C4 **Pontypool** Wales
7C4 **Pontypridd** Wales
16C2 **Ponziane, I** Italy
7D4 **Poole** England
  **Poona = Pune**
34B2 **Pooncarie** Australia
34B2 **Poopelloe,L** Australia
72E7 **Poopó, Lago** Bolivia
54C3 **Poorman** USA
72C3 **Popayán** Colombia
13B2 **Poperinge** Belgium
34B2 **Popilta L** Australia
60B1 **Poplar** USA
63D1 **Poplar Bluff** USA
63E2 **Poplarville** USA
70C3 **Popocatepetl** *Vol* Mexico
50B4 **Popokabaka** Zaïre
27H7 **Popondetta** Papua New Guinea
17F2 **Popovo** Bulgaria
75C1 **Porangatu** Brazil
42B4 **Porbandar** India
75C1 **Porcos** *R* Brazil
54D3 **Porcupine** *R* Canada/ USA
16C1 **Poreč** Croatia
75B3 **Porecatu** Brazil
12J6 **Pori** Finland
35B2 **Porirua** New Zealand
12H5 **Porjus** Sweden
69E4 **Porlamar** Venezuela
26H2 **Poronaysk** Russian Federation
20E3 **Porosozero** Russian Federation
12K4 **Porsangen** *Inlet* Norway
12F7 **Porsgrunn** Norway
9C2 **Portadown** Northern Ireland
9D2 **Portaferry** Northern Ireland
64B2 **Portage** USA
60C1 **Portal** USA
54F5 **Port Alberni** Canada
15A2 **Portalegre** Portugal
62B2 **Portales** USA
47D3 **Port Alfred** South Africa
54F4 **Port Alice** Canada
68A2 **Port Allegany** USA
63D2 **Port Allen** USA
58B1 **Port Angeles** USA
69B3 **Port Antonio** Jamaica
9C3 **Portarlington** Irish Republic
63D3 **Port Arthur** USA
8B4 **Port Askaig** Scotland
32C4 **Port Augusta** Australia
69C3 **Port-au-Prince** Haiti
64C2 **Port Austin** USA
44E3 **Port Blair** Andaman Islands
34B3 **Port Campbell** Australia
43F4 **Port Canning** India
55M5 **Port Cartier** Canada
35B3 **Port Chalmers** New Zealand
67B3 **Port Charlotte** USA
68D2 **Port Chester** USA
64C2 **Port Clinton** USA
65D2 **Port Colborne** Canada
34C4 **Port Davey** *B* Australia
69C3 **Port-de-Paix** Haiti
30C5 **Port Dickson** Malaysia
47E3 **Port Edward** South Africa
75D2 **Porteirinha** Brazil
64C2 **Port Elgin** Canada
47D3 **Port Elizabeth** South Africa
8B4 **Port Ellen** Scotland
6B2 **Port Erin** Isle of Man, British Isles
69N2 **Porter Pt** St Vincent
66C2 **Porterville** USA
32D4 **Port Fairy** Australia
50A4 **Port Gentil** Gabon
63D2 **Port Gibson** USA
58B1 **Port Hammond** Canada
48C4 **Port Harcourt** Nigeria
54F4 **Port Hardy** Canada
55M5 **Port Hawkesbury** Canada

7C4 **Porthcawl** Wales
32A3 **Port Hedland** Australia
7B3 **Porthmadog** Wales
55N4 **Port Hope Simpson** Canada
66C3 **Port Hueneme** USA
64C2 **Port Huron** USA
15A2 **Portimão** Portugal
34D2 **Port Jackson** *B* Australia
68D2 **Port Jefferson** USA
68C2 **Port Jervis** USA
34D2 **Port Kembla** Australia
7C4 **Portland** England
64C2 **Portland** Indiana, USA
65E2 **Portland** Maine, USA
34C2 **Portland** New South Wales, Australia
58B1 **Portland** Oregon, USA
34B3 **Portland** Victoria, Australia
69H2 **Portland Bight** *B* Jamaica
7C4 **Portland Bill** *Pt* England
34C4 **Portland,C** Australia
35C1 **Portland I** New Zealand
69H2 **Portland Pt** Jamaica
9C3 **Port Laoise** Irish Republic
63C3 **Port Lavaca** USA
32C4 **Port Lincoln** Australia
48A4 **Port Loko** Sierra Leone
51F6 **Port Louis** Mauritius
34B3 **Port MacDonnell** Australia
34D2 **Port Macquarie** Australia
68A2 **Port Matilda** USA
32D1 **Port Moresby** Papua New Guinea
47B2 **Port Nolloth** South Africa
68C3 **Port Norris** USA
  **Porto = Oporto**
74F4 **Pôrto Alegre** Brazil
  **Porto Alexandre = Tombua**
69A5 **Porto Armuelles** Panama
75A1 **Pôrto Artur** Brazil
75B3 **Pôrto 15 de Novembro** Brazil
75B1 **Pôrto dos Meinacos** Brazil
74F2 **Pôrto E Cunha** Brazil
75A2 **Pôrto Esperança** Brazil
16C2 **Portoferraio** Italy
69L1 **Port of Spain** Trinidad
75A2 **Pôrto Jofre** Brazil
75B3 **Pôrto Mendez** Brazil
75A3 **Pôrto Murtinho** Brazil
48C4 **Porto Novo** Benin
75B3 **Pôrto Primavera, Reprêsa** *Res* Brazil
58B1 **Port Orchard** USA
58B2 **Port Orford** USA
75B3 **Pôrto Santa Helena** Brazil
48A1 **Porto Santo** *I* Madeira
75B3 **Pôrto São José** Brazil
73L7 **Pôrto Seguro** Brazil
16B2 **Porto Torres** Sardinia, Italy
75B4 **Pôrto União** Brazil
16B2 **Porto Vecchio** Corsica, France
72F5 **Pôrto Velho** Brazil
8C4 **Portpatrick** Scotland
35A3 **Port Pegasus** *B* New Zealand
34B3 **Port Phillip B** Australia
34A2 **Port Pirie** Australia
8B3 **Portree** Scotland
58B1 **Port Renfrew** Canada
69J2 **Port Royal** Jamaica
67B2 **Port Royal Sd** USA
9C2 **Portrush** Northern Ireland
45B3 **Port Said** Egypt
67A3 **Port St Joe** USA
47D3 **Port St Johns** South Africa
55N4 **Port Saunders** Canada
47E3 **Port Shepstone** South Africa
69Q2 **Portsmouth** Dominica
7D4 **Portsmouth** England
68E1 **Portsmouth** New Hampshire, USA
64C3 **Portsmouth** Ohio, USA
65D3 **Portsmouth** Virginia, USA
34D2 **Port Stephens** *B* Australia
9C2 **Portstewart** Northern Ireland
50D2 **Port Sudan** Sudan
63E3 **Port Sulphur** USA
12K5 **Porttipahdan Tekojärvi** *Res* Finland
15A2 **Portugal** *Republic* Europe
9B3 **Portumna** Irish Republic
68A1 **Portville** USA
64B2 **Port Washington** USA
30C5 **Port Weld** Malaysia
72E6 **Porvenir** Bolivia
12K6 **Porvoo** Finland
74E3 **Posadas** Argentina
15A2 **Posadas** Spain
41G3 **Posht-e Badam** Iran
27F7 **Poso** Indonesia
28A4 **Posŏng** S Korea

20M2 **Pos Poluy** Russian Federation
75C1 **Posse** Brazil
62B2 **Post** USA
19F1 **Postavy** Belorussia
47C2 **Postmasburg** South Africa
16C1 **Postojna** Slovenia
28C2 **Pos'yet** Russian Federation
47D2 **Potchefstroom** South Africa
63D1 **Poteau** USA
16D2 **Potenza** Italy
47D1 **Potgietersrus** South Africa
62C3 **Poth** USA
21G7 **Poti** Georgia
48D3 **Potiskum** Nigeria
58C1 **Potlatch** USA
47C3 **Potloer** *Mt* South Africa
58C1 **Pot Mt** USA
65D3 **Potomac** *R* USA
72E7 **Potosí** Bolivia
74C3 **Potrerillos** Chile
18C2 **Potsdam** Germany
60C2 **Potter** USA
68C2 **Pottstown** USA
68B2 **Pottsville** USA
68D2 **Poughkeepsie** USA
75C3 **Pouso Alegre** Brazil
35C1 **Poverty B** New Zealand
20F3 **Povonets** Russian Federation
21G5 **Povorino** Russian Federation
55L4 **Povungnituk** Canada
60B1 **Powder** *R* USA
60B2 **Powder River** USA
58E2 **Powell** USA
32C2 **Powell Creek** Australia
59D3 **Powell,L** USA
54F5 **Powell River** Canada
7C3 **Powys** *County* Wales
75B2 **Poxoréo** Brazil
31D4 **Poyang Hu** *L* China
40C2 **Pozanti** Turkey
70C2 **Poza Rica** Mexico
18D2 **Poznań** Poland
74E2 **Pozo Colorado** Paraguay
16C2 **Pozzuoli** Italy
48B4 **Pra** *R* Ghana
30C3 **Prachin Buri** Thailand
30B3 **Prachuap Khiri Khan** Thailand
18D2 **Praděd** *Mt* Czechoslovakia
14C3 **Pradelles** France
75E2 **Prado** Brazil
18C2 **Prague** Czechoslovakia
  **Praha = Prague**
48A4 **Praia** Cape Verde
75A1 **Praia Rica** Brazil
72F5 **Prainha** Brazil
62B2 **Prairie Dog Town Fork** *R* USA
64A2 **Prairie du Chien** USA
61E3 **Prairie Village** USA
30C3 **Prakhon Chai** Thailand
75C2 **Prata** Brazil
75C2 **Prata** *R* Brazil
  **Prates** *I* = **Dongsha Qundao**
16C2 **Prato** Italy
68C1 **Prattsville** USA
67A2 **Prattville** USA
14B1 **Prawle Pt** England
25L4 **Predivinsk** Russian Federation
25Q3 **Predporozhnyy** Russian Federation
19E2 **Pregolyu** *R* Russian Federation
30D3 **Prek Kak** Cambodia
64A1 **Prentice** USA
18C2 **Prenzlau** Germany
44E3 **Preparis I** Burma
18D3 **Přerov** Czechoslovakia
59D4 **Prescott** Arizona, USA
63D2 **Prescott** Arkansas, USA
65D2 **Prescott** Canada
60C2 **Presho** USA
74D3 **Presidencia Roque Sáenz Peña** Argentina
75B3 **Presidente Epitácio** Brazil
75B2 **Presidente Murtinho** Brazil
75B3 **Presidente Prudente** Brazil
75B3 **Presidente Venceslau** Brazil
62B3 **Presidio** USA
19E3 **Prešov** Czechoslovakia
65F1 **Presque Isle** USA
6C3 **Preston** England
56B2 **Preston** Idaho, USA
61E2 **Preston** Minnesota, USA
63D1 **Preston** Missouri, USA
8C4 **Prestwick** Scotland
73J8 **Prêto** Brazil
75C2 **Prêto** *R* Brazil
47D2 **Pretoria** South Africa
17E3 **Préveza** Greece

30D3 **Prey Veng** Cambodia
59D3 **Price** USA
63E2 **Prichard** USA
21E6 **Prichernomorskaya Nizmennost'** *Lowland* Ukraine
69M2 **Prickly Pt** Grenada
19F3 **Pridneprovskaya Vozvyshennost'** *Upland* Ukraine
19E1 **Priekule** Lithuania
47C2 **Prieska** South Africa
58C1 **Priest L** USA
58C1 **Priest River** USA
21H6 **Prikaspiyskaya Nizmennost'** *Region* Kazakhstan
17E2 **Prilep** Macedonia, Yugoslavia
21E5 **Priluki** Ukraine
76G3 **Primavera** *Base* Antarctica
12K6 **Primorsk** Russian Federation
21F6 **Primorsko-Akhtarsk** Russian Federation
54H4 **Prince Albert** Canada
47C3 **Prince Albert** South Africa
54F2 **Prince Albert,C** Canada
54G2 **Prince Albert Pen** Canada
54G2 **Prince Albert Sd** Canada
55L3 **Prince Charles I** Canada
76F10 **Prince Charles Mts** Antarctica
55M5 **Prince Edward I** *Province* Canada
36C7 **Prince Edward Is** Indian Ocean
54F4 **Prince George** Canada
54H2 **Prince Gustaf Adolf Sea** Canada
27H8 **Prince of Wales I** Australia
54H2 **Prince of Wales I** Canada
54E4 **Prince of Wales I** USA
54G2 **Prince of Wales Str** Canada
54G2 **Prince Patrick I** Canada
55J2 **Prince Regent Inlet** *Str* Canada
54E4 **Prince Rupert** Canada
32D2 **Princess Charlotte B** Australia
69L1 **Princes Town** Trinidad
54F5 **Princeton** Canada
64B2 **Princeton** Illinois, USA
64B3 **Princeton** Kentucky, USA
61E2 **Princeton** Missouri, USA
68C2 **Princeton** New Jersey, USA
64C3 **Princeton** W Virginia, USA
54D3 **Prince William Sd** USA
48C4 **Príncipe** *I* Sao Tome & Principe
58B2 **Prineville** USA
55O3 **Prins Christian Sund** Greenland
76F12 **Prinsesse Astrid Kyst** *Region* Antarctica
76F12 **Prinsesse Ragnhild Kyst** *Region* Antarctica
24C2 **Prins Karls Forland** *I* Svalbard, Norway
70D3 **Prinzapolca** Nicaragua
20E3 **Priozersk** Russian Federation
19F2 **Pripyat'** *R* Belorussia
17E2 **Prispansko Jezero** *L* Yugoslavia
17E2 **Priština** Serbia, Yugoslavia
18C2 **Pritzwalk** Germany
20G5 **Privolzhskaya Vozvyshennost'** *Upland* Russian Federation
17E2 **Prizren** Serbia, Yugoslavia
27E7 **Probolinggo** Indonesia
61E1 **Proctor** USA
44B3 **Proddatūr** India
70D2 **Progreso** Mexico
58B2 **Project City** USA
21G7 **Prokhladnyy** Russian Federation
24K4 **Prokop'yevsk** Russian Federation
21G6 **Proletarskaya** Russian Federation
43H5 **Prome** Burma
75A2 **Promissão** Brazil
19G2 **Pronya** *R* Belorussia
73L6 **Propriá** Brazil
32D3 **Proserpine** Australia
68C1 **Prospect** New York, USA
58B2 **Prospect** Oregon, USA
18D3 **Prostějov** Czechoslovakia
55N2 **Prøven** Greenland
14D3 **Provence** *Region* France

68E2 **Providence** USA
69A4 **Providencia, Isla de** Caribbean Sea
25U3 **Provideniya** Russian Federation
68E1 **Provincetown** USA
13B3 **Provins** France
59D2 **Provo** USA
54G4 **Provost** Canada
75B4 **Prudentópolis** Brazil
54D2 **Prudhoe Bay** USA
55M2 **Prudhoe Land** *Region* Greenland
19E2 **Pruszkow** Poland
19F3 **Prut** *R* Moldavia/ Romania
21D6 **Prutul** *R* Romania
19E2 **Pruzhany** Belorussia
63C1 **Pryor** USA
19E3 **Przemys'l** Poland
17F3 **Psará** *I* Greece
20D4 **Pskov** Russian Federation
19F2 **Ptich** *R* Belorussia
17E2 **Ptolemaïs** Greece
28A3 **Puan** S Korea
72D5 **Pucallpa** Peru
31D4 **Pucheng** China
12K5 **Pudasjärvi** Finland
20F3 **Pudozh** Russian Federation
44B3 **Pudukkottai** India
70C3 **Puebla** Mexico
15A1 **Puebla de Sanabria** Spain
15A1 **Puebla de Trives** Spain
62B1 **Pueblo** USA
73L5 **Puerta do Calcanhar** *Pt* Brazil
47E2 **Puerta do Oro** *Pt* South Africa
75B3 **Puerto Adela** Brazil
74B7 **Puerto Aisén** Chile
70D4 **Puerto Armuelles** Panama
73G6 **Puerto Artur** Brazil
72C3 **Puerto Asis** Colombia
72E2 **Puerto Ayacucho** Venezuela
70D3 **Puerto Barrios** Guatemala
72D2 **Puerto Berrio** Colombia
72E1 **Puerto Cabello** Venezuela
70D3 **Puerto Cabezas** Nicaragua
72E2 **Puerto Carreňo** Colombia
75A3 **Puerto Casado** Brazil
75A3 **Puerto Cooper** Brazil
70D4 **Puerto Cortés** Costa Rica
70D3 **Puerto Cortés** Honduras
48A2 **Puerto del Rosario** Canary Islands
73H8 **Puerto E. Cunha** Brazil
72D1 **Puerto Fijo** Venezuela
73J5 **Puerto Franco** Brazil
75A3 **Puerto Guaraní** Brazil
72E6 **Puerto Heath** Bolivia
70D2 **Puerto Juárez** Mexico
72F1 **Puerto la Cruz** Venezuela
15B2 **Puertollano** Spain
69C4 **Puerto López** Colombia
74D6 **Puerto Madryn** Argentina
72E6 **Puerto Maldonado** Peru
74B6 **Puerto Montt** Chile
73G8 **Puerto Murtinho** Brazil
74B8 **Puerto Natales** Chile
70A1 **Puerto Peñasco** Mexico
75A3 **Puerto Pinasco** Brazil
74D6 **Puerto Pirámides** Argentina
69C3 **Puerto Plata** Dominican Republic
74F3 **Puerto Presidente Stroessner** Brazil
27E6 **Puerto Princesa** Philippines
72C3 **Puerto Rico** Colombia
69D3 **Puerto Rico** *I* Caribbean Sea
69D3 **Puerto Rico Trench** Caribbean Sea
73H4 **Puerto Santana** Brazil
75A3 **Puerto Sastre** Brazil
74E1 **Puerto Suárez** Bolivia
70B2 **Puerto Vallarta** Mexico
74B6 **Puerto Varas** Chile
72F7 **Puerto Villarroel** Bolivia
21H5 **Pugachev** Russian Federation
42C3 **Pūgal** India
15C1 **Puigcerdá** Spain
28A2 **Pujŏn** N Korea
28A2 **Pujŏn Res** N Korea
35B2 **Pukaki,L** *L* New Zealand
28A2 **Pukchin** N Korea
28B2 **Pukch'ŏng** N Korea
35B1 **Pukekohe** New Zealand
35B2 **Puketeraki Range** *Mts* New Zealand
20G3 **Puksoozero** Russian Federation
16C2 **Pula** Croatia
65D2 **Pulaski** New York, USA
67A1 **Pulaski** Tennessee, USA
64C3 **Pulaski** Virginia, USA

Pulau Kolepom Razim


27G7 **Pulau Kolepom** *I* Indonesia
27C7 **Pulau Pulau Batu** *Is* Indonesia
**Pulau Pulau Macan - Kepulauan = Takabonerate**
19E2 **Puławy** Poland
44C3 **Pulicat L** India
42B1 **Pul-i-Khumri** Afghanistan
44B4 **Puliyangudi** India
58C1 **Pullman** USA
27G6 **Pulo Anna** *I* Pacific Ocean
12L5 **Pulozero** Russian Federation
19E2 **Pułtusk** Poland
74C3 **Puna de Atacama** Argentina
72B4 **Puná, Isla** Ecuador
43F3 **Punakha** Bhutan
42C2 **Pūnch** Pakistan
47E1 **Punda Milia** South Africa
44A2 **Pune** India
28A2 **Pungsan** N Korea
28A2 **Pungso** N Korea
50C4 **Punia** Zaïre
74B4 **Punitaqui** Chile
42C2 **Punjab** *Province* Pakistan
42D2 **Punjab** *State* India
72D7 **Puno** Peru
74D5 **Punta Alta** Argentina
74B8 **Punta Arenas** Chile
59C4 **Punta Banda, Cabo** *C* Mexico
74F4 **Punta del Este** Uruguay
70D3 **Punta Gorda** Belize
67B3 **Punta Gorda** USA
72B1 **Puntarenas** Costa Rica
31C4 **Puqi** China
24J3 **Pur** *R* Russian Federation
72C3 **Purace, Vol** Colombia
63C1 **Purcell** USA
62B1 **Purgatoire** *R* USA
43F5 **Puri** India
44B2 **Pūrna** India
43F3 **Pūrnia** India
30C3 **Pursat** Cambodia
72F4 **Purus** *R* Brazil
63E2 **Purvis** USA
27D7 **Purwokerto** Indonesia
28B2 **Puryŏng** N Korea
42D5 **Pusad** India
28B3 **Pusan** S Korea
20E4 **Pushkin** Russian Federation
20F3 **Pushlakhta** Russian Federation
19F1 **Pustoshka** Russian Federation
43H3 **Putao** Burma
35C1 **Putaruru** New Zealand
31D4 **Putian** China
27E7 **Puting, Tanjung** *C* Indonesia
68E2 **Putnam** USA
68D1 **Putney** USA
44B4 **Puttalam** Sri Lanka
18C2 **Puttgarden** Germany
72C4 **Putumayo** *R* Colombia/ Ecuador/Peru
27E6 **Putussiban** Indonesia
12K6 **Puulavesi** *L* Finland
58B1 **Puyallup** USA
35A3 **Puysegur Pt** New Zealand
51C4 **Pweto** Zaïre
7B3 **Pwllheli** Wales
20F3 **Pyal'ma** Russian Federation
20E2 **Pyaozero, Ozero** *L* Russian Federation
30B2 **Pyapon** Burma
25K2 **Pyasina** *R* Russian Federation
21G7 **Pyatigorsk** Russian Federation
12K6 **Pyhäselkä** *L* Finland
30B2 **Pyinmana** Burma
28A2 **Pyŏktong** N Korea
28A3 **Pyonggang** N Korea
28A3 **Pyŏnggok-dong** S Korea
28A3 **P'yŏngsan** N Korea
28A3 **P'yŏngt'aek** S Korea
28B3 **P'yŏngyang** N Korea
34B3 **Pyramid Hill** Australia
59C2 **Pyramid L** USA
35A2 **Pyramid,Mt** New Zealand
14B3 **Pyrénées** *Mts* France/ Spain
19F1 **Pytalovo** Russian Federation
30B2 **Pyu** Burma

## Q

45D4 **Qa'ash Shubyk, Wadi** Jordan
45C2 **Qabatiya** Israel
45D3 **Qā'el Hafīra** *Mud Flats* Jordan
45D3 **Qa'el Jinz** *Mud Flats* Jordan
55O3 **Qagssimiut** Greenland
26C3 **Qaidam Pendi** *Salt Flat* China
45D2 **Qa Khanna** *Salt Marsh* Jordan
50D2 **Qala'en Nahl** Sudan
42B2 **Qalat** Afghanistan
45D1 **Qal'at al Ḥiṣn** Syria
45C1 **Qal'at al Marqab** *Hist Site* Syria
50E2 **Qal'at Bīshah** Saudi Arabia
41E3 **Qal'at Sālih** Iraq
26C3 **Qamdo** Tibet, China
**Qaqortoq = Julianehåb**
50E2 **Qandala** Somalia
49E2 **Qara** Egypt
50E3 **Qardho** Somalia
21H8 **Qareh Dāgh** *Mts* Iran
41E4 **Qaryat al Ulyā** Saudi Arabia
45C3 **Qasr ed Deir, Jebel** *Mt* Jordan
45D3 **Qasr el Kharana** Jordan
41E3 **Qāṣr e Shīrīn** Iran
49E2 **Qasr Farâfra** Egypt
45D2 **Qaṭanā** Syria
41F4 **Qatar** *Emirate* Arabian Pen
45C4 **Qatim, Jebel** *Mt* Jordan
45D3 **Qatrāna** Jordan
49E2 **Qattâra Depression** Egypt
41G3 **Qāyen** Iran
41F2 **Qazvīn** Iran
40B4 **Qena** Egypt
**Qeqertarsuaq = Julianehåb**
41E2 **Qeydār** Iran
41F4 **Qeys** *I* Iran
21H8 **Qezel Owzan** *R* Iran
45C3 **Qeziot** Israel
31B5 **Qian Jiang** *R* China
31E1 **Qian Shan** *Upland* China
31E3 **Qidong** China
31B4 **Qijiang** China
26C2 **Qijiaojing** China
42B2 **Qila Saifullah** Pakistan
31A2 **Qilian** China
26C3 **Qilian Shan** China
25L6 **Qilian Shan** *Mts* China
31B3 **Qin'an** China
31E2 **Qingdao** China
28A3 **Qingduizi** China
31A2 **Qinghai** *Province* China
26C3 **Qinghai Hu** *L* China
31D3 **Qingjiang** Jiangsu, China
31D4 **Qingjiang** Jiangxi, China
31B3 **Qing Jiang** *R* China
31C2 **Qingshuihe** China
31B2 **Qingshui He** *R* China
31B2 **Qingtongxia** China
31B2 **Qingyang** China
28A2 **Qingyuan** China
31D4 **Qingyuan** Zhejiang, China
39G2 **Qing Zang** *Upland* China
31B5 **Qingzhou** China
31D2 **Qinhuangdao** China
31B3 **Qin Ling** *Mts* China
30D1 **Qinzhou** China
30E2 **Qionghai** China
31A3 **Qionglai Shan** *Upland* China
30D1 **Qiongzhou Haixia** *Str* China
26F2 **Qiqihar** China
45C3 **Qîraîya, Wadi** Egypt
45C2 **Qiryat Ata** Israel
45C3 **Qiryat Gat** Israel
45C2 **Qiryat Shemona** Israel
45C2 **Qiryat Yam** Israel
45C2 **Qishon** *R* Israel
25K5 **Qitai** China
31C4 **Qiyang** China
31B1 **Qog Qi** China
41F2 **Qolleh-ye Damavand** *Mt* Iran
41F3 **Qom** Iran
41F3 **Qomisheh** Iran
**Qomolangma Feng** *Mt* **= Everest,Mt**
45D1 **Qornet es Saouda** *Mt* Lebanon
55N3 **Qôrnoq** Greenland
41E2 **Qorveh** Iran
41G4 **Qotbābad** Iran
21H8 **Qotur** *R* Iran
68D1 **Quabbin Res** USA
47C2 **Quaggablat** South Africa
13D1 **Quakenbrück** Germany
68C2 **Quakertown** USA
30C3 **Quam Phu Quoc** *I* Vietnam
62C2 **Quanah** USA
30D2 **Quang Ngai** Vietnam
30D2 **Quang Tri** Vietnam
30D4 **Quan Long** Vietnam
31D5 **Quanzhou** Fujian, China
31C4 **Quanzhou** Guangxi, China
54H4 **Qu' Appelle** *R* Canada
59D4 **Quartzsite** USA
41G2 **Quchan** Iran
34C3 **Queanbeyan** Australia
65E1 **Québec** Canada
55L4 **Quebec** *Province* Canada
75C2 **Quebra-Anzol** *R* Brazil
74F3 **Quedas do Iguaçu** *Falls* Argentina/Brazil
68C3 **Queen Anne** USA
54E4 **Queen Charlotte Is** Canada
54F4 **Queen Charlotte Sd** Canada
54F4 **Queen Charlotte Str** Canada
54H1 **Queen Elizabeth Is** Canada
76F9 **Queen Mary Land** *Region* Antarctica
54H3 **Queen Maud G** Canada
76E6 **Queen Maud Mts** Antarctica
68D2 **Queens** *Borough* New York, USA
27F8 **Queen's Ch** Australia
34B3 **Queenscliff** Australia
32D3 **Queensland** *State* Australia
34C4 **Queenstown** Australia
35A3 **Queenstown** New Zealand
47D3 **Queenstown** South Africa
68B3 **Queenstown** USA
51B4 **Quela** Angola
51D5 **Quelimane** Mozambique
62A2 **Quemado** USA
70B2 **Querétaro** Mexico
42B2 **Quetta** Pakistan
70C3 **Quezaltenango** Guatemala
27F5 **Quezon City** Philippines
51B5 **Quibala** Angola
51B4 **Quibaxe** Angola
72C2 **Quibdó** Colombia
14B2 **Quiberon** France
51B4 **Quicama Nat Pk** Angola
75A4 **Quiindy** Paraguay
72D6 **Quillabamba** Peru
72E7 **Quillacollo** Bolivia
14C3 **Quillan** France
54H4 **Quill Lakes** Canada
74B4 **Quillota** Chile
34B1 **Quilpie** Australia
51B4 **Quimbele** Angola
14B2 **Quimper** France
14B2 **Quimperlé** France
59B3 **Quincy** California, USA
64A3 **Quincy** Illinois, USA
68E1 **Quincy** Massachusetts, USA
30D3 **Qui Nhon** Vietnam
15B2 **Quintanar de la Orden** Spain
51B5 **Quirima** Angola
34D2 **Quirindi** Australia
51E5 **Quissanga** Mozambique
51D6 **Quissico** Mozambique
72C4 **Quito** Ecuador
73L4 **Quixadá** Brazil
31A4 **Qujing** China
47D3 **Qumbu** South Africa
32C4 **Quorn** Australia
40B4 **Qus** Egypt
40B4 **Quseir** Egypt
55N3 **Qutdligssat** Greenland
**Quthing = Moyeni**
31B3 **Qu Xian** Sichuan, China
31D4 **Qu Xian** Zhejiang, China
30D2 **Quynh Luu** Vietnam
31C2 **Quzhou** China
43G3 **Qūzū** China

## R

12J6 **Raahe** Finland
8B3 **Raasay** *I* Scotland
8B3 **Raasay,Sound of** *Chan* Scotland
50F2 **Raas Caseyr** Somalia
16C2 **Rab** *I* Croatia
27E7 **Raba** Indonesia
18D3 **Rába** *R* Hungary
48B1 **Rabat** Morocco
32E1 **Rabaul** Papua New Guinea
45C3 **Rabba** Jordan
40C5 **Rābigh** Saudi Arabia
55N5 **Race,C** Canada
68E1 **Race Pt** USA
45C2 **Rachaya** Lebanon
18C3 **Rachel** *Mt* Germany
30D3 **Rach Gia** Vietnam
64B2 **Racine** USA
19F3 **Rădăuți** Romania
64B3 **Radcliff** USA
64C3 **Radford** USA
42C4 **Radhanpur** India
69L1 **Radix,Pt** Trinidad
19E2 **Radom** Poland
19D2 **Radomsko** Poland
19F2 **Radomyshl'** Ukraine
18C3 **Radstad** Austria
19E1 **Radviliškis** Lithuania
54G3 **Rae** Canada
43E3 **Rāe Bareli** India
55K3 **Rae Isthmus** Canada
54G3 **Rae L** Canada
35C1 **Raetihi** New Zealand
74D4 **Rafaela** Argentina
45C3 **Rafah** Egypt
50C3 **Rafai** Central African Republic
41D3 **Rafhā** Saudi Arabia
41G3 **Rafsanjān** Iran
50C3 **Raga** Sudan
69Q2 **Ragged Pt** Barbados
16C3 **Ragusa** Sicily, Italy
50D2 **Rahad** *R* Sudan
42C3 **Rahimyar Khan** Pakistan
41F3 **Rāhjerd** Iran
44B2 **Rāichur** India
43E4 **Raigarh** India
34B3 **Rainbow** Australia
67A2 **Rainbow City** USA
58B1 **Rainier** USA
58B1 **Rainier,Mt** USA
61E1 **Rainy** *R* Canada/USA
55J5 **Rainy L** Canada
61E1 **Rainy L** Canada/USA
61E1 **Rainy River** Canada
43E4 **Raipur** India
44C2 **Rājahmundry** India
27E6 **Rajang** *R* Malaysia
42C3 **Rajanpur** Pakistan
44B4 **Rājapālaiyam** India
42C3 **Rājasthān** *State* India
42D4 **Rājgarh** Madhya Pradesh, India
42D3 **Rājgarh** Rājasthān, India
42C4 **Rājkot** India
43F4 **Rājmahāl Hills** India
43E4 **Raj Nāndgaon** India
42C4 **Rājpīpla** India
43F4 **Rajshahi** Bangladesh
42D4 **Rājur** India
35B2 **Rakaia** *R* New Zealand
39G3 **Raka Zangbo** *R* China
19E3 **Rakhov** Ukraine
42A3 **Rakhshan** *R* Pakistan
47C1 **Rakops** Botswana
19F2 **Rakov** Belorussia
67C1 **Raleigh** USA
45C4 **Ram** Jordan
45C2 **Rama** Israel
75D1 **Ramalho, Serra do** *Mts* Brazil
45C3 **Ramallah** Israel
44B4 **Rāmanāthapuram** India
26H3 **Ramapo Deep** Pacific Ocean
45C2 **Ramat Gan** Israel
13D3 **Rambervillers** France
14C2 **Rambouillet** France
43F4 **Rāmgarh** Bihār, India
42C3 **Rāmgarh** Rājasthān, India
41E3 **Rāmhormoz** Iran
45C4 **Ram, Jebel** *Mt* Jordan
45C3 **Ramla** Israel
59C4 **Ramona** USA
42D3 **Rāmpur** India
42D4 **Rāmpura** India
43G5 **Ramree I** Burma
21J8 **Rāmsar** Iran
6B2 **Ramsey** Isle of Man, British Isles
68C2 **Ramsey** USA
7B4 **Ramsey I** Wales
7E4 **Ramsgate** England
45D2 **Ramtha** Jordan
32D1 **Ramu** *R* Papua New Guinea
27E6 **Ranau** Malaysia
74B4 **Rancagua** Chile
60B2 **Ranchester** USA
43F4 **Rānchi** India
43E4 **Rānchi Plat** India
74B6 **Ranco, Lago** Chile
47D2 **Randburg** South Africa
12F7 **Randers** Denmark
47D2 **Randfontein** South Africa
65E2 **Randolph** Vermont, USA
66D3 **Randsburg** USA
35B3 **Ranfurly** New Zealand
43G4 **Rangamati** Bangladesh
60B2 **Rangely** USA
35B2 **Rangiora** New Zealand
35C1 **Rangitaiki** *R* New Zealand
35B2 **Rangitata** *R* New Zealand
35C1 **Rangitikei** *R* New Zealand
30B2 **Rangoon** Burma
43F3 **Rangpur** Bangladesh
44B3 **Rānībennur** India
43F4 **Rānīganj** India
55J3 **Rankin Inlet** Canada
34C2 **Rankins Springs** Australia
8C3 **Rannoch, Loch** *L* Scotland
42B4 **Rann of Kachchh** *Flood Area* India
30B4 **Ranong** Thailand
27C6 **Rantauparapat** Indonesia
27F7 **Rantekombola, G** *Mt* Indonesia
64B2 **Rantoul** USA
75B1 **Ranuro** *R* Brazil
13D3 **Raon-l'Etape** France
33H3 **Raoul** *I* Pacific Ocean
16B2 **Rapallo** Italy
55M3 **Raper,C** Canada
60C2 **Rapid City** USA
64B1 **Rapid River** USA
65D3 **Rappahannock** *R* USA
43M2 **Rapti** *R* India
68C2 **Raritan B** USA
40C5 **Ras Abû Dâra** *C* Egypt
40C5 **Ra's Abu Madd** *C* Saudi Arabia
50D1 **Ras Abu Shagara** *C* Sudan
40D2 **Ra's al 'Ayn** Syria
41G4 **Ras al Khaimah** UAE
38D4 **Ra's al Madrakah** *C* Oman
50E2 **Ras Andadda** *C* Ethiopia
41E4 **Ra's az Zawr** *C* Saudi Arabia
40C5 **Râs Banâs** *C* Egypt
45B3 **Râs Burûn** *C* Egypt
50D2 **Ras Dashan** *Mt* Ethiopia
41E3 **Ra's-e Barkan** *Pt* Iran
45A3 **Râs el Barr** *C* Egypt
16B3 **Ras El Hadid** Algeria
40A3 **Râs el Kenâyis** *Pt* Egypt
45C4 **Râs el Nafas** *Mt* Egypt
45B4 **Râs el Sudr** *C* Egypt
45C4 **Ras en Naqb** *Upland* Jordan
38D4 **Ra's Fartak** *C* Yemen
40B4 **Râs Ghârib** Egypt
50D2 **Rashad** Sudan
45C3 **Rashādīya** Jordan
40B3 **Rashîd** Egypt
41E2 **Rasht** Iran
45C1 **Ra's ibn Hāni'** *C* Syria
50E2 **Ras Khanzira** *C* Somalia
42B3 **Ras Koh** *Mt* Pakistan
45B4 **Râs Matarma** *C* Egypt
40B4 **Râs Muhammad** *C* Egypt
48A2 **Ras Nouadhibou** *C* Mauritius/Morocco
26J2 **Rasshua** *I* Kuril Is, Russian Federation
21G5 **Rasskazovo** Russian Federation
41E4 **Ra's Tanāqib** *C* Saudi Arabia
41F4 **Ra's Tannūrah** Saudi Arabia
18B3 **Rastatt** Germany
**Ras Uarc = Tres Forcas, Cabo**
45C4 **Ras Um Seisabān** *Mt* Jordan
50E2 **Ras Xaafuun** *C* Somalia
42C3 **Ratangarh** India
30B3 **Rat Buri** Thailand
42D3 **Rāth** India
18C2 **Rathenow** Germany
9C2 **Rathfriland** Northern Ireland
9C2 **Rathlin I** Northern Ireland
9C2 **Rathmelton** Irish Republic
45D4 **Ratiyah, Wadi** Jordan
42C4 **Ratlām** India
44A2 **Ratnāgiri** India
44C4 **Ratnapura** Sri Lanka
19E2 **Ratno** Ukraine
62B1 **Raton** USA
12H6 **Rättvik** Sweden
35C1 **Raukumara Range** *Mts* New Zealand
75D3 **Raul Soares** Brazil
12J6 **Rauma** Finland
43E4 **Raurkela** India
41E3 **Ravānsar** Iran
41G3 **Rāvar** Iran
19E2 **Rava Russkaya** Ukraine
68D1 **Ravena** USA
16C2 **Ravenna** Italy
18B3 **Ravensburg** Germany
32D2 **Ravenshoe** Australia
6E2 **Ravenspurn** *Oilfield* N Sea
42C2 **Ravi** *R* Pakistan
55Q3 **Ravn Kap** *C* Greenland
42C2 **Rawalpindi** Pakistan
41D2 **Rawāndiz** Iraq
18D2 **Rawicz** Poland
32B4 **Rawlinna** Australia
56C2 **Rawlins** USA
74D6 **Rawson** Argentina
6C3 **Rawtenstall** England
44B3 **Rāyadurg** India
44C2 **Rāyagada** India
45D2 **Rayak** Lebanon
55N5 **Ray,C** Canada
41G4 **Rāyen** Iran
66C2 **Raymond** California, USA
58D1 **Raymond** Canada
68E1 **Raymond** New Hampshire, USA
58B1 **Raymond** Washington, USA
34D2 **Raymond Terrace** Australia
63C3 **Raymondville** USA
41E2 **Razan** Iran
19G3 **Razdel'naya** Ukraine
28C2 **Razdol'noye** Russian Federation
17F2 **Razgrad** Bulgaria
17F2 **Razim** *L* Romania

**Salem** **São João do Paraíso**


68D1 **Salem** New York, USA
58B2 **Salem** Oregon, USA
64C3 **Salem** Virginia, USA
12G6 **Sälen** Sweden
16C2 **Salerno** Italy
7C3 **Salford** England
17D1 **Salgót** Hungary
19D3 **Salgótarján** Hungary
73L5 **Salgueiro** Brazil
60B3 **Salida** USA
17F3 **Salihli** Turkey
51D5 **Salima** Malawi
61D3 **Salina** Kansas, USA
59D3 **Salina** Utah, USA
16C3 **Salina** *I* Italy
70C3 **Salina Cruz** Mexico
75D2 **Salinas** Brazil
66B2 **Salinas** USA
66B2 **Salinas** *R* USA
15C2 **Salinas, Cabo de** *C* Spain
74D3 **Salinas Grandes** *Salt Pans* Argentina
62A2 **Salinas Peak** *Mt* USA
63D2 **Saline** *R* Arkansas, USA
60C3 **Saline** *R* Kansas, USA
69M2 **Salines,Pt** Grenada
66D2 **Saline V** USA
73J4 **Salinópolis** Brazil
**Salisbury = Harare**
7D4 **Salisbury** England
65D3 **Salisbury** Maryland, USA
67B1 **Salisbury** North Carolina, USA
55L3 **Salisbury I** Canada
7D4 **Salisbury Plain** England
45D2 **Şalkhad** Syria
12K5 **Salla** Finland
63D1 **Sallisaw** USA
55L3 **Salluit** Canada
43E3 **Sallyana** Nepal
41D2 **Salmas** Iran
12L6 **Salmi** Russian Federation
58C1 **Salmo** Canada
58D1 **Salmon** USA
58C1 **Salmon** *R* USA
54G4 **Salmon Arm** Canada
58C1 **Salmon River Mts** USA
12J6 **Salo** Finland
14D3 **Salon-de-Provence** France
**Salonica = Thessaloníki**
17E1 **Salonta** Romania
12K6 **Salpausselkä** *Region* Finland
21G6 **Sal'sk** Russian Federation
45C2 **Salt** Jordan
47C3 **Salt** *R* South Africa
59D4 **Salt** *R* USA
74C2 **Salta** Argentina
74C2 **Salta** *State* Argentina
7B4 **Saltash** England
9C3 **Saltee, I** Irish Republic
70B2 **Saltillo** Mexico
58D2 **Salt Lake City** USA
72D3 **Salto Angostura** *Waterfall* Colombia
75E2 **Salto da Divisa** Brazil
75B3 **Salto das Sete Quedas** Brazil
72F2 **Salto del Angel** *Waterfall* Venezuela
74E2 **Salto del Guaíra** *Waterfall* Brazil
72D4 **Salto Grande** *Waterfall* Colombia
59C4 **Salton S** USA
75B4 **Saltos do Iguaçu** *Waterfall* Argentina
74E4 **Salto Tacuarembó** Uruguay
42C2 **Salt Range** *Mts* Pakistan
69H2 **Salt River** Jamaica
67B2 **Saluda** USA
44C2 **Sālūr** India
73L6 **Salvador** Brazil
63D3 **Salvador,L** USA
41F5 **Salwah** Qatar
30B1 **Salween** *R* Burma
21H8 **Sal'yany** Azerbaijan
64C3 **Salyersville** USA
18C3 **Salzburg** Austria
18C2 **Salzgitter** Germany
18C2 **Salzwedel** Germany
26C1 **Samagaltay** Russian Federation
69D3 **Samaná** Dominican Republic
40C2 **Samandaği** Turkey
42B1 **Samangan** Afghanistan
29D2 **Samani** Japan
45A3 **Samannûd** Egypt
27F5 **Samar** *I* Philippines
20J5 **Samara** Russian Federation
32E2 **Samarai** Papua New Guinea
27E7 **Samarinda** Indonesia
38E2 **Samarkand** Uzbekistan
41D3 **Sāmarrā'** Iraq
43E4 **Sambalpur** India
27D6 **Sambas** Indonesia
51F5 **Sambava** Madagascar
42D3 **Sambhal** India
19E3 **Sambor** Ukraine
13B2 **Sambre** *R* France
28B3 **Samch'ŏk** S Korea
28A4 **Samch'ŏnp'o** S Korea
28A3 **Samdŭng** N Korea
50D4 **Same** Tanzania
51C5 **Samfya** Zambia
30B1 **Samka** Burma
30C1 **Sam Neua** Laos
33H2 **Samoan Is** Pacific Ocean
17F3 **Sámos** *I* Greece
17F2 **Samothráki** *I* Greece
27E7 **Sampit** Indonesia
63D2 **Sam Rayburn Res** USA
30C3 **Samrong** Cambodia
18C1 **Samsø** *I* Denmark
28A2 **Samsu** N Korea
40C1 **Samsun** Turkey
48B3 **San** Mali
30D3 **San** *R* Cambodia
19E2 **San** *R* Poland
50E2 **San'ā** Yemen
50B3 **Sanaga** *R* Cameroon
74C4 **San Agustín** Argentina
52D6 **San Ambrosia, Isla** Pacific Ocean
41E2 **Sanandaj** Iran
66B1 **San Andreas** USA
69A4 **San Andres, Isla de** Caribbean Sea
62A2 **San Andres Mts** USA
70C3 **San Andrés Tuxtla** Mexico
62B2 **San Angelo** USA
16B3 **San Antioco** Sardinia, Italy
16B3 **San Antioco** *I* Sardinia, Italy
56B4 **San Antonia, Pt** Mexico
74B4 **San Antonio** Chile
62A2 **San Antonio** New Mexico, USA
62C3 **San Antonio** Texas, USA
66B2 **San Antonio** *R* California, USA
63C3 **San Antonio** *R* Texas, USA
15C2 **San Antonio Abad** Spain
69A2 **San Antonio, Cabo** *C* Cuba
62B2 **San Antonio de Bravo** Mexico
69A2 **San Antonio de los Banos** Cuba
66D3 **San Antonio,Mt** USA
74D6 **San Antonio Oeste** Argentina
66B3 **San Antonio Res** USA
66B2 **San Ardo** USA
42D4 **Sanāwad** India
70A3 **San Benedicto** *I* Mexico
63C3 **San Benito** USA
66B2 **San Benito** *R* USA
66B2 **San Benito Mt** USA
66D3 **San Bernardino** USA
74B4 **San Bernardo** Chile
59C4 **San Bernardo Mts** USA
67A3 **San Blas,C** USA
70E4 **San Blas, Puerta** *Pt* Panama
74E3 **San Borja** Brazil
74B5 **San Carlos** Chile
72B1 **San Carlos** Nicaragua
59D4 **San Carlos** USA
74B6 **San Carlos de Bariloche** Argentina
20H4 **Sanchursk** Russian Federation
66D4 **San Clemente** USA
59C4 **San Clemente I** USA
70C3 **San Cristóbal** Mexico
72D2 **San Cristóbal** Venezuela
33F2 **San Cristobal** *I* Solomon Islands
70E2 **Sancti Spíritus** Cuba
14C2 **Sancy, Puy de** *Mt* France
47D1 **Sand** *R* South Africa
8C4 **Sanda, I** Scotland
27E6 **Sandakan** Malaysia
8D2 **Sanday** *I* Scotland
62B2 **Sanderson** USA
7E4 **Sandgate** England
59C4 **San Diego** USA
74C8 **San Diego, Cabo** Argentina
40B2 **Sandikli** Turkey
43E3 **Sandīla** India
12F7 **Sandnes** Norway
12G5 **Sandnessjøen** Norway
51C4 **Sandoa** Zaïre
19E2 **Sandomierz** Poland
43G5 **Sandoway** Burma
7D4 **Sandown** England
12D3 **Sandoy** *I* Faeroes
58C1 **Sandpoint** USA
63C1 **Sand Springs** USA
32A3 **Sandstone** Australia
61E1 **Sandstone** USA
31C4 **Sandu** China
64C2 **Sandusky** USA
12H6 **Sandviken** Sweden
68E2 **Sandwich** USA
55J4 **Sandy L** Canada
75A3 **San Estanislao** Paraguay
56B3 **San Felipe** Baja Cal, Mexico
74B4 **San Felipe** Chile
69D4 **San Felipe** Venezuela
15C1 **San Felíu de Guixols** Spain
52D6 **San Felix, Isla** Pacific Ocean
74B4 **San Fernando** Chile
27F5 **San Fernando** Philippines
15A2 **San Fernando** Spain
69L2 **San Fernando** Trinidad
66C3 **San Fernando** USA
72E2 **San Fernando** Venezuela
67B3 **Sanford** Florida, USA
65E2 **Sanford** Maine, USA
67C1 **Sanford** N Carolina, USA
57E4 **Sanford** USA
54D3 **Sanford, Mt** USA
74D4 **San Francisco** Argentina
69C3 **San Francisco** Dominican Republic
66A2 **San Francisco** USA
66A2 **San Francisco B** USA
70B2 **San Francisco del Oro** Mexico
66D3 **San Gabriel Mts** USA
42C5 **Sangamner** India
64B3 **Sangamon** *R* USA
25O3 **Sangar** Russian Federation
44B2 **Sangāreddi** India
66C2 **Sanger** USA
31C2 **Sanggan He** *R* China
27E6 **Sanggau** Indonesia
50B3 **Sangha** *R* Congo
42B3 **Sanghar** Pakistan
27F6 **Sangir** *I* Indonesia
27F6 **Sangir, Kepulauan** *Is* Indonesia
30B3 **Sangkhla Buri** Thailand
27E6 **Sangkulirang** Indonesia
44A2 **Sāngli** India
50B3 **Sangmélima** Cameroon
56B3 **San Gorgonio Mt** USA
62A1 **Sangre de Cristo Mts** USA
66A2 **San Gregorio** USA
42D2 **Sangrūr** India
47E1 **Sangutane** *R* Mozambique
74E3 **San Ignacio** Argentina
72D2 **San Jacinto** Colombia
59C4 **San Jacinto Peak** *Mt* USA
28A2 **Sanjiangkou** China
29D3 **Sanjō** Japan
74H2 **San João del Rei** Brazil
66B2 **San Joaquin** *R* USA
66B2 **San Joaquin Valley** USA
62B1 **San Jon** USA
74C7 **San Jorge, Golfo** *G* Argentina
15C1 **San Jorge, Golfo de** *G* Spain
72B1 **San José** Costa Rica
70C3 **San José** Guatemala
66B2 **San Jose** USA
56B4 **San José** *I* Mexico
72F7 **San José de Chiquitos** Bolivia
56C4 **San José del Cabo** Mexico
74G2 **San José do Rio Prêto** Brazil
70B2 **San Joseé del Cabo** Mexico
28A3 **Sanju** S Korea
74C4 **San Juan** Argentina
69D3 **San Juan** Puerto Rico
69L1 **San Juan** Trinidad
72E2 **San Juan** Venezuela
69B2 **San Juan** *Mt* Cuba
66B3 **San Juan** *R* California, USA
70D3 **San Juan** *R* Costa Rica/Nicaragua
59D3 **San Juan** *R* Utah, USA
74C4 **San Juan** *State* Argentina
74E3 **San Juan Bautista** Paraguay
66B2 **San Juan Bautista** USA
70D3 **San Juan del Norte** Nicaragua
69D4 **San Juan de los Cayos** Venezuela
70D3 **San Juan del Sur** Nicaragua
58B1 **San Juan Is** USA
62A1 **San Juan Mts** USA
74C7 **San Julián** Argentina
50C4 **Sankuru** *R* Zaïre
66A2 **San Leandro** USA
40C2 **Sanliurfa** Turkey
72C3 **San Lorenzo** Colombia
72B4 **San Lorenzo, Cabo** *C* Ecuador
15B1 **San Lorenzo de Escorial** Spain
66B2 **San Lucas** USA
74C4 **San Luis** Argentina
59D4 **San Luis** USA
74C4 **San Luis** *State* Argentina
66B2 **San Luis Canal** USA
66B3 **San Luis Obispo** USA
66B3 **San Luis Obispo B** USA
70B2 **San Luis Potosí** Mexico
66B2 **San Luis Res** USA
16B3 **Sanluri** Sardinia, Italy
72E2 **San Maigualida** *Mts* Venezuela
63C3 **San Marcos** USA
76G3 **San Martin** *Base* Antarctica
74B7 **San Martin, Lago** Argentina/Chile
66A2 **San Mateo** USA
73G7 **San Matías** Bolivia
74D6 **San Matías, Golfo** *G* Argentina
31C3 **Sanmenxia** China
70D3 **San Miguel** El Salvador
66B3 **San Miguel** USA
66B3 **San Miguel** *I* USA
74C3 **San Miguel de Tucumán** Argentina
74F3 **San Miguel d'Oeste** Brazil
31D4 **Sanming** China
74D4 **San Nicolas** Argentina
56B3 **San Nicolas** *I* USA
47D2 **Sannieshof** South Africa
48B4 **Sanniquellie** Liberia
19E3 **Sanok** Poland
69B5 **San Onofore** Colombia
66D4 **San Onofre** USA
27F5 **San Pablo** Philippines
66A1 **San Pablo B** USA
48B4 **San Pédro** Ivory Coast
74D2 **San Pedro** Jujuy, Argentina
74E2 **San Pedro** Paraguay
59D4 **San Pedro** *R* USA
66C4 **San Pedro Chan** USA
56C4 **San Pedro de los Colonias** Mexico
70D3 **San Pedro Sula** Honduras
16B3 **San Pietro** *I* Sardinia, Italy
8D4 **Sanquar** Scotland
70A1 **San Quintin** Mexico
74C4 **San Rafael** Argentina
66A2 **San Rafael** USA
66C3 **San Rafael Mts** USA
16B2 **San Remo** Italy
62C2 **San Saba** *R* USA
71B2 **San Salvador** El Salvador
69C2 **San Salvador** *I* The Bahamas
74C2 **San Salvador de Jujuy** Argentina
15B1 **San Sebastián** Spain
16D2 **San Severo** Italy
66B3 **San Simeon** USA
72E7 **Santa Ana** Bolivia
70C3 **Santa Ana** Guatemala
66D4 **Santa Ana** USA
66D4 **Santa Ana Mts** USA
62C2 **Santa Anna** USA
70B2 **Santa Barbara** Mexico
66C3 **Santa Barbara** USA
66C4 **Santa Barbara** *I* USA
66B3 **Santa Barbara Chan** USA
66C3 **Santa Barbara Res** USA
66C4 **Santa Catalina** *I* USA
66C4 **Santa Catalina,G of** USA
74F3 **Santa Catarina** *State* Brazil
74G3 **Santa Catarina, Isla de** Brazil
69B2 **Santa Clara** Cuba
66B2 **Santa Clara** USA
66C3 **Santa Clara** *R* USA
74C8 **Santa Cruz** Argentina
72F7 **Santa Cruz** Bolivia
27F5 **Santa Cruz** Philippines
66A2 **Santa Cruz** USA
66C4 **Santa Cruz** *I* USA
59D4 **Santa Cruz** *R* USA
74B7 **Santa Cruz** *State* Argentina
75E2 **Santa Cruz Cabrália** Brazil
66C3 **Santa Cruz Chan** USA
48A2 **Santa Cruz de la Palma** Canary Islands
69B2 **Santa Cruz del Sur** Cuba
48A2 **Santa Cruz de Tenerife** Canary Islands
51C5 **Santa Cruz do Cuando** Angola
75C3 **Santa Cruz do Rio Pardo** Brazil
33F2 **Santa Cruz Is** Solomon Islands
66A2 **Santa Cruz Mts** USA
72F3 **Santa Elena** Venezuela
74D4 **Santa Fe** Argentina
62A1 **Santa Fe** USA
74D3 **Santa Fe** *State* Argentina
75B2 **Santa Helena de Goiás** Brazil
31B3 **Santai** China
74B8 **Santa Inés** *I* Chile
33E1 **Santa Isabel** *I* Solomon Islands
66B2 **Santa Lucia Range** *Mts* USA
48A4 **Santa Luzia** *I* Cape Verde
66B3 **Santa Margarita** USA
66D4 **Santa Margarita** *R* USA
70A2 **Santa Margarita, Isla** Mexico
74F3 **Santa Maria** Brazil
66B3 **Santa Maria** USA
48A1 **Santa Maria** *I* Azores
62A2 **Santa María** *R* Chihuahua, Mexico
47E2 **Santa Maria, Cabo de** *C* Mozambique
75D1 **Santa Maria da Vitória** Brazil
17D3 **Santa Maria di Leuca, Capo** *C* Italy
62A2 **Santa María Laguna de** *L* Mexico
69C4 **Santa Marta** Colombia
72D1 **Santa Marta, Sierra Nevada de** *Mts* Colombia
66C3 **Santa Monica** USA
66C4 **Santa Monica B** USA
75D1 **Santana** Brazil
74E4 **Santana do Livramento** Brazil
72C3 **Santander** Colombia
15B1 **Santander** Spain
15C2 **Santañy** Spain
66C3 **Santa Paula** USA
73K4 **Santa Quitéria** Brazil
73H4 **Santarém** Brazil
15A2 **Santarém** Portugal
75B2 **Santa Rita do Araguaia** Brazil
74D5 **Santa Rosa** Argentina
66A1 **Santa Rosa** California, USA
70D3 **Santa Rosa** Honduras
62B2 **Santa Rosa** New Mexico, USA
66B3 **Santa Rosa** *I* USA
70A2 **Santa Rosalía** Mexico
58C2 **Santa Rosa Range** *Mts* USA
73L5 **Santa Talhada** Brazil
75D2 **Santa Teresa** Brazil
16B2 **Santa Teresa di Gallura** Sardinia, Italy
66B3 **Santa Ynez** *R* USA
66B3 **Santa Ynez Mts** USA
67C2 **Santee** *R* USA
74B4 **Santiago** Chile
69C3 **Santiago** Dominican Republic
72B2 **Santiago** Panama
72C4 **Santiago** *R* Peru
15A1 **Santiago de Compostela** Spain
69B2 **Santiago de Cuba** Cuba
74D3 **Santiago del Estero** Argentina
74D3 **Santiago del Estero** *State* Argentina
66D4 **Santiago Peak** *Mt* USA
33F2 **Santo** Vanuatu
75C3 **Santo Amaro, Ilha** Brazil
75B3 **Santo Anastatácio** Brazil
74F3 **Santo Angelo** Brazil
48A4 **Santo Antão** *I* Cape Verde
75B3 **Santo Antônio da Platina** Brazil
75E1 **Santo Antônio de Jesus** Brazil
75A2 **Santo Antônio do Leverger** Brazil
69D3 **Santo Domingo** Dominican Republic
75C3 **Santos** Brazil
75D3 **Santos Dumont** Brazil
59C4 **Santo Tomas** Mexico
74E3 **Santo Tomé** Argentina
74B7 **San Valentin** *Mt* Chile
16C3 **San Vito, C** Sicily, Italy
28B2 **Sanyuanpu** China
51B4 **Sanza Pomba** Angola
75C3 **São Carlos** Brazil
75C1 **São Domingos** Brazil
73H5 **São Félix** Mato Grosso, Brazil
75D3 **São Fidélis** Brazil
75D2 **São Francisco** Brazil
73L5 **São Francisco** *R* Brazil
74G3 **São Francisco do Sul** Brazil
75C4 **São Francisco, Ilha de** Brazil
75C2 **São Gotardo** Brazil
51D4 **Sao Hill** Tanzania
75A2 **São Jerônimo, Serra de** *Mts* Brazil
75D3 **São João da Barra** Brazil
75C3 **São João da Boa Vista** Brazil
75C1 **São João d'Aliança** Brazil
75D2 **São João da Ponte** Brazil
75D3 **São João del Rei** Brazil
75D2 **São João do Paraíso** Brazil

**Skokie** **Stapleton**


64B2 **Skokie** USA
17E3 **Skópelos** *I* Greece
17E2 **Skopje** Macedonia, Yugoslavia
12G7 **Skövde** Sweden
25O4 **Skovorodino** Russian Federation
65F2 **Skowhegan** USA
47E1 **Skukuza** South Africa
54C3 **Skwentna** USA
18D2 **Skwierzyna** Poland
10B2 **Skye** *I* Scotland
12G7 **Slagelse** Denmark
27D7 **Slamet** *Mt* Indonesia
9C3 **Slaney** *R* Irish Republic
17E2 **Slatina** Romania
54G3 **Slave** *R* Canada
19G2 **Slavgorod** Belorussia
24J4 **Slavgorod** Russian Federation
19F2 **Slavuta** Ukraine
21F6 **Slavyansk** Ukraine
18D2 **Sławno** Poland
7D3 **Sleaford** England
8C3 **Sleat,Sound of** *Chan* Scotland
54C3 **Sleetmute** USA
63E2 **Slidell** USA
68C2 **Slide Mt** USA
9B3 **Slieve Aughty Mts** Irish Republic
9C3 **Slieve Bloom** *Mts* Irish Republic
10B3 **Sligo** Irish Republic
10B3 **Sligo B** Irish Republic
17F2 **Sliven** Bulgaria
59C3 **Sloan** USA
17F2 **Slobozia** Romania
19F2 **Slonim** Belorussia
7D4 **Slough** England
66B2 **Slough** *R* USA
16C1 **Slovenia** *Republic* Europe
19D3 **Slovensko** *Region* Czechoslovakia
18C2 **Słubice** Poland
19F2 **Sluch'** *R* Ukraine
18D2 **Słupsk** Poland
19F2 **Slutsk** Belorussia
19F2 **Slutsk** *R* Belorussia
10A3 **Slyne Head** *Pt* Irish Republic
25M4 **Slyudyanka** Russian Federation
55M4 **Smallwood Res** Canada
48A2 **Smara** Morocco
17E2 **Smederevo** Serbia, Yugoslavia
17E2 **Smederevska Palanka** Serbia, Yugoslavia
21E6 **Smela** Ukraine
68A2 **Smethport** USA
66C1 **Smith** USA
54F3 **Smith Arm** *B* Canada
54F4 **Smithers** Canada
67C1 **Smithfield** N Carolina, USA
47D3 **Smithfield** South Africa
58D2 **Smithfield** Utah, USA
55L3 **Smith I** Canada
65D2 **Smiths Falls** Canada
34C4 **Smithton** Australia
60C3 **Smoky** *R* USA
34D2 **Smoky C** Australia
60D3 **Smoky Hills** USA
58D2 **Smoky Mts** USA
12F6 **Smøla** *I* Norway
20E5 **Smolensk** Russian Federation
17E2 **Smólikas** *Mt* Greece
17E2 **Smolyan** Bulgaria
19F2 **Smorgon'** Belorussia
**Smyrna = Izmir**
68C3 **Smyrna** Delaware, USA
67B2 **Smyrna** Georgia, USA
12B2 **Snæfell** *Mt* Iceland
6B2 **Snaefell** *Mt* Isle of Man, British Isles
58C1 **Snake** *R* USA
56B2 **Snake River Canyon** USA
58D2 **Snake River Plain** USA
33F5 **Snares Is** New Zealand
18B2 **Sneek** Netherlands
66B2 **Snelling** USA
18D2 **Sněžka** *Mt* Czechoslovakia/Poland
8B3 **Snizort, Loch** *Inlet* Scotland
12F6 **Snøhetta** *Mt* Norway
58B1 **Snohomish** USA
58B1 **Snoqualmie P** USA
30D3 **Snoul** Cambodia
7B3 **Snowdon** *Mt* Wales
7B3 **Snowdonia Nat Pk** Wales
54G3 **Snowdrift** Canada
59D4 **Snowflake** USA
54H4 **Snow Lake** Canada
68B2 **Snow Shoe** USA
34A2 **Snowtown** Australia
58D2 **Snowville** USA
34C3 **Snowy Mts** Australia
62B2 **Snyder** USA
28B4 **Soan Kundo** *Is* S Korea
8B3 **Soay, I** Scotland
28A3 **Sobaek Sanmaek** *Mts* S Korea
50D3 **Sobat** *R* Sudan
73K4 **Sobral** Brazil
19E2 **Sochaczew** Poland
21F7 **Sochi** Russian Federation
28A3 **Söch'on** S Korea
37M5 **Société, Îles de la** Pacific Ocean
49D2 **Socna** Libya
62A2 **Socorro** USA
70A3 **Socorro** *I* Mexico
38D4 **Socotra** *I* Yemen
66C3 **Soda L** USA
12K5 **Sodankylä** Finland
58D2 **Soda Springs** USA
50D3 **Soddo** Ethiopia
12H6 **Söderhamn** Sweden
12H7 **Södertälje** Sweden
50C2 **Sodiri** Sudan
50D3 **Sodo** Ethiopia
68B1 **Sodus Point** USA
13E2 **Soest** Germany
51D5 **Sofala** Mozambique
17E2 **Sofia** Bulgaria
**Sofiya = Sofia**
20E2 **Sofporog** Russian Federation
26H4 **Sofu Gan** *I* Japan
72D2 **Sogamoso** Colombia
12F6 **Sognefjorden** *Inlet* Norway
28A4 **Sŏgwi-ri** S Korea
39H2 **Sog Xian** China
40B4 **Sohâg** Egypt
33E1 **Sohano** Papua New Guinea
13B2 **Soignies** Belgium
13B3 **Soissons** France
42C3 **Sojat** India
28A3 **Sokcho** S Korea
40A2 **Söke** Turkey
19E2 **Sokołka** Poland
48C4 **Sokodé** Togo
20G4 **Sokol** Russian Federation
48B3 **Sokolo** Mali
55Q3 **Søkongens Øy** *I* Greenland
48C3 **Sokoto** Nigeria
48C3 **Sokoto** *R* Nigeria
35A3 **Solander I** New Zealand
44B2 **Solāpur** India
69C4 **Soledad** Colombia
66B2 **Soledad** USA
7D4 **Solent** *Sd* England
13B2 **Solesmes** France
19F2 **Soligorsk** Belorussia
20K4 **Solikamsk** Russian Federation
21J5 **Sol'Iletsk** Russian Federation
72D4 **Solimões** Peru
13D2 **Solingen** Germany
47B1 **Solitaire** Namibia
12H6 **Sollefteå** Sweden
27D7 **Solok** Indonesia
33E1 **Solomon Is** Pacific Ocean
64A1 **Solon Springs** USA
20F2 **Solovetskiye, Ostrova** *I* Russian Federation
12F8 **Soltau** Germany
66B3 **Solvang** USA
68B1 **Solvay** USA
8D4 **Solway Firth** *Estuary* England/Scotland
51C5 **Solwezi** Zambia
29D3 **Sōma** Japan
17F3 **Soma** Turkey
38C5 **Somalia** *Republic* EAfrica
36D4 **Somali Basin** Indian Ocean
17D1 **Sombor** Serbia, Yugoslavia
44E4 **Sombrero Chan** Nicobar Is, Indian Ocean
32D2 **Somerset** Australia
64C3 **Somerset** Kentucky, USA
68E2 **Somerset** Massachusetts, USA
65D2 **Somerset** Pennsylvania, USA
7C4 **Somerset** *County* England
47D3 **Somerset East** South Africa
55J2 **Somerset I** Canada
68D1 **Somerset Res** USA
68C3 **Somers Point** USA
68E1 **Somersworth** USA
63C2 **Somerville** USA
68C2 **Somerville Res** USA
17E1 **Someş** *R* Romania
13B3 **Somme** *Department* France
13B3 **Somme** *R* France
13C3 **Sommesous** France
72A1 **Somoto** Nicaragua
43E4 **Son** *R* India
28A3 **Sŏnch'ŏn** N Korea
47D3 **Sondags** *R* South Africa
12F8 **Sønderborg** Denmark
55N3 **Søndre Strømfjord** Greenland
55N2 **Søndre Upernavik** Greenland
14D2 **Sondrio** Italy
30D3 **Song Ba** *R* Vietnam
30D3 **Song Cau** Vietnam
28A3 **Sŏngch'ŏn** N Korea
51D5 **Songea** Tanzania
28A2 **Songgan** N Korea
26F2 **Songhua** *R* China
31E3 **Songjiang** China
28A3 **Songjŏng** S Korea
30C4 **Songkhla** Thailand
30C5 **Sông Pahang** *R* Malaysia
31A3 **Songpan** China
28A4 **Sŏngsan-ni** S Korea
31C1 **Sonid Youqi** China
42D3 **Sonīpat** India
30C1 **Son La** Vietnam
42B3 **Sonmiani** Pakistan
42B3 **Sonmiani Bay** Pakistan
59D4 **Sonoita** Mexico
66A1 **Sonoma** USA
66B2 **Sonora** California, USA
62B2 **Sonora** Texas, USA
70A2 **Sonora** *R* Mexico
59D4 **Sonora** *State* Mexico
56B3 **Sonoran Desert** USA
66C1 **Sonora P** USA
70D3 **Sonsonate** El Salvador
27G6 **Sonsorol** *I* Pacific Ocean
57E2 **Soo Canals** Canada/USA
19D2 **Sopot** Poland
18D3 **Sopron** Hungary
66B2 **Soquel** USA
16C2 **Sora** Italy
45C3 **Sored** *R* Israel
65E1 **Sorel** Canada
34C4 **Sorell** Australia
40C2 **Sorgun** Turkey
15B1 **Soria** Spain
24C2 **Sørkapp** *I* Barents Sea
12J5 **Sørkjosen** Norway
21J6 **Sor Mertvyy Kultuk** *Plain* Kazakhstan
75C3 **Sorocaba** Brazil
20J5 **Sorochinsk** Moldavia
19F3 **Soroki** Russian Federation
27H6 **Sorol** *I* Pacific Ocean
29D2 **Soroma-ko** *L* Japan
27G7 **Sorong** Indonesia
50D3 **Soroti** Uganda
12J4 **Sørøya** *I* Norway
16C2 **Sorrento** Italy
12K5 **Sorsatunturi** *Mt* Finland
12H5 **Sorsele** Sweden
20E3 **Sortavala** Russian Federation
28B3 **Sŏsan** S Korea
19D2 **Sosnowiec** Poland
20L4 **Sos'va** Russian Federation
50B3 **Souanké** Congo
48B4 **Soubré** Ivory Coast
68C2 **Souderton** USA
69P2 **Soufrière** St Lucia
69N2 **Soufrière** *Mt* St Vincent
14C3 **Souillac** France
16B3 **Souk Ahras** Algeria
**Sŏul = Seoul**
15C2 **Soummam** *R* Algeria
**Sour = Tyre**
47D2 **Sources,Mt aux** Lesotho
60C1 **Souris** Manitoba, Canada
60C1 **Souris** *R* Canada/USA
73L5 **Sousa** Brazil
16C3 **Sousse** Tunisia
51C7 **South Africa** *Republic* Africa
68C2 **S Amboy** USA
64C2 **Southampton** Canada
7D4 **Southampton** England
68D2 **Southampton** USA
55K3 **Southampton I** Canada
44E3 **South Andaman** *I* Indian Ocean
55M4 **South Aulatsivik I** Canada
32C3 **South Australia** *State* Australia
36H6 **South Australian Basin** Indian Ocean
63E2 **Southaven** USA
62A2 **South Baldy** *Mt* USA
67B3 **South Bay** USA
64C1 **South Baymouth** Canada
64B2 **South Bend** Indiana, USA
58B1 **South Bend** Washington, USA
65D3 **South Boston** USA
68E1 **Southbridge** USA
**South Cape = Ka Lae**
57E3 **South Carolina** *State* USA
27E5 **South China S** SE Asia
56C2 **South Dakota** *State* USA
68D1 **South Deerfield** USA
7D4 **South Downs** England
34C4 **South East C** Australia
37O7 **South East Pacific Basin** Pacific Ocean
54H4 **Southend** Canada
7E4 **Southend-on-Sea** England
35A2 **Southern Alps** *Mts* New Zealand
32A4 **Southern Cross** Australia
54J4 **Southern Indian L** Canada
67C1 **Southern Pines** USA
69H2 **Southfield** Jamaica
37K6 **South Fiji Basin** Pacific Ocean
7E4 **South Foreland** *Pt* England
62A1 **South Fork** USA
66B1 **South Fork** *R* California, USA
66B1 **South Fork American** *R* USA
66C3 **South Fork Kern** *R* USA
71G9 **South Georgia** *I* S Atlantic Ocean
7C4 **South Glamorgan** *County* Wales
64B2 **South Haven** USA
54J3 **South Henik L** Canada
65D3 **South Hill** USA
36J3 **South Honshu Ridge** Pacific Ocean
35A2 **South I** New Zealand
68D2 **Southington** USA
28B3 **South Korea** *Republic* S Korea
59B3 **South Lake Tahoe** USA
36D6 **South Madagascar Ridge** Indian Ocean
76G8 **South Magnetic Pole** Antarctica
67B3 **South Miami** USA
68B3 **South Mt** USA
54F3 **South Nahanni** *R* Canada
69G1 **South Negril Pt** Jamaica
52F8 **South Orkney Is** Atlantic Ocean
71B5 **South Pacific O**
60C2 **South Platte** *R* USA
76E **South Pole** Antarctica
64C1 **South Porcupine** Canada
7C3 **Southport** England
69Q2 **South Pt** Barbados
68C2 **South River** USA
8D2 **South Ronaldsay** *I* Scotland
52G7 **South Sandwich Trench** Atlantic Ocean
66A2 **South San Francisco** USA
54H4 **South Saskatchewan** *R* Canada
6D2 **South Shields** England
35B1 **South Taranaki Bight** *B* New Zealand
8B3 **South Uist** *I* Scotland
**South West Africa = Namibia**
32D5 **South West C** Australia
36D6 **South West Indian Ridge** Indian Ocean
37M6 **South West Pacific Basin** Pacific Ocean
52D5 **South West Peru Ridge** Pacific Ocean
7E3 **Southwold** England
7D3 **South Yorkshire** *County* England
47D1 **Soutpansberg** *Mts* South Africa
19E1 **Sovetsk** Russian Federation
20H4 **Sovetsk** Russian Federation
26G2 **Sovetskaya Gavan'** Russian Federation
20L3 **Sovetskiy** Russian Federation
47D2 **Soweto** South Africa
29D1 **Sōya-misaki** *C* Japan
51B4 **Soyo Congo** Angola
19G2 **Sozh** *R* Belorussia
13C2 **Spa** Belgium
15 **Spain** *Kingdom* SW Europe
**Spalato = Split**
7D3 **Spalding** England
64C1 **Spanish** *R* Canada
59D2 **Spanish Fork** USA
69J1 **Spanish Town** Jamaica
59C3 **Sparks** USA
64A2 **Sparta** USA
67B2 **Spartanburg** USA
17E3 **Spárti** Greece
16D3 **Spartivento, C** Italy
26G2 **Spassk Dal'niy** Russian Federation
60C2 **Spearfish** USA
62B1 **Spearman** USA
69R2 **Speightstown** Barbados
54D3 **Spenard** USA
55J3 **Spence Bay** Canada
64B3 **Spencer** Indiana, USA
61D2 **Spencer** Iowa, USA
32C4 **Spencer G** Australia
55L3 **Spencer Is** Canada
35B2 **Spenser Mts** New Zealand
9C2 **Sperrin Mts** Northern Ireland
8D3 **Spey** *R* Scotland
18B3 **Speyer** Germany
69K1 **Speyside** Tobago
58C1 **Spirit Lake** USA
54G4 **Spirit River** Canada
24C2 **Spitsbergen** *I* Svalbard, Norway
**Spitsbergen** *Is* **= Svalbard**
18C3 **Spittal** Austria
13D1 **Spjekeroog** *I* Germany
12F6 **Spjelkavik** Norway
16D2 **Split** Croatia
58C1 **Spokane** USA
64A1 **Spooner** USA
**Sporádhes** *Is* **= Dodecanese**
27E6 **Spratly** *I* S China Sea
27E6 **Spratly Is** S China Sea
58C2 **Spray** USA
18C2 **Spree** *R* Germany
47B2 **Springbok** South Africa
63D1 **Springdale** USA
62B1 **Springer** USA
59E4 **Springerville** USA
62B1 **Springfield** Colorado, USA
64B3 **Springfield** Illinois, USA
68D1 **Springfield** Massachusetts, USA
61E2 **Springfield** Minnesota, USA
63D1 **Springfield** Missouri, USA
64C3 **Springfield** Ohio, USA
58B2 **Springfield** Oregon, USA
67A1 **Springfield** Tennessee, USA
65E2 **Springfield** Vermont, USA
47D3 **Springfontein** South Africa
59C3 **Spring Mts** USA
47D2 **Springs** South Africa
68A1 **Springville** New York, USA
59D2 **Springville** Utah, USA
68B1 **Springwater** USA
58D2 **Spruce Mt** USA
7E3 **Spurn Head** *C* England
58B1 **Spuzzum** Canada
16D3 **Squillace, G di** Italy
25S4 **Sredinnyy Khrebet** *Mts* Russian Federation
25R3 **Srednekolymsk** Russian Federation
20F5 **Sredne-Russkaya Vozvyshennost'** *Upland* Russian Federation
25M3 **Sredne Sibirskoye Ploskogorye** *Tableland* Russian Federation
20K4 **Sredniy Ural** *Mts* Russian Federation
30D3 **Srepok** *R* Cambodia
26E1 **Sretensk** Russian Federation
30C3 **Sre Umbell** Cambodia
44C2 **Srīkākulam** India
44B3 **Sri Kālahasti** India
39G5 **Sri Lanka** *Republic* SAsia
42C2 **Srīnagar** Pakistan
44A2 **Srīvardhan** India
18D2 **Sroda** Poland
8C2 **Stack Skerry** *I* Scotland
13E1 **Stade** Germany
13E1 **Stadthagen** Germany
8B3 **Staffa** *I* Scotland
7C3 **Stafford** England
7C3 **Stafford** *County* England
68D2 **Stafford Springs** USA
**Stalingrad = Volgograd**
47B3 **Stallberg** *Mt* South Africa
55J1 **Stallworthy,C** Canada
19E2 **Stalowa Wola** Poland
68D2 **Stamford** Connecticut, USA
7D3 **Stamford** England
68C1 **Stamford** New York, USA
62C2 **Stamford** Texas, USA
47B1 **Stampriet** Namibia
47D2 **Standerton** South Africa
64C2 **Standish** USA
58D1 **Stanford** USA
47E2 **Stanger** South Africa
6C2 **Stanhope** England
66B2 **Stanislaus** *R* USA
17E2 **Stanke Dimitrov** Bulgaria
34C4 **Stanley** Australia
74E8 **Stanley** Falkland Islands
58D2 **Stanley** Idaho, USA
60C1 **Stanley** N Dakota, USA
44B3 **Stanley Res** India
**Stanleyville = Kisangani**
70D3 **Stann Creek** Belize
26F1 **Stanovoy Khrebet** *Mts* Russian Federation
34D1 **Stanthorpe** Australia
8A3 **Stanton Banks** *Sand-bank* Scotland
60C2 **Stapleton** USA

Starachowice Taiyuan


19E2 **Starachowice** Poland
17E2 **Stara Planiná** *Mts* Bulgaria
20E4 **Staraya Russa** Russian Federation
17F2 **Stara Zagora** Bulgaria
18D2 **Stargard** Poland
63E2 **Starkville** USA
18C3 **Starnberg** Germany
19D2 **Starogard Gdański** Poland
19F3 **Starokonstantinov** Ukraine
7C4 **Start Pt** England
21F5 **Staryy Oskol** Russian Federation
68B2 **State College** USA
68C2 **Staten I** USA
67B2 **Statesboro** USA
67B1 **Statesville** USA
65D3 **Staunton** USA
12F7 **Stavanger** Norway
13C2 **Stavelot** Belgium
13C1 **Stavoren** Netherlands
21G6 **Stavropol'** Russian Federation
34B3 **Stawell** Australia
58B2 **Stayton** USA
60B2 **Steamboat Springs** USA
68B2 **Steelton** USA
58C2 **Steens Mt** USA
55N2 **Steenstrups Gletscher** *Gl* Greenland
13D1 **Steenwijk** Netherlands
54H2 **Stefansson I** Canada
47E2 **Stegi** Swaziland
61D1 **Steinbach** Canada
12G6 **Steinkjer** Norway
47B2 **Steinkopf** South Africa
47C2 **Stella** South Africa
47B3 **Stellenbosch** South Africa
13C3 **Stenay** France
18C2 **Stendal** Germany
21H8 **Stepanakert** Azerbaijan
61D1 **Stephen** USA
35B2 **Stephens,C** New Zealand
34B2 **Stephens Creek** Australia
64B1 **Stephenson** USA
55N5 **Stephenville** Canada
62C2 **Stephenville** USA
47D3 **Sterkstroom** South Africa
60C2 **Sterling** Colorado, USA
64B2 **Sterling** Illinois, USA
62C1 **Sterling** Kansas, USA
60C1 **Sterling** N Dakota, USA
62B2 **Sterling City** USA
64C2 **Sterling Heights** USA
20K5 **Sterlitamak** Russian Federation
54G4 **Stettler** Canada
64C2 **Steubenville** USA
7D4 **Stevenage** England
64B2 **Stevens Point** USA
54D3 **Stevens Village** USA
54F4 **Stewart** Canada
59C3 **Stewart** USA
54E3 **Stewart** *R* Canada
35A3 **Stewart I** New Zealand
33F1 **Stewart Is** Solomon Islands
8C4 **Stewarton** Scotland
54E3 **Stewart River** Canada
68B3 **Stewartstown** USA
61E2 **Stewartville** USA
47D3 **Steynsburg** South Africa
18C3 **Steyr** Austria
47C3 **Steytlerville** South Africa
54F4 **Stikine** *R* Canada
61E1 **Stillwater** Minnesota, USA
63C1 **Stillwater** Oklahoma, USA
59C3 **Stillwater Range** *Mts* USA
62B1 **Stinnett** USA
34A2 **Stirling** Australia
8D3 **Stirling** Scotland
12G6 **Stjørdal** Norway
13E4 **Stockach** Germany
68D1 **Stockbridge** USA
18D3 **Stockerau** Austria
12H7 **Stockholm** Sweden
7C3 **Stockport** England
66B2 **Stockton** California, USA
6D2 **Stockton** England
60D3 **Stockton** Kansas, USA
63D1 **Stockton L** USA
7C3 **Stoke-on-Trent** England
12G5 **Stokmarknes** Norway
25P2 **Stolbovoy, Ostrov** *I* Russian Federation
12K8 **Stolbtsy** Russian Federation
19F2 **Stolin** Belorussia
7C3 **Stone** England
68C3 **Stone Harbor** USA
8D3 **Stonehaven** Scotland
63C2 **Stonewall** USA
7D3 **Stony Stratford** England
12H5 **Storavan** *L* Sweden
12G6 **Støren** Norway
34C4 **Storm B** Australia
61D2 **Storm Lake** USA
8B2 **Stornoway** Scotland
19F3 **Storozhinets** Ukraine
68D2 **Storrs** USA
12G6 **Storsjön** *L* Sweden
12H5 **Storuman** Sweden
60B2 **Story** USA
68E1 **Stoughton** USA
7E4 **Stour** *R* England
7C3 **Stourbridge** England
7C3 **Stourport** England
7E3 **Stowmarket** England
9C2 **Strabane** Northern Ireland
34C4 **Strahan** Australia
18C2 **Stralsund** Germany
47B3 **Strand** South Africa
12F6 **Stranda** Norway
9D2 **Strangford Lough** *L* Irish Republic
12H7 **Strängnäs** Sweden
8C4 **Stranraer** Scotland
14D2 **Strasbourg** France
65D3 **Strasburg** USA
66C2 **Stratford** California, USA
64C2 **Stratford** Canada
68D2 **Stratford** Connecticut, USA
35B1 **Stratford** New Zealand
62B1 **Stratford** Texas, USA
7D3 **Stratford-on-Avon** England
34A3 **Strathalbyn** Australia
8C4 **Strathclyde** *Region* Scotland
65E1 **Stratton** USA
64B2 **Streator** USA
8D2 **Stroma, I** Scotland
16D3 **Stromboli** *I* Italy
8D2 **Stromness** Scotland
61D2 **Stromsburg** USA
12H6 **Strömsund** Sweden
12G6 **Ströms Vattudal** *L* Sweden
8D2 **Stronsay** *I* Scotland
7C4 **Stroud** England
68C2 **Stroudsburg** USA
17E2 **Struma** *R* Bulgaria
7B3 **Strumble Head** *Pt* Wales
17E2 **Strumica** Macedonia, Yugoslavia
19E3 **Stryy** Ukraine
19E3 **Stryy** *R* Ukraine
34B1 **Strzelecki Creek** *R* Australia
67B3 **Stuart** Florida, USA
60D2 **Stuart** Nebraska, USA
54F4 **Stuart L** Canada
12G8 **Stubice** Poland
30D3 **Stung Sen** *R* Cambodia
30D3 **Stung Treng** Cambodia
16B2 **Stura** *R* Italy
76G7 **Sturge I** Antarctica
64B2 **Sturgeon Bay** USA
65D1 **Sturgeon Falls** Canada
64B3 **Sturgis** Kentucky, USA
64B2 **Sturgis** Michigan, USA
60C2 **Sturgis** S Dakota, USA
32B2 **Sturt Creek** *R* Australia
34B1 **Sturt Desert** Australia
47D3 **Stutterheim** South Africa
63D2 **Stuttgart** USA
18B3 **Stuttgart** Germany
12A1 **Stykkishólmur** Iceland
19F2 **Styr'** *R* Ukraine
75D2 **Suaçuí Grande** *R* Brazil
50D2 **Suakin** Sudan
28A3 **Suan** N Korea
31E5 **Suao** Taiwan
17D1 **Subotica** Serbia, Yugoslavia
21D6 **Suceava** Romania
72E7 **Sucre** Bolivia
75B2 **Sucuriú** *R* Brazil
50C2 **Sudan** *Republic* Africa
64C1 **Sudbury** Canada
7E3 **Sudbury** England
50C3 **Sudd** *Swamp* Sudan
73G2 **Suddie** Guyana
45B4 **Sudr** Egypt
50C3 **Sue** *R* Sudan
40B4 **Suez** Egypt
40B3 **Suez Canal** Egypt
40B4 **Suez,G of** Egypt
68C2 **Suffern** USA
65D3 **Suffolk** USA
7E3 **Suffolk** *County* England
65E2 **Sugarloaf Mt** USA
34D2 **Sugarloaf Pt** Australia
25R3 **Sugoy** *R* Russian Federation
41G5 **Suhār** Oman
26D1 **Sühbaatar** Mongolia
42B3 **Sui** Pakistan
31C2 **Suide** China
28C2 **Suifen He** *R* China
26F2 **Suihua** China
31B3 **Suining** China
13C3 **Suippes** France
10B3 **Suir** *R* Irish Republic
31C3 **Sui Xian** China
31E1 **Suizhong** China
42C3 **Sujāngarh** India
27D7 **Sukadana** Indonesia
29E3 **Sukagawa** Japan
26C3 **Sukai Hu** *L* China
28B3 **Sukch'ŏn** N Korea
20F5 **Sukhinichi** Russian Federation
20G4 **Sukhona** *R* Russian Federation
21G7 **Sukhumi** Georgia
55N3 **Sukkertoppen** Greenland
55N3 **Sukkertoppen Isflade** *Ice field* Greenland
12L6 **Sukkozero** Russian Federation
42B3 **Sukkur** Pakistan
44C2 **Sukma** India
51B6 **Sukses** Namibia
28B4 **Sukumo** Japan
21F5 **Sula** *R* Russian Federation
42B3 **Sulaiman Range** *Mts* Pakistan
32B1 **Sula, Kepulauan** *I* Indonesia
8B2 **Sula Sgeir** *I* Scotland
27E7 **Sulawesi** *Is* Indonesia
41E2 **Sulaymānīyah** Iraq
8C2 **Sule Skerry** *I* Scotland
17F1 **Sulina** Romania
13E1 **Sulingen** Germany
12H5 **Sulitjelma** Norway
72B4 **Sullana** Peru
63D1 **Sullivan** USA
13B4 **Sully-sur-Loire** France
16C2 **Sulmona** Italy
63D2 **Sulphur** Louisiana, USA
63C2 **Sulphur** Oklahoma, USA
63C2 **Sulphur Springs** USA
21E8 **Sultan Dağlari** *Mts* Turkey
43E3 **Sultānpur** India
27F6 **Sulu Arch** *Is* Philippines
27E6 **Sulu S** Philip
13E3 **Sulz** Germany
74D3 **Sumampa** Argentina
27C6 **Sumatera** *I* Indonesia
27E8 **Sumba** *I* Indonesia
27E7 **Sumbawa** *I* Indonesia
27E7 **Sumbawa Besar** Indonesia
51D4 **Sumbawanga** Tanzania
51B5 **Sumbe** Angola
8E2 **Sumburgh Head** *Pt* Scotland
43N2 **Sumesar Ra** *Mts* Nepal
21H7 **Sumgait** Azerbaijan
26H3 **Sumisu** *I* Japan
54F4 **Summit Lake** Canada
59C3 **Summit Mt** USA
35B2 **Sumner,L** New Zealand
29B4 **Sumoto** Japan
67B2 **Sumter** USA
21E5 **Sumy** Ukraine
58D1 **Sun** *R* USA
29D2 **Sunagawa** Japan
28A3 **Sunan** N Korea
8C3 **Sunart, Loch** *Inlet* Scotland
68B2 **Sunbury** USA
28B3 **Sunch'ŏn** N Korea
28B4 **Sunch'ŏn** S Korea
60C2 **Sundance** USA
43E4 **Sundargarh** India
43F4 **Sunderbans** *Swamp* Bangladesh/India
6D2 **Sunderland** England
65D1 **Sundridge** Canada
12H6 **Sundsvall** Sweden
58C1 **Sunnyside** USA
59B3 **Sunnyvale** USA
64B2 **Sun Prairie** USA
25N3 **Suntar** Russian Federation
58D2 **Sun Valley** USA
48B4 **Sunyani** Ghana
20E3 **Suojarvi** Russian Federation
28B4 **Suō-nada** *B* Japan
12K6 **Suonenjoki** Finland
43F3 **Supaul** India
59D4 **Superior** Arizona, USA
61D2 **Superior** Nebraska, USA
64A1 **Superior** Wisconsin, USA
64B1 **Superior,L** Canada/USA
30C3 **Suphan Buri** Thailand
40D2 **Süphan Dağ** *Mt* Turkey
27G7 **Supiori** *I* Indonesia
41E3 **Sūq ash Suyūkh** Iraq
45D1 **Şuqaylibīyah** Syria
31D3 **Suqian** China
**Suqutra = Socotra**
38D3 **Sūr** Oman
20H5 **Sura** *R* Russian Federation
27E7 **Surabaya** Indonesia
29C4 **Suraga-wan** *B* Japan
27E7 **Surakarta** Indonesia
45D1 **Şūrān** Syria
34C1 **Surat** Australia
42C4 **Sūrat** India
42C3 **Sūratgarh** India
30B4 **Surat Thani** Thailand
42C4 **Surendranagar** India
68C3 **Surf City** USA
24J3 **Surgut** Russian Federation
44B2 **Suriāpet** India
27F6 **Surigao** Philippines
30C3 **Surin** Thailand
73G3 **Surinam** *Republic* S America
66B2 **Sur,Pt** USA
7D4 **Surrey** *County* England
49D1 **Surt** Libya
12A2 **Surtsey** *I* Iceland
16B1 **Susa** Italy
28B4 **Susa** Japan
29B4 **Susaki** Japan
59B2 **Susanville** USA
68C2 **Susquehanna** USA
68B3 **Susquehanna** *R* USA
68C2 **Sussex** USA
7D4 **Sussex West** England
47C3 **Sutherland** South Africa
60C2 **Sutherland** USA
42C2 **Sutlej** *R* Pakistan
59B3 **Sutter Creek** USA
64C3 **Sutton** USA
29D2 **Suttsu** Japan
29D3 **Suwa** Japan
19E2 **Suwałki** Poland
67B3 **Suwannee** *R* USA
45C2 **Suweilih** Jordan
28B3 **Suwŏn** S Korea
31D3 **Su Xian** China
29C3 **Suzaka** Japan
31E3 **Suzhou** China
29D3 **Suzu** Japan
29C4 **Suzuka** Japan
29C3 **Suzu-misaki** *C* Japan
24C2 **Svalbard** *Is* Barents Sea
19E3 **Svalyava** Ukraine
55N2 **Svartenhuk Halvø** *Region* Greenland
12G5 **Svartisen** *Mt* Norway
30D3 **Svay Rieng** Cambodia
12G6 **Sveg** Sweden
12G7 **Svendborg** Denmark
55J1 **Sverdrup Chan** Canada
54H2 **Sverdrup Is** Canada
26G2 **Svetlaya** Russian Federation
19E2 **Svetlogorsk** Russian Federation
12K6 **Svetogorsk** Russian Federation
17E2 **Svetozarevo** Serbia, Yugoslavia
17F2 **Svilengrad** Bulgaria
19F2 **Svir'** Belorussia
20E3 **Svir'** *R* Russian Federation
18D3 **Švitavy** Czechoslovakia
26F1 **Svobodnyy** Russian Federation
12G5 **Svolvær** Norway
7E3 **Swaffam** England
33E3 **Swain Reefs** Australia
67B2 **Swainsboro** USA
33H2 **Swains I** American Samoa
47B1 **Swakop** *R* Namibia
47A1 **Swakopmund** Namibia
6D2 **Swale** *R* England
27E6 **Swallow Reef** S China Sea
44B3 **Swāmihalli** India
70D3 **Swan** *I* Honduras
7D4 **Swanage** England
34B3 **Swan Hill** Australia
69A3 **Swan I** Caribbean Sea
54H4 **Swan River** Canada
7C4 **Swansea** Wales
7C4 **Swansea B** Wales
47C3 **Swartberge** *Mts* South Africa
47D2 **Swartruggens** South Africa
**Swatow = Shantou**
47E2 **Swaziland** *Kingdom* South Africa
12G7 **Sweden** *Kingdom* N Europe
58B2 **Sweet Home** USA
62B2 **Sweetwater** USA
60B2 **Sweetwater** *R* USA
47C3 **Swellendam** South Africa
18D2 **Świdnica** Poland
18D2 **Świdwin** Poland
18D2 **Świebodzin** Poland
19D2 **Świecie** Poland
54H4 **Swift Current** Canada
9C2 **Swilly, Lough** *Estuary* Irish Republic
7D4 **Swindon** England
18C2 **Świnoujście** Poland
14D2 **Switzerland** Europe
9C3 **Swords** Irish Republic
43M1 **Syang** Nepal
9A3 **Sybil Pt** Irish Republic
34D2 **Sydney** Australia
20H3 **Syktyvkar** Russian Federation
67A2 **Sylacauga** USA
12G6 **Sylarna** *Mt* Sweden
43G4 **Sylhet** Bangladesh
18B1 **Sylt** *I* Germany
64C2 **Sylvania** USA
76G11 **Syowa** *Base* Antarctica
16D3 **Syracuse** Italy
62B1 **Syracuse** Kansas, USA
68B1 **Syracuse** New York, USA
65D2 **Syracuse** USA
24H5 **Syrdar'ya** *R* Kazakhstan
40C2 **Syria** *Republic* SW Asia
20L4 **Sysert'** Russian Federation
20H5 **Syzran'** Russian Federation
18C2 **Szczecin** Poland
18D2 **Szczecinek** Poland
19E2 **Szczytno** Poland
19E3 **Szeged** Hungary
19D3 **Székesfehérvar** Hungary
19D3 **Szekszárd** Hungary
19D3 **Szolnok** Hungary
18D3 **Szombathely** Hungary
18D2 **Szprotawa** Poland


## T


47D3 **Tabankulu** South Africa
32E1 **Tabar Is** Papua New Guinea
16B3 **Tabarka** Tunisia
41G3 **Tabas** Iran
72E4 **Tabatinga** Brazil
48B2 **Tabelbala** Algeria
30C3 **Tabeng** Cambodia
54G5 **Taber** Canada
47B3 **Table Mt** South Africa
63D1 **Table Rock Res** USA
18C3 **Tábor** Czechoslovakia
50D4 **Tabora** Tanzania
20L4 **Tabory** Russian Federation
48B4 **Tabou** Ivory Coast
41E2 **Tabrīz** Iran
40C4 **Tabūk** Saudi Arabia
39G1 **Tacheng** China
27F5 **Tacloban** Philippines
72D7 **Tacna** Peru
59D4 **Tacna** USA
56A2 **Tacoma** USA
68D1 **Taconic Range** USA
75A3 **Tacuatí** Paraguay
48C2 **Tademait, Plateau du** Algeria
50E2 **Tadjoura** Djibouti
65F1 **Tadoussac** Canada
44B3 **Tādpatri** India
28B3 **Taebaek Sanmaek** *Mts* N Korea/S Korea
28B3 **T'aech'ŏn** N Korea
28A3 **Taech'on** S Korea
28A3 **Taedasa-Do** N Korea
28A3 **Taedong** *R* N Korea
28A3 **Taegang-got** *Pen* N Korea
28B3 **Taegu** S Korea
28A2 **Taehung** N Korea
28B3 **Taejŏn** S Korea
15B1 **Tafalla** Spain
48C2 **Tafasaset** *Watercourse* Algeria
7C4 **Taff** *R* Wales
45C3 **Tafila** Jordan
66C3 **Taft** USA
21F6 **Taganrog** Russian Federation
48A3 **Tagant** *Region* Mauritius
48B2 **Taguenout Hagguerete** *Well* Mali
33E2 **Tagula** *I* Papua New Guinea
**Tagus = Tejo**
48C2 **Tahat** *Mt* Algeria
37M5 **Tahiti** *I* Pacific Ocean
63C1 **Tahlequah** USA
59B3 **Tahoe City** USA
59B3 **Tahoe,L** USA
62B2 **Tahoka** USA
48C3 **Tahoua** Niger
40B4 **Tahta** Egypt
27F6 **Tahuna** Indonesia
31D2 **Tai'an** China
28A2 **Tai'an** China
31B3 **Taibai Shan** *Mt* China
31D1 **Taibus Qi** China
31E5 **Taichung** Taiwan
35B3 **Taieri** *R* New Zealand
31C2 **Taihang Shan** *Upland* China
35C1 **Taihape** New Zealand
31E3 **Tai Hu** *L* China
29D2 **Taiki** Japan
34A3 **Tailem Bend** Australia
8C3 **Tain** Scotland
31E5 **Tainan** Taiwan
75D2 **Taiobeiras** Brazil
31E5 **Taipei** Taiwan
30C5 **Taiping** Malaysia
29D3 **Taira** Japan
28B3 **Taisha** Japan
74B7 **Taitao,Pen de** Chile
31E5 **Taitung** Taiwan
12K5 **Taivalkoski** Finland
26F4 **Taiwan** *Republic* China
31D5 **Taiwan Str** China/Taiwan
45C3 **Taiyiba** Jordan
31C2 **Taiyuan** China

Toyama Um ed Daraj, Jebel


29D3 **Toyama** Japan
29C3 **Toyama-wan** *B* Japan
29C4 **Toyohashi** Japan
29C4 **Toyonaka** Japan
29B3 **Toyooka** Japan
29D3 **Toyota** Japan
48C1 **Tozeur** Tunisia
13D3 **Traben-Trarbach** Germany
**Trâblous = Tripoli**
40C1 **Trabzon** Turkey
61D2 **Tracy** Minnesota, USA
66B2 **Tracy** USA
15A2 **Trafalgar, Cabo** *C* Spain
54G5 **Trail** Canada
10B3 **Tralee** Irish Republic
9C3 **Tramore** Irish Republic
12G7 **Tranås** Sweden
30B4 **Trang** Thailand
27G7 **Trangan** *I* Indonesia
34C2 **Trangie** Australia
76E3 **Transantarctic Mts** Antarctica
47D3 **Transkei** *Self-governing homeland* South Africa
47D1 **Transvaal** *Province* South Africa
**Transylvanian Alps** *Mts* **= Munţii Carpaţii Meridionali**
16C3 **Trapani** Italy
34C3 **Traralgon** Australia
48A3 **Trarza** *Region* Mauritius
30C3 **Trat** Thailand
34B2 **Traveller's L** Australia
18C2 **Travemünde** Germany
64B2 **Traverse City** USA
35B2 **Travers,Mt** New Zealand
62C2 **Travis,L** USA
18D3 **Třebíč** Czechoslovakia
17D2 **Trebinje** Bosnia & Herzegovina, Yugoslavia
18C3 **Trebon** Czechoslovakia
74F4 **Treinta y Tres** Uruguay
74C6 **Trelew** Argentina
12G7 **Trelleborg** Sweden
7B3 **Tremadog B** Wales
65E1 **Tremblant,Mt** Canada
16D2 **Tremiti, Is** Italy
68B2 **Tremont** USA
58D2 **Tremonton** USA
19D3 **Trenčín** Czechoslovakia
74D5 **Trenque Lauquén** Argentina
7D3 **Trent** *R* England
16C1 **Trento** Italy
65D2 **Trenton** Canada
61E2 **Trenton** Missouri, USA
68C2 **Trenton** New Jersey, USA
55N5 **Trepassey** Canada
74D5 **Tres Arroyos** Argentina
75C3 **Três Corações** Brazil
15B2 **Tres Forcas, Cabo** *C* Morocco
75B2 **Três Irmãos, Represa** *Res* Brazil
74F2 **Três Lagoas** Brazil
66B2 **Tres Pinos** USA
74C7 **Tres Puntas, Cabo** Argentina
75D3 **Três Rios** Brazil
16C1 **Treviso** Italy
7B4 **Trevose Hd** *Pt* England
13E2 **Treysa** Germany
62B1 **Tribune** USA
44B3 **Trichūr** India
34C2 **Trida** Australia
13D3 **Trier** Germany
16C1 **Trieste** Italy
45B1 **Trikomo** Cyprus
9C3 **Trim** Irish Republic
44C4 **Trincomalee** Sri Lanka
52G6 **Trindade** *I* Atlantic Ocean
72F6 **Trinidad** Bolivia
74E4 **Trinidad** Uruguay
62B1 **Trinidad** USA
69E4 **Trinidad** *I* Caribbean Sea
69E4 **Trinidad & Tobago** *Is Republic* Caribbean Sea
63C2 **Trinity** USA
56D3 **Trinity** *R* USA
55N5 **Trinity B** Canada
47C2 **Trion** USA
45C1 **Tripoli** Lebanon
49D1 **Tripoli** Libya
17E3 **Trípolis** Greece
43G4 **Tripura** *State* India
52H6 **Tristan da Cunha** *Is* Atlantic Ocean
19D3 **Trnava** Czechoslovakia
32E1 **Trobriand Is** Papua New Guinea
65F1 **Trois Pistoles** Canada
65E1 **Trois-Riviéres** Canada
20L5 **Troitsk** Russian Federation
20K3 **Troitsko Pechorsk** Russian Federation
12G7 **Trollhättan** Sweden
12F6 **Trollheimen** *Mt* Norway
46K9 **Tromelin** *I* Indian Ocean
47D3 **Trompsburg** South Africa
12H5 **Tromsø** Norway
66D3 **Trona** USA
12G6 **Trondheim** Norway
12G6 **Trondheimfjord** *Inlet* Norway
45B1 **Troödos Range** *Mts* Cyprus
8C4 **Troon** Scotland
52J3 **Tropic of Cancer**
52K6 **Tropic of Capricorn**
48B2 **Troudenni** Mali
55J4 **Trout L** Ontario, Canada
58E2 **Trout Peak** *Mt* USA
68B2 **Trout Run** USA
7C4 **Trowbridge** England
67A2 **Troy** Alabama, USA
58C1 **Troy** Montana, USA
68D1 **Troy** New York, USA
64C2 **Troy** Ohio, USA
68B2 **Troy** Pennsylvania, USA
17E2 **Troyan** Bulgaria
13C3 **Troyes** France
59C3 **Troy Peak** *Mt* USA
41F5 **Trucial Coast** *Region* UAE
59B3 **Truckee** *R* USA
70D3 **Trujillo** Honduras
72C5 **Trujillo** Peru
15A2 **Trujillo** Spain
72D2 **Trujillo** Venezuela
59D3 **Trumbull,Mt** USA
34C2 **Trundle** Australia
55M5 **Truro** Canada
7B4 **Truro** England
62A2 **Truth or Consequences** USA
26C2 **Tsagaan Nuur** *L* Mongolia
26C1 **Tsagan-Tologoy** Russian Federation
51E5 **Tsaratanana** Madagascar
51C6 **Tsau** Botswana
50D4 **Tsavo** Kenya
50D4 **Tsavo Nat Pk** Kenya
60C1 **Tschida,L** USA
24J4 **Tselinograd** Kazakhstan
47B2 **Tses** Namibia
26D2 **Tsetserleg** Mongolia
48C4 **Tsévié** Togo
47C2 **Tshabong** Botswana
47C1 **Tshane** Botswana
21F6 **Tshchikskoye Vdkhr** *Res* Russian Federation
50B4 **Tshela** Zaïre
51C4 **Tshibala** Zaïre
50C4 **Tshikapa** Zaïre
50C4 **Tshuapa** *R* Zaïre
21G6 **Tsimlyanskoye Vodokhranilishche** *Res* Russian Federation
**Tsinan = Jinan**
**Tsingtao = Qingdao**
51E6 **Tsiombe** Madagascar
51E5 **Tsiroanomandidy** Madagascar
19F2 **Tsna** *R* Belorussia
31B1 **Tsogt Ovoo** Mongolia
47D3 **Tsomo** South Africa
26D2 **Tsomog** Mongolia
29C4 **Tsu** Japan
29C3 **Tsubata** Japan
29E3 **Tsuchiura** Japan
29E2 **Tsugarū-kaikyō** *Str* Japan
51B5 **Tsumeb** Namibia
51B6 **Tsumis** Namibia
29D3 **Tsuruga** Japan
29C3 **Tsurugi** Japan
29D3 **Tsuruoka** Japan
29C3 **Tsushima** Japan
28B4 **Tsushima** *Is* Japan
**Tsushima-Kaikyō = Korea Str**
29C3 **Tsuyama** Japan
15A1 **Tua** *R* Portugal
37M5 **Tuamotu, Îles** Pacific Ocean
21F7 **Tuapse** Russian Federation
35A3 **Tuatapere** New Zealand
59D3 **Tuba City** USA
37M6 **Tubai, Îles** Pacific Ocean
74G3 **Tubarão** Brazil
45C2 **Tubas** Israel
18B3 **Tübingen** Germany
49E1 **Tubruq** Libya
68C3 **Tuckerton** USA
59D4 **Tucson** USA
74C3 **Tucumán** *State* Argentina
62B1 **Tucumcari** USA
72F2 **Tucupita** Venezuela
15B1 **Tudela** Spain
40C3 **Tudmur** Syria
47E2 **Tugela** *R* South Africa
34D2 **Tuggerah L** Australia
27F5 **Tuguegarao** Philippines
25P4 **Tugur** Russian Federation
31D2 **Tuhai He** *R* China
27F7 **Tukangbesi, Kepulauan** *Is* Indonesia
54E3 **Tuktoyaktuk** Canada
19E1 **Tukums** Latvia
25O4 **Tukuringra, Khrebet** *Mts* Russian Federation
51D4 **Tukuyu** Tanzania
42B1 **Tukzar** Afghanistan
20F5 **Tula** Russian Federation
66C2 **Tulare** USA
66C2 **Tulare Lake Bed** USA
62A2 **Tularosa** USA
72C3 **Tulcán** Ecuador
21D6 **Tulcea** Romania
19F3 **Tul'chin** Ukraine
66C2 **Tule** *R* USA
51C6 **Tuli** Zimbabwe
47D1 **Tuli** *R* Zimbabwe
62B2 **Tulia** USA
45C2 **Tulkarm** Israel
67A1 **Tullahoma** USA
9C3 **Tullarnore** Irish Republic
14C2 **Tulle** France
63D2 **Tullos** USA
9C3 **Tullow** Irish Republic
68B1 **Tully** USA
63C1 **Tulsa** USA
72C3 **Tuluá** Colombia
40C3 **Tulūl ash Shāmīyah** *Desert Region* Iran/Syria
25M4 **Tulun** Russian Federation
72C3 **Tumaco** Colombia
25R3 **Tumany** Russian Federation
34C3 **Tumbarumba** Australia
72B4 **Tumbes** Ecuador
28B2 **Tumen** China
28B2 **Tumen** *R* China/N Korea
44B3 **Tumkūr** India
30C4 **Tumpat** Malaysia
42D4 **Tumsar** India
48B3 **Tumu** Ghana
73H3 **Tumucumaque, Serra** *Mts* Brazil
34C3 **Tumut** Australia
34C3 **Tumut** *R* Australia
69L1 **Tunapuna** Trinidad
7E4 **Tunbridge Wells, Royal** England
40C2 **Tunceli** Turkey
51D4 **Tunduma** Zambia
51D5 **Tunduru** Tanzania
17F2 **Tundzha** *R* Bulgaria
44B2 **Tungabhadra** *R* India
26E4 **Tungkang** Taiwan
12B2 **Tungnafellsjökull** *Mts* Iceland
25M3 **Tunguska** *R* Russian Federation
44C2 **Tuni** India
16C3 **Tunis** Tunisia
16C3 **Tunis, G de** Tunisia
48C1 **Tunisia** *Republic* N Africa
72D2 **Tunja** Colombia
68C2 **Tunkhannock** USA
31D4 **Tunxi** China
66C2 **Tuolumne Meadows** USA
75B3 **Tupã** Brazil
75C2 **Tupaciguara** Brazil
63E2 **Tupelo** USA
19G1 **Tupik** Russian Federation
72E8 **Tupiza** Bolivia
66C3 **Tupman** USA
65E2 **Tupper Lake** USA
74C4 **Tupungato** *Mt* Argentina
43L3 **Tura** India
25L3 **Tura** Russian Federation
20L4 **Tura** *R* Russian Federation
41G2 **Turān** Iran
25L4 **Turan** Russian Federation
40C3 **Turayf** Saudi Arabia
38E3 **Turbat** Pakistan
72C2 **Turbo** Colombia
17E1 **Turda** Romania
24K5 **Turfan Depression** China
24H5 **Turgay** Kazakhstan
25L5 **Turgen Uul** *Mt* Mongolia
40A2 **Turgutlu** Turkey
40C1 **Turhal** Turkey
12K7 **Türi** Estonia
15B2 **Turia** *R* Spain
16B1 **Turin** Italy
20L4 **Turinsk** Russian Federation
26G2 **Turiy Rog** Russian Federation
50D3 **Turkana, L** Ethiopia/Kenya
38E1 **Turkestan** *Region* C Asia
40C2 **Turkey** *Republic* W Asia
38D1 **Turkmenistan** *Republic* Asia
41F2 **Turkmenskiy Zaliv** *B* Turkmenistan
69C2 **Turks Is** Caribbean Sea
12J6 **Turku** Finland
50D3 **Turkwel** *R* Kenya
66B2 **Turlock** USA
66B2 **Turlock L** USA
35C2 **Turnagain,C** New Zealand
70D3 **Turneffe I** Belize
68D1 **Turners Falls** USA
13C2 **Turnhout** Belgium
17E2 **Turnu Măgurele** Romania
17E2 **Turnu-Severin** Romania
25K5 **Turpan** China
69B2 **Turquino** *Mt* Cuba
8D3 **Turriff** Scotland
38E1 **Turtkul'** Uzbekistan
61D3 **Turtle Creek Res** USA
25K3 **Turukhansk** Russian Federation
26D1 **Turuntayevo** Russian Federation
75B2 **Turvo** *R* Goias, Brazil
75C3 **Turvo** *R* São Paulo, Brazil
19E2 **Tur'ya** *R* Ukraine
63E2 **Tuscaloosa** USA
68B2 **Tuscarora Mt** USA
64B3 **Tuscola** Illinois, USA
62C2 **Tuscola** Texas, USA
63E2 **Tuscumbia** USA
41G3 **Tusharīk** Iran
68A2 **Tussey Mt** USA
**Tutera = Tudela**
44B4 **Tuticorin** India
17F2 **Tutrakan** Bulgaria
18B3 **Tuttlingen** Germany
33H2 **Tutuila** *I* American Samoa
26D2 **Tuul Gol** *R* Mongolia
25L4 **Tuva Republic** Russian Federation
33G1 **Tuvalu** *Is* Pacific Ocean
45C4 **Tuwayīlel Hāj** *Mt* Jordan
70B2 **Tuxpan** Mexico
70C2 **Tuxpan** Mexico
70C3 **Tuxtla Gutiérrez** Mexico
15A1 **Túy** Spain
30D3 **Tuy Hoa** Vietnam
40B2 **Tuz Gölü** *Salt L* Turkey
41D3 **Tuz Khurmātū** Iraq
17D2 **Tuzla** Bosnia & Herzegovina, Yugoslavia
20F4 **Tver'** Russian Federation
8D4 **Tweed** *R* England/Scotland
34D1 **Tweed Heads** Australia
8D4 **Tweedsmuir Hills** Scotland
59C4 **Twentynine Palms** USA
55N5 **Twillingate** Canada
58D1 **Twin Bridges** USA
62B2 **Twin Buttes Res** USA
58D2 **Twin Falls** USA
35B2 **Twins,The** *Mt* New Zealand
66B3 **Twitchell Res** USA
64A1 **Two Harbors** USA
58D1 **Two Medicine** *R* USA
64B2 **Two Rivers** USA
25O4 **Tygda** Russian Federation
63C2 **Tyler** USA
26H1 **Tymovskoye** Russian Federation
26F1 **Tynda** Russian Federation
6D2 **Tyne** *R* England
6D2 **Tyne and Wear** *Metropolitan County* England
6D2 **Tynemouth** England
12G6 **Tynset** Norway
**Tyr = Tyre**
45C2 **Tyre** Lebanon
62A2 **Tyrone** New Mexico, USA
68A2 **Tyrone** Pennsylvania, USA
9C2 **Tyrone** *County* Northern Ireland
34B3 **Tyrrell,L** Australia
16C2 **Tyrrhenian S**Italy
21J7 **Tyuleni, Ova** *Is* Kazakhstan
24H4 **Tyumen'** Russian Federation
25O3 **Tyung** *R* Russian Federation
7B3 **Tywyn** Wales
47E1 **Tzaneen** South Africa
17E3 **Tzoumérka** *Mt* Greece


## U


75D3 **Ubá** Brazil
75D2 **Ubaí** Brazil
75E1 **Ubaitaba** Brazil
50B3 **Ubangi** *R* Central African Republic/Congo/Zaïre
40D3 **Ubayyid, Wadi al** *Watercourse* Iraq
28B4 **Ube** Japan
15B2 **Ubeda** Spain
55N2 **Ubekendt Ejland** *I* Greenland
75C2 **Uberaba** Brazil
75A2 **Uberaba, Lagoa** Brazil
75C2 **Uberlândia** Brazil
30D2 **Ubon Ratchathani** Thailand
19F2 **Ubort** *R* Belorussia
50C4 **Ubundu** Zaïre
72D5 **Ucayali** *R* Peru
42C3 **Uch** Pakistan
25P4 **Uchar** *R* Russian Federation
29E2 **Uchiura-wan** *B* Japan
13E1 **Uchte** Germany
58A1 **Ucluelet** Canada
25L4 **Uda** *R* Russian Federation
42C4 **Udaipur** India
43F3 **Udaipur Garhi** Nepal
12G7 **Uddevalla** Sweden
12H5 **Uddjaur** *L* Sweden
44B2 **Udgir** India
42D2 **Udhampur** India
16C1 **Udine** Italy
20J4 **Udmurt Republic** Russian Federation
30C2 **Udon Thani** Thailand
25P4 **Udskaya Guba** *B* Russian Federation
44A3 **Udupi** India
25N2 **Udzha** Russian Federation
29C3 **Ueda** Japan
50C3 **Uele** *R* Zaïre
25U3 **Uelen** Russian Federation
18C2 **Uelzen** Germany
50C3 **Uere** *R* Zaïre
20K5 **Ufa** Russian Federation
20K4 **Ufa** *R* Russian Federation
51B6 **Ugab** *R* Namibia
50D4 **Ugaila** *R* Tanzania
50D3 **Uganda** *Republic* Africa
45C3 **'Ugeiqa, Wadi** Jordan
26H2 **Uglegorsk** Russian Federation
20F4 **Uglich** Russian Federation
28C2 **Uglovoye** Russian Federation
20F5 **Ugra** *R* Russian Federation
8B3 **Uig** Scotland
51B4 **Uige** Angola
28A3 **Ŭijŏngbu** S Korea
21J6 **Uil** Kazakhstan
58D2 **Uinta Mts** USA
28A3 **Ŭiryŏng** S Korea
28A3 **Uisŏng** S Korea
47D3 **Uitenhage** South Africa
19E3 **Újfehértó** Hungary
29C4 **Uji** Japan
50C4 **Ujiji** Tanzania
74C2 **Ujina** Chile
42D4 **Ujjain** India
32A1 **Ujung Pandang** Indonesia
50D4 **Ukerewe I** Tanzania
43G3 **Ukhrul** India
20J3 **Ukhta** Russian Federation
59B3 **Ukiah** California, USA
58C1 **Ukiah** Oregon, USA
56A3 **Ukiah** USA
19E1 **Ukmerge** Lithuania
21D6 **Ukraine** *Republic* Europe
28A4 **Uku-jima** *I* Japan
26D2 **Ulaanbaatar** Mongolia
26C2 **Ulaangom** Mongolia
31C1 **Ulaan Uul** Mongolia
**Ulan Bator = Ulaanbaatar**
39G1 **Ulangar Hu** *L* China
26F2 **Ulanhot** China
26D1 **Ulan Ude** Russian Federation
26C3 **Ulan Ul Hu** *L* China
25Q3 **Ul'beya** *R* Russian Federation
28B3 **Ulchin** S Korea
17D2 **Ulcinj** Montenegro, Yugoslavia
26E2 **Uldz** Mongolia
26C2 **Uliastay** Mongolia
27G5 **Ulithi** *I* Pacific Ocean
19F1 **Ulla** Belorussia
34D3 **Ulladulla** Australia
8C3 **Ullapool** Scotland
12H5 **Ullsfjorden** *Inlet* Norway
6C2 **Ullswater** *L* England
28C3 **Ullung-do** *I* Japan
18C3 **Ulm** Germany
34A1 **Uloowaranie,L** Australia
28B3 **Ulsan** S Korea
9C2 **Ulster** *Region* Northern Ireland
24K5 **Ulungur He** *R* China
24K5 **Ulungur Hu** *L* China
8B3 **Ulva** *I* Scotland
6C2 **Ulverston** England
34C4 **Ulverstone** Australia
25Q4 **Ulya** *R* Russian Federation
19G3 **Ulyanovka** Ukraine
20H5 **Ul'yanovsk** Russian Federation
62B1 **Ulysses** USA
21E6 **Uman'** Ukraine
55N2 **Umanak** Greenland
43E4 **Umaria** India
42B3 **Umarkot** Pakistan
58C1 **Umatilla** USA
20E2 **Umba** Russian Federation
50D4 **Umba** *R* Kenya/Tanzania
32D1 **Umboi I** Papua New Guinea
12H6 **Ume** *R* Sweden
12J6 **Umea** Sweden
45C2 **Um ed Daraj, Jebel** *Mt* Jordan

Um el Hashīm, Jebel Viareggio


45C4 **Um el Hashīm, Jebel** *Mt* Jordan
47E2 **Umfolozi** *R* South Africa
54C3 **Umiat** USA
45C4 **Um Ishrīn, Jebel** *Mt* Jordan
47E3 **Umkomaas** *R* South Africa
41G4 **Umm al Qaiwain** UAE
50C2 **Umm Bell** Sudan
50C2 **Umm Keddada** Sudan
40C4 **Umm Lajj** Saudi Arabia
50D2 **Umm Ruwaba** Sudan
41F5 **Umm Sa'id** Qatar
51C5 **Umniaiti** *R* Zimbabwe
58B2 **Umpqua** *R* USA
42D4 **Umred** India
**Umtali = Mutare**
47D3 **Umtata** South Africa
75B3 **Umuarama** Brazil
47D3 **Umzimkulu** South Africa
47E3 **Umzimkulu** *R* South Africa
47D3 **Umzimvubu** *R* South Africa
47D1 **Umzingwane** *R* Zimbabwe
75E2 **Una** Brazil
16D1 **Una** *R* Bosnia & Herzegovina, Yugoslavia/Croatia
68C1 **Unadilla** USA
68C1 **Unadilla** *R* USA
75C2 **Unaí** Brazil
54B3 **Unalakleet** USA
41D4 **Unayzah** Saudi Arabia
60D2 **Uncasville** USA
60B3 **Uncompahgre Plat** USA
47D2 **Underberg** South Africa
60C1 **Underwood** USA
20E5 **Unecha** Russian Federation
45C3 **Uneisa** Jordan
55M4 **Ungava B** Canada
28C2 **Unggi** N Korea
74F3 **União de Vitória** Brazil
63D1 **Union** Missouri, USA
67B2 **Union** S Carolina, USA
65D2 **Union City** Pennsylvania, USA
63E1 **Union City** Tennessee, USA
47C3 **Uniondale** South Africa
67A2 **Union Springs** USA
65D3 **Uniontown** USA
41F5 **United Arab Emirates** Arabian Pen
4E3 **United Kingdom of Gt Britain & N Ireland** NW Europe
53H4 **United States of America**
55K1 **United States Range** *Mts* Canada
58C2 **Unity** USA
62A2 **University Park** USA
13D2 **Unna** Germany
43E3 **Unnão** India
28A2 **Unsan** N Korea
8E1 **Unst** *I* Scotland
40C1 **Ünye** Turkey
20G4 **Unzha** *R* Russian Federation
72F2 **Upata** Venezuela
51C4 **Upemba Nat Pk** Zaïre
55N2 **Upernavik** Greenland
47C2 **Upington** South Africa
66D3 **Upland** USA
33H2 **Upolu** *I* Western Samoa
35C2 **Upper Hutt** New Zealand
58B2 **Upper Klamath L** USA
58B2 **Upper L** USA
9C2 **Upper Lough Erne** *L* Northern Ireland
69L1 **Upper Manzanilla** Trinidad
61E1 **Upper Red L** USA
68B3 **Upperville** USA
12H7 **Uppsala** Sweden
61E1 **Upsala** Canada
60C2 **Upton** USA
40D4 **'Uqlat as Suqūr** Saudi Arabia
72C2 **Uraba, Golfo de** Colombia
31B1 **Urad Qianqi** China
41E4 **Urairah** Saudi Arabia
29D2 **Urakawa** Japan
21J5 **Ural** *R* Kazakhstan
34D2 **Uralla** Australia
20M4 **Ural Mts** Russian Federation
21J5 **Ural'sk** Kazakhstan
24G4 **Ural'skiy Khrebet** *Mts* Russian Federation
75D1 **Urandi** Brazil
54H4 **Uranium City** Canada
27G8 **Urapunga** Australia
60B3 **Uravan** USA
29C3 **Urawa** Japan
20L3 **Uray** Russian Federation
64B2 **Urbana** Illinois, USA
64C2 **Urbana** Ohio, USA
16C2 **Urbino** Italy
15B1 **Urbion, Sierra de** *Mt* Spain
6C2 **Ure** *R* England
20H4 **Uren'** Russian Federation
38E1 **Urgench** Uzbekistan
24J3 **Urengoy** Russian Federation
42B2 **Urgun** Afghanistan
17F3 **Urla** Turkey
17E2 **Uroševac** Serbia, Yugoslavia
75C1 **Uruaçu** Brazil
70B3 **Uruapan** Mexico
75C2 **Urucuia** *R* Brazil
74E3 **Uruguaiana** Brazil
74E4 **Uruguay** *R* Argentina/Uruguay
74E4 **Uruguay** *Republic* S America
41E2 **Urumīyeh** Iran
39G1 **Ürümqi** China
26J2 **Urup** *I* Kuril Is, Russian Federation
24J1 **Urup, Ostrov** *I* Russian Federation
42B2 **Uruzgan** Afghanistan
29D2 **Uryū-ko** *L* Japan
21G5 **Uryupinsk** Russian Federation
20J4 **Urzhum** Russian Federation
17F2 **Urziceni** Romania
39G1 **Usa** China
28B4 **Usa** Japan
20L2 **Usa** *R* Russian Federation
40A2 **Uşak** Turkey
47B1 **Usakos** Namibia
24J1 **Ushakova, Ostrov** *I* Russian Federation
50D4 **Ushashi** Tanzania
24J5 **Ush Tobe** Kazakhstan
74C8 **Ushuaia** Argentina
25O4 **Ushumun** Russian Federation
7C4 **Usk** *R* Wales
40A1 **Üsküdar** Turkey
20H3 **Usogorsk** Russian Federation
25M4 **Usolye Sibirskoye** Russian Federation
26G2 **Ussuri** *R* China/Russian Federation
28C2 **Ussuriysk** Russian Federation
25T3 **Ust'-Belaya** Russian Federation
25R4 **Ust'Bol'sheretsk** Russian Federation
16C3 **Ustica** *I* Sicily, Italy
18C2 **Ústi-nad-Laben** Czechoslovakia
24J4 **Ust'Ishim** Russian Federation
18D2 **Ustka** Poland
25S4 **Ust'Kamchatsk** Russian Federation
24K5 **Ust'-Kamenogorsk** Kazakhstan
20L2 **Ust' Kara** Russian Federation
25L4 **Ust Karabula** Russian Federation
20K5 **Ust' Katav** Russian Federation
25M4 **Ust'-Kut** Russian Federation
21F6 **Ust Labinsk** Russian Federation
25P3 **Ust'Maya** Russian Federation
20K3 **Ust' Nem** Russian Federation
25Q3 **Ust'Nera** Russian Federation
25O4 **Ust'Nyukzha** Russian Federation
25M4 **Ust'Ordynskiy** Russian Federation
20J2 **Ust' Tsil'ma** Russian Federation
25P4 **Ust-'Umal'tu** Russian Federation
20G3 **Ust'ya** *R* Russian Federation
20M2 **Ust' Yuribey** Russian Federation
21J7 **Ustyurt, Plato** *Plat* Kazakhstan
28B4 **Usuki** Japan
70C3 **Usumacinta** *R* Guatemala/Mexico
47E2 **Usutu** *R* Swaziland
28A4 **Usuyŏng** S Korea
19G1 **Usvyaty** Russian Federation
56B3 **Utah** *State* USA
59D2 **Utah L** USA
19F1 **Utena** Lithuania
42B3 **Uthal** Pakistan
68C1 **Utica** USA
15B2 **Utiel** Spain
18B2 **Utrecht** Netherlands
47E2 **Utrecht** South Africa
15A2 **Utrera** Spain
12K5 **Utsjoki** Finland
29D3 **Utsonomiya** Japan
30C2 **Uttaradit** Thailand
43E3 **Uttar Pradesh** *State* India
7D3 **Uttoxeter** England
12J6 **Uusikaupunki** Finland
62C3 **Uvalde** USA
24H4 **Uvat** Russian Federation
33F3 **Uvéa** *I* New Caledonia
50D4 **Uvinza** Tanzania
50C4 **Uvira** Zaïre
55N2 **Uvkusigssat** Greenland
26C1 **Uvs Nuur** *L* Mongolia
28C4 **Uwajima** Japan
50C1 **Uweinat, Jebel** *Mt* Sudan
31B2 **Uxin Qi** China
25Q3 **Uyandina** *R* Russian Federation
25L4 **Uyar** Russian Federation
72E8 **Uyuni** Bolivia
45B4 **Uyûn Mûsa** *Well* Egypt
38E1 **Uzbekistan** *Republic* Asia
14C2 **Uzerche** France
19F2 **Uzh** *R* Ukraine
19E3 **Uzhgorod** Ukraine
20F5 **Uzlovaya** Russian Federation
40A1 **Uzunköprü** Turkey


## V


47C2 **Vaal** *R* South Africa
47D2 **Vaal Dam** *Res* South Africa
47D1 **Vaalwater** South Africa
12J6 **Vaasa** Finland
19D3 **Vác** Hungary
74F3 **Vacaria** Brazil
75B3 **Vacaria** *R* Mato Grosso do, Brazil
75D2 **Vacaria** *R* Minas Gerais, Brazil
59B3 **Vacaville** USA
42C4 **Vadodara** India
12K4 **Vadsø** Norway
16B1 **Vaduz** Liechtenstein
20G3 **Vaga** *R* Russian Federation
19D3 **Váh** *R* Czechoslovakia
45C3 **Vahel** Israel
44B3 **Vaigai** *R* India
8E1 **Vaila, I** Scotland
33G1 **Vaitupu** *I* Tuvalu
74C6 **Valcheta** Argentina
20E4 **Valday** Russian Federation
20E4 **Valdayskaya Vozvyshennost'** *Upland* Russian Federation
72E2 **Val de la Pascua** Venezuela
15B2 **Valdepeñas** Spain
54D3 **Valdez** USA
74B5 **Valdivia** Chile
13B3 **Val d'Oise** *Department* France
65D1 **Val-d'Or** Canada
67B2 **Valdosta** USA
58C2 **Vale** USA
75E1 **Valença** Bahia, Brazil
75D3 **Valença** Rio de Janeiro, Brazil
14C3 **Valence** France
15B2 **Valencia** Spain
72E1 **Valencia** Venezuela
**Valencia** *Region* **= Comunidad Valenciana**
15A2 **Valencia de Alcantara** Spain
15C2 **Valencia, Golfo de** *G* Spain
13B2 **Valenciennes** France
60C2 **Valentine** Nebraska, USA
62B2 **Valentine** Texas, USA
6D2 **Vale of Pickering** England
6D2 **Vale of York** England
72D2 **Valera** Venezuela
12K7 **Valga** Russian Federation
7E3 **Valiant** *Oilfield* N Sea
17D2 **Valjevo** Serbia, Yugoslavia
12J6 **Valkeakoski** Finland
70D2 **Valladolid** Mexico
15B1 **Valladolid** Spain
69D5 **Valle de la Pascua** Venezuela
72D1 **Valledupar** Colombia
72F7 **Valle Grande** Bolivia
66A1 **Vallejo** USA
74B3 **Vallenar** Chile
75D1 **Valle Pequeno** Brazil
61D1 **Valley City** USA
58B2 **Valley Falls** USA
65E1 **Valleyfield** Canada
15C1 **Valls** Spain
19F1 **Valmiera** Latvia
14B2 **Valognes** France
75B3 **Valparaíso** Brazil
74B4 **Valparaíso** Chile
67A2 **Valparaíso** USA
47D2 **Vals** *R* South Africa
42C4 **Valsād** India
21F5 **Valuyki** Russian Federation
15A2 **Valverde del Camino** Spain
12J6 **Vammala** Finland
41D2 **Van** Turkey
25M3 **Vanavara** Russian Federation
63D1 **Van Buren** Arkansas, USA
65F1 **Van Buren** Maine, USA
13C3 **Vancouleurs** France
54F5 **Vancouver** Canada
58B1 **Vancouver** USA
54F5 **Vancouver I** Canada
64B3 **Vandalia** Illinois, USA
64C3 **Vandalia** Ohio, USA
54F4 **Vanderhoof** Canada
27G8 **Van Diemen,C** Australia
32C2 **Van Diemen G** Australia
12G7 **Vänern** *L* Sweden
12G7 **Vänersborg** Sweden
68B1 **Van Etten** USA
51E6 **Vangaindrano** Madagascar
40D2 **Van Gölü** *Salt L* Turkey
29C2 **Vangou** Russian Federation
30C2 **Vang Vieng** Laos
62B2 **Van Horn** USA
65D1 **Vanier** Canada
33F2 **Vanikoro** *I* Solomon Islands
26G2 **Vanino** Russian Federation
25U3 **Vankarem** Russian Federation
12H6 **Vännäs** Sweden
14B2 **Vannes** France
47B3 **Vanrhynsdorp** South Africa
55K3 **Vansittart I** Canada
33F2 **Vanua Lava** *I* Vanuatu
33G2 **Vanua Levu** *I* Fiji
37K5 **Vanuatu** *Is, Republic* Pacific Ocean
64C2 **Van Wert** USA
47C3 **Vanwyksvlei** South Africa
14D3 **Var** *R* France
41F2 **Varāmīn** Iran
43E3 **Vārānasi** India
20K2 **Varandey** Russian Federation
12K4 **Varangerfjord** *Inlet* Norway
12L4 **Varangerhalvøya** *Pen* Norway
16D1 **Varazdin** Croatia
12G7 **Varberg** Sweden
12F7 **Varde** Denmark
12L4 **Vardø** Norway
13E1 **Varel** Germany
19E2 **Varéna** Lithuania
16B1 **Varese** Italy
75C3 **Varginha** Brazil
12K6 **Varkaus** Finland
17F2 **Varna** Bulgaria
12G7 **Värnamo** Sweden
20K2 **Varnek** Russian Federation
67B2 **Varnville** USA
75D2 **Várzea da Palma** Brazil
20H3 **Vashka** *R* Russian Federation
21E5 **Vasil'kov** Ukraine
64C2 **Vassar** USA
12H7 **Västerås** Sweden
12H7 **Västervik** Sweden
16C2 **Vasto** Italy
16C2 **Vaticano, Citta del** Italy
12B2 **Vatnajökull** *Mts* Iceland
17F1 **Vatra Dornei** Romania
12G7 **Vättern** *L* Sweden
62A2 **Vaughn** USA
72D3 **Vaupés** *R* Colombia
33H2 **Vava'u Group** *Is* Tonga
44C4 **Vavuniya** Sri Lanka
12G7 **Växjö** Sweden
20K1 **Vaygach, Ostrov** *I* Russian Federation
13D1 **Vecht** *R* Germany/Netherlands
13E1 **Vechta** Germany
13D1 **Veendam** Netherlands
62B1 **Vega** USA
12G5 **Vega** *I* Norway
15A2 **Vejer de la Frontera** Spain
12F7 **Vejle** Denmark
47B3 **Velddrif** South Africa
16D2 **Velebit** *Mts* Croatia
16D1 **Velenje** Slovenia
75D2 **Velhas** *R* Brazil
25T3 **Velikaya** *R* Russian Federation
19F1 **Velikaya** *R* Russian Federation
12K7 **Velikaya** *R* Russian Federation
20E4 **Velikiye Luki** Russian Federation
20H3 **Velikiy Ustyug** Russian Federation
17F2 **Veliko Tŭrnovo** Bulgaria
48A3 **Vélingara** Senegal
19G1 **Velizh** Russian Federation
33E1 **Vella Lavella** *I* Solomon Islands
44B3 **Vellore** India
13E2 **Velmerstat** *Mt* Germany
20G3 **Vel'sk** Russian Federation
13C1 **Veluwe** *Region* Netherlands
60C1 **Velva** USA
44B4 **Vembanad L** India
74D4 **Venado Tuerto** Argentina
75C3 **Vençeslau Braz** Brazil
13C3 **Vendeuvre-sur-Barse** France
14C2 **Vendôme** France
**Venezia = Venice**
16C1 **Venezia, G di** Italy
72E2 **Venezuela** *Republic* S America
69C4 **Venezuela,G de** Venezuela
44A2 **Vengurla** India
16C1 **Venice** Italy
44B3 **Venkatagiri** India
18B2 **Venlo** Netherlands
19E1 **Venta** *R* Latvia
47D2 **Ventersburg** South Africa
7D4 **Ventnor** England
19E1 **Ventspils** Latvia
72E3 **Ventuarí** *R* Venezuela
66C3 **Ventura** USA
20E3 **Vepsovskaya Vozvyshennost'** *Upland* Russian Federation
74D3 **Vera** Argentina
15B2 **Vera** Spain
70C3 **Veracruz** Mexico
75A4 **Verá, L** Paraguay
42C4 **Verāval** India
16B1 **Vercelli** Italy
75A1 **Vérde** *R* Brazil
75B2 **Verde** *R* Goias, Brazil
75B2 **Verde** *R* Mato Grosso do Sul, Brazil
59D4 **Verde** *R* USA
**Verde,C = Cap Vert**
75D2 **Verde Grande** *R* Brazil
13E1 **Verden** Germany
14D3 **Verdon** *R* France
13C3 **Verdun** France
47D2 **Vereeniging** South Africa
20J4 **Vereshchagino** Russian Federation
48A3 **Verga,C** Guinea
15A1 **Verin** Spain
25N4 **Verkh Angara** *R* Russian Federation
20K5 **Verkhneural'sk** Russian Federation
25O3 **Verkhnevilyuysk** Russian Federation
20H3 **Verkhnyaya Toyma** Russian Federation
25P3 **Verkhoyansk** Russian Federation
25O3 **Verkhoyanskiy Khrebet** *Mts* Russian Federation
25K3 **Verkneimbatskoye** Russian Federation
20H3 **Verkola** Russian Federation
75B2 **Vermelho** *R* Brazil
13B4 **Vermenton** France
54G4 **Vermilion** Canada
61E1 **Vermilion L** USA
61D2 **Vermillion** USA
57F2 **Vermont** *State* USA
58E2 **Vernal** USA
66B2 **Vernalis** USA
47C3 **Verneuk Pan** *Salt L* South Africa
54G4 **Vernon** Canada
62C2 **Vernon** USA
67B3 **Vero Beach** USA
17E2 **Véroia** Greece
16C1 **Verona** Italy
13B3 **Versailles** France
48A3 **Vert, Cap** *C* Senegal
47E2 **Verulam** South Africa
13C2 **Verviers** Belgium
13B3 **Vervins** France
19G3 **Veselinovo** Ukraine
13C3 **Vesle** *R* France
14D2 **Vesoul** France
12G5 **Vesterålen** *Is* Norway
12G5 **Vestfjorden** *Inlet* Norway
12A2 **Vestmannaeyjar** Iceland
16C2 **Vesuvio** *Vol* Italy
19D3 **Veszprém** Hungary
12H7 **Vetlanda** Sweden
20G4 **Vetluga** *R* Russian Federation
13B2 **Veurne** Belgium
16B1 **Vevey** Switzerland
13C3 **Vézelise** France
**Viangchan = Vientiane**
15A1 **Viana do Castelo** Portugal
16C2 **Viareggio** Italy

## ACKNOWLEDGEMENTS

**PICTURE CREDITS**
The sources for the
photographs and illustrations
appearing in the atlas are
listed below.

page
48-61    Physical maps by
         Duncan Mackay,
         copyright © Times
         Books., London

62       *Mercury* NSSDC/NASA
         *Venus* NASA/Science Photo Library
         *Mars* NASA/Science Photo Library
         *Neptune* NASA/Science Photo Library
         *Uranus* Jet Propulsion Laboratory/NASA
         *Saturn* NASA

63       *Rock and*
         *Hydrological Cycles*
         Encyclopaedia Universalis
         Editeur, Paris

90       *Manhattan* Adapted
         from map by
         Nicholson
         Publications Ltd.

94-99    Robert Harding
         Picture Library Ltd.

Rear     G.L. Fitzpatrick and M.J.
Endpaper Modlin: *Direct Line Distances.*
         *International Edition* Metuchen
         N.J. and London, 1986